Mediating Criticism

Mediating Criticism
Literary Education Humanized

Roger D. Sell

John Benjamins Publishing Company
Amsterdam / Philadelphia

™ The paper used in this publication meets the minimum requirements of American National Standard for Information Sciences – Permanence of Paper for Printed Library Materials, ANSI z39.48-1984.

Library of Congress Cataloging-in-Publication Data

Sell, Roger D.
     Mediating Criticism : Literary Education Humanized / Roger D. Sell.
          p. cm.
     Includes bibliographical references and index.
          1. English literature--History and criticism. 2 American poetry--20th century--History and criticism. 3. Literature--Study and teaching. I. Title.

PR99.S466   2001
820.9'00071--dc21   2001037882
ISBN 90 272 2582 6 (Eur.) / 1 58811 104 0 (US) (Hb; alk. paper)
ISBN 90 272 2583 4 (Eur.) / 1 58811 105 9 (US) (Pb; alk. paper)

John Benjamins Publishing Co. · P.O. Box 36224 · 1020 ME Amsterdam · The Netherlands
John Benjamins North America · P.O. Box 27519 · Philadelphia PA 19118-0519 · USA

To Tia
with love

Acknowledgements

Robert Frost's "The Lockless Door" and "To Earthward" are reprinted by permission of Henry Holt & Co., LLC, from *The Complete Poetry of Robert Frost*, edited by Edward Connery Lathem, © 1951 by Robert Frost, copyright 1928, 1969 by Henry Holt & Company. Poems by Andrew Young are quoted by permission of Carcanet Press Limited from *Andrew Young: Selected Poems*, 1998.

Revised versions of passages from my own earlier writings are incorporated by permission of the original publishers. Specifically: from *Trespassing Ghost: A Critical Study of Andrew Young, Acta Academiae Aboensis ser. A* vol. 56: 1, Åbo 1978; from *Robert Frost: Four Studies, Acta Academiae Aboensis ser. A* vol. 57: 2, Åbo 1980; from *The Reluctant Naturalism of Amelia: an Essay on the Modern Reading of Fielding, Acta Academiae Aboensis ser. A* vol. 63: 3, Åbo 1983; from "Projection Characters in *David Copperfield*", *Studia Neophilologica* 55 (1983) 19–30; from "Dickens and the New Historicism: the Polyvocal Audience and Discourse of *Dombey and Son*", in Jeremy Hawthorn (ed.), *The Nineteenth-Century British Novel: Stratford-upon-Avon Studies*, Edward Arnold Limited, London 1986, pp. 62–79; from "The Unstable Discourse of Henry Vaughan: A Literary-Pragmatic Account", in Alan Rudrum (ed.), *Essential Articles for the Study of Henry Vaughan*, Archon, Hamden, Conn. 1987, pp. 311–32; from "Gerhardie's Chekhovian Debut", *Essays in Criticism* 41 (1991) 28–50, Oxford University Press; from "Literary Texts and Diachronic Aspects of Politeness", in Richard J. Watts, Sachiko Ide, Konrad Ehlich (eds), *Politeness in Language: Studies in its History Theory and Practice*, Mouton de Gruyter, Berlin 1992, pp. 109–29; and from "The Difficult Style of *The Waste Land*: a Literary-Pragmatic Perspective on Modernist Poetry", in Peter Verdonk (ed.), *Twentieth-Century Poetry: From Text to Context*. Routledge, London 1993, pp. 134–58.

As will be seen, I have been working on the authors discussed in this book for many years. For most of this time I have been based in the English Department of Åbo Akademi University, to which I owe thanks for repeated study leaves for research in Britain and the United States. I am indebted to the Åbo Akademi Foundation for sustained and very generous financial support from the H.W. Donner Fund, and to the staff of Åbo Akademi Library for their unfailing friendliness and remarkable efficiency.

Thanks are also due to the staffs of The Bodleian Library, Oxford, of Cambridge University Library, of The National Library of Scotland, Edinburgh, of The National Library of Wales, Aberystwyth, of The Baker Memorial Library at Dartmouth College, of The Clifton Waller Barret Library at the University of Virginia, of the Robert Frost Library at Amherst College, and of The Jones Library, Amherst.

For comments on drafts of various sections I am grateful to Bernard Bergonzi, Gerald Doherty, Nils Erik Enkvist, Jeremy Hawthorn, Anthony Johnson, Ulla Ora-Nikulainen, Alan Rudrum, Gunnar Sorelius, Peter Verdonk, Stephen Wall, and Richard J. Watts. For help on particular points I am indebted to Julius Barclay, Edmund Berkeley, Philip P. Cronenwett, Edward Connery Lathem, Edward Lowbury, Alan P. F. Sell, S.M. Simpson, Joan St. C. Crane, Alison Young, and Anthony Young. The remaining shortcomings are all my own.

Contents

Introduction

Retrospect and prospect

For reasons which will soon emerge, I begin with my own beginning. I was born in England in 1944, which meant that I could profit from the Butler Education Act of the same year. Having passed the eleven-plus examination, in other words, I went to grammar school. From there, or rather from the comprehensive school which my grammar school subsequently became, I went on to study English at university. In this way I developed an interest in literature which has stayed with me ever since, and which has even helped me earn a living. It led me to become, in fact, a literary scholar by profession.

Yet it is an interest which, in a longer perspective, could perhaps turn out to have been particularly distinctive of my generation. Certainly my grandparents did not read very widely, and for all I know *their* grandparents may not have read at all. My own family's history mirrors the more general spread of literacy and the rise of the meritocracy. Nor can I be absolutely sure that my taste for literature will carry on down to my great-grandchildren, supposing that I have some. If it did not, this, too, might be part of a larger social pattern. After all, present-day media technologies could conceivably be shifting the balance from literate forms of cultural production to a re-vamped orality and visuality. In that case, the middle years of my own life would have coincided with literary culture's high-water mark, and the tide would now be on the ebb. This would merely confirm the observations and predictions of a fair number of writers and critics already.[1]

In my own view, such a scenario is just possible, but by no means inevitable. That future generations will engage in kinds of activity, entertainment and communication which would leave my contemporaries and me non-plussed is quite certain. Peoples' lives will be none the less rewarding for that, just as my generation has greatly benefited from pursuits and technologies which were unavailable to our own grandparents. But the death of the book has been prophesied before — in the nineteenth century, there were those who thought that journalism was taking over.[2] And alongside everything which people of my age would find new and strange in the life-world of the future, literature could still have a place, and not only in symbiosis with the new media. Even if the "film-of-the-novel" phenomenon becomes still more frequent, for instance, with more and more novels written to be filmed rather than read, some writers will always write unfilmable texts, and readers will continue to recognize that films and novels offer two different kinds of experience.[3] Although two somewhat different kinds of interpretative skill are also involved, many young and not so young people are already proficient in both.

Hopes for literature's survival can, I think, be confidently pinned on its sheer human value, and on human beings' capacity to respond accordingly. What also helps is that literature's human dimension is something we can openly compare notes about, and to which young minds can be sensitized. Perhaps the only real threat has come, not from the new forms of cultural production, but from the way literature itself has sometimes been dealt with in schools and universities. As compared with the age of the great Victorian reviews, the twentieth century was arguably less hospitable to serious literary discussion in *non*-academic fora, and there were clear signs of scholasticism. In addition to a geometrically accelerating increase in the sheer quantity of academic criticism published, there was also a certain over-dependence on a just few authorities, plus a rather frequent appeal to attitudes which, for literature lovers who were not themselves scholastics, did not come very naturally. On the other hand, much twentieth-century commentary was at least as intelligent, timely, and sensitive as anything that had gone before, and there is no reason why, as scholars, critics and teachers entering upon a new century, we should not follow this better example. In the present book, I shall be trying to suggest what we could do to leave scholasticism well behind us.

Literary scholasticism

At the very moment in Western history when literacy skills were becoming almost universal, three other highly significant developments were also under way. First, vernacular literatures were beginning to replace Greek and Latin literature as a scholarly and educational focus. Within the culture as a whole, then, spontaneous responses to the literature ordinary people were most likely to read for pleasure ran up against a type of commentary on it that was increasingly sophisticated and specialized. Secondly, the new specialization of literary scholarship, the staking out of the larger area into many distinct fields of expertise, went together with a wholly unprecedented level of professional organization. Not only was there the huge increase in scholarly publications, plus a steady proliferation of specialist journals, bibliographies, networks and conferences. From now on literary scholars, like scholars in general, were usually in receipt of a salary, most typically for services rendered in colleges and universities. Especially in large departments, they were often assigned to one or two particular fields of expertise — early Milton, pre-Romanticism, Tragedy, and so on — and were climbing what was recognizably a career ladder. In other words, the days of the omnivorous "man of letters", who had often been a freelance journalist or gentleman-amateur, were drawing to a close.[4] Thirdly, well into the 1960s the new breed of literary-academic professionals tended to derive their attitudes from the Modernist intelligentsia. In reaction against the crasser forms of nineteenth century literary appreciation and biographical commentary, much of their criticism emphasized, not literature's human interest, but its self-renewing artistic energies, its differentness from other discourse types, and its sometimes strong, and even strongly unpleasant challenge to modes of thought and feeling which were comfortable and conventional.

The intensification of research activity led to a whole new wealth of detailed knowledge, which in principle can place our general understanding of literature on a much firmer footing. The present book is itself very heavily dependent on specialist findings, and even makes some specialist contributions of its own. Yet in social terms, the role of professional literary scholarship has not been very straightforward. Specialists can hardly be blamed for addressing most of what they write to other specialists. How else could their specialisms be developed? But if that is all they do, if no attempt is made to relate their specialist knowledge to a broader range of interests, and if their literary-critical commentaries actually lose touch with what non-academic readers experience as reality, then their new insights will remain dead and inert within the culture as a whole, and the profession of scholarship be landed with problems of legitimation.[5]

According to sociologists, professionalization involves "an occupational strategy which is chiefly directed towards the achievement of upward collective social mobility and, once achieved [sic], it is concerned with the maintenance of superior remuneration and status."[6] George Bernard Shaw said much the same thing, but without resorting to sociology's own professionalese. All professions, he remarked, are "conspiracies against the laity."[7] Throughout the ages, professionals have been satirized for snapping up pretty pickings, for living off of other people's need, for amassing power into monopolistic systems

of market control, and for using their mystifying or pompous jargon to rein-
force their privilege and prestige. As literary scholars, I hasten to add, we shall
hardly recognize ourselves in such accusations, and might well claim that our
scholarship is completely disinterested, that it has no directly marketable utilitarian function, and that our teaching activities are pure altruism on behalf of
the common good. Indeed, we still tend to think of ourselves as very much
amateurs. This, though, is somewhat at odds with our current economic status.
We do the things we love to do. But we do them *as a living*. Somebody else pays
us for it, usually in the form of those salaried posts in colleges and universities.
In point of fact, then, we do need to be able to explain and justify ourselves,
by presenting our specialist perceptions, and any attendant professional jargon,
as a contribution which is in some way socially valuable, and unavailable from
other sources. This is where, as compared with doctors, soldiers or lawyers, for
instance, we are doubly disadvantaged. Our professional embarrassment is
not merely that we never save lives or help to win wars or cases in court. There
will always be a lurking suspicion that our undertakings might be carried out
just as well by *non*-professionals, and that if this is not in fact the case, then
the undertakings can hardly be worthwhile. Literary texts, the very focus of
our research, are thought of as not just in the public domain, but as positively
accessible to a general readership, which may have insights of its own. So the
charge that literary scholarship was more appropriately organized in the days
when most scholars really were amateurs, and that professional literary analysis actually murders to dissect, will always lie close to hand. As for professionalist commentary of a Modernist persuasion, this, even at its finest, was bound to
raise some hackles.

Modernist writers and intellectuals were just as gifted and significant as
the writers and intellectuals of other periods. At the time, their creations and
insights were wonderfully liberating to those who grasped what was at issue,
and their most valuable impact on the human life-world has in fact been permanent. The present book will be focussing on two of the most distinctive
styles of Modernist interpretation: the formalist tendency to de-personalize
and de-historicize literature; and the tendency to read it in a rather grim and
gloomy expectation of unpleasantness. Although I shall be arguing that these
reading habits do now need to be seriously qualified, in their different ways
they substantially enhanced readers' experience. In discussing beauties and
complexities of form, even today we cannot always improve on the Russian
Formalists or the New Critics, some of whose insights seem freshly topical.[8] An
expectation of unpleasantness, similarly, can still be a most effective catalyst,

not least within the more generally humanizing kind of approach I shall be suggesting to Frost, Dickens and Fielding.

Yet the *de*-humanizing aspects of Modernism cannot simply be discounted. And Modernist achievements, no less than the older achievements to which they offered valuable complements, ran the risk of oversimplification. When an intelligentsia's ideas get translated into a more widely assimilable form, they can easily lose important layers of nuance and qualification, so becoming almost a kind of self-parody. As finally institutionalized within schools and universities, the somewhat a-human ethos of Modernism, like the ethos of earlier major movements, was reduced to a number of fossilized dogmas which did service as the latest form of common sense, thereby challenging those who disagreed to come up with an alternative common sense, which was always likely to turn out just as fossilized and unsubtle.

The poetics of the novel deriving from the essays and prefaces of Henry James, for example, having been rigidified into Modernist orthodoxy by Percy Lubbock in 1921,[9] was not seriously challenged until forty years later, by Wayne C. Booth.[10] But once Booth had said his piece, a non-Modernist orthodoxy sprang up almost immediately, so that the two opposed kinds of common sense for many years ran in parallel, the one admiring the technically sophisticated and sometimes painfully unpleasant dramatizations of novelists who were apparently self-effacing, the other preferring the apparently laid-back joviality, frankness and omniscience of more obviously intrusive novelists. Many literary scholastics came to believe, not only that they had to take sides here, but that any novel in which dramatization and omniscience co-existed must be fundamentally flawed. Hence, as we shall see, some of the confusion surrounding Fielding's *Amelia*. Or to take the case of Dickens, one orthodoxy was that his novels were sophisticated works of art, in which unconscious sources of inspiration were of no importance, while an alternative orthodoxy was the exact reverse. This schism, I shall argue, at least did nothing to illuminate either *Dombey and Son* or *David Copperfield*. As for poetry again, many scholastics seemed to think that a poem must be either an impersonal work of art or the work of a particular human being in a particular time and place. As I shall try to show, this conflict between the common sense of Modernist formalism and the common sense of a more traditional approach was singularly unhelpful to an appreciation of Henry Vaughan.

Not that common sense is without its value. On the contrary, Hans-Georg Gadamer can nowadays help us to see that the stock responses and prejudices of our historically situated common sense are the necessary condition for our understanding anything at all. Under circumstances demanding an unreflecting instantaneous response, common sense is a useful support. In our exploration of the unfamiliar, it is our only possible starting point. Nor, in the light of the new experience, is it unsusceptible to change.[11] The only trouble with common sense of the scholastic Modernist variety was that it involved the prejudice against common sense in any other form, a prejudice, moreover, which was *not* laid open to revision. So much so, that Modernist attitudes in general proved very resilient. Albeit under different ideological and literary-theoretical banners, there were still some rather routinely de-humanizing and gloomy attitudes among scholars, critics and teachers even at the end of the twentieth century, and hence among many ordinary readers as well — or were some of them already, therefore, merely might-have-been readers?

That Modernist attitudes eventually had such an impact on the general reading public is itself something of a paradox. How, for the early twentieth century, can we conceptualize a general reading public at all? — a general public, that is, which was likely to have read the texts of the high Modernists. Was Modernist literature even intended for ordinary people? In our own postmodern age, the distinction between high-brow and low-brow is perhaps disappearing.[12] But if so, this is the culmination of more than half a century of Western history. Since the Second World War, the distribution of material prosperity and educational opportunity has radically changed; advanced urban societies have become self-consciously multicultural, embracing many new forms of personal and communal identity;[13] and some of the most vital cultural production has been channelled into the composite genres and styles associated with the new media technologies. All of which has been part and parcel of a general challenge to traditional social gradations and types of legitimacy. By comparison, the world-view of Modernist writers can now seem extremely hierarchical.

"Much too many live and hang much too long upon their boughs. Would there came some storm to shake all these rotten and maggoty ones from the tree!" Thus spake the mouthpiece of Nietzsche, who elsewhere proposed a "declaration of war on the masses by higher men".[14] Goethe had already feared that "the progressively conscious participation of the masses in public life" would lead to a shallower intellectuality, with "nothing to make up for the loss".[15] And well into the twentieth century, in countries with widely differing histories, European intellectuals frequently returned to the same complex of issues: the population explosion, education, and the strain between masses and elites.[16] José Ortega y Gasset, whose *La rebellion de las masas* (1929–30) portrayed the intellectually inferior "mass-man" as the world's new, unchallenged master, else-where described Modernist forms of art as the understandable reaction.[17] On this view, writers, painters, sculptors and musicians, by consciously going in for a de-humanizing aesthetic, were refusing to give the people what they wanted. In Modernist literary texts, in particular, the use of metaphor, the experiments with perspective, and the rejection of realism were all symptoms of an elitist iconoclasm. Ortega was not quite sure as to the general mood of this. Perhaps it connoted an utter weariness with civilization. Or perhaps it was merely play-ful — ironical, suspicious of sham, and full of youthful high spirits. Either way, though, it hardly gave rise to art-works for mass consumption, and Bonamy Dobrée was not alone in regretting that ordinary people and poets now seemed to have very little to do with each other.[18]

But when, exactly, had they ever been in touch? It depends on what we mean by "ordinary people". At least in England, the debate was probably at its fiercest during the 1930s and 1940s, when F. R. Leavis was linking his concern for the plight of minority culture within mass civilization[19] to "the decay of the Common [sic] Reader [sic]". This Common Reader was the reader on whom Dr. Johnson could still rely: a competent, cultivated reader, whose good taste involved the "more-than-individual judgement" of "a homogeneous culture".[20] Such a view of things, though it spurred on Leavis and others to what they thought of as a crusade of educational recuperation, involved a nostalgic myth. Very many of Johnson's contemporaries had not been members of the said homogeneous culture, because they could not read. Without its economic and political dominance, the culture of the Common Reader would have been noth-ing more than a deviant sub-culture within a culture that was still strongly oral. Not even the Education Acts of 1870 and 1880 brought total change. The 1870 Act made state education available, for a fee, to children unreached by voluntary schools, while the Act of 1880 went on to make school attendance theoretically obligatory for all five- to ten-year-olds. In practice, many children remained outside of these arrangements, often because their families could not afford the fee (still payable until 1891), and because school attendance would have reduced the number of hours children could work for much needed wages. Although by the turn of the century the literacy rate in England and Wales is sometimes reported to have been 97 percent, this was merely the per-centage of men and women who could sign their own names on getting mar-ried.[21] Reading, we may be sure, could not yet be a form of mass entertainment.

But however slowly, English culture did make the shift to a more widespread literacy. In the late nineteenth century various forms of post-elementary education began to be available, and more people now had the money and time to spend on books, plus the physical living space and lighting conditions in which to read them. Circulating libraries were having a major impact; there was a continuing increase in the total number of books published; and new trends in pricing were making them purchasable by less affluent readers. In particular, classic texts were becoming available in series of cheap reprints, and the expensive (guinea-and-a-half) three-decker novel was no longer the Procrustean bed for new fiction. As a young man, George Bernard Shaw was able to identify "readers who had never before bought books, nor could have read them if they had", an observation which influenced his own decision to go in for journalism, a field expanding no less dynamically than book-publishing.[22] By 1900 there certainly were a fair number of working-class readers, and a much larger number of lower-middle-class ones. Now more than ever, participation in print culture was actually an indicator of upward social mobility.

As well as readers whose ancestors had "always" read, then, the potential audience for early Modernist writers included readers with no long family tradition of literary experience behind them. Nor was this the only complication, since Modernist writing was something of a challenge to both these kinds of reader. If first- and second-generation readers were encouraged to see themselves as just a vulgar mass, more firmly established readers were given to understand that their taste was somewhat antiquated. Both groups were often represented as in their different ways too easily satisfied with cliché, derivative mediocrity and stock response. Faced for the first time with Modernist texts, a majority of readers probably felt baffled or downright insulted. The only ones likely to feel otherwise were those belonging or aspiring to the literary intelligentsia itself.

Even so, Modernist literary texts did get read. The complete *Ulysses* was admittedly first published as an expensive limited edition, and *The Waste Land* came out in *The Dial* rather than in *Vanity Fair*. At the time this was the way for Joyce and Eliot to make most money, and there was a clear parallel with marketing in the visual arts: the forms of patronage tended to bring avant-garde texts before collector-investors and the connoisseurs who read the little magazines.[23] But Modernist ideas and types of writing did gradually permeate more widely,[24] and writers such as Dreiser, Dos Passos and Nathaniel West, though cultivating ideas and forms which were fairly esoteric, were to some degree caught up in mass civilization itself.[25] If we borrow the Modernists' own hierarchism and think of this as writers being levelled down, then readers were just as surely being levelled up. However little love was lost between writers and public at first, in the long run Modernist trends did have an impact on many, if not most of the people who took an interest in literature.

The dissemination of Modernist reading habits is actually more germane to the present discussion than is their intellectual origin.[26] The main relevance of genealogical details would be to confirm Modernism's fundamental variety. Its political colour could range from the feudal to the revolutionary, and the diversity of aesthetic doctrine is apparent from the career of Eliot alone: at one extreme, an anti-humanist aspiration to impersonal literary autonomy, involving an abstraction of geometric form and anti-vital bareness which would have appealed to Worringer; at the opposite extreme, an emphasis on individualistic will and expressive impressionism, something more reminiscent of Max Stirner and Bergson. More generally, much of Eliot's, Hulme's, Richards's, and the American New Critics' theorization was strongly aestheticizing, while in other parts of Eliot, Hulme and Richards, as also in Empson, Leavis, Edmund Wilson and Lionel Trilling, there were strong interests in psychology, morality and society.

This broad difference can still be traced in the reading styles associated with Modernism's wider assimilation. As I say, on the one hand there was the tendency to de-personalize and de-historicize literature, and this was associated with a formalist aesthetics; on the other hand, readers could also entertain a more affective view of literature as promoting painful mental re-adjustments, together with a more mimetic view of it as a source of unflattering home truths. This was simply the way in which Modernist literary theorizing and its varying emphases came to be naturalized and spread through the media and educational institutions, including not only the universities within which literary scholarship was becoming more and more professionalized, but the grammar schools which Butler had opened up to eleven-plussers such as myself.

In a sense, the contradictions were only to be expected. Intelligentsias have always managed to find arguments to privilege their own creative practice; their creativity has seldom fitted under just a single argument; and the various arguments, on achieving a wider dominance within the culture, have become more superficial and even more randomly coherent as well — as was noted by Modernist critics themselves when they confronted debased forms of nineteenth-century aesthetics. For twentieth century readers, as for readers of any other period, literary theoretical consistency was not a main consideration, the human mind being well able to hold conflicting aesthetic dogmas in suspension. So when adopted by a broader reading public, the Modernist stance became a kind of rough and ready orthodoxy, a reading kit consisting of little more than a handful of uncoordinated stock responses.

Not least, there was that unreasoning aversion to stock responses. Gadamer's arguments in mitigation of prejudice, not published until 1960, were still not general currency even during the century's last decade,[27] and if Modernism did have a common denominator, it was the one suggested by its title: an emphasis on the present moment *without* its historical roots, and if on old things at all, then on making them new. There was a much stronger interest in using what was deemed to be the usable past than in entering into a two-way dialogue with the past in its full complexity. Just as twentieth-century linguistic scholarship moved from nineteenth-century comparative philology to a synchronically oriented structuralism, so literary history became rather unfashionable, with critics tending to see only a very small segment of the past as still worthy of emulation — in Eliot's view of English literature, the period immediately prior to the seventeenth century's alleged dissociation of sensibility. Within schools and universities, horizons of understanding were still further restricted, in that this narrow canon was subjected to an a-historical practical criticism, which sometimes nudged literary–historical survey courses right off the curriculum. As a result, information on provenances was increasingly marginalized, and there was little concern for the workings of texts in any but the here-and-now twentieth-century context of reading. This is what underlay both the aestheticizing reading habit and the more gloomy reading habit involving a sharper affective or mimetic focus. Literary works could only be viewed as symbols, well-wrought urns or verbal icons by uprooting them from their temporal habitat. And the grimmest of twentieth-century experiences and perceptions could not be read back onto earlier periods except by way of a colonizing anachronism.

The presentism of such deracinations and impositions involved a sheer failure of empathy. So has the supply of empathy more recently improved? Certainly not across the board, it seems to me. By the year 2050, the watershed between the Modernists' de-humanizing formalism and the more recent Barthesian paradigm, as we can call it, may seem much less pronounced. Critical and pedagogical practices following in the wake of cultural structuralism and poststructuralism — approaches such as Marxist and post-Marxist criticism, new historicism, cultural materialism, feminist criticism, gay and lesbian criticism, postcolonial criticism, ethnic criticism, and eco-criticism — have been immensely valuable, not least in bringing history back into the picture. But in their more scholastically fossilized forms they, too, have tended to depersonalize literature, by encouraging assumptions about human nature that are too deterministic. Thanks to their de-centring of the human subject, agency and responsibility have sometimes been transferred from real writers and readers to language, society, or culture, animistic abstractions for which literary activity has been regarded as the mere channel. Furthermore, this element of determinism often belongs to a dystopian and demoralizing world-view which can be partly traced back to Modernist gloom, and which is similarly universalized to other times and places.[28]

The failure of empathy endorsed by so many twentieth-century critics, scholars and teachers was a kind of masochism. As pointed out by Wayne C. Booth,[29] Christopher Ricks,[30] Frank Kermode,[31] John Carey[32] and even Frank Lentricchia,[33] literary discussion was tending to restrict readers' sheer enjoyment. Some twentieth century critics, if we are to believe them, did not know how to function when their reading was delightful. Leavis, though often so exemplary in his sheer involvement in literature, for much of his professional career "remembered Dickens as the classic it was perhaps on the whole best to leave, piously and affectionately, to the memory and associations of the early acquaintance [during childhood]".[34]

Deeper symptoms are hard to demonstrate. But such self-denying ordinances could well have had knock-on effects in other spheres. De-historicizing, de-personalizing and pessimistically de-centring critiques of literature, by undervaluing the human achievement entailed by a major deed of writing, left readers that much less prepared for relationships and responsibilities in life at large. To point this out is not to plead for a return to nineteenth-century bardolatry, nor any other form of hero-worship. The iconoclasm of Lytton Strachey's *Eminent Victorians* (1918) was more than understandable in its immediate context, and by 1932, the year of Strachey's death and of Hitler's manoeuvring for the Chancellorship, perhaps made even better sense. Yet even if seen as an indirect precaution against dictatorship, types of criticism which fundamentally disregard literary authors are hardly unproblematic. For all we know, readers encouraged to abstain from genuine dialogue with, say, Shakespeare or George Eliot could end up treating their own nearest and dearest in the same spirit. And by homing in too exclusively on literature's unpleasantness, by refusing to see that even the most unpleasant text can pulse, as I shall argue, with a certain kind of hopefulness, they might be that much less motivated to constructive undertakings in real life. If some young people are now inclined to reject the past few centuries' book culture in favour of a time-honoured yet technologically re-vamped orality and visuality, they should perhaps be congratulated on a healthy instinct for self-preservation.

The postmodern hedonism developing out of non-Modernist common sense is now associated with the new media and their genres, and with ever more frequent conflations of up- and down-market. Already, then, there is a heavy counterbalance to the Modernist legacy. Yet thoroughly to obliterate Modernism from our cultural memory is not a possibility, and mercifully so. T. S. Eliot, for instance, was a most remarkable poet, whose work, like that of other Modernist writers, is in the long run not well served by the Modernist reading habits his own criticism did so much to instigate. And as cannot be repeated too often, even those same Modernist reading habits did bring their own range of pleasures and perceptions. Literary works do have a certain autotelic otherness, and to view them as aesthetic objects, paying little or no attention to their personal or historical penumbra, is by no means impossible, uninteresting or undelightful. Equally, great literature certainly can be most profoundly disturbing and unpleasant, and an essay such as Edmund Wilson's "Dickens: the Two Scrooges" can open our eyes to a major writer's challenge. To insist on literature's underlying hopefulness is not to claim that it always suggests *grounds* for hope. On the contrary, Modernist expectations of difficulty, unpleasantness and pain are often very *à propos*. In such cases, hopefulness is little more than a sense that the world will be improved if the bleak insights can at least be shared through communication.

But although this may not seem much, it is a great deal more than nothing at all. At bottom, the hope implied by literature is the hope which distinguishes any genuine attempt at communication from solipsistic despair: the hope of dialogue, and even the hope of fellowship. In undervaluing this, Modernist common sense entailed a human impoverishment which went hand in hand with those two other traits: the refusal of empathy, and the refusal to acknowledge significant human engagement in history. These three anti-human tendencies, which subsequently enjoyed a fresh lease of life within the Barthesian paradigm of literary studies, represented the least fortunate side-effects of the spread of more advanced literacy. Each of them is therefore directly countered by one of the present book's three main parts.

Their threat was not intrinsic to literacy *per se*. Even if writing was a technology designed to take the place of speech and memory, it had always represented most significant opportunities to improve the quality of life. Not least for knowledge, for reasoning, and for justice, the implications of literacy are enormous.[35] But reading and writing, for most of their brief five-thousand-year history, have been mainly confined to elitist groupings, and even their much more general spread in the twentieth century had its unmistakable down-side.

Especially insofar as mass literacy coincided with the scholastic rigidification of the Modernist and Barthesian attitudes towards literate art forms, human considerations were actually undervalued.

Human nature

If, as I expect, future generations do have some form of literary culture, it will mean that they really are picking up literature's human dimension. Given appropriate encouragement from within the educational system, the chances of their doing so must surely be good. What school pupils and university students most need to be exposed to is, I suggest, a generously humanizing literary appreciation.

At first this might sound like turning the clock back to the age of George Saintsbury. And certainly, literary appreciation today still needs a Saintsburian energy, enthusiasm and breadth. But it will also have to be intellectually self-conscious. It will adopt positions on more than a century of intense literary theoretical discussion, and its assumptions will be up-to-date and coherent. One proposal as to what such assumptions might be is contained in my *Literature as Communication: The Foundations of Mediating Criticism*,[36] the main ideas of which the present book will be trying out in practice.

To begin with one of the basic terms, a lot will obviously depend on what is meant by "human". For Saintsbury and his contemporaries, human nature was a universal. Nor, existentially speaking, were they wrong. All human beings are born, live in societies, and die, and they also share certain basic needs and physiological sensations. Psychologically, too, there is at least one common denominator that most people still agree on: a preference for pleasure, joy and satisfaction, together with hopes and fantasies of bringing such experiences about. If we borrow from Freud and label this as Eros, we shall also remember Freud's claim, so seminal for literary interpretation of the more gloomily Modernist variety, that Thanatos is just as fundamental. But that may already be stretching things a bit, and any further generalizations would certainly be problematic. On the one hand, the fact that many different kinds of people can understand each other could perhaps mean that they perceive human life and society in some basically similar way. On the other hand, what happens here could also be a matter of their imaginatively empathizing with perceptions very different from their own. Nowadays, differences between one human grouping and another, far from being swept under the carpet, are the explicit theme of a postmodern politics of recognition.[37]

If we still want to talk about a general human sameness, the best bet is probably some kind of paradox: a sameness-that-is-difference. Although, culturally speaking, all human beings are born as *tabulae rasae*, they rapidly acquire a social formation which reflects the time and place and exact circumstances of their living. One of the great services of the structuralist and poststructuralist de-centring of human identity has been to emphasize that social formations really do differentiate.

This, though, does not mean that a social formation *completely determines* a grouping's members. Saintsbury, like other liberal humanists, might have doubted that human beings are socially determined at all. For his generation, human identity was highly centred, and great writers, in particular, seemed heroically singular. "The essential qualities of literature, as of all art, are communicated," said Saintsbury, "by the individual, they depend upon idiosyncrasy".[38] This view now sounds old-fashioned and extreme, especially when coupled, as it sometimes was, to the bardolatrous view of major authors as infallibly brilliant, wise and virtuous. Indeed, to many late-twentieth-century commentators, the slightest hint of author criticism, as they called it, was like a red rag to a bull. As far as they were concerned, any kind of focus on authors implied that a human individual could have a much greater originary power and influence than, in the age of Barthes and Foucault,[39] was really credible. Yet many other commentators have long been complaining that Barthes and Foucault's kind of structuralist and poststructuralist de-centring can also be carried much too far. As Raymond Tallis points out, what has often been forgotten is the following statement by de Saussure, so often invoked as a founding father:

> Language [*langue*] is not a function of the speaker; it is a product that is passively assimilated by the individual . . . . Speech [*parole*], on the contrary, is an individual act. It is wilful and intellectual.[40]

As Tallis argues, the point here can be generalized. No matter whether the structured system be that of language, the psyche, society, or culture, human beings *operate* the system, and are not to be conflated with it. Even if there can be no re-instatement of "the transparent, self-possessed, controlling Cartesian *cogito*",[41] what Tallis does object to is Lévi-Strauss's enormously influential talk of myths "think[ing] themselves out in the men and without men's knowledge".[42] His own project is to re-assert

> the centrality of individual consciousness, of undeceived deliberateness, in the daily life of human beings. We are not absolutely transparent to ourselves

but we are not utterly opaque either; we are not totally self-present in all our actions but nor are we absent from them; we are not complete masters of our fates, shaping our lives according to our utterly unique and original wishes, but neither are we the empty playthings of historical, political, social, semiological or instinctual forces.[43]

Seen this way, *homo sapiens* is certainly a social being, but is actually a social *individual*, with at least a certain degree of temperamental, imaginative, intellectual and moral autonomy. That is why some feminist critics are seeking to develop what they call "persona criticism", a persona being precisely a mixture of publicly scripted stereotypes and something rather more personal.[44] Even some of the critics who have most firmly rejected the older notions of writerly authority are beginning to borrow the term *auteur* from film studies, where it has been able to describe a film-maker not only as the product of the entire culture of the film industry, but as a creator whose own oeuvre is nevertheless distinctly recognizable.[45]

An account of the human being as a social individual can help to explain how communicative interaction between the self and the other is actually possible in the first place. People can positively go against the grain of their own social formation, and by using their imagination may not only empathize with formations altogether different, but actually undergo some kind of change as a result. Despite their situationality, their personal identity is something of a wild card. From cradle to grave, they remain impressionable, and their formation is seldom unambiguous. Especially as a response to the complex experience of postmodernity, they may muster different kinds of cultural allegiance in different contexts, and can mentally distance themselves from the allegiances which are most habitual. Their customary rationality is something they can assess from the viewpoint of some completely other rationality, quite possibly with a view to reforming their own society. Without this kind of tension between a social and an individual dimension of the self, social reforms would be hard to account for, and especially reforms arising from the grass-roots level. People totally determined by their society would not even be able to criticize it.

Although, in order to do or say anything at all, people have no choice but to adapt themselves to prevailing social norms, those norms can themselves be changed in consequence. In effect, our individual dimension and our social dimension can enter into co-adaptation, with individuality adjusting to society, and society adjusting to individuality. Social innovation is never a matter of total discontinuity. Rather, the non-existent has to be coaxed forth from the preexistent. By meeting other people half-way, we may be able to persuade them to change, so that the old becomes the foundation for the new. Successful rhetoric, as Aristotle clearly saw, is co-adaptive in just this sense. So Oscar Wilde, even if during his last years he was a social outcast, had as a younger man sufficiently adapted to society's norms to persuade many people to depart from them, at least in matters of taste and style. The social norms themselves had become somewhat more adapted to the still deferential Oscar Wilde. When Dickens paid his respects to Mrs Grundy, similarly, it was with the long-term aim of de-throning her.

A view of literature as human in this socially contextualizing yet highly dynamic sense is irreconcilable with the dogmatically fossilized reading habits of scholastic Modernism. Aestheticizing interpreters, hardly concerning them-selves with the interpersonal dimension of literature at all, turned Dickens's novels into autotelic symbolism. Gloomy interpreters, though certainly fas-tening on literature's psychological, social and moral implications, could see Dickens too exclusively as society's helpless, twisted victim, revengefully per-petuating the kinds of violence and repression from which he himself had suffered. As for the later structuralist and poststructuralist de-centrings, their altered ideological and literary-theoretical premises did not hinder them from a depersonalization and gloom of their own. In extreme forms, they altogether eliminated the scope for Dickens's personal agency, viewing Dickens himself, and everything he wrote, as simply a text by Mrs Grundy. In point of fact, Dick-ens was able to achieve far more than any of these lines of interpretation could ever suggest, and despite his grimmest insights can even today arouse the kind of hope that helps to keep us going.

Hopefulness can be of three main kinds. Sometimes we hope that things will get better thanks to circumstances beyond our own control. Sometimes we hope for improvements as a result of our own interventions as relatively autono-mous social individuals. Sometimes we hope that sorrows and distresses may be alleviated by communication with other people. Hope of all three kinds can turn out to have been well founded. And even when we tell somebody that our hopes of the first two kinds have been utterly dashed, our hope of the other per-son's communicative fellowship is still a totally different emotion from suicidal despair. In a sense, to communicate *is* to hope, and when human beings cease to communicate, both their hope and their humanity may be coming to an end.

With a poet such as Henry Vaughan, one kind of hopefulness that may get communicated is religious in character: a faith that life's trials and tribula-tions will eventually be superceded by an eternity of bliss in God. With Dickens, there are also gestures in this direction, but his life and works more typically bespeak a faith in human interventions. Yet both religious and secular kinds of optimism do often fail. Vaughan's glimpse of a higher happiness is clouded over, as loved ones die and worldly enemies prevail. Dickens knows a very great deal about human wilfulness and weakness, and clearly sees the rot in society as a whole. Even so, and precisely by communicating their very bleakest perceptions, both Vaughan and Dickens can forge a kind of bond between writer and reader, and between one reader and another. The hopefulness they inspire is the hopefulness which comes from not being alone.

Communicative interaction and writer–reader parity

This has already brought us to "literature", another of this book's main terms. The phenomenon to which it refers is multi-faceted, and critics will always tend to emphasize some facets at the expense of others. Saintsbury's generation often stressed literature's entertainment value, Saintsbury himself being remembered as a *bon vivant* who read poetry in much the same spirit as he would have tasted fine wine. It was partly in protest against this ethos that Modernist gloom developed: the recognition that literature's insights into human nature and society can be very unpleasant and disturbing. Also fairly common among literary scholars of Saintsbury's day was a certain historical positivism and biographical reductionism, to which a natural reaction was Modernist aestheticization, with its emphasis on literature's formal properties. Structuralist and poststructuralist approaches, in their turn, sought to qualify the formalist New Critics' accounts of literature as an aesthetic heterocosm. They re-located writers and readers in language-culture-society.

All these literary-theoretical and critical tendencies made good sense in their precise contexts of intellectual history, and many of the attendant insights and terminologies will still inform the commentaries I shall be offering here. What has often remained hidden from view, however, is the extent to which literary writing and reading are forms of interaction. Any fuller recognition of literature's human dimension will certainly entail a much sharper focus on its communicative pragmatics. The literary *logos* is a form of voluntaristic *pragma* which can bond communities together, can urge readers towards personal change, and may even change society as a whole.

Among the twentieth-century approaches which did touch on this were the psychologism of I.A. Richards and its offshoots in Leavisian evaluation and the Empsonian exploration of ambiguity. In their different ways, Richards, Leavis and Empson all shared that typically Modernist sense of the major literary work as a radical challenge to stock responses. In their view, great literature constantly urged readers towards new and more complex types of psychological organiza- tion, albeit at the cost of some difficulty, unpleasantness and even pain.

At the beginning of the new millennium, our emphasis is unlikely to be quite so anti-hedonistic. We shall not want to restrict the new states of mind induced by literature to the adult, the mature, the responsible, the stoically unillusioned. They can just as easily amount to an extension of being that feels positively pleasurable and empowering. Indeed, our ethical stance may well be altogether more relativistic. Despite Richards's modern-sounding talk of com- plex psychological organizations, he and his followers were in some ways basi- cally Victorian. Their assumption was that great literature *improved* its readers, and even if such improvement involved a heightened awareness of complex ten- sions and ambiguities, a further assumption was that these complexities were basically the same for everyone. Nowadays, we can perhaps admit that the effect of literature can be either positive or negative, and that as Milton so clearly explained in *Areopagitica*, readers' only moral defence lies in their own personal powers of judgement. To say that literature consists only of texts which have an improving influence would seriously limit its scope as one genuine form of communication among others. And besides, who would decide on which texts are improving and which are deleterious? That type of judgemental criticism is pre-postmodern. Any recommendation or castigation of a text in such terms today would be seen as the opinion of just one particularly sited individual. Tossed as we are amid the so-called culture wars of a self-consciously hetero- geneous society, we cannot help knowing that one and the same literary work may seem either beneficial or harmful, depending on who is reading it.

Our ethical relativism can be one aspect of an approach that is fundamen- tally historical. Richards, by contrast, was the pioneer of practical criticism, that criticial and pedagogical method which had such enormous pay-offs in terms of detailed attention to language, but which also tended to uproot an act of writing or reading from its specific context. The student guinea-pigs on whose protocols he based his conclusions in the seminal *Practical Criticism* (1929) were told nothing about the provenance of the texts they were asked to com- ment on, and many teachers drew the conclusion that the literature classroom could be a kind of laboratory, artificially sealed off from social change. As a result, the analyses of complex psychological organizations were only some- what shakily grounded in the real worlds of writers and readers. Instead, commentary in this tradition went in for a non-empathetic presentism, universalizing the perceptions, experiences and values of its own Modernist here-and-now to sociocultural milieus which were very different. The fact that certain practical critics, and especially Leavis and Empson, nevertheless wrote some of the finest criticism we shall ever have was always in spite of their underlying theory and methodology, and not because of it. As readers, they could be wonderfully intelligent, and even sensitive to history.[46] But sensitivity to history will always be more consistent for being intellectually self-conscious.

Given some such modifications of the Ricardian tradition, we arrive at a literary criticism which is highly attuned to literature as *pragma*, but which, vis-à-vis authors at least, is not judgemental, and which specially focuses on differences of milieu and world-view between particular authors and the current reader. Precisely by highlighting this kind of difference, a critic may suggest new directions for an extension of the current reader's being. This, if anywhere, is where judgementalism comes in: in the critic's relationship with the current reader. The most helpful critics do not waste time damning the authors they find uninteresting. But they can very well write from a sense that the people they themselves are addressing have missed out on something, and that literature, especially literature from a different cultural milieu, could help to fill the gaps. So yes, perhaps literature does improve its readers after all, or at least improve their quality of life. But not necessarily. And certainly not by casting them in just some single human mould.

Differences of society, culture and ideology can affect communication of every kind. Nor are they always differences between entire communities. Even two people apparently belonging to one and the same grouping will in fact not share exactly the same experiential background and awareness. The differences, no matter how slight, will give their membership of the grouping dissimilar inflections, which are both an obstacle and a stimulus to mutual understanding. Between individuals whose situationalities are obviously very distant from each other, the communicative obstacles and stimuli are merely easier to notice.

In every case, human beings have, as social individuals, sufficient powers of empathetic imagination to get beyond their own personal life- and thought-world. Communication can be seen as a semiotic process by which differences between one person's milieu and world-view and another's are actually negotiated, as they try to come to an understanding of each other's perceptions, experiences and values. It is as a result of this communicative process that personal change can take place, for as Charles Taylor has remarked, human individuation is essentially dialogic. We become the people we become as the result of our encounters with significant others.[47] Communication is the catalyst to human growth.

True, one feature of *literary* communication is that the things and people a work of literature discusses are usually mainly fictional. Plato said that poets are actually liars, and many literary texts clearly do flout one of H. P. Grice's maxims for cooperative communication, the so-called maxim of quality,[48] by displaying an untruthfulness that is both specific and episodic: they mention things and places and people that have never really existed; and they narrate events that have never really happened. But this feature is not peculiar to literature, and fictional discourse is no less communicative than non-fictional. Aristotle soon countered Plato by suggesting that historians are distinctly handicapped as compared with poets, in that a narratation which is specifically and episodically true may convey very little impression of life in general — of the things which will *most typically* be and happen. To which Sir Philip Sidney later added that a poet's fiction can also convey an honestly moral sense of how life *ought* to be — or ought *not* to be. John Searle has had some inkling of these matters, for he remarked that the "undeceptive non-truth" of literary texts can communicate what somehow feels like a "serious" speech act.[49] As Grice might have said, fiction's disregard of specific and episodic truth is actually not a suspension of the cooperative principle, but an *implication* of truths of other kinds: of general truth and moral truth. And if, under conditions of postmodernity, we hesitate to speak of such truths in Aristotle and Sidney's way as totally universal, we are only the more likely to regard the fiction of a poem, play or novel as representing the intuitions of general or moral truth that are characteristic of some particular person or community. A tale can very much embody its teller's own sense of the world, and can in effect be an invitation to compare notes. Having done so, a listener or a reader may find its assessment of life significantly other in the most challenging sense.

True, too, in the case of literary communication there is usually no feedback channel. As readers we cannot tell the author what we think or feel, and the author may in any case be a complete alien, or long since dead and buried. Most linguists, however, would nowadays recognize that an act of writing is inherently dialogic even so.[50] Nor, communicationally speaking, is a literary tradition at all the same thing as a tradition of oral transmission. Although literary authors are social beings who bear the inflection of their particular sitedness, and although their texts have unwitting intertextualities with every other use of the same language, a literate culture in which those texts come down to us with their author's name on them, and which also promotes highly developed forms of historical, biographical and philological scholarship, does tend to recognize authors as individuals, even when, as in the case of Shakespeare, their intentions have become so obviously interwoven with the intentions of countless intermediaries — publishers, editors, directors, producers, actors, film-makers, critics, teachers, politicians, at the very least.[51] This interweaving of subsequent intentions with an authorial intention never results in the impersonal kind of effect associated with, say, an anonymous ballad. A published author's individuality remains a personal hallmark, and authors from the past are experienced as having written their own words, as having had their own meanings, and often, indeed, as having actually entered into dialogue with each other as relatively free agents, so that critics may need to speak of influences, sources, allusions or parody. As with many other forms of written communication, the lack of a feedback channel simply means that a reader's attention to every such sign of potentially significant otherness is only the more intense.

A written text can indeed have a continuing human potentiality, such that the act of reading it will involve a real ethical dimension. This is very much a matter of maintaining writer–reader parity. On the one hand, the relationship between the two halves of the linguistic sign — the signified and the signifier — is arbitrary. As Part I of this book will illustrate, this means that the only way for a reader to get some idea of what the writer meant is by an empathetic effort to relate the text to the full circumstances under which it was written. Even though this is increasingly difficult as the sociocultural gap widens between the context of writing and the current context of reading, good readers are very conscientious in their hermeneutic effort, in the first instance out of an obligation to the writer as another human being, but also out of self-obligation, for fear of obfuscating the potentially valuable challenge of the writer's alterity. On the other hand, the attitudes, values and knowledge which are present to the reader in the current context of reading really will be different — however greatly or slightly different — from those which were present to the writer in the context of writing, and a text's precise interpersonal valency does necessarily vary from one context to another. To claim that we owe other human beings, alive or dead, an effort of empathetic understanding is not to say that empathy will always turn into sympathy. To empathize is not to disclaim judgement, and readers of literature will inevitably be influenced by their own positionality, even if they are not completely determined by it, and even if they sometimes end up trying to shift it somewhat. Having tested what it means to agree with an author, they may finally *dis*-agree, and even *dis*-approve. Styles of reading involving some kind of historical or cultural purism — the assumption that a text's significance is never more than its significance in its original context — are unconducive to the dialogicality of genuine communication.

Changes to readers and their life-world

According to a communicational view of literature, then, what is a genuine encounter with an author really like? And how is it that reading literature can actually lead to change? Answers to these questions will underlie all my commentaries here, and will in some places become quite explicit. The two most fundamental points have to do with the nature of communicative situations in general, and the relationship between a communicative situation and the actual words that are used in it.

Communicative situations are triangular. Two parties will always be in communication about some third entity. The basic situation can still be thought of in this way even when the two parties are the two halves of one and the same self-communing individual, as when we talk to ourselves or write a diary, and even when the third entity also includes one or both of the communicating parties, who in that case speak of "me" or "you" or "us". Equally well, the third entity can be somebody or something quite unconnected with the communicants themselves, and can furthermore involve an element of hypotheticality or even fiction, as with much gossip about celebrities, and as with most literary communication. To begin with, change to the status quo has to do with the way the third entity is perceived and assessed. As they think about it, communicants lay themselves open to the possibility of mental re-adjustments, whose scope can range from the merely very minimal to the absolutely all-embracing. Directly or indirectly, these mental goings-on can also lead to actions of a tangibly physical kind, and ultimately may even contribute to changes in an entire communal thought- and life-world.

So much for communicative situations. The second fundamental point is that the situational triangle, through the actual words used, is replicated as a kind of mental model of it. The words express or imply a representation, not only of the real, hypothetical or fictional things or people under discussion, but also of the communicants themselves.

That the words have to give a representation of the things or people talked about is obvious enough. How else could they be talked about? Nor, at least for some of this book's readers, will it come as much of a surprise that representations of the communicants themselves are expressed or implied as well. Critics have long since recognized this phenomenon, often speaking of it in terms of an implied author and an implied reader.

All such communicative personae are constructed in the same way. Thanks to textual features which linguists refer to as deixis, the speaker- or writer persona and the listener- or reader persona will both be rooted in temporal, spatial and social dimensions. Tacitly or overtly, they will also be associated with particular cultural and ideological backgrounds, plus certain ranges of general and more specialized knowledge, and quite possibly characteristics of gender, age, and so on as well.

People who are communicating, including literary writers, are likely to make the match between the communicative situation and the communicative act's representation of it a fairly close one. A literary text's implied author will be as genuine an aspect of the writer's personality as any other self-presentation, and the implied reader can only be based on the writer's honest sense of who the real readers are likely to be, or at least *could* be. For much of the time, moreover, communication takes place between people belonging to some single community, so that the two communicative personae may seem in many ways identical.

Admittedly, there have been New Critics and narratologists who claimed that the implied author and implied reader of literature were entirely fictional. Sometimes they even said that it was inappropriate to speak of a literary author's sincerity. This, though, was precisely one of the ways in which Modernist literary formalism tended to de-humanize literature. Even though most literary works are largely fictional in terms of the things and people actually discussed, their implied author and implied reader are neither more nor less fictional than the representation of the participants in any other kind of communication.

This applies even in the abnormal case of irony, since if irony is actually perceived as irony, the real listener or reader still knows what the real speaker or writer means. The communicative act's tri-componential structure remains unaffected. The basic, non-ironic speaker- or writer persona and listener- or reader persona are also still notionally in place, and may also be partly textualized. The only difference is that additional, *ironic* personae can be thought of as inserted in between them — either an ironic speaker- or writer persona, or an ironic listener- or reader persona, or ironic personae of both kinds.

So when people are in communication with each other, not only do they say whatever they want to say about the topic under discussion. Their words also model the communicative situation itself. As stepping stones to communication, they offer a speaker- or writer persona which images themselves, and a listener- or reader persona which they invite their communication partner to enter into. When, as in face-to-face informal conversation, there is a feed-back channel, one of the areas of negotiation can even be these personae themselves. We sometimes feel that the listener persona our conversation partner is proposing for us is simply inaccurate — or rather unflattering. In that case we have the option of saying, "Wait a minute! You've got me wrong. I don't think like that."

Yet even when an objection of this kind would be well warranted, we do not always make one, and herein lies an insight that is absolutely crucial for an understanding of literary interaction. We can go on participating in a process of communication even if the persona we are offered is totally unrecognizable as an image of ourself. Indeed, there are many situations in which we *cannot* seek to redress it. Most obviously, there may be no feed-back channel, as with most written texts, including literary ones. What can then happen instead is that we use our powers of flexibly empathetic imagination. With however little enjoyment or approval, a feminist is perfectly capable of reading a text that is written as from one male chauvinist pig to another. Without even thinking about it, readers can project themselves into an inaccurate reader persona for the purposes and duration of communication. Or for an even longer time as well! Even though readers never disclaim their right to criticize, even though no feminist reader is going to become a male chauvinist pig on a permanent basis, communicational activities, including the reading of literature, can actually be heuristic. A reader persona in which we do not recognize ourselves allows us to try on the different identity formation for size, so to speak, and in this way can serve as the stimulus to change. In other words, the offered persona reflects the speaker or writer's persuasive intention for us. The otherness of a persona whose formation we try on for size may well turn out to be significant for us, suggesting possibilities for a more long-term self-extension. Nor need the transformation stop there, since if enough people like ourselves are feeling the same way about a text, then the change it induces will be not only personal, but ultimately social, a change to the entire life-world within which we have our being.

Influential communicators, both literary and non-literary, appeal to their audience's power of imaginative self-projection. This is what they rely on when trying to shape the world to their own liking. What they do is to propose a listener- or reader persona which, rather than exactly corresponding to their likely audience as it is at present, is a pattern to which the audience *could* perhaps conform, as the result of an open-minded effort of empathy. Co-adaptively, then, the implied reader of a literary text can combine the socially familiar with something more individual and unexpected. Dickens invited his readers both to sympathize with Mrs Grundy, and to condemn her. This is how literature can signpost new directions for the course of sociocultural history.

The faith of authors

A powerful literary text is one whose co-adaptations between the social and the individual do actually change a human life-world, or offer hints for sheer survival. And although we shall always want to talk about the beauties of literary form, the dynamics of literary *pragma* can move us to praise beauties of literary deed as well. As Part II of this book will illustrate in detail, beauty of this kind relates to the author's skill in co-adaption with prevailing circumstances. The achievement to be recognized stems from a moral trajectory which is at once bold and well judged.

Writers could never be so inspiring unless they had faith: faith to write in the first place; faith in what they want to write; faith in the readers they want to write for; faith in the final outcome of their communication. Such faith is by no means peculiar to literature, however, but is what, at the most fundamentally human level, makes literature one among many forms of communication. To use a rhyme-pair which has sometimes fascinated English poets, words are better than swords. Words are better, too, than introverted solipsism. As long as people go on exchanging words, there is still a chance that life may improve. Even a bitter pessimist, by going public, is inviting refutation, or is challenging others to steel themselves to endurance, or perhaps to turn over a new leaf. The pessimism which still makes itself heard is simply not pessimism of the darkest dye.

As if to corroborate this, in even the grimmest of literary texts the tragedy is seldom unrelieved. However fitfully, however much against the odds, literature, like human interchange in general, does pulse with the hope of joy. At the very least, it entails an assumption that life would certainly be improved if joy were possible. As Part III of this book will suggest, this is how literature endorses attempts to see the world as humanly meaningful, potentially forging a powerful bond between people of widely differing backgrounds and experience. This in itself changes the world for the better. Even when opening our eyes to the very worst things in life, a writer's own deed of communication can attune us to this universal pulse of human hopefulness, inviting us into the circle of its ameliorating commonality, even when hope's justifications or imagery are extremely insubstantial.

Mediating criticism

Seen in this way, the biggest drawback of some of the reading styles promoted by literary education in the twentieth century was that their failure of empathy was a blindness to the historical complexities and interpersonal force of literary *pragma*. No less within Barthesian accounts of literature as a social, cultural or linguistic construction than within the earlier Modernist accounts of symbolic wholes, the concern was with what literature *is*. Writers and readers were somewhat marginalized. Even the pyrotechnics of poststructuralist reader response criticism tended to attribute the process of semiosis entirely to language itself. In Modernist and still later accounts of literature's disturbing unpleasantness, meanwhile, as also in much evaluative criticism, the interest was largely in what texts *say*. If our understanding of literature is to be fully humanizing, we also need to consider what, in the there-and-then, texts actually *did* and what, in the here-and-now, they still *can do*.

The double focus is crucial: what the particular literary text has done hitherto; and what it can now do in our own present. Over distances of time or culture, formal, affective and ethical horizons of expectation do vary, together with other contextual circumstances as well. Justifiably, some literary authors have made no bones about writing for posterity, or for readers in many different countries, and an appreciative critic will always try to keep the channels for such communication as clear as possible. Yet interpretations which rest content with historical or cultural purism stifle communication's true dialogicality. Although a scholarly critic can help readers to react, as much as is ever possible, to the writer's literary deed as it really was in context, its human value will also have to be re-assessed from within the current circumstances of reading. In order to respond to its humanity at all, we need to understand it as a deed in the there-and-then. But the only way for us to re-affirm its human potential is within our own here-and-now. Necessarily, its precise valency will have become different.

To bring home literature's human dimension, therefore, the appreciative critic will engage in mediation between the writerly there-and-then and some current readership's here-and-now. For this task, the theoretical unpinning will be a historical yet non-determinist literary pragmatics of the kind I have outlined. Universalist notions of humanity such as those assumed within Saints-burian appreciation, Ricardian psychologism, Leavisian evaluation, or formalist New Criticism can no longer apply. Instead, there will be a sharp focus on socio-cultural differentiation. Sociocultural disparities between the context of writing and the current context of reading will be seen as both an obstacle and a stimulus to communication. At the same time, this sociocultural relativism will not take the form of a historicist determinism. In contrast to extremist forms of structuralist and poststructuralist de-centring, a mediating approach will see human beings as not entirely confined to their own sociocultural formation, and as perfectly capable of communicating with somebody whose formation is not the same. There will be a firm belief in their imaginative, intellectual and moral ability to negotiate such differences, with personal and even social change as one of the possible outcomes. The critic's first assumption will be that readers of literature are in this sense well equipped to vindicate an author's faith in them.

In presenting any given writer to any given current readership, the critic will have to start, explicitly or implicitly, from a cross-cultural analysis. The basic task, after all, is to ensure the communicative parity between a writer's context of writing and the current context of reading, so maximizing the chances that current readers will at least meet the author half-way. In essence, the mediating critic will be offering them assistance — historical, literary–historical, biographical, philological — in their efforts to empathize with the writer's difference from themselves, together with suggestions as to how the encounter might now modify their own life- and thought-world.

But as I say, differences between one human being and another can vary in magnitude. There are not only the widely recognized differences between whole communities or epochs. Even within one and the same grouping at one and the same time, a social formation can be differently inflected. This means that the mediating critic's task can range from a kind of ethnography to a kind of talent-scouting. Ethnographical mediation promotes understanding across the more marked kind of divide: understanding between two or more different reading communities,[52] or understanding for earlier historical phases of a community's own tradition. The present book, for instance, addresses a broad community of readers who might read literature in English, and discusses seven writers who have been dead for between 25 and 300 years, five of them already well established: T. S. Eliot, Henry Vaughan, Dickens, Frost and Fielding. As for talent-scouting mediation, this tends to be more uni-focally involved with the present cultural phase of some single community, and tries to win appreciation for those of its writers who are in some way out of the ordinary. This will obviously be an important additional element in dealing with non-canonical authors, as in this book's chapters on the novelist William Gerhardie and the poet Andrew Young. In point of fact, talent-scouting and ethnography readily complement each other. Those members of a community who are out of the ordinary are the ones most likely to contribute to its understanding of other communities. Conversely, a community which comes to a better understanding of some other community is more likely to understand those of its own members who are out of the ordinary.

Whoever the author dealt with, mediating criticism will seek to help readers negotiate departures from the norms to which they are accustomed. It will work by providing explanatory information and perspectives, so encouraging readers to bring into play their own powers of imaginative self-projection into otherness. The aim is neither bardolatrous hero-worship, nor the promotion of some grand human consensus. Given that reading is fundamentally dialogic, and that empathy does not necessarily lead to sympathy, readers may in the end be keen to re-assert a certain distance. But what the critic certainly will emphasize is the ideal of reasonable discussion, so that even dis-agreement and dis-approval will be very well understood. The critic is not out to give a "fix" on a writer, and has no compulsion to talk for victory and say the last word. To at least fifty percent the task is rather to exhibit and encourage *self*-criticism, quite simply because of the main goals: the negotiation of difference, and the facilitation of communication. What the mediating critic explores are simply relationships with an "other" which at any point may suddenly turn out to be a *significant* other.

Suitably developed within schools and universities, a mediating appreciation along these lines could, I think, help to guarantee a flourishing literary culture, in a future for which the tension between social fragmentation and globalization seems set to become still more acute. Above all, this kind of education would encourage a sense that literary texts of widely diverse provenance are human documents, and would do so precisely by redressing the deficiencies of some of the criticism written during the twentieth century. While fully recognizing that a genuine effort of appreciation may end in dis-agreement and even dis-approval, the appreciative mediator's three main hallmarks would be: an empathy that is sensitive to differences between one grouping or epoque and another; a recognition of writers' historical achievements of communication, understood as an inspiration whose precise valency is always new in every new set of historical circumstances; and a responsiveness to literature's under-lying hopefulness.

In all this there would be the additional the advantage of psychological coherence. Regardless of whether readers' final assessment is positive or nega-tive, they can never truly empathize with writers without granting due recogni-tion to their particular historical achievement. Nor can they truly recognize that achievement without an empathetic effort of historical imagination. No less inevitably, their recognition of the writerly achievement, and of the com-municative faith from which it springs, can prevent them from sinking into introverted despair. They will register both the inspiration, polyvalent but con-tinuing, and the invitation to communion, even when full communion with the particular author is something they in the end reject.

So although empathy, recognition, and responsiveness to hope each receives special emphasis in one of this book's three main parts, their separa-tion from each other will be a purely artificial measure, for the purposes of exposition only. To some extent all three features are involved at every point. Not only that, but the book's successive parts will get progressively longer, and two of the writers examined in Part II will come in for further discussion from the slightly different but related point of view developed in Part III. In these ways, I am hoping to suggest how the three main qualities of a mediating criti-cism can complement each other in a kind of appreciative *allargando*.

PART I

Empathizing

Summary

Readers can neither admire nor criticize an author's achievement until they have tried to experience it for what it really was. And twentieth century readers, when influenced by the literary scholastic orthodoxies of their own time, were all too likely to undervalue authors whose otherness might have been significant for them. Two authors somewhat marginalized in this way were themselves themselves twentieth century figures, the novelist William Gerhardie and the poet Andrew Young, whose early readers, not fully aware of the circumstances and literary traditions within which they were writing, thought of them as failing to achieve something they had not in fact attempted. In such cases, and without in any sense reducing or disnaturing the literary works under discussion, a mediating critic may be able to use biographical and literary–historical information as a way of narrowing the gap between an author's context of writing and a current reader's context of reading. Symptomatically, both biography and the study of sources and influences became rather unfashionable during the twentieth century. Yet now as always, they can do much to promote the movement of empathy so necessary to any genuine assessment, favourable or otherwise.

In Chapter 1, I frankly recognize how difficult it was for Gerhardie's first readers to project themselves into his partly Russian thought-world. Even today, the Chekhovian connection is something a mediating critic still needs to underline. It is most clearly noticeable in Gerhardie's tone of voice, in his interest in the continuing fortunes and ethos of a certain segment of Russian society, in his predilection for randomly inconsequential plots, and in his self-conscious metafictionality. At the same time, there were other important sides to his writerly personality as well, and in particular a certain epicureanism, which in his later work blossomed forth under the influence of Proust. His response to both his Russian and French predecessors resulted in a writerly personality that resembled neither of them exclusively. Taken as a whole, then, his writing illustrates a complex link between an author's love of literature and the processes of the same author's own personal individuation. A critic or teacher making this kind of point may well be able to help new readers come to terms with features they might otherwise overlook or find anomalous.

In Chapter 2, I go on to explain how the same consideration applies in the case of Andrew Young. Young's poetry was sometimes interpreted in terms of the de-personalizing Modernist aestheticism, sometimes in terms of the Modernist emphasis on gloom and the death instinct. But although both these types of reading were partly justified, his best work is in direct descent from Vaughan, Wordsworth and Dante, in being fundamentally self-expressive, with a sadness that occasionally gives way to moments of radiant vision. Mediation here will be a matter of improving this personal note's audibility, a task in which literary–historical and biographical considerations strongly complement each other. One reader who would have known how to take him was A. E. Housman, who spoke of poetry as a kind of secretion: as the noticeable issue of a private inner drama. This is very much the case with many of Young's short nature poems, for which he does have some slight reputation. But it is no less true of his verse play *Nicodemus* and his eschatalogical poem *Into Hades*, which have been even more seriously underrated.

CHAPTER 1

William Gerhardie's Chekhovianism

Who shall cast the first stone? Modernist readers' powers of empathy may have been somewhat under-used. Yet even today, we can be blind and deaf to people who are "other". The cultural blinkers which prevented an appreciation of Gerhardie; the narrow range of literary–historical and biographical considerations which led to confusion about Andrew Young: these are the kinds of limitation which will always take their toll, irrespective of whether we are reading literary authors or engaging in some other form of human relations. To study the cases of Gerhardie and Young will be to acknowledge empathy's continuing and paramount importance in communication of any kind whatever.

Granted, a failure by readers to empathize with contemporary writers belonging to their own culture can seem rather odd. But with Gerhardie, it was not that simple, and even now, a mediating critic will still have to act as both talent scout and ethnographer. Gerhardie's early readers were aware of a strangeness which they thought of as vaguely exotic. What has to be very well understood is precisely his Russian background, and especially the Chekhovian connection.

This need not entail a detailed study of his entire career. All in all, he wrote seven novels, a number of short stories and stage comedies, plus a considerable amount of criticism, autobiography and biographical history. But his relationship with both Chekhov and an English-speaking public are immediately clear from the case of *Futility*, his debut novel of 1922.[1]

It was certainly not a flop. Some reviewers hailed it with astonished delight,[2] and Gerhardie became, for a number of years at any rate, a minor celebrity — a conspicuously gifted writer, still surrounded by the mystique of that foreign past, and patronized by Beaverbrook. Nor has he ever been entirely lost from view. In the late 1940s, and again in the early 1970s, there were collected editions of his works. In the 1980s *Futility* and *Of Mortal Love* (1936) were available as Penguin Modern Classics, and in 1990 his fortunes took another turn for the better when *Futility*, the autobiographical *Memoirs of a Polyglot* (1931) and the posthumous *God's Fifth Column: A Biography of the Age 1890–1940*

(1981) were all re-issued.[3] On top of everything else, the year 1990 also saw the publication of Dido Davies's excellent biography.[4] Reviewers of these volumes were intrigued by the riddle of Gerhardie's personality, and praised his best works almost without reservation.[5] Since then, Bo Gunnarsson has written the first book-length critical study, published to mark the Gerhardie centenary in November 1995.[6]

Yet for all that, even as early as 1923 H. G. Wells was lamenting that *Futility* was not enough shouted about,[7] and seven decades later it is still not mentioned in accounts of the Modernist *annus mirabilis*. The truth is that Gerhardie's most faithful devotees have always been found among other novelists. On Graham Greene, just going up to Oxford, *Futility* made an "indelible impression": "To those of my generation . . . [Gerhardie] was the most important new novelist to appear in our young lives".[8] Olivia Manning went further still: "He is one of the immortals. He is our Gogol's *Overcoat*. We all came out of him".[9] Evelyn Waugh, in a letter to Gerhardie, made a similar point in more temperate language — "As you no doubt recognized I learned a great deal of my trade from your novels" —, but in conversation with somebody else was frankly envious: "I shall never be as good as he [Gerhardie]. I know I have great talent, but he has genius."[10]

Gerhardie's difficulty in becoming something more than a novelist's novelist had a lot to do with most readers' failure to bridge the gap to his context of writing. In fairness to them, though, the gap's width must be acknowledged. His writerly personality and its associated cultural milieu were sufficiently alien to make the business of reading him rather awkward. As Marlene Dolitsky would put it, reading Gerhardie was not, for English readers, an automatic process.[11]

❧

Part of the problem was his choice of materials, which in the case of *Futility* was positively unwelcome. The third of the novel's four parts, and roughly half the total length, touched a very raw nerve in the national psyche. Under the heading "Intervening in Siberia", it told of events which really took place and in which Gerhardie himself had had a role. The intervention in question was that of the British Mission (1918–20), a military operation in which the Middlesex and Hampshire regiments were supposed to cooperate with Czech, Canadian and American forces in order to help Admiral Kolchak crush the Bolsheviks and restore the Romanoffs. It so happens that my own father, born in the same year as Gerhardie, was present in Siberia under the same auspices. In 1971, he watched a BBC television account of the episode and wrote to me about it shortly afterwards. His letter documents the nation-wide willingness to blot out, for half a century, the events to which Gerhardie's novel relates. My father himself had never discussed these experiences with me before, and may have been writing with a sense of his own approaching death. His view of the operation is that of an ordinary soldier, English born and bred, and as he recalls old memories his tone is one of straightforward moral indignation. In its own way, this can help to explain the problematic reception of Gerhardie's *Futility*.

The television programme, appropriately called "The Forgotten War", was based on old films taken on the spot. My father commented:

> It was all pretty grim. There were the old cattle-trucks clanking along and in which we lived for 21 days in getting from Vladivostok to what was to be our head-quarters at Omsk. These trucks were the usual things with sliding doors plus a wood-burning stove in the middle and shelves at both ends for sleeping on. Each truck took 20 men. I could still smell the woodsmoke, feel the cold of the inch of frost on the walls when we woke and hear the grind of the woodsaw as we cut our ration of black rye bread.
>
> Arrived at Omsk they showed the thousands of peasants drawn in from the countryside answering the call to save their country for the Romanoffs or perhaps to get food and clothing. The cold was intense. My diary says that in Jan. of that year, 1919, the thermometer showed 80 degrees of frost.
>
> And this is where that Corporal Sell, Signalling Instructor came in. They promoted him to Temporary Acting Sergeant Major, put a little brass crown on his sleeve, gave him some sheets of paper with (1) a list of peasant names, Yacob this, Gregori that (2) a list of duties and (3) some 100 or so Russian words and how to say them. Armed thus this boy of 24 gathered his platoon of Russian peasants and proceeded to wash, clothe and feed them. They were a filthy stinking lot but seemed to change miraculously after a few days into docile, cheerful idiots, always eager to obey. They seemed to worship me as dogs would, because I suppose, like dogs I kept their bellies full and life was certainly more clean and comfortable for them.
>
> And in this fearful cold there was Serg. Maj. Sell with his list of commands square-bashing on a piece of spare ground, strutting and bawling his orders. I have often wondered since why they did not chuck their rifles at me and shout the equivalent of "Don't talk so bloody wet." My "KROOGOM MARSH!" must have sounded a horrible outrage on the language. But they didn't and by the time they were ready to join a company, for a battalion, for a brigade, for Admiral Kolchak I had grown to love them.
>
> This process lasted only a few days and then along came another platoon for similar treatment. Later we went further up the line as far as Ekaterinburgh in the Urals doing the same job. We were closing in on the Bolsheviks! Against millions of them? Over thousands of square miles? We were soon hastily flying for our cattle trucks, first back to Omsk and then to Vladivostok.

Did I realise what I had been doing? Training Russians to kill their own countrymen and in the end being [*sic*] annihilated. Of course I didn't. In the army you do not consider the political reasons for actions but do as you're told and get on with it — just as our boys are doing in Ireland.

I found the film very disturbing and in places could have wept. For Gregori and Jacob? Perhaps. But more I think for the senseless and cruel planning of the politicians who killed them. A more evil and unrighteous war was never planned and no wonder we never boast about it and no wonder no-one in that war got a medal! When we win there is always a medal, but never when we lose. But we did get 6d. a day Arctic Allowance![12]

∾

Gerhardie could scarcely have realized that his first novel, in dragging up such shameful recent memories, was risking outright rejection. What made things even worse was his own apparent attitude towards the British Mission. This is where we get still closer to his writerly personality and to his own background, both biographical and literary.

When John Rothenstein suggested "Futility" as a title for Gerhardie's manuscript[13] he may have been thinking of Wilfred Owen's poem of the same name — published in the posthumous collection edited by Sassoon in 1920 and reprinted in 1921. But Gerhardie, in his physical descriptions, was more seemly than the war poets, and the tone in which he discusses the Mission has nothing of my father's indignation, an indignation which Owen would certainly have shared.

Andrei Andreiech, the first-person-singular narrator in *Futility*, is present in Siberia in a mainly administrative and advisory capacity, as was Gerhardie himself; his forte is his knowledge of the Russian language and frame of mind. His main companions during "working" hours are Admiral Butt, the diplomat Sir Hugo, and a Russian general vaguely attached to their party, and "work" itself consists of banquets, inebriated discussions of the fair sex —

"Russian girls," I continued, "are far more interesting and clever than other girls."
"All girls," the Admiral replied, "are stupid."[14]

— and chasing the dog that chased the cat that chased the rat under the Admiral's bed, an exploit just as hopeless as the British Mission's advance on the Bolsheviks. The experience and thoughts of the common soldier, whether British or Russian, are never as close in *Futility* as in my father's letter; when Andrei Andreiech travels up-line to Omsk it is in the luxury of one of the Admiral's personal coupés. In any case, much of "Intervening in Siberia" deals with Andrei's wide circle of acquaintances in private life, who are even more prominent in the other three parts of the novel.

In a way, though, Gerhardie could be more unnerving than Owen. Underlying the "Intervening" section was the feeling that the position of the British was militarily absurd and morally wrong; despite the difference in tone, it does have this in common with my father's letter. Owen might suggest that it was not *dulce et decorum* to be killed for one's country in the trenches of France. But that was surely much better than inciting and training the people of another country to kill each other. Gerhardie, with his broad cultural horizons, somewhat divided in his loyalties, and not, like my father, under orders to do dirty work, thought this from the first. But in *Memoirs of a Polyglot*, rather than being solemn about it, he quickly sidetracks into a joke at his own expense:

> We remained in Siberia exactly two years. My inmost beliefs not being bound up with the re-establishing of an obsolete régime in Russia, my efforts were chiefly directed to resisting the perfidious attempts of senior newcomers from England to oust me from my influential post as the officer in charge of the "General Staff Office", an appointment largely of my own invention.[15]

In *Futility*, Andrei Andreiech, who is equally well placed to observe some of the men generating policy at the top, on one occasion parades the insight so acquired to his friend, Fanny Ivanovna:

> "Horrible!" she said. "It's shameful! The Whites kill the Reds, the Reds kill the Whites . . . and nobody is any the farther. . . . Why can't human beings settle things by conference?"
> "They must be human beings for that, Fanny Ivanovna."
> "Sir Hugo surely — "
> "Sir Hugo's chief preoccupation at a conference is to commit another allied gentleman into saying 'Yes' on any given point, and then by a series of masterful, elaborate and elusive thrusts of speech to commit him into saying 'No'; and then to point out the contradiction. It is what Sir Hugo calls 'displaying the good old fighting spirit'. His attention is essentially devoted to the careful recording of documents that find their way into our office accidentally, documents which in themselves he regards as inessential and unimportant. And the Admiral hates Sir Hugo's love of detail and exactitude which seems bent on proving to him very clearly and precisely the uncertainty and vagueness of his own position."

And this time the seriousness is deprived of satirical edge by a no less Gerhardiesque twist of humorous pathos:-

> She sighed.
> "It's a consolation," said she, "to think that there are other useless people in the world besides ourselves. . ."[16]

Yet what was a consolation to Fanny Ivanovna in her personal sorrows, on a more comprehensive view of the world and its future was cause for concern. As its title suggests, the novel's most insistent theme is an aimless triviality that runs through private and public spheres alike, making the distinction between the two rather hazy; civilians and military spend many hours just wining and dining each other. Least purposeful of all, however, is battle:

> "What are you firing at?" the Admiral asked.
> The man pointed at the tree.
> "Are there any Reds behind?"
> The man shrugged his shoulders. The question to him seemed immaterial.[17]

Set beside Gerhardie's clear-sighted farce, even *A Farewell to Arms* (1929) could seem less disturbing. Hemingway shows intensely private lives being grievously impinged upon by events of war, but those events are mainly beyond the protagonists' ken; on some larger view they might even make sense. With Hemingway, too, it was easier to relate to the novel's central consciousness. The tough guy with the soft centre was not exactly British, but was certainly recognizable — let's say, a transatlantic cousin — whereas Gerhardie's humorous pathos was simply odd. Granted, "Intervening in Siberia" raised a serious issue. But was raising it the same as actually *being* serious, or was Gerhardie essentially flippant and even perverse? Perhaps Fanny Ivanovna's denunciations of the Whites killing the Reds and the Reds killing the Whites were too swiftly left behind as the utterance of a particular, fallible character. How could Gerhardie anatomize the inhumanity and folly of Sir Hugo and the Admiral without personally getting hotter under the collar? For admirers of Owen, Hemingway, or section IV of Pound's "Hugh Selwyn Mauberley", it could easily have seemed that Gerhardie was trying to take some of the gloom out of Modernist gloom, and at exactly one of the points where gloom was most appropriate.

This problem, the problem of Gerhardie's tone, was bound to recur, not only elsewhere in *Futility* but with almost every sentence he ever wrote. It is partly to be explained, not so much in terms of the sentences themselves, as pragmatically, by the cultural and intellectual endowment brought to bear on them by a certain kind of reader. The bafflement experienced by many English readers in face of the true polyglot's spiritual heterogeneity is something Gerhardie himself seems to have thought about, but from his own end of things, composing *Futility* in a Russian and an English version simultaneously, presumably unsure exactly whom he should be writing for.[18] He even gets Andrei

Andreiech, the narrator-hero of *Futility* and himself a budding novelist, to comment on his own work in progress — a manuscript which Gerhardie's fiction requires us to think of as the first version of *Futility* itself:

> The quite indefinably peculiar atmosphere of it seemed to defy the choice of language. For I happen to belong to that elusive class of people knowing several languages who, when challenged in one tongue, find it convenient to assure you that their knowledge is all in another. And I am one of those uncomfortable people whose national "atmosphere" had been somewhat knocked on the head — an Englishman brought up and schooled in Russia, and born there, incidentally, of British parents . . .[19]

The phrasing here exactly describes Gerhardie's own origins. Not that English Moderns had to be English in the narrowest sense. But for those who were not, things usually worked in the same fashion as for Hemingway. James, Eliot and Pound, Yeats and Joyce, were, for all their talent at foreign languages, native speakers of English who were not truly bilingual in any other language, and they belonged to easily classifiable English-speaking communities. Even Conrad had made his reputation as the novelist not of Poland but of the sea, a topic perfectly congenial to British readers. His foreignness was too obvious to be worrying, and his written English almost too beautiful.

Futility was bound to catch most English readers off balance. Unlike the author of *The Waste Land*, Gerhardie had not established a central position in London literary life, had not moulded his own audience with critical essays, and had not been championed for several years by Ezra Pound. Unlike *Ulysses*, the novel did not have to be smuggled in to the country, a forbidden fruit that was already legendary. Yet its originality was sharply defamiliarizing, most of all by giving English expression to a temperament and aesthetic of a Chekhovian cast. This was perhaps the single greatest obstacle for Gerhardie's earliest English readers, even if at our present distance in time their difficulties are hard to imagine, since Chekhov has subsequently become more central to English-speaking readers' cultural context. True, his plays had been staged in English versions from 1909 onwards, and the translations of his tales by Constance Garnett, appearing between 1916 and 1922, were already creating a stir. But an English Chekhov had yet to be acclaimed, and there was not even a sense that such a thing might be desirable. It is mainly more recent commentators who have discovered Chekhovian features in *Dubliners*;[20] Joyce himself said he had not read Chekhov before he wrote it.[21] Shaw, who did write *Heartbreak House: A Fantasia in the Russian Manner on English Themes* (1919) in response to Chekhov's plays, captured the inconsequentialities but lost the light-handed poignancy. And Katherine Mansfield, whose short stories were Chekhovian enough for Gerhardie to seek her out as a kindred spirit, to whom he dedicated *Futility*, was generally regarded as merely antipodean.

Gerhardie's *Anton Chehov* [*sic*]: *A Critical Study*, which could have been the decisive exercise in public relations, did not come out until 1923, the year *after* the publication of *Futility*, by which time *The Waste Land* and *Ulysses* were already stealing the limelight. The book was the first extended critical study of Chekhov in a language other than Russian, and Desmond MacCarthy and others praised it as one of the finest pieces of literary criticism on any topic.[22] From the point of view of Gerhardie's own reception, it was probably two or three years too late. Faced with *Futility*, the only clues his earliest readers had were a number of metafictional ones, planted by the self-conscious Andrei Andreiech himself.

If Gerhardie had not been exiled from his land of birth by the Revolution, if he had published, as he so nearly did, in Russian, it might long ago have been realized that he was carrying the Chekhovian inspiration in directions not previously explored even in Russia. His subject-matter, for instance, involved a new phase of history. The Revolution, in one sense the ruin of his career, was in this sense its making: he could write about the same Russian social class as Chekhov, but about that class as responding to the mighty events which threatened to destroy it and which Chekhov never saw. Artistically, he showed that a Chekhovian temperament and aesthetic could be extended beyond the dimensions of the short story and four-act stage play, to those of the novel.

In *Anton Chehov* he outlines what a Chekhovian novel would be like. The passage is immediately followed by a characteristic debunking of this and every other recipe for writing — "The writer is himself one quarter unaware as to whither he is steering. It is the critics who will afterwards discover 'tendencies' and rules and method and hidden implications"[23] — but for Gerhardie's own sake we should not take this too seriously. It represents a disinclination to *use* his beloved Chekhov, and a distaste for manifestos which merely compounded the misfortune of the study's date of publication. (Contrast Eliot, the year *before* the publication of *The Waste Land*, on the Metaphysical poets: "We can only say that it appears likely that poets in our civilization, as it exists at present, must be *difficult*.")[24] Gerhardie's crucial statement is clear enough even so:

> Chehov has written no novels. He called *The Duel* a novel, but it is really too short for a novel. But that he wrote short and long stories should not be taken to mean that his method of dispensing with the visible event-plot was unsuitable for the novel. The formula for the modern novel and story, short or long, would be something like this: That things — psychological, "atmospheric", and other — must arise out of one another with, and to, some significance. The longer the story, therefore, the more space there is for things, for more things, to arise out of one another — even to a greater significance. This formula would mean that the novel has both form and plot — though it may be implicit rather than obtrusive.[25]

This proposition was the climax of several pages of argument in which careful contrasts were drawn with notable English contemporaries. Henry James's realism was a realism of detail only; his plots were based on symmetrical patterns of a simply fantastic order, while Arnold Bennett quite openly confessed that the story of a so-called realistic novel, in real life, would never happen. What Chekhov offered, on the other hand, was not only realistic details, but plots drawn from direct observation, which meant that their psychology was right as well. Chekhov caught the fluidity of life itself, and the plot ran on beneath that surface, rendering life intelligible by artistic form.

In many respects *Futility* follows Gerhardie's Chekhovian prescription to the letter. It obviously includes much direct observation from life, and the main significance arising is the deeply Chekhovian sense that life resists any kind of tidy ordering apart from the merely chronological. Day follows day, and month month; a few things happen which find their way into history books; and other things can be located as either before or after them. More specifically, Part I is set in St Petersburg before the Revolution, Part II describes the Petrograd of revolutionary days, Part III deals with the British Mission to Siberia, and Part IV is located in Vladivostok some time later. But otherwise, the events of history are seen as non-events in a way that Chekhov, as Gerhardie describes him, might have found sympathetic.

> Imagine Mr. Shaw being perpetually contradicted by Mr. Chesterton, and the resulting neutralization is approximately what has been going on in Chehov's mind. Imagine the revolutionary and the monk both shouting "Forward!" in the mind of a single man, and you will not be astonished by Chehov's choice of standing still.[26]

The vagaries of the British Mission will already be apparent, and not even the Revolution is very clear-cut:

> Crossing a bridge I passed a company of soldiers newly revolted. They marched alert and joyous to the sound of some old familiar marching song till

they came to the words "for the Czar". Having sung these words they stopped
somewhat abruptly and perplexed. "*How* for the Czar?" one of them asked.
"*How* for the Czar?" they repeated, looking at each other sheepishly. Then they
marched on without singing. There were peasants who did not know the
word "revolution" and thought it was a woman who would supersede the Czar.
Others wanted a republic with a czar. And there were others still who interpreted the word republic as "rieszshpublicoo", thinking that it meant "cut up
the public".[27]

Nor is the impact of history on private individuals any more determinate.
Nikolai Vasilievich, in many ways the central character, explains that he has
left Petrograd for Vladivostok because ever since the Bolshevik revolution his
house has been invaded by a host of undesirable people. Strictly speaking, however, and as he also mentions, the house was no longer his anyway. He has
had to mortgage it in order to pay for the all too human nonsensicalities of
his family life. Moreover: "the Bolshevik authorities had restricted individuals
from drawing on their current accounts in the banks; and what was more
important still, Nikolai Vasilievich had really nothing left in the bank to draw
upon".[28] His life has been a sequence of helpless infatuations accompanied by
guilty conscience, a formula sufficient in itself for chronic economic decline.
He now has three "wives" — past and present — to support, plus their innumerable relatives, their subsequent spouses, and his own children, an entourage
which cheerfully clings to him on his travels from Petrograd, to Vladivostok, to
Omsk, begging accommodation in the Admiral's personal coupés, though they
almost need a train just to themselves. He hopes that one day his gold mine in
Siberia will provide an income on the scale required, but it did not do so before
the Revolution, and at the end of the book he is still hoping.

Every other character has hopes and dreams which are just as resilient
and unrealistic. The novel's four parts, like the four acts of a Chekhov play,
catch these people in shifting lights, but although we see them under changing circumstances, nothing ever really happens except that they go on being
themselves. They go on nursing their fantasies while life gets neither better
nor worse. Without their urge to envisage happy endings, they would be inani-
mate, less than human. But life would not be life if their dreams came true
upon request. The artistic structure is largely made up of *Leitmotifs*, and "these
themes are principally determined by the fact that each character . . . is . . . an isolated soul that, in essentials, lives alone in a world of its own creation through
which it looks upon the life 'that is' in a misty, half-uncomprehending way; and
the blend, the clash, the incongruity of it is what moves us: there is beauty in

that blend of comicality and pathos" — words borrowed from Gerhardie's own description of Chekhov's plays.[29]

Not only does the new range of subject-matter not break the continuity with Chekhov. In their ideology and lack of historical realism, the class Gerhardie describes are what they always were. Admittedly, Prince Borisov, alias Kniaz and one of Nikolai Vasilievich's most steadfast dependents, eventually breaks his decades-long silence in order to ask the Admiral and Sir Hugo what they really think the British Mission will achieve. They say that it is working for "one indivisible national Russia by creating one strong united Russian Army", to which Kniaz replies: "Excuse me, but — but — but — but if there is any national Russia today it is all on the other side. As for the Russian Army, the only Russian Army now is the Bolshevik Army. The others have all melted away".[30] But this, which makes the Admiral and Sir Hugo walk out in absurdly dignified protest, is even less acceptable to Kniaz's fellow-countrymen. They twist his words and hoot with laughter: "Ho! Kniaz is a Bolshevik!"

As for his use of genre, Gerhardie's achievement is certainly striking. One can say that he adds extra length, and an almost Dickensian breadth, to the Chekhovian short story, or that he converts the Chekhovian four-act play to non-dramatic first-person-singular narration with several changes of setting. Either way, though, the plot is still a Chekhovian affair of a story that is not a story, capturing an essential unshapability in life, despite an incorrigible desire in human beings to shape it. Paradoxically, such a rendering into art is itself a shaping of the unshapable, and a patently successful one, as Chekhov might also have intimated.

Chekhov's own probing of such relationships between literature and life is especially marked in *The Seagull*, which clearly fascinated the author of *Futility*. Two of the play's characters are themselves writers — the young aspirant Trepliov and the older, well established Trigorin — but their rivalry extends from their literary careers to their private lives. Trepliov, hopelessly in love with Nina, gives her a part to act in a Maeterlinckian fantasy he has written, a play within the play on which Chekhov's "own" characters comment and which, by comparison with them, seems highly abstract and artificial. Trepliov subsequently presents Nina with a seagull he has shot, solemnly explaining it as a proleptic symbol of his own suicide. Trigorin, contemplating Nina and the same shot seagull, conceives a realistic story of an innocent young girl betrayed and destroyed by a cynical seducer. He himself later deserts Nina, who has borne his child and hopelessly worships him. Given all this, plus the subsequent turns of the story, the play's audience, on hearing the offstage shot just before the final curtain, cannot but wonder whether Trepliov or Nina is to be the victim. In other words, which writer's interpretation of the seagull symbol has come true, Trepliov's or Trigorin's?

The metafictional element in *Futility*, which involves the allusions to Chekhov, is bound up with the complex role of Gerhardie's *alter ego*, Andrei Andreiech, who in each and every grouping is both insider and outsider. He "works" with the Admiral and Sir Hugo, yet is intimate with the Russian characters, though not, like most of them, financially dependent on Nikolai Vasilievich. He has English parents, and by the time of the Revolution he has even spent a short period up at Oxford. For much of the novel his attention, at once freely empathizing and cooly objective, is trained upon the Russian characters, yet he also reports upon himself in much the same tone. His own frustrated desire to shape life according to his wishes is perhaps the novel's most comical hubris, and it is evident in two different areas.

The title of Part I, in which he dreams of helping his Russian friends re-organize their chaotic existence along more sensible lines, is "The Three Sisters", which has obvious Chekhovian associations. Andrei Andreiech sometimes uses the expression to refer to the three daughters of Nikolai Vasilievich, but these girls are kittenish teenagers and by no means as central as the three sisters in Chekhov's play. Much more to the point is that in Part I the family actually goes to see *The Three Sisters* at the theatre. Young Andrei Andreiech protests at the absurd futility of the characters' lives:

> ... "How can there be such people, Nikolai Vasilievich? Think of it! They can't do what they want. They can't get where they want. They don't even know what they want! ..."

Nikolai Vasilievich does not agree.

> ... He shook his head gravely and his face darkened.
> "It's all very well," he said slowly, "to *talk*. Life is not so simple. There are complications, so to speak, entanglements. It cuts all ways, till ... till you don't know where you are. Yes, Andrei Andreiech ...."
> He sighed and paused before he spoke again.
> "Chehov," he said at last, "is a great artist ..."[31]

After learning more of Nikolai Vasilievich's own "entanglements", Andrei Andreiech "understood ... why ... [he] sympathized so heartily with the people in the play".[32] Yet he still spends a whole night planning a wonderfully rational

scheme to bring everybody amorous fulfilment and at the same time redistrib-
ute economic responsibility. When he unveils his master-plan, his friends think
he is mocking them. He surely cannot *believe* in such simplistic solutions!

Secondly, there is the question of his own love life, which dominates Part
IV of the novel, entitled "Nina" after Nikolai Vasilievich's eldest daughter. Like
Chekhov's Nina in *The Seagull*, Gerhardie's Nina does not love the young
writer, but Andrei Andreiech's ardour continues unabated. After the withdrawal of the British Mission, he returns to Vladivostok from England in order
to pay suit yet again, but just as fruitlessly as ever. The novel ends with his
gloomy reflections upon her departure, together with her two sisters, to a
doubtless very jolly life in Japan.

Unlike Chekhov's Trepliov, Andrei Andreiech has the robustness to survive
his unrequited love, but partly because his feelings are not aggravated by professional jealousy, whereas Trepliov cannot forget that Trigorin is not only Nina's
seducer but a literary lion as well. Of the seriousness of Andrei Andreiech's literary ambition there can be no doubt, and this is what makes his role still more
complex. It is the one thing about him which is not subjected to his own gentle
ridicule, the one respect in which he is not an ineffectual and ordinarily Chekhovian mortal. On the contrary, as a writer he actually grows, sets himself a
goal, and achieves it. His friends' rejection of his very sensible scheme for their
future sets him on the path towards a more down-to-earth and Chekhovian
view of human nature, which is also his path towards being a novelist. His
development is handled only obliquely, yet it contrasts eloquently with Uncle
Kostia, another of Nikolai Vasilievich's dependents and also a would-be writer;
it is perhaps not accidental that "Kostia" is also the pet-name of Chekhov's
Trepliov. Gerhardie's Kostia is both sublime and ridiculous. His literary aspirations are treated by the other characters with solemn respect, but in fact
he never manages to write anything at all, and on the train to Omsk has a
moment of vision which makes him feel he was wrong even to try: life is simply
too futile and too magnificent for words, too subtle and too beautiful. Andrei
Andreiech is not unsympathetic to this insight, but neither is he cushioned by
subsidies from Nikolai Vasilievich. Still more to the point, he actually has a
streak of iron determination. He succeeds, like neither of the Kostias, but perhaps in the manner of Trigorin, in producing, not vague abstractions, but the
concrete realism of the text we are reading.

The metafictional dimension of the novel's plotting is that it implies this history of its own genesis. Like *Finnegans Wake* it ends where it began and begins
where it ended. When the steamship taking the three sisters away to Japan has

completely disappeared from view, the very last words are: "I peered at the horizon to see if I could spot the smoke from its two funnels. But there was none".[33] A most desolating farewell. Except that the novel's opening words are the direct continuation:

> And then it struck me that the only thing to do was to fit all this into a book. It is the classic way of treating life. For my ineffectual return to Vladivostock is the effectual conclusion of my theme. And the harbour has been strangely, knowingly responsive.[34]

Consolation for the farcical anguish of this futile *vita brevis* is to be sought in the realm of *ars longa*, the "ineffectual" in the former becoming the "effectual" in the latter.

An account of Gerhardie's relationship with *The Seagull* must proceed with caution, however. Chekhov's play, even on its metafictional level, is replete with paradoxes, loose ends, unshapable contradictions. Ironically enough, it is Trepliov's interpretation of the seagull symbol which comes true — Trepliov, who as a writer is *less* successful than Trigorin. But then again, the vindication of Trepliov's symbolism is brought about only by his own act of suicide: he forces life to be like bad literature, which is what his own biography would have been if he and not Chekhov had dramatized it. Trigorin's story of the ruined maid does not come wholly true, and he himself apparently forgets about the seagull that had prompted it. But it does come true in part, since Nina is definitely deranged by his treatment of her, and his literary ideals are much closer to those of Chekhov. Gerhardie noted that "Trigorin is the completest picture of himself that the 'objective-minded' Chehov ever cared to paint, and, within limits, can be safely taken to be Chehov himself".[35] Yet even if Trigorin does perhaps win the literary battle — and he is still alive at the end, which means he will go on writing — his art brings him no lasting satisfaction, either as art for art's sake or as a relief from his humiliating sexual enslavement to his *femme fatale* (who happens to be Trepliov's mother). For Trigorin, writing is mainly a matter of sheer hard slog, and *The Seagull* resists symmetry, resists a soothing aestheticization of life, to an extent which makes the circular organization of Gerhardie's novel seem decidedly polished, and perhaps even self-indulgent.

In his later work, too, Gerhardie sometimes veers away from the quotidian imperfections of the human world around him, responding to fresh experience with a less than Chekhovian openness. Some of the characters and situations in his delightful second novel, *The Polyglots* (1925), are difficult to remember separately from *Futility*, and although he did broaden his range to include the flappers, artists and press lords of the English jazz age, his novels, always partly autobiographical, also tell of Byronic wanderings in search of loves unimaginable in England, and unrealizable anywhere. When, in *Resurrection* (1934), he intensified still further his questioning of all apparent shape and purpose in life, he did so by drawing on congenial experiences of living outside his own body in a state of astral projection. His fastidious self-distancing attains its natural culmination in *Of Mortal Love*, where his feelings towards both his readers and his characters include as much coolness as warmth, and where the characters themselves are similarly close to and far from each other. The exquisite beauty, wit and pathos of the writing are beyond all question, but go hand in hand with a sense that human individuality entails this sheer separateness. Chekhov too, on Gerhardie's interpretation, sees each character as "an isolated soul that, in essentials, lives in a world of its own creation",[36] but to Gerhardie, a lasting harmonization of viewpoints seems not only impossible, but not quite desirable — "the inadequacy of all human contacts . . . throws one back on oneself, and makes the artist".[37]

The un-Chekhovian circularity of *Futility* was the first instance of a retreat into art which held a special fascination for Gerhardie, something closely associated with his long-standing stylistic imitation of Wilde, and with his growing love of Proust, who in the end became as important an influence on him as Chekhov. By the same token, as a writer of autobiography, biography and history he came to offer unusual angles on the people trying to dictate, or simply caught up in, great events, precisely because, unlike the common herd, he never quite saw life as ultimately important, or himself as a participant in it. When he does seem "of" his own time, it is because he catches the note of nineteen-twenties frivolity, for which, however, he seems to hint a metaphysical validification.

Throughout his career, then, his Chekhovianism must be weighed against a certain epicureanism: a dandyish and self-contained aloofness. In some ways this side of his work tallies with his own life-story, on which the harshest verdict would be that, whereas Chekhov was a loving husband, a doer of charitable works, a practising doctor despite his own illness, and an active man of the theatre, Gerhardie took six decades to grow up, by which time he was already a recluse. Always capable of affection and great kindness, not least to children and to those dependent on him, always energetic to secure the comfort and well-being of his sisters and of his adored mother, he remained a bachelor who fought shy of other emotional commitments and acquired a reputation as a philanderer. His social life was certainly restricted by his chronic shortage of cash. But between the two wars he did not actively seek employment other than writing, and in Anthony Powell's opinion was actually "one of these people who really remained a foreigner"; he "had no kind of feeling for living in England. I think he'd have been much more at ease in some continental capital."[38]

This could be seen as the *emigré's* bad luck. *Anton Chehov* may have paid tribute to a humanity which, in the new country, he already despaired of sustaining in his own work, and it was not necessarily his fault when English readers found his materials odd or even unwelcome, or when his tone was misheard. Yet whereas Conrad probably wanted nothing more than to address a large English public, Gerhardie, linguistically and culturally so much closer to assimilation, seems to have had an ultimate diffidence, almost as if there were still the option of addressing a pre-Revolutionary Russian one.

But why *should* he assimilate, why even try to become something other than he "really" was? "The manner, the style of the man, is plainly the influence of early environment. That I have spent my first eighteen years in St. Petersburg is something which five years in the British Army, three years at Oxford and the rest of my life in England can never undo".[39] Even if the change of milieu called for a certain adaptation, he might have argued that to assimilate beyond a certain point would have been suicidal for him, especially as a writer, and that comparisons with the outgoingness of Chekhov and Conrad are an ungrateful refusal to take him as he comes. In any case, his epicureanism should not be overemphasized. There is much about him that certainly is outgoing, and especially in his early work.

As an interpreter of Chekhov, he himself has a sharp appreciation of life's oddities and unshapabilities. He praises Chekhov for *Leitmotifs* which are grounded in real people — for a passionate curiosity about real people that fuels an overwhelming compulsion to tell stories, to communicate observations to others. Chekhov, he says, never fusses about technique, which would be the sign of deficient genius, and Chekhov's style, although restrained, merely increases the intensity of the feelings conveyed, his supreme subject being the theme of farewell. The psychology is accurate, he continues, because it is drawn from life, yet does not involve a stream of consciousness technique like that of *Ulysses*, which gets boring, and is not as profound as it seems. Psychology, Gerhardie insists, is not an end in itself, but a means, like paint to a painter. It has to be *used*, with discrimination, restraint, proportion, and humour. Since the time of Chekhov, he maintains, only Katherine Mansfield has succeeded in using psychology for artistic ends, and whereas Chekhov expresses subtle things simply, Henry James expresses simple things subtly.[40]

In the London of the early 1920's, Gerhardie's ideal of writing was in some respects traditional and even old-fashioned. Although he rejected conventional notions of plot, he admired a strong human interest; "character" was not a dirty word for him; and he had a care for the reader's entertainment. Not only that, but long sections of *Anton Chehov* are taken up with biography and an appraisal of Chekhov's qualities as a doctor, as a friend, as a husband, as a judge of others. The basic assumption is the profoundly un-Modernist and anti-Barthesian one that in reading Chekhov's works we encounter Chekhov the man, and that his greatness as an artist is inseparable from his qualities of mind and feeling. This is a type of argument which the present book is seeking to rehabilitate, and Chapter 2 of *Anton Chehov* is a magnificent precedent, constantly moving between the life and the writings, and offering an unforgettable account of Chekhov's sensibility — his steadiness of judgement, his refraining from optimism and pessimism, his distrust of truth-in-a-nutshell, his passion for dispassion.

And often, in writing about Chekhov, Gerhardie was also writing about the author of *Futility*, a novel which emulates, for one thing, Chekhov's straightforwardness. The departure of the British Mission from Vladisvostok involves a farewell that is as unashamedly poignant as the one at the end of *The Three Sisters*, and the precision of Andrei Andreiech's character portraits is not a sophisticated matter of stream of consciousness but of faithfully rendered speech. For another thing, neither Chekhov nor Gerhardie allowed their straightforwardness to eliminate insights that were both subtle and unconventional. Contrasting Chekhov with Tolstoy, he remarks that whereas Tolstoy indignantly saw the lie behind everything, Chekhov's searching curiosity helped him to find the truth behind the lie. He then quotes a letter of Chekhov to Suvorin:

> You would have me, when I describe horse-stealers, say: "Stealing horses is an evil." But that has been known for ages without my saying so. Let the jury judge them; it's my job simply to show what sort of people they are.[41]

This is where Gerhardie's own refusal to get hot under the collar while describing the British Mission, his unimpassioned amusement in the presence of the appalling, slots into place. For all his refined self-irony and epigrammatic exuberance of expression, his eye is steadily on human behaviour, including, as it were, the behaviour of his readers. While I hope he would find nothing false in the open expression of moral indignation in my father's letter, he nevertheless suspects, like Chekhov, that our cries of outrage sometimes verge on hypocrisy. Forgetting that we share the human frailties of the people we are blaming, we "present ourselves to our fellows in a stiff intellectual shirt-front". Gerhardie, no less than Chekhov, has "eased our joints with candour".[42]

∽

In addition to the less precisely specifiable interest in human nature, Gerhardie's Chekhovianism is therefore made up of four main strands: similarities of tone; an interest in the continuing fortunes and ethos of a certain segment of Russian society; a predilection for the Chekhovian type of plotting, which catches the inconsequentiality and unshapability of life, and which he adapted to the dimensions of the novel; and a preoccupation with the kind of metafictional issues raised by *The Seagull*. Taken together with the circumstantial evidence of his intimate acquaintance with Chekhov's works and of his desire to interpret them for English readers, all this confirms that he was actually influenced by Chekhov, and can help us as readers in our empathetic attempts to grasp his literary personality, and to merge our horizon of expectations with his own.

If we acknowledge the strong influence of Chekhov, however, might there not be a danger of reducing Gerhardie to a Chekhovian clone, to a mere anonymous construction of his early milieu, in which Chekhovianism was such a pervasive force? Might it not make him a social being who is *not* also, to use my term, a social individual? How does it square with the literature lover's sense of a significant author's unmistakable uniqueness?

Well, how would Gerhardie himself reply? On the one hand, his Romantic view of the original artist as a genius who produces one-offs, a view not out of key with Modernist dogma either, is at times interestingly qualified. Behind any given author he is always aware of other authors hovering in the background, so many of them, indeed, that one might almost begin to think less in terms of influence than of a synthetic intertextuality. Certainly he always sees an author as part of a social milieu, with all its traditions and conventions, and his personal testimony to the impact of a St. Petersburg upbringing is frank enough. On the other hand, he still takes for granted that a genuine author does have a personal hallmark: "Barring royalties, what has any original artist, if we come to think of it, in common with another? Originality, that is all".[43] By the same token, when one author influences another, neither party will be obscured.

Gerhardie needs an inordinately long sentence to cover a decent number of his own literary debts. Yet his generous admiration is well salted:

> One hopes — and on what little ground! — that one incorporates the lucid sanity of a Bertrand Russell, without any of his liberal smugness; the bitter incisiveness of Bernard Shaw, without his sterility; the rich humanity of H.G. Wells, without his splashing-over; the analytical profundity of Proust, without his mawkish snobbism; the elemental sweep of D.H. Lawrence, without his gawky bitterness; the miraculous naturalness of Tchehov [*sic*], without that sorry echo of the consumptive's cough . . .[44]

And so on and so forth. Altogether he mentions twenty great writers who are reincarnated but improved upon in his own work, and the listing is quintessentially Gerhardie in combining the self-mocking boast with an element of sober reasonableness. While acknowledging his predecessors, he will still be himself. And his predecessors, although critically filtered and creatively intermixed in his own sensibility, will somehow still be "there", and recognizable. Viewed in this light, a writer's genius is certainly not a matter of pure individuality. But if what Gerhardie is talking about is intertextuality, it is not intertextuality as envisaged by the most rigidly de-personalizing kind of linguistic and cultural determinism. His reasons for including Chekhov in the list of admired yet transmuted precursors were intimately personal. The relationship, albeit between two social beings, was one in which individual characteristics were very strongly involved. Ultimately, it was an affinity of temperament.

Ironically enough, even a temperamental trait can be more fashionable in one milieu than another, so that it may actually seem less personal. In the England of Addison and Steele, for instance, there was a collectively scripted identity which included the quality of being witty, whereas "a wit" today would be something of an oddity.[45] Similarly, the traits shared by Chekhov and Gerhardie were perhaps more in keeping with the manners of *fin de siècle* St. Petersburg than of post-war London, which could only increase the strain on English readers' non-automatic processing of *Futility*.

Yet temperament is not the same thing as social formation, and goes deeper, even when its manifestations coincide with collective scripts. Influence, in a case like this, is a relationship between writers of a somewhat similar bent, neither of whom could ever impinge upon the other's relative autonomy, even though the junior feels confirmed and encouraged by what he finds in the senior, and grateful for what amounts to a partial revelation of his own disposition. As noted in my Introduction, Charles Taylor suggests that it is only

through exchanges with other people of a very particular kind that we learn
our own modes of expression.

> People do not acquire the languages needed for self-definition on their own.
> Rather, we are introduced to them through interaction with others who matter
> to us — what George Herbert Mead called "significant others".[46] The genesis of
> the human mind is in this sense not monological, not something each person
> accomplishes in his or her own right, but dialogical.[47]

And although Taylor does not himself put this the other way round, one certainly
can: our individuation is a social process; yet each of us does have something
potentially distinctive, which only an interchange with certain very specific significant others will bring out in us, and which will mark us off even from the
significant others themselves. The Chekhovianism of Gerhardie's writing was
not un-self-consciously mandatory, but more in the nature of a joyously impro-
vised duet with his great predecessor. It was a positively liberating self-discovery,
which was also a self-creation. He emulated Chekhov, obviously. But in some
respects he happily out-Chekhoved him, or simply went his own way. The sorry
echo of the consumptive's cough may not be the only absence noted by connoisseurs of Chekhov, and whole sides of his work are positively un-Chekhovian.
In particular, there is the increasingly salient Proustian dimension, and what I
have called Gerhardie's epicureanism, already evident in *Futility*.

It was this stance of exquisite aestheticism, in some ways so reminiscent of
Pater, Wilde and even Stephen Dedalus, which to the twentieth century's new
breed of literary scholastics would have seemed to invite a formalist analysis. In
England, such an analysis was bound to come to the conclusion that Gerhardie
was less truly a Modernist than Eliot, Pound or Joyce. Yet attempts to force him
into the most familiar paradigms of Anglo-Saxon Modernism have persisted,
sometimes in unexpected places. This present chapter has to some extent been
anticipated by two helpful articles by Randall Craig, one on Gerhardie's early
fiction in general, the other on the influence of his *Polyglots* on Evelyn Waugh's
Black Magic. In both articles Craig traces features of theme, style and technique
back to Chekhov. Some of his phrasing, though, seems calculated to natural-
ize Gerhardie as a "largely unfamiliar early *English* modernist"[48] (my italics).
Most blatantly: "Gerhardie, modern in both technique and sensibility, is . . . an
important voice in a tradition of English fiction that begins with Sterne and
leads to Beckett".[49] This claim is not substantiated by anything else in Craig's
excellent commentaries, and oddly perpetuates the misguided interpretative
impulse which Craig's own emphasis on Chekhov does so much to redress.

The fact is that Gerhardie, in going counter to the patriotic, moral and aesthetic sensitivities of the British public, was also taking up and further extending certain possibilities of tone, subject-matter, plot and theme which were most readily to be found in Chekhov. After *Futility* and *Anton Chehov*, for the few who had ears to hear he was *the* English Chekhov, and the more they recognized this the more they understood him. That Chekhov is nowadays much more widely known means that there has already been a rapprochement between Gerhardie's context of writing and his potential new readers' contexts of reading. As he moves on through his second century, he should be less of a conundrum. Readers' empathy, without necessarily turning into sympathy, will be more immediate and steady, giving that much less occasion for ethnographical mediation.

CHAPTER 2

Andrew Young's poetic secretion

As with Gerhardie's novels, so with the poetry of Andrew Young, a mediating critic can try to encourage readers to empathize by means of literary–historical and biographical considerations. Indeed, a particular emphasis will have to fall on the ways in which the literary and the biographical are, in Young's case, interwoven. This is not to suggest that his poetry is actually *auto*biography. Nor is it to deny that a fair amount of it can be interpreted along the lines of a de-humanizing Modernist formalism. On the contrary, during his late-middle phase he seems to have responded to reviewers' approval of what they saw as his work's aestheticizing impersonality by writing verse which certainly does aim at it. For what is arguably his finest poetry, however, such a reading over-looks the literary tradition within which he was writing and expecting to be read. Under the inspiration of Hardy and Edward Thomas, as also of certain earlier poets, many of his poems seek to transfer his own emotional states to the heart of the reader. This disregard of early Modernist orthodoxy may even bring to mind the solitary labours of Christopher Wood. As Sebastian Faulks has pointed out, Wood's paintings were distinctive precisely because of his interest in human figures:

> He was the only serious English painter between the two wars who continued to believe that a picture could deal with the lives of people. The dogmatic concerns of modern art as it developed in England ruled out the appearance of human beings at all, unless in some non-representational way, a mere occupation of the picture space, like a pipe-cleaner in a Cubist collage.[1]

Young's appearances within his own writing, similarly, are self-representational. They are not a mere occupation of poetic space.

So what did he actually write? Ten years older than Gerhardie, he published his first slim volume, *Songs of Night*, in 1911.[2] In 1918 there followed some "Memorial Verses" on the death of a college friend, Cecil Barclay Simpson, in the trenches of France.[3] Between 1920 and 1923 there were four small books of poems, together with some verse drama on Old Testament themes,[4] and between 1926 and 1931 three further slim volumes of poems, published by the London firm of J. and E. Bumpus: *The Bird-Cage* (1926), *The Cuckoo Clock*

(1930) and *The New Shepherd* (1931). With the Bumpus books Young began
to attract some attention, but his real breakthrough came with *Winter Harvest,*
published by the Nonesuch Press in 1933. The reputation this brought him as a
writer of short nature poems was consolidated with *The White Blackbird* (1935),
Collected Poems (1936), *Speak to the Earth* (1939) and *The Green Man* (1947).[5]
His *Nicodemus* was also well received, a mystery play with incidental music by
Imogen Holst, broadcast by the BBC and published in 1937.[6] No new nature
poems seem to have been written after 1947, but by 1945 he had already turned
to prose, with a book expressing his knowledge and love of wild flowers, *A Prospect of Flowers,* followed by *A Retrospect of Flowers* in 1950.[7] In 1956 came a
topographical book, *A Prospect of Britain;*[8] in 1962 a study of a number of writers in relation to natural environment, *The Poet and the Landscape;*[9] and in
1967 a collection of miniaturistic topographical pieces, *The New Poly-Olbion.*[10]
As for his later poetry, the new turn he had taken became evident in *Into Hades*
and *A Traveller in Time,* the former first published in 1952,[11] and then revised
for publication with the latter under the joint title of *Out of the World and Back*
in 1958.[12] These two poems, roughly 1,600 lines in all, are metaphysical narratives with roots in Dante and the mystics. His last book, again prose, expatiates
on the life of Jesus: *The Poetic Jesus* (1972), published a few months after his
death.[13] By that time there had also been two further collected editions (1950
and 1960)[14] and two selections (1959 and 1967).[15]

　　Among the tributes he received were an honorary doctorate from Edinburgh University in 1951, the Queen's Gold Medal for Poetry in 1952, and a
collection of complimentary essays, *Andrew Young: Prospect of A Poet,* edited
by Leonard Clark in 1957.[16] *A Traveller in Time* was reprinted in its entirety
in David Wright's *Longer Contemporary Poems* (1966),[17] and some of his short
poems became regular anthology pieces, as for instance in George Macbeth's
Poetry 1900 to 1965 (1967),[18] where he stood alongside Yeats, Lawrence, Muir,
Eliot, Owen, Graves, Betjeman, Empson, Auden, MacNeice, Roy Fuller, Stevie
Smith, R. S. Thomas, Dylan Thomas, Douglas, Larkin, Davie, Middleton, Gunn,
Porter, Hughes and Plath. Leonard Clark edited *Complete Poems: Andrew
Young* in 1974.[19] My own *Trespassing Ghost: A Critical Study of Andrew Young*
appeared in 1978.[20] And *Andrew Young: The Poetical Works,* edited by Edward
Lowbury and Alison Young, marked the centenary in 1985.[21]

　　Like Gerhardie's, then, Young's reputation has been respectable, although
Larkin, in a friendly enough review, doubted that *The Poetical Works* would
bring him new readers.[22] Since that time, he will have lost a good many by natural causes.

If he is beginning to drop out of sight, another reason must be that critics had been uncertain what to say about him in the first place. It would have helped, for instance, if they had known what Young himself thought about literature. Gerhardie may have published *Anton Chehov: A Critical Study* a little too late for his own good. But Young's comments on the literary past did not come until *The Poet and the Landscape* (published four years after his last poem) and *The Poetic Jesus* (posthumous).

No less unfortunate was the dearth of biographical information about him, which meant that readers already persuaded by the Modernist dogma of poetic impersonality were even less likely to catch his distinctive voice. Only in *A Prospect of Flowers* and the first version of *Into Hades* did he begin to record some personal reminiscences. "Early Days", a more extended autobiographical sketch which he tacked on to *The New Poly-Olbion*, told no more than its title promised, and was amusedly self-depreciating at that. As for third-person accounts, up until very recently the only ones worth mentioning have been a contribution to *Prospect of a Poet* from John Baillie, a contemporary at New College, Edinburgh, and a few pages by Alison Young and Edward Lowbury, his daughter and son-in-law, in their introduction to the posthumous *Poetical Works*. These can now be supplemented by a sketch in Lowbury's *Hallmarks of Poetry: Reflections on a Theme*,[23] and by Alison Young and Lowbury's full-length biography.[24]

For good measure, Young's development as a poet was effectively obscured by the way his poems came before the public. In *Trespassing Ghost* I reported on my bibliographical and textual research, which enabled me to separate his work into its different phases. In particular, there is the early-middle period from 1926 to roughly 1931, i.e. the period of the three Bumpus books, each of which can to some extent be further distinguished from the other two. And there is the late-middle period, from roughly 1933 to 1947, i.e. the period from *Winter Harvest* to *The Green Man*, during which he wrote a total of 186 new poems which, when read in order of composition, show a clear ongoing development. Early readers could not see this because the collections of the late-middle period, the books by which he became known to a wider audience, also contained a large number of poems brought forward, in random order and sometimes with little revision, from all three Bumpus books.[25] As a result, the overall impression they each gave was potentially confusing.

What with one thing and another, the reviewers were all at sea. Things came to a head with the publication of *Into Hades* and *A Traveller in Time*, at which point the *Times Literary Supplement* hazzarded the opinion that Young had produced the only impressive long poem since *Four Quartets*, but with the reservation that these poetic narratives "do not, yet, allow themselves to be 'placed'".[26] Throughout Young's career, notices and reviews had always revealed less about the particular volume under consideration than about the twists and turns of fashionable taste.

∽

So to go back to 1922, the year of *The Waste Land* and the complete *Ulysses*, the year, too, of Gerhardie's *Futility*, which in Wells's view was not enough shouted about, what was being shouted about Young?[27] Nothing much at all. Certainly nothing to distinguish him from innumerable poetasters. Eleven years earlier *Songs of Night*, published with generous financial assistance from his father, had been congratulated on "a perpetual dust of melancholy", "a twilight beauty and glamour",[28] a note of "aesthetic mysticism — expressed in stanzas of much taste",[29] all of which signalled that its late romanticism was as forgettable as any other effusion from the vanity press. Nobody was likely to catch the hint of a small Vaughan-like poem, "The Leaf", that some other mode might one day suit its author better. A few years later, the elegy on the death Cecil Barclay Simpson, part of a memorial volume published by private subscription, had been just as inconspicuous. It did have a rather interesting beginning and ending: a kind of framing narrative expressing spiritual discomfort by means of "psychologized" natural description, a feature to recur in Young's best work. But even this succumbed to the neo-Georgian taste for moonlight, and the main body of the poem was a solid mass of sincerely meant cliché — idealizing, patriotic, consolatory. As for *Thirty-One Poems*, Young's own contribution to the Modernist *annus mirabilis*, it received few notices, and their praise of the volume's Georgian features was already old-fashioned in its own phrasing.

> Mr. Young's little book . . . distinctly sets before us the antic shapes, the smells and dyes of country places. Mr. Young has a pleasant, congenial way of bringing us upon these good things unawares, as though we took a path heedless where, and found at many a turn a new enjoyment.[30]

Young himself may have taken little exception to this. Both in published and unpublished writing of this period, he was positively trying to develop a jovial Georgian persona, and did so again in his late prose books of botanophilia and topography. As a public relations exercise, it continued to be partly successful. The *Times Literary Supplement* saw fit to recommend the *Collected Poems* of 1950 to readers who were perplexed by the poetry of the present while loving the poetry of the past. Here was a poet who was a country clergyman, an expert on wild flowers, a great walker, an acute and humorous observer, and a writer of exquisite short poems in which all these aspects of his life are reflected. . . . It would be hard to find a more delightful Christmas present.[31]

No less conservative had been the same journal's remarks on the "pure poetry" of *Nicodemus*, and on Imogen Holst's incidental music: this was suitably melodious and diatonic, truly English in flavour, and suggestive of folk carol.[32] Even after his death, Young was often still thought of as basically a clergyman-cum-Georgian, sometimes inspired by a simple Christian faith, or by intimations of a love which irradiates the whole of creation.[33]

This type of commentary, though it trivialized his best work, did grasp some important points. Above all, it was not entirely deaf to the personal vibration in many poems, even if it made them sound too uniformly cheerful. One of its limitations was in not registering other, equally important emotional states. By contrast, one of the two main schools of critics trying to make Young sound more modern did this by crediting him with feelings much less pleasant. According to Norman Nicholson, when Young contemplated the world of nature he was actually a modern man facing a lost and uncomprehended inheritance. He was nothing less than a stranger to nature, since nature was no longer, as it had been to Cowper and the young Clare, "the normal, living environment of an age. It . . . [was] a place for holidays, for afternoon walks, a place to be visited, a thing to be looked at".[34] For Nicholson, one might say, nature in Young was much the same as it was in the sharply urban poetry of Auden, Spender, MacNeice and Day Lewis, a view which, as it happens, tells us less about Young's poetry than about Nicholson's own. Young's distance from nature is real enough, but is less the result of his modernity than of his humanity, of the human being's sheer existential otherness, something which Cowper and Clare, the Clare of the "I am" poems or "An invite to eternity", had also felt. In Young, moreover, the existential loneliness is sometimes compounded by a sense of loss, bitterness or separation in human relations, or by a yearning for some otherworldly kind of mystic union. Geoffrey Grigson's review of *The Poet and the Landscape* was more accurate, therefore, since he could see through the remaining traces of Georgian blitheness to a more profound disturbance. Grigson's reading, a good example of the Modernist gloom to be explored in Part III below, made Young as intensely tormented as John Berryman, Robert Lowell, Anne Sexton or Sylvia Plath, the so-called confessional poets anthologized in Al Alvarez's *The New Poetry* of the same year (1962). Young's poetry, he said, was "most uncomfortably aware of negation, farce, blankness, pain, end, and hopelessness."[35] Nor was he far wrong about this, except that Young's confessions are never quite so importunately open as those in *The New Poetry*, and his bleakness does alternate with moments of hope, and even of radiant vision, however fleeting.

Despite the huge difference between Young as an anguished and disturbing modern and Young as a bouncy Georgian clergyman, both these lines of commentary, in registering an emotional pulse in his work, overemphasized his passivity, as if he were completely at his various emotions' mercy. There was not much talk of active intellectuality or artistic creativity. For this, though, we need only turn to the other main school of modernizing commentary, which reflected the shift in taste stemming from Pound, the Imagists, T. E. Hulme, and Eliot, and which consequently underemphasized Young's feelings and personality. His three Bumpus books were discussed from this point of view, and were actually blamed for still meeting slightly dated requirements: they were found to reveal a love of beauty, and a heart which was tender at the wonder and grace of nature. Just as often, though, the same books were praised for being altogether more self-effacing, impersonal and objective. Young did not moralize nature or cloud her with "alien human emotions",[36] and natural phenomena functioned as his objective correlatives: feeling was "purely crystallized in the object or the incident".[37] He made no concessions to the reader, and there was

> no sustained feat of poetry, but only those brief incidents and accidents of poetic thought that are like the mere examples a mind gives of itself. And brief thought is whittled down to briefer words.[38]

These observations occurred in a review by Alice Meynell, a poet and close friend of Young's who, after some initial reservations of her own about Modernist impersonality,[39] may have persuaded him to aim even more deliberately at tight objectivity and self-withdrawal. In his late–middle period, both the new poems and the revisions of early-middle poems do invite this kind of praise. He avoided the "mist of personal feeling"[40] and "the heart's romantic eloquence".[41] With his "pellucid quietism"[42] and utter lack of ostentation, he simply *became* the thing he saw.[43] Rather than offering gusts of lyricism, his was often "a metaphysical poetry full of wit and intellectual conceits; a poetry very far removed from the nature-notes of his Georgian contemporaries" and recalling Donne, Herbert and Marvell.[44] His wit was said to fuel a superlative artistry, whose aims were far from straightforwardly mimetic. He did not merely re-create an experience of the world of nature. Natural images combined with language to form an aesthetic heterocosm. As George Rostrevor Hamilton put it,

The result is marvellously close to nature: not, however, as a reproduction of the scene, but as a shining analogy, in which scene and word cannot now be parted, any more than nature and art.[45]

"Andrew Young", said Ted Walker, "is a master-craftsman — a poet's poet",[46] just as Gerhardie has tended to be thought of as a novelist's novelist.

And as in Gerhardie, so in Young, there is certainly a strain of art for art's sake. This is one of the features to which we can be sensitized by biographical knowledge, for as a young man the pose of *fin de siècle* aesthete seems to have suited him. Enchanted by the music of Swinburne, he also knew his Dowson, and John Baillie remembers him devouring "many yellow-backed French poets" as well. Trying his hand at Paterian prose, he generally aspired to an exquisite life of the senses. Baillie tells of his

> ecstasy over an unusually brilliant patch of the common germander speedwell, and on another occasion his mouthing of the phrase, "blue scabious against the grey of the rocks". And there still rings in my ears his excited cry of "Oh, the colour, the colour!" as he emerged from a dive in the sea.

Having keenly participated in a Fine Arts class in Edinburgh, he won a scholarship which, supplemented by his ever-supportive father, allowed him to spend half a year in the Latin Quarter of Paris. There he studied art and church architecture, became friendly with the Beardsleyan artist and poet W. W. Peploe and his brother, the more famous artist S. J. Peploe, and attended five performances of Richard Strauss's *Salome*, with its libretto based on Wilde. When he later settled down (though not altogether!) as a married man and Presbyterian minister in Midlothian, the Manse was

> a carefully considered harmony of form and colour, the old Sheraton or Hepplewhite furniture blending admirably with the blue-and-white [French and English] china, the rugs, the hangings and the wallpapers.[47]

In point of fact, the minister had thoughts about ecclesiastical architecture south of the border, and Anglican churches were the more attractive because of the ritual practised in them. "I even cast my eye on rich vestments".[48]

This kind of sensibility, which also warmed to Keats, Tennyson, Rossetti, the Pre-Raphaelites, is what reviewers were responding to in *Songs of Night* and in his early verse drama on Old Testament themes. There are throwbacks to it in some much later work as well. Even if sometimes qualified by grimmer intuitions, Paterian ecstasy never ceased to be one of his modes of response to nature, and the miniaturistic topographical pieces of *The New Poly-Olbion* must partly represent the same ambitions as his lost Paterian apprentice work. There is also his last poem, *A Traveller in Time*, which wings its way from one exotic blotch of local colour to the next: from luxuriant vice in Baal's temple; to Jerusalem by moonlight; to white statues and dark cypresses before the hall of mysteries in Eleusis, also by moonlight; to the riotous procession of the worshippers of Iacchos; to Shechem, set on a hill, belted in by its wall, corn-cutters in the foreground; and to the dazzling splendour of a mediaeval tiltyard, with plenty of Puginism thrown in for atmosphere — stained glass windows peopled by martyrs and saints, and "columns, / Sprouting gilt foliage from the capitals".[49]

Here Pre-Raphaelitism is moving towards the genres of popular historical fiction and Hollywood epic. And why not? After all, the same accessible pictorialism is also on display in *Into Hades*. There, though, it is subordinated to a very powerful design, and the writing is simply much tighter. The revision carried out between the 1952 and 1958 versions paid rich dividends.

But it was in the late-middle period that aestheticism had first come under control. This is where Young seems to respond to reviewers espousing Modernist minimalism, impersonality and intellectuality, for here we meet Young the wizard. Metaphor becomes legerdemain, and the *raison d'être* of natural description is neither mimesis nor pathetic fallacy but witty metamorphosis. Nature is suddenly preternatural. "Stones were seen / To change to hares and rise and run".[50] Swans become lovely "high proud galleons" in "water that is mostly sky".[51] Or, in an extended conceit which is at once fantastic and hyperrealistic, a dead crab has been a "living armoury".

THE DEAD CRAB

> A rosy shield upon his back,
> That not the hardest storm could crack,
> From whose sharp edge projected out
> The long black eyes staring about;
> Beneath, the well-knit cote-armure
> That gave to its weak belly power;
> The clustered legs with plated joints
> That ended in stiletto points;
> The claws like mouths it held outside:-
> I cannot think this creature died
> By storm or fish or sea-fowl harmed
> Walking the sea so heavily armed;
> Or does it make for death to be
> Oneself a living armoury?[52]

In writing such as this, potentially disturbing questions are not exactly taboo. Did the crab's armoury actually allow him to die? Early and late, death is always close at hand in Young. Yet here the theme is little more than patter, something on which to launch the conjuring trick, and much of the effect actually hangs on the versification, which, unlike that of the early-middle period, seldom allows a stanzaic pattern to set in. Instead, a poem will consist of just a single short verse paragraph, sometimes with rhymes placed unpredictably, and some-times with variable line lengths. On the one hand, our ear never knows quite what to expect and is frequently slightly surprised. On the other hand, we also have the sense of something very deliberate being accomplished. The rhymes are strong rhymes, and can even occur in a sequence of regular octosyllabic couplets, so that "The Dead Crab" is actually a parody of a seventeenth-century epitaph. Absolute naturalness and absolute control are the order of the day. The magician's style *par excellence.*

Put another way, the poem does not mean, but is. The dogma of Modernist formalism is vindicated. In his early-middle phase, Young had conceived of two separate worlds, a world of nature and a world of man, but had tried to relate them to each other in ways that were humanly meaningful and affecting. In these late-middle poems, by contrast, the sheer divide between the human and the natural is oddly emphasized. The poem's persona is no longer an individual with personal joys and sorrows, but just a "we" or a representative everyman, who is first and foremost the denizen of an element completely different from that of the animals. A missel-thrush

> . . . from his bough
> As in deep water he looks through
> . . . sees me there
> Crawl at the bottom of the air.[53]

A "[s]trong-shouldered mole" lives very much "below the ground":

> What wonder now that being dead
> Your body lies here stout and square
> Buried within the blue vault of the air?[54]

The topsy-turvy transpositions and conceits work in two different dimensions at once: the animal's similarity with human beings is curious, and noted for the first time; but the wit always depends on a tiny sting of surprise, in being slightly far-fetched. The charting of tenuous animal-human parallels is also the recognition of intransigent difference. The crab, like a human being, may die, and a human being, like a crab, may be seemingly well protected against death. But there is about the crab an intense quiddity, a mindless self-containedness, which would be repellent if it were not so fascinating. Nature, in witty reflexive constructions reminiscent of Marvell, is figured as a wonderfully closed system that fends for itself — with "[e]ach glow-worm her own Venus in the night", or snails which have "crawled alive to their own funeral".[55] Such pathetic fallacies draw attention to their own artificiality, having no truth beyond the page. What springs from the gap between the human and the natural is precisely that third, equally autotelic system: the poem itself, which is a moulding of nature's oddities into aesthetic wonders of Young's own. The animals, plants and landscapes become part of a new totality, like stones polished and set in gold. To return to George Rostrevor Hamilton's phrasing, Young does not simply recreate his and our experience of the outside world. He is a maker, and we share his relish in what he has himself created, a richly intellectual pleasure.

Yet for the Young who wrote *The Poet and the Landscape*, Hamilton's commentary might jar somewhat. When he himself discusses writers and their relationship with nature, he is not a Modernist aesthete. He does say that Vaughan's eye was "pensive; he thought through his senses",[56] a formulation reminiscent of Eliot on Donne. He also says that Milton "was writing with his ear rather than with his eye",[57] a complaint which may seem to echo Leavis. But he documents his case in his own way, and his true models as a critic are the enthusiastic Saintsbury, who had taught him at Edinburgh, and Housman, who argued that poetry is experienced by poet and reader alike as something almost primitively physiological. For the poet, said Housman, a poem is like an intensely personal secretion, either "a natural secretion, like turpentine in the fir, or a morbid secretion, like the pearl in the oyster."[58] For the reader, it sends shivers down the spine, tightens the throat, brings tears to the eyes, pierces like a spear. Young quotes Housman on Milton's line, "Nymphs and shepherds, dance no more" —

> . . . what is it that can draw tears, as I know it can, to the eyes of more readers than one? What in the world is there to cry about?[59]

— and concludes, in the spirit of Housman, that it must be more to do with the sound than the sense. His observation about Milton writing with his ear was not altogether a complaint:

> Nature, usually regarded as feminine, is to be admired by poets rather than investigated, and Milton *sings* her charms.[60]

Young's criticism is no less old-fashioned when it gets down to technical-
ities. Smooth, mellifluous lines are better than rough or "strong" lines. Eras-
mus Darwin was not necessarily well advised to compose "verse that ran more
sweetly than Pope's; it almost ran off the page". But Waller's "smoothness of
verse helps wit, making strange things seem credible", whereas Wyatt, in his son-
nets, only stutters.[61]

We should be careful, too, in relating Young to that line of critical thought,
leading through Wordsworth and the Imagists and beyond, which values physical concreteness in writing. Although Young likes what he calls objective and
descriptive poetry, for him this entails real knowledge of nature, the seasons,
and geography. His quibble with Milton is actually that,

> whether the Pastorals were written at Horton or not, its country cannot claim
> to be their scene; as they describe no particular season, the Plowman whist-
> ling, the Mower whetting his scythe and Thestylis binding the sheaves, all
> on one day, so they describe no particular locality, for none would include a
> mountain, a castle, a cathedral and a wide-water'd shore.[62]

Of course account must be taken of Milton's poor sight. But Milton even *hears*
things at the wrong time. Leavis's criticism of Milton, one might say, is sophisticated, literary, Modernist. Leavis comes to Milton from other literary texts
and confines himself largely to versification and language. If these exhibit a
"Shakespearian life", then "the total effect is as if words as words withdrew themselves from the focus of our attention and we were directly aware of a tissue
of feelings and perceptions",[63] and Leavis never lifts his eye from the page to
see whether the perceptions are accurate. Young does, always. Though coming
partly to the same conclusion as Leavis, he is a mimetic critic of unashamed
naivety, stubbornly irrefutable on his own terms.

Then there is the question of anthropomorphism and pathetic fallacy.
Here, too, some of Young's comments have a modern ring which other comments considerably qualify. On the one hand, this is an issue on which an
Imagist would often agree with Wordsworth, and Young with both. Tennyson,
despite his excellent notebooks of natural observation, overdoes, in Young's
view, nature's cruelty; Cowper falls below himself in describing a rill as a little
naiad weeping "her impoverish'd urn/All summer long"; and Burns is blinded
by city tastes into making nature secondary, "the background to an affecting
scene":

> Ayr, gurgling, kiss'd his pebbled shore,
> O'erhung with wild-woods, thickening green;

> The fragrant birch and hawthorn hoar,
> Twin'd amorous round the raptur'd scene.

Young's praise and blame at such points are in the spirit of the Preface to the *Lyrical Ballads*:

> As a condensed description of trees putting out their leaves "thickening green" could not be bettered, but "amorous" and "raptured" show the wood is there less for its own sake than for its sentimental value.[64]

On the other hand, sentimentality may be no bad thing. One of Young's kindred spirits is another country clergyman, Gilbert White, who although he was un-Miltonic enough to teach people "to look with their eyes, not with their ears", was nevertheless "communicative of himself". His "botanical studies did not include flowers of speech". But his book certainly "is an autobiography, all the better for not being one",[65] a remark which echoes W. H. Hudson's description of himself as "writing of myself *à propos* English birds".[66] Although White wrote with the accomplished ease of an eighteenth century gentleman, his life vividly illustrates the transition to a new sensibility to which Young, with support from Emily Dickinson, declares continuing allegiance:

> We gather that latterly [White] ... gave up the gun, calling the birds "little sisters". He may also have given up asking his friends to procure him specimens, realising that his acquaintance with his little sisters did not become more intimate by examining the contents of their stomachs. He had come to share the new and more sentimental approach to Nature of his time. For the sentiment was not confined to poets; the philosopher Kant, having held a swallow in his hand and looked into its eyes, said, "As I gazed, it was as if I had seen into heaven". Sentimental is not nowadays a popular word except in a poor sense, yet any approach to Nature that is without feeling is a going farther away;
> > The ones that cite her most
> > Have never passed her haunted house,
> > Nor simplified her ghost.
> There can be no purely factual interest in birds, for the subject of interest would not be — *birds*. Nor can there be a collection of *butterflies*.[67]

Knowing when and how to be sentimental is a matter of taste, and is closely related to control of wit, a subject on which Young's remarks are again Janus-faced. No less than Eliot or Leavis, he is enthusiastic about the Metaphysicals, his warmest response being to Vaughan and Marvell. He values Vaughan for his "unusual glimpses" of the Usk, "as when we see it in winter 'slowly float / All bound up in an Icie Coat'". Vaughan "appears to mention, rather than assert, surprising things" — "stones ... deep in admiration", for instance — and he offers "quick transitions of mood, the sunlit valley darkened by a sudden cloud-shadow, the poet, his head crowned with roses, meeting with a dead man".[68] The Young of *Nicodemus*, *Into Hades* or a shorter poem such as "The Wet Day" *would* value such things, for they clearly loosened his own tongue. As for Marvell, his grasshoppers laughing at the men who look like grasshoppers in the abyss of "unfathomable grass", his "Turn me but, and you shall see/I was but an inverted tree", his soul which casts the body's vest aside to glide into the boughs, his woodbines which bind and lace him in, are all singled out for praise,[69] and are all creatively imitated in some of Young's own poems.[70] Yet when Young writes on Donne, there are shades of Johnson on Cowley —

> *The Primrose, being at Montgomery Castle, upon the hill* might be called a flower-study, having, in fact, a somewhat studied look.[71]

— and even Marvell and Vaughan are wanting. Marvell "is not a descriptive poet", and "his habit is to do natural objects the discredit of regarding them as artificial; woodland trees are "the Columnes of a Temple green", and a wood near a flooded meadow "a green, yet growing Ark"".[72] Vaughan's poems tend to fall away after a magnificent opening, perhaps because, as a Welshman, he did not "aim at organic progression in the English mode".[73] Wit, then, should not to be allowed to the exclusion of accuracy or overall structure.

All this represents criteria according to which the delightful but short-winded artificiality of Young's own late-middle wit — in "The Dead Crab", for instance — would not count as poetry at its finest. By the time of *The Poet and the Landscape*, he clearly feels that wit should not be indulged for its own sake. Vaughan's most poignant poetry is that in which he laments the passing of the "auroral vision" of childhood.[74] To Marvell, despite his not being "descriptive", "Nature in a way meant more . . . than to many Nature poets": it offered peace and sheltered seclusion from his nation's trouble.[75]

Young's criticism expresses a strong sense that the best nature poetry penetrates not only the heart of nature but the human heart as well. Nature poets write about themselves *à propos* nature, as Hudson might have remarked. Though Young never says it in so many words, the finest nature poetry has an almost religious quality for him, in that it implies and celebrates the most piercingly vivid aspects of being alive in the world. Accordingly, it is the religious impulse which he most reveres in certain predecessors. For Christopher Smart, "'apples of ten thousand tribes,/And quick peculiar quince' were created for one purpose, ADORATION. So, too, was the little bibulous man, Kit Smart".[76] True, Smart's simplistic ecstasy was not in itself enough to produce poetry. Control

— by all means witty control — there has to be, and Young even says that in Smart's case it may even have been *physical* confinement which, though a form of religious persecution, brought forth *A Song of David*. Yet without the ecstasy and its dark antithesis, there would have been nothing to bring forth in the first place.

Given all of which, we can hazzard a guess that Young ultimately came to prefer, of his own work, the more expressive poetry of the early-middle years and of *Into Hades*. Even more to the point here, his somewhat old-fashioned comments on earlier writers can open our ears to that expressivity as it really is. Both the blithely Georgianizing reviewers and the more gloomily Modernist Grigson were partly right about it, while devotees of Modernist impersonality tended to miss it altogether.

Young's implied reader, in other words, is often no different from that of many nineteenth century poets, or from that of his admired Hardy and Edward Thomas: a reader who, like Housman, catches the expressive vibration, somebody on whom the poetry's joyful or sorrowful music may actually have a physiological impact. Even in the absence of autobiographical chapter and verse, even when the writing is a secretion in the sense of using nature as an objective correlative which *conceals* the underlying source of personal feeling, this reader will take it as a secretion in the other sense as well: as a perceptible emanation from an intense spiritual life. Young's poetic secretion is in fact an impersonality that is personal. To say this is not to read the poems as an allegory of the life in the way despised by Roland Barthes.[77] The commentary to follow here will doubtless provide a stimulus to such a reading, which is actually quite feasible and justifiable; it would become despicable only by lapsing into unsympathetic prurience and/or by forcing the texts. Yet the aim will merely be to counteract a forcing of the Modernist or Barthesian varieties, which would tend to remove Young from his writing altogether.

When New Critical scholastics claimed there could be no link between the implied author of a poem and its real author, they were misrepresenting communicative pragmatics. In communication of all kinds, implied sender- and receiver personae function as the slotting-in points for the parties concerned, who by an act of imaginative self-projection shape themselves accordingly, at least for the duration of the communication.[78] Over the centuries there have obviously been countless poems whose author persona is not the vehicle for direct self-expression — perhaps "The Dead Crab", for instance, though that poem's particular brand of "grave" humour could only be Young's. There have also been numerous poems in which the "I" seems fictional or ironic. These kinds of poem we do not read as self-expressive in any very simple way. But given the flexibility of the human psyche, even here the persona is likely to have at least *some* sort of relationship with the writer who, after all, produced it. For many other poems, including some of the best of Andrew Young's, the slightest implication that their "I" is somehow not an aspect of the author is a travesty. Which is not the same as saying that we should recognize the author on the street, since there may well be other aspects to the personality as well. Despite continuities of temperamental, imaginative and moral autonomy, the social individual can be fairly chameleonic.

ᘉ

So much for mediation by way of literary–historical re-contextualization, at least for the time being. But if this alone begins to suggest that there will be a personal note to listen for in Young, further biographical considerations can tune our ears more sharply, and still without *reducing* the poetry to biography.

Take, for instance, a short personal anecdote in *A Prospect of Flowers*:

> [I]n Wild Roses,
>> Which in a blush their lives consume,
>
> no less than in longer-lived garden Roses, we may read something more than the fleetingness of time. As a child I read it first in a garden Rose. It was on the day I recovered my sight, having long lain blind with erysipelas, a disease sometimes called the rose; my father, returning from business, brought it as though to say,
>> My love is like a red, red rose.
>
> It was my first revelation of those eternal things, beauty and love.[79]

The style of this seems dated and precious now. But when read in the context of Young's entire life and work, the little story is like a signature tune. Seeing, the act and continuous experience of seeing, is crucial for him. As a poet, nothing exists for him until he has established it by a witty act of re-visualization, and he himself exists only in relation to a perceived world. Seeing can occasion aesthetic rapture, and in more mystical moments can pierce through the world of physical matter to apprehend a world of spirit. Especially in *Nicodemus*, seeing becomes an explicit theme, and the keenness of this concern is no doubt partly attributable to the childhood experience of the loss and restoration of vision.

In the telling of that episode, however, he also tells us more, by clearly associating the happy ending with his father. It was his father who gave him the rose that made his sight active for the first time, just as the same father later encouraged his aestheticism, helping him to publish *Songs of Night* and to travel to Paris as an art student. His father smoothed his path to beauty, and beauty and love inhere not only in the rose itself but in the giving of it. Burns helps him read the silent declaration.

Somewhat similarly, it was his mother who aroused his poet's passion for words. In her case, the loving gesture was to buy him the four large volumes of the Imperial Dictionary at an auction sale. Yet partly because of his parents' generosity, Young never mentions them without a twinge of pity, regret, and self-reproach. Having said that as a child he had been obliged to play with toy-men made of newspaper, he is suddenly chided by a later memory of a real toy: ". . . after . . .[Father's] death I found in his desk a little wooden engine which I seemed to remember. He had kept it there for more than fifty years".[80] And "[t]hat I now use the Oxford English Dictionary, not the Imperial, makes me feel a little unfaithful to my mother's memory."[81] On a bleaker note, there is the memory of their deaths in the first version of *Into Hades*:

> . . . I had watched the hard, humiliating struggle,
> that made me half ashamed that I, his son,
> spied on his weakness
>
> . . . [I was] the man who came too late,
> his mother dead. She had died holding my letter,
> as though her passport to heaven.[82]

His feeling that he had let his mother down is probably the more intense because he was not the first of her sons to do so. In 1907, the family had been profoundly shaken when his elder brother David, who had gone to Singapore to work as a doctor, suddenly disappeared without a trace. According to Alison Young and Edward Lowbury, David had got involved in financial irregularities and the illegal supply of morphine, but how much of the truth was known or suspected back in Edinburgh remains unclear. At all events, the effect on Andrew was bad enough. He seems have suffered a severe mental trauma at the time, followed by life-long amnesia. He came to believe that he had spent five years at university when in fact he had spent four, and that his sister, and not David, had been the first-born. He was actually unable to remember what David looked like, and as his guide to the after-life in *A Traveller in Time* chose, not David, but William, the brother who died at the age of eight months, before he himself was born.[83] His greatest suffering, however, was clearly on account of the anxiety David's disappearance caused his parents, something which affected some of his own most important decisions. Though his father would have preferred him to become a minister of religion, he had always intended to become a lawyer. Yet as he was setting out, with the strong paternal backing, for his art studies in Paris, his

> father's parting words were, "keep your eyes open for David". So hopeless a request was deeply pathetic. Later in Paris, when a Frenchman asked about my future profession, I replied, "I mean to be a minister". I remember the incident because he looked surprised; he thought I meant a Minister of State.[84]

The more amusing memory characteristically tones down the more painful one. Yet throughout his life, the filial piety and attendant guilt feelings remained central to his mental formation. The father who had helped publish the luxuriant aestheticism of *Songs of Night*, in which "beauty" is sometimes synonymous with "sin", had a small library of his own. But it was "not so much a good collection of books as a collection of good books, such as Baxter's *Saints' Rest* and Law's *Serious Call*". For Young senior, "beauty" meant more or less the same as "chastity".[85] One consequence of such tensions was that although Young moved south to become minister to the Presbyterian church in Hove, and although he was drawn to Anglican churches and their ritual, he nevertheless

> put the idea of entering the Anglican Communion out of my mind, and I kept it out. . . . I was considering my father; he was more than a Presbyterian, an Original Seceder.[86]

It was only when Young's sister married an Anglican and became one herself that his father, by then ninety-three years old, became reconciled to the idea of his changing denomination, by which time he himself was fifty-four.

The implications of this deeply personal matter for his creative life are not difficult to see. For most of the time during which he was writing his short nature poems, he was a grateful and dutiful son, a would-be lawyer who had resigned himself to becoming a minister of religion, in a church which was not his spiritual home. His finally going over to the Anglican fold coincides with important changes in his poetry, heralded by *Nicodemus*. There is a new optimism, and he is moving towards a more expansive genre.

There had been a related inhibition in his love life. He may joke that he felt unfaithful to his mother's memory in using the Oxford English Dictionary. But in "The Flood" he says that if he seems to have fallen in love with nature, this only means that his deepest underlying love continues to be for — it can only be — his mother. The phrasing, and the way her death is mentioned, allow no other identification:

> O blue-eyed one, too well I know you will not awake,
> Who waked or lay awake so often for my sake,
> Nor would I ask our last leavetaking to retake.[87]

His love for her is like the River Adur overflowing its banks, "too full to flow along", "a drowned river" which "lies in its bed concealed". In "The Burnt Leaves" he again accuses himself of too easily forgetting his "blue-eyed one", but in "After the Funeral", keeping alive what is surely the memory of his mother's funeral, he says to himself,

> ..."Not even the Milky Way
> Shines like the golden streak of clay —
> All, all of her that I could save —
> My foot has gathered from her open grave".[88]

Here his wonder is not at beauty in Pater's sense. His attention is drawn away from the stars in "the vast hollow of space" to "the stern look on that defeated face". Even on a non-biographical reading, it is difficult not to feel that her sternness is somehow directed at the speaker, as if he had been complicit in her defeat.

Had he betrayed her, then? Such evidence as there is suggests that he had been more faithful than was good for him. As a young aesthete, he had been aware of Swinburne's injunction to change "The lilies and langours of virtue / For the roses and raptures of vice", but in Paris he resisted it. Instead, he cultivated beauty not only as Pater understood it, but in his father's sense, as chastity. Apparently he had been fascinated at least as much by John the Baptist as by Salome; in *Into Hades*, he says that he himself had been "a St. John the Baptist in the Latin Quarter".[89] More specifically, he had cultivated an entirely Platonic love affair, not with a woman of flesh and blood, but with a mysterious feminine principle of purity, a kind of nameless angel, union with whom he symbolized by placing a ring "on the third finger — of my own left hand". This "she" was a "responsive silence", present on the streets of Paris, rendering him immune to their nocturnal temptations. He could also feel her nearness on hills and in mountain mists; her voice was to be heard "in the undertone of streams"; she was

> ...the charm of the woods, my Adam's rib,
> My Muse, my shadow on the sunny side.

And although she later seems to have become more elusive, his search for her goes on, even quite without hope:

> I shall see no one there
> Though I had eyes to see the air,
> But in the waving of a bough
> Shall think I see the way she went but now.[90]

According to "In the Spinney",

> A hand touched me behind;
> I turned and lo! a bough swung on the wind.[91]

The touch was not the touch he had been hoping for, and the disappointment is important enough for him to re-write the poem as "The Secret Wood":

> What is it that I seek or who,
> Fearing from passer-by
> Intrusion of a foot or eye?
> I only know
> Though all men of earth's beauty speak
> Beauty here I do not seek
> More than I sought it on my mother's cheek.[92]

Once again, it is not a question of Paterian beauty. At such points his nature walks are rather a search for communion with his mysterious feminine principle, a principle which may have — for this is surely the implication — a maternal aspect. No less than his mother's death, his loss of his Platonic soul-mate brings on self-accusation: "I had broken my noviciate's vows, / Fallen from that envied self" who had placed the ring on his own finger.[93] Perhaps his two betrayals and his two griefs are somehow one. Perhaps his Muse, the feminine spirit of nature — "Milton *sings* her charms" — and his dead mother come together, to haunt him with the might-have-been of a long preserved virginity.

For Janet Young, née Green, just one of his female spirits would have posed a formidable challenge. She had to reckon with both of them, possibly in league. In the introduction to *The Poetical Works of Andrew Young* her daughter and son-in-law say, "Her gentle, sympathetic personality, her taste and her judgement helped and supported Young for more than fifty years".[94] This wording already suggests that she had to be patient and long-suffering, and although the same authors' *To Shirk No Idleness: A Critical Biography of the Poet Andrew Young* moves more at the level of incident than underlying desire, it provides a wealth of embarrassing detail about his quirkiness. The fact is that he came to marriage with those demanding prior attachments, aspiring to a type of fulfilment which took him off to secret woods. In his home life, he was clearly just as restless as in the Presbyterian church. Some of his excruciating pre-1925 attempts at verse confess that he has to

... go a little space from men
Until I find content;
And it may be that when I come again
No man shall know I went.[95]

In other lines from the same period the jolly Georgian says that although his wife is not with him on his countryside rambles, he thinks about her all the same, and that she is with him in the spirit. The trouble with this, though, is the writing's overdependence on *Poems of 1912–13*, which makes the woman back home sound already just as dead as Hardy's loved-one. The same thing still applies to "The Star", a rather creepy later poem: when he climbed to Hawkley, the stars were like

... blest spirits
Borne upward on a wind
And the white mist the cerements
That they had left behind;
And you, your body sleeping,
In their bright numbers moved
And with raised face I questioned,
Which is my well-beloved?[96]

In the late-middle "A Prospect of Death", on the other hand, rather than prefiguring his wife's decease, he seeks to prepare her for his own. Frankly asking her forgiveness for all his coldness and anger, he says that if he does not come down to breakfast one morning, and if she cannot wake him with a kiss, she is not to worry. "While graver business makes me stay at home", his thoughts may actually be roaming "[t]hrough woods torn by a blackbird's song". In any case,

There will be time enough
To go back to the earth I love
Some other day that week,
Perhaps to find what all my life I seek.[97]

None of which is very flattering to her. But at least it is honest. The pawky humour and apparent ungraciousness may even be a form of considerateness. Like the Edward Thomas of "No One So Much as You", he could now be a truer son of Hardy, for whom looking the worst in the face is a kind of loving-kindness, even when the worst is a difficult matter of emotional stalemate. In *Into Hades*, the truth is just as unvarnished. Finding himself (like Gerhardie in *Resurrection*, as it happens) in a state of astral projection, he actually looks down at his own funeral and notices his wife and children — "the Three" — gazing into the grave.[98] He toys with the idea of haunting the Vicarage, but decides against it. If they were unable to see his ghost, it would only make him feel more sorry for himself.

At such points our sense of what is going on can be sharpened with further literary–historical help from *The Poet and the Landscape*,[99] which pinpoints the relationship with another predecessor: John Clare. Young's comments and choice of quotations can alert us to an influence that is as deep and insistent as that of Chekhov for Gerhardie. Among other things, Clare has a keen wit and an eye for plants ("Daisies button into buds"), catches the characteristic flights of birds ("The crow goes flopping from wood to wood"), enters the insect world (where every leaf is a town), and loves frogs ("All along the shaven mead, / Jumping travellers they proceed"). More than this, Clare loved to ramble out of sight in the woods, and his sense of the numinous in nature was a kind of religious experience, somehow fusing with his love of poetry. For Clare, too, there was also another love. During his youth he had had "a romantic or Platonic sort of affection" for an idealized feminine being. But like Young, he married, and spent the rest of his life lamenting his lost goddess. In Clare's nature poetry, Young catches a clear echo of this.

The world of nature has to compensate for Young's own sense of loss. Even at its harshest, nature is not necessarily inimical. Man and boy, his mountaineering always brought him close to death, but perhaps that is why he went in for it in the first place. His life-long relish for the macabre drew him to any and every form of *memento mori*, but sometimes less as a caution than as a promise. In *Into Hades* he recognizes his own body by "a white scar on my wrist". Nothing more is said about it, but he had personal problems, by no means silenced in the same poem, which were quite deep enough to make a sufferer long for release. Death might indeed bring him "what all my life I seek". In "Walking on the Cliff" he is "arm in arm with death", but "safe as a lover".[100] Though saved from falling over the edge by noticing a gull drop down "to soar beneath", he too would only have soared — "[f]arther than any wondering star has gone", as "On Middleton Edge" puts it, imagining another avoided fall.[101] In "Morning in the Combe", the downward pull of the mud is again the pull of death in all its amorous closeness.

From just as early an age, Young's experiences of nature could also be visionary. The world around him lost its material look:

> Objects of themselves
> Melted away to their own images,
> An insubstantial world.
>
> . . .

[A]ll was visionary
And I was in a waking dream.[102]

It was by thinking about his own memories, rather than by reading Berkeley, that he became a Berkeleian, and by the time he was a student he was already countering modern German theologians with his beloved mystics — their "flights, illuminations and visions of God in a point".[103] In *The Poet and the Landscape*, he inevitably turns to Wordsworth, whom he relates to Spinoza: "Each thing has a life of its own, and we are all one life".[104] Wordsworth had the wise passiveness not to murder to dissect, and Wordsworth, like Vaughan, Traherne and Blake, had "walked in an auroral vision", his boyhood days "strangely illuminated . . . by their own light, the vision splendid, . . . the fountain-light of all his days and a master-light of his seeing".[105] Young's own "Early Days", despite its self-mockery, clearly mentions the epiphanies he himself experienced as a child.

In his earliest attempts at verse, and especially in *The Adversary*, his verse play about Job, there is an unmistakable personal vibration. More specifically, there is a tension between bliss and woe. To some extent he is struggling to get a philosophical grip on it, but the stylistic echoes of Keats, the Pre-Raphaelites, Tennyson, and Swinburne render desire exotic and sensual. Some perceptive reviewers noted that his Old Testament verse drama is "a little lacking in the simplicity which the theme and period suggest".[106] *The Adversary* was said to probe "the beneficence of Providence or the omnipotence of God" in so untraditional a manner that its author "would have been wiser to create his own characters to conduct a modern debate between 'materialism' and 'idealism'".[107] His subsequent swing towards Georgianism brought him closer to landscape and simplicity, but it is a coy simplicity, and any feelings at odds with the loyal sentiments professed to wife and family were muffled by the joviality. In *Trespassing Ghost* I studied his unfortunate and largely unpublished efforts from this period in detail which does not bear repetition. He reached stylistic maturity only after an exceptionally long apprenticeship, not to Pound, the Imagists, or Eliot, writers central to the thought-world of the early literary scholastics, but to Frost, Hardy and Thomas, three poets they regarded as somewhat more marginal and a little too easily communicative, whose work Young nevertheless imitated in his early versifying, and frequently quoted in his late prose. Especially in Hardy and Thomas, he would have recognized a burden of desire and desolation somewhat similar to his own,[108] but all three of them were more concretely close to nature than Swinburne, and more austerely chaste in style and sensibility. Steering a middle course between Decadence and the Georgian "Squirearchy", they had already produced a body of poetry which in some ways resembled Young's four interesting stanzas of "psychologised" natural description in "Memorial Verses", and their influence could be readily supplemented with that of Emily Dickinson.

So it was that, in the mature work of his early-middle period, desire is usually focussed as the desire to come closer to nature. Nature is conceived as a possible source of greater comfort or release, even though such hopes are often frustrated. In one poem he watches March hares leaping and running, "Their bodies hollowed in the sun / To thin transparency" so that he could see "[t]he shallow colour of their blood / Joyous in love's full flood".[109] Such voyeurism is all there is for him, "[w]ith no more life myself than tree or bush", and sometimes even a tree or bush can make him feel inferior —

> Strength leaves the hand I lay on this beech-bole
> So great-girthed, old and high...,

— , though he does feel an affinity with a "young withered beech that keeps / Its autumn in the spring",[110] or with a tree that is *very* old:

> Even the round-faced owl
> That shakes out his long hooting
> With the moon cheek-a-jowl
> Could claw there no safe footing.
>
> Riddled by worms' small shot,
> Empty of all desire,
> It smoulders in its rot,
> A pillar of damp fire.[111]

Young's touch in all this is pretty light — modernistically impersonal, as it could easily seem. But the underlying pattern is similar to the alternation of hope and despair in Keats's "Ode to a Nightingale". His description is witty, unsentimentalized and objective, but in his own sense of these terms, which means that an affective dimension is not actually ruled out, and there can even be a kind of religious intensity. The seen and heard physicality of his owl is very different from the literariness of Gray's moping owl complaining to the moon. But to readers for whom the Modernist dogma of poetic impersonality is only a partial truth, "Empty of all desire" will readily hint the dead tree's relevance to a human predicament. His contemplation of the silvan *memento mori* is not hysterical, or is only quietly hysterical, but it makes its point, and the thrill of intellectual excitement is indistinguishable from what Housman would have called the shiver down the spine. A conceit is always a conceit. But as Young observed à propos Marvell, there can be more feeling in a conceit than we might think.[112]

A representative early-middle poem, then, is "The Ventriloquists":

THE VENTRILOQUISTS

The birds sang in the rain
That rhythmically waving its grey veil
From smoking hilltop flowed to misty plain,
Where one white house shone sharply as a sail;

But not so bright as these,
The anemones that held the wood snow-bound,
The water-drops waiting to fall from trees,
The rusty catkins crawling on the ground.

March buds give little shelter;
Better seek shelter in the open rain
Than where tree-gathered showers fall helter-skelter,
I meditated; but "Turn, turn again,"

The birds shrieked through their song;
So rooted to the leaf-soft earth I stood,
Letting my restless eye wander among
The thick sky-scrawling branches of the wood.

But no bird could I see
In criss-cross of thin twigs or sudden twists
Where branching tree interrupted branching tree;
Yet everywhere those hidden ventriloquists

Were singing in the wood,
Flinging their cheating voices here and there;
But seeing nothing though I walked or stood
I thought the singing grew out of the air.[113]

This is not about a Keatsian flight of literary imagination but a simple country walk, the descriptive accuracy characteristically enhanced by kinetic onomato-poeia — "Where branching tree interrupted branching tree". Yet the wood does also concentrate nature's appeal and resistance. Although at the literal level he is merely wondering about how to get least wet, entry into the wood could also constate his attempt to cross from humanity into something possibly less pain-ful. Unless we are positively predisposed against such a reading, "restless" is enough of a cue here. On the one hand there is the dullness outside the wood, a dullness experienced no more than visually, but a dullness inhabited, as the one house visible intimates, by human beings. On the other hand there is the preternatural brightness and unpredictability of the wood. The pull away from the dullness towards the brightness becomes as irresistible as the thought of golden pavements and the call of London's bells to Dick Whittington, an allusion which does double service: it marks the mid-way narrative turning point, his point of no re-turn; yet maintains the low key, by his self-mocking identification with a hero so crassly materialistic. In his own case there is, too, an uncertainty about the apparent promise. If he had been hoping for some kind of mystic union with the birds, it does not really happen. Still hearing but not seeing them, he is prepared to remain in a state of bemused wonder, and the last line may even have the ring of a minor epiphany. Yet for an open-minded reader, "shrieked" and "Flinging their cheating voices here and there" will again register something else as well, something analogous to Keats's disappointment with his deceiving elf of Fancy. In Young's poem the anticlimax never explicitly comes. But a reader may well ask how much longer the climax could be sustained. Why so much fuss, after all, about the English weather and a few birds? In an age not given to lush Romantic revery, Young suggests the peremptoriness of infinite desire precisely by letting us peep at his own dottiness. No less in the writing's unostentatious frankness than in the art with which it hides its art, this is a far cry from art for art's sake.

When the poems are restored to their order of composition, the differences between this early-middle work and the late-middle are fairly striking. With the tightening of the wit and the more conspicuously aesthetic appeal of many late-middle poems, there also seems to be a more robust self-confidence, a greater degree of tough-skinned human ordinariness, so that neither anguish nor hope is quite as urgent as before. When an expressive undertow does make itself felt, the sheer technical mastery tends to rein it in, even though, as Young remarked in connection with Christopher Sharp, the relationship between feeling and control can itself be interesting, and often all to the good.

"The Dunes", for example, is magnificent:

THE DUNES

These heavy hills of sand,
That marram-grasses bind

Lest they should fly off on the wind,
Hold back the sea from Sea-kings' Land.

Such a waste holds me too
From fields where shadows fly,
Wolds, woods and streams that quote the sky,
All the sweet country that is you.[114]

Biographically, the "you" could be a living but tacitly estranged wife, a dead mother, or a platonic mistress of the skies and muse of Nature. But for most readers the precise reference cannot possibly matter. What is unmistakable is the sheer weight of desire, caught in a lovely recurrence of the type of geographical and aquatic metaphor first tried in "The Flood". The poem, by its very terseness, by the sheer unexpectedness of its last word, well suggests the pent-up emotion with which he longs to flood the beautiful loved-one. The separating wasteland, so differently imaged from Eliot's, is life itself — a life of estrangement and distance, or just mere life as opposed to death — and the formal constriction is mimetic. It is a kind of stoical resignation to the emotional seizure which it also constates.

In other late-middle poems, the control is slightly less complete than this, almost as if the professed stoicism is on the point of collapsing, an effect which, intentional or otherwise, has its own fascination. Take "Passing the Graveyard":

PASSING THE GRAVEYARD

I see you did not try to save
The bouquet of white flowers I gave;
So fast they wither on your grave.

Why does it hurt the heart to think
Of that most bitter abrupt brink
Where the low-shouldered coffins sink?

These living bodies that we wear
So change by every seventh year
That in a new dress we appear;

Limbs, spongy brain and slogging heart,
No part remains the selfsame part;
Like streams they stay and still depart.

You slipped slow bodies in the past;
Then why should we be so aghast
You flung off the whole flesh at last?

Let him who loves you think instead
That like a woman who has wed
You undressed first and went to bed.[115]

The rhyme scheme of this seems natural but is very tight; in phrases such as "spongy brain and slogging heart" there is a poised balance of factuality and laconic wonder; and the cooly structured argument for consolation is well capped by the Metaphysical conceit of death as marriage-night. Yet against the grain of such serene mastery there intrudes a certain bitterness. Her death *does* hurt the heart, *does* make "us" — a euphemism for "me", perhaps? — aghast. The consolation is proposed rather than already experienced, and the language has connotations which are quietly subversive of the ostensible conclusion. She did not even try to save his bouquet. Retroactively, his flowers are almost the tribute of a rejected lover. Not to put too fine a point on it, when a man loves a woman, what comfort does he get from her marrying and going to bed with someone else?

This kind of rebellious free association is more typically excluded from late-middle work, however, and the control can almost stifle feeling altogether. As noted earlier, Young's most characteristic form during this period is a single short verse paragraph, often unpredictably rhymed but giving a sense of firm shaping purpose. The only problem is that the finely wrought miniaturism, for the visionary gleam of a poem like "Mountain View", may be too intricately witty and detached.

MOUNTAIN VIEW

Can those small hills lying below
Be mountains that some hours ago
I gazed at from beneath?
Can such intense blue be the sea's
Or that long cloud the Hebrides?
Perhaps I prayed enough
By crawling up on hands and knees
The sharp loose screes,
Sweat dripping on the lichen's scurf,
And now in answer to my prayer
A vision is laid bare;
Or on that ledge, holding my breath,
I may have even slipped past Death.[116]

It would be churlish to complain at the exquisite conceits and beauty of this, and in both theme and style the writing could only be Young's. Yet judging by the standards of his best work, one can ask whether its artistry is not achieved at the expense of a needed lyrical scope. It is almost as if a very lovely kind of stagnation is setting in. *The Green Man* (1947), the last book of nature poems, contains some very fine things, but essentially marks time.

$$\sim$$

Young did come to recognize the limitations of his later nature poems. In a prefatory note to *Out of the World and Back*, he wrote:

> When the spring of short Nature poems ran dry, I was not altogether sorry; for while my interest in Nature was intense, it was not as deep as the underlying interest that prompted me to change my style and write *Into Hades*.[117]

Even as early as "The Flood", his nature poems themselves had spoken of something underlying his love of nature. In that poem it had been his continuing love for his lost mother, of whom nature — perhaps his platonic Muse of Nature — was a kind of extension. At a higher level of generalization, we can say that in his early-middle poems he had turned to nature with a quietly religious intensity, searching for a spiritual fulfilment which materialized only fleetingly. In the late-middle nature poems, by contrast, the personal vibrations are usually under tighter control and the interest in nature more delightedly aesthetic. In a poem such as "The Dunes", the pathos and anguish of the "underlying interest" is still unabated, and indeed is highlighted by the aesthetic control. But taking his work of the mid-nineteen-thirties as a whole, the emotional atmosphere, to the extent that such a thing now registers at all, seems rather cheerful. If it were not for the aestheticism itself, Young would come across as fairly normal, and there may even be a somewhat more confident solidarity with his own kind. In his short poems, he is never what one might call a social poet. But he does now come a bit closer to writing from within a group. When I asked whether "Why should we be so aghast...?" (in "Passing the Graveyard") could be a euphemism for "Why should I be so aghast...?", I was really not sure of the answer.

Biographically, there may be an explanation, though biographical considerations are only a way, as throughout here, to sensitize us to what is going on in the poetry. Young was evidently coming closer and closer to shaking off the repressions of filial piety and going over to the Church of England: to a form of religion and religious community that more fully satisfied his needs. In the end, he was to become Vicar of Stonegate, a little village close to the Sussex-Kent border. In turn this must have meant that nature no longer had to serve as a substitute for religion, and that his poetry could be more openly religious as well. In his short nature poems of both early- and late-middle periods, by contrast, religious imagery had never been more than a dash of Christmas-card charm.

According to the prefatory note to *Out of the World and Back*, the first poetry of the new kind is *Into Hades* (1952). In point of fact, however, there is a biographical and thematic link that goes back fifteen years earlier, to *Nicodemus* (1937). At first this may seem rather unlikely. The play was published ten years before his last collection of nature poems; it also pre-dates by two years his application for admission to the Anglican priesthood; and neither *Into Hades* nor *Nicodemus* is actually an autobiography. But as with the early-middle work, if we are to recognize Young's expressivity for what it is, we need to take for granted that his writing sprang from serious personal causes. Just as he had become a minister of religion, but without declaring his true denominational colours, so his Nicodemus recognized Jesus, but was painfully silent about it, until he finally came out (not Young's expression!) and was martyred for his faith. "Killed by the Jews; his spirit fled to heaven". On hearing news of this, John the Evangelist exclaims, "O God be praised!",[118] prefiguring the joy doubtless to be felt by George Bell, Bishop of Chichester, Young's own guide to a new life. The entire play moves relentlessly towards the strongest sense of release. *Into Hades*, in its turn, is a loosening of tongue and revelation of wonders that is comparable to the eschatological gospel named after Nicodemus.

Into Hades is very different from *Nicodemus*, yet precisely in being gospel-like is also partly continuous with it. In order to spell this out, appreciative mediation can once again turn to literary genealogy, since both works draw on certain strands of Christian simplicity which are profoundly traditional.

They reflect, for one thing, Young's own tastes, not just in mystic literature, but in the mystics as human beings — not for him the formalist divorce of text from author! He found the fierce intellectuality of Meister Eckhart less congenial than the poetry of Jan Ruysbroek The Admirable, with his view of God as a principle of goodness. As for St. Teresa, St. John of the Cross and Richard Rolle, what attracted him was their endearingly practical expression of Christian love, their moments of serenity and innocent charm, their gentle humour and waywardness. St. Teresa hurried through meals so as to be first at the kitchen sink, where God "walks among the pots and pans". St. John of the Cross celebrated Christmas by dancing with a little statue of Jesus in his arms.[119]

Temperamentally very close to this, the rhetoric of Christian poetry and drama had always gone in for powerful co-adaptations with the mentality of its current audience. In *The Dream of the Rood*, for instance, the Passion is dovetailed into the thought-world of heroic epic. The traditional aim had not been to alienate the heathen or the laity, but to get as close to them as possible. And although, by the time of *Nicodemus*, new verse drama for performance in churches and cathedrals could seem more like a form of high culture, Young's play is sub-titled "A Mystery" and is quite without stilts, addressing ordinary Christians and others without the slightest condescension or embarrassment. Gone is the crampingly fine writing and lush romanticism of his earlier verse dramas; there is none of the ostentatious metaphoricality of Charles Williams's *Thomas Cranmer of Canterbury*; and unlike Eliot in *Murder in the Cathedral*, he does not go in for prickly intellectuality, or surrender the story-interest half-way through. Without being facile, *Nicodemus* is immediately gripping and intelligible. As John the Evangelist looks back on the story of Nicodemus, the contrasts between different people, alive or remembered, are clear and effective, one of the key figures being Young's beloved St John the Baptist: "a most out-spoken man, / And he is dead. It does not always do / To say too much".[120] The Baptist's words had first awoken the Evangelist to the light, and the Evangelist now helps Nicodemus to see as well, whereas the Blind Man, despite the miracle of his restored physical sight, cannot truly see, and Nicodemus, though he certainly sees, will not speak the word to awake others, until he finally takes the same risk as the Baptist. *Into Hades*, similarly, despite its extraordinary subject-matter, has an arresting story-line with an unmistakable structure, and could be partly classified as a Christianization of Young's favourite genres for light reading: science fiction, the detective story, the Gothic ghost story, and the tale of mystery and imagination. Forty years ago, this was unlikely to impress a Modernist intelligentsia. But now that high culture and other forms of cultural production are being brought together in postmodern experimentation, Young's popular leanings could well come up for re-assessment.

Ultimately, the simplicity of the Christian literary tradition stems from the poetry of Jesus himself, to which Young's posthumous book was devoted. *The Poet and the Landscape* had already faced the question of question of how, if one sees in the visionary manner of Wordsworth (or of Young himself, of course), it is possible to write about landscape and nature at all. Young noted that Blake, on reading the Preface to *The Excursion*, suffered a severe stomach upset: "Nature was the Devil's work, and Wordsworth an Atheist. Natural objects deadened & obliterated the Imagination; the Corporal or Vegetative Eye was like a window, not to be used for sight, but looked thro".[121] Young's own short nature poems did take a good look at the physical world of nature, so satisfying his own simple mimetic standards as a critic. But in both his prose and his poems — in "Mountain View", for instance — there are also passages which attempt to see *through* nature, usually precipitating some such formula as the one he quotes from Hudson: "[T]his natural world was changed to a supernatural, and there was no more matter nor force in sea of land nor in the heavens above, but only spirit".[122] *The Poetic Jesus* suggests a way of getting even closer still to the spiritual order, and its short comment on New Testament parables sums up the method of *Into Hades* in a nutshell:

> [T]he parables, apart from a few, are not allegories; they are stories in which the material order shows some affinity with the spiritual. Some may be stories of an actual happening. . . . But to emphasize a point a story could be fantastic.[123]

Young's argument in *The Poetic Jesus*, widely implicit rather than explicit, is that the poetry of Jesus could speak of the spiritual because its grasp of the physical and the human was so extremely intimate. With truthful fiction for emphasis, Jesus found in this world an affinity with the next.

From Young's discussion, the poety of Jesus emerges as a thoroughly human product, both in its mythology and beliefs, in its tone, ranging from the sarcastic to the whimsical, and in its response to its own context — geographical, religious, national and familial. Although the respect Jesus showed for children and women was somewhat out of the ordinary, this did not affect the warm reciprocity between him and his milieu, revealed especially in details of his language and imagery. Here, as so often in *The Poet and the Landscape*, there is an uncanny similarity between Young and his subject. Jesus is the poet of sunrise and the autumn rain, of the wild flowers and the sparrows. Jesus, too, "thought much in pictures", being strongly given to concrete expression.

> *The Sower* [parable] is so true to Palestinian conditions that one feels it has a verbal authenticity. That is also true of the weather forecasts: "When ye see a cloud from the west, ye say, There cometh a shower; when ye see the south wind blow, ye say, There will be heat"; Palestine had to the west the Mediterranean Sea, the source of rain, and to the south the hot arid desert. Only one who spoke Aramaic would have said, "Behold the fowls of the air; they sow not nor reap, nor carry into barns. . . . Consider the lilies of the field, how they grow; they toil not, neither do they spin"; in Aramaic, birds, mostly called ravens, are masculine and flowers feminine. Even when we have two versions of a saying, we may tell the correct one by its more poetic quality. "If I by the

finger of God cast out demons" has been changed by St Matthew into the less vivid, "If I by the Spirit of God . . .".[124]

By becoming even more like Jesus as a poet, by actually intensifying still further the physicality of his poetry and its truthfulness to his own peculiar nook of earth, Young manages, as early as *Nicodemus*, but more fully in *Into Hades*, to suggest an affinity between the material and the spiritual. It is a rhetorical co-adaptation by which the known and the unknown meet each other halfway. Apart from adding some truthful fiction for emphasis, he leaves the temporal word perfectly recognizable, while using it to intimate something very new and strange.

In one way, then, his prefatory note to *Out of the World and Back* was completely misleading. Nature never ceased to be poetic subject-matter. Natural objects, together with the whole familial and social context in which he had lived all his life, far from deadening and obliterating the imagination, finally gave it a new lease of life.

Now in many of the short nature poems, he had been seeking to dramatize an epiphanic experience of nature's own preternaturalness, as one might put it. In early-middle poems such as "The Ventriloquists", the desire for release from a drably painful human world has a religious intensity, all the keener in that the epiphany seems so tenuous and mirage-like. In late-middle poems such as "Mountain View", the transformation of nature perhaps seems more stable, though he still may have to struggle (e.g. by climbing) for it, and the epiphany has a strongly aesthetic dimension, suggestive of countless Victorian paintings of the same Highland scenery. But in neither early- nor late-middle poems is the epiphany connected with any belief or practice that is explicitly religious. If anything, the religious intensity of "The Ventriloquists" is a matter of using the world of nature as a *substitute* for religion, while the mention of praying in "Mountain View" is actually a witty conceit for "crawling up on hands and knees / The sharp loose screes". Though so different in style and temper, both poems pointedly try to manage, as it were, without religion. Or more precisely, to manage without *theistic* religion. What does sometimes emerge, in "March Hares"[125] and a few similar poems (e.g. "The Salmon-Leap"), is a kind of pantheism, the sense of a tenderly erotic force running through the whole world of nature, a force from which mankind, however, or Young himself at least, is disconnected.

But in *Nicodemus*, the Christian simplicity is already in evidence as a very different straightforwardness and openness of affect. Nature's transfiguration is one aspect of the observer's experience of an explicitly Christian conversion, and both nature and the observer join in artless worship:

> The world is born again. Look at the stars;
> Though small they jostle in the sky for room,
> Shining so bright they drop down through the air;
> Are they not born again?
>
> . . .
>
> Why do I kneel before your empty tomb?
> You are not here, for you are everywhere;
> The grass, the trees, the air, the wind, the sky,
> Nothing can now refuse to be your home;
> Nor I. Lord, live in me and I shall live.[126]

Such writing was unlikely to appeal to critics of a Modernist persuasion. It had an unmistakable personal vibration, and without even being miserable. Vaughan's "stones … deep in admiration"[127] they could perhaps accept. Vaughan, after all, was a Metaphysical, though even he raised problems — Eliot did not mince words.[128] Young's *Nicodemus* would probably seem naive in its evangelical throb, and merely fanciful in further embroidering on Vaughan's conceit:

> … Look at the street;
> The stones are nestling down to their hard sleep,
> Stone nudging neighbour, whispering "Friend,
> Are we not born tonight?"[129]

But an I. A. Richards or an F. R. Leavis who wished to damn this would have run the risk of a category error. Young was not writing Imagist haiku, but something which he and millions of others down the ages would have felt to be infinitely more important. One comparison would be with the cheerful simplicity of St. Teresa meeting God among the pots and pans, or of St. John of the Cross dancing with the little statue of Jesus. Even closer would be Smart, perhaps, of the adoring apples and quinces. And then there are the hymns of Isaac Watts, strong in feeling, and widely accessible. Even if Watts is less playful, Young is unambiguously taking on just that type of communal role. His dramatization of Nicodemus's conversion reintroduces an expressive force into his writing, while at the same time deriving from his own personal experience a more broadly human generalizability.

The play's language and style are correspondingly down-to-earth, though its unifying metaphors of light and sight, ancient metaphors of great simplicity and power, are deployed with enough tact to avoid a bare-bones allegory. They are always grounded in a physical situation, so that the symbolic tenor and symbolizing vehicle are, as it were, in balance. When Nicodemus re-emerges into the darkness from his meeting with Jesus, he cannot quite see John, and says, "My eyes are stupid coming from the light",[130] a statement of equal literal and spiritual truth. The Sanhedrin prays to God to lighten their darkness, which is heavily ironic, yet not crudely so, since the expression figures as part of the prayer with which they always close their deliberations. This unostentatious solicitude of expression makes the climax of the play all the more forceful and believable: Nicodemus's gazing into the mystic heart of light in Christ's empty tomb. Here Young is simplicity itself, totally at ease with the timeless language of mysticism: "Light, light; nothing but light".[131] Just as unpompous is the play's humour, as when Andrew says of a dish of cooked eels, "See, they have lost their heads like John the Baptist".[132] Some of the writing is actually close to the poetry of Jesus, in intimating spiritual truth by means of simple natural analogies. Savouring the mystery of the Resurrection, Nicodemus says that Christ's body

> . . . is dissolved and risen like a dew,
> And now I know,
> As dawn forgives the night, as spring the winter,
> You have forgiven me.[133]

For the desolation of his years of self-censorship and silence Nicodemus uses the same imagery as Young's "The Dunes": it was "a wilderness / Where I must ever wander and be lost".[134] The wilderness image, and several other natural images as well, themselves have biblical overtones, not insisted on, but tacitly corroborating the spiritual application, and sometimes becoming, like the light and sight theme, structural within the play. Effortlessly, Young moves from the decapitated eels and John the Baptist, to the disciples as fishers of men, with Nicodemus a "rich lustrous fish/. . . nosing in the net".[135]

In *Into Hades*, relationships between this known, physical world and that other world of the spirit map on to the great antitheses of Christian theology and mysticism: of God as immanent in nature versus God transcendent; of the old, fleshly body versus the new body of the spirit; and of ordinary mortals versus God's saints in bliss. Intimations of the other world permeate the experience of this world, and the intensely apprehended sights and sounds of this world figure forth the other world by means of a Jesus-like poetry of analogy.

Paradoxically, the main figure of Young himself belongs to both worlds, yet also belongs to neither. He is a ghost, for ever trespassing in between, not fully at home in either Stonegate or heaven. He even has two voices, one his ordinary voice of limited worldly perception, and the other a voice he calls his Monitor, which at first seems to come upon him unawares and from the outside, yet which he finally thinks may be "myself, / The primal self who never left heaven".[136] In the same way he feels constantly drawn to the saints, whose experience is in many respects similar to his own, yet never joins them in full blessedness.

These sets of tensions, contrasts and similarities are reflected in a wonderfully simple structural division. The first seven of the poem's fourteen sections are more predominantly concerned with this world, the remaining seven with the other world. In sections 1–7, Young is a ghost who watches the funeral of his own body in his own church's churchyard; finds himself confined in a strange prison, with what seems to be a different body, a replica of the old one; wonders why nothing happens, and whether he will soon be able to reach out to a purity he dreamed of when young; suddenly finds himself haunting the Vicarage, "a trespasser in my own garden",[137] and in his own churchyard while a service is taking place inside the church; and resists the temptation to return to the body buried in the grave. Then in sections 8–14, he ventures on the unsettling possibilities of spacelessness and timelessness; has a vision of a rainbow which seems to beckon on to further insights; suddenly becomes even less substantial than a ghost, and has a vision of the New Body he will inhabit at the Resurrection; has a vision of the New Earth rising up on her way to marriage with the New Heaven; has a shattering glimpse, afterwards forgotten, of the New Heaven itself; sees a vision of three hierarchies of saints in flight to God; only to return, finally, down to the Old Earth.

In the second, even more metaphysical half of the poem, much of the imagery could hardly be more different from that of Young's short nature poems. Here the sober simplicity of *Nicodemus*, though it recurs as the stylistic ground, is overlaid with a resurgence of the rich colour of Young's earliest writing. His powers of truthful fiction for emphasis rise to their full height, bodying forth conceptions apocalyptic, hierographic, fabulous, and quite breath-taking in their beauty and sheer witty rightness. His writerly co-adaptations are very forceful, at once highly original, and deeply rooted in the Book of Revelation, *Pearl*, Spenser, Blake, and Dante, including Dante as mediated by the Pre-Raphaelites. The rainbow is

> . . . a rainbow in a foreign language,
> If rainbow it was, that overflowed with flowers,
> Amorous, dangling in a gay rebellion
> From their strict arch.[138]

The New Body is both cargo and captain of a coffin-cum-boat which, lit by St. Elmo's fire, seems to come from "anchoring off the rainbow", and it astonishingly rises like a multiplying Jesse-tree, the boughs clad with "all the bodies/I had worn on earth, child, lover, man".[139] The highest order of saints, with their "gold and purple feathers", are

> The phoenixes. They struck at the Godhead,
> One moment birds and the next moment ashes,
> Though they flocked in thousands to their immortal deaths,
> Each was God's only phoenix.[140]

In context, though, such moments do not read like an aesthete's self-indulgence. Dazzlingly lovely and intellectually intriguing, they yet develop with a quiet, steady certainty. To borrow from his own praise of Vaughan, Young seems to mention, rather than assert, surprising things. At first his love of church architecture may appear to get the better of him, even blurring distinctions between pagan and Christian —

> Lincoln's rose-window so burnt me with its beauty
> It was like broken glass; sun shining through,
> Apollo was a Christian.[141]

But in the larger design this is firmly placed, as his way of trying to cheer himself up when excluded from his own church. He confesses that "churches were my love and study, / Not theology",[142] and that Puginesque revery has been a way to *avoid* thinking about God. But this is in no way to demean beauty, and the poem itself could hardly be more lovely, its attractions including an easy intellectual control, which the cheerful lushness of *A Traveller in Time* just does not match.

The influence of Dante is reflected not only in the scope and colour of the poem's imagery, but in this organizational mastery, and particularly in the affective arrangements. Whereas *Nicodemus* dramatized the experience of conversion in the third person, the revelations of *Into Hades* are framed as a first-person dream narrative. The narrator's voice is the first of Young's two voices, the voice of limited worldly vision, and there is something of Dante's innocent spontaneousness in the way it frequently expresses fear, impatience, curiosity or astonishment. The ordinariness and frankness of this persona, inseparable from the simple, Jesus-like poetry of analogy, sets up a channel of unrestrained communication with an equally ordinary implied reader. In every section except one, there are clear emotional signposts reminiscent of Dante, with further Dantesque devices of affect, such as faintnesses, swoons, sleep-within-sleep and dream-within-dream. The psyche's oddest twists and turns are accommodated in plain statement, naturalized with homely images and allusions:

> Was Death a monster,
> A cat that toyed with a mouse, caught but not killed?
> The thought seized my brain, a fear so tumultuous
> That, afraid of itself, it died in fascination,
> A crouching, a yielding to the softened paw,
> The sense that I was safe — not to escape.[143]

The one section in which no emotion is explicitly stated is for that very reason a most effective part of the total design: the vision of the three orders of saints. Ever since the appearance of the rainbow, excitement has run high. Young's "mind began to sparkle" at the vision of the New Body, which made his eyes "sting like a jelly fish".[144] The vision of the New Heaven was an explosion, lifting him up, "Dead and alive at once, stunned by a rock, / Assaulted by the sight".[145] Like Dante after his most shattering vision, he retains no memory of it, and has no words for it except a few "foolish symbols". He has flown too high, and the Monitor charms him asleep with his soft rod, ushering in the dream of saints, which is entirely aetherial. With easy freedom of movement, Young ascends stage by stage, simply reporting the glorious sights to be seen. He familiarizes the vision by means of the natural affinities, but even these give way to the fabulous phoenixes, and it is a very human limitation which leaves his sense of relief, wonder and liberation unexpressed. His withholding from exclamation is itself a kind of dramatization, for as always in the best of Young, objectivity does not correlate with impersonality. Given the full sweep of the narrative, and all the previous signposts, there can be no doubt of how he feels. The reader's vicarious experience is all the more powerful for having to empathize more actively at the climax.

The simple, responsive narrator of *Into Hades* harks back to the sensitive persona of Young's early-middle period, and there is a fundamental thematic and structural similarity with that typically early-middle poem "The Ventriloquists". In both cases, the first half is about the pull of the ordinary and mundane, the second half about the fascination of something in an entirely different realm. In *Into Hades*, however, the unusual experience is not to be sought in the world of nature, but quite explicitly in a spiritual sphere which nature only prefigures, and the province of the ordinary and mundane is itself treated much more directly as well. In describing his sense of alienation, Young's poetry for the first time speaks quite openly of his troubled feelings at the deaths of his parents, of his young man's attempt at Platonic sublimations, of the chastity of his Muse-worship, of a sense of not belonging in his own church and vicarage, of being deposed and assassinated, even, by his parishioners, and of being left out in the cold by his own family:

> . . . For something told me
> I was warned away, a trespasser in my own garden.
> I had come to learn
> With how true an instinct I had dedicated
> The ring of twisted silver in the end.[146]

— the ring with which, in Paris, he had symbolised his union with his insubstantial Muse. Nothing could be further from the tight-lipped hints of personal anguish in the early-middle poems. Even though the writing now comes, as it did in *Nicodemus*, from within a religious community, whose culture (the church building, the ritual, the forms of words) and personnel (Fred the verger, the Rural Dean) are here well known and loved, the burden of sheer individuality and fundamental loneliness is for that very reason stronger than ever. One of the differences from Dante which Young himself registers, is that whereas Dante is once more greeted by his adored Beatrice, Young's Muse, never a woman of flesh and blood, still fails to materialize, even when he is hoping that the moment has finally come.

As in *Nicodemus*, a Jesus-like poetry of analogy helps him express emotional nuance and spiritual insight, and the analogies with nature are especially effective. As he remembers his betrayal of his chaste Platonic mistress of the skies, that love now seems to be

> . . . withered seaweed, crawled over by bleached dead crabs,
> Busy with sandhoppers; yet it had floated once,
> Waved with the water, lustrous, stranger than earth-plant.[147]

A dead man's ghost peers in through the window at his wife and children, "Face crushed against the glass, white as a mushroom, / Eyes burning like a moth's",[148] while the phoenix-saints of the third order are the more remarkable because the nature imagery did manage to find analogies for the lower orders in their ascent to God:

> . . . a waterfall, cascade after cascade,
> Made endless thunder. Pools swirled with wondering bubbles

And overflowed in wide columns of water,
That in crashing down stood still. Salmon darkened
Its white tumbling extravagance, leaping out
To fall back, curved like bows, or straight as arrows
Shot through the current.[149]

No less striking, though, is a low-keyed strain of analogies that are mundane, domestic, urban even. The Herbertian ambience of sheer day-to-day ordinariness is a further extension of the world of "A Prospect of Death", where Young's wife was potentially anxious about his breakfast getting cold, and of the disciples' goings-out and comings-in in *Nicodemus*, where they supped on eels. The style and technique are initiated on the first page:

INTO HADES

1. The Funeral

One midnight in the Paris Underground
Walking along the tunnel to a train
I saw a man leaning against the wall,
Eyes shut, head sunk on chest; selling newspapers
He had fallen asleep, but still stood on his feet.[150]

This is eschatological only by ironic parody — the Metro is our Hades now. Young calmly sets about recreating the diction, rhythm and syntax of colloquial speech, which his frankly ordinary narrating voice sustains throughout. We begin to think that, despite the title and subtitle, we are about to read a tale of the modern city. It is only with the next line that Young begins to turn the urban vignette into the vehicle of a simile; the tenor is his ambiguous sleeping-waking state as he witnesses his own funeral. That remarkable incident, and the alienation for which it is the truthful fiction for emphasis, have acquired, all unnoticed, a firm credibility. Elsewhere, in similar vein, the existential otherness for which ghosthood is a fantasy for emphasis is like arrival in hospital:

The place must have its routine, a new arrival
Causing no sensation. I should hear voices soon,
Friends at the door.[151]

It is a state represented negatively, as a distance from little household sounds never cherished until now:

I lay and listened
For night's stealthy noises, swaying curtain,
Sigh of spent cinders in a fire-place.[152]

And another down-to-earth glimpse of loneliness involves a wryly Hardyesque comparison which, we can now feel, is also deeply Youngian:

> Our universes now could no more mingle
> Than the imaginations of a man and woman
> Lying in the same bed.[153]

Thirty-three years after these lines were first published, Larkin's review of *The Poetical Works* found both *Into Hades* and *A Traveller in Time* merely confused. That *Into Hades* is magnificently organized and beautifully written quite passed him by. Instead, he dwells on Young as the solitary walker of the short nature poems, and even here he has a reservation. He admires their "compact power", and readily grants that "[t]o walk all day without meeting a soul can be refreshing and restoring", but feels bound to say that "at last one is glad to get back to humankind again".[154]

Larkin has instinctively caught, if not fully articulated, Young's note of the trespasser on earth, a trespasser who as yet belongs neither with human beings, animals, trees, nor with the saints in bliss. In his finest work, Young represents, on the contrary, the human being as a creature of fundamental isolation. The Young "in" the writing pursues a voyeuristic, vicarious existence on the peripheries of life and death, and although the possibility is never excluded that some other human beings may be more at the centre of things, more in tune with their fellows or their environment, only in *Nicodemus* does this begin to be raised to an imaginative certainty. Mostly there prevails a ghost-like sense of existential inferiority, with the epiphanies for ever fading away, the memories of the New Heaven a mere jumble of cryptic symbols. Hoping for something other than this world of here and now, his ghost furiously resists the temptation of the earthly body in *Into Hades*, and there is a constant inclination to see something else *through* the physical world — to see a view from a mountain as transparently clothing a world of spirit, to read the brushing of a branch as the touch of love. Love, in fact, never flows quite strongly enough in his direction. Vertically, so to speak, it does flow through the whole of creation, up and down between God and creatures, including Young. But this is as nothing to the hoped-for final union, and horizontally, though there is love between March hare and March hare, Young's love flows only to an aetherial Muse, to a dead mother or dead friend, to a tree or bird or salmon, and is not reciprocated. The world and the creatures in it, or Young's own attitude towards them, resists any real involvement. Action and moral choice would be impossibly problematic and probably delusive. For most of the time Nicodemus tries to act both ways at once, or to act and not to act. What happens in the end happens *to* him; his sense of sin, and with it his sense of responsibility, just melts away like dew. *Into Hades*, even more obviously, is a poem of waiting, of waiting for death, and as always in Young, the high-spots of joy are moments of rapt contemplation, abstracted from the flux of life.

Even so, Larkin's critique is no more adequate than many earlier ones, and his missing the point of *Into Hades* is not the worst of it. He is still guilty of the Modernist critic's de-historicizing failure of empathy. He not only describes Young as a solitary human being, but makes his solitude a double one, as if no other poet had ever written on quite this wavelength. Amazingly, it is as if Larkin failed to recognize the continuity between Hardy and Young's view of the marriage bed and his own poem, "Talking in Bed". Even in poems more thickly populated by other people than most of Young's, Larkin himself voices a loneliness which has the cumulative force of centuries of poetry behind it, and to which some of the very greatest writers have contributed.

Clearly, many authors have bodied forth an image of life that is totally different from Young's. Chaucer and Shakespeare, Donne and Pope, Byron and the classical English novel are all more solidly *of* this world, more consistently alive to possibilities and consequences of involvement and action. Literature can suggest our capability to win the world or lose it, throbbing with the zest for living here and now, or weeping at the grief of it. Even Frost, though such a crucial stylistic influence on Young, was on an entirely different wavelength. To Young, the closing lines of "Birches" can only have seemed wrong-headed:

> . . . Earth's the right place for love:
> I don't know where it's likely to go better.
> I'd like to go by climbing a birch tree,
> And climb black branches up a snow-white trunk
> *Towards* heaven, till the tree could bear no more,
> But dipped its top and set me down again.
> That would be good both going and coming back.[155]

Young had no taste for coming back.

But equally clearly, there have been other writers whose image of life does resemble his. As he himself points out, Wordsworth, Vaughan and Traherne share a sense of human life as a continuous retreat from an early condition of simplicity and beauty.[156] Their attempts to recover the "auroral vision" anticipate his own, entailing a similar effort to transfigure the physical. Especially close is Vaughan's peep into a better world of light, which also brings to mind

Edwin Muir, with one foot in the labyrinth of life, the other foot in Eden, where reality is more ghostly.[157] Clare, whose existential uncertainties are so like Young's, also confuses, like Young, a muse of nature with a more aetherial inspiration. Clare and, with him, Hardy and Edward Thomas anticipate, too, Young's sense of marriage as a kind of second best, where the greatest hope lies in affection, tolerance, understanding, honesty, none of which is somehow enough. With varying degrees of intensity and clarity, they all yearn for some kind of body-and-soul rapture, which no human lover could ever give or receive. Their persistent desire for "home" and love, all unattached to anything or anybody here and now, renders strangely indeterminate the boundaries between physical and metaphysical, bodily and ghostly, or past, present and future. And for each and all, the blandishments of the temporal order emanate from the great city, which is why they stick to the countryside and their own dreamworlds. This is the fraternity of the unfraternal in which Young, once a Parisian flaneur, but with a head full of Platonism, would be most at home, if being at home came naturally. As his son-in-law has recorded,

> [a]t meals he sat on his own at a small table in the window bay while the rest of the family sat round the dining table in the same room; this enabled him to escape the necessity to join in table chatter, while still being able to overhear and, when necessary, comment on what was being said.[158]

Not that the Chaucer–Shakespeare image of life and the Vaughan–Wordsworth image are mutually exclusive, either in the production of an entire cultural epoque or in the life, work and sensibility of a single writer. As with the ancient distinction between the way of action and the way of contemplation, there can be both purely single manifestations and mixtures of the two. A person who "belongs" to the world is not necessarily incapable of meditative abstraction from it, and during the interstices of meditation a contemplative person may act. Some literature can alert us to the rewards and intuitions of one or the other life-image, but life as a whole may tend towards a balance. In educational arrangements for a ruling class, such balance has sometimes been positively cultivated, and in poetry, too, balance can be programmatic, as in the paired *L'Allegro* and *Il Penseroso*, or in Yeats's use of different masks. For greater complexity, we can perhaps turn to *Four Quartets*, which for some readers has figured a veritable struggle between a professed *contemptus mundi* and an enthralled apprehension of sensuous life,[159] just as the eschatology of Dante embraces the Italy he knew in all its crassness.

In the present book I am assuming that human beings are social individuals, with a continuity of imaginative, temperamental and moral autonomy attached to a mind that is otherwise infinitely flexible between different formations. In all the poets mentioned so far, the life-image, whether Shakespearian–Chaucerian, Vaughanian–Wordsworthian, or balanced-between-the-two, is ultimately an inexplicable matter of temperament. But one or another life-image can also operate at the level of social formation, being "fashionable" in a particular milieu, or less than fundamental in its exponent. Many readers have felt that Tennyson's role of public engagement is somehow shallower than his more private song of endless grief and waiting, of self-contained lethargy and dream. Auden's contemporary commitments, likewise, have been read as a symbolism that is intensely personal.[160] His organizing antithesis between an actual social sickness and a just conceivable social health may imply an experience not totally unlike Young's, with his sense of two worlds and torn allegiances. Such an affinity seems still more likely from a reading of Edwin Muir's "The Good Town", "The Transfiguration" or "The Labyrinth", where Audenesque settings are more explicitly fused with Vaughan–Wordsworth landscape and concerns. It could be, then, that in Tennyson and Auden the belonging-in-the-world is a socially acquired positionality, while a certain not-belonging is more mysteriously individual. In other poets the same thing may happen the other way round. However paradoxically, alienation may be fashionable, and social integration deeply individualistic.

Temperamentally, Young has no truck with the Shakespeare–Chaucer–Frost party. Nor is he "balanced". He is pure Vaughan–Wordsworth. True, writers not "of" this world do not go around with their eyes shut. Young and his fellows have even helped to clinch their readers' sense of what the natural world is like. All the same, his beech tree only accentuates his own insubstantiality ("Strength leaves the hand I lay on this beech-bole/So great-girthed, old and high"), and his close knowledge of his own peculiar nook of earth always hints his desire for, at times his vision of, a very different body and a very different place. True again, a significant amount of his work, comprising the wittily aesthete poetry of his late-middle period, *Nicodemus*, and *Into Hades*, suggests that in some senses he has come in from the cold. Nicodemus himself does join John the Evangelist and other witnesses to Christ. But what happens to Young himself here is merely a matter of social conformity. The witty late-middle poems did not finally satisfy him, and although the longer, explicitly religious works express his joys and sorrows in a communal language, so generalizing his predicament and even, in *Into Hades,* giving it a familial and wider social setting, this only makes its tensions more powerful.

And how do we tune in to them? If the empathizing reader of Gerhardie will catch the Chekhovian dimension, the secretion of Andrew Young becomes recognizable as such by falling into place alongside those of certain other poets, including Jesus Christ. At the same time, it will also be perceived as intimately personal. What we have here are in fact the two sides of a fascinating co-adaptation between literary tradition and an individual writer. As a mediating critic, I have been assuming that literary history can sensitize readers to the tradition, and biography to the individuality, so clarifying the co-adaptive *tertium quid* of the writing's particular historical achievement.

PART II

Recognizing achievement

Summary

Readers' attempts at empathy will not always result in sympathy. The point is rather that in genuine communication the relation between the "sender" and the "receiver" is one of human parity. Readers of literature, then, will have their own response, which may be critical, and even severely critical. But equally, parity does require of them the empathetic effort, and their next step will sometimes be to recognize an author's communicative achievement as a real historical act. Here the central perception will be of the author's skill in co-adaptation within the original milieu, which as a result may not have remained unchanged. But then again, over the course of time the writing's interpersonal effect will not have persisted as an invariable constant. As the current context of reading has moved further and further away from the context of writing, a whole new range of implications and applications will have emerged. As we re-read T. S. Eliot, Henry Vaughan, Dickens or Robert Frost at the beginning of the new millennium, what transmits itself is not only a certain historical form of life and human identity, but an energy of moral, intellectual and imaginative accomplishment whose inspirational power is really multivalent.

As I note in Chapter 3, the poetry of Eliot has usually been valued for what it is or what it says. More relevant to the present book's communicational concerns, are the questions of what it did and what it does. In *The Waste Land*, for instance, Eliot's co-adaptation between the individual and the social was very readily to be felt as a mode of address that was at once offensive and conciliatory. An iconoclastic making-new can seem very insulting, albeit exciting, while social conformity tends to be experienced as polite, albeit sometimes dull. But Eliot was a conforming iconoclast, or an iconoclastic conformist. His communicative success was in modulating the persona of a hyper-correct Edwardian gentleman with that of brash young American Modernist. Seven decades further on, in one part of our mind it is no longer possible to respond to this. His work soon lost its unfamiliarity, and we inevitably read it in our own very different context of reading. Yet with the help of historical considerations, we can still grasp something of the huge difference he made to his contemporaries' life-world, through a force for change which will always remain infectious, though in ways he could never have predicted.

In Chapter 4, I further examine historical co-adaptation, this time in the case of Henry Vaughan. Twentieth century discussion of Vaughan's religious poetry often tended to de-personalize and de-historicize it. But originally it was a very specific response to the Puritan Commonwealth's repression of the Anglican church, within which Vaughan himself had been brought up. What his writing offered his co-religionists was a substitute for institutionalized worship. Here co-adaptation was a matter of obeying the letter of the laws restricting religious expression while undermining their spirit. In the process, his somewhat unpredictable style became the sounding-board for the types of experience which were officially marginalized, thereby consolidating his own readership as a community. In its own time, then, his poetry had, like Eliot's, a beauty of exemplary deed, relating not to Kant's realm of the aesthetic, but to the realm of ethics. Several centuries further on, for readers caught up in the cultural threats and excitements of postmodernity it represents a suggestive instance of a threatened form of identity which resists, recoups, and endures by making new.

In Chapter 5, I point out that Dickens's *Dombey and Son*, at the hands of many twentieth century critics, was de-humanized and aestheticized no less completely than the poetry of Vaughan. Even some of the more historical readings tended to oversimplify both the Victorian middle class, and Dickens himself as a middle-class writer. The suffocating kind of bourgeois decorum was merely one of a whole range of Victorian cultural formations. Though amply deferred to by Dickens in his (to us) rather boring main charaters, it was in constant counterpoint with an abundant heteroglossia of other voices and mindsets, which Dickens channels through his caricatures. His method here is quite unrelated to traditional notions of literary form, whether Aristotelian or post-Romantic. Instead, it is simply a matter of endlessly differential alternation between the decorum and its subversion. Such is the rhetorical co-adaptation whereby he defers to Mrs Grundy in order to outwit her. Some recent critics, blinded by the decorum, anachronistically accuse him of doing nothing to improve the plight of women or the poor. Much closer to the mark was George Gissing, who stressed Dickens's enormous force for change. The inspiration he still offers is that of a resolutely active diplomacy: of an abundant readiness to compromise, in conjunction with a restlessly individual creativity. It was an achievement which will always prodigally confirm the human capacity for moving from old to new.

In Chapter 6, I apply a somewhat similar cultural analysis to the poetry of Robert Frost. Frost's work needs to be related to American social contexts which both the New Critics and the ideologists of the republican melting-pot tended to neglect. Not only was the United States always torn apart by real cultural divisions. Some of these were a crucial challenge to Frost's own sense of personal identity. He ended up feeling that he was neither urban nor rural, neither lettered nor unlettered, neither artistic nor philistine. For him, various ways of being in the world could only be tried on as a kind of disguise for a fundamental inner formlessness. Although his writing did communicate a very powerful individuality, this resulted from a sheer effort of will. His whole life's struggle was to create an identity out of nonentity, and then just hang on tight. In our postmodern age of sociocultural fragmentation, the force of this example could be very telling.

CHAPTER 3

The impoliteness of *The Waste Land*

Given empathy, the next step, already partly taken in the previous chapters on Gerhardie and Young, is to accord the writerly achievement due recognition as a form of action. Empathy and recognition are two of the inseparable ingredients of a humanizing literary appreciation. A reader cannot truly empathize with writers of any merit without recognizing the precise moral valency of their historical deeds of writing. And such recognition is most adequate when it springs from an empathy of the fullest kind.

Recognition is not a matter of putting authors on Victorian pedestals. Empathy does not always lead to sympathy, or even to admiration of a more objective kind. For a critic to pretend that authors never nod, or never give grounds for disagreement or disapproval, is a surrender of responsibility. Authors who are credited with superhuman knowledge, intelligence and virtue may do a lot of harm, and an indiscriminate reverence for anything and everything they write will also cloud perceptions of those aspects of their work which may be really valuable. Bardolatry can even be a version of that presentism which universalizes the values of the here and now to contexts that were very different. As such, it is a way for readers to *avoid* real reading, by re-creating authors in their own favourite self-image.

Anachronistic, uncircumstantial readings have no place in appreciative mediation. But to assume that a text's significance is frozen once and for all within its original context of writing would be just as inappropriate. No less than the universalizing presentism, such historical or cultural purism basically rules out the dialogical parity of true communication. The only difference is that historical and cultural purists are not egotistical. Instead of silencing authors, they silence themselves. Their way of rejecting literature's dialogicality is to undervalue their own judgement and human dignity.

No matter how individual a literary work may be, it does come from its own time and place, within which even its individuality has had its particular valency. But if, when read in some other milieu, its force continues to be felt, it will have new social implications, which its author could never have foreseen or controlled. If it goes on serving as an inspiration, this will be mainly through its example of sheer moral energy. Far from being a fund of eternal wisdom whose precise bearing has remained unchanged from day 1, it will work in different ways under different circumstances. This means that the onus is always on readers themselves, and for their own sake, first to empathize as much as possible with the writerly deed in its context of writing, and secondly to perceive any relevance it may have to projects and concerns within their current context of reading. This double approach, which is actually a kind of parallel processing, is the only way for readers to be sure that they are both confronting authors in something like their full otherness, and giving that otherness a chance to become significant for them within their own life-world.

To repeat, empathy does not always become sympathy, and I am not recommending a stance of unquestioning admiration. But neither shall I be hauling anyone over the coals. At the hands of some of the previous century's literary scholastics, authors could have a bad enough time already, and sometimes their very existence was quite forgotten. Aestheticizing Modernist readings could de-personalize the act of writing altogether, and the de-centrings of the later, Barthesian paradigm, though in one sense restoring literature to history, did nothing to sharpen our sense of writers as agents. On the contrary, the re-historicization could involve a reductive determinism which made literature a purely social product. As a result, the achievement of writers' co-adaptations between the social and the individual tended to escape notice. What got lost from view was that writers such as Eliot, Vaughan, Dickens and Frost, in engaging with prevailing social scripts, were not only endorsing but transforming them, and with a moral energy that can remain unpredictably infectious under very different circumstances. In order to redress the balance, we do need to praise where praise is due.

To begin with Eliot, he was his own talent scout. So persuasive were his critical writings, and his poetry apparently so affirmative of the implied claims, that his current standing is very different from that of Gerhardie and Young. Instead, he suffers from the opposite problem, of being too well known. One of appreciative mediation's tasks must be to make him strange again, which cannot be done except by imagining his life's work away: by an ethnographic re-creation of the phase of Anglo-American culture prior to his astonishing co-adaptation with it. This is the only way to divert attention from what his poetry was or said to what it did — to the force by which it brought about cultural change. *The Waste Land*, in particular, though often thought of as the quintessentially

Modernist poem in English, was a making-new whose enormous vigour has still to be fully appreciated. Whereas the most obvious clue to poetry as *pragma* lies in its affective impact, twentieth century commentary on this poem always centred on issues of form and expressivity.

Very broadly speaking, the first phase of commentary saw *The Waste Land* in terms suggested by Eliot's own early criticism. Most seminal were his account of poetic impersonality in the essay "Tradition and the Individual Talent", and his related ideas about objective correlatives, and about the dissociation of sensibility allegedly setting in with Milton and Dryden. Most critics concluded that *The Waste Land* was not, in fact, expressive; that it was rather a triumph of form; and that it therein satisfied the reading habit of Modernist aestheticization. This interpretation, and the Eliotian claims and assumptions on which it was based, were actually key factors in the rise of twentieth-century literary scholasticism.

No less broadly speaking, during the last three decades of the century critics argued that the poem could be read in a quite different way, with support from Eliot's own later criticism. The consensus now was that the poem is expressive after all, and expressive, on the whole, in the gloomily unpleasant way expected by that other main Modernist reading habit.

Because this rejection of depersonalizing interpretations still marginalized affect, it could not catch the full interactive valency of Eliot's writerly deed. All the same, it was a crucial step in the right direction, on which an obvious gloss is suggested by the title of my previous chapter. There I was drawing on Housman's remark, well known to Andrew Young, that poetry is like an intensely personal secretion — either "a natural secretion, like turpentine in the fir, or a morbid secretion, like the pearl in the oyster". Housman continues: "I think that my own case, though I may not deal with the matter so cleverly as the oyster does, is the latter; because I have seldom written poetry unless I was rather out of health, and the experience, though pleasurable, was generally agitating and exhausting."[1] Another poet on whom Housman's words were not lost was the middle-aged Eliot, who said he thought he understood them, and that they revealed "authentic processes of a real poet".[2] In *The Use of Poetry and the Use of Criticism* (1933) he quoted the entire passage from "The Name and Nature of Poetry" in a footnote, as a way of corroborating the following observations of his own:

> I know ... that some forms of ill-health, debility or anaemia, may (if other circumstances are favourable) produce an efflux of poetry in a way approaching the condition of automatic writing — though, in contrast to the claims some-

times made for the latter, the material has obviously been incubating within the poet, and cannot be suspected of being a present from a friendly or impertinent demon. What one writes in this way may succeed in standing the examination of a more normal state of mind; it gives me the impression, as I have just said, of having undergone a long incubation, though we do not know until the shell breaks what kind of egg we have been sitting on. To me it seems that at these moments, which are characterised by the sudden lifting of the burden of anxiety and fear which presses upon our daily life so steadily that we are unaware of it, what happens is something *negative*; that is to say, not "inspiration" as we commonly think of it, but the breaking down of strong habitual barriers, which tend to re-form very quickly. Some obstruction is momentarily whisked away. The accompanying feeling is less like what we know as positive pleasure, than a sudden relief from an intolerable burden.[3]

In republishing *The Use of Poetry and the Use of Criticism* in 1964, Eliot expresses "the faint hope that one of these lectures may be taken instead of *Tradition and the Individual Talent* [*sic*] by some anthologist of the future".[4] The words just quoted do indeed create a different impression from that earlier essay, with its talk of poetry as "not a turning loose of emotion, but an escape from emotion; . . . not the expression of personality, but an escape from personality".[5] Though still careful to add that poetry hatched out from such long and intensely private incubation may not be poetry of the highest order, Eliot is unmistakably fed up with being invoked as the authority for the concepts promoted by his earlier criticism. He mentions dissociation of sensibility and objective correlative quite specifically.

Interpreters of Eliot took him — once again — at his word, partly, no doubt, because critical fashion was in any case changing, not least in response to the confessional poetry of Berryman, Lowell, Sexton and Plath. By the 1970s, commentary was regularly seeing his early criticism as a kind of smokescreen, and his poems as decidedly intimate documents. The most controversial account from that decade was James E. Miller's, who described *The Waste Land* as the exorcism of a demon of grief for the death of Jean Verdenal, allegedly Eliot's homosexual lover.[6] But in the mid-1980s F. T. Prince was still very forthright:

> In spite of the mask of ordinariness, nothing about him was ordinary — neither his mind nor his personality, nor the circumstances of his early life, nor his life as it took shape when he came to England and married. His poetry was born and developed through crisis, the crisis first of a prolonged inexperienced adolescence, then of prolonged frustration in marriage; the crises of the First World War and its aftermath, and of the Second World War and its preliminaries. . . . The power and fascination of his poetry lie in its use of a

subdued rational manner of speaking to deal with the violent irrational forces of human experience, whether of darkness or light — whether opening up abysses of horror and suffering or pointing to "the heart of light, the silence".[7]

Although it was far too late for the flood of such personalizing interpretations to be stemmed by re-affirmations of formalist dogma, some literary-theoretical commentary argued for impersonality of a de-centred structuralist or poststructuralist variety. Andrew Ross, for instance, introduced a Lacanian framework, which shifted attention away from Eliot's own personal experience of sex to the representation of sex within the culture as a whole.[8] The taste for such readings was relatively short-lived, however, and in 1990 Jewel Spears Brooker and Joseph Bentley were quite emphatic about what they saw as the three historical phases of Eliot criticism: New Critical close reading; the literary-theoretical phase, involving less close reading; and now, a return to close reading as enhanced by biographical and other historical considerations.[9]

Prince's antithesis between the "subdued rational manner of speaking" and "the violent irrational forces of human experience" echoed similar antitheses in numerous other late-twentieth-century commentators. The underlying argument was always the same: Eliot's early talk of impersonality was not the whole truth; it was precisely half the truth. Discussing his endorsement of Housman, Maud Ellmann anticipated my own remarks *à propos* Andrew Young.[10] The term "secretion" can mean either "exposed" and "secreting", or "in reserve" and "in secret". In this way, said Ellmann, it captures Eliot's own interweaving of personal and impersonal, in both his poetic practice and his theory. As she put it, he "insists that poetry originates in personal emotion, implying that the author's subjectivity pervades the text, yet at the same time he deplores this intervention".[11] For Ronald Bush, the tension was between, on the one hand, a Puritan restraint coupled to Symbolist notions of a poetry aspiring to music and, on the other hand, a natural strength of feelings harnessed to a Wordsworthian fidelity of self-expression. So the imagery of *The Waste Land*, said Bush, has a nightmarish quality which could only emerge when Eliot's normal restraint had been relaxed — a reading which was clearly influenced by Eliot's "incubation" passage, with its talk of the sudden lifting of the burden of anxiety and fear, and of the "breaking down of strong habitual barriers". Afterwards, according to Bush, Eliot tried to re-impose restraint, by adding the poem's mythological apparatus.[12] For Sanford Schwartz, again, Eliot's emotionality was in conflict with the element of dry factuality.[13] Or as Erik Svarny put it, the associations with Pound, Gautier, and Wyndam Lewis are actually deceptive. No matter how cooly satirical, aesthetic or antihumanistic Eliot may seem to be, there is always a personal reverberation, and *The Waste Land*, while aspiring to the impersonality of myth or tradition, has the poignant undertow of an "almost concealed autobiographical implication".[14] For Michael H. Levenson, similarly, *The Waste Land* was the culmination of a tension between life and form which was already evident in Eliot's earlier alternation between expressive monologues and tightly experimental quatrains.[15]

These personalizing readings of Eliot came *pari passu* with a reassessment of his relationship with earlier writers. As far as the English tradition goes, one of the key figures was still Donne, but now there was also frequent mention of Tennyson, whose influence the young Eliot had seen as Modernism's bane, but in whom Carol C. Christ was finding an ur-Eliotian anxiety about cultural disintegration, leading to an ur-Eliotian sacrifice of fine poetic and emotional impulses to political conservatism. Whereas Eliot's early criticism had hinted that his own roots were mainly in the allegedly unified sensibility of the Metaphysicals, Christ detected a unified sensibility in the Victorian poetry of the picturesque. With support from Arthur Hallam's remarkable review of *Poems, Chiefly Lyrical* (1830), he argued that Tennyson's sensuous word-pictures amount to nothing less than a coherence-giving formula for non-rational states of being. When Walter Pater used a chemical metaphor to describe the combinatory power of the artist's mind, he was in Christ's view merely articulating what the Pre-Raphaelites had learnt from Tennyson here. And despite Eliot's disclaimer, the notorious catalyst analogy in "Tradition and the Individual Talent" was, for Christ, a continuation of the same line.[16]

Another aspect of the *fin de siècle* reassessment was to grasp the connection between literary form and communicative pragmatics. The dramatized personae of Eliot's poems were no longer seen as autotelic constructs within an aesthetic heterocosm, but were taken to have a distinct relation to Eliot himself. Reading Eliot's essay on *In Memoriam* as covert self-description, Christ saw his use of the dramatic monologue as a way of transcending personality yet still remaining personal. Pound was wrong, that is to say, when he detected an indebtedness to Browning. Pound's own poems have firmer historical settings and a more conspicuous artistry, for which Browning was obviously seminal. But in Christ's view Eliot, like Tennyson, had an overall mood of despairing impotence, and Tennysonian monologue was the perfect receptacle for the fragments of his self-styled rhythmical grumbling.[17] The melancholy sense of doubt and general disintegration prevented any strong discursive or narrative

line, so leaving us with little more than the voice or the voices. In which connection critics now invoked Eliot's own suggestion that the voices of poetry are
actually three-fold:

> The first voice is the voice of the poet talking to himself — or to nobody. The
> second is the voice of the poet addressing an audience, whether large or small.
> The third is the voice of the poet when he attempts to create a dramatic char-
> acter speaking in verse; when he is saying, not what he would say in his own
> person, but only what he can say within the limits of one imaginary character
> addressing another imaginary character.[18]

For Richard Badenhausen, *Murder in the Cathedral* developed the third voice
(in Thomas, the Priests, and the Knights), but still countenanced the first voice
(in the Chorus), so recalling earlier Eliotic speakers such as Prufrock, Gerontion, and Tiresias.[19] The rise of Tiresias's voice was traced by Hirofumi Iwamassu, from the early unpublished poems onwards, as a voice in which Eliot's
own private grumbling is sublimated and gains impersonality. "Tiresias can be
called . . . a persona of Eliot, and the voice of Tiresias proves to be none other
than that of Eliot".[20] As Calvin Bedient was hearing them, *all* the voices in *The
Waste Land* were "the performances of a single protagonist, not Tiresias but a
nameless stand-in for Eliot himself".[21]

Often taking their cue from Eliot's own later prose writings, then, late-twentieth-century critics tended to see the pragmatics of *The Waste Land* as far less
exceptional than did their predecessors fifty years earlier. For one thing, Eliot
was now assumed to be actually communicating. For another, to know something about the literary–historical and personal context within which he was
writing was taken to be helpful, since the gap between that context and our
own context of reading is both an obstacle and a stimulus to communication.
Lastly, the voices of some of the poem's dramatized personae were coming to
be heard as Eliot's own self-projections for communication's sake. New Critical
warnings about an intentional fallacy simply faded away, and so did all talk of
the implied writer and implied reader as dramatis personae which hermetically
seal the poem off from life.

〜

So as Keir Elam might say, illocution is taken care of, and at the beginning of a
new century we finally extend the poem's pragmatic normalization to *per-
locution*.[22] In more old-fashioned language, New Critical diatribes against the
so-called affective fallacy can also be forgotten. What calls for special attention
is the feelings Eliot's poem aroused in early readers, in particular about itself as

a poem, and about Eliot himself as a writer. We need to take very seriously the experience of shock and indignation to which many of their comments bore witness. Coupled with the fact that the poem is still widely read today, the early protests at its extreme impoliteness give the strongest hint that his contribution to historical change was indeed on a major scale.[23] Empty gestures of cultural conformism do not excite controversy, and fairly soon sink into oblivion.

Here the mediating critic's distinction between context of writing and current context of reading has important methodological implications. What we *cannot* do is to read a literary text from an earlier period, focus the politeness issues it raised, and then turn to the responses of earlier readers to see what was said about them. This would be to put the cart before the horse. Perceptions of politeness do change. We ourselves are historical beings, tending to respond according to the criteria of our own reading community, criteria which are themselves being co-adaptively changed all the time. The only way to find out about the interpersonal impact of *The Waste Land* in 1922 is to study those earliest responses first.

What once seemed outrageous is hardest to guess when the text in question has subsequently become part of cultural tradition. That profoundly original works of literature can be surprising and even shocking seems obvious enough, and Modernist works were emphatically no exception.[24] But with the passing of the years, what at first seemed very unexpected can become more familiar. As we move on through the new millennium, we cannot possibly be upset on a perusal of the *The Waste Land*, and Eliot's niche in the pantheon now seems secure. In point of fact, it is *too* secure, too secure, that is, for his work to be fully appreciated, and therefore too secure for our own good. We are just as likely to come to his poetry as to Wordsworth's or to Shakespeare's, and may easily take it, like theirs, for granted. At school we have probably listened to teachers talking about it, and we may even know some passages off by heart. Eliot attracted the attention of our ancestors by being outrageous. When he first attracts ours, it is because he is a classic — and "attention" may nowadays be a misnomer.

Not that classics necessarily seem polite. Again because perceptions of politeness do change, classic writers can come to seem offensive in ways which their own contemporaries could never have predicted. When, in the mid-1990's, certain of Eliot's writings came in for a Jewish critique, the point was not that his thoughts and feelings about Jews were suddenly seen as essentially different from what they were always taken to be before, nor that they had never offended earlier readers at all. It was rather that such attitudes could no longer be made public today without attracting more grave and widespread condemnation.[25] For historical reasons, they had become less acceptable.

As it happens, however, this does not apply to *The Waste Land* in its published form. On the contrary, the poem's affective impact has been successively de-charged. Even if we know about the perturbation it caused when it first came out, we have to make a considerable effort of historical imagination in order to understand it. We perhaps talk fluently enough of Eliot's originality of intellect, vision or versification. But to bring alive the early interpersonal dynamics, we probably have to turn to the relevant volumes of the *Critical Heritage* series.[26]

Sometimes the shock was evidently a matter of *selectional politeness*: of Eliot's choice of subject-matter and language. Many an early reader blamed him for a baffling and allegedly over-learned use of quotations and allusions, lots of them involving foreign languages, and not much explained by the end-notes. No less annoyance was expressed at a destabilizing alternation from grand style to Cockney slang. Worst of all, though, was the poem's subject-matter, which many readers found fundamentally unpleasant. Its very first line inverted joyful associations of spring, associations at least as ancient as the first line of *The Canterbury Tales*; the talk of the human mind or human life as a heap of broken images was no less depressing; and this was only the beginning. Not that earlier poetry had been completely free of grimmer insights. Even if Arnold had removed the distressing "Empedocles on Etna" from his collection of 1853, Tennyson, still deeply venerated by ordinary readers in 1922, was in places just as bleak as Eliot's later essay was to admit. Even the poetry of Masefield and the Georgians, sometimes remembered today as all hearty seafaring and blithe pastoralism, had stretches of very dour realism. Yet Eliot did seem to be raising miserableness to new heights, and to be miserable most of the time. Readers complained of an endless sordid sterility and blank despair, whose effect was all the more shattering because of fleeting lyrical hints of love or beauty or fulfilment.

Then there were questions of *presentational politeness*, which has to do with the manner of conveying the subject-matter. Is the writer being helpful towards readers? Is it easy for them to see what the point is, what is happening, what the general bearings are? Here the basic problem was one of coherence, a problem which the end-notes were often felt to aggravate. As one commentator put it, "a poem that has to be explained in notes is not unlike a picture with 'This is a dog' inscribed underneath. Not, indeed, that Mr Eliot's notes succeed in explaining anything, being as muddled as incomplete".[27] Not only did Eliot not translate the foreign quotations. He did not make it clear how they fitted in with everything else, or, indeed, how *anything* fitted. There was no overall story: although the notes suggested that everything tied in with the Fisher King myth, passages such as the pub scene, the rape of the river nymphs, or the coupling of the typist and the young man carbuncular seemed to dramatize episodes in several separate narratives. There was no clear sense of who was speaking: although the notes hinted that all the voices somehow belonged to Tiresias, Tiresias seemed a shadowy figure, who did not help one to move from, say, "April is the cruellest month" to "Bin gar keine Russin, stamm' aus Litauen, echt deutsch." There was no clear line of discursive argument: there were only snatches of thought and apparently random juxtapositions of images. And to repeat a point that also counts under selectional politeness, there was not even a consistent verse form or level of style. A more chaotic composition — if that was the right word — was difficult to imagine.

For very many early readers, then, *The Waste Land* seemed quite shockingly impolite in both its selection of language and subject matter and in its style of presentation. Although Pound's "Hugh Selwyn Mauberley" and Eliot's own "The Love Song of J. Alfred Prufrock" and "Gerontion" had already shocked them in somewhat the same way, early responses clearly suggest that the stakes were now being raised far higher.

Yet as time passed, objections were overcome. Readers getting to grips with the poem today will probably take for granted that its text can indeed be read, and even read with profit. Between the society's dominant reading styles and Eliot's startlingly personal intervention, a co-adaptation has taken place.

This was at the heart of his historical achievement. But before examining how it came about, we do well to remember some of the implications for the way readers actually read. What is it, exactly, that readers of the poem have been persuaded to do? In particular, how do they nowadays handle those aspects of its address which were once experienced as so woundingly impolite?

As far as the most distressing selectional feature goes, readers have come to see the poem's element of Modernist gloom as either positively interesting, or only part of a rather larger picture. The best way to study this development would be within a cultural history and history of ideas far broader than my present scope. One important consideration would be the continuing influence of the poem's least pleasant details on writers and artists today: the indebtedness of Francis Bacon's *Painting* (1978; private collector) to the lines, "*Dayad-*

hvam: I have heard the key/Turn in the door once and turn once only", or of images in Lucian Freud to the poem's moments of panic and confrontation.[28] But especially after the publication of *Four Quartets*, some critics actually saw Eliot's early work less in terms of a shocking and depressing bleakness, than of an anguished spiritual search.[29] In time, this led to comparisons with Heidegger: Eliot, too, has been said to understand that a "thrown" contingency is always less than Being;[30] he is seen to demonstrate a sense of "relative truth" that is ur-postmodern in its scepticism towards absolutes.[31] A parallel suggestion has been that the early poems' disturbing unpleasantness merely paved the way for a valorization of love which became increasingly mawkish — for instance in the lines addressed to his second wife.[32] And certainly, there *was* a mellowing, including a mellowing of Eliot and his readers to each other. The ageing poet and West End dramatist became a familiar and even loveable figure to an ever larger circle. The disobliging directness of the earlier young Turk was remembered in a more indulgent light.

Much easier to pin down is the way readers have come to negotiate presentational features. Not that the sense of difficulty completely disappeared. Fifty years and more after the poem's first appearance, Clare R. Kinney was still saying that readers of *The Waste Land* are tempted to discover a narrative of quest or pilgrimage, but are constantly thwarted,[33] a comment amounting to a kind of narratological extension of Denis Donoghue's remark that the poem exhibits, not formlessness, but "a passion for form, largely unfulfilled".[34] Chong-Ho Lee, too, has described the poem as a puzzle: no story-line, no *telos*, no single meaning, and no single author (Eliot? Pound? the writers of the quotes? the reader?). All the same, Lee did say that this indefiniteness was precociously ur-postmodern, which perhaps made it acceptable after all.[35] Ruth Nevo, at any rate, had no doubts. Though a New Critic by training, she was grateful to Derridean poststructuralism for weakening the stranglehold of the New Critical reading by Cleanth Brooks. Whereas Brooks had declared *The Waste Land* a unified aesthetic whole, Nevo said that it positively self-deconstructs. It is a poem "against itself", producing a force of dislocation which spreads in all directions.[36] Even if Nevo is herself a professional literary scholar and critic, her attitude reflects the biggest single difference between readers of 1922 and most readers later on. That the poem knocks the ball squarely into the reader's court is nowadays taken for granted. The presentational features are no longer blamed as sins of either omission or commission, and readers rise to the challenge.

But this change of attitude, though crucial for an understanding of Eliot's co-adaptative achievement, does not of itself reveal how readers actually *make sense* of the text's presentation. This is a matter of their basic attempt to empathize with Eliot's writing and its circumstances. So although they will also want to relate his words to their own life-world in the here-and-now, we first need to consider, in the somewhat rarefied manner of Wolfgang Iser, those cognitive moves which a reader would *always and at the very least* have to engage in, whether reading in 1922 or 2022, and whether well-disposed to the poem or not.[37]

Iser does recognize the distinction between a text's implied reader and any particular real reader. But his analytical method does not bring it sharply into focus, and in this sense is not fully historical. In practice, the distinction can even be collapsed, so that the Iserian critic figures as a kind of representative "Everyreader", whose own powers of intuition and judgement can always safely be relied on. All the same, the approach can still capture a very wide range of effects. Nor, despite appearances, is it prescriptive. Even if my next few pages will be liberally peppered with "we" and "the reader", this does not entail a behaviouristic assumption that all readers will respond in a robotically similar manner. Granted, all responsible readers certainly do try to inhabit the reader persona which Eliot offers them, and will not adopt a more critical stance without a duly empathetic trial. But even their movement of empathy will be always already affected by the situationality from within which it commences. In addition, they are not only social beings, but social *individuals*, with a core of moral and temperamental mystery. No commentator can ever *really* be an Everyreader. In the last analysis, any interpreter is as representative as any other, in that all readers, however similar to some other readers, are also different as well. In certain respects, then, my own personal sense-making will inevitably differ from that of many other interpreters. But for present purposes, my suggestions will be neither better nor worse than anybody else's. At least for a little while, my discussion of different readers' historically different situationalities can be suspended.

So with all due reservations, the immediate question is: As readers empathize their way into *The Waste Land*, what mental operations have they actually been persuaded to engage in? What about Part II, for instance, "A Game of Chess"?[38]

Well, Part II is normally approached from Part I, "The Burial of the Dead", and the transition between the two Parts is abrupt and mystifying. This need not detain us here, however, since readers deal with it in basically the same way as the transitions between the main passages *within* Part II. In any case, a reader's earliest concern with "A Game of Chess" will probably be to get just some very general idea of what it is about.

In effect, such preliminary impressions might well centre on selectional unpleasantnesses. The poem seems to introduce us to two main female characters, one a lady (or "lady") placed in a setting with some claims (or pretensions) to elegance, the other a Cockney in a pub at closing time. Their moves are restricted by the somewhat sinister "game of chess" into which they are both locked, a demeaning sexual determinism of which we see another version in the mechanical copulation of the typist and the "young man carbuncular" in Part III. In the lady, the degraded sexuality expresses itself as neurosis, a fantasy of street-walking, and a kind of strained expectancy. In the Cockney woman, there is the gossipy prurience, and the predatoriness of her self-righteous threat to seduce an unfortunate friend's husband.

In order to get even this much out of the writing, we have already had to engage with Eliot's style of presentational politeness, a distinctive way of handling his materials which a purely "eyes-on-the-page" stylistics cannot fully deal with. Useful here is H. P. Grice's suggestion that all linguistic interchanges work according to a Cooperative Principle, involving four maxims for helpful communication.[39] Eliot plays havoc with all four maxims and in this way challenges readers to do a lot of the sense-making for themselves. So consistently does he do this that it can be seen as his style's superordinate impulse. Since he also flouts more than one maxim at a time, a cut-and-dried discussion of each maxim in turn will not always be possible. Some linguists would in any case say that one of the maxims, the so-called maxim of relation, is more important than the other three, and that they can actually be reduced to it.[40] But by retaining all four of them, and by trying to keep them at least partly separate, I shall perhaps catch something of Eliot's interpersonal complexity.

According to Grice's maxim of relation, communicators need to be sure that the things they say have a clear bearing — that a listener or reader will be able to see why they are relevant. As it happens, Eliot sometimes writes whole passages which, with the possible exception of a few lines or phrases here and there, seem to be more or less about one and the same thing, and to hang together fairly well. The real problem of relevance comes at higher levels of coherence, between the poem's five Parts, and between the main passages within those Parts. Furthermore, the problem is immediately aggravated by simultaneous floutings of Grice's maxim of manner. Among other things, this maxim states that a helpful communicator goes about things in an orderly way. Eliot's presentation is disorderly, in the sense that from one main passage to the next he switches viewpoint, verse-form, stylistic level, and general mood.

"The Game of Chess" seems to fall into three main passages, which on the page are typographically marked by line-spacing. Lines 1–34 are all about the lady sitting at a dressing table in a large room with ornate but possibly tawdry decor — by the time we get to the footsteps shuffling on the stairs (line 31) things sound almost sordid. This first passage is a third-person-singular description and contains run-on iambic pentameters somewhat reminiscent of late Shakespeare, with fairly elaborate long sentences and a smattering of rare words. The second main passage is lines 35–61. This switches to a partly dramatic method of presentation, with what we can take to be the same lady's words directly reported; more surrealistically, the words are spoken by her hair as she brushes it (lines 32–4). But there is also what seems to be a second voice, though in view of the lack of inverted commas it may not actually speak aloud. Many of the lines are short and colloquial, and there are some decidedly un-Shakespearian rhythms. The third main passage is from line 62 to the end, and dramatizes the pub scene. Interrupted only by the barman's calling time, the Cockney woman in effect speaks a dramatic monologue, printed on the page as verse, but with many short lines, and with the Shakespearian style completely forgotten amid the non-standard syntax and colloquial stress and intonation patterns. Other voices again emerge with the farewells as the pub empties.

The transition from the first main passage to the second is somewhat puzzling. The lady herself provides some continuity, but whose is the "other" voice? Is she replying to her own questions? Is it perhaps a male visitor, who will not tell her what he really thinks about her situation? Is it the poet, and if so, during an earlier visit to her, or as he now describes her to us in retrospect or imagination? But the break between the second and third main passage is even sharper. There is an abrupt change of both physical location and social ambience, with no apparent continuity in the characters involved.

But Grice's idea was not simply that there are maxims which a communicator can either observe or flout. Even if the maxims do appear to be flouted, the recipients of a communication nevertheless tend to assume that its sender is still trying to be cooperative. They conclude that the flouting is actually an economical or powerful way of making some kind of point, for instance by irony or understatement. Flouting the maxims can thus amount to an *implicature* of such a meaning, a meaning which listeners or readers have a natural curiosity to ferret out. This is precisely how Eliot's abrupt transitions work. They are not cooperative in the usual way, but challenge us to make connections for ourselves.

My earlier summary has already suggested one kind of overall relation which we can impose on "The Game of Chess", and also one of the links that can be made with the typist and her carbuncular lover in the next Part. In moving from the lady to the Cockney in the pub, we see no immediate connection, but assume that in fact there must be one, even though the two women belong to rather different worlds and stories. Given this generous assumption on our part, the sordid sex issue is what we are likely to take as a common denominator. Many of the allusions, such as to the rape of Philomel (lines 22–7), seem to be in key with it, and the very title of Part II supports such an interpretation by suggesting an all-encompassing metaphor for sexual determinism. Eliot has a note explaining that the title is based on the chess scene in Middleton's *Women Beware Women*, and this in itself is enough to tune us in to the sinister sexual undertone, and not least to the Cockney woman's designs on Lil's Albert. Such a use of Eliot's notes in interpretation might not have been in key with the strictest dictates of Modernist literary formalism, according to which readers should pay attention only to the actual text of the poem. But in the pragmatics of normal reading, Eliot's notes will play a central role, being part of the circumstances of publication and interpretation.

The note on *Women Beware Women* is *enough* to help us establish a relevance, but both here and throughout we do have to be active. What we do can be discussed partly in terms of Grice's maxim of quantity, which says that a helpful communicator gives neither too much nor too little information, but just the right amount for the purpose in hand. Eliot's abrupt transitions at first make us feel that he has left something out, and the main tendency of his revisions to the manuscript, many of them proposed by Ezra Pound, was indeed to make cuts — in Eliot and other writers of the same period, the Modernist concern for elliptical economy could also result in the minimalist art of Imagist poems and haikus. But as with the relation maxim, so with quantity: despite the unusual demands made upon us, we are still prepared to assume that Eliot is trying to communicate. If necessary, we supply things ourself, making such use of his footnotes as we can. Most obviously, perhaps, he never really gives us much of a story. What about the two women's previous history, for instance? Does the knock on the door (line 61) usually come? Does it come today? Who is it who knocks? Where do the gossipers go when the pub closes? What happened after the gammon dinner? *Did* Lil lose her Albert to the speaker? All

Eliot does is to place the two women in certain settings and let them talk. The rest we can make up for ourselves.

Not that much of our energy goes to embroidering on the stories. Although we may venture our own guesses, we quickly begin to assume that Eliot has already given what from his own point of view is the most important part, and that the characters' own spoken words somehow encapsulate the significance of their entire lives, as in a dramatic monologue by Tennyson. In the end we may accept the notes' hint that the Fisher King myth provides a kind of master narrative. But we come to see this as a thematic cohesion in terms of the sterility motif. It is not a framing plot for tightly interconnected subplots. We very soon stop wondering "What happened next?"

Rather, by expanding such information and hints as Eliot does supply we begin to create-or-discover significances and patterns that are rather different from a straightforwardly coherent argument or narrative. My hyphenated expression "create-or-discover" signals that in any interpretation, and especially in interpretations of Modernist poetry, there is a pragmatic reciprocity between text and reader. As a compensation for Eliot's apparent shortfall as far as the quantity maxim goes, we bring to the text our own familiarity with other texts and with many different spheres of real life. The poem can be read as full of both intertextual and extratextual allusions, and it is our own imaginative-or-recognizing "ear" which helps us find a path through it.

One of the configurations we may create-or-discover involves some blatant enough Shakespearian allusions. The very first line is an almost exact quotation of the beginning of Enobarbus's famous speech describing Cleopatra coming on her barge of state to meet Antony for the first time. The very last line is Ophelia's farewell. And line 49, almost the very middle of "A Game of Chess", is from Ariel's song to Ferdinand, alluded to in other Parts as well. Yet although in this numerological (first-middle-last) sense Part II has a clear Shakespearian framework, the fate of the Shakespearian pentameter is, as I say, precarious. "The Chair she sat in, like a burnished throne" is firm enough, but even in the first passage there are the obvious breakdowns of the short lines (lines 27, 31, 33). In the second passage, even the central Shakespearian line itself ("Those are pearls that were his eyes") is trochaic and a tetrameter, and there are further short lines. In particular there is the burlesque rhythm of the nineteen-twenties-style rag (lines 51–3), which adds insult to injury by commenting on bardolatry as if from the lips of a flapper.[41] In the third passage, the iambic pentameter is vaguer still, and the rhythms of Ophelia's last words are a reminder that under psychic strain it could give way to something very different even in Shakespeare.[42] As we process the verse, then, we are structuring a kind of formal correlative to the increasingly unsettling subject-matter. Though "A Game of Chess" has no argument or sustained story in the conventional sense, it can be experienced as moving towards its own kind of climax, and this is partly thanks to the verse form's apparently disorderly flouting of the maxim of manner. The flouting, one might say, helps to set up affective implicatures.

Our sense of the same movement is reinforced by our simultaneous processing of another aspect of Eliot's discourse. Here again his disorderliness flouts the maxim of manner: there is no stability in the relationship between his own voice and those of the two women characters. At the beginning we realize that we are dealing with a piece of third-person description; perhaps we remember Homeric descriptions of warriors offering prayers at an altar on the morning of battle, or Pope's description of Belinda at her dressing table. In the second passage, the lady's or her hair's direct speech suddenly forces her and her predicament upon us with much greater immediacy. But there is still the "other" voice, which could be the same narrator's, even though the running commentary is now more openly cynical and even macabre. And in the last passage, the extensive dramatic monologue confronts us with the callousness of predatory lust in all its naked ugliness, as if making any narratorial comment supererogatory, and leaving us to draw our own sickened conclusions. Once again, then, we can recuperate the presentational disorderliness as a kind of affective crescendo.

Various other patterns emerge as well. We shall never know how many patterns Eliot expected us to find. We may miss much that he intended, but there is also the possibility that we find some things which would have surprised him. All we can say with certainty is that countless things do register with our literary memories and general life experience, and that we do pattern them. All the time we are making things fit, not only from one line to the next but within the larger affective dynamics as well. "The strange synthetic perfumes" (line 11), for instance, with its parody of "the strange invisible perfumes" mentioned by Enobarbus, is one of the first sly suggestions that this modern Cleopatra may be not quite so amazing as her great predecessor, and "Drowned the sense in odours" (line 13), though it still sounds Shakespearian enough, could also be a Decadent poet the 1890s, thereby harmonizing with the Beardesleyesque imagery of the boudoir. The instability of the iambic pentameter, then, is only one of several hints, on several different levels, that the twentieth century represents an unhealthy falling away from pristine certainties.

Other patterns strengthen the links between the three main passages. We can work out, for example, that the lady's jewels, perfumes and cosmetics (lines

7–13), and poor Lil's false teeth (lines 65–9) — unless she spent the money on food for the five kids — are simply the accoutrements of different pieces in the same old "game of chess", and at several points tawdry or frustrated love is connected with war or a post-war era. The love of Antony and Cleopatra was interwoven with thoughts and deeds of war. If we follow up Eliot's note, we shall find that "laquearia" (line 16) is borrowed from Virgil's description of the ceiling of Dido's hall, where, already falling in love with Aeneas, she invites him to tell of his experiences of the fall of Troy. Lil is a woman whose husband has been away at war, presumably in the trenches of France. Given all of which, we perhaps supply the idea that the unhappiness of the lady brushing her hair is connected with the absence or death of an officer husband.

Yet the main passages never coalesce, and much of our patterning-work has to do with strong contrasts between them. Some of these arise when intertextual and extratextual echoes combine with iconic or quasi-onomatopoeic effects. Just as the lady's "My nerves are bad to-night" (line 35) and the Cockney woman's "Oh is there, she said. Something o' that, I said" (line 73) belong to two completely different sociolects, so the lady does not speak much, but her repetitions and rhythms precisely suggest, not only her physical movements in brushing her hair, but her nervous agitation. The Cockney woman, by contrast, has all the volubility of her nasty self-righteousness.

Eliot does not rub things in, but there is still plenty for readers to pick up on. To take one small example: he rejected a suggestion that "Something o' that" should be spelt "Somethink o' that". In refraining for the most part from showing pronunciation by spelling, Eliot differed from writers such as George Eliot, Kipling, Conrad and Lawrence. On the one hand, no readable writing convention will ever capture every aspect of speech, and Eliot may have feared that an attempt at phonetic accuracy would distract from the things actually being said. On the other hand, his imitation of the rhythms, idiom and syntax of Cockney speech, though not at all the same thing as a transcription by a linguist, may strike us with the same more-real-than-real quality of non-standard speech in Dickens. Given these fundamentals, we hear the rest for ourselves.

The comparison with Dickens is worth dwelling on. As will later emerge in connection with *Dombey and Son*, one can speak in Bakhtinian terms of a Dickensian heteroglossia: the novels acquire a many-tongued life by holding the different ranges of speech in tension with each other, just as they were within society and culture generally. Similarly Eliot is for ever quoting or alluding to other people's texts, and adopting other people's styles; the poem has various characters of its own, some, like the two women here, with their own voices;

and it has its narrator or narrators, with their own voices as well. Like Eliot's note on the Fisher King myth, his note about the voices as somehow belonging to Tiresias may well point to some general mood or theme. Yet no theme or mood can ultimately assimilate all the different voices to each other.

Where Eliot and Dickens differ is in their reporting conventions. Even though Dickens's late novels make frequent use of free indirect speech, the transition from the words or thoughts of one character to those of another character or the narrator is usually very clear, sometimes with explicit authorial remarks. In *The Waste Land*, the abruptness with which the voices are introduced is yet another flouting of the maxim of manner, and was one of the things which caused the first readers most difficulty.

Their problem was all the greater because there are simultaneous floutings of Grice's fourth maxim, the maxim of quality, which states that one should only say that which one believes to be true. Now in a story, whether told in casual conversation or in the form of a literary work, this maxim applies in a particular way. Even though some of the people, places and events mentioned may be real, many others will most probably not be. We do accept fiction, on the understanding that it has its own kind of interest and even truth; for instance, it may suggest something typical of life in general, or it may mark a moral point. But we can certainly speak of a story as flouting the maxim of quality, if we feel that the teller is not being frank about his or her own personal judgement and feelings as regards the story. It is precisely here that *The Waste Land* has always seemed such a riddle. How much do we hear of Eliot's own "true" voice? On the one hand, Eliot himself is presumably the narrator of the first passage in "The Game of Chess", and only Eliot could have brought about the poem's juxtapositions. Often they are juxtapositions of allusions, but the paradox is that Eliot's own voice is nothing if not allusive. On the other hand, whose *is* the "other" voice in the second passage? *Could* it be Eliot himself in some sense? If so, he would be no less intrusive a narrator than Dickens, except that we can never be in much doubt that Dickens is addressing us. Similarly, what do we do with the last line of Part II (the borrowing of Ophelia's last words)? The gross inappropriateness of "sweet ladies" as a description of either of this Part's two main characters, or of the other denizens of the pub, can be taken as a flouting of the quality maxim on Eliot's part, setting up an ironic implicature. But whether we hear the words as actually spoken by Eliot himself, by Ophelia or her ghost, or by somebody from the pub is a matter of choice. All in all, then, now we hear him, now we don't.

I say "we". The immediate point has been to suggest how any reader at all will get to grips with Eliot's impolitely unhelpful presentation. Yet this a-historical, Iserian style of analysis is in the long run artificial, and the present chapter's larger argument is that the experience of reading *The Waste Land* has actually changed over time, partly as a result of the co-adaptation initiated by Eliot himself between accepted social norms and his own intervention.

By way of concretizing the pragmatic fact that reading styles do change, here are two very slight examples which have nothing at all to do with politeness. First, many present-day readers of *The Waste Land* will know that in 1971 Eliot's widow, his second wife, published the original typescripts of the poem. From these it emerges that an earlier title Eliot had thought of for Part II was "In the Cage", an allusion to the passage from Petronius which subsequently became the epigraph for the entire poem — in English: "I saw with my own eyes the Sybil at Cumae hanging in a cage, and when the boys said to her: 'Sybil, what do you want?' she answered: 'I want to die'".[43] Knowing this, it is almost impossible for a reader not to see ways in which it, too, can suggest an organizing metaphor for the whole of Part II. Secondly, in our ceaseless efforts to pin down the poem's voice or voices, the parenthesis of line 5 —

> ...fruited vines
> From which a golden Cupidon peeped out
> (Another hid his eyes behind his wing)

— almost inevitably reminds us of the pawky humour of *Old Possum's Book of Practical Cats*, first published in 1939. Neither of these references was available to the first readers, then. But today they both seem so entirely natural that it would be absurd to try and stop ourselves using them as at least part of the way in which we relate to the poem.

The same point can be generalized to the entire interpersonal dynamics of Eliot's style. Not only is his style not straightforwardly "there on the page". A pragmatic account must stress that it never has been, in that reading is always as much a bringing-to the text as a taking-from it. During the course of time, or as the text passes from one culture to another, it actually comes to work in different ways. Readers' reactions to a literary style are bound up with their taste in aesthetic matters generally, which has a very powerful psychological reality. People genuinely believe that certain things are beautiful, shapely, artistic, special. But such convictions are partly affected — though not rigidly *determined* — by cultural conditioning, and important consequences stem from the simple fact that all new styles, and even styles as radically revolutionary as the Modernist ones, are only new until the next new style is introduced. The difficulties of a high Modernist poem such as *The Waste Land* are experienced as such by its readers, and have not simply disappeared. Yet as we continue to move into the future, the poem may actually be less baffling than at first. Although readers still have to perform the cognitive operations just illustrated in much the same way as its earliest audience did, their minds may do the job more quickly. Modernist styles, like other styles, have been part of our pluralist culture for a long time now. The kinds of connectivity involved have become very familiar, not least from films, pop videos, and television commercials.

In difficult undertakings of all kinds, the level of human achievement seems to get constantly higher. There are connoisseurs of crossword puzzles who never attempt *The Times* crossword until the day *after* it has been published, claiming that it will be easier once it has already been solved by many other people. One of the life scientists who take this kind of thing seriously is Rupert Sheldrake, who suggests that there must be some sort of supra-personal, extended mind. This would take the form of morphogenetic, behavioural, mental and social fields, within which there would be a kind of cumulative collective memory of habits and skills, so influencing and shaping individuals through "morphic resonance".[44] Whether Sheldrake's hypothesis is correct is neither here nor there. The point is only that there are tendencies in human behaviours that have led him to put it forward. An increasing facility in readers of difficult Modernist texts would be part of the larger anthropological trend.

This brings us back to changes of attitude. When people learn to do something difficult, the sense of achievement is enjoyable. The mastery of a difficult skill — whether it be playing the violin or downhill skiing — brings with it a pleasure that is quite specific to the skill in question, and sometimes it is only the anticipation of such delights which can persuade people to slog on with training or learning. If few of the earliest readers of *The Waste Land* would have foreseen the pleasure with which Ruth Nevo would later approach the text, this was because the difficulties were apparently of a new kind, and deeply confusing and offensive in ways which present-day readers may find hard to grasp.

Even so, many readers had already stopped complaining in the 1920s and 1930s, from which point onwards the poem's claim to a place in literary history was more or less unchallenged. Nothing had happened to its text on the page. But "off the page", things could hardly have been more different. The crucial change was to the ethos within which poetry was being read.

To examine the altered attitudes in more detail will bring the historical achievement of Eliot's co-adaptation under direct scrutiny. How, exactly, did society make concessions to his individuality? And how did his individuality make concessions to society? How was it that his outrageousness was not only gradually mitigated, but assimilated to the point at which society's notions of decorum could themselves be said to have changed? No answer can be complete. But we can get at least some idea of how the shift took place by relating certain features of the poem itself to certain trends in the more favourable early comments on it, and to certain things which Eliot himself did or said in other contexts.

One of the ways in which selectional offensiveness was mitigated apparently had to do with those fleeting hints of love, beauty or fulfilment. As noted, these partly worked as a foil which made the sordid sterility and blank despair seem even more distressing. Yet at the same time they could clearly be read in their own right, and the poet of

> — Yet when we came back, late, from the hyacinth garden,
> Your arms full, and your hair wet, I could not
> Speak, and my eyes failed, I was neither
> Living nor dead, and I knew nothing,
> Looking into the heart of the light, the silence.[45]

could meet admirers of Dante or Rossetti half-way — perhaps more than half-way. Indeed, an odd kind of *gestalt*-switch could occur, whereby all the sordidness and sterility themselves became a foil to such beautiful moments of dawning vision. This was all the more likely in that such a reading style already had very strong precedents within cultural tradition, one well-known example being Keats's remark on *King Lear*:

> ...the excellence of every Art is in its intensity, capable of making all disagreeables evaporate, from their being in close relationship with Beauty and Truth...[46]

A still more immediate stimulus was Eliot's own earliest criticism, for instance the essay on Dante that concluded *The Sacred Wood*, published only two years before *The Waste Land*:

> The contemplation of the horrid or sordid or disgusting, by an artist, is the necessary and negative aspect of the impulse toward the pursuit of beauty.[47]

After the publication of *Ash Wednesday* and the news of Eliot's Anglican confirmation, interpretations of *The Waste Land* along these lines were well on their way to becoming orthodox. Commenting on *Four Quartets* in 1947, Helen

Gardner said it was now widely recognized that the first critics of *The Waste Land* had misread it, unable to realize that it was an *Inferno* which would lead on to a *Purgatorio*.[48]

The other main form of selectional mitigation was for a different kind of reader, and "mitigation" is perhaps a misnomer. The point is that there were readers who positively acquiesced in the poem's offensiveness of theme because it seemed to them, not misplaced but clairvoyant. These were readers for whom the First World War had brought an end to civilization and hope, for whom the present was a barren wilderness or meaningless charade, for whom modern technology and society represented a betrayal of mankind's ancient sources of strength. Alternatively, they were readers who came to see things this way as they contemplated *The Waste Land*. And once again, the reading strategy was reinforced by things quite external to the text of the particular poem. Eliot's own early criticism often seemed to take "the horrid or sordid or disgusting" as the basic fact of modern life. Soon "The Hollow Men" seemed to pinpoint still more sharply the age's blank futility, and by 1931 Edmund Wilson was persuasively seeing Eliot's "poetry of drouth" as post-war society's most truthful mirror.[49] Leavis's influential gloss of 1932 was to similar effect:

> In considering our present plight we have ... to take account of the incessant rapid change that characterizes the Machine Age. The result is breach of continuity and the uprooting of life. This last metaphor has a peculiar aptness, for what we are witnessing today is the final uprooting of the immemorial ways of life, of life deeply rooted in the soil.[50]

A kind of confirmation for such readings could be drawn from accounts of contemporary life in, say, the novels of Lawrence and Huxley.

As for the poem's presentational impoliteness, even the most cursory examination revealed one feature which sharply qualified the impression of overall incoherence. Locally, *The Waste Land* could have a perspicuousness of almost unbearable intensity. This alone was presumably enough to keep many readers reading.

> A rat crept softly through the vegetation
> Dragging its slimy belly on the bank
> While I was fishing in the dull canal
> On a winter evening round behind the gashouse.[51]

About this and numerous other phrases, lines and passages there was, quite simply, nothing unclear. On the contrary, there was much that was not only clear but strangely fascinating. Nor did this paradoxical state of affairs pass without comment. For some readers, the local clarity has never wholly redeemed the impression of overall confusion. In 1960, Graham Hough was still describing the poem as basically belonging to the Imagist tradition, and consequently unable to rise above brilliant flashes and strange short-term effects of madness and dream.[52] But for early champions of Eliot such as Pound, I. A. Richards, Conrad Aiken, Leavis and Cleanth Brooks, various rationalizations did seem possible, partly suggested, as we should already expect, by Eliot's own criticism. Three in particular assimilated presentational offensiveness very effectively.

One argument was that Eliot had chosen the only form capable of revealing the nature of modern life. This claim was anticipated by Eliot's immensely influential essay on the Metaphysical poets, published just a year before *The Waste Land*:

> We can only say that it appears likely that poets in our civilization, as it exists at present, must be *difficult*. Our civilization comprehends great variety and complexity, and this variety and complexity, playing upon a refined sensibility, must produce various and complex results. The poet must become more and more comprehensive, more allusive, more indirect, in order to force, to dislocate if necessary, language into his meaning.[53]

In 1943 Yvor Winters was to attack this argument as an example of the fallacy of imitative form: "Eliot, in dealing with debased and stupid material, felt himself obliged to seek his form in this matter: the result is confusion and journalistic reproduction of detail".[54] Yet many other readers came to feel that Eliot's very theme required that the poem itself be "a heap of broken images", "fragments ... shored against my ruins". The abrupt transitions from one thing to the next were sometimes justified as a collage technique like that used, for similar reasons, in Modernist visual art.

A second rationalization developed the implications of that "refined sensibility" of the poet on which the variety and complexity of contemporary civilization "plays". Here again the essay on the Metaphysical poets was seminal, in effect giving a new lease of life to Coleridge's account of poetic imagination as manifested in reconciliations of opposite and discordant qualities:

> When a poet's mind is perfectly equipped for its work, it is constantly amalgamating disparate experience; the ordinary man's experience is chaotic, irregular, fragmentary. The latter falls in love, or reads Spinoza, and these two experiences have nothing to do with each other, or with the noise of the typewriter or the smell of cooking; in the mind of the poet these experiences are always forming new wholes.[55]

This and similar formulations led American New Critics to search, beneath apparent ironies, ambiguities, paradoxes, tensions, discords, for wonderful new unities. The aesthetic wholes they came up with were supposed to be autotelically impersonal, which is why their commentary can often seem rather *anaesthetic*. In Cleanth Brooks's a ccount of *The Waste Land*, later experienced by Ruth Nevo as a such a straitjacket, presentational offensiveness was smoothly defused. Having argued that the poem's multi-layered ironies and incongruous juxtapositions prompt a sense of the oneness of experience and the unity of all historical periods, Brooks concluded by rebutting readers' protests at presentational incoherence and selectional unpleasantness in a single sentence: Eliot's "statement of beliefs emerges *through* confusion and cynicism — not in spite of them".[56]

Thirdly, there was the argument that to look for a narrative or discursive thread in a poem is at once too simple and too sophisticated a procedure. One of the precedents in Eliot's own criticism was from *The Use of Poetry and the Use of Criticism* (1933) and ran as follows:

> The chief use of the "meaning" of a poem, in the ordinary sense, may be . . . to satisfy one habit of the reader, to keep his mind diverted and quiet, while the poem does its work upon him: much as the imaginary burglar is always provided with a bit of nice meat for the house-dog. This is a normal situation of which I approve. But the minds of all poets do not work that way; some of them, assuming that there are other minds like their own, become impatient of this "meaning" which seems superfluous, and perceive possibilities of intensity through its elimination.[57]

This line of argument was parallel to the contemporary dogmas of psychoanalysis and Surrealism. But Eliot, more characteristically, saw the "possibilities of intensity" in terms of "The Music of Poetry" — this being the title of a lecture he gave on the subject in 1942.[58] Poetry's music could originate, before words, in a rhythm. Nor did the reader need to understand the words in order to appreciate it. As early as 1926, I. A. Richards had expatiated on the complex psychological organization of *The Waste Land*'s "music of ideas",[59] and many subsequent commentators dwelt on subtle interweavings of mood and tone. In time, the poem's five parts came to be compared with the movements of a Beethoven string quartet, an interpretative strategy further encouraged by "The Music of Poetry" and by the title and structure of *Four Quartets*.

Actively encouraged by Eliot himself, then, there grew up around *The Waste Land* a body of commentary which served to soften the poem's offensiveness. Even though most critics did not directly discuss affect, preferring, as we have seen, to concentrate on questions of form and expressivity, their own writings actually had an affective function, helping to normalize relations between the writer and his audience, in practice by getting the audience to change its attitudes. Selectional impoliteness was in point of fact weighed against a perceived desire for spiritual wholeness, or against an acclaimed honesty about the modern condition. Presentational impoliteness came to be taken as a formal equivalent to the poem's modern themes, as the expression of a refined and ultimately unifying sensibility, and as the expression of deeper, non-cerebral modes of knowing and being. With both kinds of politeness, the discussion revealed some sense of Eliot's gamble, and there was also a co-adaptive tension between different aspects of one and the same text: between the images of sordidness or futility and the images of love and thirst; and between an overall incoherence and the intense local clarities.

Nor was this all. Over and above such literary-critical considerations, there were always aspects of the communicative relationship between Eliot and readers by which first impressions of his inconsiderateness could be further modified. In particular, his own attitude towards the general public was not conspicuously hostile. On the contrary, he had always been fascinated by the intimate relation between performer and audience in the music hall,[60] and in striking contrast to Pound, his own aspirations became steadily less elitist.[61] *Murder in the Cathedral* may lack the unpretentious ease of Andrew Young's *Nicodemus*. But Eliot did realize that writing plays demanded a wide appeal, and he was ready to oblige. As he said in an interview for the BBC at the outbreak of World War II, "I don't want you to think of the literary artist as a man who writes for a select few, either deliberately or because he can't help himself".[62]

By that time he had long been a living legend. As the editor of *Criterion* he was held in considerable esteem, and his job with the Fabers publishing house made him the single most important arbiter and patron of contemporary poetry. In his public self-presentation there could be something rather benign and even slightly comical, despite, or perhaps because of, his authoritarian manner. He was not slow to associate himself with conservative and even reactionary sentiments, but deliberately cultivated an old-fogey persona to boot. Jokes and stories about him flourished accordingly. Virginia Woolf once wrote to her brother-in-law: "Come to dinner. Eliot will be there in a four-piece suit".[63] And in 1923, he astonished Richard Aldington by raising his hat to a sentry on duty outside Malborough House.[64]

How could anybody so important, so old-fashioned, so amiably bumbling, so over-correct, be impolite? The public persona was an inseparable part of the co-adaptative process whereby he and his audience met each other half-way. Not least, it could highlight a certain aspect of his poetry itself. There, too, could be detected a disarming posture of amusingly extreme propriety. Indeed, readers' outraged protests at the writing's impoliteness might not unreasonably have given way to something more like pity. Peter Ackroyd, one of his biographers, has interpreted his salutation to the sentry as residual American ignorance of British customs. But underneath the bowler hat and dark suit there was apparently another Eliot, one of whose emanations was Prufrock, who had seen "the eternal Footman hold my coat, and snicker, / And in short, I was afraid". From Prufrock's sense of inferiority before social inferiors to the self-abasement before God in *Four Quartets*, the poetry presents a long sequence of characters, personae or voices caught in the throes of an almost crippling humility.

Here, then, the writing itself was again co-adaptive. The politeness *in* (i.e. within the world created by) the writing, like the hyper-politeness Eliot cultivated in everyday life, was completely at odds with the politeness *of* the writing, which could be aggressively *im*polite. The politeness *in* the poetry endorsed the hierarchies of an older generation, and was an important aspect of the reassurance Eliot could offer those offended by the impoliteness *of* the poetry. His management of politeness as a whole, therefore, was at once shockingly individual and socially acceptable. His deferential offensiveness or offensive deference suggests how, in a major author's historical co-adaption, the horizons of expectations associated with different historical periods are always already merged. Eliot expected himself to be, and expected his readers to find him, not only a brash young American Modernist, but a genteel Victorian or Edwardian, a veritable pillar of society.

◦∾

Today, *The Waste Land* has been in print for almost eighty years, and Eliot himself has been dead for over thirty. For more than two decades, young readers have been coming to the poem who have never been its author's contemporary. For them, it is just as distant in time as was *In Memoriam* from Eliot's first readers. This in itself would de-fuse much of its original offensiveness.

Even earlier on, to the many readers — including schoolteachers, university teachers, and their pupils' pupils — who became well acquainted with Eliot's critical essays, any suggestion that he was downright impolite would already have seemed anomalous. To recapitulate for a moment, his early comments on other poets suggested, not only reasons why poetry had to be unpleasant, but a threefold mitigation for his own work's difficulty: the difficulty is the reaction of a refined sensibility to modern life's complexity; the odd juxtapositions represent new poetic wholes; and the apparent lack of coherence stems from deeper, non-cerebral modes of being and knowing. More generally, his early criticism's pragmatic impact was to make his own poetry the very last place in which one would expect to find serious impoliteness. Our responses to impoliteness involve an assessment of whether the perpetrator really meant it, as we say. The impoliteness of a madman, a drunk, an absent-minded professor, a person in a great hurry, counsel for the prosecution, a very close friend or loved-one, is simply not offensive. As the result of essays such as "Tradition and the Individual Talent", Eliot's poetry was similarly perceived to be not wholly expressive of him as a man. His most seminal idea about poetry was that it is impersonal. Swallow that, as most of his early champions did swallow it, and you cannot go on thinking that *The Waste Land* is full-bloodedly rude, no matter how upset you were at first.

Nor did the pragmatic changes stop there. Eliot's early critical writings started a tradition of scholastic commentary which assumed massive proportions, as twentieth-century poetry came to occupy a central place in the syllabuses of schools and universities. Nowadays many readers first confront *The Waste Land* in a student's edition which offers not only a helpful introduction but notes that are much more detailed than Eliot's own. In this situation, new readers can be forgiven for thinking that, no matter how difficult Eliot's style may seem at first, it probably just had to be that way, and that it will be all plain sailing once they have learned the ropes. In almost any bookshop, they can pick up some study guide which will sort it all out for them, just as they could buy a guide to home brewing. Most explicators speak in tones of such reassuring matter-of-factness, and with such flattering confidence in novices' ability to get the point, that readers may even imagine that they have done so without noticing. Eliot without tears, as it were. There may even be a possibility that the difficulty of Modernist texts will become not only not shocking, which is inevitable, but not really arresting in any way at all. Just more lecture fodder, as Lionel Trilling might have said.[65]

Middle-aged and older readers who have always admired Eliot may find this a distressing prospect, but can perhaps take comfort. The overkill delivered by the twentieth-century "lit. crit." industry has merely accelerated the normal progress of fame. New writers have always had to win acceptance; established writers usually become less fashionable after a time; and after a further lapse of years, they are sometimes rediscovered. Readers approaching them with the preconceptions of an entirely different world view may find a new significance in them.

During the last three decades of the twentieth century, this, too, was happening to Eliot. Despite the elusiveness of his own voice in *The Waste Land*, despite his own early theory of the impersonality of poetry, despite his efforts to keep his own private life private, despite literary structuralists' obituaries on the author, readers were now avidly reading many excellent author biographies, including biographies of Eliot.[66] As a result, it became widely known that he was very unhappy in his first marriage. Confronted with his wife's mental illness, he was loyal and long-suffering, but the strain was enormous, and he drafted the final sections of *The Waste Land* while himself undergoing psychological treatment in the clinic of Dr Roger Vittoz in Lausanne. Whatever else the writing of the poem entailed for him, it was also therapeutic. Even seventy years after first publication, it still did not allow itself to be read in the way he warned against in "Tradition and the Individual Talent", as a straightforward expression of its author's suffering. But readers' new awareness of that suffering was inevitably recovering a reverberation. As always, a pragmatic link could forge itself between literary interpretation and biographical considerations. There was now a firmer sense that *The Waste Land* is "for real". As we saw, from the late 1960s onwards its expressivity became the major theme of critical commentary.

As a corollary, in our new century the poem's impoliteness could well regain — despite the overhelpfulness of the "lit. crit." industry — something of its conspicuousness, so that the stylistic difficulties, no longer simply insulting, would in the end be pleasurable. Carol C. Christ's emphasis on the note of Tennysonian melancholy would have to be qualified with a sense of Eliot's Tennysonian delight in sheer verbal mastery. The beginnings of such a change were already clear in Ruth Nevo's reading. With time, Eliot's floutings of Grice's four maxims could increasingly seem like a cat-and-mouse game with readers, a game which they will happily indulge. The poem's manifold voices would be relished as a ventriloquistic tour de force, reminiscent of a fast-changing series of cabaret sketches, so giving point to the original title for Parts I and II together: "He do the Police in different voices". This particular nugget of Cockney speech had already been made literary by Dickens, and Eliot may have cut it out only because too few clues are better than too many. It was first spoken by old Betty Higden in *Our Mutual Friend*, the adoptive parent of Sloppy, the foundling. "And I do love a newspaper," she says. "You mightn't think it, but Sloppy is a beautiful reader of a newspaper. He do the Police in different voices".[67] Throughout *The Waste Land*, Eliot himself, no less than Sloppy, no less than Dickens in public readings of his own works, is for ever doing people in different voices, echoing, quoting, parodying. As a performance which shores words against ruin, it is an amazing feat of vocal conservation and creation.

For readers hearing the poem in this way, the evident hedonism and the changed perceptions of the subject matter could have a particular bearing on each other. This was already hinted by Calvin Bedient (1986), whose attempt to connect the poem's manifold voices to Eliot's own spiritual predicament brought in Bakhtin on polyvocalism, Julia Kristeva on abjection, Angus Fletcher on allegory, and Freud on just about everything.[68] Calvin's procedure was a bit on the solemn side. Making the poem too frontally biographical, he also weighed it down with late-twentieth-century guru-babble. All the same, he was beginning to pick up something new: a boldness and a gaiety which go just as deep as the anguish, perhaps deeper, and which are quite at odds with the humbly old-fashioned, polite personae *in* Eliot's writing.

Eliot the tiger! Promethean Eliot! The impoliteness *of* the writing, positively valorized! This could be the emphasis now. Yes, the suffering was real enough. Yes, the suffering got expressed. Yes, the suffering remains. But in the midst of it, Eliot had broken through to an ecstasy of style, leaving readers to catch up with him. The shock to them was inevitable, just as was the shock to viewers of great early-modern painting. But that painting was not *only* shocking, and at least Robert Hughes finds the culture of the late twentieth century quite drab and directionless by comparison:

> What has our culture lost in 1980 that the *avant-garde* had in 1890? Ebullience, idealism, confidence, the belief that there was plenty of territory to explore, and above all the sense that art, in the most disinterested and noble way, could find the metaphors by which a radically changing culture could be explained to its inhabitants.[69]

In Eliot, even after the war, even after his personal agonies, exactly the same virtues have their force: not only the explanatory drive (which in one sense did depersonalize his experience), but also ebullience, idealism, confidence, a sense of creative possibilities, disinterestedness (which was not an absence of human vibration), nobility.

Some of the usual pointers from his early criticism still give a lead. Others can no longer. Musical analogies will always help with the non-cerebral dynamics. Less relevant is talk of amalgamations of disparate experience in aesthetic

heterocosms, or of stylistic difficulty as a necessary homologue to the difficulty of modern life. Eliot's puckish style can now be read as the product of
resistance, opposition, victory even, a reading which chimes with a rather different set of his own apophthegms. In 1931, he wrote to Stephen Spender about
Beethoven's Quartet in A minor:

> There is a sort of heavenly or at least more than human gaiety about some of
> his later things which one imagines might come to oneself as the fruit of rec-
> onciliation and relief after immense suffering; I should like to get something
> of that into verse before I die.[70]

Perhaps he need not have worried. The very wording hints that such gaiety
would not necessarily be predicated on an autumnal serenity, but could just as
easily signal the kind of release — the sudden lifting of the burden of anxiety
and fear — of which, two years later, he was to speak *à propos* Housman's and
his own poetic secretions. His thoughts had already been moving in the direction of a kind of pregnant frivolity at least a year before the publication of *The
Waste Land*, for it was in the essay on Marvell (1921) that he spoke of an "alliance of levity and seriousness (by which the seriousness is intensified)".[71] *The
Waste Land* can be read as just that sort of poetry.

Distinctions between tragedy and comedy break down, confirming that
remark from *The Sacred Wood* (1920): "The contemplation of the horrid or
sordid or disgusting, by an artist, is the necessary and negative aspect of the
impulse toward the pursuit of beauty."[72] What originally seemed impolite, what
still seems impolite in an interpretation which empathizes with the context of
the writing, is no longer simply impolite. As context of writing and context of
current reading are juxtaposed through interpretative mediation, the impoliteness is also enjoyable. The poem comes to have the edifying exemplariness of
playfulness in a Stoic, or even of a style learnt from despair. Eliot emerges, not
only as a major artist, but as a fuller historical personality than a Modernist
artist was perhaps supposed to be. There is still no need to worship him. One
can still reject his politics. It is still regrettable that his personality, paradoxically bolstered by his dogma of impersonality, eclipsed the Gerhardies and the
Andrew Youngs. But for all that, the personality was energetic and inspiring.
Challenging the horrid, the sordid, the disgusting in his own life, and in the
dreadful age in which he lived, he tirelessly hoped for new kinds of satisfaction
and meaningfulness, artistic and other.

In the short run, the impoliteness was hurtful and iconoclastic. We still
have to read it that way, if need be with assistance from the *Critical Heritage*

volumes, in order to see it for what it was. Without this historical perspective, we shall not appreciate the force of the impoliteness as it becomes, in the long run, simultaneously something else as well. The offensive hedonism becomes, in fact, Eliot's sheer refusal to accept things as they are; his insistence on his right to try and change anything and everything, no matter how distressing; his determination to change, above all, the culture to which he will remain grateful and ungrateful for his own formation.

Seen this way, the specific tension between the shocking impoliteness *of* the poem and the humble politeness *in* it comes across as a most beautiful co-adaptation with history. The beauty has a prodigious and continuing moral force, and not least for our own postmodern society, divided along multiple fault-lines, yet pressured towards a homogenizing globalization.[73] So placed, our anxieties are very basic. Who are we? Where do we belong? What to believe? What to value? From *The Waste Land*, we can take to ourselves, not some single fool-proof model of human identity, but an inspiration for living through chaotic times that is strongly polyvalent. What we find in Eliot is an unbending urge, as civilization and love both fall away, to change things, if need be with a disconcerting vigour, and so break through to joy.

CHAPTER 4

Henry Vaughan's unexpectedness

In the twentieth century Henry Vaughan, like Eliot, was much read through the spectacles of Modernist aestheticization. Partly for this reason, the full force of his literary deed, no less than Eliot's, was lost. But here, too, an appreciatively mediating critic can now seek to raise readers' powers of empathy ethnographically, by studying the writing's stylistic features within its distant sociocultural context. In this way, the boldness of Vaughan's historical co-adaption may once more become a challenge. Again as with Eliot, we shall be able to speak of a beauty pertaining, not to Kant's realm of the aesthetic, but to the ethical realm of practical reason: of a co-adaptation of the individual and the social which amounts to a beauty of deed.

Most of Vaughan's poems, secular and religious, still tend to get dismissed as merely competent and readable. Their diction echoes other poets, both Cavalier and Metaphysical, and their themes and modes are the familiar ones of love, satire, retirement, and devotion. In the devotional poems, there are also marked overtones of the Bible and hermetic writers, and the memories of Herbert are especially strong. Perhaps all this can most readily be discussed in terms of a communal intertextuality. Certainly an explication of *Silex Scintillans* as a distinctive and sustained achievement of the same order as *The Temple* would be rather unconvincing, and the Herbertian traits are for the most part not at all the same sort of thing as Gerhardie's transformation of Chekhov. We are more likely to speak of derivativeness, and of conventionality in the negative sense.

But to complain about a lack of originality here may be excessively Romantic. It runs the risk of valorizing the individual element in the human make-up at the expense of the social, so failing acknowledge that Barthes, in his famous essay "The Death of the Author",[1] was making an important point, even if his valorization of the social went too far in the opposite direction. That Vaughan's poetry was emerging from within an entire community's intertextuality was the most precious thing it could communicate to its first readers. Like the ballads, nursery rhymes and other forms of popular culture — literate, oral, visual — which so readily lend themselves to Barthesian analysis, Vaughan's poems were sometimes representative to the point of anonymity. But given the aims he had in view, this was *necessary*. As I shall try to suggest, it was a crucial part of his writing's beauty of deed.

Then again, *Silex Scintillans* does also contain a smallish number of poems in which, by general consent, Vaughan puts his borrowings to his own uses. These poems, without ceasing to be social documents, are more markedly individual as well. The co-adaptive tension between the social and the individual is much stronger.

Here too, though, his reputation has not been straightforward. If the strong social dimension of his writing has been misunderstood, then the individuality of these more distinctive poems has proved open to different interpretations. As a result, his communicative achievement has been even more likely to be neglected. True, one line of commentary, leading back through nineteenth century historical approaches and the Romantic interest in literary authors, has treated him as both a creative artist and a real person, with a spiritual life of his own, and responding to particular circumstances in a particular time and place. This we can call the traditionalist interpretation, since it became somewhat less fashionable during the twentieth century, and cannot be all that different from the way Vaughan must have been seen by his earliest readers, whose own positionality it has to some extent always borne in mind. Yet the Modernist style of reading, which goes back through the Symbolists and the Aesthetes to another side of Romantic thought, was more exclusively interested in artistic form, which it tended to de-contextualize and de-humanize.

Both the traditionalist and the Modernist approach rest on two main theses.[2] Traditionalist readings tend, first, to describe Vaughan's best passages as a kind of Longinian sublimity, spasmodic as flashes of lightening, and secondly, to see this as reflecting the high points of the poet's own spiritual life, a life whose ups and downs therefore become a matter of considerable interest. Was there a sudden religious conversion?[3] Did illness play a part?[4] Was he a mystic?[5] Critics interpreting him in the Modernist way, by contrast, in the first place praise him for an imaginative force resulting in sustained organic wholes, and in the second place see this as quite impersonal. In keeping with Eliot's famous dictum, they separate the man who suffers from the mind which creates, and concern themselves mainly with the latter.[6]

At first it may seem that these two critical tendencies would always have to be mutually exclusive, and that the two theses of each tendency are closely interdependent. If, with the traditionalists, you believe that Vaughan's poetry is true to autobiographical origins, then erratic splendours will make it seem all the more authentic, the wind of the spirit blowing as it lists through the Aeolian lyre of his sensibility. Conversely, if, with the Modernists, you believe that none of Vaughan's poetry is in a real sense autobiographical and you account for the best of it in terms of artistry, then the more artistry you can find the better. Every lapse from the perfect form of the aesthetic heterocosm is presumably a lapse into something else, which might just be life.

In point of fact, both critical tendencies have sometimes been represented by only one of their two theses, and sometimes a thesis of the one tendency has even been run together with a thesis of the other. Frank Kermode, for instance, wrote a perfectly reasonable sentence which at one and the same time took up the traditionalist topic of Vaughan's personal religious life — "he is in no sense at all a mystic" — and forcefully proposed the Modernist claim that *Silex Scintillans* is a purely literary monument — "he makes a poet's use of the mystic's language".[7]

As this begins to suggest, the entire traditionalist-Modernist dichotomy is something of a red herring, tending to underestimate the mental flexibility of poet and readers alike. It is a typical result of literary scholasticism's rigidly oversimplified and false dichotomies, and a mediating critic's first move must be to loosen things up. Vaughan's best poems do have something of the formal coherence proposed by Modernist critics, yet here and there can nevertheless rise to a sublimity that is higher. Similarly, his best poems do have the breadth of generalization and relevance which distinguishes literature from therapeutic writing, yet, like the best poetry of Andrew Young, can only be assumed to have had a personal origin. Readers can operate in the Modernist and traditionalist modes simultaneously, in other words, and will receive an impoverished reading experience if they do not. They can see highpoints even within an artistic unity. They can also see the impersonal in the personal, or the personal in the impersonal.

Even so, the red herring of a disagreement is very much a fact in the history of Vaughan criticism, and as in the case of Andrew Young, it is the traditionalist kind of understanding which at present needs more emphasis. For Vaughan, this will give an especially well rounded account of both expressivity and affect, and precisely by linking them together. What a traditionalist interpretation recognizes is an element of individual expression whose affective force was appropriate to a particular social grouping. The poems are taken to represent Vaughan's own feelings and devotions, which could then serve as a consolation or sounding-board for his co-religionists. Some such coherently communicational approach still gives scope for fresh insights, not only into personal individuality, but into communal intertextualities and interaction as well. Nor need this undermine our sense of the greatest poems' artistry.

∾

An added richness of a traditionally communicational approach is its compatibility with Vaughan's own ideas about his work. In the preliminaries to both the first and expanded editions of *Silex Scintillans* (1650 and 1655), he gives a clear statement of the poems' autobiographical corollary, and he is no less explicit in sub-titling the entire collection as "private ejaculations". Exclusively Modernist readings tended to reject such prefatory statements as external to the poetry itself. Yet even more obviously than the notes to *The Waste Land*, they are offered to readers as guidance, their importance being marked by their position in the book and by differences of format: in the first edition, the title page and an emblem with an italicized Latin poem; in the second edition, a discursive prose preface directly addressing the reader. What this can do is to sensitize readers to the autobiographical undercurrent, and convey the hope that they will themselves find spiritual nourishment here. Up until the early twentieth century, most readers took the poetry at this face value, and even non-religious readers could take it as a moving expression of Vaughan's emotional highs and lows.

This would never have happened unless the writing were felt to come from the heart. Although the second edition's preface admits that "the *history* or *reason*" for some passages "may seem something remote", it nevertheless continues:

> Were they [the poems' history or reason] brought *nearer*, and plainly exposed to your view, (though that (perhaps) might quiet your *curiosity*) yet would it not conduce to your greater *advantage*. And therefore I must desire you to accept them in that *latitude*, which is already allowed them.[8]

Vaughan, like Andrew Young in his short nature poems, is reluctant to disclose very intimate personal details, yet still assumes that the personal vibration will register. The poems do not necessarily record a sudden religious conversion or all five steps of the *via mystica*, and in order to be an act of devotion or exhortation they do not have to be "action poems". As much as anything, they probably draw on experience that is remembered and re-created. The point is merely that Modernist readers who took them as non-expressive were obeying a rule to the following effect: When authors preface a text with statements of sincerity, and actually seem in the text to be sincere, you must not take them literally, but must read their works as the unreliable narrations of a text-internal persona.

Such a rule certainly works for some of Swift, since in Swift there are ironic narrator and narratee personae, clearly distinguishable from the basic communicative personae of the implied sender and receiver.[9] In Vaughan's poems, as in countless other literary texts and most ordinary communication, this is not the case. His writing is directly personal, its implied sender being a very close counterpart to its real one.

In valuing the poetry's personal element at least as much as its aesthetic form, a traditionalist interpretation will also tend to question the Modernist claims about organic unity, again with support from the prefatory materials. The first edition's emblematic conceit of the flashing heart-cum-flint suggests an intensity that is intermittent (*"En lacerum! coelosque tuos ardentia tandem / Fragmenta"*), and the second edition's preface even says that the poems' artistry is not all that important. Far more crucial, we are told, is the perfection and holiness of spirit in which Vaughan has tried to conceive them. Mentioning Herbert as the first "that with any effectual success attempted a diversion of . . . [the] foul and overflowing *stream*" of vicious and sensual verse, Vaughan says that Herbert's record in winning over "pious *converts*" has not been matched by those aiming

> more at *verse*, than perfection; . . . for not flowing from a true, practic piety, it was impossible they should effect those things abroad, which they never had acquaintance with at home.[10]

There is more than a hint here that artistic excellence and perfection of spirit may not go hand in hand. Accomplished artistry can perhaps be insincere and unconvincing. This, the attitude of countless statements of pious intention from Southwell, Sir John Beaumont and Herbert up to hymnbooks published in our own time, again corroborates the traditionalist account of Vaughan, with its squarely interactive pragmatics. Given the discoursal circumstances, most of Vaughan's poems have precisely the degree of formal excellence one might expect. Writers of texts intended as vehicles of devotion for an entire community perhaps do well to stick to essentials. Too many refinements might almost amount to bad taste. Seen in this light, that merely respectable level of workmanship in most of Vaughan's religious poems seems more of a merit, just like the evangelical simplicity of Young's *Nicodemus*. This is not to deny that some of Vaughan's devotional poems have an intensity far more impressive than others. Nor does it rule out the possibility that some of them are a matter, not only of sublime flashes, but of sustained wholes. But the onus of proof here was certainly on the Modernists.

❧

When it came down to it, the kind of unity for which Modernist critics argued was a unity of thought: a thematic unity in the arrangement of ideas and sub-ject-matter. George Williamson said that many of Vaughan's poems depend on the witty exploration of contrasts, religious ideas and paradoxes.[11] And as if to prove the speciousness of the interpretative dichotomy between Modernists and traditionalists, some very fine scholars combined the Modernist attitudes with a strong historical orientation. Here the stress on the poems' discursive arguments became, if anything, even more marked, especially when Louis L. Martz traced their structures back to well established practices of devotional meditation. "I walked the other day (to spend my hour)", for instance, a most remarkable poem which is re-printed on pp. 156–8 below, falls into three groups of three stanzas: 1–3, the evocation of the image for analysis; 4–6, the process of understanding; and 7–9, the colloquy with God. This, Martz showed, precisely corresponds to a traditional contemplative pattern.[12]

Yet while Vaughan's best work certainly relies on such conventional con-tainers, they are not what takes a reader's breath away. Similar containers also operate for his more run-of-the-mill pieces of "practic piety", and to talk as if his best writing were strictly tidy gives the wrong idea. In his most distinctive poems, there is something peculiarly unaccountable and disconcerting, a qual-ity, very difficult to imitate, that does not need an extensive structure to make its presence felt. Sometimes it has to do with his use of a short line after a long. Often we feel it in just a single line or phrase, or even in a pause.[13]

Let me give three examples (1c, 2c, 3c), each of them preceded by two alter-natives of my own fabrication (1a & b, 2a & b, 3a & b) as a way of making Vaughan's peculiarity more obvious:

>1a. And peep into the box
>1b. And into glory soar
>1c. And into glory peep[14]
>
>2a. You two villains, get you packing
>2b. Death and darkness, be not proud
>2c. Death and darkness, get you packing[15]
>
>3a. I saw your grandmother the other night
>3b. And with Eternity my sight was dazzled
>3c. I saw Eternity the other night[16]

In each case, the colloquial-mundane of the first alternative (a) and the escha-tological-sublime of the second (b) are juxtaposed in Vaughan's own collo-quial-sublime (c). "Juxtaposed". Not "fused". As readers, we do not necessarily experience such items as a reconciliation of opposites made possible in an aesthetic heterocosm. The two types of perception are just as likely to remain in friction for us. As a result, Vaughan emerges as somebody who, envisaging or recording something astonishing, is himself astonishing by apparently being unastonished. Astonishing, and a source of potential strength to others, through his example of metaphysics domesticated. Whereas the wit and resonance of Donne's "Death be not proud" seeks to lord it over death for fourteen magnificent lines, the stylistic surprise of a single line by Vaughan — "Death and darkness, get you packing" — seems to have won without a thought.

Larger unities such as those correctly described by Williamson and Martz are the moulds from which Vaughan's elusive best overflows. Martz himself clearly had some sense of this, for his discussion of "I walked the other day" was a little non-plussed at stanza 5. This stanza seems to contain a sudden switch from the doctrinal considerations so appropriate to the middle, "understanding" stage of meditation into a passionate personal outburst. Martz described the shift as natural, and was able to point out that stanza 6 concludes the "understanding" part with greater objectivity. But he did seem to feel that a passionate personal outburst should not really have been admitted until phase three, the colloquy with God. My own suggestion will be that this poem is one of Vaughan's distinctive best precisely because it thwarts such conventional expectations, both here and elsewhere. One critic responsive to its quality has contrasted it with Herbert's "Peace", from which its trope of digging up a bulb is drawn: Herbert is more cerebral, whereas Vaughan seems to be closer to lived experience.[17] And I shall soon be trying to elucidate the paradox that stanza 5's tonal switch from objectivity to subjectivity is at once a switch and not a switch. Often, and in many different ways, Vaughan is irreducibly and *simultaneously* polyvocal.

Another astonishing poem that was sadly reduced by Modernist commentary is "The World", from which example no. 3c above was taken.

THE WORLD

1

I saw Eternity the other night
Like a great *Ring* of pure and endless light,
All calm, as it was bright,
And round beneath it, Time in hours, days, years
Driven by the spheres
Like a vast shadow moved, in which the world
And all her train were hurled;
The doting love in his quaintest strain

Did there complain,
Near him, his lute, his fancy, and his flights,
Wit's sour delights,
With gloves, and knots the silly snares of pleasure
Yet his dear treasure
All scattered lay, while he his eyes did pour
Upon a flower.

2

The darksome states-man hung with weights and woe
Like a thick midnight-fog moved there so slow
He did not stay, nor go;
Condemning thoughts (like sad eclipses) scowl
Upon his soul,
And clouds of crying witnesses without
Pursued him with one shout.
Yet digged the mole, and lest his ways be found
Worked under ground,
Where he did clutch his prey, but one did see
That policy,
Churches and altars fed him, perjuries
Were gnats and flies,
It rained about him blood and tears, but he
Drank them as free.

3

The fearful miser on a heap of rust
Sat pining all his life there, did scarce trust
His own hands with the dust,
Yet would not place one piece above, but lives
In fear of thieves.
Thousands there were as frantic as himself
And hugged each one his pelf,
The down-right epicure placed heaven in sense
And scorned pretence
While others slipped into a wide excess
Said little less;
The weaker sort slight, trivial wares enslave
Who think them brave,
And poor, despised truth sat counting by
Their victory.

4

Yet some, who all this while did weep and sing,
And sing, and weep, soared up into the *Ring*,

But most would use no wing.
O fools (said I,) thus to prefer dark night
Before true light,
To live in grots, and caves, and hate the day
Because it shows the way,
The way which from this dead and dark abode
Leads up to God,
A way where you might tread the Sun, and be
More bright than he.
But as I did their madness so discuss
One whispered thus,
This ring the bride-groom did for none provide
But for his bride.[18]

One of the things a mainly Modernist critic — Frank Kermode, in particular — effectually said here was, "Wait a minute! Don't let the opening lines reverberate too much. They don't mean what they say. Vaughan is not Dante. He's not a mystic either, and even if he were his poems are purely literary. The ring is a conceit which he uses in several other contexts as well. In this poem, he cleverly resumes it at the end, as the ring which Christ the bridegroom places on the finger of his bride, the Church."

Once again, a traditionalist reader will be perfectly willing to accept the broad outline of the structure described. It is impossible to read the poem without registering the witty turn of the close. Yet the turn at the close is precisely that, a turn *at the close*. Here some light is shed by Stanley Fish's affective stylistics,[19] which seeks to trace the ins and outs of a reader's response as it goes along. As regards our processing of individual sentences, Fish is admittedly rather misleading. What he fails to note is that we can hold our perception of meaning and syntax in suspense until we reach a pause and punctuation. But Fishian considerations certainly apply to a poem in its entirety. In "The World", Eternity is first perceived as a great ring of pure and endless light, and nothing can prevent us from responding accordingly, and at once. The witty turn fifty-eight lines later cannot possibly erase the experience. What could, ever? The poem has us, rather, responding in two different ways at two different points. Or, to be more accurate, three different ways at three different points, since the central Juvenalian section has its own most stirring severity of tone. So: first mystical serenity; then *saeva indignatio*; then devout wit. "Decorum" or "artistic unity" are the last labels we can apply to such a poem. They would obscure what is surely our strongest impression: the interpersonal challenge of a writer who is oddly unpredictable. The constant slight breaches of convention have all the eloquence of a personal touch. The co-adaptive tension between the individual and the social is what brings the style alive.

∽

So do the best poems have a coherence which derives, not so much from organic artistic form, as from the poet's very individuality? In part, yes. A traditionalist account, especially when strengthened by insights into communicative pragmatics, will not wholly endorse either the formalist idea that the poem does not mean but is, or the extremist Barthesian idea about the death of the author. Instead, it will regard a developing sense of Vaughan's own personality as part of the mental baggage which the reader brings to each new poem in succession. It is one of the things which give the poetry's wording significance, an exemplary significance whose force, with changing valencies, can carry to readers, profane or religious, in any time or place.

Up until now, however, my hints as to Vaughan's personal significance have been rather general. They may possibly cater for the domestication of metaphysics in a phrase like "into glory peep", or for a bi-vocality of mystic serenity and devout wit. But "The World", it would seem, is at least tri-vocal, and some poems go even further. What rhyme or reason can there be to such an individual? Or is his writing just a random flood of words, a mere parade of poses?

Not really. But the only way of restoring a significant coherence to it, apart from the argumentative coherence suggested by Williamson and Martz in the name of organic form, is through an exercise of empathetic historical imagination. "The World" — the poem as a whole, that is — does have a kind of beauty. But beauty is sometimes of history, and what needs to be brought into sharper focus here is the unique engagement of Vaughan's writing with the larger situation in which he lived. Knowledge of that situation, now available in the first instance from history books, can enter into a reader's experience of the poetry, restoring the larger dimension of exemplariness in poems bi-vocal and poly-vocal alike. As a response to the historical situation, Vaughan's writing had a comeliness of spiritual strength. It is this which still deserves recognition, and which may still inspire readers in a totally different world today. Given the potential significance for them of Vaughan's sheer otherness, they owe it to themselves to appreciate him, if need be with the help of an ethnographically mediating critic.

The historical situation was the period of rule by the Puritans, whose politicians and acquistive merchants the middle part of "The World" can perhaps be read as satirizing, and whose parliament and city had certainly impinged on

hitherto uncommercialized parts of the Welsh countryside, violently antagon-
izing the grass-roots social order and the ingrained practice of Anglicanism.
No sooner had the Book of Common Prayer been declared illegal on January
3rd, 1645 than Archbishop Laud was executed in the following week. For small
Welsh squires like Vaughan, this was a severe blow, even if they were undaz-
zled by Cavalier swagger and unenamoured of the episcopacy. For them, it was
the Anglican church itself that mattered, the church of Grindal, Abbott, Ussher,
Spenser, Quarles, Herbert. They saw it as a form of civilization which differentiated them from papists and Celtic pagans alike, and its doctrines of salvation
and Calvinist predestinarianism never lost their force, not even for Vaughan,
who flirted with Hermeticism.[20] As a person whose whole world was Brecon-
shire (from which he almost never travelled), he was particularly aggrieved
when, in 1648, Colonel Horton set up the parliamentarian power base in
Brecon. Nor could he and his fellow-religionists be unaffected by the regicide
of 1649, or by the 1650 Act for better Propagation and Preaching the Gospel
in Wales. On the contrary, Horton's ruthless enforcement of the latter included:
the ejection of Vaughan's brother Thomas from his living at St Bride's Church,
Llansantffraed; the replacement of him and his ilk by preachers more to Round-
head taste; the total suppression of Anglican forms of worship; and the closure
and devastation of many church buildings. In Vaughan's own *The Mount of
Olives* (1652), intended as a kind of devotional substitute for the forbidden
prayerbook, the distress is unmistakable:

> The wayes of *Zion* do mourne, our beautiful gates are shut up, and the Com-
> forter that should relieve our souls is gone far from us. Thy Service and thy
> Sabbaths, thy own sacred Institutions and the pledges of thy love are denied
> unto us; Thy Ministers are trodden down, and the basest of the people are set
> up in thy holy place ..... [R]eturn and restore us, that joy and gladness may be
> heard in our dwellings, and the voyce of the Turtle in all our land.[21]

Surprised at being suddenly cast in the role of dissenters, forced now to rely,
as Puritan dissenters had always been pleased to do, on inner light, Vaughan
and his readers were experiencing the same kind of marginalization and communal disintegration which their own establishment had forced upon earlier
nonconformists, whose turn it now was to harass Anglicans with measures
reminiscent of the Elizabethan settlement. The threat to spiritual fellowship
was similar to that which had hung over Catholic recusants all along, under
Anglican and Puritan regimes alike.[22] *Silex Scintillans* was addressed to fellow-
sufferers who were wondering when, if ever, it would all end.

Scholars have already done much to contextualize Vaughan's satirical and devotional poems, his treatises and translations, making clear that they were a concerted effort to minister to Anglicans in their time of troubles. His writings about figures such as Paulinus and Nicodemus have been linked to the predicament of a private life at odds with the official public order,[23] and his pastoralism has been seen as a matter, not of epicurean escape, but of spiritual husbandry and self-discipline: a girding of loins in the difficult situation.[24] One of the things Vaughan found unacceptable was the Puritan taste for extemporary prayers and ecstasies.[25] Although his own greatest poems are magnificent *in spite of* meditational discipline, and although *Silex Scintillans* as a whole, unlike earlier religious poetry, did not reflect the liturgy, the Eucharist and the life of communal worship, being necessarily more private, with a focus on the Bible, nature, and the inner self,[26] Vaughan did realize the importance of traditional structures of regulated worship and devotion. These were his fellow-religionists' best hope of self-preservation, and his own echoes of Herbert can perhaps be taken as a reminder of the happier and more orderly days of 1633, the intertextuality very much serving as part of the community's spiritual cement. As Chris Fitter shows, in a fine piece of historical materialist criticism that is unusually sensitive to language, Vaughan's poetic landscapes were "moulded from the bones and blood of war and military occupation".[27] The poems he published in 1650 involved a profound sense of loss, and a defiant search for new assurance. The new poems in the 1655 edition sounded a note of expectation; were decidedly more angry; blamed other people much more roundly; and called for action still more passionately,[28] sometimes seeing parallels between Christ and Charles in their sufferings, and in their possible future reincarnation.[29]

Scholars have also not hesitated to say that in real life Vaughan could be unprepossessingly bad-tempered — he was to spend many years feuding with his own children. And a seething frustration did get into the poems. Some of them, however, are more than just invective. "The World" raged, and showed how to rage, but was able to suggest alternatives to rage in its opening serenity and concluding wit. It set an example of mental flexibility that was probably far more effective than Vaughan's narrowly didactic prose translations and treatises on retirement, devotion, and how to benefit by one's enemies. The poem's fuller historical significance, once we have begun to grasp it, far from explaining the writing's strangenesses away, only makes it more surprising. The unsettling resistance to discoursal decorum is one aspect of a larger and no less unpredictable resilience that has considerable moral beauty.

Vaughan's co-adaptation with contemporary history and literary norms is un-usual in another way as well. The pragmatic point I have just been illustrating is that any text, whether written or spoken, needs to be contextualized before some sort of significance can be clinched. A second point is that this necessity is something to which the text itself must pay a kind of linguistic deference. At least a minimal amount of context has to be actually encoded. This is because the text's recipients, in their hermeneutic circling between the wording and its possible meanings in possible worlds, need somewhere to begin. The encoded context is part of the way in which a speaker or writer proposes a model of dialogic interchange. It is closely bound up with the proposed sender- and receiver personae.[30]

This self-contextualization of texts, known to linguists as deixis, can be explained in just a page or two. The critical payoffs will be for our understand-ing of yet another kind of unexpectedness by which Vaughan's poetry channels its historical beauty of deed. Here, as in a communicational-cum-traditional-ist approach generally, the links between the individual and the social, and between the expressive and the affective, will be very clear. On the one hand, Vaughan's odd deixis helped to convey his own truthfulness to circumstance; it partly explains why some readers find him so much closer than Herbert to lived experience.[31] On the other hand, the deictic peculiarities unobtrusively extended the application of his words for readers in their own lives.

The term *deixis* derives from the Greek word for "a showing", "a pointing out", "an indication".[32] Four of the types of deixis recognized by linguists directly "indicate" certain aspects of the communicative situation, so helping listeners or readers get their bearings and form a mental model their relationship with the speaker or writer. Here there will always be a kind of linguistic replica of the communicative situation's triangularity.[33] The whole point of *person deixis* is to situate the text in relation to the addresser, who has the first person role, to the addressee, who has the second person role, and to the content, i.e. to the people or things discussed in the third person role, though we must also note that the third person role can actually be filled by a first- or second person pronoun, as in, respectively, "Do I look nice?" and "What do you want?" And as well as through pronouns, person deixis is realized through other nominal expressions, and through concordant verb forms ("I *am*" but "he *is*"). *Place deixis* assigns separate spatial locations to the three role-players just mentioned. To use a simple terminology, the addresser will be in addresser-space, the addressee in addressee-space, and third-person beings or happenings in con-tent-space. Place deixis is realized mainly through place adverbials and various types of definite expression, in which an important function is served by so-called *semes of proximateness and non-proximateness*. These are elements of meaning distinguishing something closer to from something further away, as in the contrast between "here" and "there" or "hither" and "thither". *Time deixis*, similarly, assigns a time for the making of the utterance, which we can call addresser-time; a time for the receiving of the utterance, or addressee-time; and a time belonging to the third-person beings or happenings under discussion, or content-time. Time deixis is achieved largely through the tenses of verbs and through adverbials of time, where semes of proximateness and non-proximateness are again important, as for instance in "now" (which feels close to us) and "then" (more distant). *Social deixis*, lastly, models relationships within the communicative triangle from the point of view of politeness. How much respect does the addresser seem to expect from the addressee? How much respect does the addresser seem prepared to show in return? How much respect does the addresser show towards the things and people discussed as part of the content? Languages tend to include certain more or less formulaic expressions whose function is almost entirely a matter of registering some level of politeness or impoliteness. Clearly, though, an assessment of social relationships and appropriate degrees of courtesy can be reflected by almost any verb, adverb, adjective or noun whatever. So a guide who says to a group of foreign visitors, "If any of you lot have got more money than sense, you'll probably end up in one of those tourist traps over there", is not proposing at all the same set of relationships as a guide who says, "If anyone would like some souvenirs, there are some nice little boutiques over there."

A rather different kind of deixis is *discourse deixis*, in that it is reflexive or metadiscoursal. In other words, what it "indicates" is a relationship, not between the wording and the communicative situation, but between different stretches of the wording itself. It helps listeners or readers get themselves oriented within the text-internal context, so to speak. For instance, it can alert them to some sort of argumentational relationship between one thing and another. A sentence containing a discoursally deictic "thus", for instance, may essentially be summing up the meaning of a whole sequence of sentences that have gone before.

Now the deixis of utterances tends to anchor them, not randomly, but in such a way that the anchorage points constitute what linguists call a *deictic centre*. In spoken and written texts of most kinds, the central person tends to be the addresser, the central time addresser-time, and the central place addresser-place. In shorthand form, the deixis of a lot of the things we say and write is: "I, in the here and now". Discourse deixis tends to follow the same pattern. In other words, another aspect of the deictic centre is usually the point in the discourse at which the addresser has now arrived: "I, in the here and now, and saying these words". This is especially the case with face-to-face oral communication, a communicative situation in which addresser-time and addresser-space of course coincide with addressee-time and addressee-space.

As for Vaughan, one aspect of his deixis is very stable: his social deixis. This is even rather black-and-white, as one might say, in the reliable straightforwardness with which it assesses degrees of appropriate politeness. Unsurprisingly so, really, since social deixis is in a way the most directly interpersonal dimension of deixis. It actually involves gut feelings about oneself and others, feelings which do not fluctuate all that much. In Vaughan's case, what it captures are the fundamental continuities of both his spiritual life as an individual and his relationship with his community of readers. On the one hand, God is always unquestioningly looked up to as a higher being; death and darkness are always brusquely told to get packing, as it were; and Puritan politicians or misers may at any point be exposed to a deluge of Juvenalian contempt. On the other hand, his readers are always addressed as equals deserving love and respect. They are his fellows in joy and sorrow. So God or the poem's reader are extremely unlikely to be treated impolitely, and sin, death, darkness and the Puritans are just as unlikely to be treated politely. The only apparent exceptions will be for the purposes of irony, or will occur in the middle of a dramatized narrative, which will then go on to restore the status quo. Recognizing such temporary deviations for what they are, a reader's sense of who is friend and who is foe will remain unconfused.

But speakers and writers certainly do produce unstable deixis sometimes, especially person, place and time deixis. In such cases, the deictic centre can actually be shifted around or projected.[34] This is even fairly common in the case of written texts, since one aspect of their function as writing is after all to bridge real gaps in time and space between addresser and addressee. In no period of literary history has frequent or complicated deictic shifting been regarded as a feature of normally good writing. Necessarily, readers tend to find it rather disorienting. But there have always have been at least some writers who, for that very reason, have resorted to it modernistically, so to speak, for special effects.

Few of them seize on such possibilities with the opportunistic brio of Laurence Sterne, but Vaughan comes pretty close. One sentence in the preface to the second edition of *Silex Scintillans* could almost be straight from *Tristram Shandy*:

> By the last *poems* in the book (were not that mistake here prevented) you would judge all to be *fatherless*, and the *edition* posthume; for (indeed) *I was nigh unto death*, and am still at no great distance from it; which was the necessary reason for that solemn and accomplished *dress*, you will now find this *impression* in.[35]

The deictic oddity of this is in the *temporal* shifts and ambiguities. To spell it out, the movement is from the reader reading the last pages of the book at some time in the future (the future from Vaughan's own point of view, but also from the point of view of the reader who begins by reading the preface); to the reader reading the preface "here" (the single word "here" being ambiguous between Vaughan's writing time and the current reader's reading time); to Vaughan almost dead at some time prior to writing the preface; back to Vaughan still rather feeble while actually writing it; to the reader's having noticed the book's format before even reading the preface. All of which can sensitize readers to further deictic projections in the poems themselves.

Take a typical piece of "practic piety" such as "The Search". This opens in the present tense:

> 'Tis now clear day: I see a Rose
> Bud in the bright East, and disclose
> The Pilgrim-Sun; . . .

The addresser, then, is part of the content ("I" speaks about what "I" is doing), and addresser-time and content-time are purportedly the same. Lines 3–65, however, separate the two times and places from each other ("I see a Rose / . . . disclose / The Pilgrim-Sun; all night have I / Spent in roving ecstasy"), describing in past tenses how the "I" has reached this, the poem's apparent time centre, by wandering in search of his Saviour. By lines 65–6 he has brought the account up to date, as it seems, and we again have the present tense and a purported concurrence of addresser-time and content-time:

> . . . see, it is day,
> The sun's broke through to guide my way.

But then, in a move strongly reminiscent of Herbert's "The Collar", but with a shift of deictic centre which in Herbert was ruled out by the use of the past tense *throughout* a characteristically much more stable discourse, Vaughan starts a new verse paragraph:

> . . . see, it is day,
> The sun's broke through to guide my way.
>   But as I urged thus and write down
> What pleasures should my journey crown . . ..

Addresser-time is again separated from content-time, but on this occasion through the setting up of a *new* addresser-time subsequent to the previous one. Person deixis, on the other hand, remains the same as in lines 3–65: both the first person role and the third person role are still filled by "I", while the reader fills the second person role. Then, however, comes yet another deictic shift:

> But as I urged thus and write down
> What pleasures should my journey crown, . . .
> Me thought I heard one singing thus;
>
> 1
>
> Leave, leave, thy gadding thoughts;
> Who pores
> and spies
> Still out of doors
> descries
> Within them nought.[36]

The shift is a shift in person deixis, the first person role now being taken over by the singer of the monitory song (God? an angel? the Christian church? Wisdom?), while the original "I" takes the second person role as listener to the song, or *part* of the second person role, rather, since the reader has already been established in this role and is not explicitly released from it. The reader, in other words, has to attend to the warning as well. Or to express it the other way round, the deictic shift unites the poem's "I" with other people, with the poem's readers, more or less as their representative. The "I" is now clearly experiencing and expressing things *on behalf of* contemporaries, fellow-religionists and other people as well, both elsewhere and in the future. The feeling of solidarity with a circle of readers, more usually projected by Vaughan's very stable social deixis, is thus reinforced in an unexpected way.

Something rather similar happens in poems where the deictic shifts give Vaughan's human representativeness a retrospective dimension. The most obvious case is "Man's Fall, and Recovery". Here, with the help of several shifts of time deixis, the "I" is at once Vaughan himself, Adam, and everybody else in between — or rather, everybody else except Jesus Christ, who came to save the human "I". In some poems, again, the "you" or implied "you" actually merges with the "I" to give "we", and the second person role is taken over by God. So in shorthand form, a frequent devotional movement is "I/me . . . O God . . . we/us". Shorthand examples would be: "I have sinned. O God, forgive us!" or "I rejoice in my Saviour. O God, accept our thanks". Deictic place centre often shifts just as conspicuously, with addresser-time "here" merging with addressee-time "there". And so on. In every case, the net result is the same: the poetry expresses Vaughan's personal relationship with God as something in which his fellows — his readers — can vicariously share. The deixis pulls them in, so to speak.

Some such marked deictic shifting is not all that uncommon in religious poetry. Vaughan could have learnt the "I/me . . . O God . . . we/us" movement (along with some other things as well) from John Beaumont, for instance.[37] More distinctive of him at his disconcerting best are less self-advertizing shifts, so rapid as to be hardly noticeable. By this means, the field of interpersonal activity between writer and readers is electrified. Readers are for ever drawn into the communicative act, partly through sheer curiosity as to its deictic bearing, never quite sure where they will be led, and often unable to remember, when they seem to arrive somewhere, exactly how they got there.

Vaughan's most miraculous oddity of this kind is probably "I walked the other day", the deixis of which will repay some detailed analysis.

¶

1

I walked the other day (to spend my hour)
Into a field
Where I sometimes had seen the soil to yield
A gallant flower,
But winter now had ruffled all the bower   5
And curious store
I knew there heretofore.

2

Yet I whose search loved not to peep and peer
I'the face of things
Thought with my self, there might be other springs   10

Besides this here
Which, like cold friends, sees us but once a year,
And so the flower
Might have some other bower.

3

Then taking up what I should nearest spy   15
I digged about
That place where I had seen him to grow out,
And by and by
I saw the warm recluse alone to lie
Where fresh and green   20
He lived of us unseen.

4

Many a question intricate and rare
Did I there strow,
But all I could extort was, that he now
Did there repair   25
Such losses as befell him in this air
And would ere long
Come forth most fair and young.

5

This passed, I threw the clothes quite o'er his head,
And stung with fear   30
Of my own frailty dropped down many a tear
Upon his bed,
Then sighing whispered, *Happy are the dead!*
What peace doth now
Rock him asleep below?   35

6

And yet, how few believe such doctrine springs
From a poor root
Which all the winter sleeps here under foot
And hath no wings
To raise it to the truth and light of things,   40
But is still trod
By every wandering clod.

7

O thou! whose spirit did at first inflame
And warm the dead,

And by a sacred incubation fed   45
With life this frame
Which once had neither being, form, nor name,
Grant I may so
Thy steps track here below,

8

That in these masques and shadow I may see   50
Thy sacred way,
And by those hid ascents climb to that day
Which breaks from thee
Who art in all things, though invisibly;
Show me they peace,   55
Thy mercy, love, and ease,

9

And from this cave where dreams and sorrows reign
Lead me above
Where light, joy, leisure, and true comforts move
Without all pain,   60
There, hid in thee, show me his life again
At whose dumb urn
Thus all the year I mourn.[38]

This is obviously not chaotic. The poem has precisely the three-part disposition of which Martz speaks, and a reader who recognizes this immediately gets
one kind of grip on it. It also has an even more basic kind of coherence, perhaps
the most common kind of all in colloquial speech: there is first the narrative
of an event, and then the record of a response to it. Even readers who miss
the meditational pattern will pick up this. In addition, the poem has Vaughan's
usual helpful stability of social deixis. His fellowship with a community of other
sufferers is succinctly suggested in the wry mention of "cold friends" which
see "us but once a year" (l. 12), the "us" just hinting at a select circle of warmer
friends: his readers. Outside that circle, people can apparently be pretty obtuse
as well: "How few believe such doctrine springs / From a poor root" (ll. 36–7).
Vaughan is *not* addressing "every wandering clod"! And the switch from the
contemptible "clod" to the reverent colloquy with God — "O thou!" — makes
his usual discriminations in the matter of politeness with the utmost clarity.
Gut feelings about the relationships involved are unmistakable and consistent.

All this can help readers on their way. But in other respects the deixis could
hardly be more irregular. One of the very few more explicit responses to this
comes from Thomas A. Calhoun:

[T]he earth [in stanza 5] becomes "Clothes", a hole dug in the ground becomes a bed, and the reburied "Recluse" is fully personified. The logic of these shifting terms is made apparent at the end of the poem. The poet has been, all along, meditating and mourning before the burial urn of a dead companion. But in the movement of the verse there is no clear transition from past to present, from field and flower to funeral urn. *Two places, times, and objects merge.* [My italics.] The poet elides whatever verbal directions are necessary for a sense of metaphor. The narrative action cannot be designated as an explanatory fiction or parable, since it is inseparable from the present, reflective experience.[39]

But as we shall see, things are a good deal more unsettled than even this, and with significant expressive and affective consequences.

The first line of the poem leads us to expect that, as in other poems, Vaughan himself is going to play both first and third person roles, and we ourselves the second person role: that he will tell us about something he himself did in a content-time prior to addresser-time. The pilcrow, which we have already seen at the head of the collection's most personal poems, serves to strengthen this expectation, and line 2 sets up the content-place naturally enough: a field, which is neither the addresser-place nor our addressee-place. But then line 3's pluperfect tense thrusts our thoughts immediately further back to a *second* content time, earlier than the first one. In line 5, "winter now had ruffled" seems to bring us back to the first content-time, yet the *erlebte Rede* of the "now" also narrows the gap between that first content-time and addresser-time, an effect which is heightened by the remarkable jumble of proximateness and non-proximateness semes in line 7's "I knew there heretofore". What the first stanza's dizzying deixis finally brings us to in this phrase is the possibility that the gap between addresser-time and addressee-time could be narrowed: that writer and reader could come closer together.

In what follows, Vaughan's relation to his reader is indeed increasingly close. A reader's involvement in the story is bound to be somewhat intensified by the shift to direct speech in lines 10–14, with the forms "this here" and "sees" both marked for proximateness ("sees" because it is present tense, not past), and there is even a hint of the first and second person roles coalescing, a social deixis whose bonding I have already noted: "sees *us* but once a year" (my italics). This hint is still developing in line 21 ("He lived of us unseen."), and by then content-time has already been separated off by a whole sequence of words carrying non-proximateness semes ("Then", "could", "digged", "That place", "saw"[the verbs here being in past tense rather than present]), so that the author-in-first-person-role and the reader seem to be standing in a shared time and place, contemplating the author-in-third-person-role in the first content-time of "the other day" (line 1). Typically for his poetry, then, Vaughan is at one and the same time an individual and a member of the group, a group for whom his individuality has a potential interest and value.

The author-in-third-person-role in the first content time contemplates, in his turn, the emergence of a new third-person item: the bulb. This, very unexpectedly for twentieth-century users of English, but a little less so for seventeenth-century users, which was characteristic of the *slight* unease Vaughan created at his best, is referred to by the humanizing masculine pronoun (lines 17, 21, 24, 26). The bulb even teeters on the brink of a first-person role: the "that" of line 24 introduces an indirect speech construction which holds the bulb to content-time, but without preventing it from becoming the subject of the verbs in lines 25–8, temporarily replacing the author. Nor do the complications stop here, since although the "there" in line 23 and line 25 again suggests content-time, "this air" in line 26, disconcertingly, is at once content-air, addresser-air, and addressee-air, just as "ere long come forth" in line 27 relates to a future soon after content-time, to addresser-time, and to addressee-time. The "This passed" of line 29 seems firmly to separate content-time off again, yet from line 33 to line 42 the direct speech, with its present tenses and the proximateness semes in "now" and "here" (lines 34 and 38), brings about both a temporal and a spatial coalescence. Again there is continuing oddity in the lexicalization of the bulb and its immediate surroundings. A reader could even be forgiven for wondering whether the content-place has shifted from the field to a deathbed. In the diction of line 42 there seems to be an equal and opposite *de*-humanization of real people, or at least of the stupid people outside the circle of warm friends: they are referred to as a clod of earth, with eternal-present time reference. All in all, then, by this stage it is as if the story is happening in more than one place, in more that one simple time, and with agents of oddly shifting quality. Vaughan seems to be questioning some pretty basic distinctions between dead and living, human and non-human, or past, present and future, and even more to the point here, to be generalizing the relevance of what he is thinking to various possible human worlds.

No less polyvalent are lines 33–5, the passage which Martz described as simply a passionate deviation from the expected objective doctrine. It certainly *is* a passionate deviation. But at the same time, it is still also doctrine as well — and this is only the start of it! Compare *Revelation* XIV 13: "And I heard a voice from heaven saying unto me, Write, Blessed are the dead which die in the Lord from henceforth: Yea, saith the Spirit, that they may rest from their labours . . .".

Who, then, speaks these lines in Vaughan? In one sense, certainly, the poet in content-time ("I" in line 29). But we surely hear other voices as well: the voice from heaven, the voice of the spirit, as mentioned in Revelation; the voice of the writer of Revelation himself; the voice of Vaughan in addresser-time; and the voices of all Christians, always. Such allusiveness is clearly different from the use of an ironic narrator persona, and much more subtle. Pragmaticists have defined irony as the mention of an utterance that is not an actual use of it: if, in pouring rain, somebody says, "Nice day!", this is the mention of an utterance that would be more accurate in other circumstances, and it is interpreted by the hearer as ironically not meaning what it seems to say in the abstract.[40] What Vaughan is doing is not only mentioning the biblical idea, but using it as well. In other words, the wish he addresses to the Bible in his poem "Holy Scriptures" has been fulfilled:

> O that I had deep cut in my hard heart
> Each line in thee![41]

He can now speak "in lines of my Lord's penning". All of which means that the words we read are of more than one time as well. The poem's deixis is increasingly multivalent. In consequence, the human worlds to which its constatation of individual experience has outreach are increasingly manifold.

At line 43 there is some sharp deictic switching, as the second person role is transferred to God and we are referred back to an earliest time of all. "This frame" (line 46) seems to refer to the created universe in which both addresser-place and addressee-place have hitherto been located, but the "I" in lines 48 to 63 still keeps the speaker separate from the "other" recipient (that reader or "overhearer" who is not God Himself) and at addresser-time only. Nevertheless, the invocation of God is so sustained, with God actually becoming the subject of many verbs from line 43 to 61, that real readers will be almost forced, as at the end of "The Search", to align with the "I", associating themselves in the pious ejaculation. Sustained proximateness semes assist this ("here below", "in these masks", "this care"), especially in contrast with the non-proximateness semes used of heaven ("those hid ascents", "that day", "above", "there"), and the point of future time in which the "I" hopes the spiritual uplifting will take place is capaciously unspecific. It could be between addresser-time and addressee-time, but it could just as well be after addressee-time, so that readers could share in it too. In that future time, access will be achieved to a realm in which God's glory can only be expressed in the eternal present ("breaks", "art", "move"), so occasioning the poem its most striking deictic shift so far.

After this glowing prospect of union in God, the poem's last three lines are extremely disconcerting. First, the focus suddenly shifts right back, to before addressee-time, to addresser-time. Secondly, though, there is a slight surprise when the strange earlier references to the bulb are suddenly recycled as what, remembering previous poems in the collection, we might already suspect: metaphor for a dead loved-one. It is this which finally precipitates the dismaying moment of truth: Vaughan himself is suddenly highlighted in a very sharp isolation from all the sources of love and joy already mentioned — from God, from the bulb, from the loved-one, and, most oddly of all, from us, the readers. The colloquy with God, the emotional upsurge which Martz rightly detected as part of the larger structure, and in which the deixis encouraged the reader to participate, unaccountably tails off. We feel left up in the air, awkward and embarrassed for Vaughan's sake. We half look up towards God. We half look down at Vaughan, so inveterately fixed in his eternal present of grief. An hour in the field the other day has been only the briefest intermission. In the poem's last two lines its deictic centre finally comes to rest: a grieving "I" in the first person role, a grieving "I" in the third person role, with no very definite second person to hear him (God? us?), in the eternity of grief, and at the particular place of grief: beside the urn. The entire poem's only instance of discourse deixis, the "Thus" of the last line, sets the seal on this chilling anticlimax. It tells us that mourning is really what he has been doing all along, even when it seemed to be something else, even when the "him" rocked peacefully asleep below (l. 35) might still have been the bulb. By the same token, the poem comes to an abrupt end. No further search for consolation on Vaughan's part, no further deictic projection from his heavy reality, can for the moment be sustained.

If there is to be any further movement at all, then this poem seems to be saying that it cannot come from Vaughan himself. Vaughan and the reader will have to change person-roles. Whereas Vaughan, all along, and as in so many of his poems, has been generalizing the reference of his experience outwards, to become something of value within a whole community, it is now he himself who needs to hear something. The urn is all too "dumb" — as well as cold and hard and bloodless, obviously. What he direly needs is a reciprocating human gesture: a gesture of understanding. In this respect, too, then, the poem communicates in a very literal and full sense of the word: it tends to *make* a community, into which the reader is drawn to participate, not only vicariously through the example of Vaughan's own spiritual life, but ultimately in a personal, self-originating movement of commiseration. Every time the poem is sensitively read, the world becomes, to this extent, a better place, however grim the sufferings to be borne in it. As the result of Vaughan's writing and readers' reading, the grief is *shared*.

The poem's last lines give us Vaughan at a low spiritual ebb which may seem quite unthinkable in the author of "The World", with its no less intimately personal but upbeat opening. Yet despite the difference in mood, both poems were inseparable from the historical context of the puritan ascendancy. While "The World" invited Vaughan's persecuted co-religionists to share an unexpected amalgam of spiritual serenity, fiery resistance and devout wit, "I walked the other day" was beautiful in the sheer amplitude of its truth to circumstance. Its first Anglican readers would have recognized the demoralizing isolation of a solitary grief, which can find no outlet in public customs of religion and fellowship. In their mind's ear they might have heard, too, the words of comfort they themselves would have liked to offer. In this way they would have entered into a communion which, nourished only by the imagination, and by the memory and hope of better times, was spiritually far more meaningful than many a Puritan's regular church attendance.

In a sense which Arnold did not intend, "I walked the other day" was a case of poetry as a substitute for religion or, more exactly, as a substitute for public religious practices. The same applied to *Silex Scintillans* as a whole. Vaughan by writing, H. Blunden by publishing, and Vaughan's co-religionists by reading this poetry were compensating for the serious gap in the communal life permitted them. As the book's preface so clearly hinted, here was an invitation to fellowship, not through church-going but through reading. Even the poems which come closest to dejection clearly illustrate the genuine communicator's hope of finding or creating a like-minded audience. The underlying assumption is that the very sharing of sufferings tends to alleviate them and give strength for the future. This is one reason why the deixis so often collapses "I" into "we" and addresser-time and -space into addressee-time and -space. Throughout, the politically imposed separation is overcome by a deed of literary re-union. Vaughan's curiously individual co-adaptations with both stylistic decorum and contemporary history left nothing quite the same. He was positively strengthening bonds that had a real historical role.

The only way Modernist critics could deny such beauties was by turning a blind eye to history, by refusing to make the empathetic movement out of their own context of reading into Vaughan's context of writing, in the orthodox formalist belief that a poem's "I" is "only" an implied author, and its situation a mere feat of dramatizing imagination. Vaughan's poems certainly can be read that way, but they have never asked for it to be the only way. The beauty of his most extraordinary writing is not narrowly artificial and aesthetic but, as the preface to *Silex Scintillens* hints, is a "perfection" of mind and spirit, a beauty which in the first instance stemmed from the communal value of his response to his own personal situation and to the larger historical one as well, a response which itself invited a response from readers.

And still invites. For us today, caught up as we are in the sociocultural tensions of postmodernity, the continuing inspiration could well spring from the example of a threatened and marginalised identity which resists, recoups, and endures by making new. Where, in ways that Modernist critics failed to appreciate, Vaughan modernistically thwarted conventional artistic decorum in matters of coherence and deixis, the spiritual beauty of his reaction to circumstance now seems compelling. It has little to do with artistry as understood by Modernist formalism. Artistic form does give coherence, both to run-of-the-mill pieces of "practic piety" and to poems altogether more astonishing, and Modernist scholars such as Williamson and Martz, by pinpointing argumentative structures, performed a valuable service. Today, though, we can also grant due recognition to Vaughan himself, as it were, and to his historical feat of communication — of community-making. This we shall do with still no trace of bardolatry. His writing is very much a human achievement and, thanks to all the anger and self-pity, is human in the lesser sense as well.

CHAPTER 5

Decorum *versus* indecorum
in *Dombey and Son*

As a result of Modernist ideas, novels, no less than poems, came to be read as impersonal, a-historical wholes. By the middle of the twentieth century, even Dickens ran the risk of being described as an artist in, say, Stephen Dedalus's sense of the term. That Dickens offered an "esthetic [*sic*] image in the dramatic form", an image of "life purified and re-projected from the human imagination", was in effect the claim of many a scholastic critic. An author whose work had earlier seemed so obviously embroiled in the bustling life of London, whose nickname, "the Inimitable", had spoken of him as every reader's prized personal acquaintance, was now sometimes virtually dissolved into "a fluid, lambent narrative", "invisible, refined out of existence, indifferent, paring his fingernails".[1] As late as 1970, Barbara Hardy still needed to say the obvious: that Dickens is personally involved, both in history and in his own writing, and that his novels are not purely unitary. They have a complexity which begins in a "series of separately assertive intents, passions, statements."[2]

In the last three decades of the twentieth century, historians and critics did much to return Dickens and his work to history, but sometimes by oversimplifying the Victorian middle class and seeing him as its cut and dried product. If his exemplary force is once more to be recognized and released as a real potentiality, ethnographic mediation will have to bring into view a most fascinating co-adaptation: his simultaneous endorsement and subversion of a homogenizing bourgeois decorum.

To return for a moment to scholastics of a formalist orientation, what many of them found in Dickens's novels were symbolic wholes, describable in terms of imagery, mythical elements and atmospheric details. Wielding the New Critical weaponry of irony, paradox, tension and ambiguity, they staunchly defended Dickens's every inclusion and exclusion. Disunity or discontinuity was not what they were looking for. As for New Critical narratologists, their talk of a formalist *concordia discors* could involve a distinction between an anonymous narrator and Dickens himself, who was supposed to be quite outside his own writing, as it were. Or rather, the *concordia discors* was often *semi-formalist*, because at least some of Dickens's readers were said to catch him winking behind the narrator's back. In an otherwise brilliant study that was far ahead of its time, even Richard J. Watts fell into this mode, when he detected an ironic narrator persona in *Hard Times*. As described by Watts, this narrator does not practise what he preaches about human sympathy, is unhealthily fascinated by the aristocracy, and can see no justification in the cause of the trades unions. One of Watts's suggestions was that such a benighted teller would specially appeal to the prejudices of the first readers of the novel's weekly installments in *Household Words*. His other suggestion was that, for those who have ears to hear, the real Dickens actually condemns this narrator, and is also addressing a second audience, enlightened enough to pick up such a message as well.[3] For Watts, the novel was an artistic whole precisely by carrying both messages at once. Formalist commentary could only paper over Dickens's ideological inconsistencies and randomness of construction by turning him into a prodigy of calculation, who sustained extended symbolisms or cunning ambiguities at every point.

Not that formalist approaches were without their value. Especially in his later novels, Dickens did use features of theme, imagery, myth and atmosphere to bundle his copious materials more tightly together, and he was perfectly capable of using ironic narrator personae. But to switch to one of his own metaphors, the weave of his stories is not without its loose ends. Many pre-formalist admirers had not worried about these, and post-formalists were often delighted at what they saw as the creative fecundity of a negative capability,[4] or as the stimulus to an ever-proliferating semiosis.[5]

The first novel to be written on a more deliberate plan was *Dombey and Son*. But from publication onwards, its architectonics proved controversial. Many critics spoke of an artistry which, though aspiring to completeness, nevertheless fell short. For some, the book simply split in two: a finely controlled opening part which ended with the death of little Paul, and "the rest", which was hardly controlled at all.[6] For William Axton, in a New Critical article which was typical of 1960s scholasticism, the novel's imagery did give it an all-embracing unity of tone,[7] and other critics have even complained that the control was actually much too tight, inhibiting the free creative play of author and readers alike.[8] But for Barthesian scholastics, the *scriptible* flourished at the expense of the *lisible*: an infinite number of readings multiplied quite beyond either Dickens's own control or a reader's power of determinate interpretation.[9] Then there was a *media via* position, represented by Steven Connor, who saw a tension between texture and structure, or between the syntagmatic and the para-digmatic. A randomly metonymic drift was in play with a metaphorical urge towards closure, shape, significance.[10]

According to some Victorian critics, Dickens's problems of organization stemmed from the special requirements of serial publication. But although there was an element of truth in this, for other early commentators his artistry seldom faltered. Forster, in his *Life* of Dickens, said there was a clear blueprint for *Dombey and Son* from a very early stage, one piece of evidence being a letter Dickens wrote to Forster himself on July 25th, 1846.[11] As for Dickens's own view of the matter, he did acknowledge certain problems in serial publication, but only at the reader's end of things. The story-weaver himself knows exactly what is what. As the Postscript to *Our Mutual Friend* puts it,

> it would be very unreasonable to expect that many readers, pursuing a story in portions from month to month through nineteen months, will, until they have it before them complete, perceive the relations of its finer threads to the whole pattern which is always before the eyes of the story-weaver at his loom.[12]

During the heyday of New Criticism, even historical scholars gave further weight to arguments for design and aesthetic unity. John Butt and Kathleen Tillotson adduced, not only the letter to Forster, but other letters, the title, the cover design, the manuscripts (including the plans for each number), and the proof sheets.[13]

Butt and Tillotson's combination of formalist attitudes with detailed histor-ical research represented exactly the same scholarly paradigm as L.L. Martz's commentaries on Vaughan and the meditational tradition, published three years earlier.[14] As in Martz, moreover, there was an uneasy tension between the proposed artistic frameworks and the actual details of the texts as historical deeds. Both from Forster's and from Butt and Tillotson's own accounts, it was clear that important ideas for *Dombey and Son* came to Dickens as he went along. In places he was actually uncertain how to proceed and turned to For-ster for advice. Elsewhere a particular emphasis or lack of emphasis could stem from his adjustment to the 31-page limit of the monthly number. Nor, on reflec-tion, is a degree of randomness all that surprising. More remarkable in such a huge text would be an unfailing homogeneity at every cross-section. In order either to write or to read any such self-consisent *magnum opus*, a human being would have to sacrifice much flexibility of mind, so inviting the censure of *Dombey and Son*'s fascinating minor character, Morfin. As Morfin is acutely aware, there is a less than human way of responding to the passing of time, by becoming a fossilized creature of habit, which "hardens us, from day to day, according to the temper of our clay, like images, and leaves us susceptible as images to new impressions and convictions".[15] The most obvious resistance to change-through-time that we confront in Dickens is in his caricatures, in whom it is the mainspring of absurdity. Serial publication over nineteen months merely increased the chances that inconsistencies in Dickens's own design or attitudes would come out into the open.

Not least, this applied to socio-ideological inconsistencies of the kind Richard J. Watts was trying to neutralize in *Hard Times*. For Modernist New Critics, these represented the most unwelcome disunity of all — the prime candidates for aestheticizing resolution — precisely because of their profound historicity. For that same reason, in a mediating critic's attempt to re-humanize Dickens they must receive strong emphasis, and be clearly seen for what they are.

Once serialization had allowed these socio-ideological tensions to emerge, they were recognizably the instabilities and self-contradictions of Victorian readers themselves. Literary texts, far from being aesthetic heterocosms cut off from the rest of life, may actually play an active part in the day-to-day give-and-take of social discourse. This claim was already part of my previous chapter's argument about the devotional poems of Henry Vaughan. In the case of Dickens, Modernist arguments for a special aesthetic unity turned a deaf ear to Victorian society's many different voices, which in their own historical context had an audibility which no artistry could muffle.

By the last two decades of the twentieth century, some Dickens critics were beginning to discuss this in the light of a Bakhtinian socio-poetics. Roger Fowler's pioneering analysis of *Hard Times*, for instance, detected a quite specific clash of idiolects and sociolects. Here, according to Fowler, we can speak only of polyphony and problematic: of ideological tensions that remained unresolved. Within the context of his own culture, Dickens meant several things at once, discretely interpretable and self-contradictory.[16]

Fowler's argument is also suggestive for *Dombey and Son*, which is more typically Dickensian than *Hard Times,* in being a long serial novel published over nineteen months. No less than *The Waste Land* or "I walked the other day (to spend my hour)", it is also a deed of co-adaptation between the social and the individual. Dickens's reaction to his milieu resulted in two fundamentally different types of textual beauty: a (to us) lesser beauty, which is monologically bourgeois, culturally homogenizing, conventional; and a (to us) greater beauty, which is an ecstatic immersion in the polyphony of a richly differentiated cultural reality. Yet there can also be a (to us) still greater beauty, a beauty of sheer

historical deed, in the force with which Dickens clashed these different textualities against each other. The patent disunity, the refusal of both total homogenization and total differentiation, is precisely the point. Although we can never
know how much Dickens consciously thought about such things, the constant
see-saw between conformity and rebellious variety, mirroring as it did the
awesome tension between the social and the individual in his own personal
make-up, was a most powerfully co-adaptive rhetoric, whose force can still
carry on into our own time, with its very different clichés, stereotypes and
social constructions.

But before the bourgeois and non-bourgeois textual beauties can be compared
and contrasted, we need a firm sense of Dickens's own historical formation.
One of the cardinal facts of literary pragmatics is that reading a text is a matter,
not only of taking something from it, but of bringing something to it: an understanding, for one thing, of the context in which it was written. Indeed, the taking-from is in no small part dependent on the way the reader actually carries
this process of contextualization out. In the case of Dickens, my insistence here
may seem surprising, since reading Dickens, one might think, is a very different proposition from reading Vaughan. Vaughan lived three hundred years ago,
and to readers without the benefit of historical knowledge the relation of *Silex
Scintillans* to his particular community of would-be worshippers will not be
apparent from the texts themselves. For uninformed readers who applied the
eyes-on-the-page reading styles of Modernist practical criticism or New Criticism, Vaughan's historical beauties could simply have no impact. Dickens, by
contrast, lived only one hundred and fifty years ago; wrote novels which are
directly *about* the society in which he lived; and played a part in the entertainment and edification of his audience which is still a theme of our literary gossip.
To describe his novels in terms of timelessly symbolic form must have required,
one might conclude, unusually effective blinkers. As it happens, however, one
hundred and fifty years is more than enough time to blur some nice distinctions. After all, a mere fifty or sixty years obscured the shockingness of *The
Waste Land*. By the second half of the twentieth century, not even the critics
trying to re-introduce some historical perspective were always fully aware of
Dickens's social complexity. As a result, discussion of his class feelings polar-
ized into two very different accounts.

On the one hand, he was often described as having belonged to, and as
having written for, a middle class whose traits can be totted up readily enough:

class pedantry; prudishness; a taste for domestic comfort and for novels such as *David Copperfield*; and so on.[17] Middle-class readers of this stamp were said to have admired him as an ordinary man of good humour, a benevolent friend of the family, and to have been faithful to him throughout his career.[18]

On the other hand, he was just as often described as stopping short of full solidarity with such a grouping. His central characters may huddle round a middle-class hearth. But he always intimates, either through strange characters glimpsed only once, or through "irrelevant" circumstances narrated "parenthetically", peripheral worlds of misery and squalor.[19] He may be a practical man of the world, who defers to the standards of taste and decorum of the middle class on which he is financially dependent. But he can be unmerciful towards middle-class hypocrisy[20] and, especially from *Dombey and Son* onwards, draws on the grotesque contortions of the bourgeoisie for much of his comedy.[21] The impression given by this second type of account was that, while the public was relatively stable, Dickens himself was ambiguous, undecided or subversive.

The trouble with both accounts was that they froze the Victorian middle class in a single narrow stereotype. The truth is that both the public and Dickens, like audiences and writers of other periods, were not inflexible. They were involved in volatile processes of historical interaction and change. So Victorian commentary on Dickens's own work was always far from unanimous, and became even less so as his career continued. The point is not so much that the Brontës, Thackeray and George Eliot started to suggest different forms of novelistic achievement, though this was certainly important.[22] There were also readerly correlatives to Dickens's own increasing explicitness of social trajectory. Arnold found in Dickens an ally against the Philistines, while Trollope thought of him as a radical with no true understanding of political process. The middle class was always capable of both accepting and rejecting criticism, and even this is too simple a paradox. Bourgeois attitudes involved manifest and constant contradictions, not only *vis à vis* Dickens's novels, but in matters of more general ideological importance, contradictions which are fully apparent in Dickens himself.

In questions of sexual morality, for instance, by 1850 the middle class was certainly coming to embrace the "Victorian" clichés about domestic bliss and the sanctity of marriage. These doubtless seemed to represent the higher wisdom, an ideal always to be held in view even if never wholly attained, or at any rate to be held in view of the countless children in the Victorian audience — Dickens had a strong sense of authorial responsibility on this point.[23] Equally, however, nobody with Dickens's own experience, marital and extra-

marital, could adopt the clichés without some inner doubt, and the potentiality for such unsettling experience would be ever present to the imagination of
Dickens and his readers alike, casting that shadow of darker knowledge which
we shall later see haunting even David Copperfield. Again, the clichés could be
undermined by an awareness of the role that marriage might play in schemes
for social betterment, power and prestige, through which the wives, daughters
and sisters of ambitious men often lost out. The hardships and injustices suffered by women were already a theme of both public debate and popular
novels. Dickens, like most of his contemporaries of both sexes, was unwilling
or unable to imagine what many readers today would regard as a true emanci-
pation. But in describing the submission of conventionally feminine wives to
Murdstone and to David Copperfield he did show an unsettling insight into
the humiliations of emotional and economic dependency. Even when writing
at a lower level of imaginative accomplishment, as in his portrayal of Edith and
Florence Dombey, he was unmistakably outraged by their victimization, and
some of his lapses into melodrama and mawkish sentimentality here may even
have done Victorian women a service. After all, it was pitched at the intellectual
level of many of those, both men and women, who needed to be roused from
their selfishness, complacency or defeatism.

Other self-contradictions affected middle-class attitudes to the national
economy. In fact there were three main responses here, which in the day-to-day
give-and-take of social discourse could be juxtaposed in no very logical fashion.

First, there was the traditional bourgeois spirit of entrepreneurial keenness
for new technology and new markets. This was what lay behind the growth of
cities and factories, the two railways booms (1835–7 and 1845–7), the repeal
of the Corn Laws and Navigation Acts in the interests of free trade (1846 and
1849), and the many British engineering achievements which won prizes at
the Great Exhibition (1851). Such enthusiasm readily embraced the age's "new
men", the ironmasters and captains of industry, who for the first time were
combining the roles of engineer, manager, capitalist and merchant, so ensuring
Britain's pre-eminence in industry and trade. That Ruskin should have felt that
Dickens himself, with the ironmaster as his hero, was "a leader of the steam-
whistle party *par excellence*" reminds us of the favourable characterization of
Doyce in *Little Dorrit* or of Rouncewell in *Bleak House*.[24]

> [Rouncewell] is a little over fifty perhaps, of a good figure, . . . and has a clear
> voice, a broad forehead from which his dark hair has retired, and a shrewd
> though open face. He is a responsible-looking gentleman dressed in black,
> portly enough, but strong and active.[25]

For Dickens, Rouncewell is not just a self-made man, but a "gentleman", whose bodily presence creates a pleasant impression, captured in uncategorical modal expressions ("a little", "perhaps"), with any potentially negative overtones ("shrewd", "portly") immediately outbalanced by more positive ones ("open", "strong and active"). The epithets also catch the powerful masculinity of the ideal Rouncewell stands for, and the complementary roles available for women could certainly include a feminity that was circumscribed and passivizing. But at least by contrast with patriarchal formations of an older date, bourgeois manhood did have its legitimation. In the confrontation between Rouncewell and Sir Leicester Dedlock, Sir Leicester blatantly presumes upon a social rank that is inherited rather than earned. Also, there were countless middle class schemes for utilitarian reform. Dickens himself got involved in ventures such as Urania Cottage, sewer improvements, and Nova Scotia Gardens, commitments with which his novel-writing was partly continuous. *Little Dorrit*, for instance, campaigned for sanitary engineering, and against bureaucratic red tape.

Secondly, however, the utilitarian stress on economic and material criteria was challenged throughout the period by spiritual and emotional considerations. This middle class critique of middle class activities drew support from traditional Christian and moral teachings, sometimes voiced by poets and sages such as Wordsworth, Carlyle and Ruskin.[26] Even John Stuart Mill, as a young man, had a period of disaffection with utilitarianism, a crisis which made the poetry of Wordsworth seem specially important to him. As for Dickens, this is one of the points at which *Hard Times* is of interest. Dedicated to Carlyle, the novel denounced utilitarian "facts" and included a condemnation of a captain of industry which can seem rather odd from the creator of Doyce and Rouncewell. That Bounderby "could never sufficiently vaunt himself a self-made man" brings down on him the full weight of Dickens's vituperation, expressed in the most categorical style of loaded assertion, to which the lack of main verbs gives an almost exclamatory force.

> A big, loud man, with a stare, and a metallic laugh. A man made out of a coarse material.... A man with a great puffed head and forehead, swelled veins in his temples.... A man with a pervading appearance on him of being inflated like a balloon, and ready to start.[27]

Socio-economically, Bounderby is pretty much the same as Rouncewell, and even in physical appearance they are somewhat similar. The main difference is in the description itself, and in the attitude informing its social deixis.[28] In *Hard Times*, the response to engineering progress and economic growth is closer to that of the nightmare industrial landscapes in *The Old Curiosity Shop*, or of Wordsworth's sonnet "On the projected Kendal and Windemere Railway" (1844).

Thirdly, the middle class increasingly distanced itself even further still from industrialization and the city, in its aspirations to the life-style of the next class up, the class which Rouncewell challenges in his confrontation with Sir Leicester. Science, technology, industry, commerce, on which middle-class prosperity and the future of the country depended, were sometimes among the great unmentionables. Sons were sent to private schools where, far from dirtying their hands with the practical subjects taught at Owen's College or the Mechanics' Institutes, they acquired a veneer of Latin and Greek.[29] Dickens laughed heartily at the foibles of the would-be genteel, created Doyce and Rouncewell, and was associated with the adult education movement. Yet much of the force of *Great Expectations* sprang from his ability, not only to critique the parvenu hero's pride of place, but to render it understandable. His other heroes' tendency to end up in feather-bed respectability and radiant idleness was sharply noted by George Orwell,[30] and some of his reflexes were clearly those of the middle-class territorial instinct.[31] Although *Dombey and Son* and *David Copperfield* satirized the ideological subjection of the lower orders by charity schools, the revelation of 'umble Uriah's crimes only confirmed David and Dickens's deep prejudice against him.[32] Some people were not really welcome in the meritocracy of hard work, and this same class defensiveness gave a certain edge to descriptions of crowds and riots in *A Tale of Two Cities* and *Barnaby Rudge*.[33]

Both the Victorian middle class and Dickens himself, then, were more complicated than twentieth century literary scholarship sometimes allowed. Dickens was neither simply endorsing nor simply criticizing middle class ideology, and middle class ideology was itself not fixed in some single narrow mould.

At the same time, and as part and parcel of middle class attitudes themselves, there certainly was, in Dickens's own time, a tendency to simplifying homogenization. One of the symptoms is a certain narrowness of public persona which I shall later point out in the character of David Copperfield. As a result, some middle-class ideas and speech habits became more dominant than others, and there are very long stretches of Dickens's own fiction for which the clichés about Victorian mental and cultural life do apply, not only to the first public which read them, but to Dickens himself as their author. This is where we face the (to us) more boring kind of textual beauty: a decorum convention-alized in ways that are stuffily bourgeois.

Even here, or rather, *especially* here, a mediating critic will try to ensure fair play. Perhaps the greatest risk of unfairness was for late-twentieth-century criticism written within a paradigm of deterministic structuralism. This tended to minimize the distinction between the individual and the social in Dickens's own personal make-up, and even suggested that *all* of his writing was in the stuffy vein, and that it positively endorsed social injustice. More particularly, some critics gave the impression that Dickens was quite happy to turn a blind eye to the plight of women and the poor.[34] Well, he was not a twentieth-century feminist or socialist. But could we really expect him to be? And what about his ceaseless efforts, both as a writer and in hands-on social work, to combat inhumanity, exploitation, suffering, humbug, and systematic hypocrisy? In an appreciatively mediating criticism, anachronistic point-scoring and foregone conclusions will have no place, and political correctness in the here-and-now will not be allowed to malign an author who speaks only from the grave. On the contrary, every attempt will be made to understand a dead author's other-ness in its full historical context, not only out of respect for the author's own rights as a human being, but with an alert awareness that, in later contexts, the author's otherness may take on surprising new significances.

That Dickens's social criticism made concessions to the narrowness of middle class ideology is perfectly true. But he himself regarded such conces-sions as lamentable, and his persistance in them merely revealed his unrivalled gift, whether conscious or instinctive, for the arts of persuasion. In any society whatever, there are going to be issues which are sensitive. Even today, when we want to secure attention for something that needs saying, we may have to refrain from the plainest language. As Aristotle remarked in defence of rhet-oric, the truth may need to be "helped" if it is to be recognized and accepted. Whatever we say, the words we use have to construct a model of the com-municative situation in which we find ourselves, suggesting personae both for ourselves and our recipients, and in such a way that our own ends will be co-adaptively furthered. We tune our utterances to suit the circumstances, sometimes embracing, however reluctantly and temporarily, the values of our addressees. So if Dickens now seems even more deviously indirect than we ourselves, this is only because of our own angle of vision. Taboos and related notions of directness and indirectness of speech, just like the criteria for *décolle-tage* and hemlines (with which there has often been a link), change over time, and from culture to culture. Nowadays, Dickens's novels, because of their tensions between criticism and diplomacy, revelation and concealment, can certainly seem ideologically encumbered. But if Dickens had been as forthright as some twentieth century critics anachronistically demanded, his perlocutionary effect would have been nil. The fate of women and the poor would have remained exactly as it was.

As throughout the present book, my emphasis on co-adaptivity is crucial. On the one hand, Dickens endorsed bourgeois ideology. On the other hand, he crucially exploited it, stepped outside of it, worked to change it. Some late-twentieth-century scholastics of a structuralist orientation, by contrast, and particularly some of those who interpreted him in the light of Foucault, could quite deny him this relative flexibility and freedom of manoeuvre. For their rigid sociocultural determinism, he was merely the bourgeois ideology's passive, and even unconscious channel.

According to David Trotter, for example, Dickens willy-nilly transmitted the bourgeois discourse of economic modernity; more particularly, he was obsessed by the notion of circulation. The scientific backing for this was in Adam Smith's advocacy of *laissez faire*, the theory that goods and services should be traded without any restrictions. But other areas of life, and other discourses, had also been affected. Trotter said that Dickens's own restless mobility sprang from his belief that people, air, and information should all flow about freely. He lived in constant fear of any kind of stagnation, physical or spiritual, and his association with the "Moral Police" was an attempt to bring about social reforms by dispelling concentrations of disease or ignorance, for instance by proper sanitation or circulating libraries. In his novels, prostitutes and secretive lawyers are among those who cause blockages, whereas the detective police and the science of physiognomy open things up by allowing meanings to circulate freely from signs.[35] In all of which Trotter was absolutely right and very illuminating, except that this is not the *only* way Dickens thinks. A more sophisticated account of his reaction to modernity was offered by Jeremy Tambling, who saw, in *Dombey and Son* especially, the desire for openness and progress coming up against a conservative desire for concealment and preservation. Dickens's fascination with railways as the instrument of change is complemented by his concern for those ways of life and forms of experience which the railways were destroying.[36]

Philip W. Martin's commentary also calls for qualification. Martin linked Dickens to medical discourse, particularly as regards mental illness, a topic on which Foucault wrote one of his monumental studies. Above all Martin was interested in peculiarly female varieties of madness, sexuality being another of

Foucault's major concerns. The claim was that Dickens actually regressed to patterns of thought far older than Victorianism. Since ancient times, female insanity had been put down to a moving of the uterus, and the best remedy was said to be pregnancy or, better still, regular sexual intercourse. The fundamental cause was supposed be the lack or loss of a man. Victorian doctors were gradually beginning to mention educational background and social roles as important factors, and treatment was beginning to move away from physical restraint towards positive environmental influences. Yet there was still a sense in which to be a single woman *was* to be ill. Taking his examples from *Great Expectations*, Martin said that Mrs Joe, Miss Havisham and Molly are basically conceived according to the ancient stereotype of the sex-starved witch,[37] an observation that was perfectly correct, but only as far as it went. Dickens's portraits of these and other "eccentric" women include more perception than some of his explicit statements allow, plus an honesty of male trepidation at their formidable vitality.[38]

To stay with *Great Expectations* for a moment, the Foucault-inspired interpretations of Jeremy Tambling and Pam Morris were a good bit nearer the mark. Tambling argued that *Great Expectations* is about subject formation by criminalization, the theme of yet another of Foucault's major works. For Tambling this explained the element of first-person-singular confessional narration: delinquents have to pour out their souls into society's pre-structured moulds in order to be rendered harmless.[39] Morris, similarly, saw Jaggers as the arch-observer and -classifier of delinquents, and she emphasized that criminalization had been reinforced by the evangelical doctrines of sin and damnation. She also described the discoursal regulation of the poor as undergoing, during the 1860s, a subtle shift. Quoting extensively from the *Christian Observer*, the *Methodist Magazine*, *The Times* and the great Victorian reviews, she detected a new rhetoric which spoke of everybody as bound together by social chains, and of a prosperity that was open to all. The impression given was that nobody need ever again be "common", a hint which, analysed as a kind of corporate deception, makes the Victorian ideal of gentility look very sinister. In *Great Expectations*, Morris saw both criminalization and the fantasy of riches as part of the system of social control. When the poor starving Magwitch was forced into a criminalizing association, it was with Compeyson the forger.[40] Yet although the social formation of human subjects is certainly very central to the novel, the human subjects actually discussed by both Tambling and Morris were its fictional characters. Both critics implied that Dickens himself was at least partly superior to social formation, and was able to communicate insights into the very phenomenon of social formation itself. Far from extending their de-centring critique from the novel's characters to its author, they credited Dickens with considerable powers of perception and writerly control, as in their basic suggestion that his ideological critique is an anticipation of Foucault. As in much earlier sociological criticism, Dickens's own complicity in Victorian ways of thought was not so much denied, as felt to make his insights all the more penetrating.

To be fair to Dickens, however, is not to put him on a pedestal. In *Dombey and Son*, the complicity simply cannot be ignored, since it is all too visible in most of the "main" characters, some of the clearest manifestations being a matter of language. The English spoken by Edith, Carker, Walter and Florence leaves little scope for idiolectal or sociolectal variation, being an homogenized, standardized English, and very boring at that.[41] Correspondingly, these characters invited a highly generalized ideological response from Dickens's first readers, softly cushioning them against the true detail of social reality. Dickens's offering was tinged with melodrama, pantomime comedy, fairy-tale pathos, and did little to challenge either the cliché about the sanctity of marriage or the more vulgarized forms of Wordsworthian spirituality. Modernist critics who tried to whitewash this populist streak away, for instance by translating the pantomime into mythical archetypes,[42] were closing their eyes to an aspect of his relationship with his audience which he himself found stultifying.

The melodrama centred on Edith. All flashing eye and curling lip, all heaving bosom and fustian language, she is, in Kathleen Tillotson's words, "not a tragic heroine, but a tragedy queen".[43] This meant she could be reassuring to those who wished to remain complacent about the clichés of marital bliss, for in this role she resisted, not without a certain stagey nobility, both the sexual threat ostensibly embodied in Carker, and Dombey's own self-aggrandizing exploitation of her pedigree and beauty. In addition, these two men in her life were so thoroughly monstrous that readers might easily allow themselves to assume that other middle-class wives were better off.

At the same time, Dickens's authorial endorsement of Edith's bid for autonomy was passionately indignant, and there was just a chance that the histrionics might entrap some readers into profounder thought than they had bargained for. Sometimes even Dickens himself seems unwilling to keep the bourgeois stylization going. The writing, that is to say, perks up a bit, as the treatment of Edith becomes lighter, less a matter of fustian direct speech, more a matter of acutely observed behaviour. There is the way she twists a bracelet on her arm, for instance, "not winding it about with a light, womanly touch, but pressing and dragging it over the smooth skin, until the white limb showed a bar of red".[44] There is also the way in which, on three significant nights of her progress (if that is the word) from nubility to wifehood — the eve of the wedding, the night of the homecoming from the honeymoon, the night of the housewarming party — she is drawn away from thoughts of Dombey and, on the last two occasions, drawn away from the marriage bed as well, receiving more comfort and human warmth from Florence, an intimacy his suspicion of which makes Dombey blush and blanch. Alan Horsman asks whether, in Dombey's second marriage, the opportunity to father a son ever actually arose.[45] Given the spirit of these three episodes of chapter-final emphasis, an explicit statement was hardly necessary. The decorum required for the middle-class family audience did not wipe out the shadow of darker knowledge.

But that is as far as it goes. Dickens sensed, he communicated, the crushing despair of Edith's position. And then he had her shedding harmless tears with little Florence, in episodes whose critical implications readers could easily defuse. In a letter to Dickens, Judge Francis Jeffrey indulged in an aestheticization which left the necessity of ladylike subjection quite unquestioned:

> [T]he scenes with *Florence* and *Edith*, are done with your finest and happiest hand; so soft and so graceful, and with such delicate touches of deep feeling, and passing intimations of coming griefs, and woman's loveliness, and loving nature, shown in such contrasted embodiments of gentle innocence and passionate pride; and yet all brought under the potent spell of one great master, and harmonised by the grace as well as the power of his genius, into a picture in which every one must recognise, not only the truth of each individual figure, but the magic effect of their grouping.[46]

In such a response, innocent or proud feminity is not a call to reform but a stimulus to masculine pleasure. It is so much material to be shaped by a masterly male artist into an exquisite tableau. The response was predictable, because rather than openly exploring a more "feminist" reaction in Edith herself, and even though Edith dimly recognized Alice as a sister in mortification, Dickens had her sublimate her own drives in the Wordsworthian emotions needed for the gratifying reversal of the cruel-stepmother motif. Similarly, the sexual opening represented by Carker is, as I say, merely ostensible. Although the manuscript notes suggest that Dickens suddenly decided to make Edith "*not* . . . [Carker's] mistress",[47] what is truly surprising is that he had ever imagined his treatment of Carker could make consummated adultery a possibility. The notes merely reflect the way his inbuilt censor had been operating throughout, a point easily confirmed by comparison with Galsworthy. Although *Dombey and Son* clearly lies behind the portrayal of Soames and Irene, Galsworthy was not only cruder but more honest than Dickens. Dickens may not have needed to show Dombey attempting marital rape. But Galsworthy was not afraid to make Bossiney attractive.

Carker, apart from some of his speeches of hypocritical adulation addressed to Dombey, remained unreal throughout. Dickens had him meditatively eyeing Edith, and gave a notion of his voluptuary tastes in the refinement of his home and his connoisseurship of painting. Yet such coding did not rise above the theatrical, and even Carker's business abilities were defused of real interest. Instead of sexual and socio-economic insight, Dickens consistently gave his readers Carker the cat, Carker the card-player, or simply Carker's teeth. Carker is a pantomime villain, Edith does not fall, and Gissing was right: "The 'realist' in fiction says to himself: Given such and such circumstances, what would be the probable issue? Dickens, on the other hand, was wont to ask: What would be the pleasant issue?"[48]

Another case in point is Walter, who is pure pantomime hero: all standardized diction, no angles, no humour, no change. This is where Dickens himself rebelled most strongly against the bourgeois stuffiness of his conception, as we know from his query to Forster. Would it be possible, he wondered, to show Walter "gradually and naturally trailing away . . . into negligence, idleness, dissipation, dishonesty, and ruin. To show, in short, that common, every-day, miserable declension of which we know so much in our ordinary life." Could it be done "without making people angry"?[49] After he accepted Forster's warning against such a development, whole sections of the novel had to proceed at a level of benign simplicity worthy of Captain Cuttle, whose fantasies follow the same Whittingtonian legend. That Dickens made Cuttle so much a presiding spirit, instead of developing him as a foil to a socio-economic vision of a more tragic cast,[50] is of a piece with the refusal to articulate some of the more hard-nosed counterpoints existing within the society of the time.

Florence, finally, is unreal in the same ways as Walter, and the thinness of socio-economic notation is even more apparent because of her central role. She always has just enough money to give to the poor, or to take a hackney to Old Sol's, or to buy a few clothes, and it would have been easy enough for Dickens to have said that Dombey is too proud to begrudge even a daughter the pocket money decorum requires, but he remained silent. As a result, her funding comes to seem like a personal attribute, something she inalienably has as if by magic, and the same is true of her breeding. Contemplating her sufferings, Walter exclaims, "To think that she, so young, so good, and beautiful, . . . *so delicately brought up*, and born to such a different fortune, should strive with the rough world!"[51] The phrase I have italicized is just the problem. Nobody has done much about making a lady of Florence at all, as Susan Nipper, the main adult companion of her youth — we are never told of a governess — is too aware of her own social status not to recognize: "I've seen her, with no encouragement and no help, grow up to be a lady, thank God! that is the grace and pride of every company she goes in".[52] Florence's maturation is depicted entirely as an initiation in unrequited daughterly love, a process in which normal educational pursuits, on the single occasion when they are mentioned at all — "her books, her music, and her work" —, are entirely secondary to her engrossing efforts "to learn the road to a hard parent's heart".[53] Some scholarship she had acquired, like Maggie Tulliver, from helping her brother with his studies. Yet the comparison only reminds us of the overall difference between George Eliot's finely judged observation and Dickens's fairytale here.

As in the case of Edith, Dickens's righteous indignation at Dombey's treatment of women is unmistakable, and might even hijack some readers into serious thought. But the abstract emotionality of the victim's sufferings made it unlikely that readers would define themselves in contradistinction from her, just as no reader could entirely claim or disavow her standardized English. No less to the point, no reader was positively forced to feel *responsible* for such misery. Especially after Dickens shifted the emphasis on to her after the death of Paul, Florence was simply nobody in particular. The only exceptions were when she promoted a response in Dombey, Paul, Toots or Nipper, thus acquiring a vicarious reality that had to substitute for a more opaque form of her own. All too often, she was so unreservedly accessible, her soul so frontally presented, and in such homogenized language, that both writer and reader were absolved from all obligation to use their brains, whether in self-judgement or in an effort of imaginative empathy. Readers could merely endow her with a fantasy existence woven out of their own self-pity. Even in the 1970s, she was still inspiring the odd gush of cheapened Wordsworthianism.[54]

The price exacted by the long serial novel was correspondingly high. Florence's existence through time is one of the most serious problems Dickens had to grapple with. Whereas the caricature characters are each sharply fixed in a definite social attitude and intonation, Florence, for the entire length of the novel, has to be nothing in particular, nothing, that is, apart from the depersonalizing yearning for love. Dickens's own sense of the difficulty is reflected in the special "mems" he had to make to remind himself of her precise age at various points. In the first chapter of Number Eight, describing "Florence Solitary" while Dombey is in Leamington, he tried to dodge the entire issue, by noting the ravages of time upon the Dombey mansion, with which Florence is still associated — the pace of dereliction is simply spanking! But an even greater strain is felt at those moments when Florence, by persisting in her unwavering nonentity of loyal devotion to Dombey, comes to seem either masochistic or downright stupid. When Edith, to protect Florence from Dombey's jealousy, becomes less familiar with her, Florence sometimes wonders what has caused the change. But "in the calm of its abandonment once more to silent grief and loneliness, . . . [hers] was not a curious mind. Florence had only to remember that her star of promise was clouded in the general gloom that hung upon the house, and to weep and be resigned".[55] No, not a curious mind. And because the mimetic and rhetorical conventions are not those of, say, Chaucer's *Clerk's Tale*, Dickens and some of his readers, if they relished such passages, were indulging in what other readers would want to call bad taste. The invitation was to admire the masochism and stupidity he did not refuse or qualify himself.

This streak of middle-class populism in Dickens cannot be argued away. On the contrary, it is one kind of Dickensian beauty, and something in the nature of a co-adaptive rhetorical concession: the decorum of an artist who, deliberately or instinctively, gives the public what it thinks it wants — the decorum, here, of respectable family entertainment — because he is also going to give them something else as well.

Even at this lower level of achievement, Dickens was not unambiguously endorsing the social status quo. As in his own life-story, so in his writing, there are clear enough signs that he found the narrower forms of middle-class mental cultivation quite insufferable. As for his writing at its most distinctive, it is open to a far wider range of social and ideological diversification. Without the stuffily decorous palliatives, its liberating potential might actually have been too intoxicating for a middle-of-the-road Victorian reader, just as the offensive hedonism of *The Waste Land*, so sharply Dickensian in its virtuoso polyvocality, also called for polite sops to conformity — the politeness *in* the poem, as opposed to the impoliteness *of* it. Dickens's co-adaptation with the novel, the central bourgeois genre, was both socially regulated and, yes, inimitably individual. It amounted to a deed of persuasive ethical beauty.

As I hinted earlier, a helpful way to discuss the difference between bourgeois decorum and the manifold challenge to it is in terms of the sociolinguistic poetics of Bakhtin, with its strong emphasis on heteroglossia: on the fact that, in any given culture at any given time, there is not just one language, one

voice, but many. On its own level, this chimes with the complications of Victor-
rian ideology.

But although Bakhtin's account of the novel as a genre makes heteroglossia
the master concept, he also says that "the novel can be defined as a diversity
of social speech types . . . and a diversity of individual voices, *artistically organized*" (my italics).[56] When he goes on to speak of the novel as "orchestrating"
its themes and "dialogizing" the various social voices present, we might easily
jump to the conclusion that the process he has in mind is broadly analogous
to the imagination's reconciliation of opposites as conceived by Coleridge, or
by Coleridge's Modernist descendants, the New Critical proponents of the
tensions, ambiguities, paradoxes, and ironies of symbolic form. If so, Bakhtin
would be sublimating social reality in an aesthetic realm that is ultimately
a-historical.

What Bakhtin is thinking of in his account of "hybridization" is certainly a
kind of irony. Hybridization is the mixing within a single utterance of at least
two linguistic consciousnesses, often widely separated in social space. It is similar, then, to the stylistic unpredictability of Vaughan in a phrase such as "Into
glory peep". For a Dickensian example, Bakhtin turns to the description of Mr
Merdle in *Little Dorrit*:

> That illustrious man and great national ornament, Mr Merdle, continued his
> shining course. It began to be widely understood that one who had done soci-
> ety the admirable service *of making so much money out of it*, could not be suf-
> fered to remain a commoner. A baronetcy was spoken of with confidence; a
> peerage was frequently mentioned.[57]

The italics are Bakhtin's, drawing attention to what we should normally describe
as the ironical solidarity of all the other phrasing in this passage with the hypo-
critically ceremonial and "official" view of Merdle. "Making so much money out
of it" is a different, undercutting, outsider's voice, which we tend to attribute
here to Dickens himself, and which points up the irony of the rest.

Yet the irony in such cases seems to be more a process for the invention of
copy than a principle by which to organize the copy into a book. The clash of
voices generates a certain texture rather than a structure. As far as Dickens is
concerned, Bakhtin's "organization", "orchestration" and "dialogization" do *not*
ultimately amount to a larger unity of the kind to satisfy Modernist critics in
the Romantic-Symbolist tradition. Nor does it have anything to do with artistic
wholeness as Aristotle understood it. Bakhtin does not ask whether a novel's
action has a satisfying beginning, middle and end based on genuine necessi-

ties and probabilities. For him, the crucial principle is one of sustained differentiality, which is neither a principle of relevance for determining what shall be included and excluded, nor a principle of linearization for determining an order of presentation.

It goes without saying that Dickens did submit his copy to principles of relevance and linearization. But the principle of differentiality, so closely bound up with the *invention* of copy, was more fundamental, and fundamental to his challenge to bourgeois decorum. Differentiality is ultimately a matter of sustained sharpness of observation, a readiness to celebrate first one thing and then some quite different thing. At any given point, there is no particular reason why this capacity should be turned on or turned off, and although the present discussion is mainly about *Dombey and Son*, I am not endorsing New Critical claims for the unity of the individual novels. Some of them are certainly more unified than others, and are stronger on relevance and linear drive. But the non-bourgeois beauty of differentialization simply jumps across from one novel to another.

As G. K. Chesterton remarked, we can easily come to feel that Dickens did not actually write *novels*. What we have is just Dickens, and what at first seem to be separate novels are merely lengths cut off from "that flowing and mixed substance".[58] Chesterton was teased by the paradox that the things which in any other novelist would be rather important, in Dickens are more or less irrelevant. The story can involve a huge amount of secrecy about the tamest of secrets, so that as soon as we know the whole truth of the intrigue, it is also the first thing we forget. In much the same way, the minor characters in a Dickens novel often seem far more important than the main ones, overburdened as the latter are with bourgeois cliché. A so-called caricature can be the tail which wags the dog. It is the caricatures, too, who carry much of the more ecstatic kind of beauty.

Dickens was not the only Victorian serial novelist. Yet perhaps because he was hypersensitive about his own class position, and because of a strong hunch that his own instabilities were those of large sections of his reading public, his participation in the heteroglossia of his day became very marked, especially when allowed scope over the long months of serialization. So sharp was Dickens's own sense of the manifold options of attitude and tone available, and of a writer's opportunities for highlighting and extending them, that at least when he was reading novels by other people, he found respectably standardized English too insipid. Some novels were "so infernally conversational, that I forget who the people are before they have done talking, and don't in the least remember what they talked about before when they begin talking again",[59] a criticism which could also be applied to the language spoken by Edith, Carker, Walter and Florence. The more distinctively Dickensian babel, which in its own way was no less consubstantial with contemporary social history, has colour, flavour, energy.

Not a single line of Cousin Feenix would let us forget who he is, and Cousin Feenix could never be mistaken for Major Bagstock, or Captain Cuttle for Mrs Skewton. In each Dickens caricature, one option from heteroglossia is refined, is frozen in time, so as to be always sharply, absurdly recognizable. When Dickens claimed that his fictional people were based on real people, he was not exactly being untruthful. But the lady on whom he based Mrs Nickleby was quite correct when she told Dickens that nobody like Mrs Nickleby had ever existed. By the same token, we cannot imagine Mrs Nickleby or any other Dickens caricature sitting down and reading a novel by Charles Dickens. In order to empathize with a Dickens text, a reader had to be capable, and with the help of a historical perspective can still be capable today, of sounding different sociocultural options in a way that Dickens's caricatures, if they were real people, would not be. As Morfin would put it, the caricatures are as inflexible as clay images. Seen more positively, they represent a triumph of the compulsion to form over the tendency to drift, a "momentary stay against confusion" (in Robert Frost's phrase), which helped to clarify perceptions of contemporary social reality.

In doing so, moreover, they also assigned a place within that reality to Dickens and his readers themselves. An account of Dickens's characterization focusing exclusively on his ventriloquistic powers of theatrical empathy would overlook this essential psychological complement.[60] Each caricature was constantly freezing Dickens and his readers in some single response: the response of one of that particular caricature's opposite numbers and judges within heteroglossia. The caricature's distinctiveness would provoke a pleasing but illusory superiority of unconfused opposition, which would work as a principle of temporary self-definition. As long as readers were empathizing with Major Bagstock, they were also defining themselves in purest contradistinction from the name-dropping, self-important parasitism of which Bagstock was the quintessentialization. For the time being, their nearest class equal was perhaps even Dombey himself, whose blindness to Bagstock's insincerity, impositions and exploitiveness they could pity as a brother's.

Or take the case of Cousin Feenix. Chesterton said that Dickens, despite much adverse criticism to the contrary, certainly could portray the gentry and aristocracy, but not as they themselves liked to be portrayed.[61] Precisely: Feenix was consistently seen through the eyes of a more intelligent member of Dombey's own class. What comes across is an amusedly cynical attitude towards an old-boy network which was being rapidly outpaced or infiltrated, plus a large recognition of Feenix's genuine decency of feeling. Feenix represented an antiquated power factor with which, for the moment, Dickens and his readers, like Dombey but with more self-awareness, could unhesitatingly strike an alliance, gently bending it to their own purposes.

Yet all such frozen postures of response were only temporary. Captain Cuttle's unaspiring naturalness was constantly inviting judgement from a genteel sophistication worthy of Mrs Skewton. But Mrs Skewton's artificiality and ambition constantly roused a Wordsworthian naturalness not unlike Captain Cuttle's. Exactly because the book contained not only Captain Cuttle but also Mrs Skewton, plus a great many other caricatures as well, and because throughout the nineteen months of serialization the different caricatures were all constantly coming and going and coming back, each single frozen posture of response was also contantly thawing out into some other no less distinctive posture. Dickens's novels, not only as mimesis but also as expressive and affective discourse, are remarkable for an endlessly scintillating flux within heteroglossia. Such was their beautiful challenge to bourgeois decorum.

Nor are Paul and Dombey as much affected by the bourgeois homogenization as Edith, Carker, Walter and Florence. Here the simplified view of Dickens as toadying to a middle-class audience again breaks down, because the pressures of heteroglossia are still so much in evidence.

Admittedly, Paul offered a feast to moralizing sentimentalists. With all the echoes of the immortal sea that brought us hither, his portrayal certainly cashed in on Wordsworthianism. For this child on the shore, the mighty waters rolled quite deafeningly. This was not the whole story, though, and the difference between Paul and Florence was most immediately a matter of presentation. Paul was altogether more angled, with his own individual speech and core of mystery. Readers of the novel, just like Mrs Pipchin *in* the novel, could never be sure what he was going to say next, and Dickens felt no obligation to turn the first four numbers into a psychologically explicit *Bildungsroman*. Indeed, it was the Paul of Number Five who acted as a catalyst to that genre in *Jane Eyre* and *David Copperfield* in the following quinquennium. Paul in any case had an advantage over Florence, in not having to be authorially sustained beyond the novel's first five issues or his own childhood. If he had failed to cotton on to the full extent of his father's inhumanity, this would not have seemed masochistic or stupid, but merely appropriate to his years. Dickens deals with Paul's thoughts on such matters by means of a suggestive concealment, and the risk, if there is one, is that Paul will seem prematurely wise. Even Number Five, for which the mansucript notes record Dickens's intention that "his illness only [be] expressed in the child's own feelings",[62] preserved Paul's autonomy. Readers could never be sure what way his feelings would tend, and whereas Florence's later sufferings are, in Gérard Genette's terminology,[63] focalized by Florence but vocalized by the adult, platitudinous author, much of Paul's illness is both focalized and poignantly vocalized by Paul himself.

Such presentational distinctiveness would have helped to force a response which, in social terms, was more complex than sentimentality. As a matter of fact, this child's sufferings quietly controverted the fairytale plot of the Florence story, being caused, not by parental neglect, but by a particular type of parental concern. Not even Blimber is wilfully cruel to Paul. In himself, Blimber is not actually evil, and in one part of his mind regards his remunerative trade as the highest of callings. Dickens's socio-economic observation, as fine, here, as anything in George Eliot, unerringly registers the sheer failure of imagination within the class system on which Blimber thrives. Blimber's veneering of middle-class boys with the classics answers all too exactly to Dombey's own disastrous conception of his son's needs, and Dombey is representative. Many of Dickens's readers, in shedding Wordsworthian tears at the fate of Paul, would find themselves condemning their own aspirations to gentility.

At this point, in other words, the novel is so alive with the counterpointings of the bourgeoisie's own heteroglossia that to think of it as "only" a novel would be a mistake. A live novel is a microcosm of the forces at work within its culture, and is charged with a social dynamism of its own. One of the essential points was again understood by Gissing:

> We may feel assured that many an English paterfamilias, who gave his opinion in favour of the modern against the ancient, and helped on the new spirit in matters educational was more or less consciously influenced by the reading of *Dombey and Son*.[64]

Whereas the treatment of Edith and Florence highlighted injustices to women without really forcing readers to serious introspection, the treatment of Paul, in making all England weep, was subjecting genteel perversifications to the first of a series of bodyblows which culminated in *Great Expectations*.

Already I have begun to speak of Dombey himself, who, in his relations with his wives no less than in his ambitions for Paul, must have triggered in Victorian readers the same tension between moralization and gentility throughout. According to Philip Collins's stereotyping view of the book and its audience, the moralization had a free run. Combatting, not unreasonably, Modernist claims that *Dombey and Son* appealed to its contemporaries as a symbolic structure or as a wholesale critique of industrialization, Collins reduced it to a traditional sermon about pride and riches.[65] Obviously, there was much in the novel that asked to be read this way. Yet Dickens sometimes parodied such an understanding, for instance in his supercilious reports from the servants' kitchen: "'We are all brethren,' says Mrs. Perch, in a pause of her drink. 'Except the sisters,' says Mr. Perch. 'How are the mighty fallen!' remarks the Cook. 'Pride shall have a fall, and it always was and will be so!' observes the Housemaid".[66] Here and at many other points, the class pride of Dickens and his readers would prompt them to feel that, whatever Dombey's own personal failings, there were certain things he stood for which should not be traduced by easy didacticism: dignity, style, keeping the lower orders in their place. The clear moral judgements invited by his behaviour would be attended with a reservation: "I myself could occupy, *do* perhaps occupy, a similar position, without making similar mistakes." Without some half-secret sense, in author and readers alike, of a rationale behind Dombey's pride, Dombey would have evaporated into a cloud of sheer impossibility before the end of Number Two.

Over and above class pride, the moralizing option had to face another challenge. This brings us back to the nature and effects of time. The concept of a person's "own" time had been one of the main issues during the debates about the Factory Acts. *Was* time essentially a worker's own? Was it something given for the worker's own personal life and enjoyment? Those who thought that it was can be credited with a Wordsworthian view of things: life is significant by its spiritual and emotional qualities. Or was time money? Should there be a direct correlation between what a person did with time and the amount of money earned? If so, time had to do with the ethics of enterprise, and would lend itself to utilitarian measurement.[67] Dombey and Blimber, in trying to force Paul's development, and in being associated with clocks or watches which tick off the seconds, were close to this second view and, through the dynamics of heteroglossia, were judged by the standards of the other view. Yet when Dombey himself stayed away from his office, brooding over his emotional life in his private room at home, so allowing the energetic Carker to outwit him in business matters, he was clearly wasting commodity-time, and the novel was prompting reproof according to the criteria of enterprise and utility.

For many readers, the same would have applied to Dombey's courtship of Edith at Leamington. They would have had little sympathy for the scheme of a third-generation head of a family firm to link himself with the outdated oligarchy. He would have done much better to have stayed in London and cultivated the acquaintance of a "new" man — somebody like Joseph Paxton, say, the railway tycoon. Dombey's failure to respond to the economic potential of the railways, his defensively genteel attempts to force the Toodles into the paradigm of service, showed that the entrepreneurial spirit of his grandfather had atrophied in him.

Dombey's frontal exposure to the various types of ideological scrutiny was ensured by the presentation. He is usually seen quite from the outside,[68] and has the same firmness of outline as the caricatures, plus a no less unmistakable idiolect. He is static. He is absurd. And Dickens, by regularly refusing us admission to Dombey's soul, astonishes us by what seems its awe-inspiring shallowness, blindness and predictability. We can almost guess what he will say in any situation, and he constantly flabbergasts us by living up to our expectations. In Edwin Muir's terms, the Dombey plot is not so much dramatic as choreographic.[69] It is less a matter of keeping Dombey acting than of keeping him moving. He comes on and does his bit again and again, acquiring the same inflexible permanence as a Feenix or a Bagstock. However common the failings he typifies, he is thus rendered curious, alien. Dickens's readers were forced to meet him — and to meet, in him, something of themselves — head-on.

Then at the end of the novel something happens. But what, exactly? Shall we say that Dickens again settles for a (to us) lesser kind of beauty, switching to the decorum of middle-class respectability? Certainly Dombey himself seems to change — in Taine's opinion, "becomes the best of fathers, and spoils a fine novel".[70] Or shall we say, more charitably, that the final pages are themselves a kind of challenge to the bourgeoisie? — that they give us Dombey's and Dickens's own tentative experiment with a new kind of male self-image, softer and less dominating.

The heavily underlined parallels with King Lear's reconciliation to Cordelia could well point in this direction, and late-twentieth-century feminist critics actually detected a half-articulate revolutionary potential. According to Lyda Zwingler, in the Victorian scheme of things the only people for whom daughters were supposed to serve as mother substitutes and angels of the hearth were impotent old fathers or young male ingenues. Dombey, not seeing himself in either of those roles, had rejected Florence, accusing her of betraying him. Later, Florence is no longer his daughter as far as he is concerned, but somebody else's wife, and mother of the new little Dombey. The bourgeois patriarchy, in other words, is preserved, with Edith "confessing" to Florence, Florence to Dombey, and Dombey to God. Even when women conform to the images men have prescribed,

> men do not like women; yet women seem to like men. In the Dombey world women *have* to like men; men do not have to like women. Until Dombey loses the last vestiges of his patriarchal, socially constructed power, he need not treat his daughter (who is all women) or any other women (who are all daughters) with anything other than a lordly contempt, a contempt that masks the fear generated by any surpressed domestic population.

Given all this, Zwingler found Dombey's final appearance rather remarkable.

> Everyone "knows" that domestic influence is not stronger than capitalistic power, that sentimental hierarchies are not superior to patriarchal ones, and, from the standpoint of that knowledge, Dombey's end looks not only like capitulation but an unnecessary and rather frightening one.[71]

Seen this way, the end of the novel is tending towards utopianism. Dickens is making an admirable, albeit necessarily unsuccessful effort to envisage a world based on new types of relationship.

From as early as the letter of July 25th, 1846 he had certainly planned a peripeteia here. What the letter proposed was a convincing enough tale of filial and paternal love, a kind of Wordsworthian lyrical ballad in town clothes. In its exposition of this, however, the letter's discussion of Dombey was uniformly introspective, and the same was true of Dickens's attempt to meet criticism of Dombey's end in the preface to the cheap edition of 1858. Both the letter and the preface could therefore make Dombey's change seem less psychologically radical than appeared in the novel itself. The idea was that Dombey had always had a shamed consciousness of the injustice of his treatment of Florence, and that he finally did something about it.

The novel itself, before the last section, did not probe such depths. If it had, it would have lost the force of Dombey's being so sheerly "other" — while also so much "the same" as some of its readers. At two or three points, admittedly, its descriptions of Dombey had dropped the categorical language for linguistic forms that were mitigatingly modalized; "may do" and "perhaps is" took the place of "does" and "is", and questions were even formulated about Dombey's inner life:

> He goes on, without deviation, keeping his thoughts and feelings close within his own breast, and imparting them to no one. He makes no search for his daughter. He may think that she is with his sister, or that she is under his own roof. He may think of her constantly, or he may never think about her. It is all one for any sign he makes.[72]

But Dickens's return to categoricality had always been very quick and assertive:

> But this is sure; he does *not* think that he has lost her. He has no suspicion of the truth. He has lived too long shut up in his towering supremacy, seeing her, a patient gentle creature, in the path below it, to have any fear of that. Shaken as he is by his disgrace, he is not yet humbled to the level earth.[73]

If anything, the temporary modalizations had only emphasized Dombey's areas of opaqueness by acknowledging their impenetrability ("He may think . . ., or he may never think . . .").[74]

    If there is a problem with Dombey at the end of the novel, it is connected with Dickens's change of technique: his move from the brilliantly superficial style of choreographic caricature to that of the standardizing emotionalism he has used for Florence throughout. Readers can interpret this in two ways. Either "Dombey the man" was not really so fixed in attitude and tone as Dickens's earlier presentation made him appear; in which case, the 1858 preface, though essentially right, is also a tacit admission of a tendency to falsification in the earlier caricature. Or else there was now a genuine personality change in Dombey; in Jungian terms, the persona Dombey had cultivated for many years was giving way to the shadow of his common spiritual humanity; in which case, the 1858 preface is essentially wrong, and the earlier caricature was not without all foundation in reality. Either way, though, the change of technique can easily be read as a final capitulation to the cheaper kind of Wordsworthianism. On the utopianly feminist interpretation of the novel's last pages, Dombey's loss of strong individuality is of course precisely the point. But especially given the contrast with the figure Dombey cut earlier in the novel, Dickens has in that case landed himself with the old problem of how to make virtue interesting, which was always the basic problem with Florence. For present-day readers who find the utopian reading an insufficient or unconvincing compensation, the loss of individuality in Dombey may also be a loss of individuality for Dickens.

Or will it? And *is* the end of the novel problematic? Even if it is, there is really nothing new about it. The switch of presentational style is a reversion to Dickens's manner with Florence throughout, and a fluctuation between the lesser, bourgeois and the greater, ecstatic beauties is exactly what we have got used to. Perhaps the whole secret of Dickens's novelistic co-adaptation is that neither type of beauty finally wins, and that linearization is of secondary importance — as Chesterton said, we soon forget the story. To say that the last chapter is a *loss* of individuality for Dombey and Dickens might be to confuse a mere token story-line with the novel's overall effect. It might be no less of a mistake than to confuse the discursive argument of Vaughan's "The World" with its actual impact — to suggest that the poem's astonishing opening is somehow toned down by the witty conceit at the close, which is simply not the way readers read. The beginning of *Dombey and Son*, a dazzling achievement in which the unregenerate Dombey is in full command, and in which Dickens, too, is at his most rumbustiously individual, is at least as likely to stick in the memory as is the novel's end. Beginning and end, one might say, complement each other, as extreme versions of the two so different beauties which clash throughout. In this sense, then, it makes no difference which beauty comes first and which last. Both these positions lend themselves to very strong emphasis, and to wish that either the beginning or the end were different would be to wish for a *totally* different book, which Dickens, consciously or unconsciously, was too astute to waste his time on. If he had made the end more like the beginning, many of his own contemporaries would have damned it as too unremittingly outrageous. If he had tuned the beginning to the end, few twentieth-century readers, and perhaps not all that many Victorians, would have got beyond the first pages.

Here it may seem that the concept of co-adaptation is tidying up an untidy text no less briskly than did the concepts of the New Critical scholasticism which I mentioned at the outset — irony, paradox, tension, ambiguity, narrator-versus-author. But I am not seeing the text as unified, but as first one thing, then another, and then the first thing again, and so on, the two different things never ceasing to jar against each other. This is not particularly tidy at all, and the bottom line is simply Dickens's sense, conscious or unconcious, that too much of the one thing at the expense of the other thing would have made the novel either not worth writing or a historical impossibility.

If he did get things wrong, we would nowadays tend to assume that he was overgenerous with the homogenizing, bourgeois decorum. Many readers have been tempted to think of that decorum as Dickens's historical feet of clay, and of the other, ecstatic beauty as something more universal. Certainly hitherto, his riotous immersion in cultural difference seems to have pleasured all his readers, and will probably continue to do so.

But what are the preconditions for such pleasurable riot? Here we return to the principle of differentiality, which has found its way into literary thought from structuralist linguistics. That the word "bat" is not the word "bar", for instance, is due to differentiating phonemes. The Russian Formalists applied this principle to our perceptions of poetry, and in some of their later work began to make it the basis for a history of literary form. Whole genres define themselves in differential opposition to other genres, and a genuinely new poem is new by differentiation from current norms. Although I did not spell it out at the time, this kind of insight was implicit in my discussion of Vaughan: Vaughan curiously deviates from stylistic, argumentative and deictic conventions, and without the conventions his oddities would not have been oddities in the first place. A similar point applies to Eliot's impoliteness, which is why I recommended the *Critical Heritage* volumes as a way of re-activating it now that norms have changed. As for Dickens, his riotous variety similarly presupposes bounds to be broken — presupposes something narrower and restraining. And in each and every case, the norm from which the writing deviates is also firmly established in the writing itself: in Vaughan there is run-of-the-mill practic piety, in Eliot the politeness *in* the poems, and in Dickens the bourgeois decorum. Over and above the rhetorical need for palliatives, these (to us) more boring features have always had an even more basic necessity, as the foil without which the less stereotyped features would have been less sharply visible. Here again, this has had nothing to do with linearity. It did not matter that *Dombey and Son* begins with the riotous deviation from bourgeois norms. The norms were already abundantly in evidence within the culture, and the novel was well able to recuperate them for confirmatory and more specific differentiation in due course.

The co-existence of decorum and indecorum has another kind of psychological inevitability as well. Quite simply, the human mind is perfectly capable of oscillating between opposites, and actually does so on a regular basis. As I pointed out earlier, bourgeois decorum was itself a simplifying narrowing-down of Victorian attitudes which were varied and self-contradictory. It was a straitjacket even for the bourgeoisie, which must go a long way to explaining Dickens's appeal to his earliest readers. Obviously enough, thousands of them were willing to pay for an easy pathos and black-and-white moralizing worthy of the Cook and the Housemaid. But many of those same patrons were also among the first to enjoy the mysterious subtlety of little Paul or the more external, but bizarrely beautiful treatment of Dombey and the caricatures. As for Dickens himself, he could not only provide, but use, everything he ever wrote. The combination of his own ideological complexity with his prodigious talent for acting enabled him to animate every area of his texts, every voice of every character, homogenized or differentiated, and every response accordingly.

So his fingernails, which he was not indifferently paring, had all sorts of Victorian mud under them. There are aspects of his work which can only depress us, as evidence of the sheer weight of social formation on even the boldest spirit. Social formation is something none of us is free from, and my next chapter deals with Robert Frost's troubled sense that the only alternative would be a kind of spiritual, or even literal extinction. Dickens, despite the streak of rebelliousness so tellingly diagnosed by Edmund Wilson,[75] fully accepted that society is our element. Yet at the same time, nobody did more to bring the Victorians to their own attention, a feat which required a certain distance, and which, as Gissing clearly saw, was likely to promote change. Profoundly at one with his society, Dickens was able, consciously or unconsciously, to turn this known allegiance to rhetorical advantage. Demonstratively agreeing with Mrs Grundy, he started to de-throne her.

The tension between the two decorums, between human formations that were homogenized and narrowly centred and formations far more rich and manifold, uncannily prefigured the tension between globalization and fragmentation in our own postmodern age. Now as then, there is disagreement about the relative benefits of the centripetal and the centrifugal, but human life in society has to continue anyway. The inspiration offered by Dickens is that of a superlatively practical and dynamic diplomacy: of a genius for compromise in conjunction with a restless individuality and prodigious creativity. What his achievement suggests is the feasibility of navigation through powerful social cross-currents, on a course which moves co-adaptively from old to new, with no lasting opposition or loss, and fairly fast as well.

CHAPTER 6

Robert Frost's hiding and altering

Robert Frost's poems, no less than Eliot's and Vaughan's, no less than Dickens's novels, though in a very different way, represent a powerful co-adaptation between the social and the individual. Necessarily, it was a co-adaptation specific to a particular phase of a particular culture. Up until twenty-five or thirty years ago, however, many American and British critics still saw Frost as the wise bard of a universal humanity. Even readers persuaded by his self-representation as a Yankee farmer tended to take this, not as a limitation, but as the guarantee of a sagacity that knew no bounds. This view of him was also easily reconcilable with the scholastics' steady stream of New-Critical readings, which saw his poems as the timeless and placeless exponents of symbolic form. Again as in the cases of Eliot, Vaughan and Dickens, then, the solid reputation did not mean that readers had grasped the true historical achievement.

In order to uncover this for the suggestiveness it could have for our own postmodern age, ethnographical mediation can point out certain features of American social history, features which American citizens perhaps once tended not to recognize, but of which Frost himself was keenly aware. Today, such awareness is much more widespread within American culture at large. Yet the relevance of sociohistorical considerations to the poetry of Frost would sometimes be hard to guess from the way it has been discussed, or from its influence on other poets.

Take, for instance, the following:

IN TEESDALE

No, not to-night,
Not by this fading light,
Not by those high fells where the forces
Fall from the mist like the white tails of horses.

From that dark slack
Where peat-hags gape too black
I turn to where the lighted farm
Holds out through the open door a golden arm.

No, not tonight,
To-morrow by daylight;
To-night I fear the fabulous horses
Whose white tails flash down the steep watercourses.[1]

This was published in 1935, twelve years after Frost's "Stopping by Woods on a Snowy Evening", and belongs to the late–middle period of Andrew Young (compare pp. 64–6 and 81–4 above), for whom Frost's plain language and rejection of plangent sentiment were so crucial. Yet although Young's earliest work was marred by late-Romantic cliché, it had sometimes voiced a genuine enough anguish, which in his early-middle period could mutate into a distinctively macabre preoccupation with death, the preoccupation of a poem such as "The Old Tree" (quoted on p. 79 above). In his late-middle period, by contrast, as the Frostian discipline of language and versification became still tighter, Young's poetry became somewhat more comfortable and reassuring, with a stronger whiff of art for art's sake.

"In Teesdale", then, has little trace of the haunted, restless searching in many of Young's earlier poems. Compared with the *memento mori* of the old tree, the peat hags seem rather brittle in their threat, and the only wonder, the wonder of the "fabulous horses", will presumably have disappeared before his proposed climb in the safer light of day. The very fabulousness of the wonder, the fact that it seems to be a matter of legend, open to the entire human race, completely rules out the curious personal intimacy of the tryst Young would have desired previously. Now he is simply ordinary — cowardly but tough-skinned. What attracts him most strongly is a safety around the hearth, something which earlier poems such as "The Ventiloquists" (quoted on p. 80 above) would have rejected as bad faith, a betrayal of his mysterious mistress of the skies and muse of Nature.

So marked is the formal beauty of sound and rhythm in "In Teesdale" that the banality of his choice may escape notice. Paradoxically, the skill is in bodying forth his very complacency. The stanza's line-by-line addition of an extra foot, from two through to five, together with the ellipses and varied stresses, portray with an uncanny solidity that mundane mind at work, gradually finding the confidence of its own instinctive withdrawal from adventure. The third stanza's repetition of the first stanza's rhymes constates the psychological immobility, and the same desire for ease can even be felt in the contrasts between the poem's three pentameters. The reassuring golden arm of light is regularly iambic ("the open" elides "th'open"), whereas after "mist" and "flash" the two successive weak stresses suggest the horrendous drop of the water, and the sickening fall from which his body, at this particular moment in his life, retreats. The poem cunningly celebrates creature comforts as a way of indulging its own artistry.

"Stopping by Woods on a Snowy Evening" comes to mind irresistibly. Young's formal accomplishment reflects his careful study of Frost's highly wrought stanza with its repetend (*aaba/bbcb* etc.), and of the psychological iconicity of the poem's repeated last line. What has also carried over is the poet's portrayal of himself as a prudent conformist. Solitary between one farm or village and the next, Frost contemplates the woods, "lovely, dark and deep", with a sense of fascination similar to Young's as he contemplates the fells: it is as if the woods offer stolen, dangerous pleasures. But like Young, Frost turns away. A libidinal release into the unknown is not to be risked. His "official" self reminds him of obligations to other human beings.

Yet when, during the 1970s, I was first beginning to compare and contrast Frost and Young, "Stopping by Woods on a Snowy Evening" still seemed the better poem. It not only responded to aestheticizing readings. It could also be adapted to that more gloomy Modernist reading habit: to the expectation of unpleasantness, which in the case of "In Teesdale" would have been fairly unproductive. Young's retreat from the unknown, his turning towards the lighted farm, was likely to seem little more than a matter of course. The note of personal disturbance was far weaker than in his early-middle poems; even there it had been muffled by the confusing circumstances of publication;[2] and here it was hardly to be amplified by available biographical information. Young was mainly thought of as a Georgian nature poet and rural clergyman, who had also written two strange visionary poems, plus some prose books of topography and quaint botanophilia. Even my own more detailed examination was tending to suggest that the context within which he wrote this particular poem had not been too upsetting.[3] On the contrary, at the age of fifty he was at last beginning to be a bit happier with life, whereas Robert Frost's self-portrayal as an unflappable Yankee, certainly in the *late* 1970s, no longer seemed to tell the whole story. Especially in the United States, psychoanalytical readings of literature had long been in plentiful supply, and Lawrance Thompson's biography of Frost, the final volume of which was published in 1976,[4] suggested that his psyche was disturbingly volatile, with some very murky depths. Predictably, critics were already finding reverberations of this in his poetry, an approach which it is one of my next chapter's main aims to develop still further. As Frost knew only too well, he was not a gentle innocent, and if he despised Freud it was probably because, like D. H. Lawrence, he saw him as a rival in the exploration of unedifying secrets. True, in 1984 William H. Pritchard's *Frost: A Literary Life Reconsidered*[5] was to argue that Thompson (by then dead) had been over-zealous in the pursuit of submerged intentions, and deaf to Frost's poetry and humour. True, too, in 1994 the poet's own granddaughter would go on to give a loving description of his family life.[6] Today, such accounts support the qualification of unpleasant Modernist readings which is my next chapter's other main aim. But in the cultural context of the 1970s, disturbing psychoanalysis could carry on unchallenged, and "Stopping by Woods on a Snowy Evening" responded as required.

Altogether more surprising in American readings would have been suggestions to the effect that Frost's sense of the woods' absent owner is tinged with class feelings. Freudianism was one thing. This would have been a very different proposition, and one which most American critics, scholastic or otherwise, were unlikely to put forward, or their readers to accept. Needless to say, "Stopping by Woods" is one of many poems by Frost which give no warrant for it. The community, the obligations, and the bed to which the poem's solitary persona is himself returning do not trigger any particular sociocultural connotations, and he is not even absolutely sure who the woods' absent owner really is. He *believes* it is a man whose house is in the village, and that is that. Yet the more I thought about it, the more I felt that this un-class-conscious poem was not entirely representative. Frost's reputation, whether as the wise bard of a universal humanity, or as a skilful Modernist artist, or as the sort of Modernist who could be quietly unnerving, rested to no small part on precisely this text. But what its regular selection by anthologizers and imitators most clearly indicated was the marginalization by New Critical scholastics of literature's social dimension. More generally, it confirmed an observation of Lionel Trilling's in 1947:

> Americans have a kind of resistance to looking closely at society. They appear to believe that to touch accurately on the matter of class, to take full note of snobbery, is somehow to demean themselves. It is as if we felt that one cannot touch pitch without being defiled — which, of course, may possibly be the case. Americans will not deny that we have classes and snobbery, but they seem to hold it to be indelicate to take precise cognizance of these phenomena.[7]

As I shall later have cause to note again, Trilling himself had the flexibility of intelligence to be both of, and not of his own milieu and moment.

By the 1960s and 1970s, some American critics had actually begun to have reservations about Frost's Yankee-farmer persona, yet could nevertheless still see him as the sagely reasonable poet of a maturely egalitarian republic. This myth was not peculiar to the New Critical agrarians of the South, but was also accepted more widely, as the justification or proof of the American melting pot. In 1963 Reuben A. Brower said that, in Frost, there were no peasants. There were only Americans, living in a democracy strengthened by traditions of religious and political debate. According to Brower, Frost could therefore draw on a *rural* sophistication quite unavailable to Wordsworth, and earlier untapped by Wordsworth's American imitators.[8] Frost's work, it would seem, presupposed a shared spirit of equality, with everyone using essentially the same structures of belief, knowledge and communication, and quite unsullied by either rural superstition and brutishness or by the false sophistication of the city. Realistic reasonableness reigned supreme, within what sounded like a rather sober fraternity.

Reading Brower twenty-five years ago, I was unable to deny that such communities existed, or had existed, though I was less sure about their peculiar Americanness — I actually remembered the Presbyterian upbringing of Wordsworth's pedlar. I could see, too, that there were traces of such a community in the world of Frost; the well-intentioned Warren and Mary in "The Death of the Hired Man" could have been founder members. But even Brower himself elsewhere implied that there were American communities of different kinds, and sometimes went so far as to distinguish between Frost's "people" and Frost himself. Frost would have agreed. He always took for granted that, in America just as anywhere else, sources of income, the actual jobs people do, the actual place they live in, the actual education they have received, as well as their sex, religion and ethnic background, create strong social distinctions.[9] In particular, I could not help noticing that his poetry frequently thematized American ways of being obviously rural, obviously unlettered, and obviously neither of these.

So why did I fasten on this, when Brower, a fine scholar and suggestive commentator, did not? Throughout this book, I am allowing for mysteries of individual temperament which can make two readers with similar backgrounds react quite differently. My question for the time being, however, is about the pragmatics of cultural context. Temperamentally, I venture to think, Brower and I might even be somewhat similar. But was there, perhaps, a telling difference as regards milieu and upbringing? Did it signify, for instance, that I was British born and bred?

Not exactly, I think. In 1966 W.W. Robson, a British critic of no less distinction than Brower, certainly seemed to recognize the class element, when he described Frost's people as hard, curmudgeonly and themselves caste-conscious. American caste consciousness was something Robson refused to sentimentalize away. He pointed out that the "situation in 'A Hundred Collars', when a professor has to share a room with a travelling salesman, is just as uncomfortable as if they had been Englishmen." Even Robson, though, found in Frost a "capacity to express fellow-feeling with a deep and complete sincerity", a capacity fostered, he said, by the conditions of American life and society. British critics, then, no less than Andrew Young and other British poets, could actually echo American perceptions of Frost. American caste and caste consciousness, Robson continued, are certainly real. But what would have happened, he asked, if the situation in "A Hundred Collars" had been treated by a liberal English writer of Frost's generation, like E. M. Forster?

> The vein might well be lightly ironical; the English writer, in the person of the professor, would have been ashamed of himself, would have known what he ought to feel, and would have done his best to feel it. Frost's attitude also includes an element of irony. But whereas the English writer would know what the professor felt, but would have to guess at what the salesman felt, Frost knows both. That is the difference.[10]

My disagreement with Robson was pretty sharp. In my own study of Frost's poetry, I was increasingly struck by powers of empathy without which his finest work would be the poorer. But empathy, it seemed to me, was not the same thing as a ready supply of fellow feeling. Rather, the empathy was all the more impressive because the characters empathized with remained so incontrovertibly "other". Although Frost can himself sometimes rise to an ethnographic mediation of difference, difference is never eroded. Sometimes it actually still arouses strong feelings of dislike.

In his two unpublished prose plays, "In an Art Factory" and "The Guardeen", of which I was preparing editions,[11] a capacity for expressing fellow feeling with deep and complete sincerity is conspicuous by its absence. Both plays examine the hypothesis of a human fraternity which, however desirable in principle, to the extent that is remotely possible simply appals. "In an Art Factory", written during the 1920s, is about a sculptor who has a strained relationship with the philistine public which invests in his work. The play ends with an unsatisfactory ambiguity as to whether he will renounce them altogether, or renounce his art and join them. "The Guardeen", written between 1939 and 1941 but drawing heavily on Frost's own personal memories from 1895, is about a city boy and college student, a would-be poet, who comes to a wild spot in the New England backwoods in order to write a sociological thesis about its rough-neck inhabitants. He is at once attracted and repelled by the rustics, and at the same time develops a complementary ambivalence towards the urbane sophistication of his professor. He would like to achieve some entirely different *modus vivendi*, to create for himself an ambience, neither rustic nor urbane, whose air he could breathe more freely, and in which he could become an artist. But as in "In an Art Factory", the success of the protagonist's attempt at this remains uncertain.

What the two plays illustrate is a cultured man's burden of guilt and sheer dislike in face of the uncultured, a burden which a knowledge of how the other man feels does little to alleviate, yet which at the same time undermines confidence in his own type of culture as well. I speak of a cultured "man" here, because the writing is so close to Frost's own experience, which was gender specific. The plays are autobiographical in the bad sense that both he and his protagonists fail to master intense social conflicts, from which they perhaps think their female muses ought to release them into a world of art. A strong desire for self-reliant freedom has to contend with allegiances to a number of interest groupings which are mutually exclusive even amongst themselves. Whichever way Frost turned, personal and creative autonomy seemed threatened: threatened at least as much by the freemasonry of artists or the collegiality of academe as by the general public's philistinism or the backwardness of poor country folk. The plays even suggest the smouldering frustration to which such tensions gave rise, for the writing has a certain wilful carelessness, with ugly fantasies of homicidal and pyromanic "ways-out" — a centrally Frostian locution, this, and suggestive of an instinctive bolting away from confrontation. Although he wrote a poem called "Escapist — Never!", and although he liked to think of himself as expansively running *towards* things rather than shrinkingly running *away*,[12] his mind often swung towards an introverted unsociability.

I was sensitive to these aspects of Frost, not only because I had come across "In An Art Factory" and "The Guardeen", but also because I was slightly more of a *foreign* critic than either Brower or Robson. Even though in practice I failed to take advantage of it, I was in principle in a position to help British and American readers see themselves as others see them. Rather than being entirely restricted to an Anglo-American frame of reference, since my mid-twenties I had to some extent been Scandinavianized. I had worked in Swedish and Finnish universities, had undergone surgery in a Swedish hospital, followed by two months in a Swedish convalescence home, was reading Swedish literature in the original, was married to a Swedish-speaking Finn, and already had children who were being educated in Swedish-Finnish schools. Every time I returned to England on holiday, I was struck by the difference between rich and poor, and during the academic year 1978–9 my wife and I were both shocked by the same thing in Charlottesville, Virginia. As I worked on the Frost manuscripts in the University of Virginia Library, I knew that Charlottesville's named streets were still for whites, the numbered streets for blacks. My wife, who had a job in her own field in the University of Virginia hospital, came home with first-hand accounts of the social inequalities of American medicine, and when we toured the southern states we were amazed at the mile upon mile of rural slum. As if to prove Trilling's point, the most unforgettable example was a place called Panacea.

Frost himself was very far from euphemizing class in America. He knew, too, about his own social insecurities, though he often managed to hide them, along with other disturbing traits, beneath the persona of the Yankee farmer. Yet even before his death, and with the persistence of that image of him, his literary stock had begun to sink. Among the learned and the critical, there grew the feeling that any writer as closely identifiable with a particular region and its viewpoint as Frost seemingly wanted to be must have serious limitations. During the 1960s and 1970s there was also the possibility that the psychoanalytical critics would eventually conclude that his entire mental and emotional make-up was a serious liability.

It was at roughly this stage that American admirers such as Robert Poirier and Frank Lentricchia started to draw attention to completely different aspects of his work, and particularly to features allegedly shared with writers indisputably modern and fashionable. Poirier offered an extended comparison of *A Boy's Will* with Joyce's *Portrait of the Artist as a Young Man*,[13] while Lentricchia found similarities between Frost and Wallace Stevens. One of the words in the title of Lentricchia's book on Frost was actually "landscape", and there were whole chapters on brooks, houses, and woods. Lentricchia was not thinking of Frost as a regionalist, however, and his full title was *Robert Frost: Modern Poetics and the Landscapes of the Self*.[14] A landscape of the self was evidently no ordinary landscape. The brooks, houses and woods did not sound like the ones seen every day by a New England farmer. Instead they were said to be symbols or, rather, tentative symbols, deployed in subtle Stevens-like fictions, enquiringly juxtaposed to reality.

It seemed to me that this was still dodging the issue. Beyond a certain point, Frost and Stevens were not comparable. Granted, Frost sometimes took a self-conscious delight in fiction-making; some of his poems are decidedly *metafictional*. And yes, his delight in his craft is quite obvious enough to prevent his realism from seeming artless. But Lentricchia's comparison made Frost seem less scared, less serene, less Victorian, less courageous — less everything! — than I thought he really was, because whatever attitude or response or description Frost builds up was said to be essentially speculative and interim. It was yet to be qualified by, and enmeshed with, reality. This was one way for Lentricchia to argue that Frost's work is not — what to me it so clearly was — localized.

Localized, not regionalist. Even if Poirier and Lentriccia were unconvincing, Frost's reputation could not revert to that of the Yankee farmer pure and simple. The first volume of Thompson's biography (1966) had already shown that the Yankee image was one of Frost's carefully constructed myths. His formative years were spent in San Francisco, and before the move to Derry he had had less experience of working on the land than of working in a factory. His Derry neighbours regarded his chicken farm as a hopelessly dilettante enterprise, and without the help of his two partners and a generous allowance from his much maligned grandfather he could not have made ends meet. When, after a few years, he started teaching, the farm fell into disrepair. And when, after a few more years, he was finally able to get rid of it, he happily left for England on the proceeds. As Thompson's second volume (1979) went on to show, it was only on his return from England that he began cultivate the Yankee farmer image, as a way of capitalizing on the success of *North of Boston.*

Another challenge to the myth came 1976, from Frost's friend, the poet Archibald MacLeish, and published in *National Geographic*, presumably in the hope of reaching some of Frost's wide non-academic audience. What MacLeish objected to was the notion that Frost's poems are "of the New England scene . . . [and] of the New England mind".[15] In 1979 similar points were made by John C. Kemp, in his *Robert Frost and New England: the Poet as Regionalist.*[16] One of this book's weaknesses, it seemed to me, was its title, for its main claim was that Frost is not a regionalist in the restrictive sense. His locales and "people" are often taken from New England, but in his best poems, contained in *North of Boston* or written in the same mode, his own persona is that of a traveller, an outsider, a feminine, playful observer of the New England dourness, strictness and common sense. Kemp also argued that in the poems — not starting until "Birches" and "Christmas Trees" — in which Frost did deliberately adopt the Yankee persona, he actually sinks below his highest level; he cheapens himself for the sake of the market. There were two Frosts, in other words: one, the great poet, who in some of his finest work just happened to turn his gaze on New England; the other, the self-declared Yankee, with all the narrowness which that entails.

My own judgement often coincided with Kemp's on what was best in Frost. Especially after my study of the self-debasing artist-protagonists in "In an Art Factory" and "The Guardeen", I could agree that the Yankee persona might be a way of toadying to a large public. But this, it seemed to me, was still only part of the truth, because Frost could also adopt the very different but no less disingenuous persona of an urbane academic. Even one of the poems that Kemp ranked most highly, "The Death of the Hired Man", for me had a slight tendency in this direction. A sociological ambit was implied by the very title, and Warren and Mary's long debate about what people of their class should or should not do for people of Silas's class had a certain flatness as poetry. For me, Frost was torn in several different directions at once, while Kemp, in failing to pinpoint this, also missed the ugly passions to which it gave rise, and consequently missed Frost's most successful attempts at dealing with them.

One poem which caught my attention was "A Fountain, A Bottle, A Donkey's Ears, and Some Books". In this curious exploration of rural dereliction, Frost's social insecurities do begin to break through, but are more skilfully controlled than in the unsuccessful plays' violence, even if violence is still only just below the surface. The educated narrator tells how, in the attic of poetess long since dead, he and his uncouth guide came across a heap of slim volumes. Other people had already performed their kinds of sacrilege. Now he had a sacrilegious fantasy of his own:

> Boys and bad hunters had known what to do
> With stone and lead to unprotected glass:
> Shatter it inward on the unswept floors.
> How had the tender verse escaped their outrage?
> By being invisible for what it was,
> Or else by some remoteness that defied them
> To find out what to do to hurt a poem.
> Yet oh! the tempting flatness of a book,
> To send it sailing out the attic window
> Till it caught wind and, opening out its covers,
> Tried to improve on sailing like a tile
> By flying like a bird (silent in flight,
> But all the burden of its body song),
> Only to tumble like a stricken bird,
> And lie in stones and bushes unretrieved.[17]

Sacrilegious, yes. A powerful fantasy of how *not* to treat a book of poems. Yet the wording — the beautiful play on "burden", or the Miltonic rhythm and word-order of the last line — is the wording of a literature-lover. Momentarily, he is a vandal and not a vandal. He, and with him the poem, tensely await some single allegiance and identity.

Frost himself finally postpones a cultural choice here, and the surface of the poem is otherwise unruffled. In a similar postponement, though to different effect, the potentially violent claims of one sub-culture chafing against another are sometimes held at arm's length, with a showman's sardonic brio. "A Hundred Collars", with its professor and travelling salesman, is one case. In "A Vanishing Red", where the miller is the colonizing, mechanizing white man, and where his murder victim is the dispossessed primitive, Frost likewise refuses all responsibility for, or participation in the outcome. Instead, he attributes the sociocultural conflict entirely to the representative protagonists. Not taking sides, not choosing between principles, and least of all suggesting a compromise, he allows events themselves to decide, fastening on them an eye that is fascinated and unblinking at noxious detail, as of somebody prophesying from entrails or awaiting a pugilistic knockout. Such can be the excitements of what Yvor Winters alleged was spiritual drifting,[18] or of what others praised as flexibility and realism.[19] Either way, Frost is ready to wait, and to adjust to whatever sociocultural materiality finally confronts him, only wishing, perhaps, that history would make such materiality conveniently monistic.

Did he see any alternative to such adjustment? In his most unsettling poems, he is fascinated, as in "The Guardeen", by instances of human life lived at the most extreme verges of civilization — at the end of mountain paths, in a cliff wall, in deserts where the only observer is a census-taker or a passenger in a passing train. These remote settlements are instances of survival at its most minimal. Always the implicit question is: Will a life that borrows nothing further from the outside world, no further trappings of culture, have any real face to present? It is the question Lear asked of unaccommodated man, the naked beggar on the heath, and Frost's poetry vibrates with his fear that a man — again, always a man, I think — can lose his identity either by joining a social group or by leaving one. Sometimes the tension between socialization and individuation is so great that some such annihilation would almost be attractive.

But Frost is not Andrew Young, at least not the Andrew Young of the early-middle poems or *Into Hades*, for whom even the annihilation of death had a particular interest. The late-middle "In Teesdale", by contrast, shows Young turning from the gaping peat-hags and steep watercourses towards the reassuring lights of the farm. This is Young at his most Frostian, for Frost, by temperament, is a man who *lives*. Dying is for other people. And his poetry, a poetry which sensibly, conscientiously, leaves the lovely, dark and deep to one side, only confirms the melodramatic superficiality of the suicide threats he sometimes served upon his family. His son Carol was to commit suicide. But he himself, like William James, for the most part regarded suicide as a lamentable failure of belief.[20] Not religious belief. More a kind of gut-feeling, perhaps: a sense that there must surely be some reason for staying alive, even if it is not immediately apparent. With nothing corresponding to Young's hope of a beautiful other-life, he felt that everything that is going to happen can only happen here and now, and that putting up with life is infinitely preferable to not having any life at all. No matter how infuriating the possibility of living with no true identity of one's own, such a fate is infinitely superior to extinction.

So the archetypal Frost poem, I came to think, the poem which should replace "Stopping by Woods" in future anthologies, is "The Lockless Door". This is haunted by a personal memory from 1895 which he failed to dramatize successfully in the central scene of "The Guardeen".[21] In the poem, by contrast, the writing has the terse control and symbolic force of Blake or Emily Dickinson:

THE LOCKLESS DOOR

It went many years,
But at last came a knock,
And I thought of the door
With no lock to lock.

I blew out the light,
I tiptoed the floor,
And raised both hands
In prayer to the door.

Yet the knock came again.
My window was wide;
I climbed on the sill
And descended outside.

Back over the sill
I bade a "Come in"
To whatever the knock
At the door may have been.

So at a knock
I emptied my cage
To hide in the world
And alter with age.[22]

I have touched on the flexibility of human formation in this book's Introduction. Ervin Goffman makes the point in terms of the theatricality of our everyday self-presentation.[23] As part of the process of individuation, the histrionic self can to some extent try on different formations for size, as it were. This poem's "I", fearfully emerging into the world from a sheltered, formless privacy, adopts some currently available psychic formation, which will always remain alien, yet which can become a reassuring and deeply internalized camouflage in future dealings with other people. This is the only viable "way out". The alternative to such mundane and practical bad faith would be a quite unimaginable spiritual nudity or utter shapelessness.

That a poet so different from Andrew Young of the early-middle period and *Into Hades*, a poet so much *of* the world, a poet so fundamentally un-suicidal — that such a poet should express these unsettling anxieties as to social formation may seem strange indeed. We shall also have to ask how a person beset with so overpowering a sense of unauthenticity can come across as such a rugged individualist. For so it is. And if, as seems possible, social insecurity is an anxiety to which few human beings are altogether immune, Frost's affective power must be correspondingly general. Certainly much of his greatest poetry traces human identity back to some very unfoundational foundations. The theme is life as role-play, as we might put it.

In his work of this kind, sociocultural details are as clearly etched as ever, but his passions are at once energizing and controlled. This is precisely because he has not tried to fix his social valuations in advance. Rather, his own flexibility, his fundamental lack of solidarity with any single community, is turned to advantage. The connotations of both rusticity and urbanity can turn out to be either positive or negative, and are always interrelated with the particular poem's overall symbolic form. In many poems an urbane character or reporter has a clear advantage over the rustics he (*sic*!) encounters. Rusticity can connote a walling-in that is both physical and mental — think only of the woman in "A Servant to Servants". But in many other poems, it is urbanity which loses out. The persona of "Birches", whom I see as altogether less Yankee and more urban than Kemp did, but still decidedly limited, envies the exciting freedom of the country boy he imagines riding the trees. All in all, then, sociocultural discriminations become a suggestive symbolism for the life of the spirit, and are even thought of as inseparable from it. Different poems try on different social formations for spiritual size, and one and the same formation will sometimes fit, sometimes not. Such are Frost's most beautiful co-adaptations with history, the beauty stemming from their sheer experimentality and instability.

I came to feel that the most remarkable thing he ever wrote is the one-act play in prose, *A Way Out*[24] — again, that tell-tale phrase! Like "In an Art Factory" and "The Guardeen", it is frontally concerned with sociocultural differentiation, and, like some of his most disturbing poems, with the death-likeness of a tellingly realized loner. Here the loner's name is Asa Gorill, and his isolated farm is one day visited by a stranger, who has apparently worked in a factory, and who has, too, a smattering of literary culture. What also emerges, however, is that the visitor has ostracized himself from the social groupings this implies by murdering a fellow-worker. As these revelations are proceeding, the play is working on two levels at once. There is the "story": the sheer excitement of what happens next as the visitor plots to evade physical arrest, and as Asa's horrified suspicions develop. At the same time, the way out the visitor seeks will actually implicate him in an alternative culture. That is why he subjects Asa, his next victim and the man he is planning to supplant, to a barrage of questions worthy of a sociologist, eliciting responses from Asa that are sometimes less than serious. Diet? Potato peelings and string beans. Women? Them he would just as soon not eat. Economy? Poultry-based. Footgear? Usually none, sometimes slippers. Neighbours? None. Letters? Never. Family history? Lived with brother till brother died; brother was jilted after fifteen-year engagement to a woman who may finally have resented Asa. Superstitions? — and the visitor, with a city-dweller's offensive air of patronage, suggests some decadent possibilities. None. Any potentially literary responses to nature? Any philosophical bent? No: Asa is not pestered by ministers of religion, and he does not wonder whether he is happy or what life is all about. And while the visitor is briefing himself in this way for the new identity, he is also beginning to imitate Asa's physical appearance and voice. Finally, he and Asa perform a curious dance, round and round in the darkness, after which they are indistinguishable from each other to the audience. They exeunt, and then only one of them comes back. When a search party enters, he tells them that the fugitive has already departed, and the only clue, for the audience, that the man still on stage was originally the fugitive is that he pulls off a pair of socks and burns them in the stove. (Asa, it will be remembered, was usually barefoot or in slippers only.) There is now no material difference between the fugitive and Asa.

For me at least, the excitement of *A Way Out* remains unparalleled in Frost's work. The more characteristic features are brought into a powerful synthesis which shows how splendidly equipped he really was to vindicate his life-long passion for the stage.[25] The North-of-Boston realism creates a haunting grotesquerie which, so far from gratuitous, proposes central questions of identity. The violence is integral to the plot, and Frost's love of daring effects, which when out of control in "In an Art Factory" and "The Guardeen" runs to a kind of vandalism, is magnificently inventive in the astonishing dance, at once a war dance and a clinching stage symbol of the stranger's increased closeness to Asa. The very voice-tones of the dramatic give-and-take are not only curious and thrilling in themselves. They tell the same story as everything else, as the stranger gradually masters the phrasing, and even the whining, of Asa.

He *becomes* Asa, and the cultural inventory has helped to suggest that by becoming Asa he has become next to nothing. Put another way, there is little to choose between this "way out" via a loner's rusticity and the death penalty it has presumably helped him to evade. This is not to say that some other lifestyle would have been more satisfactory, or more difficult to adopt. The burden of the play rather seems to be that if you can move from one identity to another, then you can just as likely move to any other identity as well. Rusticity serves as the type for every conceivable camouflage under which "To hide in the world / And alter with age". Frost takes the particular case of Asa, explores the social symbolism of the linguistic and anthropological facts, and tacitly opens up this wider implication. In effect, he is piercing through all conceivable layers of social formation in a way which, if some immutable core of personal individuality is really to be found, must stand at least some chance of finding it.

Like the beauties from history discussed in my earlier chapters, the disconcerting beauty of this shocking farce, so inseparably bound up with the particularities of a distinct cultural history, has a moral dimension. Unlike Eliot, Vaughan and Dickens, however, Frost is never out to change things, and angrily rejected suggestions that he should be.[26] His successive co-adaptations with the world are, in his own words, his spirit's flight into matter.[27] His first priorities are simply to wait and see how matter turns out, and then to hang on tight, in the hope that spirit will not be altogether dissolved. He always rose to the challenge of this, for it was the one great adventure, the biggest gamble of all. Yet so intense was his desire for personal continuity and autonomy that the facts of social formation, both its unavoidability and its necessary narrowness, could never cease to irk him. That he comes across as such a rugged individualist is in the end because he so passionately *wanted* to. Although otherwise adaptable almost to the point of amorphousness, he positively willed his independence, and his will itself became his single, but formidable personal hallmark. In place after place, job after job, poem after poem, his spirit adjusted to various forms of matter, yet never with total commitment, never with final acceptance even, and always alert for some new form still untried. By running, so to speak, he did manage to stand still, which was all be wanted. Or to use his own language again, by expanding he was able to contract.[28] By descending outside, hiding in the world, altering with age, he not only managed to get by, but remained paradoxically himself, in the pure *desire* for selfhood. By venturing forth into what never ceased to be alien, he was able to build soil on the home patch.[29] The moral beauty, in short, is not moral in any normal meaning of the word. His only imperative is sheer survival. In one sense, nothing much at all, and quite a-moral. In another sense, the only thing that matters: a life-achievement through the trial and error of an endless flexibility.

It was partly along these lines that I wrote enthusiastic commentaries on Frost in the late 1970s. I sent them off to critical journals in Britain and the United States, but to no avail. Thanks to a Scandinavian university press, my ideas eventually found their way into print,[30] but my rhetoric was misjudged. I failed to get to grips with the simple fact that, for most British and American readers, a dimension of social class in major American poetry was probably still unthinkable. Certainly Americans, as Trilling said, had "a kind of resistance to looking closely at society". To readers persuaded by the formalist concerns of New Criticism, by the individualized tensions of Freudian criticism, or by the new formalism of Frost's "modernizers", Poirier and Lentricchia, my commentaries must have seemed anomalous.

Oddly enough, Lentricchia later became one of America's leading Marxist critics, in which phase of his career he contrasted Frost's "Mowing" with Wordsworth's "The Solitary Reaper". His point was that Frost's Modernism is a strongly masculine reaction against a softly feminine lyricism, which keeps a genteel distance from labour. "Mowing" reflects the

> insubordination and resentment of an economically marginal American college dropout who enjoyed none of the social privileges of the great English poets he admired, and whose class formation permitted him not even the easy pleasures of idealizing the life of his womenfolk, for the women he knew best knew only the hardest of times. For Frost the fashioning of a new lyric mode was an opening to all that his social identify had declared out of bounds. The cultural issue of manliness had for him an immediate, personal impact: it was what structured his relationship to his family, to himself as a male, and to literary history. It was not, as it would become for the institutionally powerful practice Warren helped to initiate, a symbolic issue concerning associated sensibilities and the course of English literary history in the seventeenth century.[31]

This comment still fails to catch the several conflicting pulls of Frost's social conflict, and makes "Mowing" more militantly proletarian than even Lentricchia himself might find it in his latest, post-Theory phase of joyous appreciation.[32] But it certainly registers the issue I was trying to articulate, and in concentrating on the question of gender roles does develop it.

In the late 1970s, the slightest suggestion of Marxist tendencies was still as unwelcome in the American cultural establishment as in the country's mainstream politics. I myself was not a Marxist, but I was using the word "class", which was a dirty word because class itself, as Trilling said, was pitch, which might defile. The very latest development in American literary theory was deconstruction, which, as yet uncomplemented by insights into the way language always has to be pragmatically contextualized, sought to explore a decontextualized semiosis. In effect if not in theory, this was continuous with New Criticism.

If it was my taste of nordic egalitarianism and social welfare which had first sensitized me to Frost's social concerns in the 1970s, at the beginning of the third millennium an Anglo-American readership is much more likely to get the point. Thanks to the sociolinguistic poetics of Bakhtin, literary criticism is now well equipped to respond to the heteroglossic confrontation between Asa and his visitor in *A Way Out*, and as a result of the human rights movements already under way in the 1970s there is a much fuller recognition of American diversity of every kind. In Western society generally, there is no longer a strong expectation that the state or the national culture will be monolithic. New perceptions have been fuelled by Jürgen Habermas and others, who see postmodern society as divided along multiple fault-lines, which extend into the formation of single individuals. In different contexts, one and the same person will have a different profile, different allies, different foes.

Seen in this perspective, the troubling self-division of Frost's social experience made him prophetic and suggestive. Far from allowing the inevitability of self-division to defeat him, he bodies forth the human ability to hang on tight, achieving identity by accepting that all identities have shifting foundations. What he creates is an anomalous autonomy out of an endlessly flexible nonentity, embraced as infinitely preferable to the even greater nonentity of death.

This means that, in ways for which earlier readers were perhaps unprepared, his writing is bracing, but bluntly un-improving. For him, the raw lust to live always takes precedence over the why and how of life. It means, too, that his poetry is fundamentally self-assertive, though with a self-assertion, not of saying but of brute being, the assertion of a self not actually defined or even stable. The writing represents the victories of his constant hiding and altering, perhaps communicating to readers, too, an urge to live by any "way out" whatever. If so, they will be roused to endure at any price. Inspired by Frost, they will be sheer survivors, living a life that may well be meaningless and amorphous as far as it goes, yet living it very emphatically, and always in the expectation of some new and finally significant twist of fate.

Summary

Any kind of genuine communication presupposes a hope of experiential, emotional, and intellectual fellowship, a hope which, in and of itself, tends to make the world a better place. Communication can be seen as an attempt to come closer together, and this applies to literary communication as much as to any other. In certain periods of literary history, and in certain genres, the dream of a commonality of joy, justice and beauty is expressed very openly. But even through works of a more tragic and painful cast, authors and readers are drawn together, into what we might call a circle of the benevolent. Authors such as Frost, Dickens and Fielding write on the assumption that the reader will take up this invitation, even when their writing most fully responds to the Modernist expectation of unpleasantness.

As I suggest in Chapter 7, Frost's work shows an interplay between what he himself once described as expansion and contraction: more particularly, between "old-fashioned" kinds of stoicism or delightful idyll and a more "modern" grimness, for which the unpleasant kind of reading certainly offers a rich interpretation. Especially fascinating is the way Frost heightens the contrast between these two moods by using children and childhood as a point of reference. Earlier readers tended to respond somewhat disjunctively. Those seeking refuge from the twentieth century's harsh realities fastened on his pleasantly child-like elements of pastoral. Readers of a more realistic, or even depressive disposition saw his work as confirming the most unpleasantly adult of home truths. Today, we can perhaps bring these two kinds of reading into interrelationship. Frost's hopefulness was not facile. But neither was his bleakness.

In Dickens, too, there is not only light but darkness, a conjunction I discuss in Chapter 8. As for the darkness, it was first explored in the great Modernist critique by Edmund Wilson, "Dickens: the Two Scrooges", and Wilson's style of reading "for pain" can still bring new insights. Even in *David Copperfield* some very disturbing features begin to emerge. Dickens, it would seem, was always already himself a brooding Modernist. At the same time, however, he was always still a Victorian, and his likely response to the Modernist preoccupation with Thanatos is something a mediating critic will also need to explore.

Mediation, in its central concern for communicational parity, is not just a matter of reading authors from a milieu that is different from our own, but of letting them read us, so to speak. As a result, some interesting inversions become apparent. On the one hand, a Modernist reading would see Uriah Heep as part of the shadow surrounding David's own gentlemanly persona. On the other hand, the unbridled drives represented by the Victorian shadow became the twentieth-century persona, while the generosity and decency of the Victorian persona were relegated to the twentieth-century shadow. Even today, Uriah Heep is probably closer than David to our public self-image, and it is David's sheer goodness that represents our repressed desire. Dickens, without giving us any reason for hope, can nevertheless remind us of hope's essential feel and contours — of our longing for a better life in a more beautiful world.

In Chapter 9, I push the Modernists' unpleasant reading style to its limits, by considering Fielding, so often thought of as one of the greatest of comic writers. In particular, I focus on his naturalistic view of human nature and society, a view sustained throughout his writing career, and temperamentally akin to that of Hobbes or Freud. For Fielding, human beings are propelled by drives over which both individuals and society as a whole must try to get control, with however little success. In his stage plays and in his first four novels, he certainly did manage to turn this into comedy, thereby generously recognizing his audience's desire for pleasure. But his naturalism was always reluctant, and especially in *Amelia*, his last novel, he would have preferred to think much better of human beings, and ultimately of the Providence which had brought them into existence and allowed them to continue. This makes it only the more remarkable that he still tries to unite his readers in the hope of a better world, even when hope seems least convincing. So although a Modernist reading is certainly the key to some very murky inner chambers, the human yearning for meaning, dignity, fellowship, and joy is never rudely dismissed here. In the last analysis, such tolerant understanding of our deepest aspirations is what still makes our reading of authors like Fielding, Frost and Dickens a rather heartening experience. In its own way, it confirms the possibility of communication — of "making common" —, sometimes across very clear lines of sociohistorical difference.

CHAPTER 7

Robert Frost and childhood

When authors are read with empathetic understanding, their co-adaptations between the social and the individual can be recognized as tending to change the life-world, or offering hints for sheer survival. Facing even the bleakest things in life, their artistic deed can communicate a pleasurable energy of its own, and be an inspiration under widely varying circumstances.

Such achievements spring from an underlying hopefulness. No less than other forms of genuine communication, literary writing entails a faith in human beings, in the value of communicating with them, and in communication's ultimate outcome. Even a grief, even a fear, even a sense of horror, even an insight into human nature's most ridiculous or disturbing sides, becomes, as soon as it is communicated, so totally different from suicidal despair as to make the world a better place. Very close to despair, Vaughan wrote "I walked the other day (to spend my hour)", seeking to communicate in a very full sense: to *make* a community, into which readers will be drawn through sheer human engagement, readers belonging to a fairly close circle of contemporaries to start with, but perhaps other readers as well, even though their own experience of the human condition will be different. Thanks to communication, whether non-literary or literary, people of various backgrounds can actually be brought closer together, in the very desire for joy and fulfilment, in the predisposition to give and receive comfort, and in the shared endurance of suffering, even when suffering would otherwise quite debilitate desire.

In Parts I and II above, the problematic intermediary between ourselves as readers and the humanity of literary communication has mainly been the de-personalizing reading habits of Modernist aestheticization and structuralist or poststructuralist de-centring. No less typical of twentieth-century literary scholasticism, however, was a marked despondency and anti-hedonism, which turned a deaf ear to literature's underlying hopefulness. So far I have mentioned this only in connection with Geoffrey Grigson's reading of Andrew Young ("most uncomfortably aware of negation, farce, blankness, pain, end, and hopelessness"), the many accounts of harrowing desolation in *The Waste Land*, and Freudian interpretations of Frost's "Stopping by Woods on a Snowy Evening".

For Ortega y Gasset, such unsettling readings would have been just another slap in the face for the new mass readership, with its assumed craving for easy pleasures.[1] A second gloss would have been that statement of Eliot's from 1921: "We can only say that it appears likely that poetry in our civilization, as it exists at present, must be *difficult*".[2] In 1963, Lionel Trilling's essay "The Fate of Pleasure"[3] was still pursuing the same line. According to Trilling, the truest representative of modern culture was Dostoevski's Underground Man. Why? Because the principle of pleasure had no weight for him.

In previous ages, said Trilling, people who cultivated painful and "unnatural" emotions or ways of life, people who attempted to know those "psychic energies that are not summoned up in felicity", were exceptional. In the twentieth century, "unpleasure" was itself the norm. Modern literature and the "extruded 'high' element" in the general culture had subversively undermined all ideas of peace and bliss, which now seemed utterly lifeless. According to Trilling, the only Christian concept he and his contemporaries really understood was that of the *felix culpa*, and even this they interpreted in their own way: through sin and death, the seductions of peace and bliss could be avoided. Eden was to be dreaded. Or as Trilling also put it, nothing was now more incomprehensible in Wordsworth than the talk of a "grand and elementary principle of pleasure" which constitutes "the naked and native dignity of man", by which man "knows, and feels, and lives, and moves". Pleasure nowadays, said Trilling, made people feel *un*real. As a confirmation that they actually existed, they needed the abrasions of pain.

As a nineteen-year-old who had already been exposed to the period's literary scholasticism, I had no difficulty in identifying with Trilling's "we". He seemed to be summing up an entire epoch, sounding dissonances which had become very familiar. Thomas Munro, for instance, had recently argued that the kind of good fortune whose destruction had once pained the spectators of tragedy was now quite without meaning or value.[4] This observation was corroborated by the mid-century intelligentsia's standard reaction to the great Modernist books, whose textuality they regularly praised as a kind of obstacle race, run over a course of moral, psychological and philosophical anguish, appropriately littered with difficulties of language, allusion and structure. The "extruded 'high' element" of the general culture had championed its own extrusion so vigorously that the simpler delights of older classics or best-sellers could seem unworthy of a serious mind's attention, unless dispassionately studied as the mental fodder of the permanently immature. This continued to be F. R. Leavis's view of Fielding, and, for many years, of Dickens as well (except *Hard Times*).[5]

Leavis thought that what Fielding and Dickens took to be ordinary hopes and joys were infantile and shallow. Nor was he the last to do so. Between Modernist anti-hedonism and certain aspects of our present thought-world there has been a direct continuity. This is magisterially shown by Raymond Tallis's recent *Enemies of Hope: A Critique of Contemporary Pessimism*,[6] which surveys more than a century of naturalistic, deterministic, irrationalist and nihilistic dogmas from Nietsche, Marx, and Freud, down through Lévi-Strauss and Foucault and beyond. Here, then, is one reason why the bleakly Modernist style of reading remains so persuasive. It still receives authoritative cultural endorsement.

Another reason is still more important. The Modernist expectation of unpleasure is extremely productive, highlighting and explaining the challenge of many great literary works, which certainly can be very profoundly disturbing. *Pace* Leavis, this reading habit can still open up new insights into even Fielding and Dickens.

Yet this means that their novels' underlying hopefulness emerges as all the more remarkable, and as anything but infantile and shallow. Similarly, even Trilling's diagnosis of the modern spirit expressed only one of his own period's emphases: the emphasis still favoured by the "extruded 'high' element" of the culture, the emphasis of Grigson on Young, or of the confessional poetry anthologized in Alvarez's *The New Poetry*. In point of fact, the emphasis was always liable to shift, and always qualified by the potentiality for a shift. To be modern in the Modernist way was to disapprove of the hedonism of non-Modernist literature, while at the same time overlooking the sheer comedy of Leopold Bloom or the straightforward excitements of Conrad's adventurers, spies and double agents.

Trilling himself, given his sharp historical awareness, fully understood such inconsistencies. He had the ironic flexibility of mind to be both "inside" and "outside" — both of, and not of — his own particular cultural moment. Although his account of Modernist subversiveness was representative, he also noted the phenomenon's peculiar circularity, whereby Modernism itself becomes the next candidate for subversion. Another of his essays, "On the Teaching of Modern Literature" (1961),[7] was very down to earth about this, and also sharply highlighted the consequences of literary scholasticism. When lectured on year after year by ageing academics, those "psychic energies that are not summoned up in felicity", that great modern protest against everything trite and comfortable, had itself become trite and comfortable to the point of boredom. Trilling suggested, too, that subversive "unpleasure", despite some clear political implications, had never found a real outlet in political activity. All in all, then, to talk about modern experience in the Modernist scholastic's way might be a bit one-sided. The mind-set could not last for ever.

Even when Modernist gloom was at its height, some of the most obvious riders were lodged by Modernist critics themselves. As noted from my Introduction onwards, Modernism was a by no means uniform phenomenon. One Modernist idea or attitude might easily be challenged by another. If Eliot's early criticism seemed to lay stress on "the horrid or sordid or disgusting", Virginia Woolf was no less eloquent on the common reader's sheer "passion for pure and disinterested reading", the passion of somebody who "loves the dark premises . . . of second-hand booksellers", somebody who "reads for his own pleasure".[8] Even the quotation from Eliot must itself be returned to that seminal context: "The contemplation of the horrid or sordid or disgusting, by an artist, is the necessary and negative impulse toward the pursuit of beauty."[9]

When mediated by an appreciative critic, Eliot's own *The Waste Land* can reveal, I have tried to show, a co-adaptivity of cultural intervention that is not at all depressing. In our present phase of culture, such a reading style could well become more common. Alternatives to unpleasure are now increasingly vocal, and image-makers have for some time been scripting us as both less snobbish and more up-beat than the Modernists. Even by the mid-1970s, the Victorians, the Edwardians and the Georgians were already being rescued from Modernist denigration, and popular culture, so regularly sniped at by scholastic champions of Modernist gloom, was becoming intellectually fashionable, as part of the move towards cultural studies as we have them today. Graham Greene, who, almost as if to apologize for his own readability, had earlier called some of his fictional works "entertainments", was by that time coming into his own with potent brews of travelogue, comic thriller and moral-historical commentary, so appealing to several different tastes at once. Other writers were following suit, offering unresistant story-lines, and an unabashed *mélange de genres*, which in their own way rivalled the experimental liveliness of the Modernists. There were serious thrillers, serious picaresque, serious science fiction, serious documentary fiction, serious historical fiction, serious westerns, all of it in ready supply, all of it both fairly respectable and best-selling, and clearly anticipating the postmodern challenge to traditional authority in matters of aesthetic judgement. Since then, the erosion of distinctions between genres, and between elitist "high" culture and the "low" culture of the masses, has only accelerated.

The dichotomy between Modernist unpleasure and un-Modernist pleasure may actually be breaking down. There is perhaps beginning to be a sense that one and the same human mind can pluralistically encompass both. But the problem is that in order to talk about this — about a human mobility between the values and sensibilities of different cultural epochs — we have to separate out the different states of mind in a way which feels untrue to the very simultaneities we are trying to pinpoint.

On the one hand, historians provide us with several ways of saying that "then" was not "now", as feels no less than right and reasonable. In literary history, the distinctions have been made with markers ranging from the biographical, social and political, to the intellectual (in history of ideas) and formal (in genre history). As a result, our capacity for empathy and recognition has been substantially enhanced. Our attention has been drawn to textual features and extratextual considerations which help us get a grip on our reading, so that the various kinds of periodization even become part of the way we actually experience writers. It seems perfectly natural to think that Donne is a Metaphysical, even though that scholarly label was still quite unavailable to Donne himself or his first readers.

On the other hand, and even though "then" was certainly not "now", societies have long been able to meet a present need by re-cycling the cultural emphasis of some earlier age. This has become one of our main ways of moving into the future (another way still being through changes in technology). Sometimes there is almost a sense of history falling away. What then seems to be left is simply humanity, which is not some single and unchanging essence, but something more like a space to be filled with potentialities for value and sensibility which in different times and places are realized to different degrees and in varying mixtures. In Frost's words, there are all sorts of ways in which we can "hide in the world / And alter with age", and a past realization can be thought of as no less human, and possibly even more human, than a present realization. Any adequate cross-section of a particular historical moment will show up the periodizations of historians for the simplifications they are. Necessary simplifications, of course: because period labels really are one way of getting intellectual control of human phenomena. But simplifications all the same: not least because highly esteemed writers who are representative of the agreed periods can also be unrepresentative of them as well. In any given phase of a culture, the realization of the human is always a mixture of different potentialities, some more firmly scripted than others for the time being, but never ruling out the emergence or resurgence of potentialities at present unexpressed.

Was the author of *The Waste Land* an outrageous young Turk? Or was he a pillar of society — a consummately polite relict of the Edwardian age? The disjunction is totally unreal. A literary work which does not seem to have a certain polyvocality between various realizations of the human, between the sensibilities and values of different periods, runs the risk of becoming, precisely, a period piece. In particular here, in a writer of any importance the "non-Modernist" emphasis on pleasure and the "Modernist" emphasis on unpleasure can very well alternate. The writing may powerfully channel literature's underlying hopefulness in ways which simultaneously qualify it. Taking such writers as a whole, we may feel that they come down on neither the one side nor the other.

∾

A case in point is Robert Frost, whose poems are as different from period pieces as could ever be. To a significant extent, he is modern in the way suggested by Trilling's essay: he can be very grim and gloomily unillusioned. Yet this mood would not be nearly so striking, if he were not also able to entertain very different moods as well. After my chapter on his hiding and altering, this claim for his psychic flexibility will come as no surprise. His poetry does not date, because it so seldom comes to rest. It constantly vacillates between the terms of binary oppositions such as realism/fantasy, age/youth, pain/pleasure, which can all be seen as aspects of a larger opposition between Modernist and pre-Modernist, an opposition which the vacillation actually tends to erode.

In Trilling's account of the modern mind-set, the relationship between pain and reality was very clear. Without the abrasions of pain, modern people could never be sure they even existed. To be was to suffer. Feelings of peace and joy were shunned as dangerously delusive. No less clearly, in the early twentieth century childhood and youth were often thought of as stages of development peculiarly marked by unrealistic wishful thinking. What I. A. Richards praised in the greatest literary texts, and what Leavis did not immediately find in Fielding and most of Dickens, was an austere anti-hedonism allegedly characteristic of the maturely adult psyche. By the same token, it was the Victorian novel's deference to an ideal of youthful innocence that had drawn some of Henry James's most presciently Modernist barbs.[10] Rousseauistic valorizations of childhood became unfashionable, and the literal childlessness of many great Modernists could seem no less symbolic than the aura of parenthood associated with some of the major Victorians. Dickens's persona of the benevolent paterfamilias was an essential part of his writerly self-authentification. Fifty years after his death, such a strategy would not have worked.

So one of Frost's most characteristic poems is "To Earthward" (1923).

TO EARTHWARD

Love at the lips was touch
As sweet as I could bear;
And once that seemed too much;
I lived on air

That crossed me from sweet things,
The flow of — was it musk
From hidden grapevine springs
Downhill at dusk?

I had the swirl and ache
From sprays of honeysuckle
That when they're gathered shake
Dew on the knuckle.

I craved strong sweets, but those
Seemed strong when I was young;
The petal of the rose
It was that stung.

Now no joy but lacks salt,
That is not dashed with pain
And weariness and fault;
I crave the stain

Of tears, the aftermark
Of almost too much love,
The sweet of bitter bark
And burning clove.

When stiff and sore and scarred
I take away my hand
From leaning on it hard
In grass and sand,

The hurt is not enough:
I long for weight and strength
To feel the earth as rough
To all my length.[11]

As so often in Frost, the extreme mental flexibility is positively enhanced by a
very tight formal structure. He once said that this particular poem recorded an
important stage of his development from boy to man,[12] and its balanced structuring around the contrast between youth and maturity is clearly of the essence.
The second half hints that in his earthwards movement — which is ultimately,

perhaps, a movement towards the grave — he now desires the pinch of suffering and imperfection as a proof of his continued life — Trilling's abrasions of
pain —, while the first half contrasts this with the youthful craving for "strong
sweets". Yet he does remember how the strong sweets used to feel, and he is not
so much rejecting the pleasure principle as saying that he needs to have a sense
of the real as well. Because of the linearity of language, the poem may seem to
come down in favour of reality/age/pain. But in the memorable short piece he
wrote in 1925 on the death of Amy Lowell, he himself suggests that there are
modes of life and thought which quite elude linear organization:

> The most exciting movement in nature is not progress, advance, but expansion
> and contraction, the opening and shutting of the eye, the hand, the heart, the
> mind. We throw our arms wide with a gesture of religion to the universe; we
> close them around a person. We explore and adventure for a while and then
> we draw in to consolidate our gains.[13]

The idea here has nothing to do with one state of mind having precedence over
another, in either an evaluative or a temporal sense. The emphasis is rather on
life as a constant movement between different possibilities, a dynamic opera-
tionalization, as one might say, of that capacity for mutation which he explored
in "The Lockless Door" and A Way Out. De-linearization; de-periodization;
alternating expansion and contraction: these are the keys. "To Earthward", in
order to work at all, has to be both expansive and contractionist, has to create
and sustain both pleasure and unpleasure, innocence and experience, youth
and age, un-Modernist and Modernist feelings. Confronted with writing like
this, literary historical periodization seems a useful a way of explaining what
is so extraordinary, but useful precisely because its categories are so facile. We
watch them drop away.

    At first it might seem that Frost's double-barrelled literary breakthrough
did represent a polarization. In 1913 came A Boy's Will, a collection of poems
which, despite a kind of colloquial-philosophical undertow and certain touches
of realism, are predominantly lyrical and idyllic — as boyish as the title promises. Then, only a year later, came North of Boston, a collection which, if it still
amounts to a pastoral, is a decidedly more Modernist one, low-keyed, unideal-
ized, less "poetical". The contrast between the two books is sufficiently apparent,
and the path from Frost's late-Romantic efforts in the 1890s to A Boy's Will is
basically clear. A Boy's Will is the same sort of thing, but better done.

    The genesis of North of Boston, however, has proved controversial. Whereas
Amy Lowell suggested that a crucial factor was Frost's personal contacts with

the English Georgians, Frost himself angrily insisted that *North of Boston* was the cause, not the result, of those friendships. The bulk of it, he said, he wrote in 1913, before meeting Wilfred Gibson and Lascelles Abercrombie, and he dated the beginnings of "The Death of the Hired Man", "The Housekeeper" and "The Black Cottage" as early as 1905.[14] In one sense these claims may be disingenuous. His not being personally acquainted with Gibson and Abercrombie would not have precluded him from an awareness of their publications, or of others like them. Essentially, though, he is probably being truthful here.[15] The very solidity of *North of Boston* makes a long preparation seem more likely than a sudden conversion, and he certainly had the mental flexibility to cultivate what might normally be regarded as two quite different kinds of inspiration at once.

During twenty years of writing in almost complete obscurity, that is just what he had been doing, and the fact is that each of his two first collections represents, albeit in differing degrees, both kinds of poetic impulse between a single set of covers. His earliest development as a writer is actually worth close scrutiny. Above all, what exactly was going on during his years on the Derry farm? The answer to this question will clearly illustrate the strengths and weaknesses of literary historical periodization, so creating a background to the suppleness of his most timeless work. What we shall see more clearly is that his greatest poetry, in inviting readers to join a community of the hopeful, came to use more than one mode of address. He was perfectly well aware that the justification for hope can sometimes seem self-evident, and sometimes quite non-existent.

Perhaps life on the Derry farm was an idyllic escape. Looking back on it, Frost stressed a salutary lack of newspapers and any real contact with the outside world: "The only thing we had plenty of was time and seclusion".[16] The whole episode could clearly be thought of as a Horatian rejection of contemporary civilization. But if so, the rural backwater was also the setting for important spiritual developments:

> I kept farm, so to speak, for nearly ten years, but less as farmer than as a fugitive from the world that seemed to me to "disallow" me. It was all instinctive, but I can see now that I went away to save myself and fix myself before I measured my strength against all creation.[17]

If he was contracting, this was a form of consolidation, a preparation for a subsequent expansion. Most obviously, many of his experiences from this period took deep root in his memory, to blossom forth as poems much later on.

Ideally, farming itself would have been both contraction and expansion, the farmer becoming self-sufficient by risking what he has. But Frost knew he was an agricultural failure, and for the same reason as the owner of the "Tentative Farm" he mentions in some manuscript notes from this period: "He thought he would; then he thought he wouldn't".[18] Frost had an allowance from his grandfather to fall back on, and his heart was simply not in the job. By the time a teaching post came up at Pinkerton Academy, both he and his neighbours had ceased to take his career in poultry at all seriously.[19]

Not that his aspirations were pedagogical. He knew he wanted to be a writer, and was already forming the beliefs which were to mark his most distinctive poetry. Some of his other manuscript jottings from the Derry period are shorthand for ideas on politics, on aesthetics and versification, on the value of science, and on learning and human character, which were to underpin his writing until the very end. Three beliefs in particular are very striking, closely anticipating pronouncements and poems from several decades later.

One of them is linked to the theme of my previous chapter: Frost's resilience, his rising to the sheer challenge of life. It also brings us straight to pleasure and pain, and in a sense which must immediately qualify any very sharp dichotomy between Modernist and pre-Modernist. The Modernist sensibility did involve an element of unpleasure, whereas the sensibilities of earlier periods tended not to. But what this way of putting it overlooks is that the Modernist emphasis was partly continuous with a spiritual toughness and gritting of the teeth that were very Victorian. This strand of grim determination is very much a factor in the make-up of Dickens and his creations David Copperfield and Mr Murdstone: a "thorough-going, ardent, and sincere earnestness",[20] which was as hard as iron, and which embraced life as a tremendous challenge. Still closer to Frost in his Derry years was the vigorous stoicism of William James, for whom pleasure was still the primary principle that it had been for Wordsworth, as yet unchallenged by Freud's suggestion that Eros and Thanatos are equal and coeval. In "Is Life Worth Living?" (1895), James has little doubt about the answer to his own question:

> It is, indeed, a remarkable fact that sufferings and hardships do not, as a rule, abate the love of life; they seem, on the contrary, usually to give it a keener zest.[21]

One of Frost's Derry notes reads, similarly,

> He [Man] came out of the heavy mist and contemplated the terms and accepted them. They were then as they are now: A little more pleasure than

pain, pain greater in length and breadth but exceeded by pleasure in height, one more pleasure by actual count, the pleasure of being alive.[22]

and there is a clear verbal similarity between this passage and the poem of 1938, "Happiness Makes Up in Height For What It Lacks in Length",[23] plus a more general similarity with many other passages as well. "Our Hold on the Planet", from 1940, says that the "proportion of good to ill" must be ever so slightly in favour of man, because otherwise the human race would not continue to increase its "hold and the planet",[24] and in a letter to *The Amherst Student* of 1935 Frost wrote, "It is immodest of a man to think of himself as going down before the worst forces ever mobilized by God",[25] a Victorian sentiment which recalls another note from the Derry period: "I hate most the fellow who makes common stories of the flight of man".[26] Paradoxically enough, the author of *A Way Out* did not like to think of himself as running away from things. In poems such as "A Lone Striker" of 1933 and "Escapist — Never" of 1962, he figures running as a running-*towards*, or a searching for some possible fulfilment, just as he also claims that his years as a fugitive in Derry had been a matter of fixing himself in order to measure his strength against creation.

A second belief is just as characteristic, and was also partly touched on in my previous chapter. The fulfilment he was hoping to find by running-towards was nothing less than some kind of viable selfhood. In his fierce need of personal autonomy, he was seeking a "way out" from social formations he experienced as an encroachment. Through the sheer strength of his desire for it, he eventually achieved a kind of identity out of nonentity. And even if he would have found this diagnosis unflattering, he would certainly have agreed that an identity is not given, and that the running towards it has to be a movement of creative faith. In this respect the Derry notes from the beginning of the century compare Columbus to the Wright brothers, a conjunction foreshadowing "Kitty Hawk", a poem not completed until 1963, which sees both the discovery of America and the first manned flights as examples of the human mind's ceaseless venture into matter. Once again the mood is thoroughly nineteenth-century. It is, after all, the mood of empire-builders, and another Derry note suggests the continuing affinity with William James. The note simply reads: "Believing the Future In".[27] With this we can compare what James had to say, again in "Is Life Worth Living?", about "maybe":

Not a victory is gained, not a deed of faithfulness or courage is done, except upon a maybe; not a service, not a sally of generosity, not a scientific exploration or experiment or text-book, that may not be a mistake. It is only by risk-

> ing our persons from one hour to another that we live at all. And often enough
> our faith beforehand in an uncertified result *is the only thing that makes the*
> *result come true.*[28]

Frost himself was still expressing precisely this Victorian sentiment, in remark-
ably similar language, in 1961:

> The Founding Fathers didn't believe in the future . . . . They believed it *in*. You're
> always believing ahead of your evidence . . . . The most creative thing in us is to
> believe a thing in, in love, in all else. You believe yourself into existence.[29]

Even more surprisingly, the Derry note adds some further phrases which
develop the *literary* implications of such belief, an idea which informs the lecture "Education by Poetry" of 1931 and the preface "The Figure a Poem Makes"
of 1939. The Derry note reads:

> Believing the Future In. (How soon you foresee what you are going to say. I
> thought of that poem as I wrote it. No surprise to author none to reader.[30]

Compare the lecture of 1931 and the preface of 1939:

> Then there is a literary belief. Every time a poem is written, every time a short
> story is written, it is written not by cunning, but by belief. The beauty, the some-
> thing, the little charm of the thing to be, is more felt than known.[31]

> It is but a trick poem and no poem at all if the best of it was thought of first
> and saved for the last. It [the genuine poem] finds its own name as it goes and
> discovers the best waiting for it in some final phrase at once wise and sad —
> the happy-sad blend of the drinking song.
>   No tears in the writer, no tears in the reader. No surprise for the writer, no
> surprise for the reader. . . . Step by step the wonder of unexpected supply keeps
> growing . . . .[32]

The third belief intimated by the Derry notes anticipates another leading
idea in "Education by Poetry". The Derry jotting reads:

> Metaphor [.] May not be far but is our farthest forth. Only accumulation of
> the ages.[33]

The later lecture argues that all our thinking is a metaphorical saying of one
thing in terms of another. Although all metaphors ultimately break down, they
are the intellectual aspect of man's endless thrusting into the unknown. And:

> Greatest of all attempts to say one thing in terms of another is the philosophi-
> cal attempt to say matter in terms of spirit, or spirit in terms of matter, to make
> the final unity. That is the greatest attempt that ever failed.

If he could have read Andrew Young's *The Poetic Jesus*, he might conceivably have seen the failure as less total. But be that as it may, the justification for the study of poetry was clear:

> The metaphor whose manage we are best taught in poetry — that is all there is of thinking. It may not seem far for the mind to go but it is the mind's furthest. The richest accumulation of the ages is the noble metaphors we have rolled up.[34]

When these three beliefs from the Derry notes are set beside the later statements, it is easy to see the direction his solitary rumination was taking. Life has always been grim but challenging, and the human mind, in what is commonly but misleadingly called escape, travels on from known to unknown. It finds metaphors for the unknown in the known, and it believes into existence forms of being and identity which are nevertheless unsurprising.

To repeat: the temper of these ideas would have seemed perfectly normal to any nineteenth century reader. Yet although they persisted throughout his life, their expansiveness always had to be complemented, for Frost, by a movement of contraction, just as his words on the death of Amy Lowell would lead us to expect. In 1939 he was to formulate the value of contraction in the metaphor of building soil: the farm is turned "in upon itself / Until it can contain itself no more, / But sweating full, drips wine and oil a little".[35] But once again, the first formulation was many decades earlier, in his valedictory address to his school of 1892, where William James may again be in the background. In 1881 James had published an essay in the *Unitarian Review* on "Reflex Action and Theism":

> All action is . . . *re*-action upon the outer world; and the [nervous system's] middle stage of consideration or contemplation or thinking is only a place of transit, the bottom of a loop, both whose ends have their point of application in the outer world.[36]

Frost told Lawrence High School that all original thought and action stem from "after-thought", from the individual's withdrawal into himself *after* contact with the world, and before returning to it. He continued:

> This, the supreme rise of the individual — not a conflict of consciousness, an effort to oppose, but bland forgetfulness, a life from self for the world — is the aim of existence.[37]

Compared with the notion of expansion, this notion of contraction and withdrawal seems less immediately cheerful, less immediately daring, and a lot more anti-social. It could easily be associated with a more brooding, Modernist note.

Just as clearly as in the Amy Lowell piece of 1925, the contraction-expansion cycle, the tension between "after-thought" and adventure, is already apparent in work of the Derry period. The Derry love poems figure the woman as at one and the same time safely known and dangerously unknown. "The Trial by Existence", completed in 1906, imagines brave souls returning to rest in heaven only to venture forth upon the world again. In other poems, there are returns to and wanderings from a thoroughly terrestrial home. And a similar kind of cyclical movement appears in "The Black Cottage", as revised some time after 1907, and in the children's stories composed during the severe winter of 1906–7, examples to which I shall gradually be turning.

So to trace the beliefs underlying Frost's writing is to realize that literary historical periodization is doubly difficult. For one thing, his most fundamental ideas never really changed. Still more to the point, ideas which might normally be thought of as mutually exclusive turn out, in Frost, to be simultaneously tenable. His old-fashioned impulse to acts of faith and expansive adventure, which one might be tempted to associate with the most lyrical aspects of *A Boy's Will*, alternates with moments of soil-building withdrawal and contraction, a more Modernist and realistic focus on the here and now which one might be tempted to associate with *North of Boston*. For a body of work such as his, this psychological agililty, with all its superficially contradictory simultaneities, is precisely the seedbed one would expect. His poetry is seldom if ever purely expansive-lyrical-childlike-pleasurable, and seldom if ever purely contracting-realistic-adult-painful. He is never easy to associate with just some single period emphasis, and even his responses to pain can range from the more Victorian stoicism to a more Modernist horror or desolation.

Frost's challenge to literary historical categories can be further studied in eleven prose stories, which the tentative farmer published in two New England poultry journals between 1903 and 1905.[38] With roots in Mark Twain and traditional American humour,[39] the writing shows him exploring the literary potential of back-country folk, so anticipating his later dramatic poems — in terms of particular situations and characters, there are some direct links. But more relevant to an understanding of his mental flexibility is a somewhat paradoxical juxtaposition of a realistic human interest with a taste for tall stories.

The human interest is linked to a technical interest in what Frost called the "sentence sounds" of real talk. Living on the Derry farm, driving with his helpers or neighbours along the country roads, he felt he wanted to write with the ear, as it were, rather than the eye. So how could he get the sentence sounds onto the page? He once said that when he picked up a new novel he opened it to see if it contained talk.[40] Dickens's exasperation at novels "so infernally conversational, that I forget who the people are before they have done talking, and don't in the least remember what they talked about before when they begin talking again"[41] is something he would have shared.

Like Dickens, too, the author of *A Way Out* was interested in speech as a form of sociocultural differentiation. But what most fascinated him was not a matter of dialect vocabulary and syntax, or of the exact physical properties of pitch, intonation, stress and length. Much more important was what a sentence sound or a sentence tone connoted semantically and rhetorically, as a clue to the speaker's purpose, emotion, attitude, or argumentative strategy. His analysis of "The Pasture", for instance, notes the following tones: "light, informing tone"; "'Only' tone — reservation"; "supplementary possibility"; "free tone, assuring"; "after thought, inviting".[42] In other words, he never denies that the same semantic-rhetorical function may be somewhat differently realized in the personal language systems of different speakers, and his basic interest is in speech as interaction.

This is linked to his conviction that poetry and good writing in general are fundamentally dramatic. He had already been thinking along these lines during the intervals between lamp-trimming in the Arlington Mill, Lawrence in 1893–4, when he had pored over Shakespeare.[43] In an interview three decades later, he distinguished Shakespeare's long rhetorical passages from his "speaking" passages, claiming that the latter

> are the best of Shakespeare to me — lean, sharp sentences, with the give and take [between the characters], the thread of thought and action quick, not lost in a maze of metaphor and adjective.

The very height of poetry, he concluded, is "in dramatic give-and-take. Drama is the capstone of poetry",[44] and in the 1929 preface to *A Way Out* he hopes that everything he has ever written is essentially dramatic, a give-and-take that makes itself *heard*. In for once writing a play, he has not "gone very far from where I have spent my life".[45] Appropriately, Robert Kern has argued that Frost reacted to the visuality of Imagism by developing a kind of aural primitivism,[46] and Tom Vander Ven has examined his entire production for the dramatic "oversound": "the tone of meaning but without the words", which "hovers, glides, dives among the words but never lights to be pinned, wriggling on the page".[47]

The poultryman tales do contain distinctive, dramatizing talk. One of them is even an extended monologue, the sales-talk of an agent for a poultry journal, which gives a sharp foretaste of later dramatic monologues in verse. Other tales, at carefully chosen turning points or climaxes, dramatize by means of dialogue, authentically modulating between stichomythia and more continuous runs. Sentences can be short and elliptical, and the diction and phraseology colloquial. Many remarks are introduced by "Say,. . ." and "I guess. . .", though at more solemn points there is greater formality. A representative example would be the opening of "The Cockerel Buying Habit":

> The old gentleman took his corncob out of his mouth, and leaning toward me lowered his voice almost to a whisper: "What's your opinion of inbreeding, anyway?" he said.
> "I'm a safe man to talk it over with," I laughed. "What's your opinion? There's no law against it, is there?"
> "Law of nature," he suggested.
> "I'd risk it."
> "You're not afraid of it then?"
> "Pshaw!"
> He rolled his eyes on me with unfeigned admiration of my recklessness; but he shook his head.
> "I snum I don't know," he reflected. "It's attended with awful consequences in the human family. You know how it's supposed to be when cousins marry. You can hear some awful stories against it."[48]

Yet although this is readable enough, Frost has not yet perfected his technique. A decade later, when he sent John F. Bartlett "some examples [of sentence sounds] pell-mell in prose and verse", his argument clearly reflected the Modernist preference for showing over telling. The narrator's own voice should not be intrusive, and the reported speech of conversations should not have to be propped up on the narrative base. More specifically, there should be nothing outside the inverted commas telling the reader how to take the words inside them. The writer should rather gather sentence sounds "fresh from talk", so that the reader can immediately "recognize" them. Most of the examples certainly do seem to speak for themselves —

> "You're a liar!"
> "I ain't a going [to] hurt you, so you needn't be scared."[49]

— but a later letter to Bartlett is even more emphatic:

> There are tones of voice that mean more than words. Sentences may be shaped so definitely to indicate these tones. Only when we are making sentences so shaped are we really writing. And that is flat. A sentence *must* convey a

meaning by tone of voice and it must be that particular meaning the writer intended. The reader must have no choice in the matter. The tone of voice and its meaning must be in black and white on the page.[50]

And to the objection of Gamaliel Bradford and an actress that there are many different ways of reading a line by Shakespeare, Frost replied that the fault must lie with Shakespeare.[51]

Here he may have been consciously overstating his point for the sheer fun of it. But Christopher Ricks has argued that some writing, which would include Frost's own as well as Shakespeare's, is actually the better for having tonal ambiguities. The net result of these, according to Ricks, is that a reader's everyday presuppositions as to how people think and feel and talk are thrown into question. The experience of reading will come as a constant slight shock, prompting a new openness of mind and healthy re-assessments and re-adjustments.[52]

Ricks's comments are in intellectual descent from I. A. Richards, whose psychologised aesthetics so clearly stated the Modernists' anti-hedonistic dissatisfaction with stock responses. The same critical tradition also ran through the brilliant verbal analyses of Richards's pupil William Empson, which partly explains why Ricks, one of Empson's greatest admirers, does not seek support from linguistic theory. Empson's formidably English intelligence was very down to earth, teasing out disconcerting ambiguities mainly by virtue of his personal feel for language in use.

Poststructuralist critics might well hail both Empson and Ricks as comrades in the analysis of the linguistic sign's instability. Certainly Ricks's argument is that the sentence sounds of good writing cannot be read off as definitively as Frost claims. In practice, however, both Ricks and Empson are hyper-responsive to co-text and context, which means that in any particular case they tend to recognize the limits to semiotic proliferation, so confirming another point made by Frost in a letter to Bartlett. Sometimes, he admitted, a context does have to be indicated, after which the reader will immediately know the tone:

> Suppose Henry Horne says something offensive to a young lady named Rita when her brother Charles is by to protect her. Can you hear the two different tones in which she says their respective names. "Henry Horne! Charles!" I can hear it better than I can say it.[53]

— which illustrates the principle now writ large in the findings of linguistic pragmaticists.

When we read off sentence sounds from the page, we can certainly be caught up in just the kind of tensions Ricks so tellingly illustrates. On the other hand, if the number of semantic-rhetorical sounds derivable from a piece of writing were never restricted by context and co-text, communication would break down. In point of fact, readers tend to find that the choice of sounds becomes progressively more limited as they continue reading a text; as their understanding and interpretation develops, their sense of what is likely to be meant obviously becomes stronger. Some texts, moreover, apparently offer a narrow tonal choice *from very early on*. Frost praised such tonal unmistakability in Edwin Arlington Robinson, whom he gently chided for not trusting to it. In Robinson's play *The Porcupine*, the use of italicized adverbials as directions to the actors — "*with feline demureness*" and so on — was in Frost's view quite unnecessary. "The speaking tones are all there on the printed page, nothing is left for the actor but to recognize and give them."[54] If the writer has built up the relationship between text and context with sufficient care, the reader's inner ear will seldom hesitate, and the writing will seem all the better for it. Ambiguity, albeit such a vital asset in cases discussed by Empson and Ricks, can hardly be a literary *sine qua non*, and in other types of case is a mere liability. Even if, Modernist fashion, we were to make a no less unreasonable *sine qua non* of unpleasantness, many a contextually unambiguous text could still be just as disturbing as a suggestively ambiguous one.

Tonal unmistakability was to figure at some of the high-points of Frost's own work, pleasant and unpleasant alike. In these early poultryman tales, however, he still resorts to verbs less semantically neutral than "say" — in the passage quoted above he has "laughed", "suggested" and "reflected" — and to trailing adverbial expressions *à la* Robinson — from two pages at random: "he said conservatively", "with the same cautious reserve", "said the man evasively". Another shortcoming is that in passages of straight narrative his own voice has not yet found its pitch. Although he is sometimes easy and forceful, he can also be rather prim, formal and facetious — we still catch the cleverness of the schoolboy journalist —, and at times he is simply dull. All in all, he is beginning to get "the ACTION of the voice, — sound posturing, gesture",[55] making "the ear . . . the only true writer and the only true reader".[56] But sometimes the writer's ear does not quite know what it wants to listen to. Either that, or the writing fails to tune in the reader's ear through co-text and context.

The other aspect of the tales' realistic human interest is their characterization, which calls for less discussion. As I mentioned in connection with "The Guardeen", Frost found some rural neighbours quite detestable. The poultryman stories give early signs of the unvarnished view of humanity so typical of *North of Boston*. Stupidity and pusillanimousness are subjected to unsentimental irony and firm poetic justice. Aiken, another farmer who thought he would and then he thought he wouldn't, who expected his wife to do the work which he did not believe in, finds that his hens will not lay. Having chased them all away, he is consigned for the rest of his life to a clerk's stool, writer's cramp, and indigestion. In another tale, the editor of a poultry journal smugly looks forward to visiting a farm run entirely on his own principles, only to be confronted by a human pathos which is quite beyond him, but which Frost himself finds very moving. It is connected with two unmarried sisters, one of whom is an invalid but "officially" the farmer, while the other does all the work. Their little fiction is a way of sharing and lessening the pain of the situation, and they are no less noble-minded about poultry shows. In a moment of uncertainty they ask the editor's advice, but when he prevaricates they know their answer: there shall be no cheating! They exhibit for competition an almost perfect hen, which is disqualified, as they know it will be, because of a leg feather they are too honest to pull off.

In some of the best tales, however, the tonal and psychological realism is almost deceptive, since the border between fact and fiction is playfully blurred. A case in point is "Old Welch Goes to the Show". Frost, who was later to write with fascination of the notorious Stephen Burroughs,[57] here warms to the inventive kind of villainy. Welch is an ancient reprobate and corrupter of youth, and "grooms and tames" his birds in a very different fashion from the spinster sisters. Out of sheer bravado, he once chose a thoroughly wretched specimen and quite transformed it, with the help of a glass eye, a pneumatic front, leg polishing, and corsets. The bird actually won a red ribbon. Or so 'tis said: the tale "rests on the authority of boys and not particularly good boys".[58] In another story, a 96-point hen is only just this side of the line between Real and Ideal, and Frost's whole connection with the poultry journals probably came to an end because he wrote, in an apparently straightforward report, that "Mr. Hall's geese roost in the trees even in winter." No geese roost in trees, ever, and Frost's poultrymen readers may not have taken the joke.[59] What we have here is an imaginative strain which, if it looks back to the traditional American tall story and his own mother's Celtic fairy tales, looks forward to Murphy's yarn about Paul's wife.

In his best work, Frost's adult contraction can hug the contours of human speech and emotion with a tenaciously objective and unillusioned realism that seem quintessentially Modernist. But this can suddenly give way to the expansive kind of dreams or yarns indulged in by "not particularly good boys". So perhaps the title of *A Boy's Will* really *was* prophetic. Hope sometimes knows no bounds.

✿

Having written a racy poultryman tale about John Hall's consuming passion for poultry, Frost wrote "The Housekeeper" as a poem, switching genre and perspective in order to explore the situation's human cost. If a poem such as "The Housekeeper" is prose become poetry, moreover, it is equally poetry become prosaic, so that literary historians could easily rush in with comparisons to Masefield's "The Everlasting Mercy", the first Georgian anthology or Yeats's rejection of Celtic Twilight for "the baptism of the gutter".

Yet although Frost's second collection was more predominantly "prosaic", his first was more predominantly "poetical". During his Derry years he was moving in both directions at once, and there is even one poem, "The Black Cottage", whose main direction clearly changed from poetical to prosaic. This is worth some detailed attention.

Frost's assertion that "The Housekeeper", "The Death of the Hired Man" and "The Black Cottage" date from 1905 was made in 1925.[60] On another occasion he was almost as specific, and added that in the seven years prior to the publication of *North of Boston* "The Black Cottage" was the only one which he had persistently submitted to editors, in the hope that they would see in it something for Memorial Day.[61] In 1938 he spoke of *two* versions of "The Black Cottage", however, one in rhyme, "which I lost on purpose as a failure, and the other that came down with some changes into *North of Boston*", both versions having been written in and around 1905–6.[62] The rhymed version, which actually survives in a manuscript in the Huntington Library, was submitted to the New York *Independent* in 1905 or 1906. And it turns out that the *North of Boston* version also incorporates parts of yet another early poem, "The Lost Faith", which was probably not complete until February 1907. Furthermore, it clearly suggests the influence of William James's *Pragmatism*, first published in June 1907.[63] These considerations support the suggestion of several scholars that the rhymed version came first.[64]

The rhymed version is thoroughly Victorian. It is full of poeticisms such as "perchance", "the bread of loneliness", "dim eyes" and "sweet flowers", and has a Tennysonian musicality: the eight-line stanzas have much enjambement, lyrical flow and phonetic patterning. All this harmonizes with a no less dated pathos and crepuscular melancholy. The poem tells of an old widow who chooses to live among the memories of her former joys, far from her grown-up sons, but with a near and cherished view of the graveyard where she will soon be buried alongside some other relatives and her husband. Now, as night comes on, and amid the dew-drenched grasses and silence of the elms, the cottage where she sits without a lamp is "as black as oozy meadow mould". It "sinks darkly upon darker hours".[65]

"The Lost Faith", the other piece which stands behind the final version of "The Black Cottage", was made public in early 1907, at a banquet of the Men's League of the Central Congregational Church in Derry. There is was read aloud by the Rev. Charles L. Merriam, a turn of events which could have given the idea for the minister-narrator in the final version of "The Black Cottage". It, too, is very nineteenth century. Its versification ranges from a plangent irregularity like that of "Lycidas" to resounding pentameter couplets, and Frost adopts the Victorian roles of despairing sage and celebrant of heroes. He recalls the terrible fierceness of the Union soldiers at Gettysburg —

Men knew us not until that wavering fight!

— and his lament for the fading of the Union dream gives a melancholy Arnoldian twist to wording from Cecil Frances Alexander's bouncy children's hymn —

... we saw it fade from sight,
Not while we slept, but while we strove too much
For things that were not beautiful and bright.[66]

The moralizing streak is as un-Modernist as could well be.

In one respect the final version of "The Black Cottage" shifts towards "The Lost Faith". It emphasizes, not the woman's love for her dead husband, but her continuing loyalty to the Union ideal, for which, we now learn, her husband died. There are also more detailed similarities of idea and phrasing. "The Lost Faith" reads as follows, for instance:

Who in our latter wisdom so unread
As not to know
Dark life too well for such a dream of morn,
What child so uninured to literal woe?
The Californian by the western sea
Exults, and by the Gulf they laugh,
Saying, "How can all men be free,
How equal, when God made them wheat and chaff?"

and the final version of "The Black Cottage" reads:

> You couldn't tell her what the West was saying,
> Or what the South, to her serene belief.
> She had some art of hearing and yet not
> Hearing the latter wisdom of the world.[67]

In general, though, the final Black Cottage poem differs markedly from both the earlier pieces. Its impressiveness stems neither from Victorian musical resonance nor from unmoderated gusts of Victorian pathos and heroics. It is in blank verse, is altogether more mentally alert, and much more low-key as well. Also, the unobtrusive command of voice tones in a line such as

> "Pretty," he said. "Come in. No one will care."[68]

is a very different thing from the adverbial expressions trailing after "said" in the poultryman prose.

Whereas the first version thrust the cottage and its occupant directly upon us, the final version is more dispassionate, being a post-mortem on the old lady at several removes: she has been dead some time; the poet is himself dramatized as coming upon her cottage during a walk; and her story is actually told to him by another character, the minister who is accompanying him. Philosophical and sociohistorical perspective is also introduced, for instance in the connection the minister makes between her political and her religious conservatism. If it had not been for "her old tremulous bonnet in the pew", he might have acquiesced in the demands of younger church members — "Or rather call them non-members in the church" — that he slightly alter the wording of the Creed.[69] Indeed, the situation is similar to the call paid by the cowardly poultry journalist on the two noble spinsters, since a tension develops between the sheer innocence of the lady's high old-fashioned principles — she *believed* that all men are created free and equal — and the reporting minister's drift towards the compromises and forgetfulness of an apostate generation —

> He fell at Gettysburg or Fredricksburg,
> I ought to know — it makes a difference which:
> Fredricksburg is not Gettysburg of course.[70]

The minister, whose calling might have made him more of a traditionalist than his contemporaries, in fact neither recriminates nor apologizes for them, being all hesitation and well-meaning quizzicality. Though more than half-willing to try and create the type of belief his own age lacks, he suffers no qualms over his own incapacity for Victorian pieties and afflatus.

In short, the minister resembles the reader to whom William James addresses *Pragmatism*:[71]

> You want a system that will combine both things, the scientific loyalty to facts
> and willingness to take account of them, the spirit of adaptation and accom-
> modation, in short, but also the old confidence in human values and the result-
> ant spontaneity, whether of the religious or of the romantic types.[72]

Religious or romantic confidence, together with scientific loyalty to the facts:
if James and the poem's minister can come up to scratch on these two points,
their "system" will be true to that "most exciting movement in nature", as Frost
put it — expansion and contraction, "the opening and shutting of the eye, the
heart, the mind", the exploratory adventure and the consolidating drawing in.

   The beauty of the poem's climax does have just that combination of tenderness and toughness of mind which James envisaged.[73] On the one hand, the
minister speculates that if we cling to beliefs even when they have ceased to
be true, they may become true again, just as James twice asserts in *The Will
to Believe* that if a mountaineer has faith in his ability to make a terrible, life-
saving leap, his "feet are nerved to its accomplishment".[74] In the words of Frost's
Derry note, he can believe the future *in*. The minister even dreams of being
monarch of a land entirely dedicated to "the truths we keep coming back to",[75]
almost as if their recurrent popularity ensured a grain of absolute truth. Compare the Preface to James's *The Will to Believe*:

> Religious history proves that one hypothesis after another has worked ill, has
> crumbled at contact with a widening knowledge of the world, and has lapsed
> from the minds of men. Some articles of faith, however, have maintained
> themselves through every vicissitude, and possess even more vitality today
> than ever before.[76]

On the other hand, the minister's expansive dream is also self-conscious, and
qualified by a Jamesian sense of truth. In *Pragmatism*, James argued that the
truth is not a preordained principle on which life has been based in the past,
but a belief which has to make itself true by the way it works in the ever-unfold-
ing future. It grafts itself "upon the ancient body of truth, which thus grows
much as a tree grows by the activity of a new layer of cambium". Consequently,

> Truth independent; truth that we *find* merely; truth no longer malleable to
> human need; truth incorrigible, in a word; such truth exists indeed superabun-
> dantly — or is supposed to exist by rationalistically minded thinkers; but then
> it means only that truth has its paleontology and its "prescription", and may
> grow stiff with years of veteran service and petrified in men's minds by sheer
> antiquity.[77]

— just as the old widow of the Black Cottage was herself rather stiff and antiquated. Or as the minister's Jamesian metaphor puts it, his land of ancient

beliefs would be a desert scarce habitable, where the sandstorm would "[r]etard mid-waste . . . [his] cowering caravan"[78] — and would retard on-going life in any other form as well. Expansion must be followed by contraction, and the minister returns from his flight of religious-romantic imagination, striking the clapboards to reveal the bees who have taken the lady's place in the cottage. They, and the minister himself, inhabit a new age.

So, now, does the poem. But as with much of Frost's finest work, it is difficult to decide which age exactly. To say that "The Black Cottage" and the rest of *North of Boston* are more realistic and more Modernist than *A Boy's Will* is not untrue. But it is by no means the whole truth. Despite the sense of the old woman's quaint stubbornness, she is still *there*, and so is all she stood for. Her belief is still there, despite the Modernist scepticism, a scepticism which itself feels the need of belief, and is prepared to countenance its reconstruction. The youthful hero-ism of the old lady's lost husband, though cut down to size by the long historical perspective, by grown man's wisdom of hindsight, by the low-key realism and humour of the writing, still resists extinction as a spiritual possibility. The minis-ter, remembering her half-kneeling in front of a poorly done crayon portrait of him "as he went to war", professes to doubt if "such unlifelike lines kept power to stir / Anything in her after all the years",[79] yet his own report of her idealism knows better. He is stirred himself, and the poem's verdict on the young men who gave their lives for freedom is very gentle, and even a little envious. Frost alludes to the heroic thought-world of the epic genre, and in one part of his mind may even entertain an un-Modernist faith that epic certainties and simplicities may actually be restored. If so, the future can be believed *in*, and the old lady's belief is obviously better than most other beliefs — if you can manage it.

Overtly, the poem is neither pessimistic nor optimistic. It is neither a state-ment of nineteenth-century faith in humanity nor a Modernist demolition of such faith. The minister thinks of the empty black cottage as "a sort of mark / To measure how far fifty years have brought us". Yet the poem also col-lapses historical distances, mediating between phases of culture that are very different from each other, and in a positive spirit that itself implies a kind of hopefulness.

～

No less than the final version of "The Black Cottage", the eighteen miniaturistic children's stories from the Derry years show Frost in complete mastery as a writer. They show, too, yet another permutation of expansion and contraction, pre-Modernist and Modernist, youth and age, so confirming that from very early on he was moving in what might normally be thought of as two different directions at once. On the one hand, his realistic command of the spoken voice and his feel for character are now at their height. By comparison, the poultry-man prose of two or three years earlier is naive. On the other hand, he enters into an idyllic world of childhood with only a single slight reservation.

One of the Derry jottings reads: "Accused of talking to an audience when I have none."[80] As a writer, Frost's need of the listening audience was always very strong; in his concern with sentence sounds, he had to feel sure that his words could be *heard*. Perhaps he first found the necessary catalyst in the captive audience of his own four children. Very obviously, the stories were written to be read aloud, and the text even indicates narratorial hesitations and paralinguistic "business":

> The next time . . . [Schneider the collie] lay down he only went to sleep with one eye — this one — no I guess it was this one.[81]

Frost records Schneider's hesitations and colloquial double negatives:

> "Well," Schneider said, "well — uh — that don't seem hardly right."[82]

There are experiments with imitative spelling and graphic notation:

> And the monkey said, "NO she didn't." And the baby said, "Ye-e-e-s". And the monkey said, "No-o-o. *You* come with me."[83]

Frost relies, too, on naturalizing features which were already standard in children's stories. The clauses tend to be main clauses, with the conjunctions (initial) "so", "and" and "but" in special prominence, and reported speech is usually incorporated by either an adverbially unsupported "said" or pure intonation, devices which make the stories closer to Hemingway than to his own poultry-man prose. He is aiming, in fact, to select and contextually determine speech, direct and reported alike, so as to allow the reader very few options in sentence sound. Some of his revisions show him finally clinching the elliptical tautness and colloquial sentence linkage which are so characteristic of his best work:

> *First version*
> And the other said Winter birds cant sing. They can only cheep.
> "Then lets cheep."
> And they
>
> *Second version*
> And the other said, "Winter birds can't sing — only cheep."
> "Let's cheep then."
> So they cheeped.[84]

As in the final version of "The Black Cottage", the mimetic mastery of the spoken voice is inseparable from a certain frankness. The writing has an unsentimental intimacy with the human or animal characters *in* the writing, and an equal intimacy with the young listeners, who often *are* the characters. Years later Frost wrote:

> I like the actuality of gossip, the intimacy of it. Say what you will effects of actuality and intimacy are the greatest aim an artist can have. The sense of intimacy gives the thrill of sincerity. A story must always release a meaning more readily to those who read than life itself as it goes ever releases meaning. Meaning is a great consideration. But a story must never seem to be told primarily for meaning. Anything, an inspired irrelevancy even to make it sound as if told the way it is chiefly because it happened that way.[85]

In the children's stories, Frost even tells his listeners that the dried-out skin of a frog "looked like the ends of your fingers after a bath",[86] and there is a corresponding inwardness of character portrayal. There is Lesley the eldest, for instance, and the inspired irrelevancy of her logic: when her brother Carol seems to emerge out of a tree as a little old man, she says,

> To get as old as that he would first have to grow to the size of a man and that might take five years if he eat well and then he would have to shrink back to his own size and that would take five hundred years because it takes longer to grow small than it does to grow large.[87]

Or there is Schneider the collie, outwitted by squirrels and chipmunks, nonplussed at avian anatomy and nesting habits, terrified by a cow. In accordance with Frost's usual bareness of description, the only physical details are of pose, habit or gesture, but these are very expressive. Carol is very proprietorial as "Lord Protector": he "always walked about with his chin close in to his neck and his fists in the pockets of his new trousers".[88] Irma, who "went wagging her dress out into the big pasture",[89] is immediately the pert little girl the rest of the story shows her to be.

At one point and one point only, the human realism becomes potentially sinister. The idyll of the child's world is suddenly qualified with darker knowledge which, characteristically for Frost, involves a moment of *self*-revelation. While he was picking raspberries, he also had his eye on a trembling, half-hidden rabbit, which his own continued presence kept from its burrow.[90] In Beatrix Potter or *Watership Down*, the latter a story about rabbits which belongs to that spate of popular but intelligently un-Modernist writing of the 1970s,[91] cruelty to rabbits is not normally seen from the human end of things. That, though, is precisely Frost's more Modernist way. This little detail should not be

overemphasized. But it is not without interest, since several of his most characteristic poems are about the human capacity for acts of quiet sadism. Even
children, and certainly child-like adults, can sometimes turn quite nasty.

The children's stories, despite their intimate inspired irrelevancy, do also
have "meaning", but with this one slight exception the meaning has nothing to
do with the unpleasant kind of realism. What is at issue is rather the crossing
of the realistically familiar with a certain strangeness. "Fairies live in juniper
bushes — you have to believe that".[92] Frost exploits the genre's licence to fantasy, delighting in telling for telling's sake, and sometimes springing the further surprises of metafiction. This catches the teller in the telling, or disorients
the hearer-reader with sudden switches of fictional projection. The story of
Schneider outwitted by a woodchuck concludes by exposing its own sleight of
tongue —

> Schneider was so mad that he gave up and went home.
> The woodchuck laughed and said, "Goodby Schneider. Come again."
> Schneider said, "O stop talking — woodchucks can't talk."
> And the woodchuck said, "Neither can dogs".
> That's so: they can't.[93]

— and when Baby goes for a walk, she doesn't just walk. She walks and walks
and walks and walks and walks and walks.[94] She walks far away from domestic
realities, to meet a monkey, a kangaroo, a honey-bear and an alligator. At the
same time, she seems to meet a "man", perhaps her undifferentiated father, and
the man finally escorts her back to "a Mamma", who gives her no time to finish
her extraordinary report before tucking her up in bed. Here and elsewhere, it
is as if there are stories in two completely different realms: Baby sees strange
creatures, Baby is brought home to bed. Everyday incidents and objects can
even be quite transformed, usually through Frost's own fantasy, but sometimes
through a child's as observed by him. When Irma comes back from the pasture
and wants to be made a fuss of, she tries her luck with a yarn about a fence-
post: he said his name was Old Stick-In-The-Mud; he went picking berries for
her; but he kept her waiting unconscionably long.

Here her father immediately counters: she should not be so outraged and
tearful; Old Stick-In-The-Mud is the oldest and kindest post on the farm; next
time she sees him, she ought to say thank-you for the berries.[95] What the father
does not do is to accuse the child of lying. There is no contraction, no realistic
bringing of the story down to earth. On the contrary, Frost relishes the irony of
a fantasy about something so very stuck in the mud, and playfully expands it

for pedagogical reasons which bring the metafiction close to metaphysics. As so often in his writing, the philosophical underpinning is from William James, the point being that fiction can engage with life so completely that it works in the same way as religious belief or scientific explanation. The hearing and telling of stories trains the mental flexibility needed to construct such fictions-for-living, and to keep them fresh and undogmatic. In checking the "stories" which Lesley herself wrote every day as part of his system of home education,[96] Frost was not concerned with spelling and grammar. The great value of fiction — of truth by metaphor — is that it can sustain us in life's adventure. It is actually an aspect of that "joy of life" whose zest is keener in face of difficulty, that "pleasure of being alive" which just exceeds the pain. Frost lets his characters and his audience relish their experience and work out their own whys and wherefores.

The scene for such explorations is set by the chosen narrative form. Each story posits two homes, which are normally inhabited by the two main parties to the action. The narrative point of view makes one home and its inhabitant less familiar than the other, but either party can be more aggressive than the other, though neither party need be. The action is experienced as an adventure, by either or both parties, and it takes the form of an abnormal encounter between the parties, either on intermediate territory or in one party's home. The action thus modifies the status quo of each party inhabiting his, her or its own home, and either some such modification becomes permanent, or the status quo is restored, both of which endings can figure as a victory for one party, though victory is not a *sine qua non*. All in all, then, the story type offered a congenial model of adventure: polarities between known and unknown, home and abroad, security and risk, polarities corresponding with Frost's deeply instinctive feel for contraction and expansion. The fictional microcosm presents a ceaseless alternation between the two.

He dwells not only on the fictionality of the stories themselves, but on the child-heroes' adventures in aligning experience with belief. Lesley's cogitations on Carol's apparent transformation into a little old man are not just inspired irrelevancy, and when she and Carol elsewhere try to explain mysterious changes that seem to have taken place to an apple, Carol is quick to jump to conclusions, whereas she is more sceptical:

> Carol saw them better than Lesley. "Fairies!" he cried. Lesley said, "I can't believe it." "Fairies sure," said Carol.[97]

Sometimes because of a change in external circumstances, even an instinctive belief may fail the pragmatic test. The frog who ventured forth from his stream, having at last found water again in a wooden pail, is cackled at by some chickens. He at once

> dove down to the bottom to hide in the mud but there wasn't any mud. It was wood and he bumped his nose.[98]

Sometimes, too, people show a Hegelian disposition to develop concepts which are so abstract that, in James's words, one cannot "come back into experience with" them.[99] That is why Carol interrupts the three wise men's speculations on the height of the sky by asking the farmer's question, "What's it going to do tomorrow?".[100] On the other hand, a fiction will sometimes work by being a pure inversion of the "facts", as when the little girl walks across the field and braves the four cows because she is playing mummy — a very calm and collected mummy — to her doll Rose, who is very frightened of cows.[101] Her play-acting nerves her feet just as surely as those of James's mountaineer in *his* leap of faith.

The quizzical concern with metaphysics and metafiction brings the stories close to the final version of "The Black Cottage". But they are altogether more expansive. Of course there must be some check on the thirst for risk, the courage a-bristle for opposition, the mind fluently adjusting to any new configuration. When the frog comes down, though not to earth, with a bump, Frost writes, "He couldn't do anything but wish.*" The original audience was clearly invited to guess *what* he wished, and the asterisk cues in the footnoted answer: "Wish that he hadn't come".[102] The frog has been foolish to leave his stream, and at one level the story is a cautionary tale against escapism in the normal sense, an argument for contraction and building soil. Lucky the frog if, like Baby when she walked and walked, he had had somebody to take him home. On this level, the adult mockery of children's wandering into fantasy gently reminds them of the security they will always need in their mother's arms and in their own warm beds. As Frost's most famous poem intimates, a release of libido into the lovely, dark and deep can only lengthen the miles between the traveller and rest. That poem, however, is in a different mood, and this is to take the stories' mockery at face value, whereas their real thrust is irresistibly against a narrow prudential view. The foolish frog is admired for sheer guts; the children's walks from home and flights of fancy are condoned by paternal example; escape *from* is adventure *towards*; and the prevailing mood is carefree and optimistic. With the small exception of Frost's own terrorizing of the rabbit, not only is there no evil, no hint of death. As in Lesley's own daily story, there is also a world of completely untroubled childhood, in a rural setting that could still be nineteenth century, with animal friends and berry-picking excursions. The only sadness is caused by the changing seasons themselves — an empty nest is filled with snow — and even here there is stoical consolation — two winter birds may bravely manage to cheep. It is a pastoral world of magically golden harmony, in which the child characters and audience can live bold lives, unsuffering and unsinful, a world in which children are definitely not adults.

Grimly Modernist realism would have been out of place in a children's story of this period. The point is, though, that Frost could rise to the demands of the genre with such charm and ease. On the one hand, the combination of vocal and human realism with tall stories, already tried out in the poultryman tales, now reaches perfection, and we are getting very close to *North of Boston*. On the other hand, the stories resolve the tension between courageous faith and consolidating rest in the same spirit as the recently written "The Trial by Existence". Their world is the world of the recent "A Prayer in Spring" and "The Tuft of Flowers", and these three poems are among the most uninhibitedly beautiful, and most central, in *A Boy's Will*.

In "The Trial by Existence", the brave souls return to rest in heaven, only to sally out upon the world yet again. In the children's stories, trusting believers are for ever venturing forth from the securities of home. The final version of "The Black Cottage", by contrast, though by no means a very bleak poem, does not endorse largeness of belief so straightforwardly. It suggests how the mind may draw back to a less youthful, less delectable reality.

Turning now from Frost's literary apprenticeship and his first mature work to survey his writing as a whole, much of it can be similarly related to the cycle of expansion and contraction. He himself would have known that his words on expansion and contraction in the Amy Lowell piece were an instance of thinking in metaphors, and as noted, he elsewhere warned that all metaphors ultimately break down.[103] Even so, he would certainly have felt that a metaphor as suggestive as this should be pursued, with a sort of tactful boldness, for as long as it seems to work. After all, he also said that metaphorical thinking is the only sort we have.[104] The main risk is that the metaphor will tempt us to impose a false symmetry, whereby some of his poems would be completely "contracted" and others completely "expanded". The thing to remember is his basic point in the Amy Lowell piece: that life, at its most exciting, does not progress in one direction unchangingly. If there were to be an unbroken line of either expansion or contraction with no countermovement, that would not be life.

"To Earthward" is representative of his own work in constating both directions in sequence. His mental flexibility, his equivocality as regards historical periodizations, can be thought of as a ceaseless pulsing between opposites. To see this still more clearly, we can now focus all our attention on the antithesis between youth and age. Differences between expansion and contraction can often be registered in the way he uses children and the youthful world-view as points of reference.

Here three main groups of poems can be distinguished. First, in certain poems included in *A Boy's Will* or written in what we think of as the same vein, the mood is one of sheer delight and hope, as in the children's stories. The two other groups, however, contain poems which are much less overtly optimistic, often rejecting the child-like view quite explicitly, and with a grimness which seems more adult and "contracted". In the one group this bleakness is associated with suffering at the hands of fate, and the framework of ideas remains essentially Victorian. The crucial question is whether endurance is still possible and, if so, whether the sheer joy of being alive can really compensate for all the pain. But since this question often seems, by implication at least, to be answered in the negative, it is easy to feel that the predominant mood is not so much Victorian as modern in Trilling's sense. The other group of contracted poems allows no hesitation. They offer extremely disturbing insights into the human heart, and especially into the heart of the child-like adult, and the writing seems modern through and through.

The paradox is that both these groups of more contracted poems seem so modern precisely because the idyllic child's-eye view and the bravely Victorian acts of faith, adventure, and endurance are also present or implied by way of contrast, almost as if expansion could begin anew. This again brings us back to Frost's resilience, the subject of my previous chapter. When there simply seems to be no reason for staying alive, the challenge to Victorian stoicism is at its greatest. Yet Frost, like some of his protagonists, invariably rises to that challenge, so that we have little choice but to call him a Victorian Modernist or a Modernist Victorian. Quite consciously against all the odds, he sets an example of hopefulness, which his own act of communication itself strengthens by tacitly inviting readers to join him.

∽

In the first, least troubled group of poems, there are some which straightforwardly recreate the sheltered world of childhood at home. In "Locked Out" a

248 Responding to hopefulness

father is telling a child that not only flowers, but thieves are locked out at night. In "A Girl's Garden" a neighbour fondly remembers how her father granted her wish for a little garden of her own. Sometimes the child's vision of peace, love and harmony is available to the adult as well. In "The Tuft of Flowers", a child-like, shared delight in flowers unites the hearts of two men working, and the original glosses to *A Boy's Will* drew attention to the way in which the disturbed, youthful persona, by way of becoming a man, can actually become more child-like. In his dark inner turbulence of adolescent knowledge he sometimes seeks out a frigid solitude or decay, hugging to himself the gloom. But elsewhere, he acquiesces in the great rhythms of the seasons and procreation, not childishly ignorant of the griefs they can entail, but confident of the joys as well, his attitude suffused with a child-like sense of wonder.

"In a Vale" is specially representative of *A Boy's Will*, in that the speaker's adolescent morbity is just about to yield. When he was somewhat younger, he lived with other people but was lonely, or made himself lonely. He indulged in eerie nocturnal communion with the spirit-like presences of flowers — they sound like the wraiths of so many Pre-Raphaelite Ophelias — who one at a time delivered up to him their secret. Now on the brink of manhood, he wishes to share the knowledge he has gained from this impassioned perversion with somebody else. His lover only has to ask him, and he will be drawn out of himself. Flowers, which have hitherto entwined in deathly erotic fantasies — in the poem they are pale maids in trailing garments before they are flowers —, may henceforth inspire a more straightforward delight constating a less autoerotic sex-life. Even *A Boy's Will*, then, is not all mere radiant lyricism. But its hints of Modernist unpleasantness are defined in opposition to a childlike simplicity which still offers hope.

The hope is later made good in some of the greatest poems of married love in the English language.[105] Trusting delight in nature goes with an internalized knowledge of nature's power. "The Telephone", for instance, is like a happy sequel to "In a Vale". The lover tells his love a child's story: he listened to a flower which conveyed her voice, calling him home. She, with mysterious womanly playfulness, neither denies nor admits it. He, with a man's playful confidence, insists on the reason they both know is not the literal reason for his return — and the sentence sounds are very beautiful:

> "I listened and I thought I caught the word —
> What was it? Did you call me by my name?
> Or did you say —
> *Someone* said 'Come' — I heard it as I bowed."

"I may have thought as much, but not aloud."
"Well, so I came"[106]

The child's telephone-flower game is indistinguishable from the lovely telep-athies of a mating dance, and such interweavings of innocence and experience even occur in poems where childhood is not an explicit trope, since it is present below the surface as a kind of archetype. In "Two look at Two", the lovers, like the children in Frost's children's stories, walk to the border between their own, human domain and a wilder one. But whereas the stories presented Baby's monkey, kangaroo, bear and alligator as bizarre and fantastic, the poem's buck and doe have an awe-inspiring dignity. The lovers stand gazing at them, as children might, yet with inner recognition and a sense of their contemplation being reciprocated, as if the earth returned their love.

Even earth's sadder messages, about a natural beauty that must perish and, by the ancient analogy, about the death of human beings, sometimes cannot dim the child-like eye. In "A Prayer in Spring" and "Rose Pogonias" the intima-tions of decay or imperfection only make the transitory pleasure more exqui-site, while in "Hyla Brook" and "The Oven Bird" things already past their prime are cherished for what little remains. The child-like adult keeps spring and summer more present to the mind than autumn and winter, believing them to be nature's truest self-revelation and point of departure and return, the point at which nature would come to rest — if nature were not also a cycle of expansion and contraction.

Frost seldom looked down on such faith, even when he could not share it, for the profound influence of William James never wore off. Beliefs, the fictions of faith, are experiments with reality. Some such experiment is in any case inevit-able; the only criterion is pragmatist; and for some people some of the time, an optimistic faith does work. There is also the further point that the expan-sive adventures of child-like hope can lead on to a contracting consolidation of the self, so representing a person's line of individuation. Although the author of "The Lockless Door" and *A Way Out* was acutely aware of the openness of human potential, he never ceased to hanker after some strong form of indi-viduality. This was already implicit in the children's stories, and in a poem like "The Ax-Helve" it is quite explicit. Children, like the hickory from which a good helve is made, have a predisposition for a certain form of their own, which must be recognized and developed individually. "Laid-on education" in a school may be analogous to the mass-production of helves that only snap[107]

— in "The Figure a Poem Makes" there is a related distinction between a true poem and a false.[108] Nor, in principle, is there any reason why, at least at some stage of development, a person's distinctive form should not comprise an adult child-likeness.

Even so, much of Frost's poetry seems unsure about this. Childhood or childlike-ness tends to figure as an elegiac memory. Returning to the final version of "The Black Cottage" we find, not only the consciousness of the man-made quality of beliefs, but hesitations as to both the range of imagination and the sharpness of individuality they permit. Though the poem in the end neither endorses nor criticizes the old widow's Jeffersonian faith, it does not hide the human cost. In the child-like naivety of her unwavering certainty, she was very strange and isolated,[109] whereas the minister is now moving towards a less heady expediency and sociability. Nor can "The Ax-Helve" be read without its sinister last paragraph, with its hint that the strongly profiled individual may be dangerous to others.

"Maple", the poem which immediately precedes "The Ax-Helve" in *New Hampshire*, calls for mention in the same connection. The child bearing the name Maple grows up to wonder why her mother, who died in childbirth, gave it to her. It must be a clue, she feels, to some secret essence or meaning within her. She is for ever restless, romantically trying to find some special self-belief for which her name can be the metaphor. Curiously, Frost even makes her invoke, by way of contrast, the names of his own surviving children, and of one of their dolls:

> What was it about her name? Its strangeness lay
> In having too much meaning. Other names,
> As Lesley, Carol, Irma, Marjorie,
> Signified nothing. Rose could have a meaning,
> But hadn't as it went. (She knew a Rose).[110]

True, the delicate richness of this poem stems from its finally being rather ambiguous, like so much else in Frost. Perhaps, one begins to feel, he is not saying that romantic seekers are entirely misguided. Perhaps people who are never touched by such yearnings are not fully alive. Yet seeking and yearning do cause trouble and waste a lot of time, as the poem clearly shows, and Frost doubtless hoped that his own children's adventures along the enchanted paths of belief had not closed their ears to home truths. His attacks on idiosyncrasy are sometimes quite without reservation. In his preface to Robinson's *King Jasper*, he says that only a brute fool would want to break off the correspondence between his own mind and those of other people.[111]

Frost himself usually stayed content, as he says Robinson did, with "the old-fashioned ways to be new", and not only in the question of verse form. On the one hand, critics were not exactly wrong when they compared him with Wallace Stevens in metafictional sophistication and imaginative scope.[112] He can certainly be both playful and expansive. On the other hand, his cautious retreat behind the barrier separating one person from another intensified with age. He contracts, and his power as a writer is actually bound up with a minimum of difference from other people — with being neither too extended nor too withdrawn. Sometimes capable of the child-like trust, and never quite despairing, he most typically weighs life's burdensomeness. His poetry, as bracing as a March wind, can also be as piercing. "A Boundless Moment" is characteristic in not pretending for too long that March is May, just as, for the poet of "To Earthward", joys undashed with pain are less than real.

This brings us to the first of the two groups of poems in which the dominant mood can be read as Modernist. At issue here is the human ability to endure misfortune. Although the initial frame of reference is Victorian, the question raised is whether a brave stoicism can actually be justified. The poems' Modernist mood springs from their implicit or explicit scepticism, even though Frost himself and his protagonists tend to remain stoical all the same.

The writing captures a certain unmalleable toughness in the very ground rules of life, something which resists or even negates the fancy-free view of child-like trust. In particular, physical labour, which in "Mowing" and "The Tuft of Flowers" offered mysterious oneness with nature or, through shared delight in nature, fellowship with other people, is now the condition of a fallen humanity. At best, hard work takes the mind off things more painful, but only by being a drudgery which numbs while it sustains. At root, labour is a necessity that is alien to the human spirit, symbolically maiming the body.

Nor would these poems seem so powerfully Modernist if they were not nostalgic for the child-like joy. Indeed, it would be a mistake to suggest that they are uniformly solemn, since boyishness can nearly get the better of long-in-the-tooth dejection. In two complex poems, "Mending Wall" and "The Grindstone", the neighbour with whom Frost mends wall and a "Father-Time-like" man[113] who has a boy turn a grindstone are both stern workers, whose dourness seems to be a response to the nature of work itself. Yet the Frost persona has the mischief of spring in him — "Mending Wall" alludes to the same spring-childhood archetype as in "A Prayer in Spring". His fantasy makes loaves and balls of the rocks, and a conjuring-trick of wall-building. At one and the same time, it is sheer hard slog, and fun —

> We wear our fingers rough with handling them.
> Oh, just another kind of outdoor game,
> One on a side.[114]

He half-pretends that some strange force dislikes walls, and the fact that it is frost that cracks up walls, and that Frost here sympathizes with frost, is itself a childish pun back of the poem. Similarly, although "The Grindstone" alludes to expressions such as "nose to the grindstone" and "the daily grind", and although the speaker now looks back on his first taste of work from a position of ironic habituation, his childhood self had been full of indignant resentment. His dehumanized view of his fellow-worker, his private fantasy of an accident which would injure the man and at least "postpone / What evidently nothing could conclude",[115] had been a defence mechanism which took its cue from the danger and stupification entailed by the work itself.

Looking back, however, the Frost persona's adult irony cannot ignore the stern taskmaster, just as, in "Mending Wall", there is no point in trying to engage the grim neighbour in a flight of fancy. "I could say 'Elves' to him".[116] But no. The neighbour moves in a kind of primitive darkness, incapable of any mental advance or deviation from the inherited chores. Nor is the importance of wall-mending unclear to the Frost figure himself, who actually instigates the annual task.

If even such pleasurable poems return to the starker realities of work, there are others whose humour is far more thinly spread. In "The Self-Seeker", which has a schematic structure like a morality play, a man has actually been lamed in an industrial accident, and now converses with three visitors: an insurance agent, who wants his signed acceptance of the cash settlement; a little girl, who promises to go out looking for flowers so as to help him keep up his interest in botany; and a neighbour, whose responses heighten the contrast between the other two visitors, so hinting that the child-like freedom to roam, rudely snatched away by a work injury, was a privilege for which neither money nor imaginative identification with the child can compensate.

Even bleaker is "Out, out . . .", probably Frost's most rawly shocking poem, where work's dehumanization and violence are on full display. The boy whose hand has been sawn off in another industrial accident is old enough to see his life spoiled:

... he was old enough to know, big boy
Doing man's work, though a child at heart.

But although it is in one sense his adult pre-vision of invalidism and unemploy-
ment that kills him, his death is actually represented as the death of the heart,
that seat of remaining childlikeness:

... They listened to his heart,
Little — less — nothing! — and that ended it.
No more to build on there.

— no more reserves of trust. The only survivors in such a world, the other workers, are like subhuman robots in their stoicism:

No more to build on there. And they, since they
Were not the one dead, turned to their affairs.[117]

An analogous stoicism figures in the one major poem which, in all his hun-
dreds of readings public and private, Frost never spake aloud because it was
"too sad": "Home Burial".[118] Its sadness for Frost came partly from its connection with the death of his own first-born. But there is an intensely grim and
harrowing sadness in the poem itself. This stems not only from the actual death
of the child, but from the way his death either causes or symbolizes the parents' loss of the child's-eye view, a loss which brings upon them a terrible darkness like that of the childless couples in "The Hill Wife" and "Snow", where the
more cheerful Meserve has fathered children in Dickensian superabundance.
In "Home Burial", it is the husband who responds stoically. He sees the cruel
fact as it is, yet immerses himself in mundane tasks and talk. His refusal to
dwell on grief is his only way through, and is attended by not the slightest glim-
mer of joy or hope. Life is simply an inescapable endurance test, requiring iron
self-discipline. The wife, again, is as far on the darker side of stoicism as "Hyla
Brook" is on the happier. Not only is she joyless. She is quite demented with
grief, and convinced that life is positively evil. One of the poem's most searching details — a case where voice-tones, gesture and mind are inseparable — is
that, to her, there seems to be something joyous in the husband's grimly stoical
grave-digging —

I saw you from that very window there,
Making the gravel leap and leap in air,
Leap up, like that, like that, and land so lightly.[119]

– whereas every mechanical spadeful digs deeper the grave of his own free spirit. An important part of our response can be suggested by saying that the birth of a second child, in such a marriage, would be a spiritual impossibility. The poem does *not* suggest a sheer joy in being alive which exceeds the pain.

$\sim$

The second group of Modernist poems are, through and through, modern in Trilling's sense. They contrast the child's-eye view, not so much with something inimical received at the hands of fate, as with something potentially violent and strange, dangerous or psychotic, in the nature of human beings themselves. This sheer unpleasantness, in all its un-Victorian bluntness, is the very starting point.

As if this were not enough, poems such as "The Runaway" or "The Cow in Apple Time" have situations and *dramatis personae* which would suit the Derry children's stories. The almost amused tone, the child-like attitude alluded to, is sensed as a fiction aimed at mitigating confusion, repulsion and panic. In the children's stories, the cow was certainly important to life on the farm, and milking her was symptomatic of a due order in life. Even when the cow disrupted that order by breaking out of her field, one sensed that the remedy was at hand, and only Schneider the collie was upset. Similarly, Old Stick-In-The-Mud, the fence-post, told Irma that if his vacated place in the fence were not guarded the cow might get out; if she did, she would eat the apples, go apple-crazy and have to be put in the barn for the rest of the season; but this serious blow to the farm never fell. In "The Cow in Apple Time", it does. The structure of topography and incident is identical with that of the children's story about the frog who left his stream and ended up bumping his nose at the bottom of the wooden bucket: the animal pointedly breaks the bounds of its habitat, risking serious detriment to its own well-being. But the frog was a plucky, if foolish little fellow, and his story was humorous through and through. The poem's cow, by contrast, connotes diabolic possession and licentious debauch, a disnatured frenzy of corruption, a horrendous stupidity and ultimate waste. And such a song of experience achieves its fullest impact when readers recognize a potentiality for the enormities in themselves. Sensing the gulf between the apparent and the real subject-matter, we define ourselves in contradistinction to the innocent child of Wordsworthian convention, a contrast which in "The Fear" becomes almost explicit: the woman character's sexual guilt and objectless paranoia in face of darkness are precipitated by the innocence and beauty of a father and son

Out walking. Every child should have the memory
Of at least one long-after-bedtime walk.[120]

But not even childhood itself is blamelessly innocent, though in "The Bonfire" it is the father figure who at first seems most alarming. He encourages
his children to throw discretion to the winds, to ignite their accumulated materials, and to raise a conflagration that will leave the neighbours outraged and
astonished. When the children are not sure whether to take him seriously, he
says that yes, he would be scared to commit such an act himself. Has he not
unleashed analogous forces once before? But clearly, the terror and the social
stigma would also intensify the excitement. The pyromaniac knows

That still, if I repent, I may recall it,
But in a moment not: a little spurt
Of burning fatness, and then nothing but
The fire itself can put it out, and that
By burning out, and before it burns out
It will have roared first and mixed sparks with stars.[121]

The hints here of male orgasm begin to extend the symbolic reference to all acts
of libidinous rebellion, and the poem's conclusion says that the entire human
race is biassed towards the corporate madness of war. When the children, still
hesitant, suggest that war is for men only, the father retorts, "*War is for everyone,
for children too*" (Frost's italics).[122] There have been children in the ships sunk
and towns bombed, and his own children ought to "have our fire and laugh and
be afraid"[123] — ought to accustom themselves to both the active and the passive roles ascribed by such fires-passions-wars. The implication is that children
who profess to abstain from life's great sado-masochistic cycle run the risk of
hypocrisy.

Even the heart of a child, and especially the child-like heart of an adult,
can harbour a subtle callousness which to Frost is the most vicious thing in
nature. Half-oblivious of its own cruel compulsions, it indulges them. Whereas
the Victorians, not least in developing the genre of the children's story itself,
had staked their faith on the innocent child of Wordsworth, Frost can bring
to mind Henry James's complaint about Victorian novelists' *excessive* deference
to the children in the audience. Now, James argued, "the novel is older, and so
are the young".[124] Yet not even James's own fiction is as radically modern (in
Trilling's sense) as "The Bonfire", for the idea that childhood or child-likeness
can be evil fills him with fascinated trepidation. In *The Turn of the Screw*
the children's moral monstrosity may be a figment of the adult governess's

warped imagination, and in *What Maisie Knew* the young girl, irrespective of whether her insight is normal or precocious, seems frankly of a different species from the grown-ups under her scrutiny. With Frost, there can be an unabashed return to the pre-Romantic, Augustinian sense of the babe sinning at its mother's breast. And as hinted earlier, his dislike of the proponent of infantile sexuality could easily have stemmed from the clash of like minds.

Sometimes his view of adults is not Wordsworthian either. Frost's critics can give the impression that the Frostian individual is a figure of some pathos, more or less at the mercy of the universe, and establishing no relationship with the natural environment, or at best an enigmatic one, and one involving much passive waiting on the human side of it.[125] It so happens that Frost can also be more positively Wordsworthian than this, creating, we have noticed, a harmony with nature that is imaginative and delighted. Yet he can also be more realistically ethical and "ecological" as well. Always, the confrontation with nature amounts to a choice, and as often as not the Frostian individual chooses to respond actively to what is perceived in the world of nature as a passivity. Creation is the human being's victim.

Most typically, the human being who victimizes nature is, precisely, a child or a child-like adult, so that we are now a very long way indeed from the Derry children's stories. There, this darker view was hinted only once, in the single story about the adult's child-like heart. Frost's own delighted raspberry-picking had also been a way of intimidating a rabbit and keeping it from its burrow. In the poems, such petty callousness frequently recurs. In "The Exposed Nest" a father and child discuss their puzzling capacity for saving birds from destruction and then failing to check on their continued well-being. Have they, in their cleverness, merely prolonged an agony? In "Our Singing Strength", the persona takes a child-like fascination in the confinement of birds to the road's warm mud after a snowfall, but also registers the effect of his own walking down the road:

> A few I must have driven to despair
> Made quick asides, but having done in air
> A whir among white branches great and small,
> As in some too much carven marble hall
> When one false wing beat would have brought down all,
> Came tamely back in front of me, the Drover,
> To suffer the same driven nightmare over.[126]

In "Blueberries", "The Thatch" and "Birches", such "child-like" victimization of nature can indicate an aptitude for the sado-masochistic cycle in human relations as well. One of the motifs in "Blueberries" resembles Frost's raspberry-picking in the Derry story. With an unpleasant fascination, the two speakers recall how their previous berry-picking has kept a bird from its nest. Here, though, the implications are considerably extended. The spirit in which they now plan to pick blueberries is that of a gloating rapist, or of a pervertedly whimsical and child-like aesthete. Their act is compared to a jewel robbery, and it will depredate nature like fire. Most significantly of all, it will be an act of sheer spite, because they gleefully hope to anticipate the Loren family, who are thoroughly harmless and polite, and who would positively need every last berry, either for food or so as to raise cash for clothing. Whereas to pick berries in the Lorens' spirit is to accept and prudently husband nature's gifts, the disingenuousness and cruelty of the child-like speakers is even hinted in the poem's anapaests and couplets, whose polish somehow comes across as self-satisfied and unnatural. In "The Thatch", birds are again unkindly kept from their nest, and the Frost persona is also "intent on giving and taking pain" to and from his lover. His childish self-exposure to the rain keeps the birds from the low eaves of the house and, simultaneously, is a ploy in the lovers' quarrel — "We should see which one would be first to yield".[127] In "Birches", finally, a poem whose popularity perhaps belies its fundamental unpleasantness, the male persona sees the trees as beautiful, feminine, but with necks abjectly bowed before a power of fiery energy —

> ... trailing their leaves on the ground
> Like girls on hands and knees that throw their hair
> Before them over their heads to dry in the sun.

— compare the analogous association in "A Young Birch": "Less brave than trusting are the fair".[128] Although he knows that only an ice-storm could bend them so permanently, he actually prefers a fantasy of displaced sexual tyranny. "I should prefer to have had some boy" who

> One by one ... subdued his father's trees
> By riding them down over and over again
> Until he took the stiffness out of them,
> And not one but hung limp, not one was left
> For him to conquer.

Just as in "The Bonfire", the imagined acts of juvenile nature-destruction pleasantly breaks a taboo — there are the Oedipal overtones — and the hinted male organism is exquisitely timed —

> With the same pains you use to fill a cup
> Up to the brim, and even above the brim.

The females are to reach an ecstasy of masochism, "carried away" but in utter subjection — the boy

> ... learned all there was
> To learn about not launching out too soon
> And so not carrying the tree away
> Clear to the ground

and he leaves them quite ravaged. The word "love" in the poem's crowning aphorism —

> ... Earth's the right place for love.
> I don't know where it's likely to go better.[129]

– is strictly delimited by context, through the analogy with "innocent" childhood. For both men and boys, it would seem that love and the pleasure principle are entangled with ruthless drives to power.

Confronted with this, a girl or woman may herself resort to a perversion of child-like "innocence": a festering virginity of spirit no less obscene than the male sportiveness. In "Wild Grapes", a poem which curiously varies the situation and theme of "Birches", the woman tells how as a child she was persuaded by her brother to hold the top of a bowed tree; he released it; and it carried her up into the sky. Still she hung on, refusing all persuasions to let go, until she was finally "come after like Eurydice". She was "brought down safely from the upper regions"[130] but, also like Eurydice, she looked back: she was plucked from the boughs like only the most reluctant of wild grapes, and the child is mother of the woman. Still she has not learned, and sees no reason to learn, to let go with the heart. Such a diseased chastity is also what motivates the girl and her mother in the loathsomely unpleasant poem, "The Subverted Flower." Whereas in "The Telephone" there was a paradisal interplay of adult and child flower-games, this is now ruled out by the female refusal to see in the man anything other than bestiality, though the bestiality is certainly real enough. Hence the incident's savagery. The girl's frothing-at-the-mouth revulsion and her mother's righteous reclamation of her are no less ugly than the man's predatory leer.[131]

Aware of this kind of thing, Frost did not ultimately remain young at heart. One kind of second childhood he perhaps reached, in his expansive barding around and in his missions to Washington, South America and the Soviet Union. But his sense of the boundaries between himself and others becomes especially acute when the others are children. In "A Mood Apart" it appears as a geriatric testiness that is quite unironized; he feels that the schoolboys looking over his garden fence are evil-eyed. In "Not of School Age" he querulously attributes his slowness to understand a child to the child's accent — and the writing is unusually slack. In "A Peck of Gold" he is toughly witty at the expense of his own childhood and its beliefs — the belief, no more ridiculous than those he admires in the Derry stories, that in California even the food is coated with gold-dust. In "A Record Stride" his grandfatherhood sounds decidedly arduous. And in "Directive", he envelops childhood with maudlin pathos. Contemplating the ruined playhouse, he says of the children of the past,

> Weep for the little things could make them glad,[132]

but his only tear is for himself, who envies such simplicity, and who seeks it out in a mood of gloomy nostalgia recalling the adolescent in *A Boy's Will* (cf. "Ghost House"). Most tellingly of all, poems such as "A Drumlin Woodchuck", "One More Brevity" and "Lines Written in Dejection on the Eve of a Great Success" have animal characters very close to those of the children's stories, and the last-mentioned poem even has a microcosm-macrocosm switch reminiscent of a lighthearted Derry story about President Roosevelt's wrath at the smashing of china in the Frosts' kitchen. But the only real interest is a kind of hard ingeniousness. Everything is cerebral point-scoring and old man's sardonic glitter. Child-like delight has lost its taste, and his mind is ceasing to grow, ceasing to be flexible. The days of expansion and contraction are long since past.

Still, the fact remains: those processes of ageing we all share generate contrasts and metaphors which probably enter at some level into every literary text, and into our understanding of it. We share ageing, after all, as we share few other things, and we even share it with nature. Hence, at least in some cultures,[133] such inexhaustible figures as the spring of childhood. And in Frost's greatest poetry, the use of children and of the child-like view as points of reference is symptomatic of the great expansion-contraction cycle, and of a variety for which he is not always given credit. There are poems which lovingly recreate the child's-eye view, poems which endorse a Victorian idealism and courageous stoicism, and there are the great poems of married love. To this extent he was able to sustain the mood of the Derry children's stories, and throughout his life he also constantly returned to the bold belief in belief which he first articulated under the influence of William James. This does not rule out a certain nostalgia for childhood, however, and in two main groups of poems I have noted a tone that is altogether more Modernist, largely because they test or actually negate the more old-fashioned ways of thought. One group deals with situations which make the continued will to live more difficult to understand, even though Frost and some of his protagonists still soldier stoically on. The other group exposes the vileness and violence of the human mind and heart. And the power of both groups is proportional to the attractiveness of Victorian belief and childlike innocence.

From his earliest writings, Frost developed expansionist and contraction-ist impulses simultaneously. Whichever mood he happens to be in for the moment, the opposite mood is still present to him as a point of contrast and temporary self-definition. Even his bleakest poems cannot wear down the apparently inexplicable stoicism of their author, if not of some of their drama-tized protagonists, and in poems such as "To Earthward" expansion and con-traction alternate, so that the linear mode of organization is deceptive, leaving us with the feeling that the conclusion is not a conclusion. The poetry can itself be seen as an act of positive mediation between the values and sensibilities dominant in two different periods. "Modernist" and "pre-Modernist" horizons are always already merged, in a temperament so amorphous, yet so paradoxi-cally individual in its survivor's reserves of stamina and flexibility, as to be quite irreducible to any single fashion.

So although the Modernist reading habit of expecting unpleasantness cer-tainly alerts us to Frost's profound darkness, it will not suffice on its own. Even the darkness seems all the darker in that he also lives up to other, very different expectations. There is much sheer beauty, love and joy, and when there is not, there is perhaps a memory of them, perhaps a hope of them, or just that simply inexplicable spark of life, whereby his whole career confirms his Jamesian aph-orism from Derry: "A little more pleasure than pain, pain greater in length and breadth but exceeded by pleasure in height, one more pleasure by actual count, the pleasure of being alive". In communicating this, in not only communicating it, indeed, but in making poetry out of it, Frost actually adds to pleasure's tally. The poetry, itself resisting the grief and horror it shapes, invites its readers into a communion of embattled and creative hopefulness. Silence would have been much closer to despair, and would not have enriched the human world at all, let alone so abundantly.

It is especially worthwhile to grasp this now, because the context in which Frost is read has so greatly changed. Earlier readers read him in a variety of different ways, the different readings naturally corresponding to their differing *reasons* for reading, which in turn reflected a response to the historical context in which reading was taking place. Among those various reasons there were two which, reinforced by two rather different literary scholastic orthodoxies, tended to be in disjunctive opposition. While some readers reacted to the harsh realities of the age by seeking a pleasantly pastoral relief, others, such as the psychoanalytical critics, grimly accepted literature as a source or confirmation of the most unpleasant home truths. Today, we are probably more Janus-faced. Unable to forget two World Wars, the Holocaust, Hiroshima and many other horrors besides, some of them still happening, we are also, however cautiously, millenarian, and can already point to the fall of the Iron Curtain, Apartheid's quiet demise, or the Good Friday Settlement for Northern Ireland. Frost is our poet, too: the poet, not only of Edwardian suns that never seemed to set, not only of a later weather, far more black and stormy, but of the climate now, when both extremes contend.

CHAPTER 8

The pains and pleasures of *David Copperfield*

In Modernist readings of Dickens, his own historical formation, like that of his main characters, was not fully understood, and was treated none too kindly. *David Copperfield* continued to be seen as his most typical novel, and David's childhood was still generally acknowledged to leap up off the page — was living and contemporary, to use Leavisian buzz-words. But Leavis was not alone in — for many years, at least — finding young David's creator himself a bit too childish. As for David as a grown-up, David the mid-Victorian gentleman-author, David the husband of Agnes, Modernist readers found this all a bit too stuffy, and found its creator stuffy as well.

Today, too, readers are likely to find Dickens's own unadulterated satisfaction with *David Copperfield* rather strange. He gave vent to it in the new preface he wrote for the Charles Dickens Edition of 1867, some three years before he died:

> Of all my books, I like this the best. It will be easily believed that I am a fond parent to every child of my fancy, and that no one can ever love that family as dearly as I love them. But, like many fond parents, I have in my heart of hearts a favourite child. And his name is DAVID COPPERFIELD.[1]

Looking back to Dickens across the intervening epoch of Modernism, present-day readers may well feel he is speaking a foreign language here. The view of childhood and father-child relations in Frost's "The Bonfire" will probably seem much closer to the mark.

So can David and Dickens become more rewarding for readers as a result of ethnographical mediation? In my chapter on *Dombey and Son* I have already suggested one kind of answer. The two very different textual beauties in Dickens, the bourgeois and the non-bourgeois, can be seen as the two halves of a larger, ethical beauty, a beauty from history, representing a co-adaptative adjustment between Victorian norms and a powerful challenge to them. As an instance of superlatively active diplomacy this can still inspire us as we shape our life-world today.

Another mediating ploy is to push the distinction between Dickens's own Victorianness and non-Victorianness still further. This is a natural follow-up to my discussion of Frost's expansion and contraction. It is to assume that great writers have the mental flexibility to be both "of" and not "of" their own period. Seen like this, Dickens, for all his Victorianness, was always already a Modernist. Even the (for us) most boring, distant and dead aspects of his writing will respond to expectations of unpleasantness, so vindicating the twentieth-century habit of reading for pain.

Or rather, a Modernist reading for pain can at any rate be an *opening* move. Having tried it out, a mediating critic of the twenty-first century will then be very concerned to protect Dickens's context of writing from an aggressive twentieth-century take-over. The human value of literature is not enhanced by undermining a dead author's autonomy. When an author's historical otherness is seen to be at once recognizably human and distinctly different from our own formation, what can then emerge in our present time is an impulse to self-scrutiny and change. Our own interests are best served by allowing Dickens's contribution to the writer-reader dialogue to be as freely heard as possible. Not least, we shall do well to ponder his likely response to twentieth-century readings for pain.

Older writers' underlying hopefulness was perhaps a more explicit part of their self-presentation than that of many twentieth century writers. In terms of concrete grounds for hope, or even of clear images of what to hope *for*, they may take us no further than their successors. On the contrary, their work can be profoundly grim and disturbing. The difference is more a question of frame of mind and style of address: of a frank recognition of the grand and elementary principle of pleasure. Their reader is more clearly invited to share in a desire, albeit often unsatisfied, for justice, joy and beauty. This invitation, by a reader's simply accepting it, makes the world a better place, in that the community of those allowing themselves to hope for the best is thereby enlarged. Those readers who gathered to form the Dickens Fellowship, which ever since 1905 has published *The Dickensian: A Magazine for Dickens Lovers*, were tuned in to Dickens's own wavelength here. And although we may nowadays fight shy of such openly pleasurable commitments, still valorizing alienation and Thanatos along the lines of the scholastic stock response described by Trilling,[2] there is really nothing to be ashamed of. To cherish ideals of friendliness, sincerity, and probity, to desire a world of sheer delight for all and sundry, is not a sign of madness. Nor is it incompatible with a very cool-headed sense of real-life probabilities. Far more questionable would be an insensitivity to the pulse of hope. All too easily, this could be de-motivating for an engagement with life in general, so turning into a self-fulfilling prophecy of gloom.

⁓

Although Dickens was no stranger to life's darkest sides, the child metaphor of the 1867 preface gave no hint of this. In the full circumstances as we now know them, the point is not without its interest.[3] In connection with *David Copperfield*, it is natural enough to think about childhood, because the novel's own treatment of childhood has always been felt to be what is best in it, an assessment which Dickens's comment can only have reinforced. The comment was made, however, eleven years after his public separation from his wife, and ten or eleven years after the commencement of his secret affair with Nelly Ternan.[4] The child metaphor, by contrast, continues to surround him with the aura of a jovial paterfamilias, whose only foible — that, too, very well concealed — was to love one of his (book-)children more than all the others.

His later novels, drawing partly on his personal experience of guilt and deception, had often been criticized as too depressing. In the 1867 preface he responds by specially recommending a novel from his middle period, a novel peculiarly about childhood, a novel to be thought of as itself innocently child-like and unsecretive, a novel most preeminently the work of the much loved entertainer at every family hearth. This was a recommendation which the child metaphor could only strengthen, helping to confirm *David Copperfield* as the most popular of his works, for ever afterwards a best-seller, often the top best-seller, in any publisher's series of English classics. When, within a few years of Dickens's death, Forster's *Life of Charles Dickens* sensationalistically revealed a few carefully selected biographical details, it was to this novel that attention was directed yet again. The narrative of David's social degradation in the blacking factory turned out to be — almost verbatim — the text of Dickens's own unfinished autobiography. The fondly loved child-hero in the fondly loved child-book was none other than the fondly loved author as a child.

The new preface invited a warm glow of admiring sympathy for hero, book and author alike, and nothing could be further from the literal and metaphorical childlessness we tend to associate with some of the bleakest Modernists, though not with Frost. That Modernist readers would find both the child metaphor and the kind of adulation it invited thoroughly repellent is understandable. Yet Dickens's treatment of David's childhood, and particularly of David's relations with the novel's most forceful characters, is far less sentimental than the adulation duly accorded might suggest. The writing is much closer to Frost's "The Bonfire" than may at first appear. Even David as a grown-up responds to a disturbing Modernist reading fairly readily, and so does the novel's happy ending.

In the mid-twentieth century, there were still readers who found the ending quite acceptable at its own face value. According to John Hillis Miller in 1959 and 1968, Dickens had brought David into conformity with his society, the values of that society being represented by Agnes, who had waited for him all along.[5] For Gwendolyn B. Needham in 1954, David had come to learn a simple moral fundamental, the importance of disciplining the heart, and Needham's only hesitation was as to whether David's state of mind at the end of the novel might be pure wish-fulfilment on Dickens's part, a question she decided to reject as irrelevantly biographical.[6]

But if Miller and Needham were still reading along Victorian lines, the secret about Nelly Ternan, so closely guarded by Forster, was already public knowledge in the 1930s. By the 1950s, there was actually a flourishing school of criticism for which *David Copperfield* was eclipsed by the more sombre later novels, precisely because of their disconcerting inwardness to Victorian duplicities. Modernist expectations of unpleasantness seemed amply rewarded. By comparison, David Copperfield's second marriage seemed quite unreal.

Especially *Great Expectations*, one of the least popular of Dickens's novels at the end of the nineteenth century,[7] was now attracting praise as a devastating critique of Victorian gentility. In 1947 Lionel Trilling said that the class system, and the great expectations it nourishes in Pip, are shown as ultimately rooted in "a sordid, hidden reality": "The real thing is not the gentility of Pip's life but the hulks and the murder and the rats and decay in the cellarage of the novel".[8] For critics of Trilling's persuasion, the late Dickens offered the kind of abrasive disillusion described by Trilling's own later essay on modern unpleasantness. Dickens showed that Victorian ideals, together with all the magnificent achievements of Victorian civilization, had their foundations in an unedifying underworld of disease, inhumanity, injustice and violence. Some of the underlying psychological realities were probed in Edmund Wilson's epoque-making essay of 1941, "Dickens: the Two Scrooges".[9] In an analysis reminiscent of Jung's distinction between "persona" and "shadow", Wilson suggested that Dickens was little less than a Jekyll-and-Hyde. Although his public persona brought him success and respect within his society, as a child he had been so badly damaged by that society's cruel demands that his shadow life had waged a secret rebellion against it ever since. He was restlessly caught up in a manic-depressive cycle of boisterous social cheer and malevolently anti-social gloom. On top of which, he was disturbingly fascinated by murder, a capital offence in the society.

According to Wilson's implied account of the human psyche, we sometimes project our repressed shadow self onto other people. We intensely dislike them, because they embody qualities we do not wish to recognize in ourselves. In 1950, and with the same emphasis as Trilling on *Great Expectations*, Dorothy Van Ghent began to trace this kind of unexpected tension and complementarity in Dickens's frequent pairings of characters.[10] Estella and Miss Havisham suddenly became two aspects of virtually a single psyche, as was also the case for Joe and Orlick, and for Pip and Magwitch: "the opposed extremes of spiritual possibility" actually belong on a "spiritual continuum". In 1960 Julian Moynaham took the approach still further, by linking it to a psychology of sadomasochistic power relations, so developing Wilson's point about the effects of cruelty experienced in childhood.[11] Moynaham's suggestion was that Pip has self-projecting fantasies of revengeful domination over his tormentors. Unconsciously, he endorses Orlick's attack on his sister, Drummle's brutalization of Estella, and the real burning and hallucinated hanging of Miss Havisham.

Oppositions between the public and the private selves of "split" characters in Dickens's late novels were still being analysed by Barbara Lecker in 1979,[12] and with a continuing focus on *Great Expectations*. In planning that novel, Dickens himself had been afraid that it might turn out to be too similar to *David Copperfield*, which he re-read in order to guard against "unconscious repetitions".[13] To many twentieth-century critics, Pip's narration seemed, not only sufficiently different from David's, but far more interesting and successful. Psychologically speaking, they found it more complex.

To Modernist-style readers, *David Copperfield* often seemed oversimplified. Harry Stone, also in 1979, said that David's ecstatic adoration of Agnes for her spirituality is simply the obverse of his ecstatic adoration of Dora for her sexuality, Dickens being unable to create spirituality and sexuality in one and the same female character, and therefore allowing his hero to sample each in sequence. Moreover, said Stone, whereas Dora's incompleteness is *seen*, Agnes's is not, since Dickens himself is still hopelessly committed to the genteel ideal of the wife as ministering angel.[14] In several of David's other eminently Victorian traits — in his admiration of goodness devoid of iron, in his division of nubile females into whores, dolls and saints, in his concomitant sublimation of instinct into social concern, in his sentimentalization of the poor, and, above all, in his earnestness — his resemblance to his creator is no less apparent than in his experience of child labour and young love. Both the traits themselves and the resemblance with Dickens tended to annoy Modernist critics,

who could fairly claim that Forster's warning against such hero-author identifications rings pretty hollow. The novel, purportedly David's own narration,
contains no clear irony signals apart from those put there by the almost middle-aged David at the expense of his younger self. Formally, and sentence
by sentence, there is no distinction between David the narrator and Dickens.
This being so, Modernist dissatisfaction could easily swing to a very different
charge: that the book was *insufficiently* subjective, a mere holiday on Dickens's
part. On this view, David represented nothing of the disturbing daemonism so
engrossingly discussed by Wilson. There was merely the benign comedy still
admired by Miller and Needham, and it was a good bit too insipid. David the
man, and Dickens the man here, were simply too Victorian.[15]

Of course they were Victorian! Nothing will alter that, and it is something
a mediating critic will finally come back to, so as to ensure that reading the
novel is a genuine two-way dialogue. But even so, Modernist criteria are not
entirely damaging here. The features which twentieth-century readers found
most vital in Dickens can even help to rehabilitate the things they found more
boring. The livingness of David's first-person narration, the livingness of the
grotesquely strong caricatures: this can be readily drawn on. So, too, can the
darker energies that errupted in *Great Expectations*, since *David Copperfield*,
despite appearances to the contrary, certainly is a stage towards that later
novel. Written some years before the zenith of Victorian stuffiness and mealy-
mouthed cant, it perhaps did little to slow down their ascent, and actually
strengthened some of the roles and images becoming culturally central —
Stone was quite right about Dora and Agnes. But bearing in mind that it was
also written eight years before the final break-up of Dickens's marriage, and
twenty years before the utterly disillusioning narrative of Pip, it is a good deal
more truthful than could reasonably have been expected. Its prophecy of high
Victorianism extends all the way from beautiful visions and seemly surfaces to
tempestuous inner torment.

David is more like Dickens than his gentleness would suggest. His respectable qualities, far from floating in a psychological vacuum, are in constant interplay with certain other qualities which seldom receive explicit expression in his
thought, speech or action. We become aware of them, or half aware of them,
through the way in which certain fellow-characters light up under David's
scrutiny with a peculiarly urgent energy — with that larger-than-life quality
that everybody recognizes in Dickens. This, the mediating critic can suggest, is
because these strong characters are projections of the shadow which David's
public persona refuses to acknowledge.

In other words, the type of analysis applied by Van Ghent and Moynaham to *Great Expectations* is possible here as well. While David is telling his story, his fascination with these other characters represents a steady stream of self-revelation. The result is a dramatization of him as an adult which, if allowed to register fully, represents his creator's repressed daemonism no less than his Victorian stuffiness, a human roundedness of co-adaptation no less interesting than the portrayal of David's childhood is beautiful and poignant. Given this perspective, neither the straightforwardly Victorian reading nor the Modernist dissatisfaction seems all-sufficient. Both interpretations still have their place in the cultural heritage within which we do our reading, and there will always be moments when readers feel that each of them is warranted. Yet the book will no longer seem either a straightforwardly benign comedy, or a benign comedy that has straightforwardly failed.

To simplify for a moment, the reason why the strong characters light up with such pressing vitality is that David is the kind of observer and narrator he is. His preoccupation with these characters brings into play his own sixth sense: as the sage women said at his birth, he is privileged to see ghosts and spirits. Every-day reality is for ever shading off into something else, as his psychic sensitivity floods his writing with strange hints and anticipations, so that the normal limits of time and space may fail to apply. David exhibits many of the qualities detected by Taylor Stoehr (1964) in his psychological approach to Dickens's later, darker novels, qualities characteristic of what Stoehr called a "supernaturalist", dream-er's stance in narration.[16] David's story-telling seems inspired or automatic, strongly visual and strangely animated — hallucinated, even. Parts of it seem, too, at once relevant and irrelevant. Significances tend to get displaced or con-densed, in secondary elaborations of story that cover up the meaning.

Most striking of all are David's strange identifications and juxtapositions of one character with another. Sometimes his intuition seems to be that a single character cannot take the full psychic charge, which therefore has to be drawn out in a further display of implications. Dora's inseparable companion Miss Mills is a *reductio ad absurdum* of Dora's own romanticism. Sometimes he seems to intuit that the charge runs from positive to negative by a sort of enan-tiodromia. The friendliness of Mr Mell's mother alternates with the ill will of old Mrs Fibbitson, who is huddled over the fire and "jealous even of the sauce-pan on it".[17] Both these kinds of intuition are at work in the pairings he hints between himself and his own projections as well.

Somewhat more broadly, David senses that a person's projections flow from a bottomless reservoir of personality potentials which, in an individual's everyday persona, are rejected or only secretly active, but which may also wreak a cruel revenge, as when Mr Spenlow's private chaos finally disrupts his outward orderliness. The Jungian metaphor of the shadow is already active in David's narration. When David and Steerforth see Emily and Ham pursued by Martha, Steerforth says, "That is a black shadow to be following the girl . . .; what does it mean?"[18] The shadow is a latent possibility for Emily which is subsequently realized. This hardly saves Emily from being rather melodramatic in conception. In Aunt Betsey's case, however, it is partly the fluctuations between persona and projected shadow which make the characterization so convincing. Betsey's championship of the oppressed is associated with tics, neuroses and a general overdevelopment of her psyche's masculine side. Although this enables her to outface the Murdstones,[19] it is actually rather terrifying, and is projected onto the person of her husband, whom David pairs with her as a haunting, savage ghost. She only became this way after her own sufferings as a young wife, and her soul is once more set at rest when the delicacy and affectionateness of her nature, that more feminine potential of which Mr Dick is the projection, re-emerges in her relation with Dora, at about which time her husband-shadow dies in obsurity. In the same way, the characters paired with David as *his* projections show what he too could easily become, or perhaps already is.

But even if we grant all this, did Dickens himself realize what he was making David do? Or did he create David's intuitive narrative intuitively? Certainly *Great Expectations* is not only more forthright than *David Copperfield* as a socio-ideological critique. It is also much more tightly written. It was published in shortish weekly installments, each of which had to get to the point pretty quickly, and its total length is also short by Dickens's usual standards. In *David Copperfield*, because the targets of the later novel's definitive social critique were themselves still in the making, and because he was publishing one longish installment per month for nineteen months (the last installment a double one), there was no call for such concentration, and the result is leisurely, relaxed, rambling even. The supernaturalist dreamer's stance seems to be indulged almost as a mannerism, the strange juxtapositions of projection characters proliferating so fluently that their relevance can be very hit and miss. Old Mrs Fibbitson with her saucepan is like a Gothic gargoyle, and even if old Mrs Fibbitson's bad temper is raising the question of whether the sweetness of old Mrs Mell is really credible, not even old Mrs Mell would have won a place in *Great Expectations*, where characters tend to be less incidental and more fully developed. From a reader's point of view, the later novel's discipline may well make it more impressive, but not necessarily more enjoyable. *David Copperfield* leaves more scope for what Barthes called the writerly kind of reading. There is much for the reader to work on, all of it ultimately from the same mind-set, but all of it capable of entering into constellations of meaning that are fascinatingly ever-changing.

On the other hand, we should not underestimate Dickens's control, even in *David Copperfield*. The shadow metaphor, for instance, is extremely *à propos*, and in the case of Emily actually rather cerebral, as if Dickens had studied Jung. In point of fact, his understanding of projections was increasing with time. He had often heard praise of his own ability, whether through his writing or through his reading performances, to transform himself — to be several different people at once. During the gestation period of *David Copperfield,* his insight into the hyper-real workings of the shadow self was developed still further, through his dealings with Mme de la Rue. This unfortunate lady, whose afflictions were rooted in frightening hallucinations, told Dickens under hypnosis of the faceless men and women crowding in upon her. One particular spirit was a man so terrifying that she dared not look at him[20] — one wonders whether she ever found relief, like Aunt Betsey. Then again, in equipping David with outer propriety and inner sensitivity Dickens, as so often, was both placating and outwitting Mrs Grundy, the stifling effects of whose horrible respectability on British art and civilization, and on the English novel in particular, he heartily deplored.[21] The dilemma in which some Victorian readers might already be placed by the novel's intimated truths is neatly illustrated by David himself, who shows a nervous, groping awareness of his own powers of insight. The original title included a parenthesis to the effect that David never intended his manuscript to be published on any account, a point he repeats elsewhere. But even his conscious reactions are not always *comme il faut*. So with a somewhat bashful defiance he apologizes: "What is natural in me, is natural in many other men, I infer, and so I am not afraid to write that . . . ."[22] His opening sentence actually warns us against taking the apparent for the real: "Whether I shall turn out to be the hero of my own life, or whether that station will be held by somebody else, these pages must show".[23] What they do show is that David may indeed be the hero of his own life, but in a way that is connected with other characters rather strangely, and not because of what he *wants* to say about himself, but in spite of it.

Even so, Dickens's artistic self-consciousness is probably not a constant, and different critics have arrived at overall estimates which are mutually incompatible. Q. D. Leavis argued that he deliberately treats Daniel Peggotty on two levels at once. Daniel's tireless search for his sinful niece is an instance of innocent love which, very appealing to Victorian sentimentality, is actually dangerous in its maudlin possessiveness, and Dickens set out to be both very sentimental and ruthlessly honest about sentimentality.[24] Replying to this, John Bayley argued that Dickens's true powers "are not only products of ruthlessness and sentimentality, but require that these two responses are unaware of each other". Dickens knew not what he did.[25] Again, Robin Gilmour highlighted David's prudent comments on his own subversively sensuous and evocative memories, and concluded that Dickens "*managed to*" (my italics) bring into fiction a Wordsworthian theme, the "imaginative loyalty to a past that has not been outgrown". Dickens, that is to say, deliberately shows David marooned in the narrowness of Victorian marriage, and returning for inspiration to the open and liberal state of youth.[26] Vereen M. Bell, by contrast, came close to saying that David knows more than his creator. Or at least, Dickens's archetypal power stems from his inability to substantiate his conscious design. Unlike Miller and Needham, Bell could not believe that what David *needs* in the adult world (i.e. Agnes) is also what he really wants, because the memories of his mother, little Emily and Dora are subversive, and subversive beyond Dickens's own control.[27] Taylor Stoehr, finally, who wrote so well about the supernaturalist dreamer's stance in Dickens's later novels, refused to give *David Copperfield* serious attention. Even though it deals with those problems of adjustment which are most relevant to his psychoanalytical approach — the finding of a job, a mate, a place to live, a position in the community, a goal in life — Stoehr complained that its attempt at dream is too literary and deliberate, anticipating programmatic dreaming in the surrealist works of a later age.[28] I myself have disagreed with this in print, suggesting that Stoehr correspondingly overrates the spontaneity of the novels he does consider great.[29]

But this entire debate is just a literary scholastic red herring, which, like the disagreement between the Modernist and traditionalist accounts of Henry Vaughan, badly underestimates the human flexibility of mind. What it does is to oppose artistic craftsmanship to intuitive impulse as if they were mutually exclusive. For a mediating critic, they can never be that, which is why my chapter on *Dombey and Son* did not pronounce on the degree of conscious planning in the juxtaposition of bourgeois and non-bourgeois beauty. We shall never know about such things for sure, and the main point is that their effect is interesting and important. The consequence of critical disagreements about them is merely to instantiate within our culture two lines of interpretation which, in the agile minds of readers, can hold a place simultaneously.

David Copperfield is certainly less disciplined than *Great Expectations*. That much is clear. But why bother to take it further? If Bayley was right in saying that Q. D. Leavis's analyses of artistry can render Dickens mechanical, what kind of service was Bayley himself performing? As a critic Bayley has always been wonderfully sensitive to the human flexibility of mind, and his comments on Dickens's simultaneous ruthlessness and sentimentality, and his implied account of the reader's response to them, were no exception. Yet there is one dimension of human complexity which Bayley's argument ostensibly denied, even though the fact of the argument's publication implicitly recognized it. Ostensibly, Bayley's analysis sought to enlighten by disenchanting: by making explicit those contradictory responses of ruthlessness and sentimentality which on Bayley's own account must remain unaware of each other if the Dickensian magic is to work. One might easily think, then, that Bayley was aiming to increase our understanding of Dickens so as to *reduce* our enchanted enjoyment. But that, as Bayley tacitly knew, is not the way it works, and the publication of his commentary remains a cause for rejoicing. To understand the secrets of magic is not to eliminate its experienced power. The human mind, the mind of both Dickens and his readers, is extremely primitive, extremely sophisticated, and extremely primitive and extremely sophisticated at the same time.

A novel like *David Copperfield* mobilizes our fullest capacities, conscious and unconscious alike. Perspectives often thought of as necessarily outside the reading experience — any kind of revelation of how the text "really works" — can always *enter into* that experience, and the experience itself can always be distanced at the drop of a hat, readerly inside and scholarly outside changing places. A literary critic attempting appreciative mediation will always assume that the cycle of belief and disbelief can be sustained and further developed.

One strategy is suggested by Wordsworth. Commenting on his own lyrical ballads, he said that they will be found to have a purpose which is not "distinct" and "formally conceived",[30] but which springs from a mind developed in special ways, whose slightest reflex is significant. The purpose, in this sense, of *David Copperfield*, its designing impulse of narration, can for the moment be said to lie in the sustained tension between David's respectability and his inadvertent honesty. The honesty is not in the nature of a parenthesis or postscript, but of the essence. Partly it is voiced in that pervasive double-edgedness that was studied, from contradictory and equally limited points of view, by Q.D. Leavis and John Bayley in the treatment of Daniel Peggotty, and by Robin Gilmour and Vereen Bell in David's memories. An even more important part of the same indistinct and unformalized purpose is David's intuitive pairing of his projection characters with himself. With the introduction of each projection character, there unfolds a new depth in David.

This is not what Mark Spilka had in mind when he called *David Copperfield* a "projective novel". Spilka used this term to suggest that the unarticulated problems of the child-hero affect, in a vague and general way, his perception of what goes on around him. Spilka seemed to hint, for instance, that Murdstone is in some sense a re-embodiment of the father "*murd*ered" underneath the grave*stone*: disturbing enough anyway, and also a guarantee that David will suffer from Oedipal stress.[31] Spilka was not saying, then, that Murdstone is an aspect of David's own shadow, whereas my present argument is that David's projection characters keep recurring in a kind of dream-music, and again in reports at the end of the novel, precisely because they represent possibilities for David himself. Through one or more of them, David's less obvious qualities were infiltrated into each monthly number, and the full *Copperfield* effect thereby registered.

Nor is the novel static. Far from there being a simple one-to-one relation between each such character and a particular Davidian trait, the projection characters themselves actually shift in value, sometimes even "merging into" or "clashing against" each other. Reading back into this an early-twentieth-century understanding of human nature, we begin to accept Dickens and David as human beings, even at their most Victorian. It can sensitize us to the Victorian mind's swirling complexity.

David's Murdstonianism, for instance, is partly a brute drive to dominate. When Murdstone moves into the Rookery, David finds "the empty dog-kennel . . . filled up with a great dog . . . [which] sprung out to get at me",[32] a clear enough anticipation of Murdstone's use of corporal punishment. David replies in kind, biting through Murdstone's hand, and there is enough truth in the placard he wears at Creakle's school — "*Take care of him. He bites.*"[33] — for the older David's criticism of Creakle's sadism and professional incompetence to sound almost defensive: "I am sure when I think of the fellow now, my blood rises against him with the disinterested indignation I should feel if I could have known all about him without having ever been in his power".[34] Like Jane Eyre, whose torture in the Red Room, journey to school, public shaming there, infatuation with a schoolfellow, and subsequent vagabondage David's early experiences so strongly resemble, David rapidly determines to be a winner.[35] Nor does he ever rule out violence. Even at Doctor Strong's, he not only becomes the most distinguished scholar, but throws himself into brawls between town and gown, finally vanquishing the butcher once and for all. Later still, he wildly assaults Uriah Heep.

But Murdstonianism can also take a special sexual colouring. Indeed, it was through Murdstone that David was initiated into sexual mysteries in the first place, and he himself emulates Murdstone's drive. He grudgingly sensed the attractiveness his mother must have seen, and knew that the courtship was taking place before he could put a name on it. He even tried to court her back, by reporting Murdstone and Quinion's conversation about the bewitching little widow. Although she calls it nonsense, David "knew it pleased her".[36] Its effect, of course, is only to take her further away from him: he is a go-between, a role he soon exercises more willingly, and with no little fascination, in the parodic courtship of Barkis and Peggotty. At Yarmouth, the cosy boathouse offers a womb-like security again, yet David is already set on an amatory conquest for himself. More particularly, he nourishes in Emily that desire to be a lady which was to bring about her fall, in true Murdstone fashion driving a wedge between her and her nearest and dearest, just as when he later courts Dora he is jealous of her father. Even David the narrator is conscious of this, again apologizing to Mrs Grundy for his state of mind — "not exclusively my own, I hope, but known to others".[37]

In yet another of its aspects Murdstonian firmness can come very close to the "thorough-going, ardent, and sincere earnestness" embraced by David publicly.[38] It is only through Aunt Betsey's self-damaging determination that the Murdstones were finally resisted. According to Sylvère Monod, the upbringing David receives in her care is itself wholly dominated by the Murdstonian ideal.[39] True, some critics have wondered whether David would have *turned into* a Murdstone if Dora had not died.[40] True, too, Ross H. Dabney said that although David ends up tougher, and more devoted to aggrandisement, than any other Dickens hero, some of Murdstone's cruelty is strictly irrelevant to Dickens's intention with him.[41] But such commentators were fighting shy of what the novel really registers, Dabney by one-sidedly pronouncing that it is out of Dickens's control. Dabney and, following him, Philip Collins[42] even said that Dora's death is a necessity forced on the embarrassed Dickens by the genre of the *Bildungsroman*: if David is to grow towards Agnes, Dora must be removed. Here the mediating critic, though certainly not discounting generic pressures, can continue to apply the unpleasant perspective of the Modernists, simply by responding to Murdstone, and to David as Murdstone illuminates him. The consequences of an ethic such as David's really can be disastrous, and Murdsone can key us in to them. When David starts paying suit to Dora, who should pop up again but Murdstone? — appositely taking out a new marriage licence. Soon David is trying to stiffen his beloved with some domestic science, and after the wedding he asks Aunt Betsey if she couldn't "advise and counsel Dora a little". Betsey replies, "Remember your own home, in that second marriage", refusing to be Miss Murdstone to his Murdstone.[43] Yet although this brings the danger into his own consciousness, he still cannot relent, and resolves to "form Dora's mind" himself.[44] His browbeating of her, all the more painful in view of his genuine kindness and tact, and even though he finally gives it up as useless, brings Dora's guilt feelings before himself and Agnes to a crisis which ends in her death, just as he freely says his mother was killed by Murdstone. Dora's willingness to go, her bequeathal of him to Agnes, is a terrible indictment we cannot flinch from.

Even Murdstone and David can feel such things. They are both capable of grief and shame, so that their interrelationship acquires yet another resonance. Half awaiting the news of Dora's death, David sits down

> by the fire, thinking with a blind remorse of all those secret feelings I have nourished since my marriage. I think of every little trifle between me and Dora, and feel the truth, that trifles make the sum of life.[45]

The intuitive force of David's narrative sends our minds back to Murdstone, after the death in The Rookery:

> Mr Murdstone took no heed of me when I went into the parlour where he was, but sat by the fireside, weeping silently, and pondering in his elbow-chair.[46]

The novel has turned Murdstone inside-out, in David, just as my present Modernist perspective again turns David's Victorianism inside-out by contemplating Murdstone.

As a shadow projection, Murdstone also merges into Steerforth, whose arrogant self-assurance and pride of place give a new twist to Murdstonian will. David's own dark complicity is also intensified and diversified: in the social dishabilitation of Mr Mell, David is a far more obsequious pawn than in the bullying of his mother. His "ceaseless sense of unmerited degradation"[47] in the bottle warehouse and on the nightmare walk to Dover is correspondingly sore. Even as things are, he is careful to note that as a "little gent" he nevertheless "held some station at Murdstone and Grimby's";[48] seems to register without actually noticing that the Peggotys give him special food and a privileged amount of space in their cramped boathouse; and senses, without quite diagnosing, Daniel and Ham's suppressed class anger, a point which for early readers could have had a background in the Chartist movement and the European revolutions of 1848.[49] When he is duly elevated as what Micawber calls "the pupil of Dr Strong", he is quite the Steerforth of the place, and his amusement at the headmaster beguiled of his gaiters by a beggarwoman is tinged with indignation at the latter's affrontery — even though the "little second-hand shop of no very good repute" where the gaiters are subsequently put up for sale is just the kind of place in which he himself had once sold his jacket to get money for food.[50] Realizing later that Steerforth thinks genuine work quite beneath him, he warmly accepts Steerforth's endorsement of the proctorial profession as a genteel sort of niche, from within which to lord it over Traddles's sheer hard slog. Perhaps part of the sadness of Steerforth's death for David is precisely that Steerforthian gentility has hitherto presented itself as exempt from the normal conditions of life.[51] Certainly the Steerforthian side of David is what later gives way to earnestness, and to more democratic feelings, including a utilitarian sense of the humbug and inefficiency of Doctors' Commons. Not only does David's Victorianness not float in a psychological vacuum. When Philip Collins said there is no real danger of Steerforth's character having a bearing on David's,[52] he was again short-circuiting what, within a Modernist perspective, is one of the novel's major meanings. Steerforth is crucially important, as a force of both attraction and repulsion.

David's Steerforthianism also entails further sexual implications. David the narrator begins a public recognition of Steerforth's sin, but in the same breath retracts it:

> If any one had told me, then, that all this was a brilliant game, played for the excitement of the moment, for the employment of high spirits, in the thoughtless love of superiority, in a mere wasteful careless course of winning what was worthless to him, and the next minute thrown away — I say, if any one had told me *such a lie* [my italics] that night, I wonder in what manner of receiving it my indignation would have found a vent.[53]

The sin might have been, and partly is, his own; he even acknowledges "my own unconscious part in his pollution of an honest home".[54] Consciously now, perhaps, he is thinking mainly of his having introduced Steerforth at Yarmouth in the first place. But it was also he himself who first raised Emily's thoughts above her station. He allowed himself to be the object of her first experiments in coquetry, and the entire episode, in which infantile sexual fantasy was inter-woven with an experiment in sado-masochistic power relations, was one factor in the blockage between himself and Agnes. When the dream logic brings him and Steerforth into the middle of Ham and Emily's engagement party, he "was filled with pleasure . . .; but, at first, with an indescribably sensitive pleasure, that a very little would have changed to pain".[55] At one point his unconcious com-plicity in Steerforthian depredation is guiltily hinted by his own second sight:

> [Passing] the door of my little chamber, which was dark, I had an indistinct impression of her being within it, cast down upon the floor. But, whether it was really she, or whether it was a confusion of the shadows in the room, I don't know now.[56]

Later on, he again sees Emily without seeing her, as it were, on the ship about to sail for Australia. In this and similar cases, Pam Morris detects his guilty intui-tion that gentility can mask the unkindness that goes with an impoverished sense of human solidarity.[57]

The elopement of Steerforth and Emily also brings into play another half-hidden side of David, which clashes against his Steerforthianism. Here an aspect of Rosa Dartle becomes the major projection. In stressing that the elopement severed all ties between himself and Steerforth, David's language is the language normally used to describe a break-up of the deepest, and sexual, relationships. This is not to say, obviously, that the sexuality had been physic-ally consummated. That it had not been, that it remained unconscious, is part of the point. Yet when Steerforth had long ago painted his mental image of the "pretty, timid, little, bright-eyed sort of girl" who might have been David's sister,[58] the ravishment that hung suspended in the charged atmosphere of the Salem House dormitory had been, not only of a girl such as David's actual childhood companion, but of David himself. David's unacknowledged blam-ing of Emily for stealing his loved-one is surely another factor in his quiet lapses of pity for, or even interest in her. Daniel Peggotty and, fleetingly on the ship, Agnes will take care of her, and the Micawbers' departure is infinitely more engrossing than hers — her whereabouts during the evening before is a mystery unremarked amid the celebrations. Hence, too, David's fascination with Rosa, a rival whose smouldering erotic attraction he misses as little as she misses his own more subtle appeal. Her scarred lip holds his gaze as the badge of her secret shame with Steerforth, yet his nervous prudery is merely the cor-ollary of his own would-be licence. Rosa's wild grief is humanly necessary to the book, a vital part of its honesty, as an expressed response to Steerforth's death. For at that supreme coincidence of the mighty dream, David's Victorian narrative is quite awe-inspiring in its dignified, Hopkinsian half-statement. Ham is positively transfigured as he meets the wind and waves in his fatal attempt at rescue. In David's admiration, in his identification with Ham's great gesture, there is dark, tempestuous knowledge. He himself should have ventured into the storm, as a first and last declarative act of union. By means of Rosa, the novel's one great all-consuming passion burns out a slower and less lovely death.

The fact that his infatuation with Steerforth developed before those with Miss Shepherd and Miss Larkin, coupled with the intensity of his relation with his mother, whom he recreates in Dora, probably ensured that his sexuality would never be unproblematic, so contributing to what is ultimately a self-abasing sanctification of Agnes. The novel's unobtrusively dramatizing revelations extend even here, and consequently to the calm of the ending. Read through the spectacles of Modernist anti-hedonism, the novel has met Harry Stone's objections to Agnes by anticipation. It contains them, in both senses of the word.

One of the projection characters involved here is Mr Wickfield. Agnes is idolized by her father with a love which both Wickfield and David say is diseased. Yet the pedestal Wickfield places her on is also clearly used for the same purpose by David. It raises her far above Annie, and Wickfield is so convinced of Annie's misdemeanours that he dislikes the two women to associate, something David registers with distinct comprehension. Both Wickfield and David, moreover, wallow in indignities of their own at Agnes' feet. Wickfield knows that drink is destroying him yet only accepts more port at her hand. David, at the climax of his own drunken debauch, comes to harrowing awareness of sitting in the same box of a London theatre as Agnes, who "ought" to be still in Canterbury. The case of Wickfield, so fascinating to David, underlines the unhealthiness in his own fixation on the anima figure throughout, a sexual blockage which explicitly is usually mentioned as a thing of spiritual beauty, which from the superficially Victorian point of view it perhaps is.

The side of David which for this reason fails to grow to full expression is projected in Micawber, who represents far more than the pre-Victorian enjoyment of life seen by Q. D. Leavis.[59] Micawber is essentially comic in the obvious sense, and in one of his aspects does embody a force very different from the gloomy religiousness of the Murdstones. As we should by now expect, it is a force which also wrestles for expression in David's own life, as in the struggle between Murdstonian dourness and his love of delight in his first marriage. But Micawber, whose own marriage survives not only its very fertility and the frequent pecuniary embarrassments, but even the acute strain imposed on it by Uriah Heep, evinces a fully-fledged sexuality and an enduring emotional realism. Micawber esteems Mrs Micawber as his "guide, philosopher and friend", recommending that David seek a similar match.[60] David's apparent echo of his phrase a few pages later in the same number involves a typical contradiction:

> ... Agnes — my sweet sister, as I call her in my thoughts, my counsellor and friend, the better *angel* of the lives of all who come within her calm, good, self-denying influence — is quite a *woman* [my italics].[61]

David's own intuition that Micawber "is" something he himself represses at such points emerges as a *déjà vu* experience:

> "If you had not assured us, my dear Copperfield, ... that D. was your favorite [*sic*] letter," said Mr Micawber, "I should unquestionably have supposed that A. had been so."
> We have all some experience of a feeling, that comes over us occasionally, of what we are saying and doing having been said and done before, in a remote time — of our having been surrounded, dim ages ago, by the same faces, objects, and circumstances — of our knowing perfectly what will be said next, as if we suddenly remembered it! I never had this mysterious impression more strongly in my life, than before he uttered those words.[62]

Through Micawber's energetic practical intelligence, that other idolater, Mr Wickfield, may even be restored to a proper relationship with his daughter. But the unnaturalness of David's contriving to have children by her contributes an uneasiness to the novel's closing calm that is almost conscious on David's part, thanks to the continuing tidings of Micawber.

Micawber is not only a repressed "positive", however. He also has some very particular class feelings. They are not vicious, of course. He recoils in alarm when Littimer enters, that embodiment of Steerforthian superiority at its most sinister. But he does transpose a side of Steerforth, tempering pride with insecurity. On Micawber's first appearance in the warehouse, David is still smarting from the wounds to his own Steerforthianism, and responds very warmly to "a certain condescending roll in ... [Micawber's] voice, ... a certain indescribable air of doing something very genteel".[63] But Micawber soon comes to embody all that is most dubious in his own social position, a projection of his own unease. Hence his discomfort when Micawber pops up at Uriah Heep's tea-party, an incident reminiscent of Dickens's exasperation with his own father, whose improvidence and importunity were a "damnable shadow" cast over his life[64] — again the Jungian metaphor! Micawber outside the prison, musing on the liberty and self-respect he had enjoyed as "an inmate of that retreat",[65] even contains the germ of William Dorrit; and in Micawber the novel suggests intensities, if not depths of emotion that nothing in *Little Dorrit* exceeds. His great handicap is, precisely, his great gift: the flow of polite language. He is a manic-depressive — transposing and intensifying the moody gaiety of Steerforth — trapped in his own gentility. We laugh so loud that we never quite hear what he says —

> "MY DEAR YOUNG FRIEND,
> "The die is cast — all is over. Hiding the ravages of care with a sickly mask of mirth, I . . . ."[66]

Like Q. D. Leavis, we may remember only the mirth, partly because the narrative always leaves him on a manic crest or suggests that one is just on the way — always, Micawber "might be expected to recover the blow".[67] But the miseries are there all the same; the reasoning irrationality of his devoted wife is a sufficient hint of the sharpness with which he feels them. Still more to the point, his passionateness in success or failure acts like Rosa Dartle's love of Steerforth: it amplifies its more restrained equivalent in David. Chapter 36, for instance, which is entitled "Enthusiasm", catches them both on a great wave of euphoria, David "in a state of ferocious virtue"[68] as he starts bread-winning as Dr Strong's secretary, Micawber at last able to walk erect before his fellow man by virtue of his secretariship to Uriah Heep. The alignment makes it almost predictable that the next chapter of David's adventure, which is in the same number, will be "A little Cold Water", an upset in his courtship of Dora, a matter at least as much of social as of romantic concern. Before long he is writing to Miss Mills to inform her that his reason is tottering on its throne, signing himself hers distractedly. Even David catches a whiff of his own Micawberism here.

The passion David restrains least is excited by Uriah Heep, whom he endows with superlative corporal loathsomeness, often intensified by vile animal comparisons. David's compulsive physical dislike is an attraction "in very repulsion", which rocks his own sanity.[69] When Uriah hints that he could have Mr Wickfield under his thumb, by blackmail, Uriah "stretched out his cruel-looking hand above my table, and pressed his . . . thumb down upon it, until it shook, and shook the room".[70] When Uriah goes on to indicate his designs on Agnes, David's sense of nightmare becomes almost insupportable:

> I believe I had a delirious idea of seizing the red-hot poker out of the fire, and running him through with it. . . . He seemed to swell and grow before my eyes; the room seemed full of the echoes of his voice. . .[71]

David afterwards wrestles all night with his fantasy of applying the red-hot poker. His impulse to do violence to Uriah, finally acted upon, is one of his most persistent reflexes.

But this is unrestrained without being explicit. What, after all, has Uriah done to deserve it? It cannot be that he has performed the criminal acts important to the story. Nothing is known with any certainty about those until Micawber's "explosion". Rather, there is a clue in the sequel to the passage just quoted:

> He seemed to swell and grow before my eyes; the room seemed full of the echoes of his voice; and the strange feeling (to which, perhaps, no one is quite a stranger) that all this had occurred before, at some indefinite time, and that I knew what he was going to say next, took possession of me.[72]

As elsewhere, David's *déjà vu* experience hints that what is happening is somehow an externalization of himself. His response to Uriah is the response we have to people who are more like ourselves than we care to admit, people we diabolize in our imagination because they embody a strongly rejected trait of our own shadow side. David plunging into the perplexing sea of stenography, no less than Uriah struggling with Tidd's *Practice*, is hugely keen, not only to earn a living, but eventually to better his position. In aspiring to the rank of his employer Mr Spenlow, and to the hand of his daughter in marriage, David merely takes a leaf out of Uriah's book. Not that countless bourgeois heroes had not worked their way towards the same consummation. But David's Steerforthianism makes him reluctant to be that kind of hero: two suspect traits again clash against each other. Gentility is a fine thing. But can it be genteel to aim at it with such rawness of ambition? Beyond a certain point, and even before Steerforth pooh-poohs his vague plans for hard-earned distinction, David is not quite sure he likes meritocratic ideas. It is permissible to cover himself with honours at school. But his courtship of Dora has to be as little like a scheme for self-improvement as possible, and, fatally for her, Dora is ideally suited to the romantic scenario he devises. His real aggressiveness peeps out when a young man suspiciously reminiscent of Uriah — an "imposter, three or four years my elder, with a red whisker"[73] — pays his addresses to Dora at the picnic. Somewhat similarly, the distraction of his letter to Miss Mills is partly linked with the financial losses of his aunt, which he sees as the ruin of his own prospects. For most of the time, however, Dora herself, aided by Miss Mills and Jip and the guitar, preserve the fairy-tale decorums.

His relationship with Dora is a displacement, sexually intensifying the blockage vis-à-vis Agnes, and socially, too, diverting him from what Agnes represents. Uriah has the nerve to seize the combined sexual and career opportunity that most naturally offered itself — as Betsey and Micawber both can see — to David, who proudly scruples to seize it for himself. Uriah simply "is" the possibility David represses. Hence the irrational intensity of his reaction to Uriah's designs, the farce of his offering Uriah his bed in Buckingham Street, matched by Uriah's offering David the use of his room in Canterbury, David's old room! Full of speciously 'umble disclaimers himself, Uriah finds David's apparent unambitiousness quite incredible, and keeps close watch — "like a great vulture: gorging himself on every syllable that I said to Agnes, or Agnes said to me".[74] The rivalry is close to the surface in their first conversation, when they each say that the other will one day take over the Wickfield business. And Uriah is again surprised when it is not even David who causes the "explosion" by which Betsey, Wickfield and Agnes are released from his power. Hence, perhaps, the bad temper of David the narrator's otherwise irrelevant remarks on Micawber's verbosity here. His own dealings with Uriah have been so entirely dictated by unacknowledged jealousy, which he masks as graceful deference, that he is quite incapable of constructive action.

He has fought a losing battle throughout. Ostensibly he offered to teach Uriah Latin. Both of them knew that his easiest way of humiliating Uriah is by being seen to have the means to raise him up. So Uriah refused. As narrator again, David helplessly retaliated in tasteless jokes and lazy description in the account of Uriah's tea-party. Even after Uriah had explained how humility was dinned into him and his father at a foundation school, and into his mother "at a public, sort of charitable, establishment",[75] something David could note with interest as a Victorian social critic, and which also ought to have pleased him at a deeper level, as suggesting his own superiority, he was soon struggling again with his impulse to knock Uriah down. It was monstrous that a charity boy should have come so far — "I am very umble to the present moment, Master Copperfield, but I've got a little power!"[76]

On hearing of the charity school, David suddenly comprehends "what a base, unrelenting, and revengeful spirit, must have been engendered by this early, and this long, suppression".[77] What, then, of the effects of his own suppression, under Murdstone, under Creakle, in the warehouse? Uriah, as so often, understands. During Micawber's explosion they stand face to face, as David's irrational hatred of this "other" self comes to a crisis in his nightmare vision of Uriah's malice, insolence, hatred and lust. On his side, Uriah calls David names that can interchangeably be used of either of them: the scum of society before somebody had charity upon him, an upstart — Uriah has duly noted the early association with Micawber. They have always penetrated each other's fantasies of ambition and sexuality with sickening inwardness. When Aunt Betsey seems to be ruined, David "had dreams of poverty in all sorts of shapes. . . . [N]ow I was hopelessly endeavouring to get a licence to marry Dora, having nothing but one of Uriah Heep's gloves to offer in exchange".[78] Later Uriah forces to the surface David's nasty, long-smouldering suspicion of Annie, at which stage David, having fruitlessly denied his horrible complicity in Uriah's charge against her, finally loses control and strikes him. Whereupon Uriah clinches his supreme victory. Instead of hitting back, he lets David's guilt eat inwards; he puts him "on a slow fire, on which I lay tormented half the night". Uriah "knew me better than I knew myself".[79]

At a point such as this, and when his sense of *déjà vu* almost tells him what his projections are going to say next, David comes very close to them. They know him better than he knows himself. It is not that he has suddenly become different. He is exactly the same as he has always been: a typical enough specimen of early mid-Victorianism. Yet his perception of himself falters. His works and days are not the least bit changed, but transvalued, and in a way which can affect a reader's perception of him as well. Nothing can alter his sheer historicity — everything about him that now seems Victorian, distant, dead, boring. But when we apply that Modernist sense of human nature to which *Great Expectations* speaks so immediately, there is something a good bit more to him.

∽

The time was ripe for a Modernist rehabilitation of the Victorian David as long ago as 1979, when Harry Stone partly anticipated what I have been saying about Uriah and Steerforth. Stone was mainly concerned to illustrate what he called Dickens's aura of fairy-tale, doing so with great sensitivity and impressive scope, and so lodging a valuable objection to some critics' over-intellectualization of Dickens. Ultimately, however, he too made both David, Dickens, and Dickens's early readers seem mentally inflexible. After his work, the fairy-tale reading will always be one dimension of *David Copperfield*. Yet he forced too sharp — precisely too fairy-tale — a divide between, on the one hand, David and, on the other hand, the goblin Uriah that David (with less good luck) might have become and the wicked enchanter Steerforth who enacts David's fantasies in a vicious form. Uriah and Steerforth were thereby less integral to David than in a fully Modernist account, less pressing as Davidian hypotheses, and the Dickensian novel was reduced to a simpler and more archaic genre. What sociological and psychological realism Stone did see he described mainly as a safeguard against a fairy-tale plot's being discredited. About Micawber, who was perhaps *too* real for him, he said very little, and nothing at all about the relevance of Micawber's social and sexual trajectories for David. Since he also overlooked other projections as well, much of Dickens's most disconcerting honesty, as in so many other critics, was short-circuited — the homoerotic element, for instance, and the novel's own unease at its quiet close. Having divorced David from the evil, the disturbing, the unconventional, Stone seemed to imply that the resultant Manichaeism will finally give way in an all-out victory for the good, the reassuring, the conventional. He spoke of a final exorcism of Uriah's powers, after which David would be reborn.[80]

For the mediating critic now, such a radiant vision, coming as it does so close to David's own fantasies, will always be there as a possibility in the text and as part of what goes through a reader's mind. The book will never be anything other than Victorian, and it will be important not to let a later context of reading subvert Dickens's Victorian context of writing. Yet when the Victorianism is addressed within the more recent perspective, Uriah is also seen as *a part* of David — from the beginning, always, unexorcisably. It is just as Chesterton could already see in 1906: when the story's secrets are out, some other mystery still carries on.[81] Uriah is *not* exploded, but thrives in jail, together with Littimer, and encouraged by Creakle. On David's visit there, even he can see the ultimate futility of the merely physical restraints imposed by Victorian society. Uriah and Littimer — that quintessentialization of Steerforth — are permanent spiritual possibilities, as are also Rosa (imprisoned in the Steerforth home), Micawber (in Australia) and Murdstone (with his new wife). As David once said — unguardedly and honestly, in the middle of extolling earnestness — "[t]here is no such thing as fulfilment on this earth".[82] When he tries to check or banish the energies carried by his daemons, what fulfilment, what life, can he expect? The calm at the novel's close is a state of great pathos, the calm before another storm in David's life no less than in Dickens's own, a storm in which the caul will again be useless. For those sage women were right in their other prophecy as well: "I was destined to be unlucky in life".[83] On which the Modernist gloss will be that David's fate embodies a universal truth: the narrower and more restrictive our society or our own self-image, the more painfully disruptive will be our unconscious. The book can be seen as comic, not by offering a resoundingly harmonious resolution, but in the sense perceived by Santayana, who said that Dickens's characters enact an absolute comedy by revealing the reader's own secrets: "there *are* such people; we are such people ourselves in our true moments, in our veritable impulses".[84] *David Copperfield* is much closer to such savage farce, and to the corresponding tragedy, than Dickens's Victorian talk of enlisting hearty merriment and kindly sympathies could ever suggest.

Santayana was already engaging in the Modernist exposure of an unpleasantness which lurks under pleasant surfaces, a project which derived a good part of its impetus from the work of Marx, Freud, Jung, Adler and Lawrence. Nor was the vein of psychoanalytical commentary showing much sign of abatement towards the twentieth century's close. On the contrary, dissatisfaction with *David Copperfield*'s "official" account of itself, and especially in respect of Agnes, was in some quarters becoming even more acute. Iain Crawford, still judging Dickens by the criteria of Lawrence, for whom sex was so intensely serious, reprimanded him for creating Agnes as an intensely serious character in whom sexuality is quite absent.[85] For Arlene M. Jackson, Agnes was only to be understood as a male idealization: though David does not realize it, Agnes is his attempt to re-create the maternal comfort and protection of which he had had so little as a child.[86] And Virginia Carmichael, bringing the terminology into line with later authorities such as Lacan, saw the traditional opposition between Agnes and Dora as the splitting of the Imaginary between love (or abstraction) and sex (or death) respectively.[87]

From psychoanalytical commentary, moreover, the Modernist penchant for delving beneath pleasant appearances was carried over to sociological and ideological critique. Mary Poovey's account of Victorian gender constructions, for instance, suggested that David develops a kind of self-protection which enables him to separate his own actions from his responsibility for them. Some of Poovey's comments were very close to the spirit of my own Modernist commentary above. In a key statement, she says that by the end of the nineteenth century David's inner separation

> would be reified and the "other" of the self dignified as the unsconsious; in Dickens's novel, however, the rudimentary notion of some "unconscious part" cannot account for or accommodate the difference within David. In fact, these differences do not even remain within David but reappear outside him — as if the entire landscape of the novel were a series of mirrors, each of which reflects some "unconscious part" of David Copperfield. Thus Heep is David's selfishness, Steerforth his feckless sexuality . . ..[88]

But although a twentieth-century-style hunt for unpleasantness can certainly make a Victorian novel and its hero much more interesting, no reading is duly ethical unless it involves a human parity between the writer and the current reader, and between their two historical periods. The overdominance of the past leads to historical purism. The overdominance of the present can have various outcomes: an earlier writer will either be quite neglected; or become a ventriloquist's dummy for the current reader's own values; or be castigated for *not* sharing those values. When, on the other hand, a mediating critic tries to safeguard the dialogicality of true communication, the application of a here-and-now perspective to the there-and-then will also entail a re-assessment of the here-and-now. Evaluation will be bi-directional.

Passing judgement on Dickens and his contemporaries was something that many late-twentieth-century scholastics still made no bones about. Critics with sociological and ideological interests expressed disapproval of Victorian gender arrangements, for instance, by further elaborating on the unsatisfactoriness of Agnes, and by postulating insidious linkages between gender and literary authorship.[89] Gail Turley Houston suggested that David's writing is an attempt to dress up his own very masculine sensibility in a feminine or androgynous garb. Seen this way, he tries to pass himself off as just another unsuccessful writer, like Dr Strong and Mr Dick, ostensibly attributing what literary success he does have to Agnes, a female muse. In point of fact, said Houston, David has women — and readers as well for that matter — playing the part of mere copyist. By wielding a pen which Houston saw as phallic, he achieves the same kind of fame and fortune as the Inimitable himself, in a mode of writing whose immense power was seldom challenged until Elizabeth Barrett Browning, by exploring the relationship between the artist as *rara avis* and the artist as an economic agent, posed the question: "What about *women* artists, then?"[90] For Mary Poovey, too, Dickens or David's status as the representatively national writer, highly successful and powerfully masculine, blinded readers to the operations of gender bias. In addition, Poovey accused Dickens of an insensitivity to poverty and social injustice more generally. In her view, both David's sexuality and his acquisitiveness are concealed by his marriage to an angel of the hearth who, unlike Dora, is an efficient and non-alienated housekeeper, whose sexuality victimizes neither herself nor him.

The power exerted by male authors in the Victorian period was well worth examining. Poovey and Houston convincingly showed that Victorian society left a lot to be desired, and that Dickens apparently acquiesced in it. Yet for a mediating critic, the issues are by no means straightforward. How much of a choice did Dickens have exactly? And was his apparent acquiescence a mere callousness towards women and the poor? Or was it in effect the best way to help them? — a co-adaptation with Victorian norms of expression and behaviour by which the norms themselves could perhaps be changed. Were even the norms so totally unacceptable? Or did they, for their time and place, contain a grain of wisdom? Not to put too fine a point on it: Were the Victorians simply too benighted to engage us in real dialogue?[91] Or could we actually benefit from a reconsideration of Victorian insights, solutions and achievements? — by which I am *not* recommending a selective and distorting rehabilitation of Victorian values *à la* Thatcher.

As I tried to suggest in connection with *Dombey and Son*, readers steering clear of presentist arrogance can indeed recognize in Dickens a co-adaptation that is both of, and not of, his own time. He certainly compromises, but compromises to powerful effect, and in many a good cause. In *David Copperfield*, his account of sexual and social relations does not whole-heartedly endorse a bourgeois patriarchy, and I have already hinted how a Modernist interpretation can actually underline this. Thanks to the projection characters of Mr Wickfield and Micawber, the novel itself anticipates the twentieth-century criticisms of Agnes, just as the projection character of Rosa Dartle must throw in question any view of David as aggressively masculine and unambiguously heterosexual. As for Dora, she certainly disappoints David's conventional expectations as a husband. But it is those expectations themselves which emerge from the novel's pages with most shame. Dora was not even, in any twentieth century sense, a sex object, but a Dresden shepherdess: a decorative status symbol for the upwardly mobile man, as Uriah would also have known. Even the sexual attraction of Emily, though decidedly stronger, was intermixed with class feelings, and in a very English way. Here the incipient eroticism had been inseparable from the experience of subjecting, and of self-subjection to, a social inferior, a pattern which Dickens amplifies in his usual projective manner, by having the young gent Steerforth elope with her.

A balanced critique will also scrutinize any traces of grand narratives of liberation still remaining in our own time. Even if, to our own way of thinking, everybody nowadays were materially and ideologically better off, Dickens might well have found many aspects of our societies all too familiar, and in some respects could reasonably have preferred his own. The Modernistically psychoanalyzed David and Dickens are not more fascinating in themselves than for the light which their very Victorianness can shed on Modernism, and on Modernism's heirs. Just as David can become so intimate with his projections that he sees himself afresh, so he and his creator can become our own familiars. For us now, David and Dickens are projections of *our* shadow, and with an insinuation that is quite clear enough. If the Victorian persona tended to repress raw despotism, lust, greed, passion of every kind, what are we to think of an age which, understanding or misunderstanding Marx, Freud, Jung, Adler, Lawrence, publicly instated such ruthless instincts as humanity's very foundation? As a result, the psychological basis for Santayana's absolute savage comedy of exposure may actually have disappeared. Those particular secrets have been writ large as part of the modern persona. *David Copperfield*'s strong characters, in all their bizarre energy or deformity, have assumed the livingness, the contemporaneity, the irresistible rightness — to continue with Leavisian language — of something we recognize as our own formation by the central presuppositions of twentieth century culture. By the same token, another reason why David and Dickens can seem so boring, dead and distant is that we have *wanted* them to be that way. It was the possibility of Victorian virtues that the Modernists relegated most firmly to the shadow. For good reasons, needless to say — just as the Victorians had had good reasons for *their* shadow. After a long-drawn-out process of secularization, after Nietzsche, after Freud, after war of a new kind and on a new scale, it was easy to find the Victorians' official view of humanity rather sanguine. Yet even today, we are still in search of wisdom, peace, fulfilment. Not because the daemons are still struggling to get out. But partly because they got long ago, creating havoc ever since. Not because we have beautiful visions, like David's, which may be false. But because our visions are rather few and far between.

This is how the Victorians can get under our skin at the beginning of our new millennium. After Modernism, there can be no return to the Victorian denial of libido, with all that hypocrisy and shame and suffering. Yet how much do we enjoy our disillusioned *laissez-faire*? How much happiness does it guarantee? How much freedom from suffering? Sometimes, surely, we feel jaded. Without wishing to surrender anything we may have gained, we would not be incurious about possible new role models. To be inspired to act more responsibly would at least make a change. After which, the next step might well be altruism, a step which some people have always already taken, needless to say, and which, Matt Ridley now says roundly, comes much easier to our actual genetic programming than either scientists or Modernists once believed.[92] Virtue may well be natural.

For most of us, the Victorians are no longer parents — or grandparents or great-grandparents. Our rebelliousness is more naturally directed against the intervening generations, and particularly against the Modernist detractors of Victorianism. In appealing to "Victorian values", Margaret Thatcher and Ronald Reagan were presumably calculating that "Victorian" would now win votes. That many commentators found such politics an evil travesty of the Victorians suggests that the period was coming to be remembered much more fondly than before, as late-twentieth-century fashion, design and architecture also showed. There was a new concern that the Victorians be properly understood. By now, we are probably reaching the stage at which David Copperfield will become quite admirable again. In his own time's way he is rather narrow. But wordlessly, he reminds us of the twentieth century's diametrically opposite narrowness, and knows us better than we know ourselves. After Lytton Strachey on the most eminent Victorians, after Edmund Wilson on the two Scrooges, David can never be less sinful than the rest of us. But what is increasingly difficult to deny is his sincerity of purpose. His moments of generosity and tact, of spontaneous trusting loyalty, are even making him rather loveable. And as the last great twentieth-century taboo is finally giving way, the taboo against recognizing human goodness and achievement, how loveable that dangerous man, his maker!

Everything the Modernist emphasis suggests about Dickens can remain true, redeeming areas of his text we might otherwise find unattractively — yes, stuffily! —Victorian. It opens our minds to features which he and his contemporaries backed away from. But equally, if Dickens was always already a Modernist, he is always still a Victorian. Although the human mind can adapt to any culture, so that the most active minds of all can readily echo the past and prophesy the future, even the most flexible intelligence has a local and a temporal habitation, beside which the past and the future must figure as not only different, but as either more desirable or less so. To read Dickens for pain is to recognize much that is unpleasant about human life and human nature. It is a reading experience whose benefits can be measured on Trilling's scale of abrasiveness. Yet a mediating critic cannot entertain such a reading without, as it were, reading Dickens's own reading of Modernism. As a move in a process of appreciative mediation, a Modernist reading can suspend belief in pre-Modernist assumptions, yet only through an effort of conscious will, such that suspension is not really suspension. To take Dickens at all, we take him, at the very least, on his own terms. What happens when we also apply the Modernist perspective is that our mind is working, as so very often, in more than one way at once. On the one hand, we are are under no illusion that life will ever be completely free of suffering, injustice and violent irrationality. Nor can we imagine that such an illusion ever got much hold on Dickens. On the other hand, we share in a hopefulness which is necessary to life's very continuance, and which Dickens's own life and works pre-eminently encouraged and encourage.

Chapter 9

Fielding's reluctant naturalism

Of English writers, it is Shakespeare who is usually the first to be exposed to new trends in criticism, and then often Dickens. Even so, the time-lag between the gloomily Modernist Dickens and the gloomily Modernist Fielding was rather long. Edmund Wilson's essay, "Dickens: The Two Scrooges", was first published in 1941. C. J. Rawson's *Henry Fielding and the Augustan Ideal Under Stress* did not appear until 1972.[1]

What follows here may go some way to explain this, and one main point will be that the Modernist reading of Fielding can still be further developed. As in the case of *David Copperfield*, the Modernist expectation of unpleasure serves to enliven texts from an earlier historical period. Once again, though, a qualification is necessary, in the interests of an even-handed and enriching interchange between the dead-and-buried author and present-day readers. That Fielding is not, in the last analysis, a Modernist is definitive for the benefit he now offers.

The main emphasis of a Modernist reading must be on his naturalistic view of human nature and society, a view sustained throughout his writing career, and temperamentally akin to that of Hobbes or Freud. For Fielding, human beings are propelled by drives over which both individuals and society as a whole must try to win mastery, with however little success.

This way of putting it already implies the necessary qualification. Fielding's naturalism, though for much of the time he managed to channel it into comedy, was more than a little reluctant. He would have preferred to think better of human beings, and ultimately of the Providence which had brought them into existence and allowed them to continue. Sometimes more explicitly, sometimes by implication, his portrayal of life can be pretty disturbing. Yet he never quite lost his own hopes of a world of goodness and happiness, and he ministered to such wishes in readers as well. Even today, his communication can still draw us into a kind of community of the benevolent.

At first my stress on the fundamental continuity of Fielding's naturalistic insights, and on his no less lasting reluctance to accept their full implications, may sound like a relapse into old-fashioned author criticism. Foucault might have complained that such a Fielding is merely a readerly construction: that it serves to neutralize contradictions in the texts which bear the Fielding label, by claiming that their incompatible elements "relate to one another or . . . cohere around a fundamental and originating contradiction".[2] It so happens that late-twentieth-century critiques of Fielding's textuality increasingly adopted Foucauldian and other poststructuralist perspectives, so that an account of what he was basically like could indeed seem rather quaint. To the extent that *fin-de-siècle* approaches allowed any glimpse of the textuality's producer at all, an individualization they usually avoided as a matter of principle, they suggested that he was chameleonic.

Thanks to analyses by poststructuralists of a feminist persuasion, some of the hard and fast things that used to be said about him certainly no longer apply. In 1976 Katharine M. Rogers had still used the well-worn contrast with Richardson in order to stereotype Fielding as a stereotyper of women:

> While Richardson was a radical feminist, Fielding accepted the male chauvinism of his culture. Richardson responded to the new sensibility about women by probing traditional assumptions about male-female relationships: if a woman is not to be regarded as sexual prey, perhaps she exists as a human individual apart from her sexuality: if marriage is to be more than a mercenary contract for the propagation of lawful children, perhaps it could be a partnership between equals. Fielding on the other hand incorporated the new sensibility into the old system of male dominance, so that his views remain entirely conventional.[3]

This vein of commentary, albeit somewhat modulated, continued through the 1980s,[4] but was also increasingly challenged, not only by male critics, and not only by reference to the extraordinary letter in which Fielding confessed to Richardson his unstinting admiration of *Clarissa*.[5] Just as often, there was an appeal to Richardsonian qualities in Fielding's own *Amelia*,[6] the novel on which the present chapter will also focus. Margaret Lenta pointed out the anachronism in descriptions of Richardson as a radical feminist;[7] Carolyn Williams insisted on Fielding's own positive sympathy and admiration for women, including even the would-be learned ones, whose scholarly shortcomings he both teased and understood;[8] and Angela J. Smallwood rousingly argued that liberal humanist patriarchs, as she called them, have been mistaken in making such a sharp divide between Fielding and eighteenth-century feminists such as Mary Astell.[9] In Smallwood's account, the objects of Fielding's disapproval included: domestic tyranny by either sex; the bogus rhetoric of the male establishment; gender bias in the discussion of moral conduct; and the segregating polarization of sexual roles, roles which she said Fielding saw as culturally constructed.

From this last point it was only a short step to Jill Campbell's fully-fledged poststructuralist reading of the plays and novels from the point of view of gender and identity. Under the carefully chosen title, *Natural Masques*,[10] Campbell showed that Fielding's early plays and satires, though still assuming conventional associations of masculinity with order, power and money, and of femininity with either virtue or folly, are nevertheless much preoccupied with the semiotic slippages which arise from castrato singing, from male and female impersonation, and from masks and costume. Joseph Andrews, similarly, is associated, not only with castrato singers, but with female virtue, with hair reminiscent of Milton's Eve, and with female vulnerability in general. Even though he becomes more manly when reunited with Fanny and obliged to defend *her* chastity, and even though it is the Hervey-like Beau Didapper who represents male femininity later on, Joseph's reaction to Fanny's threatened deflowering is markedly unmanly, and his own womanly features — his resemblance to his mother, his attractive strawberry mark — continue to catch the eye. Not that Tom Jones is any *less* beautiful. And as for Charles the Pretender, Fielding takes his cue from real-life history. The Stuarts and their entire following — with the exception of professional pedagogues, whose thwacking of order into their young charges perhaps activates masculine signifiers to excess — strongly connote an alluring homoeroticism in tandem with petticoat government. To cap which confusion, Sophia is endowed with both the warrior spirit of the great Jacobite heroines and the more modest womanly graces preferred by pamphleteering Whigs.

In *Masquerade and Civilization*, a book whose title suggests its anticipation of Jill Campbell's, Terry Castle related Fielding to a wider fascination with semiotic shifts of both gender, class and race.[11] On the personal level, Castle saw the period's masquerades as a matter of infantile wish-fulfilment, or of sheer discontent with civilization. As a social phenomenon, she saw them as carnivalesque; they were spoken of as both a safety-valve and a threat. Certainly their masks and costumes were experienced as immensely liberating, by participants of both sexes, and from a broad spectrum of society. Correspondingly, the masquerades described in novels, not least in *Tom Jones* and *Amelia*, were in Castle's reading important turning points. Thanks to their "disguises", fundamental truths come paradoxically into focus, an *éclaircissement* which leads to a more rapid denouement.

Corroboration of the kaleidoscopic play of signifiers within and outwith Fielding's texts was even to be had from more straightforward historians. Where Jill Campbell traced the semiotics of gender, Brian McCrea suggested that the field of politics, so intimately transversed by gender in Campbell's account, would have been quite unstable enough without that complication.[12] As with sex, so with political parties, there was an accepted wisdom. Whigs were supposed to approve of Marlborough's wars, a standing army, the funds, a national debt, and the new monied men, and they were also expected to believe that self-interest could serve the general good. Tories, thought of as belonging to the landed classes and favouring a national isolationism without a burden of debt, were assumed to have a much grimmer view of human nature, which allegedly made them nostalgic about Elizabethan order. But just as an English duchess might find pleasure in attending a masquerade disguised as a black pageboy, so Whigs bought land, and Tories speculated on the Exchange. Fielding's plays, similarly, were always a confusing mixture of allegedly Whig optimism and allegedly Tory pessimism, more markedly Whig and Cibber-like when intended for Drury Lane, more markedly Tory and Scriblerian when for the Haymarket. Although his career as a playwright is often said to have come to an end because of his Scriblerian opposition to Walpole's government, he may have been only too glad to accept Walpole's money as a reward for obeying the licensing act, and again for not publishing the satire of him in *Jonathan Wild*. Still later, the first readers of *Amelia*, faced with its mixture of bleakly realistic satire and generous sentiment,[13] again sought explanations in terms of a transgression, whether from the supposedly Tory culture of pessimism to the supposedly Whig culture of optimism, or vice versa.

The movement of multifarious cultural signifiers through Fielding's pages was most comprehensively studied by Ian A. Bell.[14] The conclusion he drew was a poststructuralist one: that ideas of authorship and authority break down. Like Foucault, he saw the author function as less a matter of production than reception; it is the reader's way of imposing order on textuality. He also noted Stanley Fish's distinction between the "serious" man and the "rhetorical" man. The serious man believes in his own irreducible singleness of identity, which involves his secure place within a knowable universe, whereas the rhetorical man "manipulates or fabricates himself, simultaneously conceiving of and occupying the roles that become first possible and then mandatory given the social structure his rhetoric has put in place".[15] For Bell, Fielding was predominantly rhetorical in this postmodern sense, which meant that his textualities also confirm Bakhtin's view of the novel genre as a dialogization of various sociolectal and ideological options — the idea which is so fruitful for Dickens criticism as well. As with Dickens's textualities, so with Fielding's, the clash of different genres and voices could even create uncertainties as to the social formation of their most likely first readers. As Bell pointed out, Fielding sometimes seems to proceed under the auspices of traditional aristocratic patronage, taking for granted that his readers can live up to the corresponding levels of taste and erudition. At other times he doubts the continued viability of such a sophisticated culture, and writes in a way that is altogether more popular and topical. So arises an ambiguity of sociocultural orientation which can actually strain politeness. In *Tom Jones*, for instance, his authorial persona wavers between that of a despot who, despite a streak of benevolence, can wonder whether his readers deserve any freedom at all, and that of the keeper of a public ordinary who will do anything to satisfy the market. The same novel's dedication to George Lyttleton similarly preaches high moral standards with little apparent confidence that the message will be grasped.

Given such uncertainty as to where Fielding himself really stands, Bell sometimes carried de-authorization to the point at which textuality itself took on animacy and responsibility. He even produced sentences such as: "*Joseph Andrews* is ... a highly self-conscious book, fully aware of its own story-telling devices, conscious of its dialogic relation with other books."[16] Usually, though, he was less extreme, and although refraining from discussion of Fielding as an author, saw no difficulty in drawing on film studies for the term *auteur*. A film buff forms an impression of the *auteur* behind a considerable oeuvre after the event, as it were, and will assume that many of its features are merely generic, part of the general culture of the film industry, and resistant to individuality. Indeed, the *auteur* may be so conspicuously polyphonic that the oeuvre's association with a particular historical individual will be less than straightforward. Even so, such identifications will always be at least partly possible. To those in the know, films are recognizably the work of the particular film-makers responsible for them.

Bell's thinking here brings to mind Cheryl Walker's attempt to develop what she calls persona criticism, a criticism which will take account, not only of textual and psychic formations that are typical of the culture as a whole, but also of ideational patterns that are more personal — "persona" being at once impersonal *and* personal.[17] Another analogy would be with my Introduction's account (pp. 13–17) of *homo sapiens* as a social being who is nevertheless a social individual.[18] On all these kinds of account, Fielding, and any other writer have a social positionality which necessarily involves them in a polyvocal shifting of cultural signifiers, yet also have a certain relative and continuing autonomy.

As for his reluctant naturalism, it is ultimately not a matter of moving signifiers but of temperament and personal disposition: of optimism and pessimism, of states of mind and feeling which are quite untied to any particular social formation. From its first publication onwards, *Amelia* has puzzled readers precisely because the emotions it expresses do not respect tidy cultural boundaries. Tories are *not* necessarily gloomier than Whigs, and Fielding, though his views on polite civilization sometimes endorse the cheerful Shaftesburian benevolism associated with the Whigs, on the whole defies such expectations, just as he liberates many other signifieds from their usual signifiers as well. Both the strengths and the weaknesses of his writing stem from the fear and aversion aroused in him by human beings, and from the hope and desire they arouse in him, too. At times he seems to lean towards the values and sensibility commonly associated with the Tories, at other times towards those associated with the Whigs. Although the social aspect of his being certainly belongs to his own time, it is the oscillation *between* the two cultural formations that is most profoundly characteristic of him. The reluctant naturalism is gut knowledge.

Nay more: it is self-knowledge. Arthur Murphy's 1762 *Essay on the Life and Genius of Henry Fielding, Esq.* did not conceal Fielding's human weaknesses. Fielding came across as a man no less subject to animal drives than any character in his own novels. Seeking to qualify this picture, Wilbur L. Cross's biography of 1918[19] stressed his virtue and benevolence, perhaps a bit too much. Then in 1989 Martin Battestin brought both sides together, in a portrait[20] which admirably captures what is most individual in the social individual whose writings have come down to us.

On balance, then, Foucault would not be completely misguided. The reluctantly naturalistic Fielding is indeed a Fielding which has to be constructed during reading, sometimes as a way of reconciling textual contradictions. On the other hand, as a social formation this Fielding is far more volatile than the one described in traditional liberal humanist criticism. And structuralist decentrings of the self, when too rigidly deterministic, can also be very reductive. Human beings do project themselves into, and identify with, attitudes, styles and life-worlds that are culturally available. But these can be very varied and even self-contradictory. As an individual temperament, moreover, the Fielding to be described here most definitely does correspond to the historical Fielding, to whom, unless we are reading very narcissistically, we shall wish to come as close as possible. This is not, as Roland Barthes might have alleged, because we are more interested in biography than in the literary texts themselves,[21] but because the texts, though inseparable from their culture's intertextualities, and though strongly affected by the literary institution and the facts of communal transmission, have nevertheless come down to us as the work of a single named person. The act of writing is never completely determined by cultural norms. As a process of co-adaptation between the social and the individual, it always leaves scope for a personal imprint. Nor, in most cases, is it solipsistic. So as a genuine form of communication, it places its readers under the obligation to make an effort of empathy, which will sometimes turn out to their own advantage.

To earlier generations of critics Fielding's personal imprint was clear enough. And not only was the gloomily Modernist reading a long time coming. Some Modernist critics had no taste for him at all. Leavis, notoriously, excluded him from his great tradition of English novelists on the grounds that, to "a mind . . . demanding more than external action", he is superficial, i.e. totally deficient in "marked moral intensity".[22] But although Leavis was by no means original in this judgement, for many other twentieth-century readers and critics Fielding was a cardinal figure. They quite saw that he is inseparable from his period, a period which in their own time felt remote. But the same was true of Dickens and, no less than Dickens, Fielding was not merely a historical curiosity, but also — to borrow language from Leavis's praise of Donne — living and contemporary. Many readers have always read him "as we read the living".[23]

A process of appreciative mediation can begin by asking how this can be so. What is it that comes alive in his writing? In tackling this question, the next few sections are inevitably based on my own responses, but as correlated with those of other critics. For a start, here is something from *Jonathan Wild*.

In III 6, Wild the thief-taker, who is himself the leader of a gang of thieves and a receiver of stolen goods, reprimands his underling Fireblood for pocketing some of the booty from the Dover stage coach. Next, Wild composes his epistle to the adwhorable (*sic*) Laeticia, whom he hopes soon to marry. Then the following chapter, entitled "*Matters preliminary to the Marriage between Mr.* Jonathan Wild *and the chaste* Laeticia", goes on to tell how Fireblood, being entrusted with Wild's letter, discharged his embassy and was received by the lady. She said

> she was not angry with him, nay, she was sorry so pretty a young Man should be employed in such an Errand. She accompanied these Words with so tender

> an Accent and so wanton a Leer, that *Fireblood*, who was no backward Youth, began to take her by the Hand, and proceeded so warmly, that, to imitate his Actions with the Rapidity of our Narration, he in a few Minutes ravished this fair Creature, or at least would have ravished her, if she had not, by a timely Compliance, prevented him.[24]

This kind of thing is what many readers have thought of as vintage Fielding, and it is a Fielding of unbridled naturalism. The springs of human action are greed, a thirst for revenge, and sexual lust, and the narrative humorously seeks to "imitate" the style of such action, its own rumbustious gusto resonating at the very pitch of Fireblood and Letty. True, the concluding verbal play, like the chapter heading, alludes to a norm of chastity from which Letty conspicuously departs. True too, such animalism, Wild's no less than Letty and Fireblood's, is comic by its very limitations. In the larger context, every instance is "judged", both by being its own reward, by the contrast with the virtuous Heartfrees, and by the steady evolution of the plot towards Wild's final apotheosis on the scaffold. After all, the book is ostensibly preaching that unprincipled egotism is not worth the candle. But even so, Fielding's tone intimates a readiness to allow egotism its hour, and none too brief an hour at that. Rawson has probably not been alone in seeing the rather solemn preface in which Fielding spells out the moral message as an irrelevant afterthought.[25]

What the preface illustrates is Fielding's reluctance to face his own perception of life in all its naturalism. In *Joseph Andrews* and *Tom Jones* this same reluctance is sometimes more immediately apparent, but the rumbustiousness can also make a mockery of moral scruple, so resulting in a sly coyness about sex, for instance. Fielding will tell us that characters are indulging their appetites, and everything in the larger sweep of narration and characterization will invite us to relish this. Yet we shall find ourselves forestalled by an indelicate delicacy of euphemistic circumlocution which, sometimes leering, sometimes poker-faced, and never really concealing a thing, hints that what's afoot is work of naughtiness and all the more fascinating for that.

Unabashed sexuality can also be treated as in the famous passage about Mrs Waters at Upton:

> She could feast heartily at the Table of Love, without reflecting that some other already had been, or hereafter might be, feasted with the same Repast. A Sentiment which, if it deals but little in Refinement, deals however much in Substance; and is less capricious, and perhaps less ill-natured and selfish than the Desires of those Females who can be contented enough to abstain from the Possession of their Lovers, provided they are sufficiently satisfied that no one else possesses them.[26]

Empson described this as "a particularly massive bit of double irony".[27] By this he meant that Fielding first makes a criticism of Mrs Waters by one criterion, but then implies a criticism of that criterion by another criterion, leaving the two criteria suspended in mutual comment, and forcing readers to make up their own mind; Fielding brings his characters to judgement, and makes the reader one of the bench. As we shall see, this mode of interpretation was very typical of a particular phase of Fielding criticism. Yet the passage's opening metaphor can also be taken as a stylistic "imitation" of the fictional character's appetite, just like the swift narration of Letty's "ravishment". The more chaste norm is clearly implied, but the first sentence resonates at Mrs Waters's own pitch. In the second sentence the more refined criterion is made explicit, ostensibly out of deference to respectability and so as to set up the judicious kind of balance of which Empson spoke, but actually more insidiously, so that it can be demolished from the very outset. The demolition takes the form of a straightforward denunciation of female mean-spiritedness, and a sting in the tail whose irony is surely fiercely single.

To take another example, the object of Miss Bridget's passion is described as follows:

> His Shape and Limbs were indeed exactly proportioned, but so large, that they denoted the Strength rather of a Ploughman than any other. His Shoulders were broad, beyond all Size, and the Calves of his Legs larger than those of a common Chairman. In short, his whole Person wanted all that Elegance and Beauty, which is the very reverse of clumsy Strength, and which so agreeably sets off most of our fine Gentlemen; being partly owing to the high Blood of their Ancestors, *viz.* Blood made of rich Sauces and generous Wines, and partly to an early Town Education.[28]

There can be no mistaking the man's sheer thrust, and Fielding again starts backing squeamishly away. Once more, though, he concludes by taking a swipe at squeamishness itself, this time in what he sees as its male form. Here it is not so much mean as effete.

All this presupposes a very straightforward kind of characterization, largely in terms of human types and their dominant passions. In the absence of a generally accepted poetics of the novel, Fielding turned to Aristotle, who, though discussing characterization in terms of the ethical qualities ("character") and the mental and verbal activity ("thought") of the personages represented, saw both these categories as less important than the action. Authors should first sketch their fable in outline, and interpolate the individuality of their people afterwards. Aristotle's notion of individuality can nowadays seem limiting, and

his stipulation that a speech should be appropriate to the circumstances and
to the person speaking it later tended to endorse the neo-classical conception
of characterization by type. In phrases that readers tend to remember, Fielding
himself explains that "I describe not Men, but Manners; not an Individual, but
a Species. . . . [My] Lawyer is not only alive, but hath been so these 4000 years . . .
[even if he] hath not indeed confined himself to one Profession, one Religion,
or one Country." Satire "can hold the Glass to thousands in their Closets".[29]

Even his heroes and heroines are not at all complex, and another aspect
of the comic rumbustiousness is that everything turns out well for them. Or
rather, turns out well for all of them except Jonathan Wild, whose execution
is nevertheless a heartening piece of poetic justice. Whereas in *Tess of the
D'Urbervilles*, an important letter pushed under a door is bound to disappear
under the inner doormat, never to be seen by the intended recipient, in *Tom
Jones*, the heroine's lost purse is bound to be discovered by the hero, because he
will just happen to be coming that way.

Fielding knew exactly what he was doing, and sometimes openly teased
his readers' thirst for romance and fantasy, even hinting that his realism could
easily take off at a tangent and become legend. In Upton, "they talk, to this Day,
of the Beauty and lovely Behaviour of the charming *Sophia*, by the Name of
the *Somersetshire* angel".[30] He was also perfectly capable of perpetrating what
Aristotle mentioned as one of the fiction-writer's most serviceable fallacies: *x*
is historically true; therefore *y* must be true as well. In introducing Mrs White-
field, landlady of The Bell, Gloucester and sister-in-law to the famous Methodist, Fielding is tempting his reader to swallow some far less likely things as well.

Granted, he did endorse Aristotle's argument that fiction is more philosophical than real history. Instead of being limited to what actually happened,
which may not be typical of life in general, fiction can give an idea of what
would normally tend to happen, so that its truth is a matter of probability. But
even Aristotle could countenance a departure from probability, anticipating a
poetics such as that of Sidney or Johnson, which transforms the generalizing
"must" of probability into a deontic or didactic "must": fiction as a golden world
of poetic justice.

In such cases, Aristotle insisted that the improbability must be made even
more convincing than the probability. This Fielding often saw to, sometimes
with history itself lending a hand, as in the poetic justice of Wild's execution:
the notorious thief-taker Jonathan Wild really existed and really was executed.
Elsewhere Fielding's method is first to maximize the happy surprise, and then
to give a resoundingly naturalistic explanation. So Squire Western, whom

we last saw fox-hunting on his way back to Somerset, suddenly turns up in London, just in time to rescue Sophia from Lord Fellamar, and the next chapter is demonstratively headed "*By what Means the Squire came to discover his Daughter*".[31] Naturalistic psychology can even account for pleasantly surprising changes in character roles. Western is Tom's enemy only for as long as he fears that Tom is making a marital bid for his land which could not be backed up in kind. As soon as Providence has instated Tom in his rightful position and prospects (for which there is also a full explanation), Western's same territorial passion makes him Tom's veritable Pandarus.

In the first four novels, Fielding's naturalistic psychology, and the neoclassical characterization and comic plotting that go with it, are for the most part cheerfully unproblematic. Hugely amused at the achievements Richardson alleges for Pamela's conscious efforts of virtue, and disliking what he saw as her creator's voyeuristic sentimentality, he starts out by offering Shamela as a more likely paragon of scheming lust. This interpretation he upholds with comic rigour, so that the character becomes mechanical and absurd in her narrow directness. In her defencelessness against her own dominant drives, and in the comic unswervingness of their direction, she is the prototype for later Fielding characters, including some of the "goodies". Much of his fiction is on a line from *Everyman in his Humour* to Dickens's very wooden Mr Dombey, a line to which Sterne, mounting his people upon their hobby-horses, also belongs. Critical talk of types, stereotypes, caricatures, humours, is quite in order.

The joke in the first ten chapters of *Joseph Andrews* is that such downright probability seems to be shunned. Lady Booby is no less flabbergasted at the notion of male chastity than Mrs Modern in Fielding's play *The Modern Husband*. The reader seems expected to believe in Joseph's firm resistance to her charms, and to attribute this to the combined influence of his sister's much celebrated example and Parson Adams's sermons. As Jill Campbell puts it, some of the signifiers associated with Joseph here would normally signify femininity. The eleventh chapter, however, having opened with the observation that "he is a sagacious Reader who can see two Chapters before him",[32] recounts that Joseph was already in love with Fanny, which is announced as the reason why he left town so hurriedly on his dismissal and did not go to his parents' home or Pamela's. Tacitly, it also sheds light on his recent resistance to Lady Booby, just as in *The Modern Husband* the wayward Bellamant's genuine devotion to his wife accounts for the chaste protestations Mrs Modern finds so strange. Char-

acteristically for Fielding, then, the surprise is naturalistically explained afterwards. Henceforth, Joseph is more obviously at the mercy of passion, as is the
lovely Fanny herself, who, unaccompanied, braves the London road in her rush
to his assistance. The picaresque journeyings structure the plot only second-
arily, the *primus motor* being a love whose erotic force is steadily intensified.
Key scenes are those where Joseph bears Fanny downhill in his arms, urges
Adams to suspend his scruples against marrying them at once, and is thwarted
by the news that Fanny is his sister. The incest taboo, ultimate restraint and
spur, makes for the suspenseful peripeteia, with Adams's sublime remarks on
platonic love and the non-existence of worldly pleasure, shortly followed by the
simpering withdrawal of the newly-wed Pamela and her husband for a rather
early night. When Joseph and Fanny's orgasmic release finally arrives, an "exquisite Repast" delayed until the penultimate page,[33] they end as they began: lovers
to the almost total exclusion of other traits.

Betty the chambermaid, Slipslop, Pamela and Lady Booby are propelled by
what in Fielding is always a closely analogous passion. To Joseph and Fanny he
would doubtless have applied the lines by Pope:

> As fruits ungrateful to the planter's care
> On savage stocks inserted learn to bear;
> The surest Virtues thus from Passions shoot,
> Wild Nature's vigor working at the root.[34]

(Compare, in *Tom Jones*: "this Love for which I am an Advocate, though it sat-
isfies itself in a much more delicate Manner, doth nevertheless seek its own
Satisfaction as much as the grossest of all our Appetites".)[35] In these other characters in *Joseph Andrews*, wild Nature is governed by no such restraints as the
situation imposes on the hero and heroine. Despite struggles with reason and
honour, struggles whose echo of Restoration tragedy is usually mock-heroic in
Fielding, nature remains wild indeed. The motivation is again purely naturalistic and comically clear.

The same is true of Parson Adams in a more complicated way, because he
is driven, not by one impulse but two. First, he is *passionately* Christian: his
goodness and lovableness are not the fruit of his very active mind. On the contrary, his very active mind largely feeds that pugnacious vanity which is his
second impulse. The comedy arises from his supreme lack of self-criticism in
Christianity and vanity alike. His passionate love of truth makes him tell the
magistrate that there are insufficient grounds for his own release from custody,
and he rages when he cannot find "a Sermon, which he thought his Master-

piece, against Vanity".[36] His relentless pride of intellect regularly disrupts social harmony — as in his quarrel with the generous landlord about book-learning versus experience —, and his intelligence is often open to question — as in his discomfiture at the hands of a young squire educated by a master at home, just after Adams's own fervent advocacy of such arrangements. He is the comic version of impulse in its most extreme form, and ultimately strains credibility. Our surprise is not at an Aristotelian wit in the plotting — not at the improbable demonstrating itself to be probable — but at the way Adams is for ever bouncing back to do exactly what we most expect of him. In him, reason and passion simply have no commerce with each other, so that human nature seems merely absurd. While we do know what to expect, moreover, and while it is what we can expect from an Adams, the absurdity is kept within the realm of comedy. The writing is boldly benign.

The drives that begin to be suggested in *Jonathan Wild* are more disturbing. Rawson pointed to Fielding's fascination with Suetonius and to his talk of "great tragical Farces in which one Half of Mankind was with much Humour put to Death and Tortures, for the Diversion of the other half".[37] Aurélien Digeon argued that Fielding is not only satirizing Walpole, but humanity at large. He

> probes deep down into our souls and there, like Swift, stirs up certain beliefs which we neither dare nor desire to disturb .... The concepts of honour, virtue, and social distinctions are roughly handled. Judged as dangerous by those who believe in "necessary prejudices", it may also shock those who accept them without believing in them, or who deem it imprudent to destroy them. Like Pascal's, his doubt sometimes leads us into depths which terrify the ordinary swimmer.[38]

On the other hand, there is no sense in which Wild is the archetype of all humankind, and he is judged within a moral framework that is fully articulated and endorsed. This may only make his fantastic playfulness and insidious attractiveness more intense. But in the end Fielding does not *fear* Wild, and consequently cannot fear humanity on his account. We laugh *at* Wild, not *with* him, and his wooing of the adwhorable Laeticia is a blithe parody of Fielding's usual courtship narratives. As a bailiff's daughter, she is certainly above him, and may well help him in his career. In Fielding, this much is commonplace. Quite extraordinary is the total lack of understanding between them: Laeticia is completely unconcerned about Wild's true character, and his attempts to read hers are very wide of the mark. His consuming passion is in any case for self-aggrandisement, and his success in love, as in all his pleasures, is minimal.

His blockheaded blindness to the deceit of other people regularly hoists him with his own petard, so that he is an automaton of evil not more menacing than preposterous. The unreflecting monomania with which he liquidates Fierce is certainly creepy. But the animal panic of his own plunge into the briny is the cretinous sublime. His only strength, and special weakness, is to reduce everybody to his own level. In Mrs Heartfree's hospitality he leeringly reads lubriciousness, and he thinks he can tempt her husband into crime. His exposition of different styles of hat as the politicians' way of hoodwinking the public into assuming real differences between their wearers represents a cynicism that is at once ingenious and humanly limiting. Coleridge said this speech "surpasses, short as it is, *Lilliput* or the *Tale of the Tub*".[39] Dramatically, though, the cynicism is Wild's, not Fielding's. Biting though the political satire is, the book has an unshakable comic buoyancy.

By the same token the Heartfrees have not a single moral struggle. Their virtue is instinctive and their mere passivity rides out every storm, with Providence and the clichés of romance doing sterling service. The lady's wifely treasure is preserved by tempests, rivalry among suitors, and noble savages. Even if this is a parody of popular genres, and the couple's bourgeois virtue rather boring to their maker, their deserving goodness is constantly asserted, and there is a riot of public acclamation to welcome the remarkable but historical poetic justice of the close. The falling-off of friends and prevarication of creditors do anticipate *Amelia*. But Fielding quickly whisks us from the brink.

Tom Jones leaves even less doubt. Fielding's naturalism is absolutely clear, but the tragic implications are, magnificently, not drawn out. There is the same unquestioning confidence in motivation by passion as in *Joseph Andrews*. But also as in *Joseph Andrews*, the passions displayed are mostly not dangerous, and the absurdity of their rule is delightful. Western, like Adams, has two passions, yet although they conflict with each other we know which one will win in the end: he greatly loves his daughter, but he loves his land much more, and all its pleasures. Where the natural is so often identical with the absurd, nothing is more natural than that Western should temporarily give up the pursuit of Sophia for the pursuit of a fox. As for Sophia and Tom, like Fanny and Joseph they are primarily lovers, and the sexuality, though delicate, is strong — when he catches her from her horse, when blood springs "from the lovely Arm of *Sophia*",[40] when Honour reports the whiteness of his skin, or when he fetishistically romanticises her muff and saddle. The opposition to their love is perhaps more serious than that confronted by Joseph and Fanny. The incest threat here is almost of Jones's own making, and they are tested, not by circumstances and third parties, but from within: Jones, like Mr Wilson in *Joseph Andrews* and Captain Booth in *Amelia*, has fine reasons of conscience for restraining himself, as has Sophia in her duty to her father. Even so, the psychology of their struggle is basically the same as Lady Booby's, and Fielding has been well praised for his gently ironical touch when Sophia is most martyr-like.[41] Thanks to "those secret spontaneous Emotions of the Soul, to which the Reason is often a Stranger", Sophia has "no great Horror at the Thoughts of being overtaken by" Jones.[42] Jones, similarly, on finding Sophia's purse, has a moment of truth no less startling than Western's on hearing the music of the hounds: he becomes "totally intent on pursuing *Sophia* without entertaining one [further] Thought" of the Jacobite rebels.[43]

Rational morality seems to figure most prominently as repentance after the event. Sophia may be prudent in a larger sense — "wise as serpents and harmless as doves" (*Matthew* 10: 16) —, but this is innate and very unusual, hardly to be acquired. On the lips of sister Western and Mr Allworthy, the word "prudence" is a mockery: on hers, because she illustrates its narrow sense of guile; on his, because all his worthiness will never make him wise. As for Jones, he is just as rashly impulsive as Adams, his friendly generosity and animal spirits always getting the better of him. Any suggestion of a reformation Fielding strongly undercuts. With his love of Sophia frustrated, Tom cannot be unsusceptible to a Mrs Waters. With his love rewarded, he can only be unwisely merciful towards the exposed Blifil. No less than Blifil's evil, Tom's ebullience will always take the line of least resistance, and the apparent exceptions merely prove the rule. His refusal of Mrs Arabella Hunt fed his comical vanity, and in fixing up the Nightingale marriage he was indulging his benevolence in an orgy of self-admiration — he particularly loves sermonising. Fielding here would agree with Booth in *Amelia*: "[A]s Men appeared to me to act entirely from their Passions, their Actions could have neither Merit nor Demerit".[44] Even virtuous love, as in *Joseph Andrews*, contains an element of lust, wild Nature feeding at the root. But Fielding is not in the least upset about this. It is, precisely, natural, and that is that.

Nor, in the first four novels, does the naturalistic psychology have disturbing implications for society as a whole. Not that Fielding was uninterested in society. His social concerns entered into all his thinking, and he even had ideas about sociolinguistics. As shown by Glenn W. Hatfield, he thought that social corruption was very much bound up with a decline in language.[45] Although suspicious of authoritarian programmes for linguistic reform, believing like Locke or our present-day pragmaticists that meanings are affected by usage, he nevertheless thought that those meanings which *can* be regarded as socially contracted should be carefully respected. Abstract words, representing thought at its highest pitch, thought at its furthest remove from objectifiable physical phenomena, called for special care, and not in philosophical debate only, but in everyday talk: it is through abstract words that we express social and moral values. But the irrationally passionate element in our language use is very insidious, and Fielding even doubted the reasonableness and responsibility of the 1689 Settlement. Wherever he turned, he saw interest, opportunism, enthusiasm, all buttressed by the euphemistic use of abstract words — in the literary world, in politics, in polite society, in the professions. Hatfield illustrated this from the entire range of his journalism, so that the sociolinguistic critique emerges as a constant, not much less central in earlier life than later on. In *Tom Jones*, too, a persistent irony shows up the emptiness of abstract words in honorific uses — "love", "merit", "virtue", "modesty", "breeding", "honour", "prudence". Time and time again, speakers' naturalistic drives are twisting language, and Hatfield also saw the novel's action as offering examples towards a more positive re-definition of terms. Such a project, however, implied a meliorism that is a good deal more hopeful than anything in the journalism. *Tom Jones* is a comic novel, and its picture of society fairly cheerful.

Although social corruption calls attention to itself, it is not perceived as structural, so that radical reform is quite uncalled for. Few readers have agreed with Arnold Kettle that Tom and Sophia are "rebels revolting against the respectably accepted domestic standards of the eighteenth century", or with Kettle's claim that this conventional society is represented by Blifil.[46] Tom does not act out of rebelliousness but love. When his love would urge him to woo Sophia against her father's wishes, he even tries to restrain himself. At some points he is certainly less prudent than Allworthy, at others more instinctively wise, and he does for a time lose Allworthy's favour. But at the end of the novel he is firmly brought back to where he and Allworthy both belong, in a large club of *viri boni*, a club of which even Lord Fellamar is a member when not led astray by Lady Bellaston. Although Tom's sins — whether in his liaison with Lady Bellaston or in his readiness, like Fellamar, for a duel — are not peculiar to him, they are encouraged by only a certain section of society, and Fielding's social criticism is not all that sweeping. Sophia, too, is emphatically not a rebel. Received opinion was not only that a daughter should not marry without parental consent, but that a parent should not force a daughter to marry against her liking.[47] Sophia takes a stand, not on marrying Tom, but on *not* marrying Blifil. So both she and Tom endorse their society's values, and it is precisely Blifil who does not. Blifil distinguishes himself as somebody whom everyone, *ceteris paribus*, will loathe, from Sophia to Allworthy to Western to Lady Bellaston herself. Tom's generosity towards Blifil at the end is depicted as the first instance of his new follies. Throughout, the cause of unhappiness has not been society at large but just this one diseased individual.

In both *Joseph Andrews* and *Tom Jones*, society at large could scarcely be more healthy. In the former, Barnabas is outraged at Wesley's attack on the luxury of the clergy, Slipslop is aware of subtle distinctions between the high and the low, Peter Pounce represents a new class of landowner, and the moral education of girls makes them dread what they most desire: a husband. Social detail, in other words, is certainly well rendered. But in the essential plot, society is neither determinant, victim, nor judge. The establishment is conceived as far too sound and stable to provide a genuine impetus to story, and Lawyer Scout, for instance, is only a local blemish on a magnificent system. In *Tom Jones*, and from the death of Captain Blifil onwards, the poetic justice is *ad hominem*, and a wider doomsday quite out of the question. Fielding is at pains to emphasize that the army and the upper classes are not as corrupt as the cases of Northerton and Lady Bellaston might suggest. Nor, as noted, is even Lord Fellamar really evil. That is why the masquerade suggests little more than the sheer boredom of high life, being mainly a colourful incident in Jones's own adventures, whose limited perspective is largely preserved. To much the same effect, although a countryside presided over by Justices such as Western will never be idyllic, Western is somewhat checked by the two informations exhibited against him in the King's Bench, and there is also the occasional Justice Allworthy, whose record shows how goodness itself can err. As for the Romany utopia, Ian A. Bell pointed out that Fielding on the one hand admires the Gypsy king's absolutist rule over a community whose members are still regulated by a sense of shame, but on the other hand dislikes the absolutism of the Jacobites.[48] At least for the time being, perhaps he even sees a certain irresponsibility and disorder as a fair price to pay for the Hanoverian alternative. Despite a fair amount of scholarly explication,[49] the Gypsy episode's net effect, in terms of either political philosophy or social critique, seems to be plus minus nothing. Like Mrs Heartfree's fantastic adventures in *Jonathan Wild*, it can easily be read just for entertainment.

The lack of radicalism is merely what one would expect from Fielding's social engagement outside his fiction. Just as *Tom Jones* XI.9 unironically distinguishes between those who enjoy and those who furnish the blessings of life, so *An Enquiry into the Causes of the Late Increase of Robbers* and *A Proposal for Making an Effectual Provision for the Poor* speak of society's stratification into the ranks of the nobility and gentry on the one hand and, on the other hand, the commonality. The higher ranks of men have traditionally had duties so arduous and full care that the labours of the lower orders seem by comparison enjoyable, light, and peaceful. The commonality should be content with their vassalage.

> To be born for no other Purpose than to consume the Fruits of the Earth is the Privilege (if it may be really called a Privilege) of very few. The greater Part of Mankind must sweat hard to produce them, or Society will no longer answer the Purposes for which it was ordained. *Six Days shalt thou labour*, was the positive Command of God in His own Republic . . ..

> Pleasure always hath been, and always will be, the principal Business of Persons of Fashion and Fortune, and more especially of the Ladies, for whom I have infinitely too great an Honour and Respect to rob them of any their least Amusement. Let them have their Plays, Operas, and Oratorios, their Masquerades and Ridottos; their Assemblies, Drums, Routs, Riots, and Hurricanes; their *Ranelagh* and *Vauxhall*; their *Bath, Tunbridge, Bristol, Scarborough*, and *Cheltenham*; and let them have their Beaus and Danglers to attend them at all these; it is the only Use for which such Beaus are fit; and I have seen, in the Course of my Life, that it is the only one to which by sensible Women they are applied.

> In Diversions, as in many other Particulars, the upper Part of Life is distinguished from the Lower. Let the Great therefore answer for the Employment of their Time, to themselves, or to their spiritual Governors. The Society will receive some temporal Advantage from their Luxury. The more Toys which Children of all Ages consume, the brisker will be the Circulation of Money, and the greater the Increase of Trade.

In fact, says Fielding, the only business of the politicians is "to prevent the Contagion from spreading to the useful Part of Mankind."[50] The root of social evils lies in the new wealth of the trading classes, resulting in the downward spread of upper class luxury and vice. Fielding's proposed remedies have little to do with reforming the upper classes themselves, and nothing at all to do with abolishing them. His main hope is in the tightening up of the law against offenders, which is where his naturalism again emerges strongly. Society must preserve itself, not by processes of self-cleansing and re-structuring, but by exploiting human beings' craven fear of punishment.

In his fiction, Fielding is correspondingly uncomfortable with characters who are socially dynamic. Especially in the first four novels, society, like human typology itself, is basically stable, or Fielding would like it to be so. Ian Watt duly noticed this as one of the chief differences between Fielding and Richardson or Defoe, and it provides a textbook example of how literary neoclassicism can correlate with upper-class ideology.[51] Tom does not *rise*. Rather, the plot unravels the secret of his birth, the ground of his natural gentility. The same is true of Joseph, who, even though he thinks himself Pamela's brother, has none of her Puritan eagerness to make virtue the passport to social betterment. Fielding's conception of manners may well be more humane than Chesterfield's, for he thinks that manners should be deeply rooted in morals and in a concern for other people.[52] Yet like Chesterfield, he has more than a dash of patrician hauteur. He can risk a laugh at the expense of Joseph, who is of gentle birth despite his menial function. But faced with the successful merchant Mr Heartfree he is solemnly sentimental, and sometimes cannot resist the temptation to make Heartfree a bit stupid in his virtuous vulnerability.

Jonathan Wild does begin to be more disturbing. It does depict a society riddled from top to bottom with callous greed, lust and deception. Friend cheats friend; husbands' advancement is secured by wives' adulteries; to become a judge or a bishop is the reward for bribery and flattery; and professed differences of political or religious principle are like so many hats to convince the vulgar that their rapscallion wearers are enemies, when they are actually fellow-plunderers. But as noted earlier, the exposition of the hats is dramatically Wild's own exposition, not Fielding's, whose cynicism does not yet have Wild's full scope. Rather, the book's running irony consistently makes cynicism seem a form of spiritual impoverishment, to be humorously relished for its self-punishing monomania. As in Fielding's stage comedies, the writing actually has a certain élan. While showing much of the seamier sides of life, it is not realist or condemnatory in the fullest sense, and the analogies between Fielding's Wild and the historical Wild or Robert Walpole are light-hearted enough. Even if, in the Wild phenomenon, society itself plays a clear role as part cause, part victim, and sole punisher, the very completeness and appropriateness of the punishment again attributes to society a fundamental stability and rightness. The evil of Wild is specific to the individual, like Blifil's, and here it is something which society easily expels from within its midst.

So much, then, for Fielding's naturalistic psychology, neoclassical characterization and comic plotting as remembered by enthusiastic readers, and so much for the unproblematic human and social comedy of the first four novels. In passing, however, I have already infiltrated a number of scholars and critics into the discussion. And now it is time to face the great Fielding controversy head-on, with all its extremes of disapproval and approval.

One of the first to disapprove was Lady Mary Mortley Montagu, who said that Fielding's happy endings "encourage young people to hope for impossible events to draw them out of the misery they chuse to plunge themselves into".[53] Other contemporaries accused Fielding of blatant immorality, Dr Johnson agreeing with Richardson that "the virtues of Fielding's heroes were the vices of a truly good man".[54] In the nineteenth century, even readers not indisposed to Fielding's subject-matter could be nervous about his tone. Thackeray described Jones as "an ordinary young fellow, ruddy-cheeked, broad-shouldered, and fond of wine and pleasure. He would not rob a church, but that is all." In which, said Thackeray, there is nothing surprising, and nothing that might not be dealt with in a novel. But to admire it so blatantly! There's the rub.[55] In the twentieth century, André Gide complained of a sheer antipathy to sanctity in Fielding; Fielding suggests that all striving towards perfection is motivated by pride, and achieved only by a loss of humanity.[56]

In many critics these kinds of disapproval went hand in hand with accusations of superficiality. Leavis's remarks belong to a long tradition of commentary, which in a way takes its cue from Fielding's own Aristotelian comments on his character types. According to Johnson, whereas Richardson has characters of nature, requiring the observer to "dive into the recesses of the human heart", Fielding's are characters of manners, entertaining but superficial — it is the difference between "a man who knew how a watch was made, and a man who could tell the hour by looking on the dial-plate".[57] Later critics elaborated the charge: in Fielding there is no "mysterious penumbra enveloping human action and human life"; Tom does not "take root in our imagination as an individual"; Tom's love for Sophia is not "felt from within as a unique experience";[58] Fielding's characters are hardly characters at all but mediaeval humours;[59] they are external, because of the demands of the plot; and the plot has more to do with manners and decorum than with either social dynamism, spiritual development or human relationships.[60] A fair number of critics evidently preferred novels that are more Puritan in seriousness, and perhaps also more tragic, novels which confront their characters with moral choices more momentous, which regard sexual relations as more profoundly significant, and which advertise more openly their exploration of character: novels, in other words, as written by Richardson or Lawrence.[61]

On any direct line from Richardson to Lawrence the Fielding of *Shamela*, *Joseph Andrews*, *Jonathan Wild*, and *Tom Jones* has no obvious place, which has won him some firm champions. Boswell said that Fielding does not encourage a "strained and rarely possible virtue", but does favour honour, honesty, benevolence and generosity. "He who is as good as Fielding will make him, is an amiable member of society".[62] For Coleridge, too, Fielding was charming. "To take him after Richardson is like emerging from a sick room heated by stoves into an open lawn on a breezy day in May".[63] Chesterton suggested that those who shy away from Fielding's realism only do so because they have lost faith in a limitless goodness existing *outside* humanity; consequently everything bad *in* humanity seems to leave goodness even less room; Fielding, however, merely gives us human nature as it really is.[64]

Gradually, though, the defence of Fielding became more solemn. At work here was a positive response to the biographical rehabilitation attempted by Wilbur C. Cross in 1918, together with a fuller understanding of Fielding's social concerns, in particular the magnitude of his achievement as a magistrate and reformer. Hardly less important were changing fashions in literary criticism itself. In the hey-day of New Criticism, Empson was not the only commentator to pore over ambiguities and ironies, and what emerged from them was sometimes felt to be profound thought. From the late fifties to the mid-seventies, many critics more or less assumed that Fielding's main aim as a novelist was to preach, and the early work of Martin C. Battestin — forty years prior to the beautifully judged balance of his *Henry Fielding: A Life* (1989) — offered a guide to the modified Pelagian and ameliorationist doctrines of latitudinarian divines such as Isaac Barrow, John Tillotson, Samuel Clarke, and Benjamin Hoadly. In their writings, said Battestin, "we may look for the sources of . . . [Fielding's] didacticism".[65] Hazlitt had complained that some readers' squeamish responses to Fielding were more "owing to an affectation of gentility than to a disgust at vice".[66] By 1960, Battestin and others[67] were turning Fielding into the sort of writer who could safely have been put into the hands of a young lady a hundred years earlier. Whereas Dickens, whom the Victorian Young Person had read with innocent delight, was described by Edmund Wilson and Lionel Trilling as a psyche of horrendous depths and darknesses, here was a group of critics turning Fielding into an Isaac Barrow *manqué*. Hence that strange delay of a disturbingly Modernist approach to his work.

All the same, there *was* a reaction, beginning with a number of neo-Aristotelian critics from Chicago. Their keynote was set by R. S. Crane's famous analysis of *Tom Jones*, according to which the book's religious and moral issues are blissfully uncomplicated, their relevance being purely secondary, within a design that is not philosophical or didactic but affective. The action is comic because: painful things happen to a man whose fundamental goodness we readily grant; yet the evil opposing him is not such a serious threat as to prevent his continued escapes; and we can easily see that his own blunders are partly to blame for his difficulties. As we read, said Crane, we do not desire his permanent humiliation, but neither can we take him very seriously.[68] All of which was in line with another Chicagoan's more general onslaught on the seriousness of mid-century novel criticism. Whereas many Modernist critics were praising Jamesian novels of dramatic presentation for placing readers themselves in the midst of moral complexities and ambiguities, Wayne C. Booth redirected attention to novels of "old-fashioned", intrusively omniscient narration, whose clear moral signposting he regarded as more responsible.[69]

It so happened that Henry James himself had discussed the comedy of Tom's "bewilderment", and praised Fielding's own very ample mind for charging Tom's shallowness with life.[70] This hint, quite lost on Leavis, was amply suggestive to Crane and Booth, and in due course bore fruit in a number of studies of Fielding's comic assumptions and narrator-reader relations. A certain amount of fairly technical narratology was involved here. But once the narratology was off their chests, such critics delighted in puncturing other critics' pomposity. Arthur Sherbo lambasted Mark Spilka for saying that during the bedroom-farce climax of *Joseph Andrews* the naked Parson Adams is intended as an all-resolving symbol of innocent virtue.[71] Other Chicagoans spelled the same message more generally: the nearest Fielding's festivities ever came to a moral centre was in the irresponsible exuberance of Jones, Partridge or Western.[72] Here, in other words, we are close to the Fielding emulated by Kingsley Amis, and the Fielding upheld by John Osborne and Tony Richardson's film of *Tom Jones*. Descriptively, Battestin's critique of the film was perfectly accurate: it has little seriousness of moral or providential concern, and Tom never matures. He has sexual prowess, simply, with a good heart and no hypocrisy.[73]

From Johnson's or Leavis's or Battestin's point of view, the Chicagoan rediscoverers of Fielding's comedy would have seemed shallow-minded. But for a twenty-first century critic attempting positive mediation, they do have a point. The fact remains that, for many readers, Fielding's story-telling has life, and whets their appetite for more. Readers are actually at Fielding's mercy here, and he doubtless banked on this. After all, he often makes vicarious participation in narrative an amusing part of his subject-matter. Partridge's repetition of Quixote's

bizarre confusion of stage and world, and Adams's lip-smacking delight in the
histories of Leonora and Mr Wilson are among his most loving touches, and he
would hardly share E.M. Forster's Modernist scorn for the "gaping audience of
cavemen or … [the] tyrannical sultan or … their modern descendant the movie-
public", who only ask "And then?"[74] Not that good breeding and an educated
mind are unfastidious. Readers longing to know the story of the bare-bosomed
woman Jones rescues from the murderous clutches of Northerton find themselves suddenly contrasted with her saviour, who was too polite to press enquir-
ies even after being lured into bed by her. But the stories do get told, and the logic
of situation can even hint that curiosity is close to common sense. *If* Jones had
got a bit more information out of Mrs Waters, his relationship with her, which for
all he knew was as incestuous as later developments at one stage suggest, might
have gone no further. A danger might have been avoided — the danger from
dubious associations, on which he has just been lecturing the Man of the Hill!

Nor is this all. Although Fielding is more tolerant than Forster of the "And
then?" in our response, he would never challenge Forster's claim that, at best, our
curiosity does extend to other questions: to the underlying human motivation
— in Johnson's metaphor, "What makes these people tick?" The actions in a story
can speak louder than words, and silences can speak loudest of all. Fielding is
fascinated by the way people telling their own life-stories actually respond to the
curiosity of their tellers. Usually, they tell their tale with a significant omission.
What they leave out is the one thing needed to make sense of it. Sophia and her
cousin Fitzpatrick are each dying to know how the other came to be on the road,
and each pledges to tell. Yet Sophia does so without a word of Tom Jones, and Mrs
Fitzpatrick without fully explaining the role of the peer, though by the time they
arrive in London Sophia has drawn her own conclusions. Mrs Fitzpatrick actually speaks this highly articulate novel's only two passages of disrupted syntax,
at the points where her omission particularly strains credibility —

> "When a Husband, therefore, ceases to be the Object of this Passion [love], it
> is most probable some other Man — I say, my dear, if your Husband grows
> indifferent to you — if you once come to despise him — I say, — that is, — if
> you have the Passion of Love in you — Lud! I have bewildered myself so, —
> but one is apt, in these abstracted Considerations, to lose the Concatenation
> of Ideas, as Mr. *Locke* says. — In short, the Truth is — In short, I scarce know
> what it is; but, as I was saying, my Husband returned …"[75]

> "— I — at a Time when I began to give Way to the utmost Despair — every
> Thing would be excusable at such a Time — at that very Time I received — But
> it would take up an Hour to tell you all Particulars. — In one Word, then, (for I

will not tire you with Circumstances), Gold, the common Key to all Padlocks, opened my Door, and set me at Liberty"[76]

— and Sophia is no stupid listener. As for Jones, his account of himself to Mrs Miller leaves out Sophia, and to Dowling he did not show matters "in the most disadvantageous Light: For though he was unwilling to cast any Blame on his former Friend and Patron [Mr Allworthy], yet he was not very desirous of heaping too much upon himself".[77] As we shall see, the implications of such discretion or self-whitewashing are vastly extended in *Amelia*, where the presentation is more Jamesianly dramatic. Much of its story is deviously narrated by the characters themselves, so that readers remain as benighted as other characters within the novel, guessing, simply, from their own sense of human nature.

The fact that characters are so tantalizing is an essential aspect of their lifelikeness for the reader, something reinforced by what seems to be Fielding's own strong sense of their human actuality. Henry James was right. Fielding *is* "handsomely possessed of a mind".[78] Without any Richardsonian peeping and prying, he seems to know his characters so well that he can give readers just the clues they need in order to draw their own inferences. One example of the important discriminations registered was noted by Coleridge:

> If I want a servant or a mechanic, I wish to know what he does: — but of a friend, I must know what he is. And in no writer is this momentous distinction so finely brought forward as by Fielding. We do not care what Blifil does; — the deed, as separate from the agent, may be good or ill; — but Blifil is a villain; — and we feel him to be so from the very moment he, the boy Blifil, restores Sophia's poor captive bird to its native and rightful liberty.[79]

According to another critic, Fielding even manages to hint that Blifil could content himself with masturbation, and that this simply proved his mean-spirited nastiness.[80] But it is not only the evil characters who have been found so interesting. Aurélien Digeon, though granting that Fielding is not a *pointilliste* in sensibility like Richardson, finds in Sophia a profound richness and psychological balance that Clarissa conspicuously lacks. Her tolerance of Tom's infidelities, her horror at his apparent bandying about of her name, reveal her as a woman "made for life", yet admirably sensitive as well.[81]

For readers who admire him, Fielding's comic plotting and professed neoclassicism of characterization do nothing to dampen interest in his people and their world. Much scholarship, similarly, has been devoted to his view of human psychology in general. The assumption that he had such a view, and that, *pace* Leavis and others, it is worth discussing, is here not questioned. The problem rather seems to be in defining just what it is. In particular, where does Fielding stand on ethics? Does he, or does he not, believe in the possibility of a behaviour rationally governed by moral considerations? According to Morris Golden's *Fielding's Moral Psychology*,[82] sometimes he does, and sometimes he does not. Sometimes he is Shaftesburian, sometimes Mandevillian. Some men are not evil, but some men are. Education and reason may help, or they may not. Other scholars plump for the one alternative or the other. So some say that Fielding is rehabilitating the notion of prudence, and must therefore presuppose that intellectual and moral effort can bear fruit,[83] while others say that Allworthy's Butlerian prudence is inferior to Tom's primitive Christianity, which in turn is inferior to what, in Sophia, is a Shaftesburian benevolence adjusted to a real society.[84]

In many places Fielding does actually suggest that actions are not to be judged by ethical rules, nor even by their consequences, but by the underlying impulse which really causes them. In other words, he can be read as having a "profound distrust of reason in ethics",[85] which, as we saw, was the essence of Gide's complaint: that he never "portrays a character who consciously aspires to self-perfection, self-conquest, painful self-denial — in short, to mortification of the flesh."[86] Other critics, detecting just this same tendency to regard goodness as a matter of instinct, strongly relish it.[87] For one thing, it has been praised for anticipating by half a century the enlightened self-interest of the Benthamites,[88] and is sometimes mentioned as a reason for preferring Fielding to the novelists of momentous moral choice from Richardson to Lawrence.

Mediating critics will take the controversy surrounding Fielding with a pinch of salt. They will be unsurprised that some interpreters find him predominantly comic and even trivial while others find him serious and even profound, and unsurprised that the ones who find him serious differ as to whether or not he believed in the power of reason to influence behaviour. All these types of reading are now well embedded in the cultural context within which we read Fielding, which means that there are likely to be moments when they are all going on in our highly flexible minds at once. Unsurprisingly, too, it was Fielding who started it all, by being just as flexible himself.

Most obviously, he was partly having fun and partly being serious, in a way that seems much more human, and also much more interesting, than trying to do just one thing all the time. Sometimes, though, these two main states of mind did conflict with each other, and there arises that odd juxtaposition of gusto and caution which is one aspect of his reluctant naturalism. This is what has given both the blithe and the solemn critics their opening. Fielding himself sometimes seems to think he ought to choose one way or the other. So far, my quotations from his novels have mainly illustrated his naturalism at its most rumbustious. But at almost any point we could dip in and find clear evidence of a willingness to believe, as much as possible, in divine providence and human virtue, and of his own Jonesian willingness to preach. Since his storylines also go in for resounding poetic justice, the Chicagoan rediscoverers of comedy and the Barrowizing exponents of Providence were partly singing, however unwillingly, the same tune.

As to the precise colour of his ethical concerns, mediating critics will carefully balance a number of opposing considerations which do not necessarily cancel each other out. His scepticism as to the sway of reason is absolutely fundamental. It is the main ground of his naturalism, one of the main sources of his comedy. Nor is there any doubt that he knows and likes a good heart when he sees one. But the suggestion that he therefore has a sentimental, or incipiently sentimental view of human nature must be carefully qualified. Often he does try to celebrate the heart's most benevolent potentialities. Even in *Tom Jones* exquisite delights accrue to the fine sensibilities of characters who are charitable and sympathetic. In *Amelia*, the *douceur de pleurer* is indulged even more extensively. Yet it is still Richardson who more fully anticipates the Victorians in this respect, whereas Fielding can still remind us of the old England of the Restoration theatre. Even if the animal spirits of Western have, in Tom, been refined by the *Spectator* and forty years of education, and even if, by the end of his life, Fielding was laying on the sentimentality a good bit thicker, his basic intuition, first and last, is that in any human group the instinctively good hearts will form a small minority. Usually people are impulsively selfish, and not in the enlightened way. All of which can also mean, of course, that although he does not really believe in rational morality, he can still write about the need for responsibility, self-discipline and prudence as if he did. What other hope is there, after all? He does contradict himself, in other words. But his contradictions make an important kind of sense. For mediating critics appealing to readers' mental flexibility, he will be a prime exhibit. At one and the same time, his work readily responds to the gloomy Modernist reading style, and is hopeful against all the odds.

The first critic to make a concerted effort to mediate between the various readings of *Tom Jones* was Irvin Ehrenpreis (1964).[89] On the one hand he made no bones about diagnosing doctrines: latitudinarian Anglicanism, with good works as the test of faith; Pelagian optimism; a belief in charity; reservations about simple Stoicism or the Shaftesburian faith in virtue's attractiveness; and so on. On the other hand, Ehrenpreis also wrote of an ultimate tolerance in Fielding; of an amusement at the ironies of politics and religion; of a self-amused recognition that many readers would oppose the establishment he supports; of stylistic fun and games; of comic plotting that minimalizes pain; of a teasing appearance of losing the reader in irrelevancies; and of a fascination with Western as a force more ancient than right or wrong. In its various perspectives, Ehrenpreis's commentary was not so much confusing as flexible and truthful, and future attempts at mediation must follow his example, extending the discussion with perspectives hitherto unapplied. As always, the only caveat will be that such new readings must respect the dead-and-buried author's autonomy, both altruistically, as that of a fellow-human being, and in the hope of spiritual benefit from his otherness.

In extending to Fielding the Modernist sort of perspective applied by Edmund Wilson and Lionel Trilling to Dickens, the main anachronism to be avoided is that of imposing on the eighteenth century those varieties of hypocrisy and unconscious repression which were more typical of the nineteenth. Especially for his novels up until *Tom Jones*, the Jungian distinction between persona and shadow, so suggestive for Dickens, yields nothing at all. Uriah is a projection of David, but Blifil is not a projection of Tom. Not that Fielding's people always acknowledge their own motives. On the contrary, the rationalization in some of their interior monologues is hilariously funny. But it would not be nearly so funny if self-deception were socially endorsed and wide-rangingly systematic. Although the main affinity with the Modernist Dickens is perhaps the sense of an evil that is widespread throughout society as a whole, and although Fielding's evil characters can be very evil indeed, when they plot to deceive their prey their mask is not actually part of their social formation, and is fairly easily detachable — sometimes literally a mask at a masquerade. Under their own scrutiny, moreover, they can be frank and naked, and the only way they themselves can become ensnared in deception is through the agency of people still more corrupt and powerful than themselves, since corruption spreads downward through society, just like the contagion of luxury. Since, in Fielding, a distinction between good and evil, albeit much confused, is still in principle possible, at least some of the people victimized and cheated are actually rather innocent.

Yet this does make their position particularly interesting, not as the objects of Fielding's sometimes lugubrious pity, but intellectually. They are frankly

honest observers in a frankly wicked world, for which they feel no real sympathy, but into which they are drawn. *Pace* Wayne C. Booth, another central
emphasis of the Modernist interpretation will be that Fielding's handling of the
moral, emotional and epistemological uncertainties of such relatively innocent
human beings anticipates the plots and narratological devices of Henry James.
And as in James, the complications are certainly very troubling. The distinction between good and evil can actually become so confused as to seem endan-
gered. Whether or not total innocence is humanly possible, a protagonist's own
merely relative innocence may sometimes leave too much to be desired. In two
of Fielding's relatively innocent male characters, moreover, the grimly Modernist reading can certainly detect repressions of a rather more Victorian scope.
Projection characters like those surrounding David Copperfield would simply
have been the next novelistic step.

If all this is beginning to sound a rather unlikely Fielding, the reason may
be that the Modernist perspective applies most obviously to his last and least
known novel, *Amelia*. Fielding is usually thought of as one of the creators of the
"traditional" English novel, the type of novel praised by Wayne C. Booth. What
has been less fully recognized is that in *Amelia* he did not so much fail to live
up to his earlier achievements, as begin to create the genre afresh. The overall
effect is very different, and some of the writing is certainly tired and wretched,
with some odd loose ends or contradictions. Yet like *David Copperfield*, *Amelia*
was its author's own most fondly loved work, and in an important sense it
remains his most complete work as well. Because the reluctant naturalism is
here at its most pronounced, the different sides of his mind are most sharply in
contrast with each other. Although some of the results are horribly embarrassing, others are very impressive.

   Those earliest readers who, according to Johnson, rushed to buy up the
entire first edition in a single day could not possibly have guessed what they
were getting. Yet even in Fielding's earlier novels, the comic mood could occasionally give way to something else. In particular, there are significant differences between Mr Wilson's digressive autobiography in *Joseph Andrews* and
that of the Man of the Hill in *Tom Jones*. In Mr Wilson's narrative, the vice and
folly of an entire society give scope to the man's own a-rationality. The rake
progresses along a path well-worn and -signposted, the realistic probabilities
showing Fielding at his most Smollett-like. But even Smollett dishes up sentimental reunions and happy endings, and Mr Wilson is finally saved by an act

of grace. Typically for Fielding, the richer and more virtuous lady stoops, raising up the despairing man to her own station, a gesture which in Richardson
would have indicated her own spiritual baseness. The sentimental comedy of
an unsuccessfully veiled mutuality of passion, even though mocked through
Parson Adams's slavering for more and more of the same, reigns supreme. And
to crown it all, at the end of the novel we learn that Joseph is none other than Mr
Wilson's long lost son. The Man of the Hill in *Tom Jones*, by contrast, remains
out of step with that novel's dominant drive. This is the more striking in that
Fielding does at least begin to pull the Man's story back towards comedy. There
are the amusing reactions of Partridge. There are Jones's reactions, ironically relevant to his own later waywardness: if he had practised what he here preaches
to the Man about the careful choice of company, he would have avoided some of
his later close shaves. And there are the parallels between Jones himself and the
Man — both of them unhappy in love, both betrayed by a friend, both march-
ing against Popery —, parallels which are shaping up for the same sort of sentimental climax which united Joseph Andrews and Mr Wilson. But even though
the Man has lived in roughly the same part of the country as Mrs Bridget, he is
not Tom's father, and the news, when it finally comes, that Tom's father is somebody hitherto quite unheard of is slightly disconcerting. This, and the bleak
misanthropy in which (despite some revisions to the text) the Man understand-
ably remains after so many trials unmitigated by grace, are the first conspicuous example of Fielding's not coming up with the comic goods.

In *Amelia*, the unease of the Man of the Hill episode is writ large, and even
a synopsis will give some sense of this. Whereas both *Joseph Andrews* and *Tom
Jones* end with a marriage, Captain and Mrs William Booth — Amelia, that is
— have already been married for some years, and the novel tells of mounting
stresses and strains in the relationship. Booth is not a bad man, but he is a dis-
believer, who blames his fate on fortune, spending time in and out of prison,
sometimes for debt, sometimes falsely convicted. At the beginning of the novel
he has been unable bribe his way out of trouble and is therefore thrown into
the Newgate. Notable among the prison's squalid denizens is Blear-eyed Moll,
of whose nose "*Venus*, envious perhaps at . . . [Moll's] former Charms, had carried off the gristly Part".[90] But another inmate is an old acquaintance of Booth's,
Miss Mathews, who has the means to arrange for a clean cell, and invites Booth
to share it with her. He accepts, albeit remorsefully, and they begin, presumably
among other things, to catch up on each other's life-stories. Booth tells Miss
Mathews how, assisted by Dr Harrison, a benevolent and energetic parson, he
had eloped with the adorable Amelia and settled down to married life in the

country. Later, when his soldiering had taken him to France, Amelia had followed him thither on receiving news that he was ill. They had shared lodgings with the fiercely proud Major Bath and his sister, who later married a certain Captain — later Colonel — James. With occasional interruptions, Booth's and Miss Mathews's very long autobiographical narratives take up most of the first three of the novel's twelve books. But then the story-line switches back to the present and reintroduces James, who turns up to bail Booth out of prison, and also takes Miss Mathews as his mistress. From this point onwards, Booth spends much of his time gambling and currying favour with the great and wealthy, in the hope of securing a commission. Meanwhile Amelia, though her more domestic existence is utterly miserable, does not complain. When Booth fails to come home to a frugal meal of lovingly hashed mutton, she forgives him without a thought, and she forgives him much else as well. Dr Harrison still tries to keep a watchful eye on the family, but then James and a powerful peer, who remains anonymous throughout, plan an assault on Amelia's virtue. Among the peer's pimps and procuresses are a Captain and Mrs Trent and a Mrs Ellison, who is the Booths' landlady. When Mrs Ellison introduces Amelia to the peer at an oratorio, he ingratiatingly promises to arrange a commission for Booth, and starts showering her children with presents. She then receives an invitation to a masquerade, but another of Mrs Ellison's lodgers, the blue-stocking widow Mrs Bennet, advises her against it. In the novel's third very long autobiographical narration, which takes up nearly a whole book, Mrs Bennet confesses to Amelia that she herself, after just such an invitation, had become prey to the peer's lust. Unbeknown to Booth, it is therefore Mrs Bennet, disguised as Amelia, who finally accompanies him to the masquerade, where her flirtatiousness, to Amelia's subsequent mortification, secures from the peer a commission for her own new husband, Captain Atkinson. (Mrs Bennet and Mrs Atkinson are one and the same woman at different stages of her marital career, and I shall be using whichever name seems more appropriate in context.) The plot has many further complications, including more time in prison for Booth. But in the end Dr Harrison, having worked hard to shake Booth out of his philosophical scepticism, pays off Booth's debts and arranges for him to return to farming. Better still, Amelia discovers that she is heiress to her mother's fortune, so that their rural retirement is likely to be a life of peace and prosperity.

At least ostensibly, then, the book has a happy ending, and even in *Amelia* Sheridan Baker found many parallels with the stories, situations and language of romance.[91] With references to *Floris and Blanchefleur*, *The Mourning Bride*, *The Fair Penitent*, *Cassandra*, and *Orlando Furioso*, Baker defined what he calls

Fielding's constant, underlying fairy-tale paradigm: a youth of hidden origins is brought by flukes of circumstance and his own natural qualities into his rightful inheritance; and the worthy man-at-arms, serving a lady seemingly above him, is rewarded by the lady, who is a kind of three-in-one: the lady of courtly love, Providence, and Our Lady the Blessed Virgin. In *Amelia*, this pattern appears in a foreshortened form, without the riddle as to the hero's origins. Yet Baker felt that it does bolster up the novel's sentimentality, as a resistance to the uncomic realism. For Carla Mulford, similarly, the happy ending was no more mechanical that those of *Tom Jones* and *Joseph Andrews*.[92]

Nor is it. The only difference is that in *Amelia* as a whole uncomic realism is far more predominant, so raising expectations of a realistic ending as well. Even in small, throw-away details, the drawing back from comedy, far stronger than in the Man of the Hill's story in *Tom Jones*, amounts to a positive refusal. Take, for instance, the unmalleable contingency of the death of Mrs Bennet's mother by falling down a well. More generally, the contrivedness of the romance ending, the providential doctrine it seeks to uphold, and the underlying dream of a retreat from the corruptions of the world are all in glaring contrast to what the book has earlier shown of human psychology, and to the corresponding dismay of Fielding's overall tone.

No wonder the book's first eager purchasers were taken aback! — so much so, by the way, that Andrew Millar postponed his plans for a second edition until 1762.[93] Many readers who had previously disapproved of Fielding now began to admire him. Johnson, heartily condoning the book's morality, claimed to have read it in one sitting. On the other hand, some earlier admirers now waxed cold, and there was real disagreement about what Fielding had actually tried to do, a controversy which still reverberates today. According to Chicagoan rediscoverers of his comedy, his wit and stylistic play were just what they had always been; some characters were still genuinely comic; and the "undertones" of injustice, venality, and corruption were nothing more than business as usual.[94] Booth's adultery, they insisted, was not much more disturbing than the peccadillos of Tom Jones, and his periods in prison were not seriously worrying either.[95] But many other commentators have gone at least as far as Johnson in reading the novel as virtually a sermon. To Thackeray, Booth was greatly preferable to Jones, because Jones gets the "plumcake and rewards of life" far too easily, whereas Booth is properly contrite, begging due pardon of the "angelic woman" he so rightly adores. So "*Amelia* perhaps is not a better story than *Tom Jones*, but it has the better ethics".[96] For several twentieth century critics, what it preached was anti-Mandevillian benevolism. It was remarkable for placing centre-stage a voluptuous woman, not, as in *Clarissa*, so that she can deny the passion she stimulates, but so that she can platonically raise it to higher goals. On this view, even if Amelia herself from time to time has doubts about religion, there is always Harrison to fall back on, a firm defender of theistic absolutes.[97]

Both the Chicagoan and Johnsonian schools exaggerated. No matter what the Chicagoans claimed, the mood of *Amelia* is very far from uniformly exuberant; there is no straightforwardly comic character — most characters are actually rather disturbing; and "*under*tones" is not the word for this society's all-pervading evil. Fielding certainly is troubled by Booth's adultery — Booth's guilty anger at Amelia (in X 10) is very finely done —, and during each of his imprisonments his marriage is at serious risk, thanks either to his own claustrophobic affair with Miss Mathews or to the unimpeded machinations of James and the peer. As for the Johnsonians, they at least had the support of Fielding's dedication to Ralph Allen: the book, he said, "is sincerely designed to promote the Cause of Virtue, and to expose some of the most glaring Evils, as well public as private, which at present infest the Country".[98] But the most consoling parts of the message had to be made up by the solemn critics themselves. In his heart of hearts, Fielding does not really believe that Amelia's example will be more infectious than the surrounding social rot, and Harrison's Christianity is little more than eschatological sticks and carrots.

Even the commentators who saw Fielding as preaching religion and constructive practical morality could not ignore the essential darkness, though their reluctance to face it recapitulates Fielding's own. They admitted that Booth's conversion is not fully rendered; that Fielding's sympathy with the benevolists was out of step with his observation of "many people who could only be moved by threats";[99] and that his call to moral energy, rationality, and religious belief is not exactly loud and clear, so that readers would just have to work it out for themselves.[100] Most interestingly of all, Martin C. Battestin, who under the influence of Cross's whitewashing had earlier emphasized the influence of Barrow, later noted that Barrow's views had been newly challenged by Hume's claim that reason "is, and ought only to be, the slave of the passions, and can never pretend to any other office than to serve and obey them".[101] Now Battestin pointed out that Booth interprets himself and others in precisely Hume's way, and that Fielding makes Booth's literal imprisonment a symbol of his intellectual bondage to such a view. In other words, Fielding would like to refute it. But Battestin was unable to report that Booth's conversion resolves the problem, because "the true and felt dilemma of the novel is Fielding's own". As already hinted, one of Harrison's arguments is that fear and hope are spurs to religion, but it is an argument which only proves, as Hume says, Hume's point. Quite simply, Fielding does *not* believe in prudence or a Popeian control of the passions, and Battestin himself was no longer beating about the bush: "Passion alone is the spring of behaviour", he remarked, and the novel's characterization is itself Humean, with an emphasis on the inerradicability of each man's character, and on the darkest of passions. Good nature is insufficient — even Amelia educates her children by fear and hope — and Fielding's own sentimental rhetoric is based on the Humean assumption that the most effective means of communication is by passionate appeal.

In other words, Battestin was now firmly on course towards the more balanced view of his magnificent *Henry Fielding: A Life*. His only remaining reluctance to face the full intensity of Fielding's naturalism was in his dating of it. He called it new with *Amelia*, "discernible in inchoate form in Fielding's earlier writings, but never before fully articulated in any work of fiction", whereas the present chapter has discerned it all along. In *Tom Jones*, for instance, it was quite unmistakable, not only in the characterization and plotting, but in countless authorial intrusions:

> This Lecture he [Parson Supple] enriched with many valuable Quotations from the Antients, particularly from *Seneca*; who hath, indeed, so well handled this Passion [anger], that none but a very angry Man can read him without great Pleasure and Profit.[102]

What has changed in *Amelia* is largely Fielding's *response* to his naturalist psychology, and not the basic perception. He sees now that it has wider implications, simply, and he no longer turns it into straightforward comedy. On the contrary, the ebullient comic tone is destabilized. Or as some critics put it, he is wavering between the novelistic and the homiletic.

In 1972 these uncertainties were brilliantly captured by Claude Rawson, who saw in the long description of Blear-eyed Moll a violated faith in order, combining "desperate bewilderment with hard finish and almost unflinching assurance of style".[103] Sometimes, Rawson said, such assurance reaches the point where the urbanity stiffens, and genial élan gives way to dogged literalness, anger, weeping, sarcasm. The mock-heroic elements are suddenly reconstituted as the serious, and the seriousness ghoulishly parodies mock-seriousness. Fielding seems to believe in both human benevolence and human depravity, in both the virtue of all classes and the criminality of the poor, in both Amelia and Moll. The Augustan dream of order is dancing its dance of death.

The Modernist reading so powerfully initiated by Rawson seems true the novel's tone. Fielding stumbles on from pained, avuncular nagging to hysterical didacticism or sentimentality. He blames Amelia for despairing too soon yet is amply tearful himself. Images of virtue as a tender — succulent! — lamb, as a frightened hare, as small fry at the mercy of voracious pike, though used casually enough in the earlier novels, have here a chilling intensity. Amelia, in her tears and faintings and lack of suspicion, is altogether less resilient than Fanny, Mrs Heartfree or Sophia, and her forgiveness of Booth may be less charitable and strong-minded than pathetic and defeatist. The very vulnerability of her soft female virtue sometimes titillates, titillates Fielding no less than it titillates Colonel James or the peer, so that *Shamela*'s critique of *Pamela* returns to plague the inventor. The lapses are all the more noticeable because of their self-distrust, and in moments of finer control Fielding himself shows that sentimentality can fuel voyeurism. From the sobbing marital fondnesses and reunions of Booth's narration, the attentive Miss Mathews squeezes every drop. The only anticipations of this novel's embarrassing pathos in *Tom Jones*, as in the tear-jerking account of the distresses of Mrs Miller's kinsfolk, were fleeting by comparison.

Above all, Fielding's insistence that men are good or bad — and usually bad — in ways quite beyond their own control is now not comic in the least. Even the professed stoic, a fellow-prisoner of Booth's, on hearing that he must immediately proceed to Newgate, is very upset that he will therefore be unable to see his wife and children. This confirms Booth's belief, quite evidently Fielding's own, that "we reason from our Heads, but act from our Hearts".[104] Booth's own reformation we might easily dismiss with the same contempt Fielding levels at similar happy turns in other writers, until we notice its curious honesty. In Booth's case, the brand of Christianity entails the unedifying morality of coercion, and even Harrison's more passionate Christianity is disconcerting. Harrison's ferocity in the cause of right convinces onlookers that he is, not simply absurd like Parson Adams, but positively mad. His fervour is no less alarming, one might say, than James's lust or Bath's pride. And whereas, in the novels containing Letty, Fireblood, Wild, Mrs Waters, Mrs Bridget, Betty the chambermaid and so on, Fielding can always toss off something such as

> O Love, what monstrous Tricks dost thou play with thy Votaries of both sexes! ... thou turnest the Heart of a Man inside-out, as a Juggler doth a Petticoat, and bringest whatsoever pleaseth thee out from it.[105]

in *Amelia*, love is far more awesome:

> [O]f all Passions there is none against which we should so strongly fortify our-
> selves as this, which is generally called Love: for no other lays before us, espe-
> cially in the tumultuous Days of Youth, such sweet, such strong and almost
> irresistible Temptations; none hath produced in private Life such fatal and
> lamentable Tragedies; and what is worst of all, there is none to whose Poison
> and Infatuation the best of Minds are so liable. Ambition scarce ever produces
> any Evil but when it reigns in cruel and savage Bosoms; and Avarice seldom
> flourishes at all but in the basest and poorest Soil. Love, on the contrary,
> sprouts usually up in the richest and noblest Minds; but there, unless nicely
> watched, pruned, and cultivated, and carefully kept clear of those vicious
> Weeds which are too apt to surround it, it branches forth into Wildness and
> Disorder, produces nothing desirable, but choaks up and kills whatever is
> good and noble in the Mind where it so abounds. In short, to drop the Alle-
> gory, not only Tenderness and Good-nature, but Bravery, Generosity, and
> every Virtue are often made the Instruments of effecting the most atrocious
> Purposes of this all-subduing Tyrant.[106]

The phenomenon so naturalistically described is the same as it always was. But
Fielding's naturalism is now as reluctant as can well be. Very uncomfortably,
he recognizes that he shares the world-view of the world's worst inhabitants —
as it were, of a Jonathan Wild. He can no longer simply attribute this view to
exceptionally wicked characters who are to be punished by poetic justice, and
nothing he finds for Harrison to say can cheer him up. Instead, in an intensely
Shavian dialogue between Harrison and a powerful lord, a terrible disquiet is
evident from the force of the lord's realism. "Do you not know, Doctor, that this
is as corrupt a Nation as ever existed under the Sun? And would you think of
governing such a People by the strict principles of Honesty and Morality?"[107]

Turning now from the book's general tone and the controversy surrounding
it, we can examine the difference from the earlier novels in more detail. There
is an important contrast, for a start, between the roles of Amelia and Sophia.
Like Amelia, Sophia is an instance of humanity at its finest but, unlike Amelia,
she is not held up as a model. Jones admires, but will never match her. Fielding
comfortably lets Sophia and everybody else in *Tom Jones* just be themselves. In
his last novel, his new horror at what human nature generally seems to entail
gives him a restless urge to change it. Amelia is a symbol of virtue that is supposed to attract love, esteem, emulation. Embodying a strongly recommended
fineness of sensibility, she is also a paragon of a wife, happily attending to her
duties, faithfully and affectionately obeying her husband, tactfully forgiving his

many lapses, all in perfect accordance with the period's standard moral treatises and manuals of domestic conduct.

Here many readers have felt that Fielding lacks the conviction to turn his
didactic will into an artistic deed. There have been frequent remarks on the
stiffness of the parable and the frozen conventionality of the poses in which
Amelia is portrayed. Many critics have also disliked the associated sentimentality, blaming its tendency to idealization for undermining the novelistic drive
towards psychological realism.[108] Towards the end of the twentieth century,
however, feminist critics were finding much to admire in Amelia, and consequently in Fielding for having created her. Amelia, they said, believes that true
Christianity would support the dignity of labour, and would militate against
class prejudice and the male worlds of learning and power.[109] Nor was that all.
As a model of goodness, tenderness and friendship she was actually found to
speak to both sexes,[110] her response to Booth's infidelity showing great maturity
and strength of character.[111] In other words, she was now getting a much better
press than Agnes Wickfield.

Irrespective of whether the feminist readings will have brought about a permanent shift of taste, Amelia is certainly an interesting creation, and especially
when she is most sorely tried, for then she gives vent to the kind of half-articulate protest which Harrison would describe as sinful doubt. Her uncertainties arise because, in the naturalistic world Fielding now conveys so clearly,
she is relatively innocent. Once again, the contrast with Sophia is illuminating.
When Sophia penetrates the sexual schemings of her cousin Fitzpatrick, Fielding does defend her against the charge of undue suspiciousness, but his defence
is a very confident one. Sophia does not have that "vast Quicksightedness into
Evil" which itself proceeds from a bad heart. Rather, there is a more commendable kind of suspiciousness, arising "from the Head", and this Sophia does have.
It is "no other than the Faculty of seeing what is before your Eyes, and of drawing Conclusions from what you see"; sometimes, too, it can take the form of
thinking "that a man is capable of doing [again] what he hath done already".[112]
In *Amelia*, this second, commendable kind of suspiciousness seems impossible.
Only the thoroughly evil are likely to see through appearances:

> [I]t is not, because Innocence is more blind than Guilt, that the former often
> overlooks and tumbles into the Pit, which the latter foresees and avoids. The
> Truth is, that it is almost impossible Guilt should miss the discovering of all
> the Snares in its Way; as it is constantly prying closely into every Corner, in
> order to lay Snares for others. Whereas Innocence, having no such Purpose,
> walks fearlessly and carelessly through Life, and is consequently liable to tread

on the Gins which Cunning hath laid to entrap it. To speak plainly, and without Allegory or Figure, it is not Want of Sense, but Want of Suspicion by which Innocence is often betrayed. Again, we often admire the Folly of the Dupe, when we should transfer our whole Surprise to the astonishing Guilt of the Betrayer. In a Word, many an innocent Person hath owed his Ruin to this Circumstance alone, that the Degree of Villainy was such as must have exceeded the Faith of every man who was not himself a Villain.[113]

Even Harrison laments that a good face is a dubious letter of recommendation — "O Nature, Nature, why art thou so dishonest, as ever to send Men with these false Recommendations into the World?" — and Amelia's rejoinder here comes from the novel's very core: "Indeed, my dear Sir, I begin to grow heartily sick of it, . . . For sure all Mankind are Villains in their Hearts".[114] Harrison may counter that it is not innate evil but bad habits, bad customs and bad education that drive men to vice. Fielding as narrator may piously remonstrate that Amelia's despair blinds her to a possible means of safety. But Amelia's anguished indignation is the natural accompaniment of a growing disillusion which constitutes the most credible of all her recurrent postures, one in which she characteristically defers to Harrison's authority, but in which, when even Harrison himself seems to have become Booth's enemy, she bewails "an End of all Goodness in the World".[115] Another of her outbursts is a bit less sweeping: "Good Heavens! . . . what are our great Men made of? Are they in Reality a distinct Species from the rest [sic] of Mankind? Are they born without Hearts?" But when Booth extends it — "all Men, as well the best as the worst, act alike from the Principle of Self-Love" — she finds herself no less tongue-tied than usual.[116] She has often wanted to convince Booth of the reality of religion and virtue, but can only wish he would discuss the matter with Harrison.

Even more upsetting, how can she, in her relative innocence, prevent what little evil she does foresee without becoming evil herself? Sometimes it seems that her only practical course is to soil herself in the manner of other people. So can an evil means be justified by a virtuous end? Or will it simply lead to *more* evil? The contrast with the earlier fiction is as instructive as ever. Sophia can extricate herself from a tight spot by being economical with the truth and flattering an aunt's vanity, exactly the same strategy as adopted by the sinful Mrs Fitzpatrick. Mrs Heartfree tricks a would-be ravisher into a drunken stupor, even sinking so low as to exclaim that "I loved a Can as well as himself, and would never grant the Favour to any Man till I had drunk a hearty Glass with him".[117] For Amelia, policy is far more problematic. In two protracted episodes, she can hold her husband back from the dangerous evil of duelling only by deceiving him into thinking that her would-be ravisher is still a friend, a deception which makes her own honour and safety more precarious, and without altogether eliminating the threat of a duel. Again, the subterfuge of letting the disguised Mrs Bennet (Mrs Atkinson, as she secretly is already) go to the masquerade in her stead is something Amelia comes bitterly to regret. At the masquerade Mrs Atkinson titillates the peer's lust in order to get her own new husband a promotion, thereby making it seem that Amelia herself trades sex as cynically as the Trents. One critic points out that there is actually a running contrast between Amelia and Mrs Atkinson, expressive of precisely this problem of the survival of innocence *as* innocence.[118] Mrs Atkinson seems at once tragic and comic, true and false, virtuous and licentious, demure and tipsy, sympathetic and corrupt. And in her compromises with morality, she has a self-reliance quite denied Amelia.

The multi-faceted Mrs Atkinson is of a piece with the world Fielding now shows so clearly, a world which seems to make his former confidence melt away. Although the action of the novel is set in the past, Mrs Atkinson's imperfections are typical the 1750's as seen through the troubled eyes of Fielding the magistrate.[119] Particularly in his treatment of sex, the bluff straightforwardness of the earlier novels has given way to odd shifts and apparent indirections, a withdrawal from watertight distinctions and neat resolutions.

An example involving Mrs Atkinson herself begins with a conversation about the mental powers of women. Here she seems to start out reasonably enough, until her streak of coarseness makes itself felt. She raves like one of the middle-aged landladies in the earlier novels, and we are given to believe that she can be pacified only by being bedded. The crudity is underlined by her own Elizabethan pun:

> [Atkinson] at last not only quieted his Wife; but she cried out with great Sincerity, "Well, my dear, I will say one thing for you, that I believe from all my Soul, though you have no Learning, you have the best Understanding of any Man on Earth."[120]

Atkinson's priapism is disconcerting because he is also portrayed as the platonic lover of the chaste Amelia, sentimentally worshipping her from afar.

Even this itself has been strangely subversive, supplementing the novel's main design with a consistent countersuggestion. To put it bluntly, readers are constantly in the position of feeling that Atkinson would be a far worthier match for Amelia than Booth is, and that the snobbish, erring Booth and the termagant Mrs Atkinson would also be an appropriate pairing. In both these counter-couples the strength of mutual attraction cannot be mistaken, and the relationship between Amelia and Atkinson is already as explicitly erotic as Fielding can make it without impugning Amelia's virtue. Following Atkinson's confession that his passionate devotion had led him to steal the miniature of her, she becomes, as Terry Castle also noted, decidedly flustered, engaging

> in hysterical disavowal, "carelessly" reaching out her hand while murmuring in confusion, "I don't know what I am doing". She betrays every sign . . . of inwardly reciprocating his transgressive desire . . . [and gets into] such a state of disorder that she sheds "plentiful" tears and has to drink "a great Glass of Water" to calm herself.

Fielding affirms that, "without any Injury to her Chastity", Atkinson's gentleness succeeded in softening her heart in a "momentary Tenderness", a liberal insight which Castle praised as "probably the most sympathetic, least ironic representation of female desire in all . . . [his] fiction"[121] One of its effects is to hint the awkwardness of Atkinson's marrying Mrs Bennet in the first place, a "betrayal" of Amelia which in its own way parallels Booth's betrayal of her with Miss Mathews. According to *Mrs* Atkinson, it is perfectly possible for "a Man who can love one Woman so well at a Distance" to

> love another better that is nearer to him . . . These [platonic] Passions, which reside only in very amorous and very delicate Minds, feed only on the Delicacies there growing; and leave all the substantial Food, and enough of the Delicacy too, for the Wife.[122]

But if Mrs Atkinson's connoisseurship of compromise at first seems to have much of the novel's weight behind it, a different tale is told by Atkinson's dream, in which his wife, sleeping at his side, becomes James, Amelia's enemy. On waking, Atkinson catches himself in the act of strangling her, which must count as one of the earliest cases of a novelist's using a dream to index secret feelings. (Fielding's compilation, at roughly this time, of cases illustrating the theme "murder will out" indicates a similar interest, an interest at least as strong as the ostensible desire to show the force of Providence and Justice.)[123] Atkinson may also be the first recorded case of a man in bondage to a Becky Sharp but adoring an Agnes Whitfield (Thackeray's word for Fielding's Amelia was "angelic").[124] The serious farce of his taking his wife's spilt cherry brandy to be her mortally shed blood is bound up with the possibility that his own hand could unbeknownst have seized the most absolute means of releasing him from her.

Earlier on in the novel, the old demarcation between love and lust was eroded even more weirdly, in an association generated between the accidentally broken nose of Amelia and the syphilitic ruin of Blear-eyed Moll's. This association, which in another novel would simply have been an infelicity, easily removed in proof-stage even, is typical of *Amelia's* unpredictability. Fielding no longer seems to care for literary decorum, perhaps because tidy art would achieve no comforting victory over life. Sometimes he still selects and patterns his materials to shape up to comedy, but there is also much that is random and disconnected. This is all the more striking, in fact, because some of the most curious questions do receive an answer. We later learn that the madman who broke into the Booths' lodgings was none other than Harrison, and we also learn, thanks to Fielding's temporary return to his old explanatory habits, why he did it. But what is the point of Booth's dying sister taking Booth for a highwayman? Is the point only that there is no point? Or who sent Amelia a letter advising her to go to Gibraltar? Or why is Mrs James so distraught when she thinks her husband and Booth may duel? Is it because she is lusting, as we later learn, for Booth? But that lust is also said to be none too peremptory. So is it because widowhood would entail an inconvenient loss of social status? Or is she genuinely concerned for Amelia's sake? At one point her friendship with Amelia is said to be mere form. Elsewhere, she is even said to have, beneath the polite veneer, a heart. Such tensions between conventional comic patterning and aleatory casualness carry novelistic realism in a direction that is arguably not resumed until *The Way of All Flesh*.

Any claims to an understanding of human nature are much less simple and assured than in the earlier novels. Miss Mathews, a fine young lady and former acquaintance of Booth, has now, Booth learns from her Newgate narrative, committed murder. Mrs Bennet, so quiet and plain, is also, she confesses to Amelia, a murderess, and an adulteress as well. The astonishment Booth and Amelia feel at these points is only an extreme case of their unease at life's defiance of order throughout, an unease in which their creator's apparent artlessness participates. Emphasizing the remarkable variations in Miss Mathews's temper, Fielding adduces violent changes in the English weather and in the moods of other women, so suggesting that such oddities are, precisely, natural. If he is still a believer in conservation of character, it is a far more complex affair than in *Tom Jones*, where, even though instinct could at first be restrained by reason and duty, an *éclaircissement* was always forthcoming, and sometimes fairly soon. In *Amelia*, the suspensions of authorial omniscience put the reader in the same doubts as the protagonists themselves, and several characters are conceived in what seems a spirit of no less perplexity on Fielding's own part: there is James, the good friend who seeks his friend's ruin, for instance, or

Bath, who is tender as a brother but quite monstrous in his pride as a man of honour. Novelistically, the gain is that critical talk of neoclassical stereotypes at last becomes invalid. As Digeon observed, Fielding's creatures now are "independent of the author and of the reader, . . . personal beings endowed with all the unforeseen spontaneities of life."[125] The only trouble with Digeon's phrasing was that it made the unforeseen spontaneities sound rather attractive.

With diagnosis of human nature so difficult, moral judgement cannot be easy either. Booth tells Miss Mathews that, out of consideration for Amelia's superior social position, he had originally tried to hide his love for her, even going so far as to announce that he loved her spiteful friend. Miss Mathews exclaims that he thereby showed himself a wonder of generosity, after which Fielding invites readers, between chapters, to consider for themselves "whether this Conduct of Mr. *Booth* was natural or no".[126] Well, clearly it is possible. But is it probable? And does "natural" here not also hint at what we should now understand by "humane" or "duly considerate"? Booth's behaviour actually pained Amelia deeply, and we may even wonder whether he really was so unattracted by the friend, who might have become spiteful only later, or only in Booth's narration. But even granting him the benefit of the doubt on this, would it not have been better to tell Amelia the truth at once, and to come to an honourable agreement to allow their love no headway until his circumstances improved? But again, would such resolution itself be natural — likely? And *isn't* the course he did choose more generous, as Miss Mathews says? Well, perhaps it is. But then again, how much should we be influenced by Miss Mathews's opinion? — or professed opinion? She is trying to ingratiate herself in Booth's affections again, here by echoing Amelia's own praise of his "deception" when she found out. Surely Amelia's judgement can be trusted, though? Or can it be trusted in everything except her adoration of Booth? And so on.

Only one critic has ever suggested that author-reader relations are the same here as in earlier novels,[127] and Fielding's handling of point-of-view has on the whole been blamed as rather confusing. Sometimes he is said to lack warmth and personal involvement: to see his characters from a certain distance; to offer no affectionate defence of Booth because it is simply undeserved; and to leave Amelia utterly helpless.[128] At other times he is said to be unable to keep his feelings, and especially his sentimentality, under control, and to commit himself too vigorously to preaching, something which readers with a Modernist preference for showing over telling are said to find distasteful.[129] Other critics, again, complain that he far too often *withdraws* from all-judging omniscience: that just when, during the early Newgate scenes, he has begun to establish his customary intimacy with the reader, he suddenly switches to the very long narrative monologues of Miss Mathews and Booth.[130] A further grouse is that Miss Mathews and Booth, even though entrusted with so much of the story-telling, are neither witty nor intelligent, and that Fielding's scrupulous verisimilitude neither raises their narratives above the commonplace of their own minds, nor offers the reader any help in assessing their motives. Because Booth is not judged beforehand by the author, this complaint continues, his narration leaves us in just as much doubt as narrations by characters in Joyce or Faulkner, but Fielding does not *use* the situation as Joyce or Faulkner would.[131] For instance, we are said to have no way of judging Booth's account of the family's horses and carriage, which originally made his rural neighbours jealous, so precipitating his fateful journey to London.[132] Critics alleging that Fielding is similarly absent during the narratives of Miss Mathews and Mrs Bennet complain that the reader has to work too hard at interpretation; that Fielding's omniscient voice, when it does return, wastes time repeating what readers have already been forced to work out for themselves; and that Miss Mathews and Mrs Bennet in any case soon retire from centre stage, so that everything seems to have been a lot of fuss about nothing.[133] The narrations of Booth, Miss Mathews and Mrs Bennet are all criticized for being far too long, for telling rather than showing, and for not even suiting their narrators' characters. What, in one of the earlier novels, would have been authorial comment from Fielding himself is said to have been transmuted into the characterization of Harrison, while the more direct of the remaining authorial remarks are tritely sentimental. All in all, the novel is condemned as, narratologically speaking, a frightful mess.

In some respects critics have been too kind. Not only is the sentimentality very trite. Harrison is actually less interesting when he is dignified and didactic than when he is rabidly undignified. His fervour for justice has the force of a quite uncontrollable, awe-inspiring passion. The passion represents Fielding's naturalistic insights, the dignified didacticism his reluctance to face them.

If we adopt the Modernist perspective, however, the critics' onslaughts do seem rather blinkered, precisely because their premise is so militantly non-Modernist. They start from the expectation that Fielding is always going to write in the omniscient mode for which he was praised by Wayne C. Booth in his critique of the Jamesian novel of dramatic presentation. The attempts to derive a critical orthodoxy from Wayne C. Booth were no less one-sided than the Modernists' earlier devaluation of omniscient narration. Both tendencies yielded prime examples of the rigidifying monoideaism of twentieth-century literary scholasticism. The task of mediation between Modernist and anti-Modernist presuppositions must be to loosen things up.

If Fielding's earlier novels were in the mode of intrusive authorial omniscience, for his stage plays that option was of course unavailable. His very apprenticeship as a writer was in dramatic presentation in the most literal sense, and there was no reason why he should always write omnisciently in *Amelia*. Ordinary readers, using their flexible powers of adaptation, have far less trouble with the novel's mixed conventions than many critics seem to imagine. To switch backwards and forwards between personal deduction and authorial guidance can be decidedly interesting, and countless subsequent novels have been written on a similar plan. Readers move from one convention to another, granting, as Coleridge might have said, willing suspension of disbelief in both cases, yet also knowing, as Johnson might have said, that a book is always a book. To deny such mental flexibility in readers is the mark of a purism as narrow as that which criticized Shakespeare for breaking the Unities or for mixing comedy and tragedy. In *Amelia*, the reader's deductions and the authorial guidance certainly overlap. But they do so less often than the critics suggest, and the authorial guidance can in any case be seen as sustaining readers on their way, helpfully confirming them in their conclusions, or reminding them of earlier conclusions. The book proposes a collaborative effort, demanding more of readers than Fielding's earlier novels did, but also implying greater respect on Fielding's part for both readers' intelligence and life's complexities.

Booth and Miss Mathews do have commonplace minds. There is no denying that, and so has Mrs Bennet. Yet during their very long narratives, those three minds do not hold unrivalled sway. Precisely because Fielding also allows his own extraordinary mind to surface, we are alerted to view their reports ironically. These three characters are among the earliest examples of what Wayne C. Booth himself defines as one of the hallmarks of the Modernist, Jamesian novel: they are unreliable narrators. Their commonplaceness is actually an aspect of their unreliability, and Fielding's handling of the ironies can be extremely skilful. Just where the critics least seem to expect it, he registers certain discriminations with firm exactness. Although the novel's dramatization shows that moral questions are desperately complex, if Wayne C. Booth had noticed the unreliable narrations here he could not have accused Fielding of moral irresponsibility. Critics arguing that Fielding is less concerned than Faulkner "with the degree of truth and partiality in any single view of a series of incidents"[134] are forgetting that such a concern was his main reason for objecting to *Pamela*, and that the concern recurs elsewhere as well. In *Tom Jones*, we have seen his fascination with the bias of narrations by Mrs Fitzpatrick, Sophia and Jones. In *Amelia*, the artistic possibilities are developed further still, not only in the treatment of Booth's courtship but throughout.

In the case of Miss Mathews's narration, there is a deliberate holding back from transparent characterization, plus considerable sophistication in the interplay of flashback, action, and teller-listener interaction. The prison colloquy between Miss Mathews and Booth has a subtlety of implication that gives a sharp foretaste of Jane Austen, registering Miss Mathews's sentimentality as a mask for her rather frightening predatoriness — their discussion of Mandeville is appropriately rich. The critic who complains that Miss Mathews's coquetry towards Booth (in IV 1) does not match the comic power and figurative richness of Mrs Waters's amorous battle at Upton is very off-key.[135] The point is not open lust but adulterous euphemism, and Fielding's allusion to *All for Love* — "she cast a Look as languishingly sweet as ever *Cleopatra* gave to *Anthony*"[136] — amply suggests the quality of the love ideal she represents, a love that is not without its poetry and passion, yet faintly tarnished all the same, and quietly callous in the wrong it does to the absent Octavia figure. Or to switch from allusions to anticipations, the golden bowl is flawed. Fielding is not repeating his earlier achievements in "straightforward" comedy, but is cultivating an underlying seriousness of tone, at once moral and tragic, a tone we have subsequently heard much more of in James, who uses similar narratological means to give it resonance. That not even *Amelia* found a place in *The Great Tradition*, that Leavis thought that Fielding had by this stage simply "gone soft",[137] is very strange indeed.

In the case of Booth's narration, the kind of detail which critics have failed to read can be easily pinpointed. Take, for instance, one of the passages adduced to prove the reader's inability to form a judgement of the controversial carriage and horses:

> [F]rom a Boy I had always been fond of driving a Coach, in which I valued myself on having some Skill. This, perhaps, was an innocent, but I allow it to have been a childish Vanity. As I had an Opportunity, therefore, of buying an old Coach and Harness very cheap (indeed they cost me but Twelve Pound) and as I considered that the same Horses which drew my Wagons would likewise draw my Coach, I resolved on indulging myself in the Purchase.
>
> "The Consequence of setting up this poor old Coach is inconceivable. Before this, as my Wife and myself had very little distinguished ourselves from the other Farmers and their Wives, either in our Dress or our Way of Living, they treated us as their Equals; but now they began to consider us as elevating ourselves into a State of Superiority, and immediately began to envy, hate, and

declare War against us. The neighbouring little Squires too were uneasy to see a poor Renter become their Equal in a Matter in which they placed so much Dignity; and not doubting but it arose in me from the same Ostentation, they began to hate me likewise, and to turn my Equipage into Ridicule, asserting that my Horses, *which were as well matched as any in the Kingdom*, were of different Colours and Sizes, with much more of that Kind of Wit, the only Basis of which is lying [my italics].[138]

The clause I have italicized indicates clearly that Booth's horses, even though also used for his waggons, had been most carefully selected for appearance. His pride in them is quite obvious, and from the whole tone of the passage we can readily draw the conclusion that his decision to buy a coach was not so disarmingly childish a vanity as, at one level, he would seem to have Miss Mathews believe. He depreciates the coach for its age and cheapness, yet states as a fact that it made him the equal of the local squires. There is more than half an understanding between himself and his tempting, sympathetic listener that, by many people's standards, he is giving a most conservative estimate of the fine impression created. His gentlemanly extravagance of self-indulgence is one of the traits by which, on his side, their present flirtation is being sustained.

As for Mrs Bennet's narration, the way in which readers build up their impression was carefully studied by John S. Coolidge (1960),[139] but other critics again seem wide of the mark. One of them complains that Fielding made a mistake in hinting that she is merely pretending when she swoons after mentioning her venereal disease. The same critic also says that her narrative does not prepare us for her later dishonesty.[140] Such commentary is quite blind to the subtle interplay of crudely animal drive and polite delicacy, as in her account of how, like Mrs Fitzpatrick in *Tom Jones*, she conducted an affair with a man who pretended to pay court to her maiden-aunt chaperone. In her own way, Mrs Bennet/Atkinson is reluctant naturalism incarnate.

From the mid-1980s onwards, a few critics finally started to emulate Coolidge's close attention to detail. Donald Fraser pointed out that even though many of the novel's characters, including Harrison and Amelia, practise deceptions, Fielding himself leads the reader astray without actually lying. The book represents a magistrate's sense of how complex and difficult it can be to ascertain the truth of a situation, and of the need, in a corrupt world, for alert judgement and keen observation.[141] Somewhat similarly, Susan K. Howard invoked Iser's account of how a reader can actively fill a narrative's gaps,[142] even if things are not quite as straightforward as Howard suggested. Like Iser himself, she was actually speaking of the text's *implied* reader, and tended to suggest that real readers will always fill in the gaps in just the one way. But her account could easily be made more sensitive to the pragmatics of real reading, for instance in ways suggested by Arlene Wilner, for whom all of Fielding's novels posed problems of interpretation and judgement, being fictions in the sense defined by Kermode: they are "for finding things out, and they change as the needs of sense-making change". They inculcate a "methodology of perception".[143]

In experimenting with an unpleasant Modernist reading, similarly, we shall not underestimate the amount of work a reader must and *can* do. We shall emphasize, too, not only the artistry with which Fielding's discriminations are sometimes conveyed, but the complexity of the resultant character deline-ations. Like Parson Adams and Squire Western, the two most powerful char-acters from the earlier novels, Miss Mathews, Booth and Mrs Atkinson are not only creatures of impulse, but creatures of conflicting impulses, impulses which in *Amelia* are interwoven with varying assays at self-control or disguise. These are characters whom we can never quite capture and quintessentialize. The only thing that seems pretty certain is that their behaviour is not dictated by reason.

This complexity obtains even in passages of non-dramatic presentation, where so many critics have suggested that Fielding is more cut and dried. One example again involves a vehicle of transportation. In the novel's penultimate chapter, Booth does not immediately inform Amelia of her restored fortunes, telling her instead that he has had a dream about a coach and four, in which the two of them embarked, together with their children and a maidservant, for Amelia's house in the country. His stated intention in making all this up is to shield her from too sudden a gust of prosperity, which might violently trans-port her mind. Fielding just leaves it at that, except that he allows Harrison to be similarly devious. But as Amelia herself says, she has already shown how well she can endure happiness, on Booth's release from prison. What we have here, surely, is yet another case of Booth's professed kindness taking the form of delaying Amelia's joy unnecessarily, sadistically almost, as during their court-ship. Moreover, the imagery of his invented dream — the coach and four — is ominous. It hints that, despite all talk of his reformation, his pride of place will continue unabated. The writing does not ironically point such possibilities in the immediate verbal texture. But in the larger context of the novel as a whole, they do suggest themselves.

In reaching towards them, readers are doing what they have been doing throughout, in passages of dramatic and omniscient presentation alike. As A. R. Humphreys very finely remarked,

> We grow into the book, testing each character at each appearance, and perpetu-
> ally making discoveries and assessments. Few novels come nearer to the tenta-
> tive and provisional adjustments we seek in life to new persons and situations;
> we advance through the book with little feeling that the material is ready made.
> The surprises come, with some exceptions, not by evident manipulation but by
> natural emergence of fresh revelation.[144]

As readers we are ourselves implicated in the plot's ambiguities, and our position is analogous to that of Booth and Amelia themselves. A critic who blamed
as improbable their belief that Atkinson is going to marry Mrs Ellison rather
than Mrs Bennet was wise after the event.[145] This was one perfectly reasonable
interpretation of the evidence as it at this stage presented itself, to the Booths
and us alike. That it was wrong, that the apparently demure Mrs Bennet goes
beyond Mrs Ellison's loose vulgarity of speech to positive predatoriness — and,
as we later learn, is hardly less devoted to the bottle — enforces the novel's
finally relentless naturalism all the more powerfully.

Here and throughout, the essential design is to involve us in Booth and
Amelia's heuristic adventure, their attempts at probable explanations of other
people's behaviour. Their speculations are not idle, but urgently necessary, providing the only basis for their own continuing choices and actions. If Booth's
suspicions of the peer lead him, despite Mrs Ellison's promptings, to veto Amelia's attendance at Ranelagh, then his own hopes of the peer's favour will be at
an end. Are the suspicions really justified, then? Earlier in the novel, it had not
taken all that long for Booth to "read" Miss Mathews. But in the central drama,
different interpretations of Mrs Ellison, Mrs Bennet, James and the peer are all
held in sustained conflict with each other. Perhaps Mrs Bennet's only reason for
advising against the masquerade is that she has received no invitation herself.
But why did Mrs Ellison, if Mrs Bennet is somehow not respectable, help her in
distress and introduce her to Amelia? Or is Mrs Ellison simply aiming to pique
Booth? On the other hand, Mrs Ellison's dislike of him is not necessarily unreasonable, and Booth's dislike of Mrs Ellison could be a sign of guilt since, *pace*
Thackeray, he does undervalue Amelia at least as much as Mrs Ellison alleges.
And Mrs Ellison did show some merit (in a chapter which, though omitted
from the second edition, is not just a parenthetical swipe at the medical profession), by helping Amelia find a good doctor for her child, an important link
in the Booths' chain of indebtedness to her. The viciousness of the peer is in
any case far less blatant than that of the corresponding peer in *The Modern
Husband*. Or rather, Amelia cannot see, and Booth cannot see for himself, what
the reader is partly told. As with Henry James's later novels, there is a vague but

ever intensifying sense of menace. The characters are writing stories, as it were, which are in dissonance with a real story that readers themselves discover only gradually.

The exact focus is constantly shifting. During Mrs Bennet's long narration, her informative value for Amelia is at once clinched and exhausted by the fearfully mounting parallel between their two histories. But at the same time she begins to be fascinating in other ways as well. As a would-be bluestocking, what are her own credentials for criticizing her bluestocking aunt? More generally, although she tries to whitewash herself, and although we do feel some sympathy for her distresses, we can easily see that her fancy was taken, like Booth's, by worldly vanities. Perhaps her readiness, like Miss Mathews, to blame her sexual fall on drink is also deceitful. On the other hand, she clearly does drink, her grossnesses placing an increasing pressure on her polite forms. Somewhat similarly, the odd association between Amelia and Blear-eyed Moll is suddenly re-charged, when we learn that the peer's chief gift to Mrs Bennet, Amelia'a predecessor in his attentions, was the pox. Mrs Bennet's narration insidiously draws us into a world from which Mr Wilson's narration in *Joseph Andrews* briskly hastened away.

To take a second variation of focus, Amelia and Booth also have secrets from each other, though she finds out about his long before Booth, or the reader, realizes. At what point she confirms Booth in his suspicions of the peer Fielding never actually tells us (though she has clearly done so by X 12). But for much of the time, and with more deeply felt perplexity than Mrs Bellamant in *The Modern Husband*, she is disguising threats to her virtue for fear that her husband may resort to a duel. The first case of this happened in France, and Booth himself reports it in his narrative to Miss Mathews. In doing so, he temporarily adopts his original, blinkered viewpoint, so that we have to read between the lines or simply wait till his narration of the full disclosure by Bath. That he should once again don the same blinkers, in not consciously noticing the machinations of James and the peer, is all too ironic, especially after he has heard some inadvertent revelations about James by Atkinson.

We are now, then, a very long way indeed from the simple character typologies of the earlier novels, and the most fascinating riddle of all is obviously Booth, himself one of the explorer-protagonists. For Robert L. Oakman, however, Booth was among the novel's chief weaknesses, largely because he has so many roles.[146] As a husband, a mere second-rate man dependent on his wife, he is on the whole unconvincing, said Oakman, because passivized by too little freedom of movement. At the same time he has to be the mouthpiece for Fielding's ideas on morality and society, and, quite inconsistently, to play the part of the godless cynic. On top of which he also has to be the representative victim of social injustice. This last point I shall return to. Suffice it here that Booth's passivization is the natural consequence of an ever-encroaching social corruption whose extent Oakham quite underestimated. We are *not* still reading *Tom Jones*. As for a more general Modernist response, it would be that Oakam was a one-track-minded critic who preferred simple stereotypes to psychological complexity. The different roles he distinguished for Booth are not only compatible with each other, but help to make Booth the supreme creation of Fielding's reluctant naturalism. The pathos of his victimization carries his creator's own recoil from the brutal forces he everywhere sees at work, and Booth is a reluctant naturalist himself. He sees the iniquities of publication by subscription: yet his experience of neglected merit forces him to toady to interest no less corruptly. He delivers a tirade on the justice which ought to befall the maid who betrays Amelia by stealing her linen: yet Oakman's reading of this as an authorial comment on the legal system was deaf to the tirade's dramatic force. Who is Booth to condemn a betrayer of Amelia, and in such a trifle? His own finer marital gestures shy away from society's prevailing evils: yet his adultery, and his general lack of consideration for Amelia, participate in them. His vacillation between Barrowistic platitudes and Humean free-thinking is frighteningly convincing.

Moved by passion? Of course he is. But exactly which passion, and when? The novel's opening situation anticipates the motif of prior amatory attachments in novels by Thomas Hardy. Despite a clearly acknowledged prior attachment to Miss Mathews, Booth has nevertheless married Amelia, whom he championed in much the same way as he had championed Miss Mathews against her spiteful friends. On now confronting his first love again, he confuses things still further by responding to her tendernesses, thus betraying his second love. His generous boldness becomes foolhardy weakness almost imperceptibly. Similarly, although he angrily rejects — out of pride, naturally — Trent's idea of sacrificing Amelia's reputation for the sake of financial gain, and although — from pride again — he is punctilious in his honour as a soldier, he is also capable of loose salaciousness and cowardly deviousness. The reader groans, finding him too, too real. His ribald waggishness at Mrs Ellison's tale of Atkinson denied her inner chamber; his guilty anger in charging Amelia herself with a breach of honour: all is equally distasteful or painful to Amelia. And when he cannot bring himself to tell her directly that he plans to go to the West Indies and leave her under the protection of James, Fielding's command of strange areas of the psyche can again have few precedents in the English novel. As in their original courtship, at one level Booth wants to spare her, but in fact he only wounds. Like the dreaming Atkinson, he has some dim sense of what he is suppressing — his waving aside of Atkinson's reluctant disclosures about James was sufficiently marked. Unconsciously he knows the danger Amelia fears, and he is forcing her to brave it. If she goes on resisting James, and if tragedy ensues, Booth's self-esteem will perhaps only be flattered. Certainly it is from Booth himself that she suffers most cruelty, and he may even goad her into inciting the cruelty's continuance. Her very goodness may almost be turning into a kind of perversion, as the dialogue again rises to an intensity that anticipates Jane Austen — or, rather, Ivy Compton-Burnett. Booth's language is replete with horrendous *double entendres*, each of which screws Amelia's anguish to a still higher pitch. The creepy echo of the Restoration stage leaves us uncertain whether to laugh or cry.

> "What can you mean, Mr. *Booth*?" cries *Amelia*, trembling.
> "Need I explain my Meaning to you more?" answered *Booth.* — "Did I not say, I must give up my *Amelia*?"
> "Give me up!" said she.
> "For a Time only, I mean", answered he: "for a short Time perhaps. The Colonel himself [James] will take Care it shall not be long — for I know his Heart; I shall scarce have more Joy in receiving you back than he will have in restoring you to my Arms. In the mean Time, he will not only be a Father to my Children, but a Husband to you."
> "A Husband to me!" said Amelia.[147]

In following the lives of this "very worthy Couple after their uniting in the State of Matrimony",[148] then, the novel resists comedy. In *Jonathan Wild*, Fielding remarked that most comedies and novels suggest that the future ensuing upon their happy endings will be like Salisbury Plain: pleasant, but always the same. In its own style, *Jonathan Wild* challenged that convention, yet did not fail to be resoundingly comic: the marital strife of Wild and Letty, yes; but also, secure poetical justice for Wild, and unassailable marital bliss for the Heartfrees. In *Amelia*, marriage, though in one sense it is the main subject, in another sense means nothing at all. A wedding introduces no change, no automatic magic, no levelling off of tension. The one wedding actually described is that of Miss Mathews's sister, which figures only as a link in the relentlessly uncoiling psychological development of Miss Mathews. Still more to the point, Booth's waverings in affection, and the lover's unkindnesses which he inflicts and Amelia forgives, persist from courtship, during the marital trials, and even to the stage when their externally imposed affliction is coming to an end. This sado-masochism represents the most disturbing of all the naturalistic insights Fielding's honesty shocks him by opening up. The text responds to a Modernist expectation of such unpleasantness just as readily as do the tales of wife-breaking in *David Copperfield*, or the contemplation of cruelty to rabbits, birds and birch trees in Robert Frost.

∽

So much for the private sphere. But as Fielding notes in his dedication to Allen, his aim is to expose "glaring Evils" that are not only private but public, and several critics have said that his view of society has now become more holistic. Robert Alter, for instance, on the basis of the treatment of marriage, found that *Amelia* "anticipates the masterful interlocking of separate lives through shared situation that gives *Middlemarch* such remarkable structural coherence".[149] A.R. Humphreys commented, similarly:

> Fielding creates a social group so fully related as to be a living society. That he can handle the abundant material of his London scenes and at the same time give the individual lives in their imaginative reality is the mark of technical strength and human understanding unparalleled in English fiction save by Thackeray, George Eliot and Henry James.[150]

Amelia, in quite new ways, is a novel *about* society. For one thing, Fielding appears to be questioning some of his earlier patrician certainties. Perhaps the status quo is not quite so stable as it seemed, and this may even be a good thing. Captain Atkinson, in particular, is a new departure, not only because he dreams, but because he at one and the same time knows his place yet actually moves up in the world. Fielding cannot help remarking, in his old fashion, on Atkinson's ungraceful deportment in polite society, and he notes Atkinson's deference towards the better-born Booth with approval. Yet there are also those hints that Atkinson may nevertheless be the worthier of the two. Fielding, who, to do him credit, thought that there are more things in life than can be learned from a gentleman dancing-master, warms to the man's natural goodness, and to his full appreciation of Amelia's beauteous virtue.

More generally, he shows a new interest in those who may be suffering from social and financial deprivation. As Digeon put it, the novel shows "the power which society endows on wealth and how difficult it is to be proud and virtuous when one is poor"; Amelia, exposed to "that insidious seduction" faced by all poor women at every step, is the first authentic case of the *tragique quotidien* to be treated in a novel. This means that money

> begins to play the important part which it was to retain in the works of our realists; money visible or hidden, is the mainspring of the action, and gives rise to all its most agonizing turns.[151]

The preoccupation with corruption is correspondingly strong, and Cynthia Griffin Wolff pointed out that Fielding, though himself a legal reformer, sometimes seems less than confident about the future. Legislators can try to curb social evils, and particular laws can be improved, as with the law relating to perjury. But whereas rewards and punishments after death are administered infallibly by God, so that religion conceivably has coercive force, the civil law is man-made, corruptible and unpredictable. Sometimes those administering it are themselves wicked. Sometimes they are virtuous, but too lenient. Innocent victims are unprotected and powerless, and infection by the social ills of the day is resistant to cure. Strict laws do not actually work.[152]

So injustice thrives. Whereas Captain Merit in *The Modern Husband* and the poor lieutenant in *Tom Jones* are minor characters whose lack of deserved advancement is soon forgotten, the focus on Booth's career makes such wrongs very central. What we see is that nobody really cares. There is a Wild-like cynicism abroad, and that tense dialogue between Harrison and the powerful nobleman shows that this attitude is as respectable as it is pervasive. With a few exceptions such as in the portrayal of Trent, Fielding's earlier easy assurance that the cynical view belongs to the spiritually deformed has disappeared. In *Tom Jones*, recommendations of prudence were cancelled out because people are so irrational as individuals. In *Amelia*, there is a further sense that, even if the protagonists were *personally* capable of prudence, society would not give them a chance to show it. Booth's sins, unlike Tom's, are the sins of that entire society. Frail though he is, his distresses, too, have a representative quality and are not altogether his own fault; his first imprisonment, quite unfairly, at the hands of Justice Thrasher sets the pattern. Whereas Lawyer Scout in *Joseph Andrews* was an exceptional blemish on a beautiful system, and whereas even Western in *Tom Jones* listened to his clerk, in *Amelia* Justice Thrasher is the stated norm, so that the fair-minded magistrates who rule on Amelia's stolen linen and a case of perjury come as a pleasant surprise, and the legal restitution of Amelia's family fortunes as nothing short of a miracle. Thanks to the frustration of the peer's wicked designs, we may begin to wonder whether Trent has been caught and brought to account. But whereas in *The Modern Husband* the discomfiture of Mr Modern, the willing cuckold who corresponds to Trent, is publicised, the world of *Amelia* is so evil that a single conviction would not be much to write home about.

Against this background the masquerade acquires a strange symbolic intensity. As noted earlier, Terry Castle saw the masquerades in both *Tom Jones* and *Amelia* as loosening things up and leading to a more rapid denouement. She also said that they suggest the fascination of evil, and tempt Fielding into moralizing. Yet the masquerade in *Tom Jones* connotes, as I say, less of high society's evil than of its sheer boredom. The one in *Amelia*, by contrast, really is disturbing, and can remind us of Dickens as seen by the Modernist critics, Edmund Wilson and Lionel Trilling. What Fielding conveys here is an arresting sense of dream or phantasmagoria, as his realism sickeningly blurs into something like surrealism. The disguises paradoxically *reveal* lust, pride and malice, and bizarrely, he arranges for Harrison's jeremiad against adultery to be declaimed by a roué. As with Atkinson's dream and some of the novel's dialogues, what seems to be forcing its way to the surface is the invincible energy of an omnipresent irrationality.

The fairytale romance of the protagonists who are finally accorded their due social position is taking on a new colouring. In the previous novels, such couples have been up against the freaks of chance and the scheming of exceptional individuals. In *Amelia*, they themselves are being turned into exceptional individuals by reason of their virtuous merit, while the threats they encounter represent an evil that is very widespread in society as a whole. We are well on the way, in other words, to some of the most disturbing insights of late Dickens. One might even argue that the anonymity of the vicious peer, and also the name "Thrasher", though lamented by some critics as lapses from an otherwise powerful realism, have a profoundly generalizing appropriateness. Compare, in *Little Dorrit*, Bishop, Bar or the Barnacles. Robert Alter already felt that evil in *Amelia* is a very nearly institutionalized, so that a turnkey and a nobleman would be functionaries of the same cynical system.[153] Even the catastrophe reminds us somewhat of Dickens: the legal cobwebs, the corrupt lawyer, the maniacally energetic detective and champion of right, the smaller criminal — a greater criminal's instrument — who repents and informs.

Throughout the novel, moreover, there is a very unsettling kind of patterning. There would seem to be a constant danger that the opposition between virtuous protagonists and evil society will be eroded. Just as William Dorrit thrives on the genteel cant which also makes him pine, so Booth and Amelia, in their struggles to escape, are for ever being sucked into the vast, immoral whirl-pool of society. Booth drinks, gambles, duels. His fickleness is not less alarming than James's. And his own experiences of, and opinion about, human psychology make him, again like James, a bold free-thinker. The only difference lies in that conscientious reluctance he shares with his creator. Amelia, similarly, by accepting the peer's gifts, and by allowing Mrs Atkinson to stand in for her at the masquerade, is implicating herself in compromises that would make her a second Mrs Atkinson. Because Fielding's account of the masquerade suddenly switches from omniscient to dramatic narration, so that the reader is no more aware than Booth that his masked companion is not his wife, it suddenly seems that Amelia really is flirting with other men like a Mrs Atkinson. Mrs Atkinson, in her turn, is only one tenuous remove from the evil Mrs Ellison. All distinction between person and person, virtue and vice, is for ever crumbling away in a relentless entelechy of all-pervading, all-moving passion, sanctioned by a God so blind and arbitrary that he can scarcely be said to exist. The natural drives of these human beings make them quite frightening enough in the private sphere. But their society, the exponential product of those same drives, hardly bears thinking about.

∾

Where does all this leave us? In part, my mediation has been between Fielding's quarrelling critics. The controversy now so deeply embedded our culture is not surprising, and can be traced back to Fielding's own flexibility of mind. Fielding himself has a very rich vein of rumbustious naturalistic comedy, involving simple character types, poetic justice, and complete acceptance of the social status quo. But he also has a highly developed philosophical disposition, and is a responsible citizen with thoughts about private and public morality and the organization of society. His gut instinct that people are moved by passion never changes, but he is not always sure that human beings are as straightforwardly understandable as his comic novels mainly suggest. Sometimes he wishes that people could control their natural drives by the exercise of reason, and that there could be some more obvious sort of justice in the world. He can even have a sense of the stable social order giving way to animalistic chaos. His tone can be very far from comic.

The first four novels are clearly more predominantly comic than *Amelia*, though they, too, have clear signs of his more serious concerns. In some respects *Amelia* attempts to sustain the comic note, but he now sees the wider, social implications of his naturalistic psychology, and the overall mood is closer to the tragic. If there had not been both the comic side and the potentially tragic side to his work, two sides which sometimes comfortably coexist in the same text but which do sometimes seem to be in tension with each other, the proposition facing readers and critics would have been more straightforward and less interesting. Either as a comic writer pure and simple, or as a serious writer pure and simple, Fielding could easily have been forgotten. As things are, he ranges between extremes of sensibility in a way that almost anticipates Robert Frost. But with notable exceptions such as Ehrenpreis, different critics, seizing on different aspects of his work, have expressed themselves over-coherently. There has been a compulsion to praise and blame Fielding by squeezing him into the mould of either a whole-heartedly jovial writer or a thoroughgoingly solemn one.

Believing in readers' imaginative flexibility, the mediating critic explores a wide range of human potentiality as a resource for the future. This means that every side of Fielding will be of interest, so that he must be thought of in more than one way at once. Given the cultural tradition within which he has come to be read, real readers are already likely to have a fairly pluralistic view of him. Although those who read him as they read the living are probably responding most immediately to his rumbustious naturalistic comedy, their response may already be partly running in other channels as well. These the mediating critic can seek to broaden and deepen.

With this goal in mind, I have occasionally drawn comparisons and contrasts with Jane Austen, Ivy Compton-Burnett, Samuel Butler, Thomas Hardy, and Richardson. But my main strategy has been to apply an unpleasant Modernist perspective, a perspective which, though it has long been applied to Dickens, was not introduced into Fielding studies until the work of Claude Rawson. In developing Rawson's line of argument I have focussed sharply on *Amelia*, and have suggested, first, that this novel strongly anticipates the Modernist novel as inaugurated by Henry James and, secondly, that it can also be illuminated by comparison with late Dickens as perceived by Modernist critics such as Wilson and Trilling.

Seeing *Amelia* as a fairly late Jamesian novel highlights its treatment of the private sphere, and in particular the despondent uncertainty of its beautiful heroine. Her dilemma is that of a relatively innocent individual in an evil world with which she is forced to have dealings, and in which the only way to prevent great evil may be by becoming slightly evil herself. This erosion of moral boundaries is a constant concern here. In Fielding's four earlier novels, Nature's vigor was always working at the root, but love was still clearly distinct from lust. In *Amelia*, and most obviously in the portrayal of the Atkinsons, such distinctions are blurred. More generally, the novel seems to have an aleatory casualness which leaves many other things unexplained as well, part of the complication coming from humanity itself as now perceived. There is no question that people are still driven by their passions. But it now seems that they usually have more than one passion at once. It is very difficult to know which passion is dominant at any given time, and since the motivation for actions is ambiguous, it becomes almost impossible for the reader to make firm moral judgements. What compounds the difficulty is that Fielding also intermixes omniscient narration with very long stretches of unreliable narration by three main characters, and that, even as an omniscient narrator, his own judgements are now less unambiguous, his characterization less straightforward, and his challenge to the reader's own powers of deduction much more apparent. Precisely as in late James, these tendencies involve the reader in the same heuristic adventure as the main characters themselves, an adventure in which there is a steadily increasing sense of menace, and in which the reader is not necessarily piecing things together in the same way as the characters. Herein lies the novel's realism: the overall effect is as interesting and problematic for a reader as is life itself to the average observer. There are constant slight shifts of perspective, throwing up new ironic parallels and interpretative cruxes, with the characterization of Booth emerging as an especially complex and sophisticated masterpiece of very pressing reality. Booth is reluctant naturalism incarnate, kind in his cruelty, cruel in his kindness, temperamentally religious in his disbelief, blindly falling into the evil he sees and shuns. Moreover, Booth is *always* like this. Despite the novel's forced happy ending, there is no real sense of a threshold having been crossed. There is no comic rounding off with a wedding. As so often in James, the plot's delights and torments are not pre-marital but marital and extramarital.

Comparing *Amelia* with the late Dickens of Edmund Wilson and Lionel Trilling, one especially notes the book's social dimension. Above all, there is beginning to be, despite some looseness and digressiveness, a sense of society as a whole, and of social phenomena which are widespread rather than particular and arbitrary. Fielding's patrician sense of the status quo has here been seriously shaken. There is a new concern with social and financial underprivilege, together with a more sympathetic response to upward social mobility, especially as represented by Atkinson. Fielding now seems far less sure than previously that those in power actually deserve to be in power. Very like the late Dickens, he thinks of the legal system as rotten through and through, and he is beginning to see that everything is held in place by greed, lust and corruption. By the same token, innocence and true merit are curiously naked and exposed, but even the victims of society are corrupted by it. Booth simply will not see what is going on in the triangle between himself, Amelia and James, and his professed concern for the well-being of his wife is potentially as sinister as David Copperfield's loving domination of Dora. In Booth, Fielding is beginning to feel his way towards individual repressions that internalize, and are structured by, the surrounding society. The next step would be to have a projection character for Booth with the same role that Murdstone has for David. Although Fielding still holds on to a difference between good and evil, his naturalistic vision is of society as a dizzyingly confused whirlpool into which everybody is drawn relentlessly. The still virtuous are a minority group which is for ever being psychologically and morally assimilated into an appalling wickedness, a pattern which a kind of surrealistic realism, as in late Dickens, sometimes presents with fearsomely heightened intensity.

So an unpleasant Modernist reading does make a kind of sense. Yet the process of mediation I have been trying to set in motion is not only between Fielding's various critics, but between our own urgently present moment and Fielding's increasingly far-away past. In order for the process to be complete it must be bi-directional. In the ways I hope to have suggested, the Modernist perspective on Fielding can help us see him differently, and can become part of the way in which we now read him. But Fielding's own eighteenth century perspective on us, as one might put it, will become part of the way in which we experience ourselves, and may well suggest some of the personal and cultural possibilities which may lie ahead. In discovering the Modernist Fielding, in emphasizing his naturalistic sense of the selfish drives underlying human behaviour, we tend to highlight what his contemporaries would have thought of as a Tory pessimism, a sensibility and set of values with which Modernist-style readers who read for pain may feel a natural affinity. But in the fullest act of mediation, we will also try to mediate between ourselves and the Fielding who does *not* seem so close, the Fielding whose see-saw temperament could also lead him to endorse the optimism sometimes labelled Whiggish. That more distant Fielding was very real for Fielding himself — an important aspect of Fielding's own Fielding, as one might say — and we should be absurdly arrogant to reject its continuing human potentiality. By confronting it head-on, we can see ourselves more clearly than through the spectacles of literary Modernism, precisely because it is now much further outside of us. Which is not to say that it should never be reintegrated into our mainstream. On the contrary, we may badly need it.

The most non-Modernist thing about Fielding is that his first four novels, despite his unswervingly naturalistic view of human psychology, are still comic. In the long run this is significant, not because he managed to render the happy endings probable — he did not, and our willing suspension of disbelief will be temporary at best — but because he so spontaneously understood and shared readers' *desire* for happy endings. If Lady Mary Mortley Montagu disliked the element of wish-fulfilment on moral grounds, on a Modernist view it is likely to seem a cheapening of Fielding's artistic integrity as well, a pandering to popular taste. Yet Fielding remains one of the most articulately self-conscious of all English novelists, and much of his art is frankly of the kind which recognizes the human right to love, laughter, happiness and fair play. This represents intellectual honesty of a kind which was seldom praised in the twentieth century. Readers influenced by the Modernist view of human life and human nature were much more likely to praise writers who show how fragile and illusory human happiness can be, writers who bring home to us life's meanness, tragedy and horror. We need such writers, obviously, and the Fielding of *Amelia* is one of the most interesting of them. Yet even work such as theirs stems from an underlying faith in communication, and we also need writers who more openly recognize the "grand and elementary principle of pleasure" and the human hope of joy. This the prodigiously gifted and many-sided Fielding did as well. His four great comic novels worked, and can still work, by binding readers together in the desire for happiness and pleasure, and by generously trying to satisfy it. In observing the comic decorums, they triumphantly assert the commonality of human aspirations, and can do this in any time and place, and despite humanity's myriad realizations. In no small part, this is what readers today still find in him who read him as they read the living, readers unlikely to be cowed into too much Modernist gloom.

Even in *Amelia*, along with all the lugubrious passages of tired despair and the willed hilarity of the happy ending, there are aspects of the old Fielding which must qualify an unpleasant reading. Despite the Dickensian range and intensity of the novel's social vision, Booth, in his repressed cruelty towards Amelia, is one of only two characters — Atkinson is the other — for whom a mask is at all internalized. As noted earlier, although most of the characters deceive each other, they do not on the whole deceive themselves. When they acquiesce in the social rot, they do so consciously, however grudgingly. To distinguish between right and wrong may be extremely difficult in practice, but is still taken to be possible in principle. This fundamental assumption on which the old society used to be grounded remains in place, even if badly shaken and soon liable to crumble away altogether. Fielding already seriously doubts the probity and effectiveness of the legal profession to which he has devoted so much of his life. But he has not quite given up the ideal of a frank and straightforward moral code.

And despite critics' comparisons with *Middlemarch*, the social vision of *Amelia* is still not quite that coherent. At times the novel reads more like Fielding's later travelogue, *A Voyage to Lisbon*, with its random observations of mainly local abuses, and its proposals for piecemeal and essentially conservative reform — when his journey brings him up against the idleness and extortionateness of the poor, for instance, he opines that a J. P. would be justified in fixing the price of labour so as to ensure that they will have to work very hard for very little pay. In *Amelia*, the problems identified include: the evils of publication by subscription; the viciousness of Ranelagh and Vauxhall; venal Justices; disrespect of the clergy; duelling; and, as in *A Voyage to Lisbon*, petty officials who abuse their authority at the expense of gentlemen. Often an appropriate specific is prescribed, and in all these cases the writing has the same static quality as in the portrayal of Amelia as ideal wife. We may also be reminded of Fielding's journalistic essays on particular cases or fashions.

So his modernistically Dickensian insights are not developed into a social critique quite comprehensive and radical enough to appeal to a Wilson or a Trilling. Instead, the assumption seems to be that, given the exercise of common sense, and given a firm treatment of the lower orders, everything will be all right. This same optimism is what underlies the book's happy ending, at which point George Sherburn (1936) accuses Fielding of turning his back on the social problems altogether, much in the manner of Smollett, Johnson and Goldsmith, all of them deeply conservative writers who, though critical of the aristocracy, had no desire to overthrow the *ancien régime*.[154] Some of the social evils in *Amelia* even prompt him to a carefree kind of brio we shall recognize from *Jonathan Wild*. The biography of Trent, especially, is a miniature masterpiece of controlled scorn, penned in full confidence of the reader's perceiving its butt as a diseased automatism who is quite outside the club of *viri boni*.

Dickens was born 23 years after the French Revolution, whereas *Amelia* was published 38 years before it. Dickens knew that the old order could collapse, and in the climaxes of some of his late novels the establishment takes some very rude knocks — Trollope's view of him as a radical was not altogether misplaced. In *Amelia*, Fielding can no longer blame the widespread social corruption onto the accident of Walpole's bad government, but is forced to consider whether a country under the leadership of Pelham, whom he genuinely admired, would have come to such a pass unless the very system itself were at fault.[155] Even so, he shows not the slightest inclination to deal the system its death-blow. This caution is well understood by Battestin, who, having compared the novel's detailed and far-reaching social insight to that of Marx, hastens to insist on Fielding's intense fear of "the Fourth Estate", as he called it: "THE MOB; which seem at present in a fair Way to get the better of all the rest",[156] and which could only be restrained — as Marx was again to argue — by religion's pledges to the unprivileged of a better life beyond the grave. In Fielding's view, the ideological weapon of religion needed strong support from the army and the Law, and the Law's efficacy needed to be demonstrated through the public spectacle of awesome hangings.[157] As for John Richetti's wish that his novels had given more of a say to the poor, it is jejunely anachronistic. A person of Fielding's class and experience would simply have had no time for it,[158] being quite unable to see how a transfer of power, if such an event could be contemplated as even remotely desirable in principle, could in practice take place without the most horrific bloodshed.

Nor would he have lacked all prescience here. On the contrary, Fielding's attitude points up a curious omission in Terry Castle's history of masquerades, in the section where, somewhat at a loss to explain why they finally went out of fashion, she merely said that they were out of key with the age of reason and the decline of old folk ways.[159] A far more significant factor is to be found in what became of the sexual, social and racial liberation prefigured by their utopian scenarios as Revolution moved inexorably to Terror. Fielding clearly saw the masquerade's breaking-down of social barriers as very threatening indeed. The only alternative to contemporary society allowed in *Amelia* is in Booth's marital bliss and rural contentment at the close, an escapist idyll of safely Horatian pedigree.

But for all that, the masquerade's hint of a different order did not pass unnoticed, and a side of Fielding's imagination was positively attracted. Here it is once again Atkinson who is interesting, since, in a world still partly feudal, he rises, so that his life is something of a masquerade mutation in itself. In a more meritocratic world, in the world for which Fielding is certainly making a plea when he laments the injustices dealt out to Booth, Atkinson would outstrip Booth altogether, and his sheer human excellence is part of what Amelia responds to in her softened heart's "momentary Tenderness". No less interestingly, a second possibility is foreshadowed by Amelia herself: a world in which the homosocial ideals which so consistently blind Booth to his own and his family's best interests would no longer hold sway. As Jill Campbell pointed out, Fielding's trajectory here is well suggested by comparison with John Hill, author of *On the Management and Education of Children* (1754). Hill, who argues that a gentleman must firmly complement a mother's instruction, thinks that *Amelia* goes too far in the maternal direction.[160]

What a better world would be like Fielding partly sensed, then. But in the nature of things, he could not foresee everything, and we still cannot do so today. We are living in a world which is partly post-feudal, partly post-bourgeois, partly post-colonial and so on, but which, above all, is still far from perfect. Even today, most of us — even that extremely small percentage of the human race likely to take an interest in Henry Fielding — shrink from imagining what universal justice would mean in practice. Since some other people's share of the cake is always bigger than our own, we easily forget those who hardly receive a crumb — and forget that such metaphors may be indistinguishable from literal reality.

Fielding has sensed that vagueness about the future is dangerous. He sees how a Booth, lacking a sustaining vision, can turn sour and cynical. Even more suggestively, he sees Atkinson, quite possibly the man of that day's tomorrow, having to make his way, having to marry, in a world that falls far short of his desire. Atkinson's true desire is not for the upward social mobility he is actually achieving, and the question of rewards for merit is in a way a side-track. What Fielding shows Atkinson trying to forget is his thirst for beauty, virtue, probity, justice. If those high ideals were to be realized, everything else would follow. As things are, Atkinson deliberately short-circuits the great human hope so generously recognized by Fielding's earlier novels. That, basically, is what he represses when he hides his love of Amelia so that it will haunt him only in his dreams. Amelia's significance, that is to say, is far greater than that of just another human being, and while Booth fails to see this, not to see it is Atkinson's whole aim. His platonic self-distancing from her would have charmed Dr Bowdler, born in 1754, the year of Fielding's death. But its implications for the grand and elementary principle of pleasure were very ominous.

Dickens, David Copperfield, Mr Whitfield and perhaps even Uriah Heep preserve, in Agnes Whitfield, something of the ideological significance of the angelic woman. But unlike Fielding or his male characters, they tend to deprive her, not only of her body, but of her interest as a person with a mind and life of her own. Agnes is far more angel than woman, which is the way Thackeray sees (Fielding's) Amelia, too. In our own time, not even her ideological significance survives, not least because feminists have helped us to see that those who serve as a society's utopian signifiers are often the people whose significance in the real world is most undervalued. Perhaps the human — not merely male — need to which Amelia might once have answered, instead of entering into some entirely new scheme of cultural figuration, has been positively repressed. As early as Fielding's day, it was certainly under threat, as when Atkinson forces it into the dream in which both she and, with her, the need itself come under attack from Colonel James. As for Fielding's own recommendation of Amelia, not even his twentieth century feminist admirers denied the moments of strain. What his pastness gives us here is a clear anticipation of the Modernist scepticism in face of hope, but at a point in time when the need that was going unsatisfied was more clearly remembered and recognized. If we read this novel in an unreservedly Modernist way, the sentimentally idealized heroine merely gets on our nerves. If we also sympathize with the feminist readings, our irritation may tend to seek relief in those aspects of her which Fielding does make more genuinely credible. What both responses leave unspoken is our own desire for a better world than any so far known.

When Rawson finally opened up the discussion of Fielding's naturalism, this was bound to appeal to readers brought up on Henry James and on Trilling and Wilson's Dickens. A return to Fielding as a kind of Isaac Barrow *manqué* no longer seems likely. All the same, and assuming that the naturalism will from now on be central to our sense of him, his own reluctance to face it may gradually arouse fresh interest. In this reluctance, in his creation of Amelia herself, as also in his four great comic novels, Fielding's instinct was to do whatever he could to make life happy. Frost and Dickens would also see the point of such a goal, and even today it is not one to shy away from. These three writers themselves are more than enough to stop us being naive about it. But even when they give no grounds or little imagery for hope, they still communicate hope's pulse, and invite an answering vibration. On their very grimmest page, what they never fail to inscribe is their belief in a reader who accepts the power of human need and desire to bond all kinds of people together, a belief which real readers owe it to themselves to vindicate, not least when the writer's life-world is quite different from their own. Such otherness may prove significant.

Epilogue

Mediating critics and common [*sic*] readers [*sic*]

As I mentioned at the outset, twentieth century criticism could be as intelligent, timely, and sensitive as the criticism of any previous age. True, it was produced in huge quantities. In 1969 John Gross was already saying,

> To . . . [take] the example of Pope: a generation or so ago very little of real note had been added to what eighteenth-century critics had said. Today there are, I suppose, at least half-a-dozen full-length critical studies which are worth reading, while a leading American scholar has edited an anthology entitled *44 Essential Articles on Pope*. None of this represents wasted labour. But what are we all going to do when there are forty-four essential *books*?[1]

Thirty years further on, and with scores and scores of books now written about every major — and many a minor — author, the answer has become obvious enough. Unless we confine our interests to just a very small number of authors, we are simply not going to read all the critical studies, and in point of fact, a few of them are far more essential than most others. For it is true, too, that quality did also become a problem. Not least, the somewhat contradictory emphases of early-to-mid-century critics on literature's formal properties and on its often disturbing unpleasantness could become exaggerated, routine and de-human-izing, as could also the later emphasis on literature's consubstantiality with language, culture, society. But to point out the drawbacks of a fossilizing scho-lasticism is not to detract from the century's finest critical writings, without whose stimulus I personally, at least, would never have devoted so much time and thought to seven literary authors. Many critics were in any case working around the edges of the dominant paradigms, or in unfashionable disregard of them. Much of the best work continued to take the form of literary biography, for instance, which was probably more widely purchased and read, in its own way doing more to promote an interest in literary texts, than all the other forms of commentary taken together. Think only of Ellmann on Wilde, Holroyd on Shaw, or Holmes on Coleridge.[2]

Yet under changing social circumstances, and in the interests of literary culture itself, we do need to take stock, just as twentieth century critics themselves provided a complement to what had gone before. In this book, I have been arguing that literary criticism could now afford to become more consciously rooted in the real life-experience of human beings, sometimes precisely through a happy reunion with biography. Although this would represent a return to the down-to-earthness of some nineteenth century critical practice, the type of commentary I have in mind would also be far from oblivious of twentieth century developments, and would be entirely of our own age in both its underlying theory and its function.

In a nutshell, my suggestion has been that literature can be viewed as one among other forms of communicative interaction between social individuals, and that such an account offers the necessary foundations for mediation as a central role in both literary criticism and literary education. A mediating commentary, even while recognizing that readers' attempts at empathy will sometimes end in disagreement or even disapproval, increases the chances of literature's remaining what, for its warmest admirers, it has always been: a vital source of inspiration and communion, and a catalyst to understanding and change. More distinctively, the mediating approach does not confine humanity to a single mould, but is postmodern in the most rewarding sense. Not only the differences between various historical periods, but also the differences between cultural and sub-cultural groupings co-existing within one and the same period, are seen as an endless resource, whose benefits a mediator's concern for communicational parity can help to maximize.

In illustrating mediation in action, I have moved sharply away from twentieth century criticism in its more de-humanizing forms. A mediating commentary's first premise is the agency of both authors and readers. It sees the writing and reading of a literary text as activities so strongly interpersonal that they can in principle establish an ever widening circle of community. This is where mediating commentators can themselves be a kind of human sounding board. By displaying qualities of empathy, generosity of acknowledgement, and responsive hopefulness — the three qualities I have emphasized in this book's three main parts — critics may be able to arouse an equivalent participation in their own audience.

By the same token, I have also been suggesting a counterbalance to that specialist professionalization of vernacular literary studies which set in after the waning of Classics.[3] By the last quarter of the twentieth century, many literary scholars read only certain journals and attended only certain kinds of conference. A large English department would duly have its Chaucer expert, its eighteenth-century satire expert, its feminist expert, and so on. And a frequent talking-point in departmental staffrooms was becoming the question of whether you needed to have read any actual literature in order to be an expert on literary theory. Under these circumstances, there was a risk that larger structures of understanding would not be developed as often as they might be, or that when they did emerge, some of the substantiating detail would be rather thin. The combination of wide perspectives and detailed nitty-gritty was increasingly likely to occur, not in the writings of scholars themselves, but somewhere else — perhaps in the private journal of one of the undergraduates shuttling between Chaucer classes, eighteenth-century satire classes, and classes on literary feminism. In the matter of actually making sense of all the different specialities and approaches, undergraduates were indeed left to their own devices. By which I am not implying that they should never have been allowed to make up their own minds. The point is merely that, to extend Gerald Graff's simile,[4] the curriculum had become too like a cafeteria counter, with no helpful waiter on hand to describe and contrast the attractions of all the various items.

A specialist cannot be blamed for preferring to communicate with other specialists, and some books and articles and notes are inevitably going to be above the non-specialist's head. This is the most likely way for a specialization to be consolidated. But to repeat my earlier observations, unless specialist findings are related to some larger view of things, they remain socially lifeless and inert; and all professions, especially those in receipt of public monies, do ultimately have to legitimate themselves in the public eye. For the profession of literary scholarship, this is specially awkward, since the expertise involved does not have a straightforwardly marketable utilitarian value, and relates to a topic on which, in principle, any ordinary member of the public may also have some insight. As scholars today, we may think of ourselves as still having, despite our economic status as professionals, a true amateur's love of the tasks we undertake. But if the love is never communicated in our actual writings, our position may be thrown in doubt. Our readers will be entitled to ask whether literature is actually real for us. Do we truly *know* the phenomenon we are purporting to discuss?

This is where twentieth-century scholarship did not always strike an appropriate balance. Sometimes scholars behaved as if a non-specialist's curiosity and enthusiasm could safely be left to one side. Not a few came to see themselves as positively superior to ordinary people, an attitude reflecting an academic culture which, still unaffected by Gadamer's rehabilitation of common sense, was particularly hospitable to certain kinds of task. To explain a poem as an impersonal verbal icon; to interpret a novel as casting unpleasant doubt on typical human responses and values; to describe a text as not the work of an author but as the product of culture; to engage in radical deconstructions: all such undertakings could in themselves be valuable enough, yet did create openings for a sort of intellectual one-up-manship. Even commentaries much less affected by the fashions for de-humanization could be produced solely for reasons of "publish or perish", in full awareness that not even scholars would take much interest in them. This was specialization driven to the point of solipsism, a mere pseudo-communication. Granted, there were also scholars who did address themselves to non-specialists by writing coursebooks. But coursebooks, too, could be rather limited in range, and were sometimes frankly downmarket, as if their likely reader was irredeemably unenlightened. As it happens, the dichotomy between the narrow-guttedly "specialist" book and the blatantly "popular" or "educational" book was by this time a basic principle of marketing for British and American publishers. Most houses' lists of books on literature for the general, cultivated reader were getting shorter and shorter. The explanation was not, I think, that increased access to higher education could only lower standards. In my own view, standards might just have easily have risen, since students and readers are what teachers and writers make them. Or rather, they can become what teachers and writers encourage them to make themselves.

But if some professionals were contemptuous of non-scholars, or simply lacked the general knowledge to make their specialist knowledge interesting, there were certainly other commentators who, like the literary journalists and gentlemen-amateurs of an earlier age, had a surer human touch. W. W. Robson, Bernard Bergonzi, Frank Kermode, Christopher Ricks, John Carey, Harold Bloom — educators like these continued to make themselves knowledgeable *in more than one area at a time*, and to write for a general, cultivated reader, who was keen for the latest information and ideas on particular topics, but who also wanted to see the larger bearings. Here literary criticism's addressee was recognizably an intelligent human being, quite clearly on a par with any critic.

This is the line I have been trying to extend. My gratitude for the work of professional specialists has, I hope, been clear in every chapter. Here and there, I have included new specialist findings of my own. But a more important aim has been to complement professionalist expertise with the enthusiasm and broader understanding of an amateur. Basically, I have been trying to place a wide variety of literary phenomena — several different authors from several different periods — within a single wide perspective, and in doing so, have assumed the possibility of a general, educated reader who will take an interest. My belief is that if, as literary scholars, we can sometimes refrain from talking above the heads of most people, or talking down to them; if, instead, we just talk *with* them, as with fellow human beings; if we assume that most readers are sensibly open to the human relevance of what they read; if we can bring out the human dimension of literature, as itself a kind of interactive communication; and if, drawing strength from a historical but non-deterministic theory of literary pragmatics, we can also mediate between writers and readers belonging to different times, places, or traditions: then our own work may well reach out to a whole company of general, cultivated readers who are merely waiting for an invitation to read themselves into existence. Teachers, too, in adapting the theory and general spirit of my proposals to the various levels of literary education, would be displaying a courteous and optimistic trust *vis à vis* their own students which would offer them this same enriching possibility.

Admittedly, for the postmodern age the notion of "the Common Reader" is just as problematic, though for different historical reasons, as for the age of Johnson.[5] In the West, the distinction between highbrow and lowbrow has lost some of its grounding in socioeconomic reality, and general, cultivated readers are nowadays bound to be cultivated in widely various ways.[6] Some single cultural literacy can no longer be a hegemonic straitjacket, which is precisely why the role of mediation has become so crucial. So here we can drop the capital letters and switch to an indefinite plural. "The Common Reader" never really existed, and even as an idea is now truly dead and buried. From now on, there can only be "common readers" of many different kinds.

Yet readers in the future, no matter how striking their differences from each other, from all of us now, and from all of our own predecessors, will be every bit as human as readers always have been. Although duly confident in their own autonomy and powers of judgement, they will also be: self-interestedly curious about the countless alternative forms of human life; fully equipped with the intellectual, imaginative and moral strength to empathize with such "otherness"; quite capable of recognizing true achievement when they see it; perfectly open to self-scrutiny, and even to re-formation; and despite any number of continuing and inevitable conflicts, potentially drawn together in their widely various dreams of joy and beauty, and in the need for fellowship and justice. This, surely, represents a humanity to which literary authors will always speak. So, too, I think, should pedagogues and critics.

Notes

Introduction

1. See discussions in Dale Sawak (ed.), *A Passion for Books* (Macmillan, Basingstoke, 1999) and Alvin Kernan, *The Death of Literature* (Yale University Press, New Haven, 1990).

2. See Elizabeth L. Eisenstein, "The End of the Book? Some Perspectives on Media Change", in Salwak, *A Passion for Books*, pp. 181–97.

3. See John Bayley, "Other Worlds to Inhabit", in Salwak, *A Passion for Books*, pp. 21–31.

4. Some men of letters were fully aware of this at the time. See especially John Gross, *The Rise and Fall of the Man of Letters: English Literary Life since 1800* ([1969] Penguin, Harmondsworth, 1973). In his "Epilogue" (pp. 310–28), Gross views the increasingly close connection between literary culture and the universities with a mixture of hope and apprehension.

5. See Roger D. Sell, "Communication: A Counterbalance to Professional Specialization", in Herbert Grabes (ed.), *Innovation and Continuity in English Studies* (Peter Lang, Frankfurt, 2001), pp. 73–89.

6. N. Parry and J. Parry, *The Rise of the Medical Profession* (London: Croom Helm, 1976), p. 79.

7. George Bernard Shaw, *The Doctor's Dilemma, Getting Married, & The Shewing-up of Blanco Posnet*, (Constable, London, 1921), p. xxii.

8. Roger D. Sell, *Literature as Communication: The Foundations of Mediating Criticism* (Benjamins, Amsterdam, 2000), p. 115.

9. *The Craft of Fiction* (Jonathan Cape, London, 1921).

10. *The Rhetoric of Fiction* (Chicago University Press, Chicago, 1941).

11. Hans-Georg Gadamer, *Truth and Method* ([1960], London, Sheed and Ward, 1989), pp. 277–307.

12. See Sell, *Literature as Communication*, pp. 271–77, and Richard Shusterman, "Don't Believe the Hype: Animadversions on the Critique of Popular Art", *Poetics Today* 14 (1993) 101–22.

13. See Eric Hobsbawm, *Age of Extremes: The Short Twentieth Century, 1914-91* (Abacus, London, 1995), pp. 287–343, and Amy Gutman (ed.), *Multiculturalism: Examining the Politics of Recognition* (Princeton University Press, Princeton, 1994).

14. Friedrich W. Nietzsche, *Thus Spake Zarathustra* ([German original 1883–92] Dent, London, 1933), p. 64, and *The Will to Power* ([German original 1888] Weidenfield & Nicolson, London, 1968), p. 77.

15. I quote from the summary of Goethe's position by Erich Auerbach. Auerbach was not anachronistic. He did not allow himself to wish that Goethe's aims and achievement had enjoyed the benefit of his own hindsight. But even so, himself an exile from Germany from 1936 onwards, he could not help wondering "what effect might have been exerted upon German literature and German society, if Goethe, with his vigorous sensuality, his mastery of life, his far-reaching and untrammeled vision, had devoted more interest and constructive effort to the emerging modern structure of life" (Erich Auerbach, *Mimesis: The Representation of Reality in Western Literature* ([1953] Doubleday, Garden City, 1957) pp. 398–9).

16. See John Carey, *The Intellectuals and the Masses: Pride and Prejudice among the Literary Intelligentsia, 1880–939* (Faber, London, 1992), esp. pp. 3–45.

17. José Ortega y Gasset, "The Dehumanization of Art", in his *The Dehumanization of Art and other Essays on Art, Culture, and Literature* ([Spanish original 1925] Princeton University Press, Princeton, 1968).

18. In his view, because poets had neglected the great themes of Stoicism, Scientism and Patriotism (his capitals). See Bonamy Dobrée, *The Broken Cistern* (Cohen and West, London, 1954).

19. Leavis's pamphlet, *Mass Civilization and Minority Culture*, was first published in 1930 (The Minority Press, Cambridge). In a slightly corrected form, it appeared as an appendix in his *Education and the University* (Chatto and Windus, London, [1943] new ed. 1948). Another important expression of the same concern was Q. D. Leavis, *Fiction and the Reading Public* (Chatto and Windus, London, 1932).

20. Phrasing taken from his "How to Teach Reading" (in *Education and the University*, pp. 106–7). The desirability of a new Common Reader continued to be urged for several decades, as for instance by Frank Kermode ("The Common Reader", *Daedalus*, Winter 1983, 1–11), who thought that educational endeavours were still very much in order, and by E. D. Hirsch, whose *Cultural Literacy* (Houghton Mifflin, Boston, 1987) had the sub-title, *What Every American Needs to Know*, provoking serious disagreement as to both the possibility and the desirability of just some single cultural norm in the United States.

21. My information on the growth of readership is mainly drawn from a series of classic studies by Richard D. Altick ("English Publishing and the Mass Audience in 1852", "The Literature of Imminent Democracy, 1859", "From Aldine to Everyman: Cheap Reprint Series of the English Classics, 1830–906", and "The Reading Public in England and America in 1900"), reprinted in Altick, *Writers, Readers, and Occasions: Selected Essays on Victorian Literature and Life* (Ohio State University Press, Columbus, 1989), pp. 141–58, 159–73, 174–95, 209–30). See also James Raven, Helen Small and Naomi Tadmor (eds.), *The Practice and Representation of Reading in England* (Cambridge University Press, Cambridge, 1996), esp. the bibliography (pp. 291–7).

22. Michael Holroyd, *Bernard Shaw, Vol.I, 1856–98. The Search for Love* (Chatto and Windus, London, 1988), p.79.

23. See Laurence Rainey, "The real scandal of *Ulysses*: How literary modernism came to retreat from the public sphere", *Times Literary Supplement*, January 31st, 1997.

24. See Ian Wilkinson, Warwick Gould and Warren Cornice (eds.), *Modernist Writers and the Marketplace* (Macmillan, London, 1996).

25. Thomas Strychacz, *Modernism, Mass Culture, and Individualism* (Cambridge University Press, Cambridge, 1993).

26. The historical task has been undertaken by, for instance: Christopher Butler, *Early Modernism: Literature, Music, and Painting in Europe, 1900-16* (Clarendon Press, Oxford, 1994); Peter Nicholls, *Modernisms: A Literary Guide* (Macmillan, London, 1995); Michael H. Levenson, *A Genealogy of Modernism: A Study of English Literary Doctrine 1908-22* (Cambridge University Press, Cambridge, 1983); Richard Shusterman, *T. S. Eliot and the Philosophy of Criticism* (Duckworth, London, 1988).

27. For instance, Christopher Ricks's *T. S. Eliot and Prejudice* of 1994 (Faber, London), though in effect arriving at Gadamerian conclusions, apparently did so in unconsciousness of Gadamer himself. But at least by that time, English-speaking readers no longer faced problems of accessibility. One helpful introduction was Kurt Meuller-Vollmer (ed.), *The Hermeneutics Reader: Texts of the German Tradition from the Englightenment to the Present* (Blackwell, Oxford, 1985), which included commentary and bibliographical information for further reading. The English translations of Gadamer's own most important writings were: *Philosophical Hermeneutics* [1962–72] (University of California Press, Berkeley, 1976); *Reason in the Age of Science* 1981[1976, 1978, 1979] (MIT Press, Cambridge, Mass., 1981); *The Relevance of the Beautiful and Other Essays* [1967, 1977, 1980] (Cambridge University Press, Cambridge, 1986); *Truth and Method* [1960] 1989. Excellent general commentaries were Joel Weinsheimer, *Gadamer's Hermeneutics: A Reading of* Truth and Method (Yale University Press, New Haven, 1985), and Georgia Warnke, *Gadamer: Hermeneutics, Tradition and Reason* (Polity Press, Cambridge, 1987). And the relevance to specifically literary concerns was discussed in: *New Literary History* 10 (Autumn 1978), a special issue on this topic; David Hoy, *The Critical Circle: Literature, History, and Philosophical Hermeneutics* (University of California Press, Berkeley, 1978); Judith Perkins, "Literary History: H.-G. Gadamer, T. S. Eliot and Virgil" (*Arethusa* 14 (1982) 241–9); and Joel Weinsheimer, *Philosophical Hermeneutics and Literary Theory* (Yale University Press, New Haven, 1991). More recently, there is Sell, *Literature as Communication*, pp. 137–45.

28. See Sell, *Literature as Communication*, pp. 88–106, and Raymond Tallis, *Enemies of Hope: A Critique of Contemporary Pessimism, Irrationalism, Anti-Humanism and Counter-Enlightenment* (Macmillan, Basingstoke, 1997).

29. Wayne C. Booth, *The Company We Keep: An Ethics of Fiction* (University of California Press, Berkeley, 1988).

30. Christopher Ricks, *Essays in Appreciation* (Clarendon Press, Oxford, 1996).

31. Frank Kermode, *An Appetite for Poetry* ([1989] Fontana, Glasgow, 1990).

32. *The Intellectuals and the Masses.*

33. Frank Lentricchia, "Last Will and Testament of an Ex-Literary Critic", *Lingua Franca*, October 1996, 59–67. I say "*even* Frank Lentricchia" because Lentricchia, during the middle part of his career, became well known as a champion of literary theory, or of Theory (as it was sometimes written).

34. F. R. Leavis, "The First Major Novel: *Dombey and Son*", in F. R. and Q. D. Leavis, *Dickens the Novelist* ([1970] Penguin, Harmondsworth, 1972), pp. 21–56, esp. 21.

35. Cf. Elizabeth L. Eisenstein, *The Printing Press as an Agent of Change* (Cambridge University Press, Cambridge, 1979); J. Goody (ed.), *Literacy in Traditional Societies* (Cambridge University Press, Cambridge, 1968); J. Goody, *The Domestication of the Savage Mind* (Cambridge University Press, Cambridge, 1977); J. Goody, *The Logic of Writing and the Organization of Society* (Cambridge University Press, Cambridge, 1986); J. Goody, *The Interface between the Written and the Oral* (Cambridge University Press, Cambridge, 1987); J. Halverson, "Havelock on Greek Orality and Literacy", *Journal of the History of Ideas* 53 (1992) 148–63; E. Havelock, *The Literate Revolution in Greece and its Cultural Consequences* (Princeton University Press, Princeton, 1982); E. Havelock, *The Muse Learns to Write* (Yale University Press, New Haven, 1986); E. Havelock, "Orality and Literacy, an Overview", *Language and Communication* 9 (1989) 87–98.

36. See also Roger D. Sell, "A Historical but Non-deterministic Pragmatics of Literary Communication", *Journal of Historical Pragmatics* 2 (2001) 1–32.

37. Cf. Gutman, *Multiculturalism*.

38. George Saintsbury, *Essays in English Literature, 1780–1860* (Percival, London, 1890), p. xii.

39. Cf. esp. Roland Barthes, "The Death of the Author" [French original, 1968], in his *Image-Music-Text: Essays Selected and Translated by Stephen Heath* (Fontana, Glasgow, 1977), pp. 142–8, and Michel Foucault, "What is an Author?" [1969], in Josué V. Harari (ed.) *Textual Strategies: Perspectives in Post-Structuralist Criticism* (Methuen, London, 1980), pp. 141–60.

40. Ferdinand de Saussure, *Course in General Linguistics* ([1916] Fontana, London, 1974), p. 14.

41. Raymond Tallis, *Enemies of Hope*, p. 228.

42. Claude Lévi-Strauss, "Overture to Le Cru et le Cuit" [1964], in Jacques Ehrmann (ed.), *Structuralism* (Anchor-Doubleday, Garden City, 1970), pp. 31–55, esp. 46.

43. Raymond Tallis, *Enemies of Hope*, p. 228. In this connection my *Literature as Communication* cites not only Tallis, but Frank Kermode, Emmanuel Levinas, Salman Rushdie, Wole Soyinka and Wilson Harris.

44. Cf. Cheryl Walker, "Persona Criticism and the Death of the Author", in William H. Epstein (ed.), *Contesting the Subject: Essays in the Postmodern Theory and Practice of Biography and Biographical Criticism* (Purdue University Press, West Lafayette, 1991), pp. 109–21.

45. Cf. Ian A. Bell, *Henry Fielding: Authorship and Authority* (Longman, London, 1994). See also pp. 294–6 below.

46. Leavis and Empson both wrote illuminatingly *about* history, of course, and sought to bring about a certain interdisciplinarity between the study of history and the study of literature. There are certainly also passages in which they recognize that "then" is not "now". More often, however, they tend to assume that a reader here and now can, should, and does read in exactly the same way as a reader in the there and then, and that the effect of any particular literary work will always be the same. See Sell, *Literature as Communication*, pp. 234–38. See also under "unitary context assumption" in the same work's Subject Index.

47. Charles Taylor, "The Politics of Recognition", in Gutman, *Multiculturalism*, pp. 25–73, esp. 32–5. Taylor acknowledges his indebtedness to George Herbert Mead's *Mind, Self, and Society* (University of Chicago Press, Chicago, 1934) for the term "significant other".

48. H. P. Grice, " Logic and Conversation" [1967], in Steven Davis (ed.). *Pragmatics: A Reader* (Oxford University Press, New York, 1991), pp. 305–15.

49. John Searle, "The Logical Status of Fictional Discourse", *New Literary History* 6 (1975) 319–92.

50. Sell, *Literature as Communication*, pp. 83–8.

51. Cf. Roger D. Sell, "*Henry V* and the Strength and Weakness of Words: Shakespearian Philology, Historicist Criticism, Communicative Pragmatics", *Neuphilologische Mitteilungen* 100 (1999) 535–63.

52. As in Gerald Graff, *Beyond the Culture Wars: How Teaching the Conflicts can Revitalize American Education* (Norton, New York, 1992) and Edward Said, *Culture and Imperialism* (Chatto and Windus, London, 1993). Graff and Said both recognize the need for a mediating criticism, and have written very directly about the condition of postmodernity: about the differences which have now so clearly defined themselves between writers and readers representing widely varied communities and sub-communities within the polycultural societies of the present. My own *Literature as Communication* has this same starting-point.

Chapter 1

1. William Gerhardie, *Futility: A Novel on Russian Themes* (Richard Cobden-Sanderson, London, 1922). Prior to the publication of *Futility*, Gerhardie had published only four short stories, totaling eleven pages, in *Oxford Fortnightly Review* and *Oxford Outlook*. For a full bibliography, see Dido Davies, *William Gerhardie: A Biography* (Oxford University Press, Oxford, 1990), pp. 394–5.

2. "His performance is, without exaggeration, astonishing" (*Times Literary Supplement*, July 20th, 1922).

3. *Futility* and *Memoirs* were republished by Robin Clark (London), and *God's Fifth Army* by The Hogarth Press (London).

4. See n. 1.

5. Frank Kermode's review of the Penguin Modern Classic edition of *Futility* for *London Review of Books* (2 April, 1981) is reprinted in his *The Uses of Error* (Fontana, London, 1991), pp. 308–16.

6. *The Novels of William Gerhardie* (Åbo Akademi University Press, Åbo, 1995).

7. In *Adelphi*, July 23rd.

8. Quoted on the dust-jacket of the revised definitive edition of Gerhardie's *Anton Chehov [sic]: a Critical Study* ([1923] Macdonald, London, 1974).

9. Ibid.

10. Davies, *William Gerhardie*, p. 313.

11. Marlene Dolitsky, *Under the Tumtum Tree: From Nonsense to Sense: A Study in Non-*

automatic Comprehension (Benjamins, Amsterdam, 1984). See also Roger D. Sell, *Literature as Communication: The Foundations of Mediation Criticism* (Benjamins, Amsterdam, 2000), pp. 132–33.

12. A. P. Sell to Roger D. Sell, September 12th, 1971. Cf. *Radio Times*, 2nd September, 1971: programmes for 4th September, and "The War We Forgot — but the Russians Didn't". The latter is an interview with Sir Brian Horrocks, who participated as a liaison officer with the First Siberian Army.

13. Davies, *William Gerhardie*, p. 100.

14. *Futility*, p. 145.

15. *Memoirs of a Polyglot* ([1931] Robin Clark, London, 1990), p. 139.

16. *Futility*, pp. 181–2.

17. *Futility*, pp. 172–3.

18. The notebooks are to be found in Box 11 of the Gerhardie Archive, Cambridge University Library (Additional Manuscript 8292).

19. *Futility*, p. 226.

20. E.g. Harry Levin, *James Joyce: A Critical Introduction* (2nd. ed., Faber, London, 1960), pp. 39–40, and Arnold Goldman, "James Joyce", in Bernard Bergonzi, *The Twentieth Century* (Sphere Books, London, 1970), pp. 75–105, esp. 85–6.

21. Richard Ellmann, *James Joyce: New and Revised Edition* (Oxford University Press, Oxford, 1982), p. 166 fn.

22. See Michael Holroyd's introduction to the 1974 edition, p. iii.

23. *Anton Chehov*, p. 86.

24. "The Metaphysical Poets", reprinted in *Selected Essays by T. S. Eliot* (Faber, London, 1951), pp. 281–91, esp. 289.

25. *Anton Chehov*, p. 85.

26. *Anton Chehov*, p. 24.

27. *Futility*, p. 86.

28. *Futility*, pp. 115–6.

29. *Anton Chehov*, p. 144.

30. *Futility*, p. 217.

31. *Futility*, pp. 16–17.

32. *Anton Chehov*, p. 44.

33. *Futility*, p. 256.

34. *Futility*, p. 11.

35. *Anton Chehov*, p. 48.

36. See p. 44 above.

37. *Memoirs of a Polyglot*, p. 257.

38. Davies, *William Gerhardie*, p. 301.

39. *Memoirs of a Polyglot*, p. 7.

40. *Anton Chehov*, pp. 144, 78–9, 110–16, 118–22, 97–104.

41. *Anton Chehov*, p. 44.

42. *Anton Chehov*, p. 8.

43. *Memoirs of a Polyglot*, p. 319.

44. *Memoirs of a Polyglot*, pp. 164–5.

45. Cf. K. Anthony Appiah, "Identity, Authenticity, Survival: Multicultural Societies and Social Reproduction", in Amy Gutman (ed.), *Multiculturalism: Examining the Politics of Recognition* (Princeton University Press, Princeton, 1994), pp. 149–63, esp. 159–60.

46. [Taylor's footnote:] George Herbert Mead, *Mind, Self and Society* (Chicago, Chicago University Press, 1934).

47. Charles Taylor, "The Politics of Recognition", in Gutman (ed.), *Multiculturalism*, pp. 25–73, esp. 32.

48. Randall Craig, "Evelyn Waugh and William Gerhardie", *Journal of Modern Literature* 16 (1990) 597–614, esp. 614.

49. Randall Craig, "The Early Fiction of William Gerhardie", *Novel: A Forum on Fiction* 15 (1982) 240–56, esp. 241.

Chapter 2

1. Sebastian Faulks, *The Fatal Englishman: Three Short Lives* ([1996] Vintage, London, 1997), p. 69.

2. De la More Press, London.

3. In *Cecil Barclay Simpson: A Memorial by Two Friends*, privately printed, Edinburgh. The other friend was D. M. Baillie, another contemporary from New College, Edinburgh, whose tribute was in prose.

4. *Boaz and Ruth and Other Poems*, (John G. Wilson, London, 1920); *The Death of Eli and Other Poems* (John G. Wilson, London, 1921); *Thirty-One Poems* (John G. Wilson, London, 1922); *The Adversary* (John G. Wilson, London, 1923).

5. All published by Jonathan Cape, London.

6. Jonathan Cape, London.

7. Both published by Jonathan Cape, London.

8. With twenty photographs by J. Allan Cash. Published by Hutchinson, London. Reprinted in 1957 by the Country Book Club.

9. Rupert Hart-Davis, London.

10. Rupert Hart-Davis, London.

11. Rupert Hart-Davis, London.

12. Rupert Hart-Davis, London.

13. S. P. C. K., London.

14. Respectively, Jonathan Cape, London and Rupert Hart-Davis, London.

15. *Quiet as Moss* (Rupert Hart-Davis, London) and *Burning as Light* (Rupert Hart-Davis, London).

16. Rupert Hart-Davis, London.

17. Penguin, Harmondsworth.

18. Longman with Faber, London.

19. Secker and Warburg, London.

20. *Acta Academiae Aboensis, ser. A. Humanoria* 56:1.

21. Secker and Warburg, London.

22. *The Observer*, 13th January, 1985.

23. "Andrew Young", *Hallmarks of Poetry: Reflections on a Theme* (University of Salzburg, 1994), pp. 68–82.

24. Edward Lowbury and Alison Young, *To Shirk no Idleness: A Critical Biography of the Poet Andrew Young* (University of Salzburg, Salzburg, 1997).

25. There were twenty-eight Bumpus poems in *Winter Harvest* and, respectively, twelve, nine, six and eleven in *The White Blackbird, Collected Poems* (1936), *Speak to the Earth*, and *The Green Man*. A further eleven Bumpus poems, finally, were included in the *Collected Poems* of 1960.

26. December 5th, 1958.

27. For a detailed account of the growth of Young's reputation, see Sell, *Trespassing Ghost*, pp. 222–38.

28. Quoted by Leonard Clark in his introduction to *Complete Poems: Andrew Young* (1974), p.16.

29. *Times Literary Supplement*, March 24th, 1910.

30. *Times Literary Supplement*, February 15th, 1923.

31. *Times Literary Supplement*, 22nd December, 1950.

32. *Times Literary Supplement*, December 11th, 1937.

33. See the tributes by Richard Church and John Betjeman in *Andrew Young: Portrait of a Poet* (pp. 46–50, 39–45). For links with Gilbert White and other country parsons see Church's review of *Collected Poems* (1950) in *The New Statesman and Nation* (December 30th, 1950, pp. 685–6); Leonard Clark and R. George Thomas, *Andrew Young and R. S. Thomas* [two separate accounts; Writers and Their Works series no. 196] (Longmans, Green & Co., London, 1964); Tom Stacey, "Andrew Young, R. S. Thomas and the Parson Poets", in Michael Holroyd (ed.), *Essays by Divers Hands 42* (Royal Society of Literature and Boydell Press, London, 1982), pp. 91–108.

34. In *Andrew Young: Prospect of a Poet*, pp. 61–8.

35. Review of *The Poet and the Landscape, New Statesman*, September 14th, 1962.

36. Review of *The Bird-Cage, Times Literary Supplement*, January 27th, 1927.

37. Review of *The New Shepherd, Times Literary Supplement*, March 10, 1932.

38. Viola Meynell, review of *The New Shepherd, The New Statesman and Nation*, May 7th, 1932.

39. Her review of *The Bird-Cage* and *The Cuckoo Clock* had found that his verse, though revealing a "disturbance" of "human consciousness", did not have "the clinching significance, and the very question asked seems to go astray, and not even tend in the direction of an answer". At that stage Meynell apparently felt that human significances were better clinched (*The New Statesman and Nation*, July 25th, 1931).

40. Review of *The White Blackbird, The Times Literary Supplement*, February 8th, 1936.

41. Review of *Collected Poems* (1950), *Times Literary Supplement*, December 22nd, 1950.

42. Christopher Hassall, in *Andrew Young: Prospect of a Poet*, p. 58.

43. Reviews of *Winter Harvest* and *Collected Poems* (1936), *Times Literary Supplement*, May 24th, 1934 and July 18th, 1936.

44. Leslie Norris, untitled essay, *Priapus*, Autumn 1965, facing pp. 10 and 11.

45. In *Andrew Young: Prospect of a Poet*, p. 101.

46. Review of *Complete Poems, New Statesman*, 22nd February, 1974.

47. John Baillie, in *Andrew Young: Prospect of a Poet*, pp. 35–8.

48. *The New Poly-Olbion*, p. 21.

49. *Poetical Works*, p. 292.

50. "Young Oats", *Poetical Works*, p. 32.

51. "The Swans", *Poetical Works*, p. 36.

52. *Poetical Works*, p. 38.

53. "The Missel-Thrush", *Poetical Works*, p. 59.

54. "A Dead Mole", *Poetical Works*, p. 63.

55. "Glow-Worms", *Poetical Works*, p. 62.

56. Andrew Young, *The Poet and the Landscape* (Rupert Hart-Davis, London, 1962), p. 52.

57. *Poet and the Landscape*, p. 60.

58. *A. E. Housman: Selected Prose*, ed. John Carter (Cambridge University Press, Cambridge, 1962), pp. 193–4.

59. *Poet and Landscape*, p. 60.

60. *Ibid*, Young's italics.

61. *Poet and the Landscape*, pp. 112, 76, 29.

62. *Poet and the Landscape*, p. 57.

63. F. R. Leavis, *Revaluation: Tradition and Development in English Poetry* ([1936] Penguin, Harmondsworth, 1964), p.47.

64. *Poet and the Landscape*, pp. 187, 106, 145.

65. *Poet and the Landscape*, pp. 97–9.

66. See W. J. Keith, *The Rural Tradition: William Cobbet, Gilbert White, and other Non-fiction Prose Writers of the English Countryside* (Harvester, London, 1975), pp. 177–84.

67. *Poet and the Landscape*, pp. 103–4.

68. *Poet and the Landscape*, pp. 48–51.

69. *Poet and the Landscape*, pp. 64–6.

70. Respectively: "The Missel-Thrush", "The Old Tree", "The Oak-Wood", "Killed by a Hawk", "The Stars", *Into Hades*, and "The Secret Wood".

71. *Poet and the Landscape*, p. 45.

72. *Poet and the Landscape*, p. 66.

73. *Poet and the Landscape*, p. 52.

74. *Poet and the Landscape*, pp. 54–5.

75. *Poet and the Landscape*, pp. 66–7.

76. *Poet and the Landscape*, p. 27.

77. Roland Barthes, "The Death of the Author" [French original, 1968], in his *Image-Music-Text: Essays Selected and Translated by Stephen Heath* (Fontana, Glasgow, 1977), pp. 142–8.

78. See pp. 22–5 above and Roger D. Sell, *Literature as Communication: The Foundations of Mediating Criticism* (2000), pp. 32, 45–7, 56–9, 78–9, 84, 88, 158–75, 206, 254, 283.

79. *A Prospect of Flowers*, p. 126.

80. *The New Poly-Olbion*, p. 10.

81. *The New Poly-Olbion*, p. 12.

82. Quoted from the first edition of *Into Hades* (1952).

83. Edward Lowbury and Alison Young, "Introduction", *The Poetical Works*, pp. xviii-xix.

84. *The New Poly-Olbion*, p. 24.

85. *The New Poly-Olbion*, p. 11.

86. *The New Poly-Olbion*, p. 29.

87. *Poetical Works*, p. 28.

88. *Poetical Works*, pp. 22, 27.

89. This phrase comes from the 1952 version but was omitted from the 1958 revision, whose text I otherwise follow here (*The Poetical Works*, p. 272).

90. "An Old Road", *Poetical Works*, p. 17.

91. *The New Shepherd*.

92. *Poetical Works*, p. 47.

93. *Into Hades*, *Poetical Works*, p. 273.

94. *Poetical Works*, p. xix.

95. "Night", *Boaz and Ruth*. Reprinted in *Complete Poems*, p. 250.

96. *Poetical Works*, p. 11.

97. *Poetical Works*, p. 82.

98. *Poetical Works*, p. 266.

99. Pp. 178–81.

100. *Poetical Works*, p. 75.

101. *Poetical Works*, p. 48.

102. *Into Hades, Poetical Works*, p. 268.

103. *The New Poly-Olbion*, p. 27.

104. *Poet and the Landscape*, p. 165.

105. *Poet and the Landscape*, p. 162.

106. Review of *Boaz and Ruth*, *Times Literary Supplement*, July 21st, 1921.

107. Review of *The Adversary*, *Times Literary Supplement*, July 17th, 1924.

108. Between Young and Frost there was a fundamental difference of temperament. See pp. 97–8, 205–7 below.

109. "March Hares", *Poetical Works*, p. 7.

110. "The Beech", *Poetical Works*, pp. 8–9.

111. "The Old Tree", *Poetical Works*, p. 5.

112. *The Poet and the Landscape*, p. 66.

113. *Poetical Works*, p. 53. In this version the poem includes a few late-middle tightenings-up for the *Collected Poems* of 1936.

114. *Poetical Works*, p. 82.

115. *Poetical Works*, pp. 73–4.

116. *Poetical Works*, p. 71.

117. *Poetical Works*, p. 331.

118. *Poetical Works*, p. 252.

119. *The New Poly-Olbion*, pp. 26–7.

120. *Poetical Works*, p. 229.

121. *Poet and the Landscape*, p. 166.

122. *The Poet and the Landscape*, p. 167.

123. *Poetic Jesus*, p. 29.

124. *Poetic Jesus*, p. 30.

125. See above, p. 79.

126. *Poetical Works*, pp. 236, 261.

127. Quoted on p. 53 of *The Poet and the Landscape*.

128. T. S. Eliot, "The Silurist", *The Dial* 83 (1927), pp. 259–63.

129. *Poetical Works*, p. 236.

130. *Poetical Works*, p. 236.

131. *Poetical Works*, p. 261.

132. *Poetical Works*, p. 228.

133. *Poetical Works*, p. 261.

134. *Poetical Works*, p. 258.

135. *Poetical Works*, p. 228.

136. *Poetical Works*, p. 286.

137. *Poetical Works*, p.274.

138. *Poetical Works*, p. 279.

139. *Poetical Works*, p. 281.

140. *Poetical Works*, p. 285.

141. *Poetical Works*, p. 276.

142. *Ibid.*

143. *Poetical Works*, p. 269.

144. *Poetical Works*, p. 281.

145. *Poetical Works*, p. 283.

146. *Poetical Works*, p. 274.

147. *Poetical Works*, p. 273.

148. *Poetical Works*, p. 269.

149. *Poetical Works*, p. 284.

150. *Poetical Works*, p. 266.

151. *Poetical Works*, pp. 267–8.

152. *Poetical Works*, p. 267.

153. *Poetical Works*, p. 280.

154. *The Observer*, 13th January, 1985.

155. *The Poetry of Robert Frost*, ed. Edward Connery Lathem (Jonathan Cape, London, 1972), p. 122.

156. *The Poet and the Landscape*, p. 168.

157. Cf. "The Labyrinth" and "One Foot in Eden", *Edwin Muir: Collected Poems* (Oxford University Press, New Jersey, 1960), pp.163–65, 227.

158. Edward Lowbury, "Andrew Young", p. 80.

159. See, for instance, C. K. Stead, *The New Poetic: Yeats to Eliot* (Harper, New York, 1964), p. 180 and F. R. Leavis, *Revaluation*, pp. 155–64.

160. John Bayley, *The Romantic Survival: A Study in Poetic Evolution* (2nd ed., Constable, London, 1969), pp. 127–85.

Chapter 3

1. "The Name and Nature of Poetry", *A. E. Housman: Selected Prose*, ed. John Carter (Cambridge University Press, Cambridge, 1962), esp. pp. 193–4.

2. Review of Housman's "The Name and Nature of Poetry", *Criterion* 13 (1933) 151–4, esp. 154.

3. T. S. Eliot, *The Use of Poetry and the Use of Criticism: Studies in the Relation of Criticism to Poetry in England* ([1933] Faber, London, 1964), pp. 144–5.

4. *The Use of Poetry*, p. 9.

5. "Tradition and the Individual Talent" [1919], in his *Selected Essays* (Faber, London, 1951), pp. 13–22, esp. 21.

6. James E. Miller, *T. S. Eliot's Personal Waste Land: Exorcism of the Demons* (University of Pennsylvania Press, University Park, 1977).

7. F. T. Prince, "The Man and the Mind", *Agenda* 23 (1985) 82–6, esp. 86.

8. See Andrew Ross, "*The Waste Land* and the Fantasy of Interpretation", *Representations* 8 (1984) 134–58.

9. Jewel Spears Brooker and Joseph Bentley, *Reading* The Waste Land: *Modernism and the Limits of Interpretation* (University of Massachusetts Press, Amherst, 1990).

10. See p. 70 above.

11. Maud Ellmann, *The Poetics of Impersonality: T. S. Eliot and Ezra Pound* (Harvester, Brighton, 1987), pp. 41, 2–3.

12. Ronald Bush, *T. S. Eliot: A Study of Character and Style* (Oxford University Press, Oxford, 1984).

13. Sanford Schwartz, "Beyond the 'Objective Correlative': Eliot and the Objectification of Emotion", in Laura Cowan (ed.), *T. S. Eliot: Man and Poet* [itself a significant title] *vol. 1* (National Poetry Foundation, University of Maine, Orono, 1990), pp. 321–41.

14. Erik Svarny, "*The Men of 1914*": T. S. Eliot and Early Modernism* (Open University Press, Milton Keynes, 1988), esp. p. 239.

15. Michael H. Levenson, *A Geneology of Modernism: A Study of English Literary Doctrine 1908–22* (Cambridge University Press, Cambridge, 1984), esp. pp. 163–4. Cf. Brian Lee, *Theory and Personality: the Significance of T.S. Eliot's Criticism* (Athlone Press, London, 1979).

16. Carol T. Christ, "T.S. Eliot and the Victorians", *Modern Philology* 79 (1981) 157–65, and "Self-Concealment and Self-Expression in Eliot's and Pound's Dramatic Monologues", *Victorian Poetry* 22 (1984) 217–26. Other examples are: David Ned Tobin, *The Present of the Past: T.S. Eliot's Victorian Inheritance* (UMI Research Press, Ann Arbor, 1985) and Carl Plasa, "Reading Tennyson in *Four Quartets*: the Example of 'East Coker'", *English: the Journal of the English Association* 40 (1991) 239–58.

17. "Various critics have done me the honour to interpret the poem [*The Waste Land*] in terms of criticism of the contemporary world, have considered it, indeed, as an important bit of social criticism. To me it was only the relief of a personal and wholly insignificant grouse

against life; it is just a piece of rhythmical grumbling." Quoted by Theodore Spencer during a lecture, recorded by Henry Ware Eliot, Eliot's brother, and printed in Valerie Eliot (ed.), *T. S. Eliot: The Waste Land: A Facsimile and Transcript of the Original Drafts Including the Annotations of Ezra Pound* (Harcourt Brace Jovanovich, New York, 1971), p. 1.

18. T.S. Eliot, *On Poetry and Poets* ([1957] London, Faber, 1985), esp. p. 56.

19. Richard Badenhausen, "'When the poet speaks only for himself': The Chorus as 'First Voice' in *Murder in the Cathedral*", in *T.S. Eliot; Man and Poet, vol. 1*, pp. 239–56.

20. Hirofumi Iwamassu, "Eliot's Personality in *The Waste Land*", *Kyushu American Literature* 27 (1986) 13–20.

21. Calvin Bedient, *"He Do the Police in Difference Voices": "The Waste Land" and Its Protagonist* (University of Chicago Press, Chicago, 1986), esp. pp. ix–x.

22. Keir Elam, "Much Ado About Doing Things With Words (and Other Means): Some Problems in the Pragmatics of Theatre and Drama", in Michael Issacharoff and Robin J. Jones (eds.) *Performing Texts* (University of Pennsylvania Press, Philadelphia, 1988), pp. 39–58.

23. For a general discussion of the politeness of literature see Roger D. Sell, *Literature as Communication: The Foundations of Mediating Criticism* (Benjamins, Amsterdam, 2000), pp. 207–30.

24. See e.g. John Press, *The Chequer'd Shade: Reflections on Obscurity in Poetry* (Oxford University Press, London, 1958).

25. Anthony Julius, *T. S. Eliot, Anti-Semitism, and Literary Form* (Cambridge University Press, Cambridge, 1995).

26. Michael Grant (ed.), *T. S. Eliot: The Critical Heritage*, vols. 1 and 2 (Routledge and Kegan Paul, London, 1982).

27. F. Lucas, review of *The Waste Land*, *New Statesman*, 3rd November, 1923.

28. See Ashley Brown, "T. S. Eliot in the Postmodern Age", *Virginian Quarterly Review* 65 (1989) 693–701.

29. E.g. T. H. B. M. Harmsen, "T. S. Eliot's Poetic Testament: the Personality of the Impersonality Seeker", *English Studies* 69 (1988) 509–17; Victor P. H. Li, "'The Poetry does not Matter': *Four Quartets* and the Rhetoric of Humility", *T.S. Eliot Annual no. 1* (Macmillan, Basingstoke, 1990), pp. 63–86; Paul Murray, *T. S. Eliot and Mysticism: The Secret History of* Four Quartets (Macmillan, Basingstoke, 1991).

30. See Harriet Davidson, *T.S. Eliot and Hermeneutics: Absence and Interpretation in "The Waste Land"* (Louisiana State University Press, Baton Rouge, 1985).

31. See Jeffrey M. Perl, *Skepticism and Modern Enmity: Before and After Eliot* (Johns Hopkins University Press, Baltimore, 1988).

32. Shyamal Bagchee, "Eliot and the Poetics of 'Unpleasantness'", in Bagchee (ed.) *T. S. Eliot: A Voice Descanting: Centenary Essays* (Macmillan, Basingstoke, 1990), pp. 255–70.

33. Clare R. Kinney, "Fragmentary Excess, Copious Death: *The Waste Land* as Anti-Narrative", *Journal of Narrative Technique* 17 (1987) 273–85.

34. Denis Donoghue, "The Word Within a Word", in A. D. Moody (ed.), *The Waste Land in*

Different Voices (Arnold, London, 1974), pp. 185–201, esp. 191.

35. Chong-Ho Lee, "Eliot and Postmodernism: Postmodernity in *The Waste Land*", *Journal of English Language and Literature* 36 (1990) 29–54.

36. Ruth Nevo, "*The Waste Land*: Ur-Text of Deconstruction", *New Literary History* 13 (1982) 453–61.

37. Cf. e.g. Wolfgang Iser, *The Implied Reader: Patterns of Communication in Prose Fiction from Bunyan to Beckett* (Johns Hopkins University Press, Baltimore, 1974).

38. All quotations of Eliot's poetry will be from T.S. Eliot, *The Complete Poems and Plays of* ... (Faber, London, 1969), in which "A Game of Chess" appears on pp. 64–6.

39. H.P. Grice, "Logic and Conversation", in Steven Davies (ed.), *Pragmatics: A Reader* (Oxford University Press, New York, 1991), pp. 305–15.

40. Dan Sperber and Deirdre Wilson, *Relevance: Communication and Cognition* ([1986] Blackwell, Oxford, 1995).

41. Terence Hawkes draws attention to the rag-time song Eliot echoes here (in his *That Shakespeherian Rag: Essays on a Critical Process* (Methuen, London, 1986)).

42. See Roger D. Sell, "Two Types of Style Contrast in *King Lear*: A Literary-Critical Appraisal", in Håkan Ringbom (ed.), *Style and Text: Studies Presented to Nils Erik Enkvist* (Scriptor, Stockholm, 1975), pp. 158–71, esp. 165–70.

43. *Waste Land Facsimile*, pp. 17, 126.

44. Rupert Sheldrake, *A New Science of Life: The Hypothesis of Formative Causation* (Blond and Briggs, London, 1981) and *The Presence of the Past: Resonance and the Habits of Nature* (Collins, London, 1988).

45. *Complete Poems and Plays*, p. 62.

46. *Letters of John Keats*, ed. Frederick Page (Oxford University Press, London, 1954), p. 52.

47. T.S. Eliot, *The Sacred Wood* ([1920] Methuen, London, 1960), p. 169.

48. Helen Gardner, "Four Quartets: A Commentary", in B. Rajan (ed.) *Focus Three: T. S. Eliot, A Study of His Writings by Several Hands* (Dennis and Dobson, London, 1947), pp. 57–77.

49. Edmund Wilson, "T.S. Eliot", in his *Axel's Castle: A Study in the Imaginative Literature of 1870–1930* ([1931] Fontana, London, 1961), pp. 80–110.

50. F.R. Leavis, *New Bearings in English Poetry* ([1932] Penguin, Harmondsworth, 1963), p. 71.

51. *Complete Poems and Plays*, p. 67.

52. Graham Hough, *Image and Experience* (Duckworth, London, 1960).

53. *Selected Essays*, p. 289.

54. Yvor Winters, *On Modern Poets* (Meridian, New York, 1959), p. 70.

55. *Selected Essays*, p. 287.

56. Cleanth Brooks, *Modern Poetry and the Tradition* ([1939] University of North Carolina Press, Chapel Hill, 1965), p. 172.

57. *The Use of Poetry*, pp. 151–2.

58. Reprinted in *On Poetry and Poets*.

59. I. A. Richards, *Principles of Literary Criticism* (Routledge and Kegan Paul, London, 1926), pp. 289–95.

60. See his "Marie Lloyd" [1923], in his *Selected Essays*, pp. 456–9.

61. See Richard Badenhausen, "'Communal Pleasure' in a Uniform Culture: T. S. Eliot's Search for an Audience", *English Language Notes* 29 (1992) 61–9.

62. "The Writer as Artist: Discussion between T. S. Eliot and Desmond Hawkins", *The Listener*, 28th November, 1940, p. 773.

63. See Lyndall Gordon, *Eliot's Early Years* (Oxford University Press, Oxford, 1977), pp. 83–4.

64. Peter Ackroyd, *T.S. Eliot* ([1984] Abacus, London, 1985), p. 166.

65. See below, p. 219.

66. The biographical details mentioned in this paragraph were covered by, for instance, Gordon, *Eliot's Early Years* and Ackroyd, *T.S. Eliot*. Interpretations of Eliot provide some of the examples in a more extensive discussion of the relationship between reading and literary gossip in Roger D. Sell, "Literary Gossip, Literary Theory, Literary Pragmatics", in Sell and Peter Verdonk (ed.), *Literature and the New Interdisciplinarity: Poetics, Linguistics, History* (Rodopi, Amsterdam, 1994), pp. 221–41.

67. Charles Dickens, *Our Mutual Friend* [1865], ed. E. Salter Savies (Oxford University Press, London, 1952), p. 198 (Chapter 16).

68. Calvin Bedient, *"He Do the Police in Different Voices"*.

69. Roger Hughes, *The Shock of the New: Art and the Century of Change* (Thames and Hudson, London, [updated and enlarged ed.] 1991), p. 9.

70. Stephen Spender, *Eliot* (Fontana/Collins, Glasgow, 1975), p. 129. Cf. C. A. Patrides, "T. S. Eliot: Alliances of Levity and Seriousness", *Sewanee Review* 96 (1988) 77–94.

71. *Selected Essays*, pp. 292–304, esp. 293, 296.

72. *The Sacred Wood*, p. 169.

73. See Sell, *Literature as Communication*, pp. 8–12, 266–71.

Chapter 4

1. Roland Barthes, "The Death of the Author" [French original, 1968], in his *Image-Music-Text: Essays Selected and Translated by Stephen Heath* (Fontana, Glasgow, 1977), pp. 142–8. Cf. Roger D. Sell, *Literature as Communication: The Foundations of Mediating Criticism* (Benjamin, Amsterdam, 2000), pp. 88–106, 199.

2. The lines of battle between traditionalists and Modernists were clearly drawn up by the middle of the century. They can be quickly traced with the help of descriptive bibliographies in Robert E. Bourdette, "Recent Studies in Henry Vaughan", *English Literary Renaissance* 4

(1974), 299–310, and Kenneth Friedenreich, *Henry Vaughan* (Twayne, Boston, 1978).

3. As will soon emerge, I endorse the general autobiographical slant of the traditional approach to Vaughan. As for his conversion, much turns on the two sets of introductory matter to *Silex Scintillans*, which for reasons soon to be given I take at their word. The emblem and the Latin poem of the 1650 edition say that Vaughan has long been so insensitive to God's approaches that God has suddenly decided upon sterner measures: "*Accedis proprior, molemque ex* saxea *rumpis/Pectora, fitque* caro, *quod fuit ante* lapsis." (All quotations from: *Henry Vaughan: The Complete Poems*, ed. Alan Rudrum ([1976] Penguin, Harmondsworth, 1983).) It seems natural to take this as an allusion to his feelings at the loss of his brother William, especially in the light of some of the opening poems such as "Thou that know'st for whom I mourn", where the grief is seen as essentially chastening, and "Joy of my life! while left me here", where the dead loved-one is said to be a "pillar-fire" which leads to the heavenly city. In the preface of 1655 Vaughan regrets his earlier non-devotional verse and speaks of himself as one who has been converted by the religious poetry of Herbert. He has tried to suppress his "greatest follies" and is glad that "those which escaped from me" are "innoxious" and "interlined with many virtuous, and some pious mixtures". One of the reasons for the new preface to the second edition may have been a desire to account in this way for the publication of *Olor Iscanus* in December 1647. In July 1648 William died. And in the publisher's note to *Olor Iscanus* it is clearly stated that Vaughan had tried to withdraw the poems and that they were being published against his will. This statement is corroborated by William R. Parker's examination of the circumstances of publication ("Henry Vaughan and his Publishers", *The Library* 20 (1940) 401–11): neither Vaughan himself nor, unusually, his brother Thomas apparently had anything to do with it. Nothing, to my own mind, could be more likely than that the impacts of Herbert's example and William's death fell within roughly the same period, a period during which he suffered other shocks as well: the execution of Charles II, the Act for the better Propagation and Preaching the Gospel in Wales (1650), and his own financial difficulties. All this could well have contributed to a fairly sudden shift in Vaughan's spiritual life and poetic aims, a likelihood which suits with other poems as well, and which also persuades Christopher Hill ("Henry Vaughan (1621 or 1622? - 1695)" in his *Collected Essays, Vol. I: Writing and Revolution in Seventeenth Century England* (Harvester, Brighton, 1985), pp. 207–25) and Stevie Davies (*Henry Vaughan*, seren, Bridgend, 1995). For a more cautious and less traditional view of the "conversion", see Jonathan F.S. Post, *Henry Vaughan: The Unfolding Vision* (Princeton University Press, Princeton, 1982), E.L. Marilla, "The Religious Conversion of Henry Vaughan", *Review of English Studies* 21 (1945) 15–22, and James D. Simmonds, *Masques of God: Form and Theme in the Poetry of Henry Vaughan* (University of Pittsburgh Press, Pittsburgh, 1972), who all argue for a much more gradual development of religious interest. There can be no denying that events of 1645 — the banning of the Prayer Book and the execution of Laud — must already have registered with him and, as will soon emerge, that the nature of his religious concerns continued to change after the first *Silex Scintillans*. But for the argument of the present chapter, it suffices that those concerns had at least begun to take shape by the time he wrote the earliest poems in *Silex Scintillans*.

4. Again, I find no reason to disbelieve the 1655 preface, which speaks of illness and is thereby concordant with some poems. Marilla is probably correct, however, in assigning the onset to 1653–54.

5. The book-length discussions of this question include: Elizabeth Holmes, *Henry Vaughan and the Hermetic Philosophy* (Blackwell, Oxford, 1932); Ross Garner, *Henry Vaughan: Experience and the Tradition* (University of Chicago Press, Chicago, 1959); E. C. Pettet, *Of Paradise and Light: A Study of Vaughan's* Silex Scintillans (Cambridge University Press, Cambridge, 1960); and R. A. Durr, *On the Mystical Poetry of Henry Vaughan* (Harvard University Press, Cambridge, Mass., 1962). All of these explicitly or implicitly take issue with the anti-autobiographical trend in Modernist criticism, Garner and Pettet with particularly sharp words on Frank Kermode (see n. 6). Holmes credits Vaughan with mystic glimpses. Garner says that the poems embody, not so much mystic experience itself, as a longing for mystic experience. Pettet finds a development towards greater peace in the edition of 1655. And Durr finds the first three stages of the traditional *via mystica* though not the last two: not the dark night and final union, but certainly the awakening, purgation and illumination.

6. Apart from a small "inconsistency" soon to be noted, Frank Kermode is a clear case of the Modernist approach ("The Private Imagery of Henry Vaughan", *Review of English Studies* 1 (1950) 206–25).

7. Kermode, "The Private Imagery of Henry Vaughan", p. 225.

8. *Complete Poems*, p. 143.

9. See Introduction, pp. 22–5 above.

10. *Complete Poems*, p. 142.

11. George Williamson, *Milton and Others* (Faber, London, 1965), pp. 165–79.

12. Louis L. Martz, *The Poetry of Meditation: A Study in English Religious Literature of the Seventeenth Century* ([1954] Yale University Press, New Haven, 1962), pp. 64–7.

13. Many details of phrasing are sensitively discussed by Gerald Hammond, "Henry Vaughan's Verbal Subtlety: Wordplay in 'Silex Scintillans'", *Modern Language Review* 79 (1984) 526–40.

14. "They are all gone into a world of light", *Complete Poems*, pp. 246–7.

15. "Easter-Hymn", *Complete Poems*, p. 216.

16. "The World", *Complete Poems*, pp. 227–8.

17. Sharon Cadmon Seelig, *The Shadow of Eternity: Belief and Structure in Herbert, Vaughan and Traherne* (University Press of Kentucky, Lexington, 1981), pp. 63–5.

18. *Ibid.*

19. Stanley Fish, *Surprised by Sin: The Reader in* Paradise Lost (Macmillan, London, 1967).

20. My description here is influenced by Christopher Hill ("Henry Vaughan"), though Vaughan is sometimes seen as more Cavalier than this.

21. *The Works of Henry Vaughan*, ed. L. C. Martin (Oxford University Press, Oxford, 1957), p. 166.

22. Cf. Janet E. Halley, "Versions of the Self and the Politics of Privacy in *Silex Scintillans*", *George Herbert Journal* 7 (1984) 51–71.

23. Halley, "Versions of the Self".

24. Friedenreich, *Henry Vaughan*.

25. Simmonds, *Masques of God*.

26. Louis L. Martz, "Henry Vaughan: The Man Within", *PMLA 78* (1963) 40–9.

27. Chris Fitter, "Henry Vaughan's Landscapes of Military Occupation", *Essays in Criticism* 43 (1992) 123–47, esp. 142–3. Fitter's brilliant reading of "The Waterfall" tends to suggest that Christopher Hill's account of the not particularly Cavalier small Welsh squire may be a bit too revisionist. The poem shows Vaughan's fascination with "a shining current of Cavalier coolness and grace, borne helplessly to its fate by time's treacherous 'stealth'" (p. 126).

28. See Boyd M. Berry, "Childhood and the Self in *Silex Scintillans*", *George Herbert Journal* 7 (1984) 73–90, and John N. Wall, *Transformations of the Word: Spenser, Herbert, Vaughan* (University of Georgia Press, Athens, 1988), pp. 293–365. Their account of the second edition modifies that of Garner (see n. 5 above).

29. See Robert Wilcher, "'Then keep the ancient way!' A Study of Henry Vaughan's *Silex Scintillans*", *Durham University Journal* 76 (1983) 11–24.

30. See Introduction, pp. 22–5 above.

31. Cf. the contrast drawn by Seelig between Herbert's "Peace" and Vaughan's "I walked the other day" (n. 17 above). Garner has a whole chapter entitled "Vaughan as the Poet of Experience" (*Henry Vaughan*, pp. 130–44).

32. My account of deixis is mainly based on Stephen Levinson, *Pragmatics* (Cambridge University Press, Cambridge, 1983), pp. 54–96, who gives further references. Early discussions of literary deixis include: Meir Sternberg, "Deictic Sequence: World, Language and Convention", in Gisa Rauh (ed.), *Essays on Deixis* (Gunter Narr, Tübingen, 1983) pp. 277–316; Balz Engler, "Deixis and the Status of Poetic Texts", in Udo Fries (ed.) *The Structure of Texts* (Gunter Narr, Tübingen, 1987), pp. 65–73; and an earlier version of the present chapter (Roger D. Sell, "The Unstable Discourse of Henry Vaughan: A Literary-Pragmatic Account", in Alan Rudrum (ed.), *Essential Articles for the Study of Henry Vaughan* (Archon, Hamden, Conn., 1987), pp. 311–32). Since then the topic has continued to attract interest. See, for instance, Keith Green (ed.) *New Essays in Deixis: Discourse, Narrative, Literature* (Rodopi, Amsterdam, 1995), and Sell, *Literature as Communication*, pp. 164–6.

33. See Introduction, pp. 22–5 above.

34. Livia Polanyi ("Literary Complexity in Everyday Storytelling", in Deborah Tannen (ed.), *Spoken and Written Language: Exploring Orality and Literacy* (Ablex, Norwood, N.J., 1982) pp. 155–70) shows that the deixis of oral narratives is a factor in setting up the intradiegetic world of the story over against the extradiegetic world of the narrator, with its own "I-now-here". She analyses the subtle ways in which an oral narrator can exploit this circumstance.

35. *Complete Poems*, p. 143.

36. *Complete Poems*, pp. 157–9.

37. Particularly from what I have elsewhere called Beaumont's sacerdotal poems (Roger D. Sell, *The Shorter Poems of Sir John Beaumont: A Critical Edition with an Introduction and Commentary*, Acta Academiae Aboensis, ser. A. Humaniora, 49 (1974), esp. pp. 40–4). As a recusant at the time of the Gunpowder Plot scare, Beaumont also had to enter on a life of rural retirement. He found that poems by Juvenal, Horace, Ausonius and Claudian spoke to

his situation, and he also translated some of them, often into iambic pentameter couplets. Vaughan likewise.

38. *Complete Poems*, pp. 240–2.

39. Thomas A. Calhoun, *Henry Vaughan: the Achievement of* Silex Scintillans (University of Delaware Press, Newark, 1981), p. 64. Fredson Bowers's article, "Henry Vaughan's Multiple Time Scheme" (*Modern Language Quarterly* 33 (1963) 291–326), has a promising title from our present point of view, but is actually about the way Vaughan uses time as an idea and as part of his Christian allegory; it is not about time as a dimension of his discourse. For pragmatic and psycholinguistic accounts of self-contextualization by narrative texts, see for instance: Wallace L. Chafe, "The Deployment of Consciousness in the Production of Narrative", in Chafe (ed.), *The Pear Stories: Cognitive, Cultural and Linguistic Aspects of Narrative Production* (Ablex, Norwood, N.J., 1980), pp. 9–50; Charles J. Fillmore, "Pragmatics and the Description of Discourse", in Peter Cole (ed.) *Radical Pragmatics* (Academic Press, New York, 1981), pp. 143–81; Margaret Rader, "Context in Written Language: The Case of Imaginative Fiction", in Deborah Tannen, *Spoken and Written Language*, pp. 185–98.

40. Dan Sperber and Deirdre Wilson, "Irony and the Use-Mention Distinction", in Cole, *Radical Pragmatics*, pp. 295–318.

41. *Complete Poems*, p. 198.

Chapter 5

1. James Joyce, *A Portrait of the Artist as a Young Man* ([1916] Penguin, Harmondsworth, 1960), pp. 214–5.

2. Barbara Hardy, "The Complexity of Dickens", in Michael Slater (ed.), *Dickens: 1970: Centennial Essays* (Chapman and Hall, London, 1970), pp. 29–51, esp. 51.

3. Richard J. Watts, *The Pragmalinguistic Analysis of Narrative Texts: Narrative Cooperation in Charles Dickens's "Hard Times"* (Gunter Nar Verlag, Tübingen, 1981). For discussion of Watts's achievement, see Roger D. Sell, *Literature as Communication: The Foundations of Mediating Criticism* (Benjamin, Amsterdam, 2000), pp. 78–80, 162–63.

4. E.g. John Bayley, *The Uses of Division: Unity and Disharmony in Literature* (Viking, New York, 1976), pp. 90–103.

5. E.g. Susan R. Horton, *Interpreting Interpreting: Interpreting Dickens's* Dombey (Johns Hopkins University Press, Baltimore, 1979) and *The Reader in the Dickens World: Style and Response* (Macmillan, London, 1981).

6. See George Gissing, *The Immortal Dickens* (Cecil Palmer, London 1925), pp. 140–63; F. R. Leavis, "The First Major Novel: *Dombey and Son*", in F. R. and Q. D. Leavis, *Dickens the Novelist* [1970] (Penguin, Harmondsworth, 1972), pp. 21–56.

7. Willaim Axton, "Tonal Unity in *Dombey and Son*", *PMLA* 78 (1963) 341–8.

8. See G. K. Chesterton, Introduction to the Everyman Edition of *Dombey and Son* (Dent, London, 1907); Gabriel Pearson, "Towards a Reading of *Dombey and Son*" in Gabriel Josipo-

vici (ed.) *The Modern English Novel: the Reader, the Writer and the Work* (Open Books, London, 1976), pp. 54–76.

9. See Horton (n.5 above).

10. Steven Connor, *Charles Dickens* (Blackwell, Oxford, 1985), e.g. p. 54.

11. John Forster, *The Life of Charles Dickens* [1872–4], ed. J. W. T. Ley (Cecil Palmer, London, 1928), pp. 472–3 (Book 4, Chapter 2).

12. *Our Mutual Friend* [1865] (Oxford University Press, London, 1952) p. 821.

13. John Butt and Kathleen Tillotson, *Dickens at Work* (Methuen, London, 1957), pp. 90–113.

14. See pp. 144–5 and 160–2 above.

15. Chapter 53, *Dombey and Son* [1848], ed. Alan Horsman (Clarendon Press, Oxford, 1974), p. 711.

16. Roger Fowler, "Polyphony and Problematic in *Hard Times*", in Robert Giddings (ed.), *The Changing World of Charles Dickens* (Barnes and Noble, London, 1983), pp. 91–108.

17. See Richard D. Altick, "Varieties of Readers' Response: the Case of *Dombey and Son*", *Yearbook of English Studies* 10 (1980) 70–94; Humphrey House, *The Dickens World* ([1941] Oxford University Press, London, 1942), pp. 133–69; J. D. Jump, "Dickens and His Readers", *Bulletin of the John Rylands Library* 54 (1971–2) 384–97.

18. See Philip Collins, "The Popularity of Dickens" *The Dickensian* 70 (1974) 5–20; George H. Ford, *Dickens and His Readers: Aspects of Novel Criticism since 1836* (Norton, New York, 1965), pp. 3–155.

19. See Horton, *The Reader in the Dickens World*.

20. See James M. Brown, *Dickens: Novelist in the Market-Place: a Sociological Reading of the Later Novels of Dickens* (Macmillan, London, 1982).

21. See Roger B. Henkle, *Comedy and Culture: England 1820–1900* (Princeton University Press, Princeton, 1980).

22. See Ford, *Dickens and His Readers*, pp. 75–155.

23. See David Paroissien, "Literature's 'Eternal Duties': Dickens's Professional Creed", in Giddings, *The Changing World of Charles Dickens*, pp. 31–50.

24. See Philip Collins, "Dickens and Industrialism", *Studies in English Literature, 1500–1900* 20 (1980) 651–73; John MacVeagh, *Tradeful Merchants: the Portrayal of the Capitalist in English Literature* (Routledge and Kegan Paul, London, 1981); Ivan Melada, *The Captain of Industry in English Fiction, 1821–71* (University of New Mexico Press, Albuquerque, 1970).

25. Chapter 28, *Bleak House* [1873], ed. Stephen Gill (Oxford University Press, Oxford, 1996), p.415.

26. See John Colmer, *Coleridge to Catch-22: Images of Society* (Macmillan, London, 1978).

27. Chapter 4, *Hard Times* [1854], ed. Dingle Foot (Oxford University Press, London, 1955), p. 14.

28. For social deixis, see pp. 152–8 above and Sell, *Literature as Communication*, pp. 164–6.

29. See Eric Ashby, *Technology and the Academics: an Essay on the Universities and the Scien-*

tific Revolution (London, Macmillan, 1958); Martin J. Wiener, *English Culture and the Decline of the Industrial Spirit, 1850–980* (Cambridge University Press, Cambridge, 1981).

30. George Orwell, "Charles Dickens" [in his *Inside the Whale*, 1940] in Stephen Wall (ed.), *Charles Dickens: A Critical Anthology* (Penguin, Harmondsworth, 1970), pp.297–313.

31. See Ivanka Kovačević, *Fact into Fiction: English Literature and the Industrial Scene* (Leicester University Press, Leicester, 1975).

32. See pp. 281–4 below.

33. See David Craig, "The Crowd in Dickens" and Thomas J. Rice, "The Politics of *Barnaby Rudge*" in Giddings, *Changing World*, pp. 75–90 and 51–74.

34. One example would be N.N. Feltes, "Realism, consensus and 'exclusion itself': Interpellating the Victorian bourgeoisie", *Textual Practice* 1 (1987) 297–308. Somewhat similarly, Robert Clark argues that in *Dombey and Son* Dickens himself represses Florence: he is committed to the great capitalist adventure, but sees women less as free-traders than as items to be traded ("Riddling the Family Firm: The Sexual Economy in *Dombey and Son*", *English Literary History* 51 (1984) 69–84).

35. David Trotter, *Circulation: Defoe, Dickens, and the Economies of the Novel* (Macmillan, London, 1988).

36. Jeremy Tambling, "Death and Modernity in *Dombey and Son*", *Essays in Criticism* 43 (1993) 308–29.

37. Philip W. Martin, *Mad Women in Romantic Writing* (Harvester, Brighton, 1987), pp. 113–22.

38. See Lucy Frost, "Taming to Improve: Dickens and the Women in *Great Expectations*", *Meridian* 1 (1982) 11–20 (reprinted in Roger D. Sell (ed.) *New Casebook: Great Expectations* (Macmillan, Basingstoke, 1995), pp. 60–78).

39. Jeremy Tambling, "Prison-Bound: Dickens and Foucault", *Essays in Criticism* 36 (1986) 11–31 (reprinted in Sell, *Great Expectations*, pp. 123–42).

40. Pam Morris, *Dickens's Class Consciousness: A Marginal View* (Macmillan, Basingstoke, 1991) pp. 103–19.

41. See Johannes Söderlind, "En språklig analys av en Dickensroman", *Annales Societas Litterarum Humaniorum Regiae Upsaliensis* (1973–4), pp. 20–33.

42. E.g. William Axton, "*Dombey and Son*: From Stereotype to Archetype", *English Literary History* 31 (1964) 301–17.

43. Kathleen Tillotson, *Novels of the Eighteen-Forties* (Oxford University Press, London, 1961), p. 179.

44. Chapter 40, *Dombey and Son*, p. 542.

45. Introduction to his 1982 edition of *Dombey and Son* (Oxford University Press, Oxford), p. x.

46. Lord Jeffrey to Charles Dickens, 12th September, 1847. In Lord Cockburn, *Life of Lord Jeffrey with a Selection from his Correspondence* (2nd ed., Adam and Charles Black, Edinburgh, 1852), vol. 2, p. 429.

47. Appendix B, Horsman's 1974 edition of *Dombey and Son*, p. 852 (p. 749 in his 1982 edition).

48. Gissing, *Immortal Dickens*, pp. 160–1.

49. Forster, *Life of Charles Dickens*, p. 473 (Book 4, Chapter 2).

50. See Julian Moynaham, "Dealings with the Firm of Dombey and Son: Dryness versus Wetness", in John Gross and Gabriel Pearson (eds.), *Dickens and the Twentieth Century* (Routledge and Kegan Paul, London, 1962), pp. 121–31.

51. Chapter 50, *Dombey and Son*, p. 669.

52. Chapter 44, *Dombey and Son*, p. 589.

53. Chapter 23, *Dombey and Son*, pp. 314–5.

54. See, for instance, Nina Auerbach, "Dickens and Dombey: a Daughter after All", *Dickens Studies Annual* 5 (1976) 95–114; Denis Donoghue, "The English Dickens and *Dombey and Son*", in Ada Nisbet and Blake Nevins (eds.), *Dickens Centennial Essays* (University of California Press, Berkeley, 1971), pp. 1–21.

55. Chapter 47, *Dombey and Son*, p. 624.

56. M. M. Bakhtin, *The Dialogic Imagination: Four Essays* (University of Texas Press, Austin, 1981), pp. 262–3.

57. As quoted by Bakhtin, *op. cit.*, p. 306.

58. G. K. Chesterton, *Charles Dickens* [1906], passage reprinted in Wall, *A Critical Anthology*, pp. 244–9.

59. Forster, *Life of Charles Dickens*, p. 744 (Book 9, Chapter 5).

60. For all that, Robert Garis, *The Dickens Theatre: a Reassessment of the Novels* (Clarendon Press, Oxford, 1965) offers a fine account of Dickens.

61. Chesterton, introduction to *Dombey and Son*.

62. Appendix B, Horsman's 1974 edition of *Dombey and Son*, p. 839 (p. 74 in his 1982 edition).

63. See Gérard Genette, *Narrative Discourse* (Cornell University Press, Ithaca, 1980).

64. Gissing, *Immortal Dickens*, p. 152. See also Philip Collins, "Special Correspondent to Posterity: How Dickens's Contemporaries saw his Fictional World", in Samuel I. Mintz *et. al.* (eds.), *From Smollett to James: Studies in the Novel and Other Essays* (University Press of Virginia, Charlottesville, 1981), pp. 157–82.

65. Philip Collins, "*Dombey and Son* — Then and Now", *The Dickensian* 63 (1967) 82–94.

66. Chapter 59, *Dombey and Son*, p. 787.

67. See N. N. Feltes, "To Saunter, to Hurry: Dickens, Time, and Industrial Capitalism", *Victorian Studies* 20 (1977) 245–67.

68. See Ian Milner, "The Dickens Drama: Mr Dombey", in Nisbet and Nevins, *Centennial Essays*, pp. 155–65.

69. Edwin Muir, *The Structure of the Novel* (Hogarth Press, London, 1928), p. 28.

70. Hippolyte Taine, *History of English Literature* [1859, English trans. 1871], passage reprinted in Alan Shelston (ed), *Charles Dickens:* Dombey and Son *and* Little Dorrit: *A Casebook* (Macmillan, Basingstoke), pp. 34–5.

71. Lyda Zwinger, "The Fear of the Father: Dombey and Daughter", *Nineteeth Century Fiction* 39 (1985) 420–40, esp. 436, 440.

72. Chapter 51, *Dombey and Son*, p. 682.

73. *Ibid.*

74. See also Patricia Ingham, "Speech and Non-Communication in *Dombey and Son*", *Review of English Studies* 30 (1979) 145–53.

75. See below, pp. 266–7.

Chapter 6

1. *The Poetical Works of Andrew Young*, ed. Edward Lowbury and Alison Young (Secker and Warburg, London, 1985), p. 43.

2. See p. 59 above.

3. Roger D. Sell, *Trespassing Ghost: A Critical Study of Andrew Young* (*Acta Academiae Aboensis, ser. A. Humanoria* 56:1, 1978), pp. 111–21.

4. Lawrance Thompson, *Robert Frost: the Earlier Years, 1874–915* (Holt, Rinehart and Winston, New York, 1966), *Robert Frost: The Years of Triumph, 1915–38* (Holt, Rinehart and Winston, New York, 1970) and *Robert Frost: The Later Years, 1938–63* (Holt, Rinhart and Winston, New York, 1976).

5. Oxford University Press, Oxford.

6. Lesley Lee Frost, *The Frost Family's Adventure in Poetry* (University of Missouri Press, Columbia).

7. Reprinted in Lionel Trilling, *The Liberal Imagination: Essays on Literature and Society* [1950] (Mercury Books, London, 1961), pp. 213–14.

8. Reuben A. Brower, *The Poetry of Robert Frost: Constellations of Intention* (Oxford University Press, New York, 1963), pp. 80–1.

9. Frost's thoughts on the American class system began at least as early as his years on the Derry farm, where he made some notes on the subject. See Roger D. Sell, "Three Separate Leaves from Frobert Frost's Derry Years: a Note and Transcriptions", *Studies in Bibliography* 36 (1983) 229–32. Frost's notes mention the "Artist's Revolt from the Middle Class", a theme which recurs, as we shall soon see, in "In An Art Factory", and they also recognize peasant, tradesmen and upper middle classes as well. Throughout his life, Frost referred to American society in these or similar terms without qualification.

10. W. W. Robson, "The Achievement of Robert Frost" [1966], reprinted as "Robert Frost" in his *The Definition of Literature and Other Essays* (Cambridge University Press, Cambridge, 1982), pp. 168–95, esp. 178–8.

11. Roger D. Sell (ed.), "Robert Frost: Two Unpublished Plays: *In an Art Factory* and *The Guardeen*", *Massachusetts Review* 26 (1985) 265–340.

12. See pp. 227–8 below.

13. Robert Poirier, *Robert Frost: the Work of Knowing* (Oxford University Press, Oxford, 1977), pp. 28–49.

14. Duke University Press, Durham, 1975. See esp. Chapter 7.

15. Archibald MacLeish, "Robert Frost and New England", *National Geographic* 149 (1976) 438–44, esp.438.

16. Princeton University Press, Princeton.

17. *The Poetry of Robert Frost*, ed. Edward Connery Lathem (Jonathan Cape, London, 1971), p. 216.

18. Yvor Winters, "Robert Frost: Or, the Spiritual Drifter as Poet" [1948], in James M. Cox (ed.), *Robert Frost: A Collection of Critical Essays* (Prentice-Hall, Englewood Cliffs, 1962), pp. 58–82.

19. E.g. David W. Wyatt, "Choosing in Frost", in Jac Tharpe (ed.), *Frost: Centennial Essays II* (University Press of Mississippi, Jackson, 1976), pp. 129–40.

20. Thompson, *The Early Years*, pp. 196–7, 308–9, 521, 537–8. For belief, see Chapter 7 below, esp. pp. 227–8, 238–40, 243–6, 249.

21. I trace this biographical background in the introduction to my edition of "The Guardeen" (*The Massachusetts Review* 26 (1985) 270–90). Donald G. Sheehy ("Robert Frost and the Lockless Door", *New England Quarterly* 56 (1983) 39–59) deals with the same materials, but whereas I place more stress on questions of social identity, Sheehy is more interested in Frost's relationship with Elinor, his wife.

22. *The Poetry of Robert Frost*, pp. 286–7.

23. Ervin Goffman, *The Presentation of the Self in Everyday Life* (Doubleday, New York, 1959).

24. First performed by Amherst students. Published in *Seven Arts* vol. 1 no. 4 (February 1917); Helen Louise Cohen (ed.), *More One-Act Plays by Modern Authors* (Harcourt Brace, New York, 1927); and Edward Connery Lathem and Lawrance Thompson (eds.), *Robert Frost: Poetry and Prose* (Holt, Rinehart and Winston, New York, 1972). Published separately by The Harbor Press, New York, 1929.

25. See p. 231 below.

26. His introduction to E. A. Robinson's *King Jasper* includes a powerful argument for "the old-fashioned way to be new", both in matters of personality and literary style (*Selected Prose of Robert Frost*, ed. Hyde Cox and Edward Connery Lathem (Macmillan, New York, 1949), pp. 59–67). As for social changes, he insisted that it was not the business of the poet to cry for reform, and poems such as "Two Tramps in Mud Time" and "A Roadside Stand" were, to say the least, satisfied with the status quo. See Thompson, *The Years of Triumph*, pp. 423–43, esp. 425.

27. See pp. 227–8 below.

28. See p. 224 below.

29. See p. 229 below.

30. Roger D. Sell, *Robert Frost: Four Studies* (*Acta Academiae Aboensis, ser. A. Humanoria* 57:2, 1980).

31. Frank Lentricchia, "The Resentments of Robert Frost" [1990], in Edwin H. Cady and Louis J. Budd (eds.), *On Frost. The Best from* American Literature (Duke University Press, Durham, 1991), pp. 222–47.

32. See p. 361 n. 33.

Chapter 7

1. See pp. 6–7 above.

2. "The Metaphysical Poets", reprinted in *Selected Essays by T.S. Eliot* (Faber, London, 1951), pp. 281–91, esp. 289.

3. Republished in Lionel Trilling, *Beyond Culture: Essays on Literature and Learning* (Penguin, Harmondsworth, 1967), pp. 62–86.

4. Thomas Munro, "The Failure Story: A Study of Contemporary Pessimism", *The Journal of Aesthetics and Art Criticism* 17 (1958) 362–87.

5. See pp. 297 below and 11 above. Leavis's appreciation of *Hard Times* formed the final chapter of *The Great Tradition* (1948).

6. Raymond Tallis, *Enemies of Hope: A Critique of Contemporary Pessimism, Irrationalism, Anti-Humanism and Counter-Enlightenment* (Macmillan, Basingstoke, 1997).

7. Reprinted in *Beyond Culture*, pp. 19–41.

8. *The Essays of Virginia Woolf*, ed. Anne Olivier Bell (5 vols., Hogarth Press, London, 1986–94), vol. 2 p. 55, vol. 4 p. 19.

9. T.S. Eliot, *The Sacred Wood* ([1920] Methuen, London, 1960), p. 169. Cf. pp. 128–9 above. For an interesting recent treatment of Eliot's paradox, see A.D. Nuttall, *Why Does Tragedy Give Pleasure?* (Clarendon Press, Oxford, 1996).

10. See this chapter below, p. 255.

11. *The Poetry of Robert Frost*, ed. Edward Connery Lathem (Jonathan Cape, London, 1972), pp. 226–7.

12. *Selected Letters of Robert Frost*, ed. Lawrance Thompson (Holt, Rinehart and Winston, New York, 1964), p. 482.

13. *Selected Prose of Robert Frost*, eds. Hyde Cox and Edward Connery Lathem (Holt, Rinehart and Winston, New York, 1966), pp. 71–2.

14. *Selected Letters*, pp. 219–20; inscription in Elizabeth Shepley Sergeant's copy of *Selected Poems* (1923), Canady Library, Bryn Mawr College.

15. William H. Pritchard seems to agree with me. He argues that Frost did not feel challenged by the Georgians because he could see — or rather, hear, since it was especially a matter of the sounds of speech — that they were less original (*Frost: A Literary Life Reconsidered* (Oxford University Press, Oxford, 1984), pp. 82–91).

16. *Selected Letters*, p. 552.

17. *Selected Letters*, p. 158.

18. See Roger D. Sell, "Three Separate Leaves from Robert Frost's Derry Years: a Note and Transcriptions", *Studies in Bibliography* 36 (1983) 229–32. The leaves are stored in the Clifton Waller Barret collection at the University of Virginia Library, accession no. 6261, box 2.

19. Lawrance Thompson, *Robert Frost: The Early Years, 1874–915* (Holt, Rinehart and Winston, New York, 1966), p. 315.

20. Charles Dickens, *David Copperfield* [1850], ed. Nina Burgis, (Clarendon Press, Oxford, 1981), p. 518 (Chapter 42).

21. Reprinted in *The Will to Believe and Other Essays in Popular Philosophy* [1897, bound here with] *Human Immortality: Two Supposed Objections to the Doctrine* [1898] (Dover, New York, 1956), p. 47.

22. Sell, "Three Separate Leaves".

23. This similarity is pointed out by Frost himself in a letter to his daughter Lesley in 1951 (Thompson, *The Early Years*, pp. 563–4; *Family Letters of Robert and Elinor Frost*, ed. Arnold Grade (State University of New York Press, Albany, 1972), p. 261). On the manuscript of the Derry notes itself Frost's late hand has added: "This is as old as Derry days [.] You can see from it where one idea started[.] R.F. 1951".

24. *The Poetry*, p. 349.

25. *Selected Prose*, pp. 105–6.

26. Sell, "Three Separate Leaves".

27. Sell, "Three Separate Leaves".

28. *The Will to Believe*, p. 8, James's italics.

29. *Interviews with Robert Frost*, ed. Edward Connery Lathem (Holt, Rinehart and Winston, New York, 1966), p. 271.

30. Sell, "Three Separate Leaves".

31. *Selected Prose*, p. 44.

32. *Selected Prose*, p. 19.

33. Sell, "Three Separate Leaves".

34. *Selected Prose*, pp. 41, 43.

35. "Build Soil: A Political Pastoral", *The Poetry*, p. 323.

36. Reprinted in *The Will to Believe*, p. 114.

37. *Robert Frost and the Lawrence, Massachusetts, "High School Bulletin": The Beginnings of a Literary Career*, eds. Edward Connery Lathem and Lawrance Thompson (The Grolier Club, New York, 1966), p. 21.

38. Collected in *Robert Frost: Farm-Poultryman: The Story of Robert Frost's Career as a Breeder and Fancier of Hens & the Texts of Eleven Long-forgotten Prose Contributions by the Poet, Which Appeared in Two New England Poultry Journals in 1903–05, during his Years of Farming at Derry, New Hampshire*, eds. Edward Connery Lathem and Lawrance Thompson (Dartmouth Publications, Hanover, 1963).

39. Cf. G.W. Geyer, "A Poulterer's Pleasure: Robert Frost as Prose Humorist", *Studies in Short Fiction* 8 (1971) 589–99.

40. *Interviews*, p. 175.

41. See pp. 183–4 above.

42. Lecture to the Browne and Nichols School, 1915, notes by George Browne in Elaine Berry, *Robert Frost on Writing* (Rutgers University Press, New Brunswick, 1973), pp. 142–4.

43. Thompson, *Early Years*, p. 155.

44. *Interviews*, pp. 59–62.

45. *A Way Out* (The Harbor Press, New York, 1929).

46. Robert Kern, "Frost and Modernism" [1988], in Edwin H. Cady and Louis J. Budd (eds.), *On Frost: the Best from* American Literature (Duke University Press, Durham, 1991), pp. 190–206.

47. Tom Vander Ven, "Robert Frost's Dramatic Principle of 'Oversound'" [1973], in Cady and Budd, *On Frost*, pp. 86–99, esp. 99. Ven borrows the word "oversound" from "Never Again Would Bird Song Be the Same", a poem which several critics have commented on for its Edenic vision of an interaction between human voice sounds (Eve's "tone of meaning but without the words") and the sounds of nature.

48. *Farm-Poultryman*, p. 84.

49. *Letters*, pp. 110–4.

50. *Selected Letters*, p. 204.

51. Thompson, *Early Years*, pp. 427, 669.

52. Christopher Ricks, *T.S. Eliot and Prejudice* (Faber, London, 1988), pp. 154–71.

53. *Selected Letters*, p. 112.

54. *Selected Letters*, p. 180.

55. *Robert Frost on Writing*, pp. 142–4.

56. *Selected Letters*, p. 113.

57. *Selected Prose*, pp. 81–4.

58. *Farm-Poultryman*, p. 63.

59. See *Farm-Poultryman*, pp. 16–21. Frost's own reflections on the fact-fiction interplay in the poultryman pieces and in his other early journalism are recorded in a letter of March 1913 to John Bartlett (*Letters*, p. 67). They show that, as one would expect, he was perfectly conscious of what he was doing.

60. Inscription dated March 1925 in Elizabeth Shepley Sergeant's copy of *Selected Poems* (1923), Canady Library, Bryn Mawr College.

61. Thompson, *Early Years*, p. 594.

62. Letter to Robert Newdick, January 18th, 1938, in *Robert Frost: A Descriptive Catalogue of Books and Manuscripts in the Clifton Waller Barrett Library, University of Virginia*, comp. Joan St. C. Crane (University Press of Virginia, Charlottesville, 1974), pp. 244–5.

63. Roger D. Sell, *Robert Frost: Four Studies (Acta Academiae Aboensis, ser. A. Humanoria* 57:2, 1980), esp. p. 25.

64. Cf. Thompson, *Early Years*, p. 59 and Andrew J. Angyal, "Robert Frost's Poetry Before 1913: A Checklist", in Joseph Katz (ed.), *Proof 5: The Yearbook of American Bibliographical and Textual Studies* (Faust, Columbia, 1977), pp. 76–125, esp. 87.

65. Quoted in Thompson, *Early Years*, pp. 592–3.

66. *The Derry News* 27/16 (Friday, March 1st, 1907), pp. 1 and 5.

67. *The Poetry*, p. 57.

68. *The Poetry*, p. 55.

69. *The Poetry*, pp. 57–8.

70. *The Poetry*, p. 56.

71. W. David Shaw, "The Poetics of Pragmatism: Robert Frost and William James" (*New England Quarterly* 59 (1986) 159–88) is one of many treatments of its topic. For another pragmatist reading of this particular poem see Lewis H. Miller, "William James, Robert Frost, and 'The Black Cottage'", in Jac Tharpe (ed.), *Frost: Centennial Essays III* (University Press of Mississippi, Jackson, 1978), pp. 368–81.

72. *Pragmatism: A New Name for Old Ways of Thinking* [1907, and] *The Meaning of Truth: a Sequel to Pragmatism* [1909] (Harvard University Press, Cambridge, 1978), p. 17.

73. *Pragmatism*, pp. 12–26, 144.

74. *The Will to Believe*, pp. 52, 96.

75. *The Poetry*, p. 58.

76. *The Will to Believe*, p. xii.

77. *Pragmatism*, pp. 36–7.

78. *The Poetry*, p. 59. Cf. *Pragmatism*, p. 104: "I have led you through a very sandy desert. But now, if I may be allowed so vulgar an expression, we begin to taste the milk of the coconut."

79. *The Poetry*, p. 56.

80. Sell, "Three Separate Leaves".

81. Robert Frost, *Stories for Lesley*, ed. Roger D. Sell (University Press of Virginia, Charlottesville, 1984), p.11. The stories are edited from the single witness of the so-called Derry notebook (Clifton Waller Barrett collection, University of Virginia Library, accession no. 6261, box 2).

82. *Stories*, p. 7.

83. *Stories*, p. 13. In this and some of the other examples quoted in this section, my edition of the stories has very slightly normalized Frost's unconventional accidentals where they were clearly not intended for special effect. (See the Editorial Notes to *Stories*, esp. pp. 71–2.) Here,

Frost's expressive spellings have been retained, but the inverted commas are an editorial insertion. This insertion, however, is one of very few exceptions to a more general editorial decision not to make the punctuation heavier than it is in the manuscript. Frost was clearly punctuating with an ear to the sounds of the sense.

84. *Stories*, p. 73.

85. *Selected Letters*, p. 159.

86. *Stories*, p. 25.

87. *Stories*, p. 46.

88. *Stories*, p. 59.

89. *Stories*, p. 52.

90. *Stories*, p. 19.

91. Richard Adams, *Watership Down* (Rex Collings, London, 1973). Cf. Roger D. Sell, "*Watership Down* and the Rehabilitation of Pleasure", *Neuphilologische Mitteilungen* 82 (1981) 28–35.

92. *Stories*, p.35.

93. *Stories*, p. 9.

94. *Stories*, p. 13.

95. *Stories*, p. 57.

96. Printed in *New Hampshire's Child: The Derry Journals of Lesley Frost*, eds. Lawrance Thompson and Arnold Grade (State University of New York Press, Albany, 1969).

97. *Stories*, p. 39.

98. *Stories*, p. 27.

99. *Pragmatism*, p. 50.

100. *Stories*, p. 51.

101. *Stories*, p. 63.

102. *Stories*, p. 27.

103. "Education by Poetry", *Selected Prose*, pp. 33–46, esp. 41.

104. Ibid.

105. Commenting on "Never Again Would Birds' Song Be the Same", Richard Poirier (*Robert Frost: The Work of Knowing* (Oxford University Press, Oxford, 1977), pp. 169) speaks of Frost's "deep commitment to married love as a precondition for discovering human 'embodiments' in nature, for discovering Adam and Eve, whose intercourse included the 'call or laughter' that was 'carried aloft' where ever since it has been 'crossed' with the song of birds". Frost's treatment of an Edenic experience of married love continues to draw sensitive comments. See, for instance, Judith Oster's *Toward Robert Frost: The Reader and the Poet* (University of Georgia Press, Athens, 1991), pp. 220–54.

106. *The Poetry*, p. 118.

107. *The Poetry*, p. 188.

108. Quoted above, p. 228.

109. Stephen J. Adams ("Black Cottages: Frost, Eliot, and the Fate of Individualism" (*Cithara: Essays in the Judaeo-Christian Tradition* 22 (1982) 39–52) says that "The Black Cottage" is one of very few American poems which can be compared with "Gerontion" as a "monument to forlorn egoism". Other such monuments are said to include *The Great Gatsby* and "The Fall of the House of Usher".

110. *The Poetry*, p. 181.

111. *Selected Prose*, pp. 60–1.

112. E.g. Reuben A. Brower, *The Poetry of Robert Frost: Constellations of Intention* (Oxford University Press, New York, 1963), Chapter 4; Frank Lentricchia, *Robert Frost: Modern Poetics and the Landscapes of the Self* (Duke University Press, Durham, 1975), Chapter 7; Robert Poirier, *Robert Frost: the Work of Knowing* (Oxford University Press, New York, 1977), Chapter 3 iii; Todd M. Lieber, "Robert Frost and Wallace Stevens: 'What to make of a diminished thing'"[1975], in Edwin H. Cady and Louis J. Budd, *On Frost: the Best from* American Literature (Duke University Press, Durham, 1991), pp. 100–19.

113. *The Poetry*, p. 189.

114. *The Poetry*, p. 33.

115. *The Poetry*, p. 190.

116. *The Poetry*, p. 34.

117. *The Poetry*, p.137.

118. Thompson, *The Early Years*, p. 598.

119. *The Poetry*, p. 53.

120. *The Poetry*, p. 92.

121. *The Poetry*, p. 130.

122. *The Poetry*, p. 133.

123. *Ibid.*

124. "The Future of the Novel" [1899], in *Henry James: Selected Literary Criticism*, ed. Morris Shapira (Penguin, Harmondsworth, 1968), pp. 218–27, esp. 226.

125. See e.g. Brower, *Constellations of Intention*, Chapter 6.

126. *The Poetry*, p. 240.

127. *The Poetry*, pp. 252–3.

128. *The Poetry*, p. 375.

129. *The Poetry*, pp. 212–2.

130. *The Poetry*, p. 196.

131. The poem has provoked biographical, including psychoanalytical interpretations. Margaret Storch ("Robert Frost's 'The Subverted Flower'", *American Imago: A Psychoanalytical Journal for Culture, Science and the Arts* 43 (1986) 295–305)) says that it re-writes an incident in Frost's courtship of Elinor, but that there is also a sense in which both of the characters

in it are Frost himself. He had to break loose from his mother's sphere of prudery (which drove his sister Jenny to madness) in order to establish his independence, which is associated with his drunken father's violence. For Storch, both characters are still struggling to get beyond the oral stage. All of which is interesting enough and may well account for the poem's genesis, but misinterprets its genre, which is not that of a first-person lyric. The poem does communicate the strongest possible feelings, but at aspects of human nature which are not taken to be merely personal to its own writer. On the uses and abuses of biographical knowledge in literary interpretation, see Roger D. Sell, *Literature as Communication: The Foundations of Mediating Criticism* (Benjamins, Amsterdam, 2000), pp. 193–207.

132. *The Poetry*, p. 378.

133. Not all parts of the world have the same four seasons as Europe. Presumably, then, seasonal metaphors of human life will not be universal, or not universal to the same effect. See Ziva Ben-Porat, "Two-Way Pragmatics: From World to Text and Back", in Roger D. Sell (ed.), *Literary Pragmatics* (Routledge, London, 1991), pp. 142–63.

Chapter 8

1. Charles Dickens, *David Copperfield* [1850] ed. Nina Burgis (Clarendon Press, Oxford, 1981), p. 750.

2. See p. 218 above.

3. Throughout his writing career Dickens, no less than Frost, used children and childhood as points of reference. For his exploration of the unresolved relationships between childhood and the world of adults, see Malcolm Andrews, *Dickens and the Grown-Up Child* (Macmillan, Basingstoke, 1994).

4. See Claire Tomalin, *The Invisible Woman: The Story of Nelly Ternan and Charles Dickens* [1990] (Penguin, Harmondsworth, 1991), pp. 130–49.

5. John Hillis Miller, *Charles Dickens: The World of his Novels* (Harvard University Press, Cambridge, 1959), p. 158 and "Three Problems of Fictional Form: First-Person Narration in *David Copperfield* and *Huckleberry Finn*", in Roy Harvey Pearce (ed.), *Experience in the Novel* (Columbia University Press, New York, 1968), pp. 21–48.

6. Gwendolyn B. Needham, "The Undisciplined Heart of David Copperfield", *Nineteenth-Century Fiction* 9 (1954) 81–107.

7. This is the assessment of Mowbray Morris, "Charles Dickens", *Fortnightly Review* 32 (1882) 762–99. Another suggestive piece of evidence is that *Great Expectations* is listed as a "minor work of fiction" in James Cook, *Bibliography of the Writings of Charles Dickens and Many Curious and Interesting Particulars Relating to His Works* (J. & J. Cook, Paisley, 1879), p. 26.

8. Lionel Trilling, "Manners, Morals, and the Novel" [1947], in his *The Liberal Imagination* [1951] (Mercury, London, 1961), pp. 205–22, esp. 211.

9. In Edmund Wilson, *The Wound and the Bow* (Houghton Mifflin, Boston, 1941), pp. 1–104.

10. Dorothy Van Ghent, "The Dickens World: A View from Todgers's", *Sewanee Review* 58

(1950) 419–38, incorporated into her *The English Novel: Form and Function* (Rinehart, New York, 1953), pp. 125–38.

11. Julian Moynaham, "The Hero's Guilt: the Case of *Great Expectations*", *Essays in Criticism* 10 (1960) 60–79.

12. Barbara Lecker, "The Split Characters of Charles Dickens", *Studies in English Literature, 1500–1900* 19 (1979) 689–704.

13. John Forster, *The Life of Charles Dickens* [1872–74] ed. J. W. T. Ley (Cecil Palmer, London, 1928), p. 734 (Book 9, Chapter 3).

14. Harry Stone, *Dickens and the Invisible World: Fairy-Tales, Fantasy, and Novel Making* (Macmillan, Basingstoke, 1979), p. 272.

15. See, for instance, Edmund Wilson's "Dickens: the Two Scrooges" and Angus Wilson, *The World of Charles Dickens* (Secker and Warburg, London, 1970), pp. 213–6.

16. Taylor Stoehr, *Dickens: The Dreamer's Stance* (Cornell University Press, Ithaca, 1964).

17. Chapter 5, *David Copperfield*, p. 64.

18. Chapter 22, *David Copperfield*, p. 227.

19. Natalie E. Schroeder and Ronald E. Schroeder even argue that Aunt Betsey and Miss Murdstone are another of Dickens's pairings, with their harshness towards Clara as a common denominator ("Betsey Trotwood and Jane Murdstone: Dickensian Doubles", *Studies in the Novel* 21 (1989) 269–78).

20. Edgar Johnson, *Charles Dickens: His Tragedy and Triumph* (Gollancz, London, 1953), pp. 541–2.

21. Johnson, *Charles Dickens*, p. 857.

22. Chapter 32, *David Copperfield*, p. 388.

23. Chapter 1, *David Copperfield*, p. 1.

24. Q. D. Leavis, "Dickens and Tolstoy: The Case for a Serious View of *David Copperfield*, in F. R. and Q. D. Leavis, *Dickens the Novelist* ([1970] Penguin, Harmondsworth, 1980), pp. 60–150, esp. 80.

25. John Bayley, *The Uses of Division: Unity and Disharmony in Literature* (Viking, New York, 1976), p. 94.

26. Robert Gilmour, "Memory in *David Copperfield*" *The Dickensian* 71 (1975) 30–42.

27. Vereen M. Bell, "The Emotional Matrix of *David Copperfield*", *Studies in English Literature, 1500–1900* 8 (1968) 633–49.

28. *Dreamer's Stance*, p. 68 n.

29. Roger D. Sell, "Projection Characters in *David Copperfield*", *Studia Neophilologica* 55 (1983) 19–30.

30. "Preface to the Second Edition of Several of the Foregoing poems Published, with an Additional Volume, under the Title of 'Lyrical Ballads'", in *The Poetical Works of Wordsworth*, ed. Thomas Hutchinson, new ed. Ernest de Selincourt ([1904] Oxford University Press, Oxford, 1950), pp. 734–41, esp. 735.

31. Mark Spilka, "*David Copperfield* as Psychological Fiction", in A. E. Dyson (ed.), *Dickens: Modern Judgements* (Macmillan, London, 1968), pp. 186–96, esp. 187.

32. Chapter 3, *David Copperfield*, p. 37.

33. Chapter 5, *David Copperfield*, p. 67.

34. Chapter 7, *David Copperfield*, p. 77.

35. Which is not to say that the two novels are identical. Most readers would probably agree with L. R. Leavis in finding *Jane Eyre* more literary, more puritan, un-comic, and the work of a woman writer ("*David Copperfield* and *Jane Eyre*", *English Studies* 67 (1986) 167–73.

36. Chapter 2, *David Copperfield*, p.21.

37. Chapter 38, *David Copperfield*, p. 475.

38. Chapter 42, *David Copperfield*, p. 518.

39. Sylvère Monod, *Dickens the Novelist* (University of Oklahoma Press, Norman, 1968), p. 359.

40. Michael Black, *The Literature of Fidelity* (Chatto and Windus, London, 1975) pp. 82–102.

41. Ross H. Dabney, *Love and Property in the Novels of Dickens* (Chatto and Windus, London, 1967), pp. 66–79.

42. Philip Collins, *Charles Dickens: David Copperfield* ([Studies in English Literature 67] Arnold, London, 1977), p. 45.

43. Chapter 44, *David Copperfield*, p. 545.

44. Chapter 48, *David Copperfield*, p. 592.

45. Chapter 53, *David Copperfield*, p. 658.

46. Chapter 9, *David Copperfield*, p. 111.

47. Chapter 11, *David Copperfield*, p. 142.

48. Chapter 11, *David Copperfield*, p.139.

49. John O. Jordan, "The Social Sub-Text of *David Copperfield*", *Dickens Studies Annual* 14 (1985) 61–92. At several points in his careful reading, Jordan refuses to say whether David is an unreliable narrator or whether his "blindnesses" are also Dickens's own. As will be clear, I think that such a refusal can be justified on the grounds that artistry and intuition are anything but mutually exclusive, and that readers are flexible enough to entertain either possibility, or both possibilities in alternating sequence.

50. Chapter 16, *David Copperfield*, p. 204.

51. Edwin E. Eigner, "*David Copperfield* as an Elegiac Romance", *Dickens Studies Annual* 16 (1987) 39–60.

52. Collins, *Charles Dickens*, p. 23.

53. Chapter 21, *David Copperfield*, p. 265.

54. Chapter 32, *David Copperfield*, p. 38.

55. Chapter 21, *David Copperfield*, p. 269.

56. Chapter 30, *David Copperfield*, p. 379.

57. Pam Morris, *Dickens's Class Consciousness: A Marginal View* (Macmillan, Basingstoke, 1991), pp. 63–80.

58. Chapter 6, *David Copperfield*, p. 76.

59. Q.D. Leavis, "Dickens and Tolstoy", pp. 87–90.

60. Chapter 17, *David Copperfield*, p. 225.

61. Chapter 18, *David Copperfield*, p. 229.

62. Chapter 39, *David Copperfield*, p. 483.

63. Chapter 11, *David Copperfield*, p. 134.

64. Johnson, *Charles Dickens*, p. 98.

65. Chapter 49, *David Copperfield*, pp. 602–3.

66. Chapter 17, *David Copperfield*, p. 225.

67. Chapter 28, *David Copperfield*, p. 366.

68. *David Copperfield*, p. 447.

69. Chapter 25, *David Copperfield*, p. 328.

70. Chapter 25, *David Copperfield*, p. 324.

71. Chapter 25, *David Copperfield*, p. 326.

72. *Ibid.*

73. Chapter 33, *David Copperfield*, p. 413.

74. Chapter 26, *David Copperfield*, p. 329.

75. Chapter 39, *David Copperfield*, p.490.

76. *Ibid.*

77. *Ibid.*

78. Chapter 35, *David Copperfield*, p. 431.

79. Chapter 42, *David Copperfield*, pp. 530–1.

80. Stone, *Dickens and the Invisible World*, pp. 220–6, 233–7.

81. G. K. Chesterton, *Charles Dickens*, extract reprinted in Stephen Wall (ed.), *Charles Dickens: A Critical Anthology* (Penguin, Harmondsworth, 1970), pp. 242–9.

82. Chapter 42, *David Copperfield*, p. 518.

83. Chapter 1, *David Copperfield*, p. 1.

84. George Santayana, "Dickens" [1921], reprinted in Wall, *Charles Dickens*, p. 265.

85. Iain Crawford, "Sex and Seriousness in *David Copperfield*", *Journal of Narrative Technique* 16 (1986) 41–54.

86. Arlene M. Jackson, "Agnes Whitfield and the Church Leitmotif in *David Copperfield*", *Dickens Studies Annual* 9 (1981) 53–65.

87. Virgina Carmichael, "*Nom/Non du Père* in *David Copperfield*", *English Literary History* 54 (1987) 653–67.

88. Mary Poovey, *Uneaven Developments: The Ideological Work of Gender in Mid-Victorian England* (University of Chicago Press, Chicago, 1988), pp. 89–125, esp. 119.

89. For a more general account of the relation between writing, civilization and the self see Murray Baumgartan, "Writing and *David Copperfield*", *Dickens Studies Annual* 14 (1985), 39–59.

90. Gail Turley Houston, "Gender Construction and the *Kunstlerroman* [*sic*]: *David Copperfield* and *Aurora Leigh*", *Philological Quarterly* 72 (1993) 213–36.

91. The same comment would apply to Irène Simon, "*David Copperfield*: A Künstlerroman", *Review of English Studies* 43 (1992) 40–56.

92. Matt Ridley, *The Origins of Virtue* (Penguin, Harmondsworth, 1997).

Chapter 9

1. Routledge and Kegan Paul, London.

2. Michel Foucault, "What is an Author?" [1969], in Josué V. Harari (ed.) *Textual Strategies: Perspectives in Post-Structuralist Criticism* (Methuen, London, 1980), pp. 141–60, esp. 151.

3. Katharine M. Rogers, "Submissive Women: Richardson and Fielding", *Novel* 9 (1976) 256–70.

4. E.g. Mary Anne Schofield, "Exploring the Woman Question: A Reading of Fielding's *Amelia*", *Ariel: A Review of International English Literature* 16 (1985) 45–57; Mona Scheuermann, "Henry Fielding's Images of Women", *The Age of Johnson: A Scholarly Journal* 3 (1990) 231–80.

5. See Martin C. Battestin, *Henry Fielding: A Life* (Routledge, London, 1989), pp. 442–3.

6. E.g. Anthony J. Hassall, "Women in Richardson and Fielding", *Novel* 14 (1981) 168–74 and Peter Sabor, "*Amelia* and *Sir Charles Grandison*: the Convergence of Fielding and Richardson", *Wascana Review* 17 (1982) 3–18.

7. Margaret Lenta, "Comedy, Tragedy and Feminism: The Novels of Richardson and Fielding", *English Studies in Africa* 26 (1983) 13–25.

8. Carolyn D. Williams, "Fielding and Half-Learned Ladies", *Essays in Criticism* 38 (1988) 22–34.

9. Angela J. Smallwood, *Fielding and the Woman Question: The Novels of Henry Fielding and the Feminist Debate 1700–50* (Prentice-Hall, Englewood Cliffs, 1989). Not the least of this book's many virtues was the very extensive bibliography of the period's writings on the woman question.

10. Jill Campbell, *Natural Masques: Gender and Identity in Fielding's Plays and Novels* (Stanford University Press, California, 1995).

11. Terry Castle, *Masquerade and Civilization: The Carnivalesque in Eighteenth-Century English Culture and Fiction* (Standford University Press, Stanford, 1986).

12. Brian McCrea, *Henry Fielding and the Politics of Mid-Eighteenth-Century England* (University of Georgia Press, Athens, 1981).

13. See Martin C. Battestin, *Henry Fielding*, pp. 531–8.

14. Ian A. Bell, *Henry Fielding: Authorship and Authority* (Longman, London, 1994).

15. Stanley Fish, "Rhetoric", in Frank Lentricchia and Thomas McLaughlin (eds.), *Critical Terms for Literary Study* (Chicago University Press, Chicago, 1990), p. 90.

16. *Henry Fielding*, p. 99.

17. Cheryl Walker, "Persona Criticism and the Death of the Author", in William Epstein (ed.), *Contesting the Subject: Essays in the Postmodern Theory and Practice of Biography and Biographical Criticism* (Purdue University Press, West Lafayette, 1991), pp. 109–21.

18. See also Roger D. Sell, *Literature as Communication: The Foundations of Mediating Criticism* (Benjamins, Amsterdam, 2000), pp. 145–58.

19. Wilbur L. Cross, *The History of Henry Fielding* (Yale University Press, New Haven, 1918).

20. Martin C. Battestin with Ruthe R. Battestin, *Henry Fielding: A Life* (Routledge, London, 1989).

21. For more detailed comments on Barthes's influential essay, "The Death of the Author", see Sell, *Literature as Communication*, pp. 89–93, 199–200.

22. F. R. Leavis, *The Great Tradition: George Eliot, Henry James, Joseph Conrad* ([1948] Penguin, Harmondsworth, 1962), pp. 11–12.

23. F. R. Leavis, *Revaluation: Tradition and Development in English Poetry* ([1936] Penguin, Harmondsworth, 1964), p. 18.

24. Henry Fielding, *Miscellanies by Henry Fielding, Esq; Volume Three* [1743], eds. Bertrand A. Goldgar and Hugh Amory (Clarendon Press, Oxford, 1997), p. 109.

25. The Preface to the *Miscellanies*. See Rawson, *Henry Fielding*, pp. 231–52.

26. Henry Fielding, *The History of Tom Jones, A Foundling* [1749] ed. Martin C. Battestin and Fredson Bowers (Clarendon Press, Oxford, 1974) p. 518 (IX 6).

27. William Empson, *"Tom Jones"* ([1958] in Neil Compton (ed.), *Henry Fielding: Tom Jones: A Casebook* (Macmillan, London, 1979), pp. 139–72.

28. I 11, *Tom Jones*, p. 66.

29. Henry Fielding, *Joseph Andrews* [1742], ed. Martin C. Battestin (Clarendon Press, Oxford, 1967), p. 189 (III 1).

30. X 7, *Tom Jones*, p. 554.

31. XV 6, *Tom Jones*, p. 803.

32. *Joseph Andrews*, p. 48.

33. IV 16, *Joseph Andrews*, p. 343.

34. "An Essay on Man", II 181–4, *The Poems of Alexander Pope: A One-Volume Edition of the Twickenham Text*, ed. John Butt (Methuen, London 1963), p. 522.

35. VI 1, *Tom Jones*, p. 270.

36. III 3, *Joseph Andrews*, p. 214.

37. Rawson, *Henry Fielding*, p. 193.

38. Aurélien Digeon, *The Novels of Fielding* (Routledge, London, 1925), pp. 127–8.

39. Note on *Jonathan Wild*, 27th February, 1832. In *Coleridge's Miscellaneous Criticism*, ed. Thomas Middleton Raysor (Constable, London, 1936), p. 306.

40. IV 14, *Tom Jones*, p. 204.

41. Robert Alter, *Fielding and the Nature of the Novel* (Harvard University Press, Cambridge, Mass., 1968), pp. 69–70.

42. XI 3, *Tom Jones*, p. 580.

43. XII 5, *Tom Jones*, p. 635.

44. Henry Fielding, *Amelia* [1751] ed. Martin C. Battestin (Clarendon Press, Oxford, 1983), p. 511 (XII 5).

45. Glenn W. Hatfield, *Henry Fielding and the Language of Irony* (Chicago University Press, Chicago, 1968).

46. Arnold Kettle, *An Introduction to the English Novel* ([1951] Arrow Books, London, 1962), vol. 1, p. 83.

47. See A. R. Towers, "*Amelia* and the State of Matrimony", *Review of English Studies* 4 (1953) 144–57.

48. Ian A. Bell, *Henry Fielding*, pp. 207–10.

49. E.g. Martin C. Battestin, "Tom Jones and 'His *Egyptian* Majesty': Fielding's Parable of Government", *PMLA* 82 (1967) 68–77.

50. Henry Fielding, *An Enquiry into the Causes of the Late Increase of Robbers* [1751] *and Related Writings*, ed. Malvin R. Zirker (Clarendon Press, Oxford, 1988), pp. 80, 83–4.

51. Ian Watt, *The Rise of the Novel: Studies in Defoe, Richardson and Fielding* ([1957] Penguin, Harmondsworth, 1963), pp. 271–92.

52. See Sell, *Literature as* Communication, pp. 213–14.

53. Letter to Lady Bute, 23rd July, 1754, in *The Complete Letters of Lady Mary Mortley Montagu*, ed. Robert Halsband, vol. III (Clarendon Press, Oxford, 1967), p. 65.

54. James Boswell, *Life of Johnson* ([1791] Dent, London, 1906), pp. 343–4.

55. William Makepeace Thackeray, from *The English Humourists* [1853], in his *Henry Esmond; The English Humourists; The Four Georges*, ed. George Saintsbury (Oxford University Press, London, no date), p. 60.

56. André Gide, "Notes for a Preface to Fielding's *Tom Jones*" [1937], in R. Paulson (ed.), *Fielding: A Collection of Critical Essays* (Prentice-Hall, Englewood Cliffs, 1962), pp. 81–3.

57. Boswell, *Life of Johnson*, vol. 1, p. 343.

58. Alan Dugald McKillow, *The Early Masters of English Fiction* (University of Kansas Press, Lawrence, 1956), pp. 120, 129.

59. Kettle, *Introduction to the English Novel*, vol. 1, p. 82.

60. See John Butt, *Fielding* ((Writers and their Work no. 57) Longman, London, 1957), p. 27

and Watt, *The Rise of the Novel*, pp.271–92.

61. Cf. Alter, *Fielding*, Chapter 1.

62. Boswell, *Life of Johnson*, p. 344.

63. A remark made 20 days before his death on July 25th, 1834, and preserved in *Table Talk Recorded by Henry Nelson Coleridge and John Taylor Coleridge*, vol. I, ed. Carl Woodring (Routledge and Princeton University Press, London and Princeton, 1960), p. 496.

64. G. K. Chesterton, from *All Things Considered* ([1908] Lane, New York, 1909), pp. 261–2, 266.

65. Martin C. Battestin, *The Moral Basis of Fielding's Art: A Study of "Joseph Andrews"* (Wesleyan University Press, Middletown, 1959), p.14.

66. William Hazlitt, "Trifles Light as Air" [1829], *The Complete Works of William Hazlitt*, vol. 20, ed. P. P. Howe (Dent, London, 1934), pp. 277–83, esp. 280.

67. E.g. Aubrey Williams, "Interpositions of Providence and the Design of Fielding's Novels", *South Atlantic Quarterly* 70 (1971) 266–86.

68. R. S. Crane, "The Plot of *Tom Jones*", in Crane (ed.) *Critics and Criticism: Ancient and Modern* (Chicago University Press, Chicago, 1952) pp. 616–47.

69. Wayne C. Booth, *The Rhetoric of Fiction* (Chicago University Press, Chicago, 1961).

70. Preface to *The Princess Casamassima* [New York ed., 1908] (Macmillan, London, 1921), p. xvii.

71. Arthur Sherbo, *Studies in the Eighteenth Century Novel* (Michigan State University Press, East Lansing, 1969). Sherbo was reacting against Spilka's "Comic Resolution in Fielding's *Joseph Andrews*" (1953), rep. in Paulson, *Fielding*, pp. 59–68.

72. Andrew Wright, *Henry Fielding: Mask and Feast*, (Chatto and Windus, London, 1965).

73. Martin C. Battestin, "Osborne's *Tom Jones*: Adapting a Classic" (1966), rep. in Compton, *Henry Fielding*, pp. 193–208.

74. E. M. Forster, *Aspects of the Novel and Related Writings*, ed. Oliver Stallybrass (Arnold, London, 1974), p. 60.

75. XI 7, *Tom Jones*, p. 599.

76. XI 7, *Tom Jones*, p. 601.

77. XII 10, *Tom Jones*, pp. 658–9.

78. Preface to *The Princess Casamassima*.

79. *Coleridge's Miscellaneous Criticism*, p. 303.

80. Alter, *Fielding*, p. 44.

81. Digeon, *The Novels of Fielding*, pp. 146–50.

82. University of Massachusetts Press, Amherst, 1966.

83. See. e.g. Hatfield, *Henry Fielding*, p. 166: Fielding "is closer to Shaftesbury than Locke in his belief in an innate potential of moral sympathy to which one can appeal directly through examples when the words that traditionally represent the moral ideas in question are too

corrupt to be depended on." That Fielding embraced latitudinarian ideas about the soul's perfectability is also suggested by Battestin (*The Moral Basis*) p. 14 and Irvin Ehrenpreis, *Fielding: Tom Jones* ([Studies in English Literature 23] Arnold, London, 1964), p. 28.

84. A.E. Dyson, from *The Crazy Fabric* (1965), rep. in Compton, *Henry Fielding*, pp. 182–92.

85. Dyson.

86. Gide, in Paulson, *Fielding*, p. 81.

87. E.g. Alter, *Fielding*; Dorothy Van Gent, *The English Novel: Form and Function* ([1953] Reinhart, New York, 1963), pp. 65–81; Empson, *"Tom Jones"*; John Middleton Murry, "In Defence of Fielding", *Unprofessional Essays* (Jonathan Cape, London, 1956), pp. 11–52.

88. Digeon, *The Novels of Fielding*, pp. 161–6.

89. See n. 83 above.

90. I 3, *Amelia*, p. 28.

91. Sheridan Baker, "Fielding's *Amelia* and the Materials of Romance", *Philological Quarterly* 41 (1962) 437–49.

92. Carla Mulford, "Booth's Progress and the Resolution of *Amelia*", *Studies in the Novel* 16 (1984) 20–31.

93. Martin C. Battestin, *Henry Fielding*, p. 533.

94. Sherbo, *Studies*.

95. Samuel E. Longmire, "*Amelia* as a Comic Action", *Tennessee Studies in English Literature* 13 (1972) 67–79.

96. Thackeray, *The English Humourists*, p. 652.

97. C.K.H. Bevan, "The Unity of Fielding's *Amelia*", *Renaissance and Modern Studies* 14 (1970) 90–110; Allan Wendt, "The Naked Virtue of Amelia", *ELH* 27 (1960) 131–48. Carla Mulford ("Booth's Progress and the Resolution of *Amelia*") also claims to be persuaded by Booth's conversion, and says that he actually discovers the art of life.

98. *Amelia*, p. 3.

99. Wendt, "Naked Virtue".

100. D.S. Thomas, "Fortune and Passions in Fielding's *Amelia*" (*Modern Language Review* 60 (1965), 176–87.

101. Martin C. Battestin, " The Problem of *Amelia*: Hume, Barrow, and the Conversion of Captain Booth", *ELH* 51 (1974) 613–48. Cynthia Griffin Wolff ("Fielding's *Amelia*: Private Virtue and Public Good", *Texas Studies in Literature and Language*, 10 (1968) 37–55) also squarely faces Fielding's insight into human depravity.

102. VI 9, *Tom Jones*, pp. 303–4.

103. Rawson, *Henry Fielding*.

104. VIII 10, *Amelia*, p. 350.

105. I 7, *Joseph Andrews*, pp. 36–7.

106. VI 1, *Amelia*, p. 233.

107. XI 2, *Amelia*, p. 460.

108. Alter and Wright are fairly representative in this respect.

109. See Jill Campbell, *Natural Masques*, pp. 204–48.

110. See Angela A. Smallwood, *Fielding and the Woman Question*, pp. 167–71.

111. See Margaret Lenta, "Comedy, Tragedy and Feminism".

112. XI 10, *Tom Jones*, pp. 615–6.

113. VIII 9, *Amelia*, p. 347.

114. IX 5, *Amelia*, p. 374.

115. VII 10, *Amelia*, p. 307.

116. X 9, *Amelia*, p. 450.

117. VII 10, *Amelia*, p. 307.

118. John S. Coolidge, "Fielding and 'Conservation of Character'" (1960), rep. in Paulson, *Fielding*, pp. 158–76.

119. See Morris Golden, "Public Context and Imagining Self in *Amelia*", *University of Toronto Quarterly* 56 (1987) 377–91, and Mona Scheuerman, "Man not Providence: Fielding's *Amelia* as a Novel of Social Criticism", *Forum for Modern Language Studies* 20 (1984) 106–23.

120. X 4, *Amelia*, p. 428.

121. Terry Castle, *Masquerade and Civilization*, pp. 240–1.

122. VII 10, *Amelia*, p. 306.

123. *Examples of the Interposition of Providence in the Detection and Punishment of Murder* (A. Millar, London, 1752).

124. Thackeray, *The English Humourists*, p. 651.

125. Digeon, *The Novels of Fielding*, p. 207.

126. II, 2, *Amelia*, p. 73.

127. Sherbo, *Studies*, p. 50.

128. Dianne Osland, "Fielding's *Amelia*: Problem Child or Problem Reader?" *Journal of Narrative Technique* 10 (1980) 56–67.

129. J. Paul Hunter, "Fielding and the Modern Reader: The Problem of Temporal Translation", in Hunter and Martin C. Battestin, *Henry Fielding in His Time and Ours* (William Andrews Clark Memorial Library, Los Angeles, 1987), pp. 1–28.

130. Charles A. Knight ("The Narrative Structure of Fielding's *Amelia*" (*Ariel: A Review of International English Literature* 11 (1980) 3–21) is one of those who say that the shifts of viewpoint, though an understandable attempt to probe society on many fronts, alienate readers and clog up the narrative drive.

131. Anthony J. Hassall, "Fielding's Amelia: Dramatic and Authorial Narration", *Novel* 5 (1972) 225–33.

132. Eustace Palmer, "*Amelia* — The Decline of Fielding's Art", *Essays in Criticism* 21 (1971) 135–51.

133. McKillop, *Early Masters*, pp. 142–3; Bevan, "The Unity".

134. Hassall, "Fielding's *Amelia*".

135. Palmer, "*Amelia*".

136. IV 1, *Amelia*, p. 150. Cf. *All for Love*, III i 169 (*The Works of John Dryden*, vol. 13, ed. Maximillian E. Novak, George R. Guffey and Alan Roper (University of California Press, Berkeley, 1984), p. 60).

137. Leavis, *The Great Tradition*, p. 12.

138. III 12, *Amelia*, pp. 148–9.

139. Coolidge, "Fielding and 'Conservation'".

140. Palmer, "*Amelia*".

141. Donald Fraser, "Lying and Concealment in *Amelia*", in K. G. Simpson (ed.) *Henry Fielding: Justice Observed* (Vision Press, London, 1985), pp. 174–98.

142. Susan K. Howard, "The Intrusive Audience in Fielding's *Amelia*", *Journal of Narrative Technique* 17 (1987) 286–95.

143. Arlene Wilner, "The Mythology of History, the Truth of Fiction: Henry Fielding and the Cases of Boavern Penlez and Elizabeth Canning", *Journal of Narrative Technique* 21 (1991) 185–201. She cites Frank Kermode from his *The Sense of an Ending: Studies in the Theory of Fiction* (Oxford University Press, Oxford, 1966), esp. p. 39.

144. Introduction to his edition of *Amelia* (Dent, London, 1962), p. ix.

145. Palmer again, "*Amelia*".

146. Robert L. Oakman, "The Character of the Hero: A Key to Fielding's *Amelia*", *Studies in English Literature 1500–1900* 16 (1976) 474–89.

147. IX 4, *Amelia*, p. 369.

148. I 1, *Amelia*, p. 15.

149. Alter, *Fielding*, p. 151.

150. Humphreys (ed.), *Amelia*, p. ix.

151. Digeon, *The Novels of Fielding*, pp. 201–2.

152. Wolff, "Fielding's *Amelia*".

153. Alter, *Fielding*, p. 173.

154. George Sherburn, "Fielding's *Amelia*: An Interpretation" (1936), rep. in Paulson, *Fielding*, pp. 146–57.

155. See Brian McCrea, "Politics and Narrative Technique in Fielding's *Amelia*", *Journal of Narrative Technique* 13 (1983) 131–40.

156. *Covent-Garden Journal*, 1st February, 1751/2, "Modern History".

157. Martin C. Battestin, *Henry Fielding*, pp. 545–6.

158. John Richetti, "The Old Order and the New Novel of the Mid-Eighteenth Century: Narrative Authority in Fielding and Smollett" *Eighteenth-Century Fiction* 2 (1990) 183–96, and

"Class Struggle without Class: Novelists and Magistrates", *The Eighteenth Century: Theory and Interpretation* 32 (1991) 203–18.

159. Terry Castle, *Masquerade and Civilization*, pp. 98–109.

160. Jill Campbell, *Natural Masques*, p. 239.

Epilogue

1. John Gross, *The Rise and Fall of the Man of Letters: English Literary Life since 1800* ([1969] Penguin, Harmondswoth, 1973), p. 319.

2. Richard Ellmann, *Oscar Wilde* (Hamish Hamilton, London, 1987), Michael Holroyd, *Bernard Shaw* ([3 vols] Chatto and Windus, London, 1988–91), Richard Holmes, *Coleridge: Early Visions* (Hodder and Stoughton, London, 1989).

3. See also Roger D. Sell, "Communication: A Counterweight to Professional Specialization", forthcoming.

4. Gerald Graff, *Beyond the Culture Wars: How Teaching the Conflicts Can Revitalize American Education* (W. W. Norton, New York, 1992), esp. pp. 125–43.

5. See p. 7 above.

6. Cf. Roger D. Sell, *Literature as Communication: The Foundations of Mediating Criticism* (Benjamins, Amsterdam, 2000), pp. 271–77.

Bibliography

Ackroyd, Peter, [1984] 1985. *T. S. Eliot* (Abacus, London)

Adams, Richard, 1973. *Watership Down* (Rex Collings, London)

Adams, Stephen J., 1982. "Black Cottages: Frost, Eliot, and the Fate of Individualism", *Cithara: Essays in the Judaeo-Christian Tradition* 22: 39–52

Alter, Robert, 1968. *Fielding and the Nature of the Novel* (Harvard University Press, Cambridge, Mass.)

Altick, Richard D. 1980. "Varieties of Readers' Response: the Case of *Dombey and Son*", *Yearbook of English Studies* 10: 70–94

Altick, Richard D., 1989. *Writers, Readers, and Occasions: Selected Essays on Victorian Literature and Life* (Ohio State University Press, Columbus)

Andrews, Malcolm, 1994. *Dickens and the Grown-Up Child* (Macmillan, Basingstoke)

Angyal, Andrew J., 1977. "Robert Frost's Poetry Before 1913: A Checklist", in Joseph Katz (ed.), *Proof 5: The Yearbook of American Bibliographical and Textual Studies* (Faust, Columbia), pp. 76–125

Anon., 1910. Review of Andrew Young's *Songs of Night*, *Times Literary Supplement*, March 24th, 1910

Anon., 1921. Review of *Boaz and Ruth*, *Times Literary Supplement*, July 21st

Anon., 1922. Review of William Gerhardie's *Futility: A Novel on Russian Themes*. *Times Literary Supplement*, July 20th

Anon., 1923. Review of Andrew Young's *Thirty-One Poems*, *Times Literary Supplement*, February 15th

Anon., 1924. Review of *The Adversary*, *Times Literary Supplement*, July 17th

Anon., 1927. Review of Andrew Young's *The Bird-Cage*, *Times Literary Supplement*, January 27th

Anon., 1932. Review of Andrew Young's *The New Shepherd*, *Times Literary Supplement*, March 10th

Anon., 1934. Review of Andrew Young's *Winter Harvest*, *Times Literary Supplement*, May 24th

Anon., 1936. Review of Andrew Young's *Collected Poems* (1936), *Times Literary Supplement*, July 18th

Anon., 1936. Review of Andrew Young's *The White Blackbird*, *The Times Literary Supplement*, February 8th

Anon., 1937. Review of Andrew Young's *Nicodemus*. *Times Literary Supplement*, December 11th

Anon., 1950. Review of Andrew Young's *Collected Poems* (1950), *Times Literary Supplement*, December 22nd

Anon., 1958. Review of Andrew Young's *Out of the World and Back*, *Times Literary Supplement*, December 5th

Appiah, K. Anthony, 1994. "Identity, Authenticity, Survival: Multicultural Societies and Social Reproduction", in Gutman, *Multiculturalism*, pp. 149–63

Ashby, Eric, 1958. *Technology and the Academics: an Essay on the Universities and the Scientific Revolution* (London, Macmillan)

Auerbach, Erich, [1953] 1957. *Mimesis: The Representation of Reality in Western Literature* (Doubleday, Garden City)

Auerbach, Nina, 1976. "Dickens and Dombey: a Daughter after All", *Dickens Studies Annual* 5: 95–114

Axton, Willaim, 1963. "Tonal Unity in *Dombey and Son*", *PMLA* 78: 341–8

Axton, William, 1964. "*Dombey and Son*: From Stereotype to Archetype", *English Literary History* 31: 301–17

Badenhausen, Richard, 1990. "'When the poet speaks only for himself': The Chorus as 'First Voice' in *Murder in the Cathedral*", in Cowan, *T. S. Eliot*, pp. 239–56

Badenhausen, Richard, 1992. "'Communal Pleasure' in a Uniform Culture: T. S. Eliot's Search for an Audience", *English Language Notes* 29: 61–9

Bagchee, Shyamal, 1990. "Eliot and the Poetics of 'Unpleasantness'", in Bagchee (ed.) *T. S. Eliot: A Voice Descanting: Centenary Essays* (Macmillan, Basingstoke), pp. 255–70

Baillie, John, 1957. Tribute to Andrew Young, in Clark, *Andrew Young*, pp. 35–8

Baker, Sheridan,1962. "Fielding's *Amelia* and the Materials of Romance", *Philological Quarterly* 41: 437–49

Bakhtin, M. M., 1981. *The Dialogic Imagination: Four Essays* (University of Texas Press, Austin)

Barthes, Roland, [1968] 1977. "The Death of the Author" in his *Image-Music-Text: Essays Selected and Translated by Stephen Heath* (Fontana, Glasgow), pp. 142–8

Battestin, Martin C., 1959. *The Moral Basis of Fielding's Art: A Study of "Joseph Andrews"* (Wesleyan University Press, Middletown)

Battestin, Martin C., [1966] 1970. "Osborne's *Tom Jones*: Adapting a Classic", in Compton, *Henry Fielding*, pp. 193–208

Battestin, Martin C., 1967. "Tom Jones and 'His *Egyptian* Majesty': Fielding's Parable of Government", *PMLA* 82: 68–77

Battestin, Martin C.,1974. " The Problem of *Amelia*: Hume, Barrow, and the Conversion of Captain Booth", *ELH* 51: 613–48

Battestin, Martin C. with Ruthe R. Battestin, 1989. *Henry Fielding: A Life* (Routledge, London)

Baumgarten, Murray, 1985. "Writing and *David Copperfield*", *Dickens Studies Annual* 14: 39–59

Bayley, John, 1969. *The Romantic Survival: A Study in Poetic Evolution* [2nd ed.] (Constable, London)

Bayley, John, 1976. *The Uses of Division: Unity and Disharmony in Literature* (Viking, New York)

Bayley, John, 1999. "Other Worlds to Inhabit", in Salwak, *A Passion for Books*, pp. 21–31

Beaumont, Sir John, 1974. *The Shorter Poems of Sir John Beaumont: A Critical Edition with an Introduction and Commentary*, ed. Roger D. Sell [*Acta Academiae Aboensis, ser. A. Humaniora*, 49], Åbo Akademi University, Åbo

Bedient, Calvin, 1986. *"He Do the Police in Difference Voices": "The Waste Land" and Its Protagonist* (University of Chicago Press, Chicago)

Bell, Ian A., 1994. *Henry Fielding: Authorship and Authority* (Longman, London)

Bell, Vereen M., 1968. "The Emotional Matrix of *David Copperfield*", *Studies in English Literature, 1500–1900* 8: 633–649

Ben-Porat, Ziva, 1991. "Two-Way Pragmatics: From World to Text and Back", in Roger D. Sell (ed.), *Literary Pragmatics* (Routledge, London), pp. 142–163

Berry, Boyd M., 1984. "Childhood and the Self in *Silex Scintillans*", *George Herbert Journal* 7: 73–90

Betjeman, John, 1957. Tribute to Andrew Young, in Clark, *Andrew Young*, pp. 39–45

Bevan, C. K. H., 1970. "The Unity of Fielding's *Amelia*", *Renaissance and Modern Studies* 14: 90–110

Black, Michael, 1975. *The Literature of Fidelity* (Chatto and Windus, London)

Booth, Wayne C., 1988. *The Company We Keep: An Ethics of Fiction* (University of California Press, Berkeley)

Booth, Wayne C., 1961. *The Rhetoric of Fiction* (Chicago University Press, Chicago)

Boswell, James, [1791] 1906. *Life of Johnson* (Dent, London)

Bourdette, Robert E., 1974. "Recent Studies in Henry Vaughan", *English Literary Renaissance* 4: 299–310

Bowers, Fredson, 1963. "Henry Vaughan's Multiple Time Scheme", *Modern Language Quarterly* 33: 291–326

Brooker, Jewel Spears and Joseph Bentley, 1990. *Reading* The Waste Land: *Modernism and the Limits of Interpretation* (University of Massachusetts Press, Amherst)

Brooks, Cleanth, [1939] 1965. *Modern Poetry and the Tradition* (University of North Carolina Press, Chapel Hill)

Brower, Reuben A., 1963. *The Poetry of Robert Frost: Constellations of Intention* (Oxford University Press, New York)

Brown, Ashley, 1989. "T. S. Eliot in the Postmodern Age", *Virginian Quarterly Review* 65: 693–701

Brown, James M., 1982. *Dickens: Novelist in the Market-Place: a Sociological Reading of the Later Novels of Dickens* (Macmillan, London)

Bush, Ronald, 1984. *T. S. Eliot: A Study of Character and Style* (Oxford University Press, Oxford)

Butler, Christopher, 1994. *Early Modernism: Literature, Music, and Painting in Europe, 1900–1916* (Clarendon Press, Oxford)

Butt, John, 1957. *Fielding* ([Writers and their Work no. 57] Longman, London)

Butt, John and Kathleen Tillotson, 1957. *Dickens at Work* (Methuen, London)

Cady, Edwin H. and Louis J. Budd (eds.), 1991. *On Frost: the Best from* American Literature (Duke University Press, Durham)

Calhoun, Thomas A., 1981. *Henry Vaughan: the Achievement of* Silex Scintillans (University of Delaware Press, Newark)

Campbell, Jill, 1995. *Natural Masques: Gender and Identity in Fielding's Plays and Novels* (Stanford University Press, California)

Carey, John, 1992. *The Intellectuals and the Masses: Pride and Prejudice among the Literary Intelligentsia, 1880–1939* (Faber, London)

Carmichael, Virgina, 1987. "*Nom/Non du Père* in *David Copperfield*", *English Literary History* 54: 653–67

Castle, Terry, 1986. *Masquerade and Civilization: The Carnivalesque in Eighteenth-Century English Culture and Fiction* (Standford University Press, Stanford)

Chafe, Wallace L., 1980. "The Deployment of Consciousness in the Production of Narrative", in Chafe (ed.), *The Pear Stories: Cognitive, Cultural and Linguistic Aspects of Narrative Production* (Ablex, Norwood, N. J.), pp. 9–50

Chesterton, G. K. [1906] 1970. Passage from his *Charles Dickens*, in Wall, *Charles Dickens*, pp. 244–9

Chesterton, G. K., 1907. Introduction to the Everyman Edition of *Dombey and Son* (Dent, London)

Chesterton, G. K., [1908] 1909. *All Things Considered* (Lane, New York)

Christ, Carol T., 1981. "T. S. Eliot and the Victorians", *Modern Philology* 79: 157–65

Christ, Carol T., 1984. "Self-Concealment and Self-Expression in Eliot's and Pound's Dramatic Monologues", *Victorian Poetry* 22: 217–26

Church, Richard, 1950. Review of Andrew Young's *Collected Poems* (1950), *The New Statesman and Nation,* December 30th

Church, Richard, 1957. Tribute to Andrew Young, in Clark, *Andrew Young,* pp. 46–50

Clark, Leonard and R. George Thomas, 1964. *Andrew Young and R. S. Thomas* ([two separate accounts; Writers and Their Works no. 196] Longmans, Green & Co., London)

Clark, Leonard (ed.), 1957. *Andrew Young: Prospect of A Poet* (Rupert Hart-Davis, London)

Clark, Robert, 1984. "Riddling the Family Firm: The Sexual Economy in *Dombey and Son*", *English Literary History* 51: 69–84

Cockburn [Lord], 1852. *Life of Lord Jeffrey with a Selection from his Correspondence* (2nd ed., Adam and Charles Black, Edinburgh)

Cole, Peter, (ed.) 1981. *Radical Pragmatics* (Academic Press, New York)

Coleridge, Samuel Taylor, 1960. *Table Talk Recorded by Henry Nelson Coleridge and John Taylor Coleridge*, vol. I, ed. Carl Woodring (Routledge and Princeton University Press, London and Princeton)

Coleridge, Samuel Taylor, 1936. *Coleridge's Miscellaneous Criticism*, ed. Thomas Middleton Raysor (Constable, London)

Collins, Philip, 1980. "Dickens and Industrialism", *Studies in English Literature, 1500–1900* 20: 651–73

Collins, Philip, 1977. *Charles Dickens: David Copperfield* ([Studies in English Literature 67] Arnold, London)

Collins, Philip, 1967. "*Dombey and Son* — Then and Now", *The Dickensian* 63: 82–94

Collins, Philip, 1974. "The Popularity of Dickens" *The Dickensian* 70: 5–20

Collins, Philip, 1981. "Special Correspondent to Posterity: How Dickens's Contemporaries saw his Fictional World", in Samuel I. Mintz *et. al.* (eds.), *From Smollett to James: Studies in the Novel and Other Essays* (University Press of Virginia, Charlottesville), pp. 157–82

Colmer, John, 1978. *Coleridge to Catch-22: Images of Society* (Macmillan, London)

Compton, Neil (ed.), 1979. *Henry Fielding: Tom Jones: A Casebook* (Macmillan, London)

Connor, Steven, 1985. *Charles Dickens* (Blackwell, Oxford)

Cook, James, 1879. *Bibliography of the Writings of Charles Dickens and Many Curious and Interesting Particulars Relating to His Works* (J. & J. Cook, Paisley)

Coolidge, John S., [1960] 1962. "Fielding and 'Conservation of Character'", in Paulson, *Fielding*, pp. 158–76

Cowan, Laura (ed.), 1990, *T. S. Eliot: Man and Poet vol. 1* (National Poetry Foundation, University of Maine, Orono)

Craig, David, 1983. "The Crowd in Dickens", in Giddings, *The Changing World*, pp. 75–90

Craig, Randall, 1982. "The Early Fiction of William Gerhardie", *Novel: A Forum on Fiction* 15: 240–56

Craig, Randall, 1990. "Evelyn Waugh and William Gerhardie", *Journal of Modern Literature* 16: 597–614

Crane, Joan St. C., 1974. *Robert Frost: A Descriptive Catalogue of Books and Manuscripts in the Clifton Waller Barrett Library, University of Virginia* (University Press of Virginia, Charlottesville)

Crane, R. S., 1952. "The Plot of *Tom Jones*", in Crane (ed.) *Critics and Criticism: Ancient and Modern* (Chicago University Press, Chicago), pp. 616–47

Crawford, Iain, 1986. "Sex and Seriousness in *David Copperfield*", *Journal of Narrative Technique* 16: 41–54

Cross, Wilbur L., 1918. *The History of Henry Fielding* (Yale University Press, New Haven)

Dabney, Ross H., 1967. *Love and Property in the Novels of Dickens* (Chatto and Windus, London)

Davidson, Harriet, 1985. *T. S. Eliot and Hermeneutics: Absence and Interpretation in "The Waste Land"* (Louisiana State University Press, Baton Rouge)

Davies, Dido, 1990. *William Gerhardie: A Biography* (Oxford University Press, Oxford)

Davies, Stevie, 1995. *Henry Vaughan* (seren, Bridgend)

de Saussure, Ferdinand, [1916] 1974. *Course in General Linguistics* (Fontana, London)

Dickens, Charles, [1848] 1974. *Dombey and Son*, ed. Alan Horsman (Clarendon Press, Oxford)

Dickens, Charles, [1850] 1981. *David Copperfield*, ed. Nina Burgis (Clarendon Press, Oxford)

Dickens, Charles, [1854] 1955. *Hard Times*, ed. Dingle Foot (Oxford University Press, London)

Dickens, Charles, [1865] 1952. *Our Mutual Friend*, ed. E. Salter Savies (Oxford University Press, London)

Dickens, Charles, [1873] 1996. *Bleak House*, ed. Stephen Gill (Oxford University Press, Oxford)

Digeon, Aurélien, 1925. *The Novels of Fielding* (Routledge, London)

Dobrée, Bonamy, 1954. *The Broken Cistern* (Cohen and West, London)

Dolitsky, Marlene, 1984. *Under the Tumtum Tree: From Nonsense to Sense: A Study in Non-automatic Comprehension* (Benjamins, Amsterdam)

Donoghue, Denis, 1974. "The Word Within a Word", in A. D. Moody (ed.), *The Waste Land in Different Voices* (Arnold, London), pp. 185–201

Donoghue, Denis, 1971. "The English Dickens and *Dombey and Son*", in Nisbet and Nevins, *Dickens Centennial Essays*, pp. 1–21

Dryden, John, 1984. *The Works of John Dryden*, vol. 13, ed. Maximillian E. Novak, George R. Guffey and Alan Roper (University of California Press, Berkeley)

Durr, R. A., 1962. *On the Mystical Poetry of Henry Vaughan* (Harvard University Press, Cambridge, Mass.)

Dyson, A. E., [1965] 1970. Passage from his *The Crazy Fabric*, in Compton, *Henry Fielding*, pp. 182–92

Ehrenpreis, Irvin, 1964. *Fielding: Tom Jones* ([Studies in English Literature 23] Arnold, London)

Eigner, Edwin E., 1987. "*David Copperfield* as an Elegiac Romance", *Dickens Studies Annual* 16: 39–60

Eisenstein, Elizabeth L., 1999. "The End of the Book? Some Perspectives on Media Change", in Salwak, *A Passion for Books*, pp. 181–97

Eisenstein, Elizabeth L., 1979. *The Printing Press as an Agent of Change* (Cambridge University Press, Cambridge)

Elam, Keir, 1988. "Much Ado About Doing Things With Words (and Other Means): Some Problems in the Pragmatics of Theatre and Drama", in Michael Issacharoff and Robin J. Jones (eds.) *Performing Texts* (University of Pennsylvania Press, Philadelphia), pp. 39–58

Eliot, T. S. [1919] 1951. "Tradition and the Individual Talent", in Eliot, *Selected Essays*, pp. 13–22

Eliot, T. S., [1920] 1960. *The Sacred Wood* (Methuen, London)

Eliot, T. S. [1921] 1951. "The Metaphysical Poets", in Eliot, *Selected Essays*, pp. 281–91

Eliot, T. S., [1923] 1953. "Marie Lloyd", in Eliot, *Selected Essays*, pp. 456–9

Eliot, T. S., 1927. "The Silurist", *The Dial* 83: 259–63.

Eliot, T. S., 1933. Review of Housman's "The Name and Nature of Poetry", *Criterion* 13: 151–4

Eliot, T. S., [1933] 1964. *The Use of Poetry and the Use of Criticism: Studies in the Relation of Criticism to Poetry in England* (Faber, London)

Eliot, T. S. 1940. "The Writer as Artist: Discussion between T. S. Eliot and Desmond Hawkins", *The Listener*, 28th November

Eliot, T. S., 1951. *Selected Essays by T. S. Eliot* (Faber, London)

Eliot, T. S. [1957] 1985. *On Poetry and Poets* (Faber, London)

Eliot, T. S. 1969. *The Complete Poems and Plays of. . .* (Faber, London)

Eliot, Valerie, 1971. *T. S. Eliot: The Waste Land: A Facsimile and Transcript of the Original Drafts Including the Annotations of Ezra Pound* (Harcourt Brace Jovanovich, New York)

Ellmann, Maud, 1987. *The Poetics of Impersonality: T. S. Eliot and Ezra Pound* (Harvester, Brighton)

Ellmann, Richard, 1982. *James Joyce: New and Revised Edition* (Oxford University Press, Oxford)

Ellmann, Richard, 1987. *Oscar Wilde* (Hamish Hamilton, London)

Empson, William, [1958] 1979. "*Tom Jones*", in Compton, *Henry Fielding*, 139–72

Engler, Balz, 1987. "Deixis and the Status of Poetic Texts" in Udo Fries (ed.) *The Structure of Texts* (Gunter Narr, Tübingen), pp. 65–73

Faulks, Sebastian, [1996] 1997. *The Fatal Englishman: Three Short Lives* (Vintage, London)

Feltes, N. N., 1977. "To Saunter, to Hurry: Dickens, Time, and Industrial Capitalism", *Victorian Studies* 20: 245–67

Feltes, N. N., 1987. "Realism, consensus and 'exclusion itself': Interpellating the Victorian bourgeoisie", *Textual Practice* 1: 297–308

Fielding, Henry, [1742] 1967. *Joseph Andrews*, ed. Martin C. Battestin (Clarendon Press, Oxford)

Fielding, Henry, [1743] 1997. *Miscellanies by Henry Fielding, Esq; Volume Three*, eds. Bertrand A. Goldgar and Hugh Amory (Clarendon Press, Oxford)

Fielding, Henry, [1749] 1974. *The History of Tom Jones, A Foundling*, ed. Martin C. Battestin and Fredson Bowers (Clarendon Press, Oxford)

Fielding, Henry, [1751] 1983. *Amelia*, ed. Martin C. Battestin (Clarendon Press, Oxford)

Fielding, Henry, 1751. *Covent-Garden Journal*, 1st February

Fielding, Henry, 1752. *Examples of the Interposition of Providence in the Detection and Punishment of Murder* (A. Millar, London)

Fielding, Henry, 1988. *An Enquiry into the Causes of the Late Increase of Robbers* [1751] *and Related Writings*, ed. Malvin R. Zirker (Clarendon Press, Oxford)

Fillmore, Charles J., 1981. "Pragmatics and the Description of Discourse", in Cole, *Radical Pragmatics*, pp. 143–81

Fish, Stanley, 1967. *Surprised by Sin: The Reader in* Paradise Lost (Macmillan, London)

Fish, Stanley, 1990. "Rhetoric", in Frank Lentricchia and Thomas McLaughlin (eds.), *Critical Terms for Literary Study* (Chicago University Press, Chicago), p. 90

Fitter, Chris, 1992. "Henry Vaughan's Landscapes of Military Occupation", *Essays in Criticism* 43:123–47

Ford, George H., 1965. *Dickens and His Readers: Aspects of Novel Criticism since 1836* (Norton, New York)

Forster, E. M., 1974. *Aspects of the Novel and Related Writings*, ed. Oliver Stallybrass (Arnold, London)

Forster, John, [1872–74] 1928. *The Life of Charles Dickens*, ed. J. W. T. Ley (Cecil Palmer, London)

Foucault, Michel, [1969] 1980. "What is an Author?", in Josué V. Harari (ed.) *Textual Strategies: Perspectives in Post-Structuralist Criticism* (Methuen, London), pp. 141–60

Fowler, Roger, 1983. "Polyphony and Problematic in *Hard Times*", in Giddings, *The Changing World*, pp. 91–108

Fraser, Donald, 1985. "Lying and Concealment in *Amelia*", in K. G. Simpson (ed.) *Henry Fielding: Justice Observed* (Vision Press, London)

Friedenreich, Kenneth, 1978. *Henry Vaughan* (Twayne, Boston)

Frost, Lesley, 1969. *New Hampshire's Child: The Derry Journals of Lesley Frost*, eds. Lawrance Thompson and Arnold Grade (State University of New York Press, Albany)

Frost, Lesley Lee, 1994. *The Frost Family's Adventure in Poetry* (University of Missouri Press, Columbia)

Frost, Lucy, 1982. "Taming to Improve: Dickens and the Women in *Great Expectations*", *Meridian* 1:11–20 [reprinted in Sell (1995), *New Casebook*, pp. 60–78]

Frost, Robert, [1903–05] 1963. *Robert Frost: Farm-Poultryman: The Story of Robert Frost's Career as a Breeder and Fancier of Hens & the Texts of Eleven Long-forgotten Prose Contributions by the Poet, Which Appeared in Two New England Poultry Journals in 1903–05, during his Years of Farming at Derry, New Hampshire*, eds. Edward Connery

Lathem and Lawrance Thompson (Dartmouth Publications, Hanover)

Frost, Robert, 1907. "The Lost Faith", *The Derry News* 27/16, Friday, March 1st, pp. 1 and 5.

Frost, Robert, 1917. *A Way Out, Seven Arts* vol. 1 no. 4 (February) [Subsequently in Helen Louise Cohen (ed.), *More One-Act Plays by Modern Authors* (Harcourt Brace, New York, 1927); and Edward Connery Lathem and Lawrance Thompson (eds.), *Robert Frost: Poetry and Prose* (Holt, Rinehart and Winston, New York, 1972). Also published separately by The Harbor Press, New York, 1929.]

Frost Robert, 1949. *Selected Prose of Robert Frost*, ed. Hyde Cox and Edward Connery Lathem (Macmillan, New York)

Frost, Robert, 1964. *Selected Letters of Robert Frost*, ed. Lawrance Thompson (Holt, Rinehart and Winston, New York)

Frost, Robert, 1966. *Interviews with Robert Frost*, ed. Edward Connery Lathem (Holt, Rinehart and Winston, New York)

Frost, Robert, 1966. *Robert Frost and the Lawrence, Massachusetts, "High School Bulletin": The Beginnings of a Literary Career*, eds. Edward Connery Lathem and Lawrance Thompson (The Grolier Club, New York)

Frost, Robert, 1972. *The Poetry of Robert Frost*, ed. Edward Connery Lathem (Jonathan Cape, London)

Frost, Robert, 1973. *Robert Frost on Writing*, ed. Elaine Berry (Rutgers University Press, New Brunswick)

Frost, Robert, 1984. *Stories for Lesley*, ed. Roger D. Sell (University Press of Virginia, Charlottesville)

Frost, Robert and Elinor, 1972. *Family Letters of Robert and Elinor Frost*, ed. Arnold Grade (State University of New York Press, Albany)

Gadamer, Hans-Georg [1960] 1989. *Truth and Method* (London, Sheed and Ward)

Gadamer, Hans-Georg [1962–72] 1976. *Philosophical Hermeneutics* (University of California Press, Berkeley)

Gadamer, Hans-Georg, [1967, 1977, 1980] 1986. *The Relevance of the Beautiful and Other Essays* (Cambridge University Press, Cambridge)

Gadamer, Hans-Georg, [1976, 1978, 1979] 1981. *Reason in the Age of Science* (MIT Press, Cambridge, Mass.)

Gardner, Helen, 1947. "Four Quartets: A Commentary", in B. Rajan (ed.) *Focus Three: T. S. Eliot, A Study of His Writings by Several Hands* (Dennis and Dobson, London), pp. 57–77

Garis, Robert, 1965. *The Dickens Theatre: a Reassessment of the Novels* (Clarendon Press, Oxford)

Garner, Ross, 1959. *Henry Vaughan: Experience and the Tradition* (University of Chicago Press, Chicago)

Genette, Gérard, 1980. *Narrative Discourse* (Cornell University Press, Ithaca)

Gerhardie, William, 1922. *Futility: A Novel on Russian Themes* (Richard Cobden-Sanderson, London)

Gerhardie, William, [1923] 1974. *Anton Chehov [sic]: a Critical Study* (Macdonald, London)

Gerhardie, William, [1931] 1990. *Memoirs of a Polyglot* (Robin Clark, London)

Gerhardie, William, [1936] 1982. *Of Mortal Love* (Penguin, Harmondsworth)

Gerhardie, William, [1981] 1990. *God's Fifth Army: A Biography of the Age 1890–1940* (The Hogarth Press, London)

Geyer, G. W., 1971. "A Poulterer's Pleasure: Robert Frost as Prose Humorist", *Studies in Short Fiction* 8: 589–99

Giddings, Robert (ed.), 1983. *The Changing World of Charles Dickens* (Barnes and Noble, London)

Gide, André, [1937] 1962. "Notes for a Preface to Fielding's *Tom Jones*", in Paulson, *Fielding*, pp. 81–3

Gilmour, Robert, 1975. "Memory in *David Copperfield*" *The Dickensian* 71: 30–42

Gissing, George, 1925. *The Immortal Dickens* (Cecil Palmer, London)

Goffman, Ervin, 1959. *The Presentation of the Self in Everyday Life* (Doubleday, New York)

Golden, Morris, 1966. *Fielding's Moral Psychology* (University of Massachusetts Press, Amherst)

Golden, Morris, 1987. "Public Context and Imagining Self in *Amelia*", *University of Toronto Quarterly* 56: 377–91

Goldman, Arnold, 1970. "James Joyce", in Bernard Bergonzi, *The Twentieth Century* (Sphere Books, London), pp. 75–105

Goody, J. (ed.), 1968. *Literacy in Traditional Societies.* (Cambridge University Press, Cambridge)

Goody, J. 1977. *The Domestication of the Savage Mind.* (Cambridge University Press, Cambridge)

Goody, J., 1986. *The Logic of Writing and the Organization of Society* (Cambridge University Press, Cambridge)

Goody, J., 1987. *The Interface between the Written and the Oral* (Cambridge: Cambridge University Press, Cambridge)

Gordon, Lyndall, 1977. *Eliot's Early Years* (Oxford University Press, Oxford)

Graff, Gerald, 1992. *Beyond the Culture Wars: How Teaching the Conflicts can Revitalize American Education* (Norton, New York)

Grant, Michael (ed.), 1982. *T. S. Eliot: The Critical Heritage*, vols. 1 and 2 (Routledge and Kegan Paul, London)

Green, Keith Green (ed.), 1995. *New Essays in Deixis: Discourse, Narrative, Literature* (Rodopi, Amsterdam)

Grice, H. P. [1967] 1991. " Logic and Conversation", in Steven Davis (ed.). *Pragmatics: A Reader* (Oxford University Press, New York), pp. 305–15

Grigson, Geoffrey, 1962. Review of Andrew Young's *The Poet and the Landscape*, *New Statesman*, September 14th

Gross, John, [1968] 1973. *The Rise and Fall of the Man of Letters: English Literary Life since 1800* (Penguin, Harmondsworth)

Gunnarsson, Bo, 1995. *The Novels of William Gerhardie* (Åbo Akademi University Press, Åbo)

Gutman, Amy (ed.), 1994. *Multiculturalism: Examining the Politics of Recognition* (Princeton University Press, Princeton)

Halley, Janet E., 1984. "Versions of the Self and the Politics of Privacy in *Silex Scintillans*", *George Herbert Journal* 7:51–71

Halverson, J., 1992. "Havelock on Greek Orality and Literacy", *Journal of the History of Ideas* 53: 148–63

Hamilton, George Rostrevor, 1957. Tribute to Andrew Young, in Clark *Andrew Young*, pp. 99–105

Hammond, Gerald, 1984. "Henry Vaughan's Verbal Subtlety: Wordplay in 'Silex Scintillans'", *Modern Language Review* 79: 526–40

Hardy, Barbara, 1970. "The Complexity of Dickens", in Michael Slater (ed.), *Dickens: 1970: Centennial Essays* (Chapman and Hall, London)

Harmsen, T. H. B. M., 1988. "T. S. Eliot's Poetic Testament: the Personality of the Impersonality Seeker", *English Studies* 69: 509–17

Hassall, Anthony J., 1972. "Fielding's Amelia: Dramatic and Authorial Narration", *Novel* 5: 225–33

Hassall, Anthony J., 1981. "Women in Richardson and Fielding", *Novel* 14: 168–74

Hassall, Christopher, 1957. Tribute to Andrew Young, in Clark, *Andrew Young*, pp. 51–60

Hatfield, Glenn W., 1968. *Henry Fielding and the Language of Irony* (Chicago University Press, Chicago)

Havelock, E., 1982. *The Literate Revolution in Greece and its Cultural Consequences* (Princeton University Press, Princeton)

Havelock, E., 1986. *The Muse Learns to Write* (Yale University Press, New Haven)

Havelock, E., 1989. "Orality and Literacy, an Overview". *Language and Communication* 9: 87–98

Hawkes, Terence, 1986. *That Shakespeherian Rag: Essays on a Critical Process* (Methuen, London,)

Hazlitt, William, [1829] 1934. "Trifles Light as Air", *The Complete Works of William Hazlitt*, vol. 20, ed. P. P. Howe (Dent, London), pp. 277–83

Henkle, Roger B., 1980. *Comedy and Culture: England 1820–1900* (Princeton University Press, Princeton)

Hill, Christopher, 1985. "Henry Vaughan (1621 or 1622?–1695)", in his *Collected Essays, Vol. I: Writing and Revolution in Seventeenth Century England* (Harvester, Brighton), pp. 207–25

Hobsbawm, Eric, 1995. *Age of Extremes: The Short Twentieth Century, 1914–1991* (Abacus, London)

Holmes, Elizabeth, 1932. *Henry Vaughan and the Hermetic Philosophy* (Blackwell, Oxford)

Holmes, Richard, 1989. *Coleridge: Early Visions* (Hodder and Stoughton, London)

Holroyd, Michael, 1988. *Bernard Shaw* ([3 vols] Chatto and Windus, London, 1988–91)

Horrocks, Sir Brian, 1971. Interview. *Radio Times*, 2nd September: programmes for 4th September, and "The War We Forgot — but the Russians Didn't"

Horsman Alan, 1982. Introduction to his edition of *Dombey and Son* (Oxford University Press, Oxford)

Horton, Susan R., 1979. *Interpreting Interpreting: Interpreting Dickens's Dombey* (Johns Hopkins University Press, Baltimore)

Horton, Susan R., 1981. *The Reader in the Dickens World: Style and Response* (Macmillan, London)

Hough, Graham, 1960. *Image and Experience* (Duckworth, London)

House, Humphrey, [1941] 1943. *The Dickens World* (Oxford University Press, London)

Housman, A. E., 1962. *A. E. Housman: Selected Prose*, ed. John Carter (Cambridge University Press, Cambridge)

Houston, Gail Turley, 1993. "Gender Construction and the *Kunstlerroman* [*sic*]: *David Copperfield* and *Aurora Leigh*", *Philological Quarterly* 72: 213–36

Howard, Susan K., 1987. "The Intrusive Audience in Fielding's *Amelia*", *Journal of Narrative Technique* 17: 286–95

Hoy, David, 1978. *The Critical Circle: Literature, History, and Philosophical Hermeneutics* (University of California Press, Berkeley)

Hughes, Roger, 1991. *The Shock of the New: Art and the Century of Change* ([updated and enlarged ed.] Thames and Hudson, London)

Humphreys, A. R., 1962. Introduction to his edition of Fielding's *Amelia* (Dent, London)

Hunter, J. Paul, 1987. "Fielding and the Modern Reader: The Problem of Temporal Translation", in Hunter and Martin C. Battestin, *Henry Fielding in His Time and Ours* (William Andrews Clark Memorial Library, Los Angeles), pp. 1–28

Ingham, Patricia, 1979. "Speech and Non-Communication in *Dombey and Son*", *Review of English Studies* 30: 145–53

Iser, Wolfgang, 1974. *The Implied Reader: Patterns of Communication in Prose Fiction from Bunyan to Beckett* (Johns Hopkins University Press, Baltimore)

Iwamassu, Hirofumi, 1986. "Eliot's Personality in *The Waste Land*", *Kyushu American Literature* 27:13–20

Jackson, Arlene M., 1981. "Agnes Whitfield and the Church Leitmotif in *David Copperfield*", *Dickens Studies Annual* 9: 53–65

James, Henry, [1899] 1968. "The Future of the Novel", in *Henry James: Selected Literary Criticism*, ed. Morris Shapira (Penguin, Harmondsworth), pp. 218–27

James, Henry, [1908] 1921. *The Princess Casamassima* [New York ed.] (Macmillan, London)

James, William, [1897 & 1898] 1956. *The Will to Believe and Other Essays in Popular Philosophy* [bound here with] *Human Immortality: Two Supposed Objections to the Doctrine* (Dover, New York)

James, William, [1907 & 1909] 1978. *Pragmatism: A New Name for Old Ways of Thinking* [and] *The Meaning of Truth: a Sequel to Pragmatism* (Harvard University Press, Cambridge)

Johnson, Edgar, 1953. *Charles Dickens: His Tragedy and Triumph* (Gollancz, London)

Jordan, John O., 1985. "The Social Sub-Text of *David Copperfield*", *Dickens Studies Annual* 14: 61–92

Joyce, James, [1916] 1960. *A Portrait of the Artist as a Young Man* (Penguin, Harmondsworth)

Julius, Anthony, 1995. *T. S. Eliot, Anti-Semitism, and Literary Form* (Cambridge University Press, Cambridge)

Jump, J. D. 1971–2. "Dickens and His Readers", *Bulletin of the John Rylands Library* 54: 384–97

Keats, John, 1954. *Letters of John Keats*, ed. Frederick Page (Oxford University Press, London)

Keith, W. J., 1975. *The Rural Tradition: William Cobbet, Gilbert White, and other Non-fiction Prose Writers of the English Countryside* (Harvester, London)

Kemp, John C., 1979. *Robert Frost and New England: the Poet as Regionalist* (Princeton University Press, Princeton)

Kermode, Frank, 1950. "The Private Imagery of Henry Vaughan", *Review of English Studies* 1: 206-25

Kermode, Frank, 1966. *The Sense of an Ending: Studies in the Theory of Fiction* (Oxford University Press, Oxford)

Kermode, Frank, [1981] 1991. Review of William Gerhardie's *Futility*, in his *The Uses of Error* (Fontana, London), pp. 308-16

Kermode, Frank, 1983. "The Common Reader", *Daedalus*, 1-11

Kermode, Frank, [1989] 1990. *An Appetite for Poetry* (Fontana, Glasgow)

Kern, Robert, [1988] 1991. "Frost and Modernism", in Cady and Budd *On Frost*, pp. 190-206

Kernan, Alvin, 1990. *The Death of Literature* (Yale University Press, New Haven)

Kettle, Arnold, [1951] 1962. *An Introduction to the English Novel* (Arrow Books, London)

Kinney, Clare R., 1987. "Fragmentary Excess, Copious Death: *The Waste Land* as Anti-Narrative", *Journal of Narrative Technique* 17: 273-85

Knight, Charles A., 1980. "The Narrative Structure of Fielding's *Amelia*", *Ariel: A Review of International English Literature* 11: 3-21

Kovačević, Ivanka, 1975. *Fact into Fiction: English Literature and the Industrial Scene* (Leicester University Press, Leicester)

Larkin, Philip, 1985. Review of *Andrew Young: The Poetical Works*, *The Observer*, January 13th

Leavis, F. R., 1930. *Mass Civilization and Minority Culture* (The Minority Press, Cambridge)

Leavis, F. R., [1932] 1963. *New Bearings in English Poetry* (Penguin, Harmondsworth)

Leavis, F. R., [1936] 1964. *Revaluation: Tradition and Development in English Poetry* (Penguin, Harmondsworth)

Leavis, F. R., [1943] 1948. *Education and the University* (Chatto and Windus, London)

Leavis, F. R., [1948] 1962. *The Great Tradition: George Eliot, Henry James, Joseph Conrad* (Penguin, Harmondsworth)

Leavis, F. R., [1970] 1972. "The First Major Novel: *Dombey and Son*", Leavis and Leavis, *Dickens the Novelist*, pp. 21-56

Leavis, F. R. and Q. D. Leavis, [1970] 1972. *Dickens the Novelist* (Penguin, Harmondsworth)

Leavis, L. R., 1986. "*David Copperfield* and *Jane Eyre*", *English Studies* 67: 167-73

Leavis, Q. D., 1932, *Fiction and the Reading Public* (Chatto and Windus, London)

Leavis, Q. D., [1970] 1980. "Dickens and Tolstoy: The Case for a Serious View of *David Copperfield*, in Leavis and Leavis, *Dickens the Novelist*, pp. 60-150

Lecker, Barbara, 1979. "The Split Characters of Charles Dickens", *Studies in English Literature, 1500-1900* 19: 689-704

Lee, Brian, 1979. *Theory and Personality: the Significance of T. S. Eliot's Criticism* (Athlone Press, London)

Lee, Chong-Ho, 1990. "Eliot and Postmodernism: Postmodernity in *The Waste Land*", *Journal of English Language and Literature* 36: 29-54

Lenta, Margaret, 1983. "Comedy, Tragedy and Feminism: The Novels of Richardson and Fielding", *English Studies in Africa* 26: 13-25

Lentricchia, Frank, 1975. *Robert Frost: Modern Poetics and the Landscapes of the Self* (Duke University Press, Durham)

Lentricchia, Frank, [1990] 1991. "The Resentments of Robert Frost", in Cady and Budd, *On Frost*, pp. 222–47

Lentricchia, Frank, 1996. "Last Will and Testament of an Ex-Literary Critic", *Lingua Franca*, 59–67

Levenson, Michael H., 1984. *A Geneology of Modernism: A Study of English Literary Doctrine 1908–1922* (Cambridge University Press, Cambridge)

Lévi-Strauss, Claude, [1964] 1970. "Overture to Le Cru et le Cuit", in Jacques Ehrmann (ed.), *Structuralism* (Anchor-Doubleday, Garden City), pp. 31–55

Levin, Harry, 1960. *James Joyce: A Critical Introduction* (2nd. ed., Faber, London)

Levinson, Stephen, 1983. *Pragmatics* (Cambridge University Press, Cambridge)

Li, Victor P. H., 1990. "'The Poetry does not Matter': *Four Quartets* and the Rhetoric of Humility", *T. S. Eliot Annual no. 1* (Macmillan, Basingstoke), pp. 63–86

Liebre, Todd M., [1975] 1991. "Robert Frost and Wallace Stevens: 'What to make of a diminished thing'", in Cady and Budd, *On Frost*, pp. 100–19

Longmire, Samuel E., 1972. "*Amelia* as a Comic Action", *Tennessee Studies in English Literature* 13: 67–79

Lowbury, Edward, 1994. "Andrew Young", in his *Hallmarks of Poetry: Reflections on a Theme* (University of Salzburg, Salzburg), pp. 68–82

Lowbury, Edward and Alison Young, 1997. *To Shirk no Idleness: A Critical Biography of the Poet Andrew Young* (University of Salzburg, Salzburg)

Lubbock, Percy, 1921. *The Craft of Fiction* (Jonathan Cape, London)

Lucas, F., 1923. Review of *The Waste Land, New Statesman*, 3rd November

Macbeth, George (ed.), 1967. *Poetry 1900 to 1965* (Longman with Faber, London)

McCrea, Brian, 1981. *Henry Fielding and the Politics of Mid-Eighteenth-Century England* (University of Georgia Press, Athens)

McCrea, Brian, 1983. "Politics and Narrative Technique in Fielding's *Amelia*", *Journal of Narrative Technique* 13: 131–40

McKillow, Alan Dugald, 1956. *The Early Masters of English Fiction* (University of Kansas Press, Lawrence)

MacLeish, Archibald, 1976. "Robert Frost and New England", *National Geographic* 149: 438–44

MacVeah, John, 1981. *Tradeful Merchants: the Portrayal of the Capitalist in English Literature* (Routledge and Kegan Paul, London)

Marilla, E. L., 1945. "The Religious Conversion of Henry Vaughan", *Review of English Studies* 21: 15–22

Martin, Philip W., 1987. *Mad Women in Romantic Writing* (Harvester, Brighton)

Martz, Louis L., [1954] 1962. *The Poetry of Meditation: A Study in English Religious Literature of the Seventeenth Century* (Yale University Press, New Haven)

Martz, Louis L., 1963. "Henry Vaughan: The Man Within", *PMLA* 78: 40–9

Mead, George Herbert, 1934. *Mind, Self, and Society* (University of Chicago Press, Chicago)

Melada, Ivan, 1970. *The Captain of Industry in English Fiction, 1821–1871* (University of New Mexico Press, Albuquerque)

Meuller-Vollmer, Kurt (ed.), 1985. *The Hermeneutics Reader: Texts of the German Tradition from the Englightenment to the Present* (Blackwell, Oxford)

Meynell, Viola, 1931. Review of Andrew Young's *The Bird-Cage* and *The Cuckoo Clock*, *The New Statesman and Nation*, July 25th

Meynell, Viola, 1932. Review of Andrew Young's *The New Shepherd*, *The New Statesman and Nation*, May 7th

Miller, James E., 1977. *T. S. Eliot's Personal Waste Land: Exorcism of the Demons* (University of Pennsylvania Press, University Park)

Miller, John Hillis, 1959. *Charles Dickens: The World of his Novels* (Harvard University Press, Cambridge)

Miller, John Hillis, 1968. "Three Problems of Fictional Form: First-Person Narration in *David Copperfield* and *Huckleberry Finn*", in Roy Harvey Pearce (ed.), *Experience in the Novel* (Columbia University Press, New York)

Miller, Lewis H., 1978. "William James, Robert Frost, and 'The Black Cottage'", in Jac Tharpe (ed.), *Frost: Centennial Essays III* (University Press of Mississippi, Jackson), pp. 368–81

Milner, Ian, 1971. "The Dickens Drama: Mr Dombey", in Nisbet and Nevins, *Dickens Centennial Essays*, pp. 155–65

Monod, Sylvère, 1968. *Dickens the Novelist* (University of Oklahoma Press, Norman)

Montague, Lady Mary Mortley, 1967. *The Complete Letters of Lady Mary Mortley Montagu*, ed. Robert Halsband, vol. III (Clarendon Press, Oxford)

Morris, Mowbray, 1882. "Charles Dickens", *Fortnightly Review* 32: 762–99

Morris, Pam, 1991. *Dickens's Class Consciousness: A Marginal View* (Macmillan, Basingstoke)

Moynaham, Julian, 1960. "The Hero's Guilt: the Case of *Great Expectations*", *Essays in Criticism* 10: 60–79

Moynaham, Julian, 1962. "Dealings with the Firm of Dombey and Son: Dryness versus Wetness", in John Gross and Gabriel Pearson (eds.), *Dickens and the Twentieth Century* (Routledge and Kegan Paul, London), pp. 121–31

Muir, Edwin, 1928. *The Structure of the Novel* (Hogarth Press, London)

Muir, Edwin, 1960. *Edwin Muir: Collected Poems* (Oxford University Press, New Jersey)

Mulford, Carla, 1984. "Booth's Progress and the Resolution of *Amelia*", *Studies in the Novel* 16: 20–31

Munro, Thomas, 1958. "The Failure Story: A Study of Contemporary Pessimism" *The Journal of Aesthetics and Art Criticism* 17 (1958) 362–87

Murray, Paul, 1991. *T. S. Eliot and Mysticism: The Secret History of* Four Quartets (Macmillan, Basingstoke), pp. 11–52.

Murry, John Middleton, 1956. "In Defence of Fielding", in his *Unprofessional Essays* (Jonathan Cape, London), pp. 11–52

Needham, Gwendolyn B., 1954. "The Undisciplined Heart of David Copperfield", *Nineteenth-Century Fiction* 9: 81–107

Nevo. Ruth, 1982. Nevo, "*The Waste Land*: Ur-Text of Deconstruction", *New Literary History* 13: 453–61

New Literary History 10 (1978). Special issue on hermeneutics and literary scholarship

Nicholls, Peter, 1995. *Modernisms: A Literary Guide* (Macmillan, London)

Nicholson, Norman, 1957. Tribute to Andrew Young, in Clark, *Andrew Young*, pp. 61–8

Nietzsche, Friedrich W. [1883–92] 1933. *Thus Spake Zarathustra* (Dent, London)

Nietzsche, Friedrich W., [1888] 1968. *The Will to Power* (Weidenfield & Nicolson, London)

Nisbet, Ada and Blake Nevins (eds.), 1971. *Dickens Centennial Essays* (University of California Press, Berkeley)

Norris, Leslie, 1965. Tribute to Andrew Young, *Priapus*, Autumn 1965, facing pp. 10 and 11

Nuttall, A. D., 1996. *Why Does Tragedy Give Pleasure?* (Clarendon Press, Oxford)

Oakman, Robert L., 1976 . "The Character of the Hero: A Key to Fielding's *Amelia*", *Studies in English Literature 1500–1900* 16: 474–89

Ortega y Gasset, José, [1925] 1968. "The Dehumanization of Art", in his *The Dehumanization of Art and other Essays on Art, Culture, and Literature* (Princeton University Press, Princeton)

Orwell, George, [1940] 1970. "Charles Dickens", in Wall, *Charles Dickens*, pp. 297–313

Osland, Dianne,1980. "Fielding's *Amelia*: Problem Child or Problem Reader?" *Journal of Narrative Technique* 10: 56–67

Oster, Judith, 1991. *Toward Robert Frost: The Reader and the Poet* (University of Georgia Press, Athens)

Palmer, Eustace, 1971. "*Amelia* — The Decline of Fielding's Art", *Essays in Criticism* 21:135–51

Parker, William R., 1940. "Henry Vaughan and his Publishers", *The Library* 20: 401–11

Paroissien,David, 1983. "Literature's 'Eternal Duties': Dickens's Professional Creed", in Giddings, *The Changing World*, pp. 31–50

Parry, N. and J. Parry, 1976. *The Rise of the Medical Profession* (London: Croom Helm, 1976)

Patrides, C. A., 1988. "T. S. Eliot: Alliances of Levity and Seriousness", *Sewanee Review* 96: 77–94

Paulson, R. (ed.), 1962. *Fielding: A Collection of Critical Essays* (Prentice-Hall, Englewood Cliffs)

Pearson, Gabriel, 1976. "Towards a Reading of *Dombey and Son*" in Gabriel Josipovici (ed.) *The Modern English Novel: the Reader, the Writer and the Work* (Open Books, London,), pp. 54–76

Perkins, Judith, 1982. "Literary History: H.-G. Gadamer, T. S. Eliot and Virgil", *Arethusa* 14: 241–9

Perl, Jeffrey M., 1988. *Skepticism and Modern Enmity: Before and After Eliot* (Johns Hopkins University Press, Baltimore)

Pettet, E. C., 1960. *Of Paradise and Light: A Study of Vaughan's* Silex Scintillans (Cambridge University Press, Cambridge)

Plasa, Carl, 1991. "Reading Tennyson in *Four Quartets*: the Example of 'East Coker'", *English: the Journal of the English Association* 40: 239–58

Poirier, Robert, 1977. *Robert Frost: the Work of Knowing* (Oxford University Press, Oxford)

Polanyi, Livia, 1982. "Literary Complexity in Everyday Storytelling", in Tannen, *Spoken and Written Language*, pp. 155–70

Poovey, Mary, 1988. *Uneaven Developments: The Ideological Work of Gender in Mid-Victorian England* (University of Chicago Press, Chicago)

Pope, Alexander, 1963. *The Poems of Alexander Pope: A One-Volume Edition of the Twickenham Text*, ed. John Butt (Methuen, London)

Post, Jonathan F. S., 1982. *Henry Vaughan: The Unfolding Vision* (Princeton University Press, Princeton)

Press, John, 1958. *The Chequer'd Shade: Reflections on Obscurity in Poetry* (Oxford University Press, London)

Prince, F. T., 1985. "The Man and the Mind", *Agenda* 23: 82–6

Pritchard, William H., 1984. *Frost: A Literary Life Reconsidered* Oxford University Press, Oxford

Rader, Margaret, 1982. "Context in Written Language: The Case of Imaginative Fiction", in Tannen, *Spoken and Written Language*, pp. 185–98

Rainey, Laurence, 1997. "The real scandal of *Ulysses*: How literary modernism came to retreat from the public sphere", *Times Literary Supplement*, January 31st

Raven, James, Helen Small and Naomi Tadmor (eds.), 1996. *The Practice and Representation of Reading in England* (Cambridge University Press, Cambridge)

Rawson, Claude, 1972. *Henry Fielding and the Augustan Ideal Under Stress: "Nature's Dance of Death" and Other Studies* (Routledge and Kegan Paul, London)

Rice, Thomas J., 1983. "The Politics of *Barnaby Rudge*", in Giddings, *The Changing World*, pp. 51–74

Richards, I. A., 1926. *Principles of Literary Criticism* (Routledge and Kegan Paul, London)

Richetti, John, 1990. "The Old Order and the New Novel of the Mid-Eighteenth Century: Narrative Authority in Fielding and Smollett" *Eighteenth-Century Fiction* 2: 183–96

Richetti, John, 1991. "Class Struggle without Class: Novelists and Magistrates", *The Eighteenth Century: Theory and Interpretation* 32: 203–18

Ricks, Christopher, 1988. *T. S. Eliot and Prejudice* (Faber, London)

Ricks, Christopher, 1996. *Essays in Appreciation* (Clarendon Press, Oxford)

Ridley, Matt, 1997. *The Origins of Virtue* (Penguin, Harmondsworth)

Robson, W. W. [1966] 1982. "Robert Frost" in his *The Definition of Literature and Other Essays* (Cambridge University Press, Cambridge), pp. 168–95

Rogers, Katharine M., 1976. "Submissive Women: Richardson and Fielding", *Novel* 9: 256–70

Ross, Andrew, 1984. "*The Waste Land* and the Fantasy of Interpretation", *Representations* 8:134–58

Sabor, Peter, 1982. "*Amelia* and *Sir Charles Grandison*: the Convergence of Fielding and Richardson", *Wascana Review* 17: 3–18

Said, Edward Said, 1993. *Culture and Imperialism* (Chatto and Windus, London)

Saintsbury, George, 1890. *Essays in English Literature, 1780–1860* (Percival, London)

Santayana, George, [1921] 1970. "Dickens", in Wall, *Charles Dickens*, p. 265

Sawak, Dale (ed.), 1999. *A Passion for Books* (Macmillan, Basingstoke)

Scheuerman, Mona, 1984. "Man not Providence: Fielding's *Amelia* as a Novel of Social Criticism", *Forum for Modern Language Studies* 20: 106–23

Scheuermann, Mona, 1990. "Henry Fielding's Images of Women", *The Age of Johnson: A Scholarly Journal* 3: 231–80

Schofield, Mary Anne, 1985. "Exploring the Woman Question: A Reading of Fielding's *Amelia*", *Ariel: A Review of International English Literature* 16: 45–57

Schroeder, Natalie E. and Ronald E. Schroeder, 1989. "Betsey Trotwood and Jane Murdstone: Dickensian Doubles", *Studies in the Novel* 21: 269–78

Schwartz, Sanford, 1990. "Beyond the 'Objective Correlative': Eliot and the Objectification of Emotion", in Cowan, *T. S. Eliot*, pp. 321–341

Searle, John, 1975. "The Logical Status of Fictional Discourse", *New Literary History* 6: 319–92

Seelig, Sharon Cadmon, 1981. *The Shadow of Eternity: Belief and Structure in Herbert, Vaughan and Traherne* (University Press of Kentucky, Lexington)

Sell, Roger D., 1975. "Two Types of Style Contrast in *King Lear*: A Literary-Critical Appraisal", in Håkan Ringbom (ed.), *Style and Text: Studies Presented to Nils Erik Enkvist* (Scriptor, Stockholm), pp. 158–71

Sell, Roger D. 1978. *Trespassing Ghost: A Critical Study of Andrew Young* ([*Acta Academiae Aboensis, ser. A. Humaniora* 56:1] Åbo Akademi University, Åbo)

Sell, Roger D., 1980. *Robert Frost: Four Studies* ([*Acta Academiae Aboensis, ser. A. Humaniora*, 57:2] Åbo Akademi University, Åbo)

Sell, Roger D., 1981. "*Watership Down* and the Rehabilitation of Pleasure", *Neuphilologische Mitteilungen* 82: 28–35

Sell, Roger D., 1983. "Projection Characters in *David Copperfield*", *Studia Neophilologica* 55: 19–30

Sell, Roger D., 1983. "Three Separate Leaves from Robert Frost's Derry Years: a Note and Transcriptions", *Studies in Bibliography* 36: 229–32

Sell, Roger D. (ed.), 1985. "Robert Frost: Two Unpublished Plays: *In an Art Factory* and *The Guardeen*", *Massachusetts Review* 26: 265–340

Sell, Roger D., 1987. "The Unstable Discourse of Henry Vaughan: A Literary-Pragmatic Account", in Alan Rudrum (ed.), *Essential Articles for the Study of Henry Vaughan* (Archon, Hamden, Conn.), pp. 311–32

Sell, Roger D., 1994. "Literary Gossip, Literary Theory, Literary Pragmatics", in Sell and Peter Verdonk (ed.), *Literature and the New Interdisciplinarity: Poetics, Linguistics, History* (Rodopi, Amsterdam), pp. 221–41

Sell, Roger D. (ed.), 1995. *New Casebook: Great Expectations* (Macmillan, Basingstoke)

Sell, Roger D., 1999. "*Henry V* and the Strength and Weakness of Words: Shakespearian Philology, Historicist Criticism, Communicative Pragmatics", *Neuphilologische Mitteilungen* 100: 535–63

Sell, Roger D., 2000. *Literature as Communication: The Foundations of Mediating Criticism* (Benjamins, Amsterdam, 2000)

Sell, Roger D., 2001. "A Historical but Non-deterministic Pragmatics of Literary Communication", *Journal of Historical Pragmatics* 2 : 1–32

Sell, Roger D., 2001. "Communication: A Counterbalance to Professional Specialization", in Herbert Grabes (ed.), *Innovation and Continuity in English Studies* (Peter Lang, Frankfurt, 2001), pp. 73–89

Shaw, George Bernard, 1921. *The Doctor's Dilemma, Getting Married, & The Shewing-up of Blanco Posnet* (Constable, London)

Shaw, W. David, 1986. "The Poetics of Pragmatism: Robert Frost and William James", *New England Quarterly* 59: 159–88

Sheehy, Donald G., 1983. "Robert Frost and the Lockless Door", *New England Quarterly* 56:39–59

Sheldrake, Rupert, 1981. *A New Science of Life: The Hypothesis of Formative Causation* (Blond and Briggs, London)

Sheldrake, Rupert, 1988. *The Presence of the Past: Resonance and the Habits of Nature* (Collins, London)

Sherbern, George, [1936] 1962. "Fielding's *Amelia*: An Interpretation", in Paulson, *Fielding*, pp. 146–57

Sherbo, Arthur, 1969. *Studies in the Eighteenth Century Novel* (Michigan State University Press, East Lansing)

Shusterman, Richard, 1988. *T. S. Eliot and the Philosophy of Criticism* (Duckworth, London)

Shusterman, Richard, 1993. "Don't Believe the Hype: Animadversions on the Critique of Popular Art", *Poetics Today* 14: 101–22

Simmonds, James D., 1972. Simmonds, *Masques of God: Form and Theme in the Poetry of Henry Vaughan* (University of Pittsburgh Press, Pittsburgh)

Simon, Irène, 1992. "*David Copperfield*: A Künstlerroman", *Review of English Studies* 43: 40–56

Söderlind, Johannes, 1973–4. "En språklig analys av en Dickensroman", *Annales Societas Litterarum Humaniorum Regiae Upsaliensis*, pp. 20–33

Smallwood, Angela J., 1989. *Fielding and the Woman Question: The Novels of Henry Fielding and the Feminist Debate 1700–1750* (Prentice-Hall, Englewood Cliffs)

Spender, Stephen, 1988, *Eliot* (Fontana/Collins, Glasgow)

Sperber, Dan and Deirdre Wilson, 1981. "Irony and the Use-Mention Distinction", in Cole, *Radical Pragmatics*, pp. 295–318

Sperber, Dan and Deirdre Wilson, [1986] 1995. *Relevance: Communication and Cognition* (Blackwell, Oxford)

Spilka, Mark, 1968. "*David Copperfield* as Psychological Fiction", in A. E. Dyson (ed.), *Dickens: Modern Judgements* (Macmillan, London), pp. 186–96

Spilka, Mark, [1953] 1962. "Comic Resolution in Fielding's *Joseph Andrews*", in Paulson, *Fielding*, pp. 59–68

Stacey, Tom, 1982. "Andrew Young, R. S. Thomas and the Parson Poets", in Michael Holroyd (ed.), *Essays by Divers Hands 42* (Royal Society of Literature and Boydell Press, London), pp. 91–108

Stead, C. K., 1964. *The New Poetic: Yeats to Eliot* (Harper, New York)

Sternberg, Meir, 1983. "Deictic Sequence: World, Language and Convention", in Gisa Rauh (ed.), *Essays on Deixis* (Gunter Narr, Tübingen) pp. 277–316

Stoehr, Taylor, 1964. *Dickens: The Dreamer's Stance* (Cornell University Press, Ithaca)

Stone, Harry, 1979. *Dickens and the Invisible World: Fairy-Tales, Fantasy, and Novel Making* (Macmillan, Basingstoke)

Storch, Margaret, 1986. "Robert Frost's 'The Subverted Flower'", *American Imago: A Psychoanalytical Journal for Culture, Science and the Arts* 43: 295–305

Strychacz, Thomas, 1993. *Modernism, Mass Culture, and Individualism* (Cambridge University Press, Cambridge)

Svarny, Erik, 1988. *"The Men of 1914": T. S. Eliot and Early Modernism* (Open University Press, Milton Keynes)

Taine, Hippolyte, [1859, 1871] 1985. Passage from his *History of English Literature* in Alan

Shelston (ed), *Charles Dickens:* Dombey and Son *and* Little Dorrit: *A Casebook* (Macmillan, Basingstoke), pp. 34–35

Tallis, Raymond, 1997. *Enemies of Hope: A Critique of Contemporary Pessimism, Irrationalism, Anti-Humanism and Counter-Enlightenment* (Macmillan, Basingstoke)

Tambling, Jeremy, 1986. "Prison-Bound: Dickens and Foucault", *Essays in Criticism* 36: 11–31 [reprinted in Sell, *New Casebook*, pp. 123–42]

Tambling, Jeremy, 1993. "Death and Modernity in *Dombey and Son*", *Essays in Criticism* 43: 308–329

Tannen, Deborah (ed.), 1982. (ed.), *Spoken and Written Language: Exploring Orality and Literacy* (Ablex, Norwood, N. J.)

Taylor, Charles, 1994. "The Politics of Recognition", in Gutman, *Multiculturalism*, pp. 25–73

Thackeray, William Makepeace, n.d. *Henry Esmond; The English Humourists; The Four Georges*, ed. George Saintsbury (Oxford University Press, London)

Thomas, D. S., 1965. "Fortune and Passions in Fielding's *Amelia*", *Modern Language Review* 60: 176–87

Thompson, Lawrance, 1966. *Robert Frost: the Earlier Years, 1874–1915* (Holt, Rinehart and Winston, New York)

Thompson, Lawrance, 1970. *Robert Frost: The Years of Triumph, 1915–1938* (Holt, Rinehart and Winston, New York)

Thompson, Lawrance, 1976. *Robert Frost: The Later Years, 1938–1963* (Holt, Rinehart and Winston, New York)

Tillotson, Kathleen,1961. *Novels of the Eighteen-Forties* (Oxford University Press, London)

Tobin, David Ned, 1985. *The Present of the Past: T. S. Eliot's Victorian Inheritance* (UMI Research Press, Ann Arbor)

Tomalin, Claire, [1990] 1991. Tomalin, *The Invisible Woman: the Story of Nelly Ternan and Charles Dickens* (Penguin, Harmondsworth)

Towers, A. R., 1953. "*Amelia* and the State of Matrimony", *Review of English Studies* 4: 144–57

Trilling, Lionel, [1947, 1951] 1961. "Manners, Morals, and the Novel", in his *The Liberal Imagination*, pp. 205–222

Trilling, Lionel, [1950] 1961. *The Liberal Imagination: Essays on Literature and Society* (Mercury Books, London)

Trilling, Lionel [1961]1967. "On the Teaching of Modern Literature", in his *Beyond Culture*, pp. 19–41

Trilling, Lionel [1963]1967. "The Fate of Pleasure", in his *Beyond Culture*, pp. 62–86

Trilling, Lionel, 1967. *Beyond Culture: Essays on Literature and Learning* (Penguin, Harmondsworth)

Trotter, David, 1988. *Circulation: Defoe, Dickens, and the Economies of the Novel* (Macmillan, London)

Van Ghent, Dorothy, 1950. "The Dickens World: A View from Todgers's", *Sewanee Review* 58: 419–38 [Incorporated into her *The English Novel: Form and Function* (Rinehart, New York, 1953), pp. 125–38.]

Vaughan, Henry, 1957. *The Works of Henry Vaughan*, ed. L. C. Martin (Oxford University Press, Oxford)

Vaughan, Henry, [1976]1983. *Henry Vaughan: The Complete Poems*, ed. Alan Rudrum (Penguin, Harmondsworth)

Ven, Tom Vander, [1973] 1991. "Robert Frost's Dramatic Principle of 'Oversound'", in Cady and Budd, *On Frost*, pp. 86–99

Walker, Cheryl, 1991. "Persona Criticism and the Death of the Author", in William H. Epstein (ed.), *Contesting the Subject: Essays in the Postmodern Theory and Practice of Biography and Biographical Criticism* (Purdue University Press, West Lafayette), pp. 109–21

Walker, Ted, 1974. Review of Andrew Young's *Complete Poems*, *New Statesman*, 22nd February

Wall, John N., 1988. *Transformations of the Word: Spenser, Herbert, Vaughan* (University of Georgia Press, Athens)

Wall, Stephen (ed.), 1970. *Charles Dickens: A Critical Anthology* (Penguin, Harmondsworth)

Warnke, Georgia, 1987. *Gadamer: Hermeneutics, Tradition and Reason* (Polity Press, Cambridge)

Watt, Ian, [1957] 1963. *The Rise of the Novel: Studies in Defoe, Richardson and Fielding* (Penguin, Harmondsworth)

Watts, Richard J., 1981. *The Pragmalinguistic Analysis of Narrative Texts: Narrative Cooperation in Charles Dickens's "Hard Times"* (Gunter Nar Verlag, Tübingen)

Wells, H. G., 1922. Review of William Gerhardie's *Futility*, in *Adelphi*, July 23rd

Weinsheimer, Joel, 1985. *Gadamer's Hermeneutics: A Reading of* Truth and Method (Yale University Press, New Haven)

Weinsheimer, Joel, 1991. *Philosophical Hermeneutics and Literary Theory* (Yale University Press, New Haven)

Wendt, Allan, 1960. "The Naked Virtue of Amelia", *ELH* 27:131–48

Wiener, Martin J., 1981. *English Culture and the Decline of the Industrial Spirit, 1850–1980* (Cambridge University Press, Cambridge)

Wilcher, Robert, 1983. "'Then keep the ancient way!' A Study of Henry Vaughan's *Silex Scintillans*", *Durham University Journal* 76:11–24

Wilkinson, Ian, Warwick Gould and Warren Cornice (eds.), 1996. *Modernist Writers and the Marketplace* (Macmillan, London)

Williams, Aubrey, 1971. "Interpositions of Providence and the Design of Fielding's Novels", *South Atlantic Quarterly* 70: 266–86

Williams, Carolyn D., 1988. "Fielding and Half-Learned Ladies", *Essays in Criticism* 38: 22–34

Williamson, George, 1965. *Milton and Others* (Faber, London)

Wilner, Arlene, 1991. "The Mythology of History, the Truth of Fiction: Henry Fielding and the Cases of Boavern Penlez and Elizabeth Canning", *Journal of Narrative Technique* 21:185–201

Wilson, Angus, 1970. *The World of Charles Dickens* (Secker and Warburg, London)

Wilson, Edmund, 1941. *The Wound and the Bow* (Houghton Mifflin, Boston)

Wilson, Edmund, [1931] 1961. "T. S. Eliot", in his *Axel's Castle: A Study in the Imaginative Literature of 1870–1930* (Fontana, London), pp. 80–110

Winters, Yvor, 1959. *On Modern Poets* (Meridian, New York)

Winters, Yvor, [1948] 1962. "Robert Frost: Or, the Spiritual Drifter as Poet", in James M. Cox (ed.), *Robert Frost: A Collection of Critical Essays* (Prentice-Hall, Englewood Cliffs), pp. 58–82

Wolff, Cynthia Griffin, 1968. "Fielding's *Amelia*: Private Virtue and Public Good", *Texas Studies in Literature and Language*, 10: 37–55

Woolf, Virginia, 1986–94. *The Essays of Virginia Woolf*, ed. Anne Olivier Bell (5 vols., Hogarth Press, London)

Wordsworth, William, [1904] 1950. "Preface to the Second Edition of Several of the Foregoing poems Published, with an Additional Volume, under the Title of 'Lyrical Ballads'", in *The Poetical Works of Wordsworth*, ed. Thomas Hutchinson, new ed. Ernest de Selincourt (Oxford University Press, Oxford), pp. 734–41

Wright, Andrew, 1965. *Henry Fielding: Mask and Feast* (Chatto and Windus, London)

Wright, David (ed.), 1966. *Longer Contemporary Poems* (Penguin, Harmondsworth)

Wyatt, David W., 1976. "Choosing in Frost", in Jac Tharpe (ed.), *Frost: Centennial Essays II* (University Press of Mississippi, Jackson), pp. 129–40

Young, A. J. [= Andrew], 1911. *Songs of Night* (De la More Press, London)

Young, A. J. [= Andrew], 1918. "Memorial Verses", in *Cecil Barclay Simpson: A Memorial by Two Friends* (privately printed, Edinburgh)

Young, A. J. [= Andrew], 1920. *Boaz and Ruth and Other Poems*, (John G. Wilson, London)

Young, A. J. [= Andrew], 1921. *The Death of Eli and Other Poems* (John G. Wilson, London)

Young, A. J. [= Andrew], 1922. *Thirty-One Poems* (John G. Wilson, London)

Young, A. J. [= Andrew], 1923. *The Adversary* (John G. Wilson, London)

Young, A. J. [= Andrew], 1926. *The Bird-Cage* (J. & E. Bumpus, London)

Young, A. J. [= Andrew], 1928. *The Cuckoo Clock* (J. & E. Bumpus, London)

Young, A. J. [= Andrew], 1931. *The New Shepherd* (J. & E. Bumpus, London)

Young, Andrew, 1933. *Winter Harvest* (Nonesuch Press, London)

Young, Andrew, 1935. *The White Blackbird* (Jonathan Cape, London)

Young, Andrew, 1936. *Collected Poems* (Jonathan Cape, London)

Young, Andrew, 1937. *Nicodemus* (Jonathan Cape, London)

Young, Andrew, 1939. *Speak to the Earth* (Jonathan Cape, London)

Young, Andrew, 1945. *A Prospect of Flowers* (Jonathan Cape, London)

Young, Andrew, 1947. *The Green Man* (Jonathan Cape, London)

Young, Andrew, 1950. *A Retrospect of Flowers* (Jonathan Cape, London)

Young, Andrew, 1950. *Collected Poems* (Jonathan Cape, London)

Young, Andrew, 1952. *Into Hades* (Rupert Hart-Davis, London)

Young, Andrew, 1956. *A Prospect of Britain* [with twenty photographs by J. Allan Cash] (Hutchinson, London) [reprinted in 1957 by the Country Book Club]

Young, Andrew, 1958. *Out of the World and Back* (Rupert Hart-Davis, London)

Young, Andrew, 1959. *Quiet as Moss* (Rupert Hart-Davis, London)

Young, Andrew, 1960. *Collected Poems* (Rupert Hart-Davis)

Young, Andrew, 1962. *The Poet and the Landscape* (Rupert Hart-Davis, London)

Young, Andrew, 1967. *Burning as Light* (Rupert Hart-Davis, London)

Young, Andrew, 1967. *The New Poly-Olbion* (Rupert Hart-Davis, London)

Young, Andrew, 1972. *The Poetic Jesus* (S. P. C. K., London)

Young, Andrew, 1974. *Complete Poems: Andrew Young* (Secker and Warburg, London)
Young, Andrew, 1985. *Andrew Young: The Poetical Works* (Secker and Warburg, London)
Zwingler, Lyda, 1985. "The Fear of the Father: Dombey and Daughter" *Nineteeth Century Fiction* 39: 420–40

Manuscripts

Frost, Robert. The Derry Notebook and separate leaves. Clifton Waller Barret collection at the University of Virginia Library, accession no. 6261, box 2
Gerhardie, William. Gerhardie Archive, Box 11. Cambridge University Library, Additional Manuscript 8292
Sell, A. P. Letter to Roger D. Sell, September 12th, 1971. Private possession

Index

Flowers, 58–9, 71; *A Retrospect of Flowers*, 58; "The Salmon-Leap", 88; "The Secret Wood", 75; *Songs of Night*, 57, 63, 72–3; *Speak to the Earth*, 58; "The Star", 76; *Thirty-One Poems*, 60; *A Traveller in Time*, 58–9, 64, 92; "The Ventriloquists", 80–1, 88, 93, 196; "Walking on the Cliff", 77; "The Wet Day", 68; *The White Blackbird*, 58; *Winter Harvest*, 58–9

Young, Andrew John (father of Andrew Young), 63, 71–4
Young, David (Andrew Young's brother), 72
Young, Janet (née Green), 75–6
Young, Margaret (Andrew Young's sister), 73
Young, Maria, (mother of Andrew Young), 72–5
Young, William (Andrew Young's brother), 72

Zwingler, Lyda, 188–9